World History Dictionary

A Student Guide

Third Edition

Elliott L. Meyrowitz
Macomb Community College

Kendall Hunt
publishing company

Cover image: Shutterstock, Inc.

Kendall Hunt
publishing company

www.kendallhunt.com
Send all inquiries to:
4050 Westmark Drive
Dubuque, IA 52004-1840

Copyright © 2009, 2012, 2017 by Elliott L. Meyrowitz

Text plus KHQ ISBN: 978-1-5249-4028-7
Text only ISBN: 978-1-5249-4528-2

Published in the United States of America

Dedication

In memory of Tommy Morales and Thomas Rogers, young men of hope, courage, and promise, whose senseless deaths many years ago in a useless and unnecessary war in Vietnam caused me to seek solutions to history's many tragedies. This book is also dedicated to Professor Richard Falk whose encouragement and intellectual insights helped me to discover a talent I never thought I possessed.

Contents

Acknowledgments

I am very grateful to attorney Steven Knox and Will Meyrowitz for their patience and understanding while editing this book. Their invaluable insights and knowledge made the definitions contained in this book more accurate and readable.

Introduction

The Importance of the Study of History

Those who can make you believe absurdities can make you commit atrocities.
Voltaire

What gets us into trouble is no what we don't know.
It's what we know for sure that just ain't so.
Mark Twain

Social responsibility is an essential ingredient in a democratic society. My primary objective in teaching history is to provide students with the skills and information necessary to contribute to the development of a truly participatory democratic society. In all of the history courses that I teach, I seek to develop the critical tools by which a student can analyze, understand, accept and challenge the various intellectual and ideological arguments or positions advocated by political candidates, journalists, pundits, commentators, professors, lawyers and political interest groups on the issues that touch our lives on a daily basis. It is my hope that such tools will provide each student with a deeper appreciation of the development, influence and limitations of our society.

The sometimes overwhelming demands and fast pace of the modern era leave little time to consider some of the fundamental questions of our existence. What things are worth striving for? What makes life worth living? Are there universal values that transcend cultural differences? What are the basic ethical values that do and should inform the range of practical decisions that we make on a daily basis? What are the underlying norms in the current political debates about such topics as war, economic inequality, the environment, civil rights, immigration, criminal punishment, health care, national economic policies, and national security strategy? A study of history reveals that there has been and continues to be a complex array of assumptions, beliefs, and values that, often unconsciously, inform policy decisions by our political leaders.

In order to understand these crucial undercurrents, I emphasize in all of my courses the meaning of words and the use of language. Why, you might ask, am I so concerned about such meaning and the use of language in history and courses—simply put, language is crucial to self-preservation. In order to survive, people must be able to correctly assess their surroundings, including any threats that may materialize. This is as true today as it has been historically.

Language is fundamental to human evolution and adaptation. The development of the human ability to speak is the functional equivalent to the "Big Bang Theory" in astrophysics.

Language, which is the keystone of human cultures around the world, helps us to think about our most basic human experiences. As humans are the conscious part of nature, we have the unique ability to construct and make sense of our lives and social interactions by the use of language. Our ability to speak, to conceptualize our understanding of the world around us is the central evolutionary development that makes us human.

English is a syncretistic language. Its vocabulary is drawn from Greek, Latin, French, Spanish, Italian, Arabic, German and Old English. Today, there are thousands of languages besides English. While each is different, they all share certain common features—the use of sounds to express thoughts. Language permits humans to fashion abstract thought and to generalize, distinguish, analyze and hypothesize. Without language there would be no art, literature, music, films, science, and technology.

History should be viewed as individuals generating, receiving and acting out of these thoughts. Since ideas, like language, change over time, ideas must be studied as historically created and not as some arbitrary and unchanging structure. Without knowledge of history, we are unable to understand ourselves and make reasoned decisions. As human beings we have been shaped by the values, customs, traditions, ideas and institutions we have inherited from the past.

From my perspective, ideas can do two things. They can build bridges by making people understand their shared sense of humanity or ideas can dig ditches making differences among people wider and deeper. Lies, myths, propaganda and pseudo-scientific arguments have been used throughout history to compel people to do what they otherwise would not do. As a result, it is imperative that we understand historically how language has shaped the ideas that we have inherited over the millennia. To do so constitutes an act of intellectual self-defense crucial to protecting one's humanity, if not the future of our species.

From ancient Greek society have come a number of concepts that have had a significant impact on our culture. Indeed, much of the history of Western societies for the past 2000 years has centered on efforts to answer the questions first raised by the ancient Greeks. What are the appropriate roles and rights of an individual in society? To whom or to what does an individual owe primary allegiance, the dictates of conscience or the laws of the state? How should the state be properly organized and governed and by whom? Who should rule and why? Do divine forces govern natural phenomena and human history?

The teaching of history emphasizes patterns, trends and processes. In order to understand the importance of contemporary world events, one must not overlook the deep causal explanations, i.e., the long-term demographic, geographical, social, cultural, economic, technological and philosophical factors that have molded our modern world. For example, how can one understand the causes for World War II, without understanding the beliefs and ideologies on both sides? How does one understand the role of nationalism in the 1800s and 1900s without having traced its emergence during the French Revolution? Can one understand the on-going conflicts in the Middle East and Central Asia without understanding the role of religions embraced by those societies. How can one understand the Holocaust, without understanding the development of anti-Judaism and its evolution into anti-Semitism? One cannot hope to understand the Vietnam War without an awareness of the effect of such ideas of imperialism, colonialism, independence, self-determination and nationalism throughout Vietnamese history. How can one understand European and American imperialism and colonialism in the 1800s and 1900s without knowledge about the various political movements that opposed such developments or about the rise and decline of past empires in world history? While one must necessarily try to understand the immediate causes that trigger a historical event or processes, one must also understand the long-term historical processes that established the foundation for such triggering events.

Today, there is an overemphasis on the "present" in news reporting about political, social, economic, cultural or technological developments. In so doing, such reporting overlooks the long-term casual explanations for current developments. Nevertheless, in all of my courses I emphasize the long-term geographical, environmental, social, political, economic, cultural, technological and scientific factors that have shaped our modern world. Rather than simply describing "what happened", I stress the "why" of things. When it comes to understanding historical events or processes, the bare facts of this or that event by themselves are simply not enough. Facts without context are worse than useless; they may be dangerous because misleading or inaccurate data will produce ill-advised decision-making. Accordingly, my approach to the study of history does not simply consist of a chronology of sequentially linked events, but rather emphasizes the on-going story of the developments that moved people and shaped events.

We must remember that when we engage in historical analysis our understanding will never be more than partial and evolving. The study of history requires an open mind as conventionally accepted "truths" may often unravel over time and require reinterpretation in light of our increasing knowledge and perspective. But, not all interpretations are equally valid. Valid interpretations are those that are based on credible, reasonable and rational evidence.

As a professor of history one is continually confronted with the question of why so many students find the study of history uninteresting or unimportant. For many students, a history course simply represents credits that must be earned as a prerequisite to the specialized training that is their primary objective. Unfortunately, some students tend to focus primarily on how much work will be required of a history course rather than the value of the substantive material covered in the course. This perspective is underscored by increasingly influential perspective that the study of history is not an important part of a student's college education.

Yet, whatever career, job or profession a person pursues, an understanding of the past is usually highly relevant and often positively essential. In our interdependent and interconnected world one needs to better understand the role that humans play in making their own cultures, social systems and forms of government and the degree to which existing preconditions such as geography and the environment influence historical developments. When we ignore why historical events and processes happened and when we dismiss drawing any lessons from those events and processes, the effect of historical under-standing on our personal lives becomes increasingly powerful in ways beyond our control or intent.

Admittedly, history can seem like an endless succession of wars, diseases, famines, natural disasters, and economic depressions. Indeed, for some people all of this pain and suffering, which seems to occur again and again, is controlled by some all-powerful outside force. Today, conspiracies are quite the fashion, the stuff of drama for TV and movies. But a sound familiarity with real world of history gives us the tools to avert the reoccurrence of such tragic events.

History should not solely be a scholarly/academic discipline with historians primarily analyzing the works and arguments of other historians. History should offer ideas and examples to help solve real-world situations. History offers guidance to understand the questions of ethics and morality that arise in our everyday situations.

From my perspective history is simply the study of the development of humanity–an epic tale of the personal experiences of human beings, in all their complexity, struggling to survive in a wide range of hospitable and inhospitable environments. Looked at from this perspective, the study of history can become a truly absorbing adventure with significant educational and practical payoffs.

History is comprised of stories about the human experience. Some of the stories are difficult to tell and some are difficult to hear, but they must be told and explained in order to gain a more accurate un-derstanding of the human experience. A fuller understanding of history will help us identify the mistakes humans have made, identify the causes for those mistakes and offer insights as to steps humans must take to guard against such mistakes in the future. An objective view of history may make us uncomfortable and even question the values upon which a society is built. Nevertheless, as a result of confronting and struggling to understand this unease, discomfort and questioning, we, hopefully, can learn how to make ourselves and our society more equitable and just. A people cannot celebrate their collective historical experience unless they are willing to confront the legacy of the negative aspects of a society's history. Such an exploration, while difficult, will yield a new and more accurate understanding of a nation's history.

Accordingly, we must confront the grave reality of the past and its continuing legacy in the present in order to understand the meaning of our individual and societal hopes for the future.

Education is the process by which a person develops his or her knowledge, skills, abilities and character. It can be accomplished by individual effort or with the assistance of a trained guide, a teacher. Education should not involve mindless obedience, but rather critical questioning. My hope is that this book will help students develop a new vocabulary by which to analyze the ideas of others; enhance a student's ability to think critically by asking relevant questions; strengthen a student's confidence to construct an argument knowing that new information might change his or her analysis; provide a student with the courage to defend his or her conclusions using relevant evidence and reasoned argumentation; and improve a student's ability to communicate his or her thinking clearly to others.

Lee Meyrowitz
May 1, 2017

Terms

A

Abaoji (872–926 CE) was the founder of the Liao Dynasty in China who reigned from 907 to 926 following the collapse of the Tang Dynasty.

Abbasid Caliphate was the dynastic name given to the caliphs (rulers) who ruled the Islamic world, except for al Andalus (Spain), from 750 until 1258. Abu al-Abbas, uncle of Muhammad, founded the Dynasty. The Abbasids overthrew the Umayyad caliphs in 750 and moved the Islamic capital from Damascus to Baghdad. While the Abbasid Caliphate flourished for two centuries, it began to decline with the rise of the Turkish army (Mamluks), which they had created. Their rule finally ended in 1258, when the Mongols sacked Baghdad.

Abbe is a French word which means abbot of a monastery. However, after the 1600s, it was the title of respect and honor that was awarded by French kings to Catholic clergymen men, whether ordained or not, who served in secular capacities as professors, lecturers, tutors to upper class families, secretaries to the nobility or writers. Clergymen who held this title were permitted by the French kings to receive income from a monastery without providing any services to the monastery.

Abbot/Abbess or Prior/Prioress was the name for the male or female head of a monastery or convent.

Abd al-Rahman III (889/91–961 CE) is considered by some historians as the greatest and most successful of the princes of the Umayyad Dynasty in Spain. He was the caliph of Cordoba from 912–961. He ascended the throne when the Spain was exhausted by more than a generation of tribal conflict among the Arabs and conflict between the Arab aristocracy and the Muslims of native Spanish descent. The Arab nobles were the most serious threat to Abd al-Rahman's rule. Next to them came the Fatimids, a rival Islamic Dynasty based in Egypt and northern Africa, who claimed the caliphate based on descent from the Muhammad, and who sought to extend their rule over the Muslim world. By declaring himself as the Caliph of Cordoba, he broke all ties with caliphs of Egypt and Syria. Traditionally, the caliphate was thought only to belong to the prince who ruled over the sacred cities of Mecca and Medina. But this tradition had been so weakened that Abd al-Rahman proclaimed himself caliph in 929. During his almost fifty year reign, he actively supported scholars making Cordoba one of the most important centers of learning in Europe in the 900s.

Abelard, Peter (1079–1142 CE) was a medieval French theologian, philosopher and teacher. Relying upon systematic doubting in his teachings and writings, he contributed to the development of scholasticism. After attending a cathedral school in Reins, he went to Paris around 1100 to study and give lectures, an activity in which only the clergy could engage in France. In Paris, he engaged in debates (called disputations) with leading theologians, began to give lectures on dialectical theology, and established his own school near Paris. His growing reputation as a teacher drew students to Paris from throughout Europe. Between 1122–1123, he wrote a textbook for his students, *Sic et Non* (*"Yes and No"*) in which he used logical reasoning in an attempt to reconcile over 150 contradictory statements found in the Bible, the writings of the Church Fathers and statements by Church councils by the use of logical reasoning to analyze such statements. His ideas expressed in his book were condemned by the Church and he was forced to burn it to avoid charges of heresy. In using dialectical reasoning to resolve contradictions, he said that "It is by doubting that we come to investigate and by investigating that we recognize the truth". As his reputation for brilliance grew, he attracted the attention of clerics associated with the Notre Dame Cathedral. Abelard was hired to teach a cleric's niece named Heloise, who had previously been taught at a convent as a young girl, and was one of the few educated women in Europe. Even though he was much older than Heloise, he fell in love with her. They married and conceived a son, even though they were living apart. Since celibacy was required of a theologian and fearful that his career as a teacher might be ruined, they kept the marriage secret as well as the birth of their son. When the love affair and marriage became known to Heloise's uncle, he hired criminals to castrate Abelard. After his castration, Abelard became a monk and an abbot at a monastery, while Heloise became a nun and entered a convent and their son was adopted by Heloise's sister. Although they loved each other deeply, they would spend the remainder their lives isolated from one another.

Abolitionists were men and women in the United States and Britain who in the late 1700s and early 1800s struggled for an end to slavery and the transatlantic slave trade.

Abraham was the patriarch of the Hebrew people who moved from Ur to Palestine in the second millennium BCE.

Absolution is a religious ritual performed by a Catholic priest who pronounces forgiveness and the remission of sins.

Absolutism is a form of government and a political theory in which sovereignty is vested in a single person, the monarch, who has complete and unlimited power to make war, tax, make and enforce laws, and coin money. Advocates for this theory argued that royal power should not be limited by any law or constitution and that hereditary monarchical rule would provide the most effective means to prevent chaos and disorder. Absolute monarchs in the 1600s and 1700s in Europe also relied upon the theory of the divine right of kings to legitimate their rule. These absolutist monarchs claimed that they had received their authority to rule from God and thus were accountable only to God. As absolute monarchs monopolized and centralized political power, such as King Louis XIV of France, they diminished the rival political power of the nobility.

Absurdism was a philosophical school of thought that emerged during the post-World War II period, which was articulated by the French philosopher and writer Albert Camus. He argued that human existence was inherently meaningless and that any effort by humans to give meaning to life was futile. He contended that humans have typically dealt in three ways with the meaningless of their existence: suicide; systems of religious or spiritual belief and morality. Camus argued that humans should directly confront the absurdity of the human condition. He further claimed that without confronting this absurdity political, social, economic and cultural oppression will continue. Absurdism has its roots in nihilism and existentialism, schools of philosophical thought that emerged in the mid-1800s and early 1900s in Europe.

Abu Bakr (573–634), who was one of the earliest followers of Muhammad, was the first caliph after the the death of Muhammad.

Abu Hureyra is an archaeological site in northern Syria near the Euphrates River where the earliest evidence of agriculture in the world has been found. Cultivated (domesticated) cereal grains, including rye, have been found at Abu Hureyra dating from about 11,000 BCE during the Paleolithic era, which is at least a thousand years before agriculture was previously thought to have begun in Mesopotamia. Previously the earliest known site for agriculture was also in Syria (Tell Aswad), which dates from about 10,000 BCE.

Academy was the name of Plato's school of philosophy that he founded circa 385 BCE in a sacred grove of olive trees dedicated to Athena, the goddess of wisdom, outside the city walls of Athens. Aristotle was a student at the Academy.

Acclimatization is the physiological process by humans to adapt to extreme climate changes.

Acculturation is the complex, interconnected psychological, cultural and sociological process by which a person or a group of people (such as immigrants, refugees and indigenous populations) adopts, willingly or unwillingly, the language, customs, values, traditions, dress and social behaviors, in whole or in part, of another person, group of people, society or culture. This process has significantly influenced the development of the societies and cultures of the United States and Europe.

Achaea was a province of ancient Greece along the northern coast of the Peloponnese where the Achaean people lived. The city-states in Achaea would form the Achaean League in the 3rd century BCE. Achaeans was the term used by Homer in the *Iliad* and the *Odyssey* collectively for the ancient Greeks who fought in the Trojan War during the 12th or 13th century BCE. The origin of the Achaeans has been debated by historians. Some scholars argue evidence exists which establishes that the ancient Achaeans were the Mycenaeans. Other scholars contend that the Achaeans were a people who entered Greece after the Dorian invasion is the 12th century BCE. Herodotus would later claim that the Achaeans who lived in Achaea in the 5th century BCE were the descendants of the Achaeans described by Homer.

Achaean League was a defensive military alliance of city-states in the Peloponnese that was first established in the 5th century BCE. While the league dissolved in 338 BCE, it was refounded in 280 BCE during the Hellenistic era and attempted to build a politically unified federation, in which each member city-state was considered equal. Even though each member city state maintained its own form of government, each member city-state was also subject to the centralized governance of the federation. The federation annually elected a chief political leader and a chief general, a governing council and a general assembly in which citizens of each member city state could participate. A uniform body of laws also applied throughout the league and every citizen of a member city state held joint citizenship. This federated league sought to ensure the political independence of its member city-states and to organize resistance to the increasing efforts by the Antigonids of Macedonia to dominate all of Greece. The league fought a war in 220 BCE against the Aetolian League to stop Aetolian raids on Achaean territory. The league's dominance in the Peloponnese declined, however, after the Roman defeat of Macedonia during the Third Macedonian War (171–168 BCE). In 146 BCE, the league fought a war against the growing Roman domination of Greece, but it was defeated at the Battle of Corinth. In the wake of that war, the Romans dissolved the league and destroyed Corinth.

Achaemenid Empire (559–330 BCE) was the first great Persian Empire founded by Cyrus the Great. It reached its height of power under Darius I. Its capital was in Susa

Acheson-Lilenthal Plan (Baruch Plan) (1946) was a proposal by the United States to the UN Atomic Energy Commission(UNAEC) in its first meeting in June 1946 to a) extend between all nations the exchange of basic scientific information about atomic energy for peaceful ends; b) implement control of atomic energy to the extent necessary to ensure its use only for peaceful purposes; c) eliminate from national armaments atomic weapons and all other major weapons adaptable to mass destruction; and d) establish effective safeguards by way of inspection and other means to protect the nations of the world against the hazards of violations and evasions. Under this plan of international control of atomic energy, the United States agreed to turn over all of its weapons on the condition that all other countries pledge not to produce them and agree to an adequate system of inspection. The Soviets rejected this plan on the grounds that the United Nations was dominated by the United States and its allies in Western Europe, and could therefore not be trusted to exercise authority over atomic weaponry in an evenhanded manner. When the Soviet Union refused to agree to this disarmament plan, American policymakers embarked on a massive nuclear weapons testing, development, and deployment program that contributed to the nuclear arms race between the Soviet Union and the United States that lasted throughout the Cold War.

Acquired Immune Deficiency Syndrome (AIDS) is a complex viral infection that attacks the body's immune system which is transmitted through intravenous drug use and sexual contact. Appearing first in the 1970s, it has developed into a global health problem affecting nations in Africa and Asia.

Acre was a port city located in Phoenicia, which played a major role in the ancient maritime trade in the Mediterranean. Because of its natural harbor, it was a frequent target of invaders over the centuries. It was conquered by Alexander the Great and it became the base from which the Romans mounted their suppression of the Jewish revolt from 66 to 70 CE. The Persians, the Arabs, and the Christian crusaders subsequently captured it and made it their capital. Its capture by the Arabs in 1291 CE marked the end of the rule of the Christian crusaders in the Holy Land.

Acropolis is literally the upper part of a town. For purposes of defense, early settlers in ancient Greece chose elevated ground, frequently a hill with precipitous sides, on which to establish a settlement. These early hilltop citadels became the beginnings of large cities that grew up on the surrounding lower ground. In ancient Greece, an acropolis was an elevated point within a city-state where temples, altars, public monuments, sanctuaries, and various dedications to the gods of the city-state stood, such as the Parthenon. The Acropolis of ancient Athens was used both for civic celebrations and defense.

Act of Supremacy (1534) was the law passed by the British parliament during the Protestant Reformation that caused the English to break with the Catholic Church. This law declared that Henry VIII, not the pope, was the head of the Church of England and that Henry had the right to determine church doctrine and practice. Henry VIII required a public oath of support for this law, but Thomas More, Henry's Lord Chancellor, refused to do so. As a result of his refusal to take such an oath, Henry had him executed for treason.

Action Française was an extreme right-wing, nationalist, promonarchy and anti-Semitic political group that was organized in France in 1898 in response to the controversy surrounding the Dreyfus Affair. It opposed parliamentary democracy in France, even calling for its violent overthrow. Action Francaise supported the restoration of the French monarchy, arguing that a monarchical government was the only institution in France that could unify a politically polarized French society. It claimed that the French government was corrupt, that democracy was unworkable, that France was in decline and that only a return to the values and institutions existing prior to the French Revolution would restore the grandeur of France. Furthermore, Action Francaise supported the restoration of Catholicism as the state religion in France, which it believed would create greater social cohesion and stability. Action Francaise was also the name of the group's newspaper, which was published daily between 1908 and 1944. Charles Maurras, a journalist, was the director of the newspaper in which he expressed the basic ideological beliefs of the group. Maurras condemned the legacy of the French Revolution, socialism and communism, French Protestants (Huguenots), Jews and foreigners residing in France. He argued that the Protestant Reformation, the Enlightenment and the French Revolution all had contributed to the emerging belief that individual rights should put ahead of the nation. Even though Action Francaise was widely supported by French Catholics, Pope Pius XI publicly condemned the group in 1926 and placed its newspaper and Maurras's writings on the Church's Index of Forbidden Books. Nevertheless, Action Francaise remained popular as increasing numbers of people in Europe supported authoritarian political movements. Many members of Action Francaise supported the growth fascism in Europe. During World War II (1940–1944), Action Francaise supported the German collaborationist Vichy government headed by Marshall Philippe Petain. After the Allied victory in France in 1944, the group ceased to exist, its newspaper was banned and Maurras was sentenced to life imprisonment for collaboration with the enemy.

Actium, Battle of (31 BCE) was the decisive military victory during the Roman Empire in the political struggle between Octavian and Mark Antony. Octavian's victory paved the way for the establishment of the Principate.

Act of Toleration (1689) was the name for the law passed by the British Parliament granting freedom of worship to Protestants such as Baptists, Congregationalists, and Quakers who dissented from the Church of England. It allowed these religious sects their own places of worship and their own teachers and preachers, so long as they took an oath of allegiance to the English monarch. This law did not apply to Catholics, who continued to be excluded from holding political office and from attending English universities.

Act of Settlement (1701) was a law passed by the English Parliament to ensure that the succession to the English throne was restricted to a Protestant monarch. The problem of succession arose because King William III and Mary II, who came to power after the Glorious Revolution of 1688, died without any surviving children. As the Bill of Rights of 1689 excluded Catholics from the throne, Parliament ruled that Mary's Protestant sister Anne would succeed William and Mary. When Queen Anne died without any surviving children and because the Bill of Rights did not provide for succession after Queen Anne, Parliament was compelled to settle the succession issue. It declared that the throne would pass to the granddaughter of King James I of England, the Electress Sophia of the Protestant House of Hanover and her non-Catholic descendants. Since Sophia died before Queen Anne, her son, the elector of Hanover, became King George I of England. He would establish the House of Hanover as the ruling dynasty in England until World War I when the name was changed to Windsor. This law and the Bill of Rights are considered today to be the two basic constitutional laws governing succession to the throne of the United Kingdom.

Act of Uniformity (1558), which is also known as the Act of Uniformity of 1549, was the law passed by Parliament that required Protestant worship in England and its territories to be conducted in accordance with the religious doctrines and practices enunciated in *The Book of Common Prayer,* which was written by Archbishop Thomas Cranmer. The purpose of this law was to establish uniform religious worship in England and its territories. Parliament also required that all church services be conducted in the English.

Acts of Attainder were laws passed by the English Parliament between the late 1400s and the late 1700s that punished an individual for an act, commonly treason, which both houses of Parliament declared to be crime. These legislative acts, which were approved by the king, were often used by Parliament and the king to eliminate a rival political faction or a minister the king distrusted.

Recognizing that such laws deprived a person of a fair trial and due process of law, the framers of the U.S. Constitution specifically prohibited the legislative issuance of a bill of attainder in Article I, Section 9 of the Constitution.

Acts of Union were two laws passed by English and Scottish Parliaments in 1706 and 1707 that joined the separate kingdoms of England and Scotland into a single united kingdom with one king and one parliament. By this law, Scotland also recognized the succession of the Protestant House of Hanover to the English throne. This new state would be called the "United Kingdom of Great Britain". While England and Scotland were ruled by the same king (James VI of Scotland was James I of England) during the 1600s, Parliament feared that an independent Scotland with a separate king might form alliances with other nations that would threaten England and its territories.

Actor is a term used by some historians to describe individuals, governments, movements and organizations that play significant roles, positively or negatively, in the process of historical development.

AD and BC are abbreviations for two dating systems traditionally used by Western historians to distinguish between periods of history. AD, which is Latin for *anno domini,* means "in the year of our lord" and BC means "before Christ." The *anno domini* dating system dates events after the birth of Christ. The "before Christ" dating system dates events before the birth of Christ. Bede the Venerable, an English monk, theologian and historian, popularized the *anno domini* dating system in the early 700s in Europe. Today, many historians tend to us CE, which means "Common Era," in place of AD and BCE, which means "Before the Common Era," in place of BC.

Aden is a port city in the country of Yemen, which was an important port for the British navy and merchant fleet in the 1800s and 1900s.

Adenuaer, Konrad (1876–1967) was the chancellor of West Germany during the Cold War from 1949 until 1963. He established an effective democracy in West Germany and the rebuilt its economy, which had been devastated by World War II. He supported the Cold War polices of the United States and Western Europe.

Adrianople, Battle of (378 CE) was an armed conflict between the army of the Eastern Roman Empire and the Germanic Visigoths of the Roman province of Thracia (modern Greece and Bulgaria). In this battle, north of Constantinople, the Roman army was decisively defeated by the Visigoths and, according to some accounts, forty thousand Roman soldiers were killed. The Eastern Roman Emperor Valens, who led the Roman army, was also killed in the battle. Some historians consider this battle to be the beginning of the process that led to the decline of the Western Roman Empire. In 375, the Visigoths, who were considered an important ally of Rome, helped Rome defeat the Ostrogoths who were threatening the Roman frontier along the Danube River. In 376, under increasing pressure from the Huns, the Visigoths petitioned Emperor Valens to let them cross the Daube River, and enter the Roman Empire. Hoping that the Visigoths would become farmers and serve as soldiers in the Roman army, Emperor Valens allowed them to enter the Roman Empire. In return for providing them with food and supplies, the Visigoths agreed to guard the Roman border along the Danube River. When corrupt local officials failed to provide the promised food and supplies even though the Visigoths were facing starvation, the Visigoths revolted. Emperor Valens tried to suppress the rebellion, but his army was ambushed by the Visigoths. The defeat at Adrianople both undercut the belief in the invincibility of Roman army and demonstrated that barbarians such as the Visigoths had become powerful adversaries.

Adversus Judaeos, which means "against the Jews" in Greek, is the title of a series of eight sermons delivered by John Chrysostom, a preacher and theologian noted for his eloquence. In his sermons to his congregation in Antioch he denounced the Jews and Judaizing Christians and claimed that the Jews were collectively responsible for the crucifixion of Jesus. He criticized those Christians he called Judaizers for continuing to observe Jewish customs and participate in Jewish festivals and observances. In his sermons, he also denounced the synagogue as a pagan temple and the source of all vices and heresies. In his attack on the synagogue and the Jews, he further declared that "demons dwell in the synagogue and in the souls of the Jews" and that Jews were "fit for slaughter". His denunciation of Jews and Judaism would be widely circulated and would contribute to the pervasiveness of anti-Judaic sentiments in Europe over the next 1500 years, until the emergence of anti-Semitism in the late 1800s. His sermons would be subsequently used by the Nazis to legitimate the persecution and murder of Jews. Even though his ideas were denounced by Christian churches after World War II and the Second Vatican Council (1965) repudiated the belief that Jews were collectively responsible for the death of Jesus, he is still considered to be one of the Church Fathers as well as a saint by the Eastern Orthodox and Catholic Churches.

Adwa or Adowa, Battle of (1896) was a military conflict precipitated by Italy's invasion of Ethiopia. Equipped with modern rifles, machine guns and artillery, the Ethiopians forces decisively defeated the outnumbered Italian invasion force. The Battle of Adwa was the first defeat of a European nation by African forces. During the late 1800s, in what historians have called the "Scramble for Africa", all of Africa had been colonized by European nations except for Liberia on the west coast of Africa and Ethiopia on the strategically important Horn of Africa, both of which retained their independence. Italy, which was a newcomer to European colonization in Africa, had conquered Eritrea and Somalia, both of which were near Ethiopia. Hoping to expand Eritrean and Somalian territories and improve its relation with Ethiopia, Italy signed the Treaty of Wuchale (1889) with Ethiopia in which Ethiopia ceded certain Ethiopian territories to Italy in return for Italian financial assistance and military supplies. Subsequently, a dispute arose over the Italian interpretation of the treaty. Italy claimed that under the treaty Ethiopia had relinquished its authority to conduct its own foreign affairs to Italy. By this Italian interpretation, Italy claimed that Ethiopia had become an Italian protectorate. In response to Ethiopia's refusal to accept the Italian interpretation of the treaty, Italy, confident in its belief that it could easily defeat the Ethiopian forces, invaded Ethiopia in 1895 with a force of 20,000 soldiers. The Ethiopian forces slaughtered the Italian invasion force killing about 8,000 soldiers. The Ethiopian victory forced Italy to sign the Treaty of Addis Ababa, which recognized Ethiopia as an independent state. While the Ethiopian victory prevented Italy from building a colonial empire in Africa, the Ethiopian victory became, more importantly, a symbol of resistance in for African nationalists in their struggles against European colonization in the 1900s.

Aedile was a governmental office of the Roman Republic created in 494 BCE, the same years as the office of tribune. In Rome, the aediles were responsible for maintenance of public buildings, regulation of public festivals, management of the plebeian and Roman games and supervision of the grain supply. They also had the power to enforce public order by exercising certain police functions and issuing fines. Half of the aediles were drawn from the ranks of plebeians and half from the patricians. Two aediles were elected annually. Young men who sought higher political office generally sought this office.

Aegean Sea is located between the Greek peninsula and western Anatolia. The Aegean Sea was the birthplace of two ancient civilizations, the Minoans of Crete and the Mycenaen civilization of the Peloponnese. The Aegean Sea facilitated contact between several diverse civilizations of the eastern Mediterranean. It is named for Aegeus, the legendary king of Athens and father of Theseus.

Aeneid is an epic poem written by Virgil between 30 and 19 BCE about the founding of Rome. It tells the legendary story of Aeneas, a Trojan who traveled to Italy, where he became the ancestor of the Romans. Aeneas was already a subject of Roman legend and myth. Virgil simply took the existing oral tales about Aeneas and wrote an epic that linked Emperor Augustus to Aeneas and the heroes and gods of Troy. The poem glorified traditional Roman virtues and legitimated the Julio-Claudian Dynasty as descendants of the founders of Rome and Troy.

Aeolians were one of the three ancient Greek tribal groups, the others being the Dorians and the Ionians. After the collapse of the Mycenaean civilization, the Dorians settled in the Peloponnese and Crete and the Ionians settled in Attica and the Aegean islands. The Aeolians, who spoke a dialect of Greek known as Aeolic, migrated to the western coast of Anatolia along the Aegean Sea as well as several off-shore islands between 1130 and 1000 BCE, where they established city-states in an area that would be later known as Aeolia. Their most famous city-state was Smyrna. The Aeolians considered themselves to be descended from Aeolus,

who fathered Helen, and was the mythological patriarch of all Hellenes.

Aeschylus (525–456 BCE) was an ancient Greek writer who was the first author of Greek tragedies. While he wrote dramatic and powerful poetry, his only surviving work is his trilogy entitled *Oresteia*.

Aesthetics is a branch of philosophy that involves the study of beauty and its embodiment in nature and works of art such as painting, sculpture, and architecture.

Aetolian League was a defensive military alliance of about 60 city-states and villages in Aetolia in central Greece that was established in the 4th century BCE to resist the growing influence of Macedonia and the Achaean League. It was organized as a federal system that consisted of a popular assembly of all male citizens that meet twice a year to elect officials and decide issues of war and peace. The League was presided over by an annually elected general. The League also had a central council in which each member city-state and village participated with voting determined by the population of each member city-state and village. While each member city-state and village had control over its the internal affairs, the council was responsible for foreign relations, raising and army and waging war. Taxes were paid both to the League and each member city-state and village. While the League was an ally of Rome during the First and Second Macedonian Wars, it later supported the resistance by the Seleucid king Antiochus II against Rome, who was defeated in 189 BCE. With the defeat of Antiochus, the League was forced to sign a peace treaty with Rome that made it Rome's ally, ending its military and political influence in Greece.

African Origins Theory (also known as the Out of Africa Theory) is the generally accepted theory developed by paleontologists and archaeologists to explain the origins of anatomically modern humans. Relying upon fossil evidence and the testing of mitochondrial DNA (which is passed only through the mother to her offspring), advocates for this theory argue that Homo sapiens ('thinking man") evolved from Homo erectus originally and exclusively in Africa and then migrated to the rest of the world between 125,000 and 60,000 years ago. Proponents of this theory also claim that any biological differences, which are relatively recent in the evolutionary process among modern humans, such as skin, eye and hair color, bone structure, body shape, body hair and hair characteristics, reflect the adaptation of human sapiens to the various environments to which they migrated. Out-of-Arica theorists further contend because of human blood types and the ability to interbreed, the diverse human groupings that have been historically labeled as "races" (which supposedly shared distinctive genetic traits and physical characteristics), the concept of "race" cannot be scientifically substantiated. Today, the earlier concept of "races" is uniformly rejected by the scientific community, who agree that there exists only one race in the world, the human race. Charles Darwin was the first person to suggest the Out of Africa hypothesis in his book *The Descent of Man* published in 1858.

African National Congress (ANC) (1912) was a multiracial political organization created to end racial discrimination in South Africa and to obtain equal voting and civil rights for the black majority in South Africa. While the South African government banned it and many of its leaders were imprisoned, it, nevertheless, played a central role in bringing majority rule to South Africa. The ANC would come to power in 1994 when apartheid was ended.

Afrikaners or Boers were citizens of South Africa who were descendants of Dutch or Huguenot (French Protestant) colonists. They arrived in South Africa in the 1600s. The language they spoke was called Afrikaans, which was derived from Dutch. They established a colony called the Cape Colony at the Cape of Good Hope on the southern tip of Africa in 1652. Initially the colony was a coastal station for the merchant ships of Dutch maritime empire. Between 1835 and the 1840s approximately 12,000 to 14,000 Boers left the Cape Colony in rebellion against the British policies and in search of new farmlands. This migration from the Cape Colony was called the "Great Trek" and the participating Boers were called Voortrekkers. As a result of the Great Trek, the migrating Boers or Voortrekkers established the new settler colonies of Transvaal and the Orange Free State in South Africa in the 1850s to assert their independence from the British colonial government in the Cape Colony. The discovery of diamonds and gold in the 1860s caused British migration into the Boer territory. After the defeat of the Boers by the British in 1902 in the South African War, the Transvaal and the Orange Free State were incorporated into the Union of South Africa, a colony of the British Empire. Although the Boers were a minority among the people of South Africa, they dominated politics and imposed a system of racial segregation in South Africa called apartheid in 1948.

Agamemnon, King was the mythical king of Mycenae who led the unified Greeks in the Trojan War to recover Helen, the wife of Menelaus, who had been kidnapped by Paris. Menelaus was the brother of Agamemnon. Agamemnon also is the husband of Clytemnestra, whose lover kills Agamemnon after his return from Troy. According to legend, he sacrificed his daughter Iphigenia before he sailed for Troy to appease the wrath of the goddess Artemis and to ensure his success in battle. The *Iliad* tells the story of the quarrel between Agamemnon and Achilles over a slave girl that he stole from Achilles. Agamemnon and his family became the subject of the tragedy *Oresteia* by Aeschylus.

Age of Revolution is a term used by historians to describe the period from the 1770s through the late 1840s when political revolutions arose in North America, Europe, the Caribbean and South America

Agnosticism is a method of philosophical analysis used to determine the truth or validity of certain claims concerning the existence of a god, gods or supernatural forces. The concept was developed in 1869 by Thomas Huxley, a British biologist. An agnostic neither believes nor disbelieves in the existence of a god, gods or supernatural forces because he or she has no credible scientific evidence upon which to draw such a conclusion.

Agoge was a rigorous education and training regime undergone by every Spartan male except for the heirs to the kingships. This educational regime trained boys from the age of seven to eighteen. It involved education, military training, hunting, dance, and social preparation. Boys were taken from the family home and from then on lived in groups where they were trained to express loyalty to their communal mess hall rather than their families. Older warriors would be paired with a teenage student. This bond was considered important in passing on knowledge and in maintaining loyalty on the battlefield. Thus, the agoge focused exclusively on producing new generations of soldiers.

Agon, which is an ancient Greek word that means to struggle or compete, was a virtue that was to be displayed by male contestants in an athletic contest, particularly the Olympic games. Ancient Greeks also believed that it meant that life was a constant struggle or competition.

Agora was the political center of an ancient Greek city-state (polis). It was comprised of temples, public buildings, a public square, and a marketplace for the citizens to gather for informal discussions, conduct business, and engage in political and judicial affairs. Agoras developed after the fall of Mycenaean civilization and were a well-established part of an ancient Greek city-state by the 8th century BCE.

Agrarian Capitalism is a form of economic organization developed by Europeans in the 1600s and 1700s in their colonies in North and South America. The system relied upon the expropriation of land from the indigenous population and the use of slave labor for the production of certain agricultural products such as tobacco, indigo, rice and sugar.

Agreements of the People (1647–1649) were three versions of a political manifesto written by the Levellers and soldiers of the New Model Army that were published during the three English Civil Wars that lasted from 1642 to 1651. These three agreements, which represent the earliest attempt to create a written constitution in England, demanded fundamental changes in the structure of the English government. The first version of the Agreement drafted in 1647 was considered too extreme by Oliver Cromwell and his supporters. It demanded the adoption of a written constitution the frequent meeting of Parliament, and freedom of religion and equality under the law. The second version stated that sovereign political power should reside in the people rather than the king or Parliament, that the existing Parliament should be dissolved, that Parliament should be elected biennially, that the franchise should be given to all adult males who should select representatives based on the proportional representation, and that Parliament should be only comprised of the House of Commons, which would have supreme political authority in England. The final version published in 1649 by the Levellers, whose movement would be subsequently crushed by Oliver Cromwell, demanded the right to vote for all adult males over the age of 21, annual elections to Parliament, equality under the law, trial by a jury of 12 men, no punishment for refusing to testify against themselves, the abolition of imprisonment for debt and the abolition of military conscription. Some historians contend that these agreements influenced the drafters of the U.S. Constitution.

Agricultural Revolution (Neolithic) is the term used by historians to describe the transition by prehistoric human societies from hunting and gathering to agricultural production. The term refers to the societal and political changes that resulted from the adoption of early farming techniques, domestication of plants and animals and crop cultivation. Those changes, which gradually evolved between 10,000 and 4000 BCE, included the development of permanent or semi-permanent settlements, human modifications to the natural environment, reliance on vegetable and cereal foods as part of a human diet, the development of social hierarchies, the division of labor, the emergence of regional trading, and the development of new farming technologies.

Agricultural Revolution (Middle Ages) is the name used by historians to describe the changes in technology, farming methods, manufacturing and transportation that occurred between 1000 and 1300 CE in Western Europe that produced a significant increase in agricultural production. First, by adopting the heavy-wheeled moldboard plow with an iron plowshare pulled by a team of oxen, a farmer was able cut through the heavy and wet soil of northern Europe more readily, which resulted in reducing the time needed to prepare a field for planting and increasing the amount of land that could be farmed. This new plow also aerated the soil and created the furrows that carried away excess water from the fields. Secondly, the replacement of the teams of oxen with tandem teams of horses that used padded horse collars which did not choke the horse, horseshoes which increased the horse's traction and harnesses all enhanced the ability of the farmer to meet the growing demand for food by the increasing populations in the urban areas. While the horses were more expensive than oxen, they were no more costly to feed and they allowed the farmer to plow more acreage in a day than oxen and haul loads farther. Thirdly, the use of harnessed teams of horses hitched in tandem, which pulled large four–wheeled carts, allowed the farmer to transport greater quantities of food faster and farther to existing and new markets. For the urban dwellers, these developments made the delivery of food more regular, predictable and offered greater diversity. Fourthly, the adoption of the three-field system of crop rotation increased the amount, quality and diversity of agricultural production. Under the three-field system, two-thirds of a farmer's land would be cultivated and one field left fallow, which was used to pasture animals whose manure would fertilize the field. In winter, a farmer would plant wheat in one field and in spring he would plant oats, barley, peas and beans. Oats would be used to feed the animals and barley would be used to make beer. Finally, the development of mechanical power such as wind mills and water wheels became the primary source of power for manufacturing. Wind mills and water wheels were increasingly used to turn grinding wheels, drive saws for lumber, process cloth, crush pulp for paper and drive oil and wine presses and iron forges. All of these developments in farming, transportation and manufacturing would spread across Europe and remain fundamentally unchanged until the Industrial Revolution, which began in the mid-1700s in England.

Agrippa, Marcus (63–12 BCE) was the military commander who was responsible for the victory at Actium against Mark Antony and Cleopatra. He was a lifelong friend of Augustus and was designated by Augustus as his successor. He married Augustus' daughter and when he died Augustus adopted all of Agrippa's children.

Aguinaldo, Emilio (1869–1964) was the leader of the Filipino independence movement between 1895 and 1898 against Spain. During the Spanish-American War, he proclaimed the independence of the Philippines in 1899. However, American military forces during the American occupation of the Philippines crushed the Filipino independence movement.

Ahmose I (reigned 1539–1514 BCE) was the name of the Egyptian pharaoh who founded the New Kingdom circa 1500 BCE. He completed the expulsion of the Hyksos (which means in Egyptian "rulers of foreign lands") who had invaded the Nile Delta region of Egypt at the end of the 16th century BCE.

Ahura Mazda, which means the "one lord" or "eternal god", was the name of the god worshipped by Zoroastrians. They believed that Ahura Mazda was the creator or all things, represented truth and goodness and was in an eternal struggle with Angra Mainyu, who represented evil.

Akhenaten (Amenhotep IV) was an Egyptian pharaoh who ruled from 1353 to 1336 BCE. Akhenaten's chief wife was Nefertiti, who has been made famous by her exquisitely painted statute. He was a religious revolutionary who in the first year of his reign introduced the previously obscure god Aten to the position of supreme deity. Aten was the name for the sun itself. Aten was by this point in Egyptian history considered to be an aspect of the composite deity Ra-Amun-Horus. These three previously separate deities had been merged with each other. Akhenaten simplified this development by proclaiming the visible sun itself to be the sole deity. He declared that Aten was not merely the supreme god, but the only god, and that he, Akhenaten, was the only intermediary between Aten and his people. He thus introduced monotheism in ancient Egypt. He began the construction of a new capital, Akhenaten ('Horizon of Aten'), at the site known today as Amarna. In the same year, Amenhotep IV officially changed his name to Akhenaten ("Effective Spirit of Aten") as evidence of his new worship. In honor of Aten, Akhenaten also oversaw the construction of some of the most massive temple complexes in ancient Egypt, including the one at Karnak.

Akkad (or Agade) was a city and its surrounding region in northern central Mesopotamia that became the capital of the Akkadian Empire and later that of the northern part of the ancient Babylonian Empire. The city was probably situated on the west bank of the Euphrates, between Sippar and Kish (in present-day Iraq, about 30 miles southwest of the center of Baghdad. Despite an extensive archaeological search, the precise location of Akkad has never been found. Akkad reached the height of its power between 2400 and 2200 BCE under the leadership of Sargon who has been traditionally cited as the first ruler of the combined empires of Akkad and Sumer. As king of Akkad and Sumer, Sargon embarked upon a career of foreign conquest. Four times he invaded Syria and Canaan, and he spent three years conquering the countries of "the west" to unite them with Mesopotamia "into a single empire." However, Sargon took this process further, conquering many of the surrounding regions to create an empire that reached as far west as the Mediterranean Sea and Anatolia and extending as far south as Magan (Oman). He ruled the Akkadian Empire for 56 years. He established a network of trade that extended from the silver mines of Anatolia to the lapis lazuli mines in Afghanistan, to the cedars of Lebanon and to the copper mines of Magan. His consolidation of the city-states of Sumer and Akkad reflected the growing economic and political power of Mesopotamia. The Empire's breadbasket was the agricultural system of northern Mesopotamia. He also built a chain of fortresses to control imperial wheat production. Within 100 years of the creation of the Akkadian Empire, it collapsed as a result of invasions by tribes from the Zagros Mountains. The population of Akkad was entirely dependent upon the agricultural production. While the Akkadian Empire had a surplus of agricultural products, it lacked almost everything else, particularly metal ores, timber and building stone, all of which had to be imported. To some degree, the spread of the Akkadian Empire to the "silver mountain"(which is believed to have been in the Taurus Mountains, in southern Anatolia), the "cedars" of Lebanon, and to the copper deposits of Magan (Oman), seems to have been motivated by the need to secure control over these imports. Because of this need for foreign imports, the Akkadian Empire was linked together by roads, along which there was a regular postal service.

Akrotiri is a well-preserved Bronze Age farming and fishing village on the Greek island of Santorini (Thera) that was discovered by archeologists in 1967. Since there is no indication what the original inhabitants called the village, archaeologists named it for a modern village located on a hill nearby. Archaeological evidence indicates that the first inhabitants at the site date from around 4000 BCE. Over the next 2000 years, the settlement grew into and important urban center for trade because of its strategic location on the sailing routes between Cyprus and Minoan Crete. Archaeologists have linked the settlement to the Minoan civilization because of the Linear A inscriptions found at the site. A volcanic eruption on Thera in the late 17th century BCE destroyed the settlement, forced the inhabitants to flee and buried the village in volcanic ash preserving most of the settlement. Excavations have revealed a large and prosperous settlement with paved streets, multi-storied buildings, an elaborate drainage system, furniture, high quality pottery used for cooking , eating and drinking and oil lamps, large pottery jars used for the storage and transportation of food, well-preserved frescoes, and various imported objects. Discovery of copper molds and crucibles indicate that the settlement was also an important center for the processing of copper. Some historians argue that the destruction and abandonment of the Akrotiri settlement was the inspiration for Plato's story of Atlantis mentioned in his dialogues *Timaeus and Critias*.

Aksum was a kingdom that emerged in northwestern Ethiopia between 100 and 800 CE. Since it was strategically located close to the entrance to the Red Sea from the Indian Ocean, it became a major center of trade between the Arabia, eastern Africa, Iran, India and Sri Lanka and the Roman and Byzantine Empires. Through its primary port of Adulis on the Red Sea, Aksum exported gold, emeralds, ivory, musk, myrrh, spices, slaves, ostrich feathers, tortoise shells and rhinoceros horns and imported glass, ceramics, sugar, olive oil, wine, cotton and linen. Aksum kings and merchants used Greek in conducting foreign trade. It minted its own bronze, silver and gold coins with Greek inscriptions that circulated among the nations with whom Aksum traded. Influenced by Christian missions, King Ezana, its most well-known king, adopted Christianity in the early 300s CE and made it the official religion of Aksum. The commercial importance of Aksum along the Red Sea declined after the expansion of Islam into northern Ethiopia in the 700s.

Aktion 14f13, which was also known as "invalid or prisoner euthanasia", was the code name adopted by the Nazis for the murder of those concentration camp prisoners who were determined by a panel of physicians to be physically incapable of working as forced labor in the factories of the German defense industry . The program was organized by

Heinrich Himmler in spring 1941 to ensure that every able-bodied concentration camp prisoner was available to work in the defense industry. This program was designed to relieve concentration camps of what the Nazis termed as "excess ballast", which meant those prisoners who were mentally or physically unable to work. Included within this group were those prisoners who were incurably sick, diseased, crippled, elderly, incapacitated, suffering from war injuries, criminals or any person deemed "asocial". Such prisoners were sent to three centers in Germany where they were killed by carbon monoxide poisoning. Their bodies were cremated in crematorium located at each center. Some historians have estimated that between 15,000 and 20,000 prisoners were killed when this program ended in 1944.

Aktion Reinhard is the code name adopted by the SS for a military operation that sought to annihilate the entire Jewish population in a portion of Poland occupied by Germany. The operation was named "Aktion Reinhard" to honor Reinhard Heydrich, the main architect of the Final Solution, who was assassinated by members of the Czech underground in June 1942. Three death camps were built by the SS to accomplish the mass murder of the Jews: Belzec, Sobibor, and Treblinka. The operation began in mid-March 1942 and ended in November 1943, during which more than two million Jews were killed.

Al Andalus in the Muslim name for the Iberian Peninsula, which encompasses most of modern-day Spain. European Christians called it Andalusia, which means "land of the Visigoths" in Arabic, during the Middle Ages. For almost six hundred years the Iberian Peninsula was a Roman province called Hispania until the Visigoths conquered it in the early 400s CE. A Muslim Berber army from North Africa conquered the Visigoths in the 711 and most of the Iberian Peninsula. The Muslim conquerors made al Andalus a province of the Umayyad Caliphate with Cordoba as its capital. During the 720s the governors of al Andalus launched several attacks into Aquitaine, but were defeated at the Battle of Toulouse. In 732, another al Andalusian attack of Aquitaine was stopped by the Carolingian king Charles Martel at the Battle of Poitiers. In 755 an Umayyad prince, Abd ar Rahman I, escaped from the Abbasids in Damascus and fled to Cordoba. In Cordoba, he assumed the title of emir (commander in Arabic) and declared the Emirate of Cordoba in 756. He and his descendants would successfully govern al Andalus for over 100 years. They transformed Cordoba into the largest (500,000 people) and the richest city in Europe during the Middle Ages. Cordoba was well-known as a center of learning and culture. The emirs of Cordoba built the largest library in Western Europe with 400,000 books, the Great Mosque of Cordoba and paved streets with lighting. Under their rule Muslims, Christians and Jews lived peacefully for over 400 years. In 929, Abd ar Rahman III, the Emir of Cordoba, assumed the title of caliph and declared the creation of the Caliphate of Cordoba. In 1031, the Caliphate of Cordoba collapsed and rulers of small independent regions called "taifas" took power in al Andalus. Over the next 400 years, the northern Christian kingdoms conquered various Muslim armies and brought the Iberian Peninsula under Christian control. The last bastion of Muslim rule, Granada, was defeated in 1492.

Alamogordo is the site in New Mexico where the world's first atomic bomb was successfully exploded by the United States on July 16, 1945. The destructive power of an atomic bomb results from fission. Fission, the splitting of the nucleus of an atom, was first produced in 1938 when Otto Hahn, a German radiochemist, bombarded the nucleus bombarded the nucleus of a Uranium 238 atom producing a chain reaction. Otto Frisch, a German experimental physicist who fled Nazi Germany in the 1930s, gave the process of splitting the nucleus of uranium atom the name "fission".

Alaric I (375–410 CE) was the chief of the Visigoths from 395 to 410. He was responsible for uniting the Visigoths who migrated into to Italy between 400 and 406. Subsequently, he led the Visigoths in sacking Rome in 410, an event that has come to symbolize the fall of the Western Roman Empire.

Albigensians, also known as Cathars, were French advocates of a dualist religion in the 1200s who were viewed as heretics by the Catholic Church. Their name was derived from their association with the city of Albi in southern France where they had the support of the local nobles and secular leaders. They considered the material world evil and renounced wealth and marriage. They advocated a pious and ascetic existence that followed the example set by Jesus and the Apostles. During the 1200s and 1300s, the Catholic Church, relying upon the military support of northern Catholic nobles and the royal army of King Louis VIII, successfully crushed the Albigensians as a popular religious movement in the Languedoc region of southern France.

Albigensian Crusade (1209–1229) was a holy war and political struggle that was initiated by Pope Innocent III against the Cathars, a heretic sect in the Languedoc region of southern France It was the first crusade in Europe. With Jerusalem and the Holy Land under the control of the crusaders by the mid-1100s, Pope Innocent III created a special class of war against enemies of the faith in Europe. For the Catholic Church, Albigensianism represented the most widespread challenge to the authority of the Catholic Church in Europe. Initially the Church sent preachers to the region to convert the Cathars to Catholicism, but they failed to root out the heresy. Even St. Dominic, who had founded the Order of Preachers (Dominicans), was unable to convince the Cathar leaders to convert to Catholicism. Pope Innocent III began the Crusade in 1208 after a papal legate sent to investigate the situation in southern France was murdered. The Crusade was especially popular with the Catholic nobles of northern France because the pope offered them both the opportunity to receive indulgences from the Church and to seize the land of the Cathars. Fearing that religious divisions could lead to civil unrest and hoping to gain control of Languedoc, King Louis VIII joined the Crusade. By 1229, the Cathars were defeated by King Louis IX. The Crusade was a brutal conflict during which the Cathars were massacred and burned at the stake. The Treaty of Meaux-Paris, which ended the conflict, allowed the French monarchy to bring Languedoc under its control. Although the Crusade was successful, Catharism still had broad popular appeal and it would not be completely eliminated in southern France until the end of the 1200s.

Al-Biruni (973–1050 CE) was a Persian Muslim astronomer, mathematician, ethnographer, anthropologist, linguist, historian and geographer. He is considered by many historians to be the most influential Islamic scholar during the Middle Ages. His writings were encyclopedic in scope. His most famous works are *Chronology of Ancient Nations, A History of India, Elements of Astrology and The Mas'undic Canon,* a major work on astronomy in which he discussed the Earth's rotation on its axis and made accurate calculations of latitude and longitude. In *Determination of the Coordinates of Places for the Correction Between Cities*, he defended the useful role of mathematical sciences in understanding the world against attacks by religious scholars and the method for determining longitudes and latitudes on land. Because of his extensive study of the cultures of various nations such as India, he is considered by some scholars to be the "first anthropologist".

Albuquerque, Alfonso da (1453–1515) was a Portuguese sea captain and soldier who created naval bases in the Indian Ocean region to facilitate Portuguese trade

Alchemy was the study of metals in the 1500s and 1600s in Europe which attempted to turn base metals such as lead and iron into precious metals such as silver and gold. Alchemy would become influential in the development of chemistry. Isaac Newton, an English mathematician and physicist who formulated the theory of universal gravitation and contributed to the development of calculus, spent thirty years studying and writing about alchemy.

Alcibiades (450–404 BCE) was an Athenian politician, general and orator who advocated the invasion of Sicily during the Peloponnesian War. He was made co-commander of the invasion, but before the invasion he fled to Sparta after his political enemies in Athens brought charges of sacrilege against him. In Sparta, he served for a number of years as a military adviser, proposing or supervising several campaigns against Athens. But, in Sparta he also made political enemies and he defected to Persia where he also served as a military adviser until his Athenian political allies could facilitate his return, Once again in Athens, her served as a general and played a significant role in a number of Athenian military victories that contributed to Sparta seeking peace with Athens. In terms of military tactics, he was unconventional relying on treachery or negotiation to defeat a city rather than siege. However, he once again made important political enemies in Athens who exiled him for the second time. He fled to Phrygia in northwestern

Asia Minor where the Persian governor had him murdered at the instigation of the Spartans.

Alcuin of York (732–804 CE) was an Anglo-Saxon scholar who was greatly influenced by intellectual revival initiated by Bede, a monk and scholar. He went to Charlemagne's court circa 786 and promoted intellectual reforms in Charlemagne's Empire. He was the Abbot of Tours from 796 to 804.

Aldeias were settlements established by Jesuits in Brazil that offered protection from slavery by the Portuguese to those indigenous peoples who converted to Christianity.

Alemanni (Alamanni or Alamani) was the name used by the Romans for a confederation of Germanic tribes located on the upper Rhine River. The Romans first became aware of the Alemanni when the Romans attacked them in 213. Subsequently, the Alemanni expanded into present-day Alsace and northern Switzerland. They were conquered by the Frankish leader Clovis in 496 and became part of his empire. Today, the French word for Germany is Allemagne, which is derived from their name.

Alesia, Battle of (52 BCE) was a major military conflict fought in Gaul by a confederation of Gallic tribes against and an invading Roman army led by Julius Caesar. Even though the Roman army was outnumbered, Caesar was able to achieve a decisive victory over the Gallic tribes. After this battle, organized resistance to the Roman invasion of Gaul ended and Gaul was made a Roman province. Some historians consider Caesar's victory at Alesia as his greatest military achievement. As result of the Gallic War, Caesar became very rich from the sale of prisoners of war. Even though the Gallic War produced enormous wealth for Rome, the Senate refused to honor Caesar's victory with a public triumphal parade in Rome, an honor typically awarded to a general at the peak of his career. Within two years of this battle, Caesar would cross the Rubicon River in Italy, which precipitated the Roman Civil War of 49–45 BCE.

Alexander I, Tsar (1777–1825) was the autocratic ruler of Russia who early in his reign advocated social political and educational reforms. While believing that Russia needed constitutional reforms

and the reform of serfdom, resistance by the nobles prevented him from initiating such reforms. During the Napoleonic Wars he was, at times, either an ally or an enemy of Napoleon. When the Napoleonic Wars began, he became an ally of Austria and Prussia and fought with them against Napoleon at the Battles of Austerlitz in 1805 and Friedland in 1807. After massive and decisive defeats in both of those battles, Tsar Alexander entered into the Treaty of Tilsit, which forced Russia to become an ally of France against Prussia and Austria. The treaty also required Russia to join Napoleon's Continental System, which created a European trade blockade against Great Britain. When the Tsar realized that joining the Napoleon's Continental System created severe economic problems for Russia, he did not enforce the blockade and began to trade secretly with Great Britain. In 1810, Tsar Alexander withdrew Russia from the Continental System and increased trade with Great Britain. In the wake of Russia's repudiation of one of the central provisions of the Treaty of Tilsit, Napoleon invaded Russia with 600,000 men and occupied and burned Moscow. After Napoleon's retreat from Russia in the fall of 1812, Tsar Alexander joined Prussia, Austria and Sweden and decisively defeated Napoleon's retreating army at the Battle of Leipzig (also known as Battle of the Nations). Between 1813 and 1815, Tsar Alexander played a prominent role in creating the coalition of European nations (Great Britain, Russia, Prussia and Austria) that defeated Napoleon. He also played an important role in the Congress of Vienna, which established a stable and peaceful system of international relations in Europe that would last for the next 100 years.

Alexander II, Tsar (1818–1881) was the Russian emperor who, during his reign from 1855 to 1881, instituted a number of significant social and political reforms to modernize and strengthen Russia. The reforms initiated by Tsar Alexander were the most significant reforms undertaken by any Russian tsar since the reign of Peter the Great. In the wake of Russia's humiliating defeat in the Crimean War by Great Britain and France, Tsar Alexander recognized that Russia was industrially and technologically backward in comparison to other European countries. Since the beginning of serfdom in 1645, Russia had been a feudal agricultural society dominated by a landowning class of nobles and gentry. Proponents of "westernization" among the educated elite believed that abolishing serfdom would be an important step in the modernization of Russia. Encouraged by this growing support for modernization and fearful that serfdom offered the potential for rebellion, Tsar Alexander issued the Emancipation Law in 1861, which freed 22 million serfs. Under the law, the peasants would be able to own the land that they had worked for their landlords and pay for it over 50 years. The law also provided that the government would compensate the landowners for the land they were required to sell to the peasants. However, the landowners kept the best land for themselves and sold poor quality land at inflated prices to the peasants. Since much of the land sold to the peasants was unable to support a family, many peasants continued to work for their former landlords as agricultural workers. Fearful that poor and uneducated freed peasants had the potential for rebellion, the Tsar Alexander created the village commune (mir) system to control the peasants. The village commune was responsible for collecting the mortgage payments and taxes imposed by the government on the peasants and determining how the peasants used their land. Furthermore, the peasants could not leave their land without the permission of the village commune. While the law freed the serfs, the nature of rural life in Russia changed very little. The peasants remained a distinct social class who were poor, uneducated and tied to the land. Tsar Alexander initiated three other important reforms. He created locally-elected district and provincial assembles (zemstvos) that built roads, schools, provided health care and educated the peasantry about new agricultural developments. He also created an independent judiciary based on equality before the law, public jury trials and uniform sentences. Finally, he instituted universal military conscription for all social classes for a period of six years. Despite Tsar Alexander's reforms, Russia remained a society ruled by an autocratic monarch who was supported by a powerful aristocracy. During his reign, he was the target of numerous assassination attempts, one of which succeeded in1881 when a member of People's Will, a revolutionary group, killed him with a bomb.

Alexander III the Great (356–323 BCE) was the King of Macedon (336–33 BCE) after his father, Philip II. He led military campaigns that defeated the Persian Empire and extended Greek influence into Central Asia. He was arguably the most successful military commander in ancient history, conquering most of the then known world before his death. Following the unification of the multiple city-states of ancient Greece under the rule of his father, Philip II of Macedon, Alexander conquered the Persian Empire, including Anatolia, Syria, Phoenicia, Gaza, Egypt, Bactria and Mesopotamia and extended the boundaries of his own empire as far as the Indus Valley (north-west India and modern-day Pakistan). As a result of his conquests, Alexander contributed to the spread Greek culture across the Middle East, founded many Greek-style cities and integrated non-Greeks into his army and administration. He encouraged marriage between Greeks and non-Greeks, and did so himself. After twelve years of constant fighting, Alexander died, possibly of malaria, typhoid or viral encephalitis. His conquests ushered in centuries of Greek settlement and rule over lands he conquered, a period described by historians as the Hellenistic Age. During his lifetime, and especially after his death, his exploits inspired a literary tradition in which he appeared as a legendary hero in the tradition of Achilles.

Alexandria, located Mediterranean coast of northern Egypt, was founded by Alexander. It became the capital of the Hellenistic kingdom of the Ptolemies who ruled Egypt after the death of Alexander. Alexandria became one of the greatest cities of the Hellenistic world, second only to Rome in size and wealth. As it contained a renowned library and museum, Alexandria became a center for leading scientific and literary figures. Its merchants engaged in trade around the Mediterranean and the Indian Ocean. However, upon the founding of Cairo by Egypt's medieval Islamic rulers its status as the country's capital was ended.

Alexius I Comnenus (1057–1118 CE) was the emperor of the Byzantine Empire who wrote Pope Urban II requesting the Pope's assistance in forming an army to defeat the Seljuk Turks who had captured Anatolia. Instead, Pope Urban II used the letter to justify the creation of the First Crusade The pope urged the European Christian nobility at the Council of Clermont in 1095 to raise an army to recapture the Holy Land and Jerusalem from the

Muslims. During his long reign of thirty-seven years from 1081 to 1118, Alexius Comnenus restored the power and prestige of the Byzantine Empire that had been in decline as a result of military defeats. He expanded the central authority of the government, strengthened the financial resources of the Byzantine Empire, built up the military, and expanded the boundaries of the empire into southern Anatolia and the eastern Mediterranean.

Alfred the Great, King (849–899 CE) was king of the southern Anglo-Saxon kingdom of Wessex from 871–899. He organized a successful defense against the Vikings, who sought to conquer England. He united Anglo-Saxon England under his leadership, which contributed to recapturing Viking-controlled territory. Alfred was the first king who considered himself "King of England." A learned man, which was rare among Christian rulers in Europe in the 800s, Alfred encouraged education and improved the kingdom's legal system. He wrote a law code for England and had *Consolation of Philosophy*, the most popular philosophical handbook of the Middle Ages, translated from Latin into Old English.

Algerian War of Independence or Algerian War (1954–1962) was the eight year guerrilla war fought against French colonial rule. Algeria became a French colony in 1834. After World War II, France in its effort to rebuild its colonial empire granted Algerians French citizenship in 1947 and made Algeria an integral part of France, unlike any other French colonial possession. A fledgling nationalist movement for independence and self-determination emerged after World War I, but it was unsuccessful. The movement for independence resurfaced with greater intensity after World War II when France's promises of independence went unfulfilled. With the defeat of France in 1954 in Vietnam by the Viet Minh and its withdrawal of French troops from Vietnam, many Algerians became more determined to wage a guerrilla war of national independence. Such a war erupted in 1954 and was led by the newly-formed National Liberation Front (FLN), an anti-colonial nationalist political party. France sent 50,000 soldiers to Algeria to suppress the rebellion. However, the war became a brutal stalemate in which the FLN used terror tactics in Algerian cities against French soldiers and colonists. And, in turn, French soldiers used torture on the FLN and its civilian supporters. News reports of the brutality of the French army in Algeria changed public opinion in France about the war. The war weakened the ability to govern of the Fourth Republic, which led to its replacement by the Fifth Republic, of which Charles De Gaulle was president. Despite resistance by the French colonists and the French army in Algeria, De Gaulle negotiated an end to the war and Algeria was granted independence in 1962. The conduct of the war by the French soldiers attracted world-wide attention, which was portrayed in the film *The Battle of Algiers*.

Alienation is the psychological belief that some part of one's self is separated from one's own identity, from other people or from meaningful activity. As a result a person exhibits apprehension about life and the future. It is a concept derived from Marxism, which argues that the impersonal nature of modern industrial societies causes the industrial worker to be disconnected or separated from the product of his or her own labor because capitalists extract profit from the objects a worker produces. Anomie, a term developed by Emile Durkheim, a sociologist, is considered to be a synonym.

Alighieri, Dante (1265–1321 CE) was an Italian poet who wrote *The Divine Comedy*, an allegorical narrative that offered a religious and political critique of contemporary society. In *The Divine Comedy*, Dante is guided through Hell and Purgatory, by Virgil the Greek poet who Dante greatly admired. In Heaven, however, Dante's guide was his dead lover Beatrice.

Allende, Salvador (1908–1973) was the socialist politician elected president of Chile in 1970. He supported peasant seizure of foreign owned lands and factories and nationalized Chilean and foreign owned banks and industries. He was overthrown and killed in a military coup in 1973 led by General Augusto Pinochet who was supported by the U.S. government under President Nixon.

All Hallows Eve, which is called Halloween today, was originally the evening before All Saints' Day. Pope Boniface VII had established All Saints' Day in the 600s to replace a pagan holiday with a religious observance. It has its origins as an end-of-summer festival by Celts in Britain and Ireland who believed that the souls of their dead returned to visit their homes. To frighten away the evil spirits such as ghosts and demons thought to be present at that time of the year, the Celts set bonfires and sometimes wore masks and disguises. As the religious observance gained wider acceptance among Christians during the Middle Ages, the evening before All Saints' Day was considered a holy or hallowed eve. While Protestants ended All Hallows Eve as a religious holiday, it continued to be celebrated in Britain as a secular holiday.

Alliance is a bilateral or multilateral agreement entered into by nations to determine the conditions under which each nation will use military force in support of the actions of one nation or all the nations who are party to the agreement.

Alliance for Progress (1961) was established by President Kennedy to facilitate economic development in Latin America. It was supposed to offer an alternative to more radical political solutions to economic development. The limited success of its development programs led to more direct intervention by the U.S. government in the internal affairs of various Latin American countries during the Cold War.

Allied Powers (also known as the Entente Powers) was the name for the coalition of states during World War I who fought against the Central Powers of Germany, Austria-Hungary, Bulgaria and Turkey. The principal Allies were Great Britain, France, Italy, Russia and Japan. The secondary Allies were Belgium, Greece, Serbia, Montenegro and Romania. When the United States entered the war in 1917, it was an "associated power" rather than as a formal ally of Great Britain and France. Although Canada, Australia, New Zealand and India also fought against the Central Powers, they were not considered allies because as territories of the British Empire (formally known as Dominions) they did not have independent foreign policies during World War I.

Allies was the term used for the coalition of states during World War II comprised of the United States, the Soviet Union, Great Britain, and France that fought against Nazi Germany, fascist Italy, and imperial Japan.

All-India Muslim League (1906) was a political organization founded by Muhammad Ali Jinnah in India in 1906 to defend the interests of India's Muslim minority. In 1940, it began demanding a separate state for Indian Muslims, which was to be called Pakistan.

Al Khwarizmi, Muhammad ibn Musa (780–850) was a Persian mathematician who studied Greek and Sanskrit scientific and mathematical manuscripts at the House of Wisdom in Baghdad, which had become a center of trade and scientific studies after the Muslim conquest of Persia. In 830 he wrote *On the Calculation with Hindu Numerals*, which was responsible for disseminating the Hindu system of numerals (1, 2, 3, 4 etc.) in Europe in the 1100s and which we now call Arabic numerals. The term algorithm, also an Arabic word, is derived from his use of Hindu numerals in making arithmetical calculations. Because his book *The Compendious Book on Calculation* by Completion and Balancing (830) offered the first systematic mathematical calculations to solve linear and quadratic equations, he is considered to be the inventor of algebra, another Arabic word. He also developed a decimal system and introduced the concept of zero. His advances in mathematics would be later be applied to solve problems in physics, astronomy and geography.

Almohads (1170–1269) was the name of a Berber family from Morocco that established a dynasty that ruled Spain from its capital in Seville. They had ousted the Almoravid rulers from North Africa and Spain. The Almohads promoted a puritanical and fundamentalist version of Islam. After their defeat of the Almoravids, they initially oppressed Spanish Jews and Christians who took refuge in Christian Portugal, Aragon and Castille. In 1195, the Almohads defeated King Alfronso VIII of Castile, temporarily halting the Christian reconquest of Spain. Subsequently a Christian coalition from Leon/Castille, Navarra and Aragon defeated the Almohads at the Battle of las Navas de Tolosa. As a result of this defeat, the Almohads were forced to return to Morocco, where they would rule until 1269.

Al-Qaeda is a terrorist organization founded in the late 1980s by Osama bin Laden and former mujahedin who had fought against the Soviet Union in Afghanistan. It was responsible for terrorist attacks on the United States embassies in Kenya and Tanzania in 1998, the U.SS. Cole, an American destroyer in Yemen in 2000, the World Trade Center and the Pentagon in the United States on September 11, 2001. It has also claimed responsibility for other terrorist attacks in Europe, Africa, the Middle East and Southeast Asia. Osama bin Laden was killed by U.S. military forces in Pakistan in 2011.

Amarna Letters refers to a large collection of cuneiform tablets that were discovered in Egypt in 1887. These tablets contain the imperial and diplomatic letters of the pharaohs from the mid-14th century BCE.

Amarna Period is a term used by historians for the period in Egyptian history, during the New Kingdom, when the pharaoh Akhenaten built a new capitol at Amarna, seized power from the temple priests, and replaced the god Amon-re with Aten. After Akhenaten's death, the Amon-Re religious cult regained its position of prominence in Egyptian society.

Ambrose of Milan, Saint (337/340–397 CE) was the Bishop of Milan from 374 to 397. Together with Augustine of Hippo, Jerome and Pope Gregory I, he is considered to be one of the "fathers" of the Catholic Church, who developed the central ideas upon which the Christian Church was built. He claimed that secular rulers were part of the Church and subject to the sacred authority of bishops and other Church leaders. Ambrose also articulated important religious arguments concerning the spiritual superiority of celibacy to marriage. Ambrose was a Roman citizen into a Christian family. He studied literature, law and rhetoric in Rome. Since he had an excellent knowledge of Greek, which was then rare in the Roman Empire, Ambrose studied the Bible and Greek authors. In 372 he was made a consular prefect in Milan, which was then considered to be the second capital in Italy. Because Ambrose was an excellent administrator, he became very popular among the populace. At the time, the diocese of Milan was deeply divided between Trinitarians and Arians. In 374, when the bishop of Milan died, those two opposing religious factions struggled for the position of bishop. While addressing Church followers who had gathered to elect the new bishop, the crowd spontaneously elected Ambrose bishop of Milan. Although he initially refused the position of bishop because he had no theological training, he accepted the position only after the intervention by the Roman Emperor. Impressed by his sermons, Augustine of Hippo, who had thought poorly of Christian preachers, began to agree with Ambrose's theological thinking. As a result of his acceptance of Ambrose's religious views, Augustine became the spiritual successor to Ambrose. While Ambrose generally supported the Roman emperors, he defied imperial authority by excommunicating Emperor Theodosius in 390 because of a massacre in Thessalonica.

American Century is a term used by Henry Luce, the publisher of *Time Magazine,* in a 1938 editorial to describe the 1900s. In that editorial, Luce advocated the entrance of the United States into World War II in order to defend democratic values. He urged the United States to reject isolationism and to spread democracy throughout the world. Today, this phrase usually represents U.S. military and economic dominance of the world during much of the 1900s beginning with the Spanish-American War and continuing during World War I, World War II and the Cold War, when the U.S. emerged as one of the world's two superpowers.

American Cultural Imperialism is a phrase that arose in the 1900s that reflected the fear among Europeans and other peoples of the world that power of American corporations, methods of production, organization, marketing and mass communication, such as films, television and music would negatively influence and perhaps even dominate the societies and cultures of other nations throughout the world.

American Dream is a national belief that freedom and equality in the United States includes the opportunity for prosperity and success and upward social mobility through diligence and hard work. According to this belief, the United States, historically, has been a place that encouraged social and economic progress in which ability and merit were more important than a person's social class, caste, religion, race or ethnicity. Unhampered by the barriers imposed by a hierarchical or aristocratic society, the United States had no predetermined ceiling for individual aspirations. The idea of an "American Dream" was popularized by James Truslow Adams in his 1931 book *Epic of America.*

American Empire and **American Imperialism** are terms used by some historians to describe the unrivaled global political, economic, military, and cultural influence of the United States since the end of the Cold War. However, some historians argue that the westward expansion of the United States in the 1800s was the beginning of the American Empire and that subsequent overseas economic expansion and foreign military interventions are part of that legacy.

American Exceptionalism is an ethnocentric worldview first articulated by Alexis de Tocqueville in 1831, which expressed belief held by many Americans that the United States differs from all other nations in the world. He contended that the American people believe that the United States holds a special place in world history because of its historical origins and distinctive political institutions. He further argued that Americans believe that the United States is morally superior to all other nations because it offers opportunity and hope for humanity based on the ideals of personal and economic freedom.

American Expeditionary Force (AEF) was the name of the U.S. military force that was sent to Europe beginning in 1918 during World War I in support of the British and French troops. The AEF was commanded by General John J. Pershing, who insisted that American military forces would not be used merely as replacements for French and British soldiers, but that the American military force be under separate command. Pershing wanted an American force that could operate independently of the other Allies. Eventually over one million American troops would be sent to Europe, of whom approximately 350,000 were African-Americans. The American troops were called "Doughboys" by other Allied troops. The AEF sustained about 360,000 casualties, including 116,000 dead—some 50,000 of them were killed in action or died of wounds—and 234,000 wounded.

Amerindian is the name used by historians to refer to the aboriginal peoples of the Americas.

Americanization is a term used by historians and anthropologists to describe the process by which American values, customs, practices popular culture, products behavior and ideas are spread through the means of mass communication.

Amun-Re, which means "hidden", was considered by Egyptian pharaohs to be the most power god of the pantheon of Egyptian gods. Ancient Egyptians believed that Amun-Re was responsible for the defeat of the Hyksos. As a polytheistic society, Egyptians worshipped many gods, the most powerful of which was Amun, the sky god who created the universe. They also believed that Re, the sun god, brought life to the land of Egypt and its people and controlled the sky, earth and the underworld. During the early New Kingdom, the pharaohs, who considered the two gods to be similar, combined them into one all-powerful god.

Amorites were a Semitic-speaking people who may have emigrated from Arabia into Mesopotamia, Syria, and Palestine. They dominated Mesopotamia, Syria, and Palestine between 2000 and 1600 BCE. During this period, virtually all of the local kings, including Hammurabi, were Amorites. They worshipped Amurru. Between 1600 and 100 BCE, the language of the Amorites disappeared from Babylonia, but became dominant in Syria and Palestine.

Amphora was a clay jar used by ancient Greeks and Romans to store and transport grain, wine, olive oil. It had handles on either side of its neck and a pointed bottom.

Amritsar Massacre (1919) was the killing of over 400 and the wounding of over 1,000 unarmed men, women, and children by British troops in the Indian city of Amritsar. Fearing a mass uprising and desiring to repress growing nationalist dissent and political activism, British troops were ordered to fire without warning on an unarmed civilian crowd who held an unauthorized political demonstration. This event heightened opposition to British imperial rule, especially when the officer in command of the firing on the Indian civilians was greeted as a hero in England. In the wake of the barbarity of this event, many Indians who considered themselves pro-British began to advocate independence and self-determination.

Amulet is any object intended to bring good luck or protection from trouble to its owner. They have been found frequently in archaeological excavations in Mesopotamia and Egypt. An amulet reflects a religious belief in supernatural powers that was common among the peoples of many ancient civilizations. An amulet could include: gems or simple stones, statues, coins, drawings, pendants, rings, plants, animals, and even words said on certain occasions to repel evil or bad luck.

Amur River is located between north China and eastern Russia. It was fought over by both nations until the Treaty of Nerchinsk of 1689 reached a settlement.

Anabaptism, which means to rebaptize or second baptism, is the ideology of those Protestant radicals in the 1500s that rejected infant baptism in favor of adult baptism. This ideology considered the Bible as a blueprint for reforming the Christian Church and European society and rejected the authority of the state. Anabaptism stressed the need for its followers to live in self-governing "holy communities".

Anabaptist was a sect of Christians who objected to the practice of infant baptisms. They claimed that infant baptisms were not valid because an infant was not capable of truly having faith and knowingly accepting baptism. While their opponents gave Anabaptists their name "rebaptizers", Anabaptists referred to themselves as brethren, believers and Christians. They believed that the Bible should be taken literally, that a second baptism should occur in adulthood and that the Second Coming of Christ was imminent. Today the descendants of the Anabaptists are the Amish and the Mennonites.

Anarchical State System is a term used in international relations to describe an international system made up of sovereign nation-states that lacks a legitimate international governmental authority to make and enforce legal norms.

Anarchism is the influential social and political ideology that emerged in Europe between the mid-1800s and early 1900s that viewed the state and existing political systems as repressive and unnecessary for acquiring social and political liberty. Rejecting all forms of government, laws, political parties, unions and other forms of mass organization, proponents of anarchism advocated the destruction of the state by the use of violence. Anarchists advocated the formation of small-scale, self-governing democratic communities based on voluntary cooperation. Mikhail Bakunin, a political writer and prominent Russian revolutionary, was the leading proponent of anarchism in Europe in the mid-1800s.

Anatolia is the ancient name for what comprises most of modern Turkey. Anatolia is a Greek word for "land of the sunrise," or the East. Because of its strategic geographic location between Europe and Asia, it has been an intersection between peoples, cultures, and civilizations since prehistoric times.

Anaximander (610–546 BCE) was a pre-Socratic Greek philosopher who lived in Miletus in Ionia who wrote about astronomy, geography and the nature of things. He studied with Thales. While little is known about his life and work, he is considered to be the first philosopher to have written down his studies. He was an early advocate for scientific thinking. He tried to observe and explain different aspects of the universe, with a particular interest in its origins. He claimed that nature is ruled by laws, just like human societies, and anything that disturbs the balance of nature does not last long. He set up a shadow-casting rod at Sparta and used it to demonstrate the equinoxes and solstices and perhaps the hours of the day. He drew a map of the known world, which was later corrected by Hecataeus and he may also have built a celestial globe. Anaximander developed an evolutionary perspective concerning living things. He argued that the first creatures originated from a moist element produced by evaporation. He also argued that humans originated from some other kind of animal, such as fish. Anaximander is significant because he tried to give a unified and rational explanation for all of nature.

Anaximenes of Miletus (585–528 BCE) was a pre-Socratic Greek philosopher from Miletus. He argued that the basic building block of all matter was *aer* (mist, vapor, air.) Thales had argued that water was basic building block of all matter. His thinking as well as that of Thales and Anaximander represents the slow and incremental transition from mythology and gods to science and rationality as explanations for natural phenomena.

Ancien Regime (Old Order) is the term used by historians to describe the pattern of social, political, economic, and cultural relations and institutions dominated by the monarchy, the clergy, and the nobility that existed in France for centuries before the French Revolution.

Angevin Empire is a term used by historians to describe the lands of Henry II of England in the 1100s. Those lands consisted of the Kingdom of England and duchies or counties of Normandy, Anjou, Poitou, Maine, Gascony, Touraine, Béarn, Toulose, Brittany and Aquitaine in France along with Wales, Scotland and Ireland. While Henry did not establish any imperial institutions to govern the lands he owned, he did create a union of his disparate territories with himself at the center of a network of kinship ties and feudal obligations. The height of the Angevin Empire was during the reign of Richard I of England ("Richard the Lionheart"), who was captured and ransomed during the Third Crusade to capture Jerusalem. King Philip II of France took the opportunity of Richard's absence to encourage rebellion among the vassals of Richard and to pursue his claims to the lands in France claimed by Richard. Upon his release from captivity, Richard spent the remainder of his reign attempting to regain the territory he had lost to France under Philip II. The end of the Angevin Empire occurred when King John, the younger brother of Richard, was unable to prevent Philip II from capturing virtually all of the land in France once controlled by Henry II.

Anglicanism is the name for the theology adopted by a branch of Christians in England during the Protestant Reformation, which claimed that it represented a middle path between Protestantism and Catholicism. It provided the ideological basis for the formation of the Church of England, which became the official church of England during the reign of Elizabeth I ((1558–1603).

Anglo-Saxon England refers to the period of English history after the invasion by the Angles and Saxons which began in the 440 and end with the Norman Conquest in 1066

Anglo-Afghan Wars (1839–1842, 1878–1880, and 1919) were three armed conflicts between Britain and Afghanistan in which Britain tried to expand its influence into Afghanistan in order to protect British rule in India. As Russia tried to expand its influence into South and Central Asia during the early 1800s, Britain feared that growing political instability in Afghanistan might cause Russia to invade the country. Since Afghanistan's ruler was unwilling to negotiate an alliance with Britain, Britain invaded Afghanistan to put in place a pro-British ruler, who was opposed by the Afghan tribes. Unable to decisively defeat resistance by Afghan tribes to the British occupation, the British withdrew their forces. Both critics in Britain and participants in the war viewed it as a disaster. By the 1870s, Britain was once again concerned about the growing influence of Russia in Afghanistan. In response to this development Britain decided to send a diplomatic mission to Afghanistan, but it was prevented from entering Afghanistan by Afghan soldiers. The Second Anglo-Afghan War began in November 1878, when British troops invaded the Afghanistan. The British force readily defeated the Afghans and forced the ruler of Afghanistan to sign the Treaty of Gandamak, which permitted Britain to establish a permanent embassy in Afghanistan and ensured British control of the foreign policy of Afghanistan. While Britain never made Afghanistan a colony, the British ensured that Afghanistan would conduct its affairs as a tributary state. After almost 40 years of peace between Britain and Afghanistan, the Third Anglo-Afghan War, which lasted only one month, began in May 1919 when a new ruler of Afghanistan declared independence from Britain. Although this brief war was inconclusive, Afghanistan, as part of an armistice between the two countries, gained the right to conduct its own foreign policy.

Animism is the religious belief based on the worship of nature, which is supposedly alive with spirits, gods and human ancestors. It imputes supernatural spirits to natural forces and objects and contends that inanimate objects and natural phenomena have souls and can influence human events. Animism was prevalent among the ancient Mesopotamian religions.

Annam, which means "pacified south", is the name used for one thousand years by successive dynasties of the Chinese Empire for the area known today as northern Vietnam After driving out the Chinese in 938 CE, the area was renamed Dai Co Viet. In the early 1800s, it was renamed Vietnam, However, when the French conquered

Vietnam in the late 1800s, they divided Vietnam into three areas: Tonkin (North Vietnam), Annam (Central Vietnam) and Cochin China (South Vietnam).

Anschluss is the German word for "union" or "connection", which was used to describe the annexation of Austria by Nazi Germany in March 1938.

Antarctic Treaty (1959) is a multilateral arms control treaty that demilitarizes Antarctica, requires that the Antarctic environment will be protected, and that Antarctica will be used exclusively for peaceful and scientific purposes. It is one of the first multilateral treaties concerning the environment. The treaty specifically prohibits the use of Antarctica for any military purpose such as the establishment of military bases, the testing of any type of weapon including nuclear weapons, the use of Antarctica for military maneuvers, the stationing of nuclear weapons, and the disposal of nuclear waste materials.

Anthony, Saint (251–356 CE) was a Christian from Alexandria who led an ascetic life as a hermit in the Egyptian desert. His conduct inspired many Christians to follow an ascetic life and became the basis for the ideals of upon which monasticism was built.

Anthropoids are one of the two major groupings of primates, which includes monkeys, apes, and humans.

Anthropomorphism means the attribution to a god, gods, or any other supernatural force of the appearance, nature and characteristics of human beings.

Antiballistic Missile (ABM) Treaty (1972) is a bilateral arms control treaty entered into by the United States and the Soviet Union that prohibits each nation from developing, testing, or deploying a ballistic missile defense system in either the United States or the Soviet Union, except for two sites in each country. In negotiating this treaty, both the United States and the Soviet Union recognized that a ballistic missile defense system would undermine the nuclear strategy for mutual assured destruction and nuclear deterrence.

Anticlericalism is the belief that emerged in Europe in the Middle Ages among some laypeople that the involvement of Catholic clergymen in all aspects of their everyday social and political lives was harmful and should be restrained. These laypeople stressed that the clergy had become corrupt. They claimed that some clergy were behaving immorally by drinking, gambling, dressing in fancy clothes and ignoring their vowel of celibacy, that some clergy were illiterate and simply mumbled the Latin words during Mass and that some clergy held more than one Church office at a time.

Anti-Comintern Pact (1936–1937) was an anti-Communist agreement concluded between Nazi Germany and Japan and then between fascist Italy, Germany, and Japan that was directed against the Soviet Union. It provided that in the event of an attack by the Soviet Union against Nazi Germany, Germany and Japan would agreed to protect their respective common interests. They also agreed that neither of them would enter into any treaties with the Soviet Union. Germany also agreed to recognize the Manchukuo, a puppet state created in Manchuria in 1932 by Japan.

Anti-Corn Law League was an organization formed in England in the early 1800s to repeal the Corns Laws, which protected farmers and landowners. In order to keep the price of bread high, Parliament had established high tariffs on imported grain. Rejecting the protectionism of the Corn Laws, the League advocated free trade.

Antigonids was the name of a dynasty of Macedonian kings founded in 276 BCE by Antigonus Gonatus, the grandson of Antigonus the One-Eyed, one of the generals of Alexander the Great. The Antigonids ruled mostly over Asia Minor and northern Syria. They would rule the Balkans until conquered by the Romans in the 100s CE. The Antigonid Empire was one of three empires created after Alexander's death by his generals, the others being the Seleucid Empire and Ptolemaic Empire. The Antigonid Dynasty ended with the Roman domination of the Macedon beginning in 168 BCE.

Antikythera Mechanism (150–100 BCE) is an ancient mechanical calculator designed to calculate astronomical positions that was discovered in a shipwreck near the Greek island of Antikythera in

1901. The mechanism is the oldest known complex scientific calculator. It contains many gears, and is considered by some scholars as the first analog computer. It appears to be constructed upon theories of astronomy and mathematics developed by Greek astronomers. Technology of similar complexity would not appear for a thousand years.

Anti-Judaism is terms used by historians to express opposition to the religion of Judaism and to Jews as adherents of that religion by individuals who accept a competing system of religious beliefs and practices. Those individuals consider Judaic beliefs and practices as inferior. Anti-Judaism is based on religious beliefs and practices and is distinguished from anti-Semitism, which is based upon racial or ethnic prejudice.

Antioch was one of the cities founded by Seleucus, a general of Alexander the Great, which was located near the present-day Turkish-Syrian border. It became one of the wealthiest and most luxurious cities of all the ancient eastern Mediterranean cities.

Antiochus IV Epiphanes (215–164 BCE) was the Seleucid king of Syria who reigned from 175 to 164 BCE. As a strong advocate for Greek culture and institutions, his attempts to suppress Judaism brought on the war with the Maccabees.

Anti-Pope was the name given by the Catholic Church to any person who challenged the authority and legitimacy of the officially elected pope located in Rome. During the 11th and 12th centuries, numerous anti-popes emerged as a result of the struggles for political dominance in Europe between the Roman Catholic Church and the Holy Roman Empire. The earliest anti-pope was Natalius, circa 200. During the Great Schism (1378–1417), there were initially two and then later three rival popes, each supported by a faction of cardinals.

Anti-Semitism is an ideology that expresses virulent hatred of, hostility toward, persecution of and discrimination against Jews. The term was originated in 1879 by Wilhelm Marr, a German writer. Anti-Semitism became especially powerful, both officially and unofficially, across Europe in the late 1800s, particularly during the Dreyfus Affair in France. Proponents of anti-Semitism, such as the Nazis, claimed that Jews were a separate race who were biologically inferior and should be eliminated and that the Jews were engaged in a global conspiracy to control the world. Anti-Semitism was influenced by the development of scientific racism and the emergence of ultranationalist and racist political movements in Europe in the late 1800s.

Antonine Age is the term used by historians to refer to the almost one hundred years of political stability in the Roman Empire that was established by Emperor Nerva and subsequently, by his adopted son and heir, Emperor Trajan.

Antonine Decree (212 CE) was law passed by Emperor Aurelius Antoninus (also known as Caracalla), that granted citizenship to all free inhabitants of the Roman Empire. As a result of this law, Roman law applied throughout the Roman Empire.

Antonine Plague is the name for the outbreak of what many historians consider to be smallpox throughout the Roman Empire during the reign of Marcus Aurelius (161–180). However, the specific cause for this pandemic remains undetermined. It is suspected that the disease was brought to Rome by Roman soldiers who were returning from military campaigns in the Middle East. The disease spread as far as Gaul and Britain in the west, Persia and Egypt in the east wiping out whole towns and villages. The disease also infected the Roman legions along the Rhine, which hampered their ability to adequately defend against the advances of the Germanic tribes along the borders of the Roman Empire. The Greek physician Galen describes the symptoms of the epidemic in his writings around 166. It is claimed by some historians that the disease may have killed Emperor Lucius Verus in 169. According to the Roman historian Cassius Dio, at its height the disease may have killed up to 25% of the population of Rome. Some historians have estimated that the disease killed about five million people throughout the Roman Empire, decimated the Roman army, weakened trade, decreased agricultural production and devastated the whole economy of the Roman Empire. Some historians consider other outbreaks of smallpox epidemics to have also occurred during the reigns of Emperor Decius (249–251), Emperor Gallus (251–253) and Emperor Claudius Gothicus (268–270), who supposedly died from the disease.

Antony, Mark (83–30 BCE) was a Roman aristocratic who fought under Julius Caesar in Gaul and supported Caesar when he became dictator of Rome. Antony was appointed consul by the Senate in 44 BCE, but opposed the rise to power of Octavian. He was a member of the Second Triumvirate along with Octavian and Lepidus that was formed in 43 BCE. As part of the Second Triumvirate, he ruled the eastern part of the Roman Empire, which included Egypt, where he had a love affair with Queen Cleopatra VII. As a result of his growing political struggle with Octavian, he was defeated at the Battle of Actium in 31 BCE after which he committed suicide in Egypt.

Anubis was the ancient Egyptian god of the dead who guided humans into the afterlife. Since he was also associated with mummification, he was also the patron god of the embalmers. He was widely-revered during the First Dynastic Period (3100–2890 BCE) and Old Kingdom ((2575–2130 BCE). During the Middle Kingdom (1938–1630–1650), he was replaced by Osiris who became ruler of the underworld. Anubis was portrayed as a jackal or as a human with a black jackal head. Anubis was also portrayed in the *Book of the Dead* as assisting in the religious ritual known as the "weighing of the heart", which determined whether a deceased person was worthy to enter the realm of the dead.

Apartheid (1948) was the policy of systematic racial segregation and discrimination, which was instituted by the Afrikaner-dominated South African government in 1948. This policy made lawful political, legal and economic discrimination against non-whites. Under apartheid, South Africans were divided into four groups according to ethnicity: white, Bantu (black Africans), colored (those of mixed descent), and Asian. As a result of this policy the black majority population of South Africa was maintained in a position of political, social, and economic subordination for nearly 50 years. President DeKlerk of South Africa began the process of ending apartheid in 1993 when he released Nelson Mandela, the leader of the anti-apartheid movement in South Africa, from prison. Apartheid was officially ended in 1994 when the African National Congress came to power.

Apocalypticism was a worldview held by many ancient Jews and Christians that maintained that the world was controlled by evil forces that God would destroy at the end of time when God would intervene in history. It claimed that important matters were hidden from view and they would soon be revealed in a major confrontation of earth-shaking magnitude that would change the course of history. According to Christians, the Apocalypse would also involve the second coming of Christ.

Apollo-Soyuz (1975) was the name for the first manned space flight conducted jointly by the United States and the Soviet Union during the era of détente. On July 17, 1975, the U.S. *Apollo* spacecraft and Soviet *Soyuz* spacecraft docked for two days of joint operations.

Apollonius of Rhodes (circa 295 BCE) was a Hellenistic Egyptian scholar and poet. He was the director of the Library of Alexandria. He is best known for his epic poem the *Argonautica*, which told the mythological story of Jason and the Argonauts' quest for the Golden Fleece.

Apollonius of Tyana was a wandering ascetic Greek philosopher and religious figure who became a mythic figure during the Roman Empire in the first century CE. He allegedly could perform miracles and deliver divinely inspired teachings. As a Pythagorean, he opposed animal sacrifice, lived fugally, and followed a vegetarian diet. He spent most of his life in the cities of Asia Minor (Turkey). His followers worshipped him and believed that he was the "son of God" and that Jesus was a fraud. His followers erected many shrines to honor him. Most of what we know about him is derived from a book titled *The Life of Apollonius*, which was written by Philostratus. Even though this book is considered a work of fiction by many scholars today, many pagans in the Roman Empire believed what was said in this book.

Apologetics is the intellectual defense of the truth of the Christian religion. Apologetists traditionally offered an argument for Christianity and a criticism of opposing religious beliefs. It sought both to strengthen the Christian believer against personal doubts and remove any skepticism that might inhibit the conversion of unbelievers to a religion based on faith. In the early Christian Church, the leading apologists were Justin Martyr, Tertullian, Origen, and Augustine. In the 1200s, the most influential apologist was Thomas Aquinas who developed an influential defense of belief in God. During the Protestant Reformation apologetics was substantially replaced by polemics, in which many Christian churches sought to defend their particular beliefs rather than Christianity as a whole.

Apostate is a person who appears to conform to the principles and rituals of a dominant religion, such as Christianity, but, in fact, practices the principles and rituals of another religion or philosophy. The Roman Emperor Julian, who reigned from 361 to 363 CE and was baptized and raised as a Christian, publicly announced his conversion to paganism in 361, even though Christianity had become the most influential religion in the Roman Empire. As a result of his conversion he became known as Julian the Apostate.

Apostle, which means "one who is sent" in Greek, was a follower of Jesus who was supposed to became a missionary for Christianity after the death of Jesus. The term is also used to refer to any of the twelve disciples chosen by Jesus (Peter, James, John, Andrew, Philip, Bartholomew, Matthew, Thomas, James, Thaddaeus, Simon and Judas). Paul, who converted to Christianity after the death of Jesus, also claimed to be an apostle.

Apostolic Poverty was the Christian belief that emerged in Europe in the 1200s by mendicant religious orders such as the Waldensians and Franciscans who repudiated ownership of land or the accumulation of wealth. They followed the monasticism of Saint Francis of Assisi and argued that virtuous Christians should live like the poor just as Jesus and his disciples had done. While this doctrine challenged the power, wealth and influence of the Church, the idea of apostolic poverty was widely accepted by the poor in Europe between the 1100s and 1300s. The Church condemned this doctrine as heresy in 1323.

Apostolic Primacy is the Christian doctrine that all popes are the direct successors to the Apostle Peter and are the head of the Catholic Church.

Apostolic Succession is the Christian doctrine that Christian bishops trace their authority back to the apostles of Jesus. This principle claims that the powers given by Jesus to his apostles have been transmitted from bishop to bishop through the process of ordination.

Appeasement was the policy of negotiating political concessions with Nazi Germany rather than engaging in a direct military confrontation. This policy was adopted by the British and the French in the 1920s and 1930s. They hoped to avoid the devastation of another world war with Germany. In the wake of Hitler's annexation of Austria in 1938, the British and the French hoped that this approach would maintain peace and stability in Europe in the face of increasing German aggression. This approach culminated in the British policy employed by Prime Minister Neville Chamberlain at the Munich Conference in 1938. In response to the demands by Nazi Germany, he agreed to the territorial expansion of Germany into the Sudetenland, which was then part of Czechoslovakia. Rather than maintaining peace in Europe, this policy permitted Hitler to militarize the Sudetenland and eventually occupy all of Czechoslovakia.

Appian Way was the road built by Rome in 312 BCE. It was named for Appius Claudius Caecus, who first proposed its construction. Originally, it ran from Rome to Capua, a distance of 132 miles. About 244 BCE, it was extended an additional 234 miles to Brundisim, a town located on the southern Adriatic coast of Italy.

Apprenticeship refers to the process used by the guilds in Europe to train young men in a particular trade or art under the supervision of master tradesmen, craftsmen, or artist. Typically, an apprentice was unpaid and they were expected, while learning their trade, to act as servants to their master, with whom they lived.

April Theses (1917) was the radical political program developed by Vladimir Lenin during the Russian Revolution of 1917 after his return from exile in Switzerland. His program called for Soviet control of state power. During the February Revolution two different political bodies had replaced the imperial government which had collapsed with the abdication of Tsar Nicholas II—the Provisional Government and the Petrograd Soviet of Workers' and Soldiers' Deputies. The Socialists who dominated the Petrograd Soviet interpreted the February Revolution as a bourgeois revolution and considered it appropriate for the bourgeoisie to hold power. They therefore submitted to the rule of the Provisional Government, formed by liberals from the Duma who wanted to continue Russia's involvement in World War I. The Petrograd Soviet agreed to cooperate with the government and to advise it in the interests of workers and soldiers. Lenin, however, viewed the two bodies as institutions representing social classes locked in the class struggle. He felt that, as one class gained dominance over the other, its governing body would crush the rival institution; thus the two could not indefinitely coexist. On the basis of this interpretation he developed his theses, in which he urged the Bolsheviks to withdraw their support from the Provisional Government and to call for immediate withdrawal from World War I and for the distribution of land among the peasantry. The Bolshevik Party was to organize workers, soldiers, and peasants and to strengthen the Soviets so that they could eventually seize power from the Provisional Government. The April Theses also called for the nationalization of banks and for Soviet control of the production and distribution of manufactured goods. Lenin first presented his April Theses to a gathering of Social Democrats and later (April 17, 1917) to a Bolshevik committee, both of which immediately rejected them. The Bolshevik newspaper *Pravda* published them, but stated that they were Lenin's personal ideas. The April Theses became very popular with the workers and soldiers of the Petrograd Soviet, who tried to force the Petrograd Soviet to take power in July 1917. The April Theses provided much of the ideological groundwork that later led to the October Revolution and it would be the basis for Leninism.

Aqueduct is an artificial channel that is constructed to convey water from one location to another. Aqueducts were typically built above the landscape resembling bridges rather than rivers. Powered entirely by gravity, aqueducts transported very large amounts of water very efficiently. The aqueduct of Pont du Gard in Provence, France carried nearly 6 million gallons a day and the Roman aqueducts combined carried over 300 million gallons a day. Although generally associated with the Romans, aqueducts were devised centuries earlier in the Middle East, where peoples such as the Babylonians and Egyptians built sophisticated irrigation systems. Roman-style aqueducts were used

as early as the 7th century BCE, when the Assyrians built a 50 mile long limestone aqueduct to carry water across a valley to their capital city, Nineveh. The Romans constructed numerous aqueducts to supply water to cities. The city of Rome had the largest concentration, with water being supplied by eleven aqueducts constructed over a period of 500 years. Their combined length was nearly 260 miles. However, only 29 miles were above ground, as most Roman aqueducts were constructed below the surface. This method of conveyance helped to keep the water free from disease (the carcasses of animals would not be able to get into the aqueduct) and helped protect Rome from enemy attack. The longest Roman aqueduct, 87 miles in length, was built in the 100s CE to supply Carthage. Roman aqueducts were extremely sophisticated constructions. They were built to remarkably fine tolerances and of a technological sophistication that was not to be equaled for over 1000 years after the fall of the Roman Empire. Much of the expertise of the Roman engineers was lost during the Middle Ages.

Aquinas, Saint Thomas (1225–1274 CE) was an Italian Dominican friar, theologian, and scholastic philosopher who wrote the *Summa theologica* and the *Summa contra gentiles*. He encouraged the study of ancient philosophy and science as a complement to theology. Aquinas argued that by the use of reason it was possible to attain a greater understanding of the natural order, moral law and the nature of God. He distinguished between natural truth, which a person could know by reasoning, and revealed truths, which could only be known through faith in God's revelation.

Aquitaine was a section of southeastern Gaul between the Pyrenees Mountains and the Garonne River conquered by Julius Caesar. Emperor Augustus made it an administrative district in the Roman Empire. By the 400s CE, it was conquered by the Visigoths, who were subsequently conquered by the Franks in 507. After Charles Martel drove the Moors out of Aquitaine, it became part of the Carolingian Empire. In 1137, Eleanor of Aquitaine united Aquitaine with France by marrying the French King Louis VII. After he divorced her, she married Henry Plantagenet in 1152, who became the King Henry II of England in 1554. Aquitaine then became part of his realm and he subsequently gave it to his son Richard I (Richard the Lion-hearted). It would remain one of the possessions of the English monarchs in France until the end of the Hundred Years War, when it was reunited with France.

Arable land is fertile ground that can be easily cultivated to produce crops and raise livestock.

Aramaic is a Semitic language originally spoken by the Aramaeans who settled in modern day Syria, Iraq and eastern Turkey between the 12th and 11th centuries BCE. It is closely related to Hebrew and was written in a script derived from the Phoenician alphabet rather than cuneiform. Over the centuries it was used by the Assyrians and became the language of commerce among Babylonian merchants. Between 559 and 330 BCE during the reign of the Achaemenid Dynasty in Persia, it became the official language of the Persian Empire. Aramaic would be replaced by Greek as the official language of the Persian Empire after the conquest of Alexander the Great. Around the 6th century BCE, Aramaic replaced Hebrew as the spoken language among the lower class Jews while Hebrew remained the language of the Jewish religion, the government of Palestine and upper class Jews. It is believed that Jesus and his Apostles spoke Aramaic. It was the language in which certain portions of the Old Testament as well as the Babylonian Talmud were originally written. Armaic was supplanted by Arabic as the dominant language of the ancient Middle East circa 650 CE.

Arab-Israeli Wars (1948–1982) were a series of five wars between Israel and Egypt, Jordan, Lebanon and Syria after the creation of the state of Israel in 1948. The first war, from 1948 to 1949, began after Britain announced in 1947 that it was withdrawing from Palestine in 1948. Britain had governed Palestine as a mandate territory under the authority of the League of Nations since 1919. In the hopes of avoiding a civil war in Palestine between Arabs and Jews, the United Nations General Assembly passed a resolution calling for the partition of Palestine two separate states (one Arab and one Jewish), which was rejected by the Arab states. Nevertheless, Jewish leaders proclaimed the creation of an independent state of Israel. On May 14, 1948, the day the British mandate ended, the surrounding Arab states of Egypt, Jordan, Lebanon and Syria attacked Israel in support of the Palestinian Arabs, but were decisively defeated by a better

trained and more determined Israeli army. As a result of their victory, the Israelis actually gained more territory than they would have received under the UN partition plan. The second war began in 1956 after Egypt nationalized the British-owned Suez Canal Company, which was viewed by Egypt as a symbol of Western imperialism. In response, the British, the French and the Israelis invaded Egypt. While the French and British air forces attacked Egyptian airfields, the Israelis invaded the Sinai Peninsula which bordered the Suez Canal. The United States, which condemned the attack on Egypt, forced the British, French and Israelis in 1957 to withdraw their military forces. The third Arab-Israeli war began in June 1967 when Egypt and Syria massed their military forces on the Israeli border to invade Israel. In response, Israel launched a surprise attack that destroyed the Egyptian, Syrian and Jordanian air forces. Over the course of five days, the Israelis again decisively defeated the Egyptian, Jordanian and Syrian armies. As a result of this victory by the Israelis in what is called the 1967 Six Day War, Israel occupied the Sinai Peninsula, the Gaza Strip in Egypt, the West Bank and East Jerusalem controlled by Jordan and the Gold Heights in Syria. The fourth war began in October 1973 on Yom Kippur, the holiest day in Judaism, when Egypt and Syria attacked Israel beginning what came to be known as the Yom Kippur War. Although the Israeli military was caught off-guard and unprepared for the surprise attack, the Israelis stopped the assault. After signing a cease-fire agreement in November 1973, Israel and Egypt signed a peace treaty in January 1974. That agreement required Israel to withdraw its military forces from the Sinai Peninsula, Egypt to reduce the size of its military forces on east bank of the Suez Canal and a UN peacekeeping force to be established as a buffer between the two armies. Israel and Syria signed separate cease-fire agreements in May 1974 under which another UN buffer zone was created to separate the militaries of both countries. With assistance from the United States, Israel and Egypt signed a peace treaty known as the Camp David Accords ending 30 years of hostilities between the two countries. Under this agreement Israel returned control of the entire Sinai Peninsula to Egypt and, in return, Egypt recognized Israel's right to exist. Nevertheless, after the Yom Kippur War, OPEC announced an embargo on oil exports to those nations who supported Israel and quadrupled the price of a barrel of oil. The fifth war began in May 1982 when Israel invaded Lebanon to stop the Palestine Liberation Organization (PLO) from launching raids into Israel. Israeli military forces occupied a large portion of Lebanon until 1985 when they were withdrawn entirely. Even though hostilities existed between Israel and the PLO during the late 1980s and early 1990s, they were able to negotiate a peace settlement. In 1993, Israel and the PLO signed the Oslo Accords in which Israel recognized the PLO as the legitimate presentative of the Palestinian people and agreed to the gradual implementation of Palestinian self-governance in the West Bank and Gaza strip. In return, the PLO recognized the right of the state of Israel to exist and renounced the use of violence and its long-held political objective of destroying Israel.

Arab Revolt (1916–1918) was the guerrilla rebellion by Arab nationalist groups in the Middle East against the Ottoman Empire during World War I. For the Arab nationalist groups the objective of the revolt was to replace Ottoman imperial rule with the establishment of independent, autonomous Arab states. For the British, who encouraged and supported the revolt, the revolt diverted the use of Ottoman troops who might have otherwise been used to attack the Suez Canal, a strategic hub in the British Empire. While the Arab Revolt did not affect the war in Europe, it did contribute to the defeat of the Ottoman Empire in Middle East.

Arab Spring (2010) is the name for the various peaceful rebellions that occurred in Arab countries in North Africa and the Middle East against dictatorial rulers. The first rebellion began in Tunisia and it inspired the outbreak of other rebellions in Yemen, Libya, Syria, Bahrain, Kuwait and Egypt. The rebellion in Libya and Egypt resulted in the overthrow of Muammar Qaddafi and Hosni Mubarak respectively. The rebellion in Syria led to the outbreak of a civil war.

Arbenz, Jacobo (1913–1971) was the democratically elected government of Guatemalan who began a sweeping land reform program. As part of his agrarian reform program, he confiscated lands owned by the U.S. based United Fruit Company and redistributed the land to the landless peasants. Because of the political influence of United Fruit Company in Washington, Arbenz's land reform program was quickly opposed by the U.S. government. In 1953 the CIA was ordered to organize a coup to overthrow Arbenz. The CIA organized a small band of rebels based in neighboring Honduras, who attacked Guatemala in June 1954. At first the rebels were not successful. However, a CIA radio propaganda campaign exaggerated the size of the rebel force and contributed to the defection of Arbenz's officer corps. Arbenz fled into exile and a military junta took control of the Guatemalan government. The success of this operation provided a blueprint that would be used by other CIA led coup attempts. For the next several decades, a succession of right-wing, military governments ruled Guatemala. Anti-Castro Cuban exiles were permitted to train in Guatemala for the ill-fated Bay of Pigs invasion in 1961. Counterinsurgency efforts by the Guatemalan military against a leftist insurgency led to the creation of death squads, which were responsible for the death of thousands of Guatemalan civilians during a 35 year of civil war. Peace talks between leftist rebels and a democratically elected government began in 1991. A peace accord was eventually signed in 1996.

Arawak were the indigenous peoples who inhabited the islands in the Caribbean at the time of Columbus.

Arcadia was a mountainous region in the central portion of the Peloponnese of ancient Greece that was cut off from the sea on all sides. Because of its isolation, it was not occupied by the Dorians during their invasion of Greece between 1100 and 1000 BCE.

Arcadian League (370–230s BCE) was a defensive military alliance established by the ancient city-states of Arcadia to protect themselves from the influence and power of Sparta in the Peloponnese. As a bulwark against the Spartans, the Arcadians built a strongly fortified capital city, Megalopolis. While the League reached the heights of its influence in the 360s BCE, it continued to exist until the 230s BCE when the Arcadian city-states joined the Achaean League.

Archaeology is the study of ancient civilizations and cultures by the discovery, examination, analysis, and interpretation of physical artifacts/remains created by humans from those civilizations and cultures.

Archaic Greece (800–500 BCE) is a term used by historians to describe a period of ancient Greek history characterized by artistic achievement, increased emphasis on individualism, and the moving away from divine explanations toward more abstract, mechanistic explanations. Historians contend that during this period of ancient Greek history the Western philosophical tradition began.

Archimedes (287–212 BCE) was a scientist, mathematician, and inventor in ancient Greece. He discovered the formulas for the surface area and the volume of a sphere, the physical law of buoyancy, and invented a machine for raising water, Archimedes' screw, which was used by the Romans. When Rome attacked Syracuse in Sicily in 213 BCE, he constructed machines that played an important part in the defense of the city. During the Roman sack of the city, he was killed.

Archimedes' screw was a simple machine used for transferring water from a low-lying body of water into irrigation ditches. It is one of several inventions and discoveries reputed to have been made by Archimedes, though writings about the Hanging Gardens of Babylon hint that a similar device was used by the Mesopotamians as early as 600 BCE, over 300 years before his birth, to irrigate their fields. Archimedes' screw consisted of a screw inside a hollow pipe. The lower end of the device is put in the water, and the screw is then turned (usually by a windmill or by animal or human labor). As the bottom end of the tube turns, it scoops up an amount of water. This water will slide up in the spiral tube as the shaft is turned, until finally it falls out from the top of the spiral tube and feeds the irrigation system.

Archon was the title of the chief Athenian magistrate elected to serve for only one year.

Areopagus was the governing council of Athens before the rise of Athenian democracy, which was the oldest political institution in Athens and was comprised only of the nobility. The nobles would annually select the nine archons and magistrates who would govern Athens. The Areopagus was named after the hill on which it met.

Arête is the Greek term for manliness, courage, and excellence, the fundamental qualities of a Greek hero. These qualities were necessary for a hero to acquire and defend his honor. Arête was considered the highest virtue in Homeric society.

Arianism was a view of Christianity held by followers of Arius (250–336 BCE), a Christian priest who lived in Alexandria, Egypt, in the early 300s CE. Arius rejected the idea that Jesus could be equal to God. He taught that Jesus was subordinate to God. He argued that Jesus was a divine being created by God, through whom God created all things. The conflict between proponents of Arianism and Trinitarianism was the first major doctrinal dispute in the Christian Church after the legalization of Christianity by Emperor Constantine I. Arianism was considered a heresy by the Church and was subsequently condemned by the Council of Nicaea in 325. However, Arianism influenced family members of Roman emperors, the imperial nobility and the clergy and was adopted by many of the Germanic tribes who entered the Roman Empire in the 300s and 400s. Trinitarianism subsequently prevailed and became the basic doctrine upon which Christianity was built.

Aristarchus of Samos (310–230 BCE) was an ancient Greek philosopher who first formulated the heliocentric theory of the universe in 275 BCE, that is the earth revolves around the sun, which is at the center of the universe.

Aristocracy is a form of government based on rule by the "best" or "most noble". It was a social class that relied upon hereditary political rule by a wealthy, warrior elite, whose wealth was based primarily on land ownership. The term aristocracy was first used to refer to young Athenian men who led armies into battle. During the Middle Ages, the term was applied in Europe to an emerging hereditary class of military leaders. One of the factors that contributed to the French Revolution was the widely held belief among the bourgeoisie, who emerged as leaders of the French Revolution, that the traditional aristocracy no longer represented the "best" and that political rule and participation should be based on merit rather than birth.

Aristophanes (450–388 BCE) was an Athenian playwright who was a contemporary of Sophocles and Euripides. He wrote forty plays, eleven of which still survive. His plays were comedies that were performed as part of religious festivals. His comedies used satire, parody, and sexual references to ridicule powerful Athenian social, political, military and cultural figures, including Socrates. He used comedy as a means to emphasize the importance of the polis and the responsibilities of citizens. During the Peloponnesian War he wrote three plays that expressed an anti-war theme, *Acharnians*, *Peace* and *Lysistrata*. In *Lysistrata*, his most well-known play, the women of Greece, whose husbands have waged a long war, refuse to have sex with their husbands until they make peace. In his plays, *Babylonians* and *Knights*, he not only attacked Cleon, the demagogue then in power in Athens, but also the allied city-states of Athens, who he portrayed as slaves of Athens. In *Clouds*, he attacked the morals taught by the Sophists and Socrates, who he portrayed as a Sophist. In his play *Knights* he addressed the issue of religion. In the play two slaves are complaining about another slave. To avoid him one slave suggests that they go to the statute of some god and prostrate themselves. Disdainfully the other slave says: "Do you really believe in gods? What is your proof?". To which the other slave says "the fact that I am cursed by them"?

Aristotle (384–322 BCE) was an ancient Greek philosopher who was a student of Plato and the teacher of Alexander. He argued that knowledge could be obtained by rational analysis of the material world and the investigation of all phenomena rather than the metaphysical speculations by Plato about Ideal Forms. In his view, the world and all of its parts had a fundamental purpose. His writings concerning science, politics, logical argumentation and ethics were perhaps the most influential philosophical works during the Middle Ages in Europe.

Ark of the Covenant was, according to the Hebrew Bible (Old Testament), an ornate, gold-plated wooden box that contained the stone tablets of the Ten Commandments that were given to Moses by God on Mount Sinai. It is considered to be the most sacred relic of the Judaism, signifying the covenant between God and the Jewish people. According to Judaic tradition, King Solomon built the Temple in Jerusalem to house it. The Ark disappeared when the Neo-Babylonian armies under King Nebuchadnezzar captured Jerusalem in 586 BCE and destroyed the Temple.

Arkwright, Richard (1732–1792) was an English inventor who became the wealthiest and most successful textile manufacturer of the early Industrial Revolution. He invented the water frame, a machine that could spin many cotton threads simultaneously.

Armada, The Spanish (1588) was the fleet of 130 ships and 30,000 men sent by the Catholic King Philip II of Spain in 1588 in a failed attempt to invade England. The Armada was defeated by a combination of the tactics of British navy and bad weather. A large part of Spanish fleet was scattered and destroyed by a hurricane on its return to Lisbon. For King Philip II of Spain, the Armada was to be a crusade against the enemies of Catholicism. This religious antagonism was increased by economic competition in trade with the Spanish Empire in America and by English privateering and piracy. The matter of England's disruption (along with France) of the annual bullion-run by the Spanish treasure fleet from Peru and Mexico to the port of Seville in Spain was of critical importance to Philip. The Spanish were also angered because of England's interference in the revolt against Spanish rule in the Netherlands. Thus, the Armada was organized, in part, to put a stop to these religious, economic and political matters.

Armenian Massacres refers to the state-planned systematic campaigns of killing the Armenian population by the Ottoman Empire in 1894–96 and 1915. In the 1880s, a nationalist Armenian movement arose that sought independence from the Ottoman Empire. It is estimated that nearly two million Christian Armenians lived in the Ottoman Empire by the late 1880s. In response to such demands, the Ottoman sultan sought to suppress nationalist sentiments by drastically raising taxes on the Armenians and encouraging resentment and hostility against the Armenians in the Kurdish community. When some Armenians refused to pay the taxes, Turkish troops and Kurdish tribesmen killed thousands of them and burned their villages in 1894. In 1896, in response to Armenian revolutionaries seizing the Ottoman Bank in Istanbul, more than 50,000 Armenians were killed by mobs of Muslim Turks whose actions were coordinated by government troops. The last and deadliest of the massacres occurred during World War I, when Armenians from the Caucasus region of the Russian Empire formed volunteer battalions to help the Russian army against the Turks. Early in 1915 these battalions attempted to recruit Turkish Armenians to fight on the side of Russia against the Ottoman Empire. In response, the Ottoman government ordered the forced deportation of about 1,750,000 Armenians to Syria and Mesopotamia. In carrying out this plan, the Ottoman military took Armenian men women and children from their homes. Depriving them of food and water, the soldiers forced them to march for hundreds of miles to the desert in what is now Syria. During the marches, the soldiers indiscriminately massacred the Armenian men, women and children regardless of age or gender. They also engaged in rape and other forms of sexual abuse. These forced marches were intended to cause the death of the Armenian population. It is estimated that between 600,000 and 1–1.5 million Armenians died of starvation or were killed by Ottoman soldiers and police during these marches. Because these killing were systematically planned, organized and carried out by the Ottoman government, many scholars consider this event in 1915–1916 to be the first modern example of genocide. The Republic of Turkey, the successor state of the Ottoman Empire, denies the word genocide is an accurate description of the events even though most genocide scholars and historians accept this view and many countries have officially recognized the events of 1915–16 as genocide.

Armenian Question (1877–1914) was a term used in the late 1800s and early 1900s by politicians and journalists after the Russo-Turkish War of 1877–78 and the Congress of Berlin of 1884–85 to describe the efforts by Great Britain, Russia and Germany to protect the rights and freedoms of the Armenian community in the Ottoman Empire and to prevent government-sponsored or condoned acts of violence and discrimination against the Armenian people.

Armistice is a cease-fire agreement negotiated by the parties to a war. During the period of an armistice, the parties to the war will attempt to negotiate an agreement ending the war and restoring peaceful relations.

Arms Control refers to the process among states to negotiate unilateral or multilateral agreements restricting and/or prohibiting the research, manufacture, possession and deployment of nuclear, biological and chemical weapons, more commonly known as weapons of mass destruction. Such agreements may also reduce or eliminate certain types of weapons as was accomplished by the Intermediate-Range Nuclear Forces (INF) Treaty of 1988 between the United States and the Soviet Union.

Arms Race is a process in which two or more nation-states build up their respective military capabilities in response to real or perceived threats posed by each other. In seeking to reduce its insecurity by the acquisition of new and more powerful weaponry, a state actually increases the level of insecurity of the other state or states. In international relations, this quest for security is never-ending and is known as the "security dilemma". The Cold War nuclear arms race began on July 16, 1945 when the United States successfully tested the first atomic bomb in Alamogordo New Mexico.

Arquebus was a portable, long-barreled gun used in the 1400s in Europe that was fired by a wheel-lock or match-lock.

Arthur, King is an important figure in the mythology of Great Britain, where he appears as the model of kingship in both war and peace. There is disagreement about whether Arthur ever actually existed. The possible historical accuracy of the King Arthur legend has long been debated by scholars. One school of thought believes Arthur to have lived sometime in the late 400s to early 500s CE, to have been of Roman-British origin, and to have fought against the pagan Saxons. His power base was probably in Wales, Cornwall or the west of what would eventually become England. However, controversy over the center of his power and the extent and kind of power he wielded continues to this day. Some historians have argued for identifying Arthur with a certain Riothamus, "King of the Brettones." Unfortunately, scholars know little about him and are uncertain as to whether the "Brettones" he led were Britons or Bretons. Other scholars have claim that Arthur was Ambrosius Aurelianus, a war Roman-British leader who won important battles against the Anglo-Saxons circa 500 CE. Another group of scholars contend that Arthur may have been a Celtic deity. However, the Arthur of legend may simply be a composite of these figures and that tales of the real Arthur's exploits may have been confused and merged with that of other war leaders of the time. Nevertheless, all of these theories fail to mention that Arthur which means "bear-man" in Welsh and Latin, could have been a fictitious name used by a leader who fought against the Saxons and whose true name is lost.

Artisan is the term used historians to refer to a skilled maker of goods. Typically, an artisan would produce goods such as pottery, tools, jewelry, clothes, furniture, and other consumer items. As a result of industrialization in the late 1700s and 1800s in Europe, the artisan would be replaced by the factory worker, who would operate machines to mass produce goods that were previously produced by hand.

Aryan is an English word derived from Indian and Persian cultures that was used originally to refer to clan or ethnic identity. Over time, the meaning of the term has evolved to be roughly similar to noble or honorable. The word first appears circa 1500 BCE in Indian and Persian sacred texts. The word Iran is derived from the word Aryan and India was called the "Land of the Aryans." Because these two peoples were the earliest speakers of "Indo-European" languages, the word Aryan was adopted to refer not only to the Indo-Iranian people, but also to Indo-European speakers, such as the Greeks, Romans, Celts, Germans and Slavs, whose languages all have a common root. Accordingly, the word Aryan is primarily a linguistic term used to refer to the Indo-European language family. It has also been used to describe a people who began to migrate from their homeland in India and Iran to Mesopotamia, Asia Minor and Europe circa 2000 BCE.

Aryan Race was an anthropological and political concept that emerged in Europe in the mid-1800s. Proponents of this idea argued that the original speakers of the Indo–European languages, who migrated into Europe from India and Iran and their descendants, constituted a master race. This

linguistic term, Indo-European, was subsequently perverted by the Nazis, who deemed those people who spoke an Indo-European language to be superior to those people who spoke a Semitic language. Thus, the Nazis claimed that Aryans constituted the original racial group in Europe as contrasted with other groups such as the Jewish people who spoke a Semitic language. Max Muller is considered to be the first writer to speak in English of an Aryan race in his book *Lectures on the Science of Language* (1861). However, the most influential proponent of the idea of an Aryan race in Europe during the mid-1800s was Joseph-Arthur, Comte de Gobineau. In his *Essay on the Inequality of Human Races* (1853–1855), he claimed that there were three major races in the world, white, black and yellow, and that the Aryans were the purest group of whites. He further argued that when Aryans intermarry with lower races, they dilute their blood, which would cause the decline of their civilization. Gobineau identified three separate races within the white race, Nordic, Alpine and Mediterranean. According to him each of them had distinct mental abilities, physical characteristics and natural abilities such as leadership, economic resourcefulness, creativity, inventiveness, morality, and aesthetic sensibilities. The tall blond Nordics, who were descendants of the ancient Germanic tribes, were the intellectuals and the leaders. The Alpines, who had brown hair and were of intermediate height, were the peasants and the workers. The Mediterraneans, who were darker and shorter, were according to Gobineau, decadent, degenerate and a mixture of "nigridize" and "semitized" races. Many proponents of German nationalism in the late 1800s were so influenced by the ideas of Gobineau that they developed a new ideology of "Aryanism" that would subsequently become the foundation for Nazi race theories in the 1900s.

Aryanization was the program established by the Nazis to expropriate Jewish businesses, enterprises and property and transfer to them "Aryan" ownership or control.

Asante was the African Kingdom on the Gold Coast of Africa that expanded rapidly after 1680. It participated in the transatlantic economic system by trading gold, slaves, and ivory. It resisted British imperialist efforts for over twenty-five years before being absorbed into the British Imperial system in 1902.

Asceticism was the Christian practice of suppressing physical needs and daily desires in an effort to achieve a spiritual union with God. It was the religious practice upon which the monastic movement was built. Saint Augustine emphasized this practice.

Ashur was the capital of the Assyrian Empire located along the banks of the Tigris River. The other principal cities in Assyria were Nimrud and Nineveh. Ashur was a center for trade. Its trade routes led to Anatolia, where Assyrian trading colonies were established to trade in tin and wool. Ashur remained the capitol of the Assyrian Empire until 706 BCE when Nineveh became the capitol. Ashur was destroyed by the Babylonians in 614 BCE.

Ashurbanirpal, King (7th century BCE) was an Assyrian king who reigned from 668 to 627 BCE. He was the last Assyrian king. He created one of the first great libraries of the ancient world, which was located in Nineveh

Asia Minor is a geographic term used by historians and geographers to describe ancient Anatolia, which constitutes the majority of the eastern part of present-day Turkey. Asia Minor is bounded by the Black Sea to the north, the Mediterranean Sea to the south and the Aegean Sea to the west. The Bosphorus, the Sea of Marmara and the Dardanelles together form the dividing line between Europe and Asia Minor.

Asian Tigers refers to those nations in East and Southeast Asia such as South Korea, Taiwan, Hong Kong, and Singapore that emerged as economic powers in the 1970s and 1980s.

Asiento is the Spanish name for the trade agreements that Spain negotiated with private contractors or another country between the early 1500s and the mid-1700s which gave the private contractor or country the exclusive contractual right to supply African slaves for sale in the Spanish colonies in the Americas. In exchange for this exclusive right, the private contractor or country agreed to pay Spain a specific amount of money annually. In 1713, after the War of Spanish Succession, the Treaty of Utrecht specifically gave Great Britain a 30 year monopoly to supply 4800 slaves annually to the Spanish colonies in the Americas, which slave markets had been traditionally closed to Great Britain.

Aspasia was born in Miletus, an Ionian Greek settlement on the coast of Western Anatolia. Aspasia's father insisted that she be educated, which was uncommon for Greek women. In Miletus, she was also exposed to a melting pot of ideas, cultures, and influences. Aspasia decided to leave Miletus and go to Athens, which was unheard of for a young, unmarried woman. Aspasia arrived in Athens probably around the middle 440s BCE. Independently minded, witty, and with a gifted intellect, she soon attracted the attention of Pericles, the city's democratic leader and became his constant companion. Pericles divorced his wife, with whom he who had two sons, so he could live with Aspasia. As the companion of Athens' leading politician, she supposedly exercised great influence over the policies of Pericles. Aspasia quickly became the target of malicious gossip. She was accused of being a hetairai, a high-class courtesan who entertained wealthy Athenian men during their dinner parties, but were not considered suitable as wives or companions. For traditional Athenian men, what was most threatening about Aspasia was the respect Pericles, the city's political leader, showed her. Traditionally, Greek women were meant to be unseen and unheard. However, Pericles treated Aspasia as an equal. He did not prevent her from interacting with important Athenian men and openly showed her great affection. Pericles never married Aspasia because of a law he enacted. In an effort to prevent aristocratic families from making alliances with other cities, he had introduced a new citizenship law in 451. Under this law, the sons of non-Athenian women could not become full citizens. If he married Aspasia, Pericles would be violating the very law he had created. With two sons already Pericles' family line seemed secure, so Aspasia lived with him as his companion. In 440 BCE, she bore him a son, named after Pericles' father. When the Peloponnesian War began between Athens and Sparta in 431 BCE, Aspasia was blamed for the war. Her critics argued that by helping her home city of Miletus ten years earlier, Pericles had provoked Sparta, who had supported Miletus' enemies. Nevertheless, having lived with Pericles for nearly two decades, Aspasia enjoyed almost all of the privileges of an Athenian noblewoman. When Pericles delivered his famous 'Funeral Oration', glorifying the war dead, Plato joked that the speech was written by Aspasia. But their lives were irreparably changed when the plague devastated Athens. Pericles became ill and struggled for months against the plague. When both of his legitimate sons died from the plague, he tried to have his son by Aspasia declared as his heir. After he died in 429 BCE, the Athenian popular assembly granted Pericles' son with Aspasia full Athenian citizenship.

Association of South-East Asian Nations (ASEAN) is a regional political and economic organization that was established by Thailand, Singapore, Indonesia and the Philippines in 1967 for the purpose of increasing economic growth, social progress and ensuring regional peace and stability in Southeast Asia. Subsequently, Brunei, Vietnam, Cambodia, Laos and Myanmar joined ASEAN. In 1992, the members of ASEAN agreed to create a free trade zone in the hopes that it would be the basis in the future for an ASEAN common market. The ASEAN has a population of approximately 625 million people. As of 2015, the combined GDF of its members was $2.6 trillion, which ranks it as the seventh largest economy in the world. The largest economies in the world ranked ahead of the ASEAN are the U.S., China, Japan, Germany, France and the United Kingdom.

Assembly of Notables (1787–1788) was an advisory body of the high-ranking nobles, clergy and public officials established by King Louis XVI for the purpose of approving royal reforms. He created it to circumvent the parlements. The Assembly refused to endorse many reforms and, with the backing of public opinion, forced the king to call for a meeting of the Estates-General. This move contributed to the outbreak of the French Revolution.

Assignants was the name for the paper money that replaced the French franc. It was issued by the French government during the early stages of the French Revolution to liquidate the national debt. It was based on the value of the land confiscated from the Catholic Church in France by the government. While assignats were not legal tender, the holders of assignats were supposed to receive interest. Because too many were issued, the assignats caused inflation and the hoarding of metal currency. In May 1797, they were withdrawn from circulation by the government in the hopes of returning to a metallic currency and greater economic stability.

Assimilation is the process by which an ethnic group loses its unique cultural identity and adopts and absorbs the culture, language, customs, traditions, values and attitudes of another dominant society.

Assur (Ashur) was the chief god of the Assyrians and considered the protector of the Assyrian state. It was believed that Assur guided the actions of the king and ensured victory in war.

Assurnasirpal II (circa 9th century BCE) was the Assyrian king who reigned from 883 to 859 BCE. He began the process of Assyrian expansion and used military terror tactics extensively.

Assyria was a region on the Upper Tigris River, named for its original capital, Ashur. Later, as a nation and empire, it also came to include roughly the northern half of Mesopotamia. There is little known of the early history of the kingdom of Assyria. According to some Judeo-Christian legends, the city-state of Ashur was founded by Ashur the son of Shem, who was deified by later generations as the city's patron god. Besides Ashur, the other three royal Assyrian cities were Calah (Nimrud), Khorsabad, and Nineveh, which later replaced Ashur as the capital of the Assyrian Empire. Assyria seems to have been ruled from Sumer, Akkad, and northern Babylonia in its earliest stages, all of which were part of Sargon the Great's empire. Assyria was founded as an independent kingdom circa 1900 BCE. The city-state of Ashur had extensive contact with cities in Anatolia having established merchant colonies between 1920–1840 BCE and 1798–1740 BCE. These colonies were attached to Anatolian cities, but physically separate, and had a special tax status. While they may have been created because of a long tradition of trade between Ashur and various Anatolian cities, there is no archaeological or written evidence to corroborate this trade. The city of Ashur was conquered by Hammurabi of Babylon.

Assyrians were a Semitic-speaking people who emerged in northern Mesopotamia circa 2400 BCE. They created a highly militaristic and well-structured empire that would dominate Mesopotamia between the 12th century BCE and 612 BCE. Assyria reached it height of power during the 800s and 700s BCE. Their military innovations included using cavalry as their main striking force and having weapons and armor made of iron.

Astell, Mary (1666–1731) was an English feminist writer who advocated for greater equality for women. In 1694, she published her *Serious Proposal to the Ladies for the Advancement of their True and Greatest Interest* in which she argued that since women were the intellectual equals of men, women should be given equal access to education and that a private women's college should be established to provide women with both a religious and secular education. She was the first English woman to advocate such ideas and to engage in a public philosophical debate about such issues. Astell concluded that "If all Men are born Free, why are all Women born Slaves?. In In 1697, she published a second book, *A Serious Proposal, Part II* in which she further argued that the education of women should be based on reason and debate rather than custom and tradition. Critics accused her of promoting ideas that were subversive and contradicted the Bible. In another book titled *Some Reflections upon Marriage*, which she published in 1706, she criticized the relationship between men and women in a marriage. In this book, she claimed that education would help women make better decisions about a marriage partner, that a marriage should be based on a lasting friendship and equality and that men should not exercise absolute sovereignty within the marriage or the family. Astell concluded that "If absolute authority be not necessary in a state, how comes it to be so in a family".

Astrolabe was navigational instrument used by European sailors between the mid-1400s and early 1700s to calculate more accurately a ship's position (latitude) at sea north or south of the equator, which was critical for long distance maritime travel. An astrolabe determined a ship's latitude by measuring the angle of the sun at noon relative to the horizon or the polestar (the North Star) relative to the horizon at night. While the astrolabe was first invented by the ancient Greeks between 220 and 150 BCE, it was used primarily to make astronomical observations and to measure the altitude of stars and planets above the horizon. Between the 700s and 1200s CE, Muslim astronomers improved the astrolabe and Muslim sailors used it to open new trade routes. By the early 1400s, the improved and more reliable astrolabe was introduced to European sailors by Muslim Spain. In the late 1400s and early 1500s, Portugal and Spain subsequently recognized that the use of such a technological innovation was critical to their plans for overseas expansion. Longitude, which involved more complicated east-west calculations, would not be used by European navigators until the invention of seaworthy clocks in the mid-1700s.

Astrology was the pseudo-scientific study of the influence of the planets on individuals and societies. During the Scientific Revolution, the study of astrology contributed to the development of astronomy as a science.

Astyages was, according to Herodotus, the legendary king of the Medes who was defeated by Cyrus the Great, the founder of the Persian Empire.

Ataturk, Kemal (1880–1938) was a Turkish army officer who led a revolt in 1923 that overthrew the sultanate in the Ottoman Empire and established the Turkish Republic. During World War I, he distinguished himself in the Turkish defense of Gallipoli. He also forced the withdrawal of the Greek army from Anatolia in 1921–1922. As the first president of the new Turkish Republic, he advocated reform of Turkish society through the adoption of Western European cultural patterns.

Aten or Aton was the name of the monotheistic god of the Egyptian pharaoh Akhenaten who reigned from 1353 to 1335 BCE. Aten is considered to be the world's first example of monotheism.

Athanasian Creed was the Catholic profession of faith believed to have been developed in the 300s CE by Saint Athanasius that supported the idea of the Trinity. Today, it is widely recognized that it was not written by Saint Athanasius, but was probably written in the 400s CE in southern France.

Athanasius, Saint (293–373 CE) was a Christian theologian, ascetic, and Bishop of Alexandria who in the 300s CE vigorously articulated the defense of the concept of the Trinity against the heretical challenges posed by Arianism. Followers of Saint Athanasius and his defense of Christian orthodoxy were known as Athanasians. One of his most important intellectual endeavors was his massive theological work *Four Orations Against Arians*.

Atheism is the ideology that rejects the existence of deities or any transcendent spiritual or supernatural force. It contends that there is no rational empirical evidence to prove the existence of polytheistic gods, the monotheistic god of Judaism, Christianity and Islam or any transcendent supernatural divine force. During the Enlightenment in France in the 1700s, Baron d'Holbach emerged as the first advocate for atheism. In the 1800s, Ludwig Feuerbach, a German philosopher and a Sigmund Freud, a Viennese physician and psychoanalyst both argued that beliefs in deities were human inventions created to address specific social and psychological needs. Influenced by the work of Feuerbach, Karl Marx and Friedrich Engels argued that religious beliefs were used by those in positions of political and economic power to manipulate and oppress the working class.

Atlantic Charter (1941) was the Allied declaration negotiated by British Prime Minister Winston Churchill and President Franklin D. Roosevelt of the United States aboard warships near Newfoundland on August 14, 1941. The Atlantic Charter established a vision for a post–World War II world, despite the fact the United States had not yet entered World War II. The Charter contained eight points: no territorial gains would be sought by the United States or the United Kingdom; postwar territorial adjustments would conform to the desires of the people involved; peoples of the world would have the right of self-determination; trade barriers would be lowered; there would be postwar disarmament; people would have freedom from want and fear; there would be freedom of the seas for the nations of the world; and an international association of nations would be created.

Atlantic Slave Trade was the forced migration between the 1600s and early 1800s of approximately twelve million Africans to serve as slave labor on the plantations in the colonies of the European powers in North and South America. By the 1780s, shipments of African men and women averaged about 80,000 per year.

Atlantic System is a term used by historians to describe the international system and network of trade in goods, resources, people, and culture that linked the Americas, Europe, and Africa that emerged between 1500s and 1700s in the wake of the European colonization of North and South America. Under this system the Europeans traded goods for slaves in western Africa, sold the slaves to the colonial plantation owners in North and South America and the Caribbean and then bought the commodities produced by those colonial plantations for resale in Europe.

Atom is the smallest component of an element possessing all of the chemical characteristics of that element. It is composed of a nucleus and one or more electrons.

Atomic Bomb is a weapon created by the splitting of the nucleus of an atom, which results in the enormous release of energy. It was the weapon that the United States dropped on Hiroshima, Japan, on August 6, 1945 and Nagasaki, Japan on August 9, 1945, ending World War II. The American development of the atomic bomb led to an arms race during the Cold War. The Soviet Union developed its first atomic bomb in 1949 and by the 1950s both nations had developed the more power hydrogen bomb. The nuclerization of modern warfare during the Cold War caused U. S. policymakers to develop four nuclear strategies: massive retaliation, flexible response, mutual assured destruction and nuclear utilization target selection.

Attila the Hun was the ruler of one of the barbarian tribes that attacked the Roman Empire during the 400s. He ruled the Huns from 434 to 453. The empire of the Huns stretched from the Alps in the west to the Baltic Sea in the north to the Caspian Sea in the east and the Roman Empire in the south. He murdered his brother with whom he co-ruled the Huns until 445. During the period of co-rule with his brother, they negotiated a peace treaty with the Eastern Roman Empire by which the Romans agreed to pay them a yearly subsidy. When the Eastern Roman Empire failed to pay the negotiated subsidies, Attila attacked the Balkan provinces of Greece. Subsequently he invaded Gaul in 451 and northern Italy in 452, but was forced to withdraw his troops from Italy because of famine and disease.

Augsburg Confession (1530) was the central document of the Lutheran reformation, which was written as a reaction against the Catholic Church. The Augsburg Confession was originally written by Philipp Melanchthon with the approval of Martin Luther. It was the most widely accepted statement of the Lutheran faith. This statement was adopted by the Schmalkaldic League, a defensive alliance of Lutheran states.

Augur was a priest in ancient Rome whose primary function was to interpret the will of the gods prior to a major public or private undertaking in Roman society such as the appointment of a magistrate, decisions by the people's assembly, the passing of laws, the decision to initiate a war, a blessing for a good harvest or a successful commercial transaction. An augur did not predict the future, but rather determined whether a proposed course of action met with approval or disapproval of the gods by studying, for example, the flight of birds. Augurs wrote books containing records of past signs, the appropriate rituals to follow and the necessary prayers to be used in order to train other augurs. Until circa 300 BCE when the plebeians were permitted to hold the office of augur, it was a position only held by patricians.

Augustine of Canterbury, Saint (died 604/605 CE) was a Benedictine monk who was chosen by Pope Gregory I in 596 to lead a mission of forty monks to England to convert the pagans to Christianity. He was the first archbishop of Canterbury.

Augustine of Hippo, Saint (354–430 CE) was a theologian in the early Christian Church. He is considered to be one of the "fathers" of the Catholic Church and one of the most influential thinkers in Christian history. His writings would influence Martin Luther and John Calvin. While raised and educated in Carthage, his mother was a devout Catholic and his father a pagan. He was educated in philosophy and rhetoric and taught in Carthage. After studying rhetoric in Rome, he was made a professor of rhetoric at the imperial court in Milan. While in Milan, he rejected Manichaeism

and converted to Neoplatonism. However, in 386, influenced by the teachings of the Ambrose, the bishop of Milan, he converted to Christianity and abandoned his teaching position in Milan. Instead, he decided to become a priest. His book *Confessions* describes his conversion to Christianity. In 388, he returned to North Africa, where he became a famous preacher noted for opposing Manichaeanism. In 396, he was made bishop of Hippo and remained in that position until his death in 430. He was greatly influenced by Stoicism, Platonism and Neoplatonism. Initially, his philosophical and religious writings focused on the human will. However, it was his arguments against the Pelagians, who did not believe in original sin, from which he developed the doctrine of original sin, a central tenet of Christianity. Augustine also developed the theory of the just war and the doctrine of divine predestination. He claimed that the Jews were the enemies of Christianity and that they should be punished by God for their denial of Jesus as the Messiah. Alongside *The Confessions*, *The City of God*, which was written in the early 400s, is considered one of Augustine's most important works. He wrote this book in response to the pagan claims that the sack of Rome was punishment of the Romans for abandoning the traditional Roman religion and the acceptance of Christianity by the Roman emperors. In response to the pagan claims, Augustine argued for the truth of Christianity as compared to other religions and philosophies and asserted that Christianity had, in fact, saved Rome from complete destruction. He further contended that the decline of Rome was the result of internal factors and moral decay. In *The City of God*, Augustine presented human history as a universal conflict between what he called the City of Man, which consisted of people only concerned with the personal matters and pleasures of the present and the City of God, which consisted of people who rejected earthly pleasures and dedicated themselves to the eternal truths of God as revealed by Christianity. Augustine's conception of world history as a universal war that would only end with the second coming of Christ was adopted as official doctrine of the Catholic Church. *The City of God* was one of the most influential writings during the Middle Ages.

Augustus, which means "divinely favored", was the title granted to Octavian by the Roman Senate in 27 BCE because of his restoration of the Roman

Republic. It was a title which became synonymous with the Roman emperor and was used by all subsequent Roman emperors. It was a semi-religious title that implied veneration, majesty and holiness.

Augustus, Caesar (63 BCE–14 CE) was honorific name of Gaius Julius Caesar Octavianus, founder of the Roman Principate, the military dictatorship that replaced the failing rule of the Roman Senate. After defeating Mark Antony and Cleopatra at the Battle of Actium in 31 BCE, he ruled the Roman Empire for forty years. During his long reign, he laid the groundwork for several centuries of stability and prosperity in the Roman Empire that became known as "Pax Romana"—the Roman peace. He was the grand-nephew and adopted heir of Julius Caesar and the first emperor of the Roman Empire.

Aurelian, Emperor (Lucius Domitius Aurelianus) (215–275 CE) was the Roman Emperor who reigned from 270–275, during the latter part of the Third Century Crisis (235–284). He began his military career as a common soldier, but successfully rose through the ranks to become a general in the Roman army. After Emperor Gallienus was murdered by some of his senior officers in 268, Aurelian was elected emperor by the Roman army. In 273, he successfully suppressed the rebellion of Queen Zenobia of Palmyra in Syria who had seized Egypt and parts of Asia Minor. Aurelian also defeated a mutiny of Roman soldiers in Britain, Gaul and Spain in 274 and protected Rome's northern and eastern borders that were threatened by invasion by the Vandals, the Alamanni and the Goths. In response to the increasing threat posed by invading barbarian armies to Rome's security, he had a massive wall built around Rome. In 275, he was assassinated by a group of army officers.

Aurelius, Marcus (121–180 CE), who reigned as the Roman Emperor from 161–180, was the last of the "Five Good Emperors" (Nerva, Trajan, Hadrian and Antonines Pius) who many historians consider to be the most capable rulers in Roman history. Historians have also argued that the "Five Good Emperors" who ruled between 96 and 180, produced nearly a century of unparalled prosperity and peaceful imperial succession. Emperor Hadrian arranged for Antoninus Pius to adopt Marcus Aurelius and Lucius Verus. When Antoninus Pius died,

Marcus Aurelius and Lucis Verus became co-emperors, which was the first time that Rome was ruled by two emperors. Verus defeated the rebellious Parthian Empire, but died when he returned to Rome in 169 to celebrate a triumph. During his reign Marcus Aurelius was confronted with serious economic problems and almost continuous wars against the Parthian Empire in Persia and Mesopotamia and raids by Germanic tribes such as the Marcomanni and the Goths along the Rhine and Danube borders of the Roman Empire. Believing that the Marcomanni could be assimilated into the Roman Empire, Marcus Aurelius offered them land within the Empire on which they could build settlements and obtain positions as soldiers in the Roman army. He was also confronted, during his reign, with a series of natural disasters such earthquakes, floods, famines and the plague (known as the Antonine Plague), which was brought to Roman by Roman soldiers returning from fighting against the Parthian Empire. Even though Christianity was growing in influence during the reign of Marcus Aurelius, he was more influenced by the Stoic philosopher Epictetus, a former slave. His book entitled *Meditations,* which was written while he was fighting against the barbarian tribes in northern Europe, provided an ethical guide to human behavior and a philosophical rationale for upholding the traditional Roman virtues of a sense of duty and self-discipline.

Auschwitz was a Nazi concentration camp established in Poland in 1940 that was designed to systematically murder European Jews, gypsies, socialists, communists, and other political opponents of the Nazis. It became an extermination camp in early 1942 and was the largest of the six Nazi extermination camps, all of which were located in Poland. The Nazis would ship Jews by train from all over Europe to Auschwitz. At the height of its operation in 1944, about 12,000 people were killed each day. Eventually, Auschwitz was comprised of three sections: Auschwitz I was the main camp; Auschwitz II (Birkenau) was an extermination camp; and Auschwitz III (Monowitz) was the I.G. Farben labor camp, also known as Buna. Auschwitz also operated a number of subsidiary camps. Between 1942 and 1944 it has been estimated that 1.1 to 1.6 million people died at the camp: 1,350,000 Jews, 70,000 to 75,000 Poles, 21,000 Gypsies, 15,000 Soviet POWs, and 5,000 other individuals. Today, it is considered by many people to be the most significant symbol of the Holocaust.

Ausgleich (1867), which means compromise in German, was the term used to describe the agreement between the Habsburg Emperor and the Hungarians to give Hungary greater political autonomy within the Habsburg Empire. This agreement gave Hungary its own parliament and constitution and created the dual monarchy of Austria-Hungary and the Austro-Hungarian Empire. This empire collapsed at the end of World War I.

Austerlitz, Battle of (1805) was one of a number of battles fought by France between 1792 and 1805 against a series of three coalitions of European nations opposed to both the French Revolution and Napoleon's efforts to expand French territory and influence in Continental Europe. In 1804, Britain, Austria and Russia formed a third coalition to contain and defeat the growing French hegemony in Europe. Even though Napoleon achieved a decisive victory over the combined larger Russian and Austrian armies at Austerlitz, Britain, nevertheless, defeated the French fleet at Battle of Trafalgar in 1805, ending any threat of a French invasion of Britain. After permitting the remaining Russian troops to retreat to Poland, Napoleon captured Vienna, the capital of the Habsburg Empire, and forced the Austrians to surrender. Napoleon required the Austrians to agree to the Treaty of Pressburg (1805), which compelled Austria to withdraw from the third coalition and to relinquish control over territory in Italy, Bavaria, and the western parts of the Habsburg monarchy in Germany. Furthermore, the defeat of Austria at Austerlitz led to the abdication of the Austrian emperor and the subsequent collapse of the Holy Roman Empire. As a result of his victory at Austerlitz, Napoleon formed the Confederation of the Rhine, a collection of smaller German states which he intended to use as a buffer between France and Central Europe. Napoleon's victory at Austerlitz was viewed by many Europeans as a symbol of his military invincibility. This reputation was reinforced with Napoleon's subsequent victories against Prussia at the Battle of Jena in 1806 and Russia at the Battle of Friedland one year later in 1807. The victories at Austerlitz, Jena and Friedland would form the basis for a French Empire that would dominate Europe until Napoleon's defeat at the Battle of

the Nations in 1814. Nevertheless, the Battle of Austerlitz is considered by many historians to be Napoleon's greatest military victory.

Australopithecus africanus is a hominid that lived in South Africa about 3.0 and 2.5 million years ago. It had humanlike characteristics such as bipedalism. However, its brain size was closer to that of chimpanzees than to humans.

Australopithecus afarensis is the best known member of hominid species. It was discovered in East Africa and dates from 3.8 to 2.9 million years ago. Its footprints, preserved in volcanic ash, are similar to those of modern humans (forward-pointing big toe, short lateral toes, and arched feet). Its skull has a crest and a projecting lower face. Its brain was about one-third the size of a modern human's.

Australopithecus anamensis is considered to be earliest member of the hominids. Its fossils were found in Kenya and date to 4.2–3.9 million years ago. It had a protruding lower face and walked upright.

Australopithecus (southern ape) is an extinct hominid that is the oldest ancestor of modern human beings. It was discovered in South Africa and lived during the Pliocene (5.3 to 2.6 million years ago) and Pleistocene (2.6 million to 11,700 years ago) eras. It had a combination of human and apelike traits. It walked on two legs (bipedalism), had a small brain and canine teeth and used simple tools. The most famous example of this species is a fossilized skeleton of an adult female known as "Lucy" (3.2 million years ago) that was found in Ethiopia. Lucy was found with the remains of nine adults and four juveniles that were buried together at the same time. They have been named the "First Family". Raymond Dart, an anthropologist, developed the name Australopithecus in 1925.

Austrasia was the eastern part of the Frankish kingdom between the 6th and 8th centuries CE during the Merovingian Dynasty. It was comprised of northeastern France, Belgium, and the old homeland of the Franks, the Rhineland, in western and central Germany. It disappeared as a separate entity during the Carolingian Dynasty.

Austro-Hungarian Empire (Dual Empire) (1867–1918) was the dual monarchy established by the Habsburg family in 1867 that eventually collapsed at the end of World War I.

Austro-Prussian War or the Seven Weeks War (June-August 1866) was initiated by Otto von Bismarck, the prime minister of Prussia, to eliminate the influence of the Austrian Empire and its ally the German Confederation in German political affairs and to unify all the northern German states under Prussian dominance. At the Congress of Vienna in 1815, 38 German states formed an alliance to protect themselves against France. Austria, who was the architect of the German Confederation, dominated the alliance. When a dispute arose between Prussia and Austria over the joint administration of Schleswig-Holstein, which they occupied after defeating Denmark in 1862, Bismarck announced that the German Confederation was to be dissolved. When Austria opposed such a plan, Bismarck declared war against Austria. Initially, Austria had the support of the German Confederation, but the Prussian army rapidly defeated several German states that supported Austria. Relying upon the introduction of universal military service, railroads to rapidly deploy Prussian troops, the telegraph to facilitate long-distance communication and breech-loading rifles and artillery, the modernized Prussian army decisively defeated the unprepared Austrian forces at the Battles of Königgrätz and Sadowa in Bohemia. As a result of this Prussian victories Austria was forced to sign the Treaty of Prague, which dissolved the German Confederation and permanently excluded Austria from any involvement in German political affairs. Furthermore, under the Treaty Prussia did not seek any Austrian territory, which made it possible for Prussia and Austria to be allies in the future. As part of Bismarck's efforts to dominate German politics, he created the North German Confederation, a union of all the German states north of the Main River. While each state in the Confederation controlled its own local affairs, Prussia controlled the army and the foreign affairs of the Confederation. The North German Confederation would become the basis upon which a unified Germany would be built in 1871.

Autarky is an economic policy of internal self-sufficiency by which a nation seeks to avoid or minimize foreign trade by using protectionism and tries to produce domestically the most vital things it may need.

Authoritarianism is a form of a centralized and dictatorial government that rules without holding free elections. Claiming to be above the law, authoritarian governments typically restrict individual civil and political rights, freedom of the speech and the press and repress any political opposition. Proponents of authoritarian governments claim that it is superior to democracy and that it is extremely effective in mobilizing the citizens of a nation. Typically, an authoritarian government is dictatorial rather than totalitarian, because it does not demand the population to be as actively involved in politics as does a totalitarian government. A modern authoritarian ruler will control the governmental bureaucracy, the means of mass communication and maintain order through the use of the military, a secret police, and paramilitary groups.

Autocracy is a form of government in which one person has unlimited and absolute political power and authority.

Autonomy, which is also known as self-determination, was the primary objective of the anti-colonial movements that arose in the European colonies beginning in the early 1800s. These movements sought political independence, self-governance, and freedom from the military control of the European colonial government.

Auto-da-fé, which means "act of faith" or "theater of faith", was a public confession of sin and a ritual act of penance imposed on heretics and apostates by the Catholic Church during the Inquisition in the 1400s in Spain and Portugal. It was designed to cause pain and humiliation for those who had supposedly sinned and to promote fear of God's judgment among those who witnessed it. It usually culminated in burning at the stake the alleged heretic or apostate.

Auxiliary were soldiers drawn from the conquered nations of the Roman Empire to supplement the regular Roman legions. Auxiliaries received Roman citizenship after their term of service.

Avant-Garde is a French phrase that means "vanguard" or "ahead of the rest". It is a term used to describe an artistic movement that emerged in the late 1800s that celebrated art considered being ahead of its time. Avant-garde artists rejected all existing forms of artistic expression. They created new forms of artistic expression that were inspired by novel or unconventional techniques. The term is also used to describe those individuals who considered themselves to be innovative and unconventional, to be at the forefront of a new style.

Averroës (1126–1198 CE) was an Islamic religious philosopher from Cordoba who integrated Islamic traditions with ancient Greek thought. He was also trained in medicine and was the chief judge of Cordoba. He was the personal physician to two caliphs, one in 1182 and the other in 1184. He produced a series of summaries and commentaries on most of Aristotle's works (1169–95) and on Plato's *Republic*, which exerted considerable influence in both the Islamic world and Christian Europe for centuries. (1179–80). Averroës' own first work, *General Medicine,* was written between 1162 and 1169. However, only a few of his legal writings and none of his theological writings have been preserved.

Avesta is the holy book of the Zoroastrian religion. It is comprised of a collection of the sacred texts that are preserved in two languages: the more ancient, in the Avestan language, the oldest Iranian language still very closely related to Sanskrit; the younger texts in Pahlavi, a Middle Iranian language. When translated into Pahlavi, the Avestan language was largely forgotten, and literal translations of some places became confusing. Therefore, the priests added commentaries to the whole Avestan text. This has become known as Send Avesta, and is often used to refer to the sacred text instead of simply Avesta. The Avestas were collated over several hundred years. The oldest portions, the Gathas, are the hymns thought to have been composed by Zoroaster himself. These portions constitute elaborations of Zoroastrian thinking along with detailed descriptions of ritual practices. The texts were transmitted orally for centuries, with the earliest written version circa 1278 BCE. According to a Parsi legend the full text of the Avesta was burned by Alexander the Great when he invaded Persia. It was later only partly reconstructed from the memories of Zoroastrian priests. This story is not generally accepted by scholars now, but it is acknowledged that the

existing text of the Avesta is a fraction of the full texts that existed in antiquity, before the decline of the Zoroastrian faith.

Avicenna of Sina (980–1037) was a Persian Muslim physician, an influential philosopher and scientist in the Islamic world. He wrote almost 450 treatises on a wide range of subjects, such as philosophy, astronomy, alchemy, geology, psychology, Islamic theology, logic, mathematics, physics, and poetry. He was particularly influential because of his writings in the fields of Aristotelian philosophy and medicine. He composed the *Book of the Cure*, a philosophical and scientific encyclopedia, and *The Canon of Medicine*, both of which are among the most famous books in the history of medicine. His writings served as an important vehicle for transmitting Hellenistic and Islamic learning to an emerging Europe. He is considered today by many scholars to be the most influential thinker of the Islamic Golden Age.

Axial Age is a term used by historians to describe the period from 800 to 200 BCE during which revolutionary thinking appeared simultaneously in China, India, ancient Greece and the Middle East. The idea of an axial age was developed by Karl Jaspers, a German philosopher in his book *The Origin and Goal of History*. In that book, he identified a number of key axial age thinkers as having had a profound influence on future philosophy and religion, and identified characteristics common to each area from which those thinkers emerged. Jaspers saw in these developments in religion and philosophy a striking parallel without any obvious direct transmission of ideas from one region to the other, having found no recorded proof of any extensive inter-communication between ancient Greece, the Middle East, India and China. Jaspers considered this age as unique, and one to which the rest of the history of human thought might be compared. Jaspers argued that during the axial age "the spiritual foundations of humanity were laid simultaneously and independently. And these are the foundations upon which humanity still subsists today". Jaspers' axial shifts included the rise of Platonism which would later become a major influence on both Christian and secular thought throughout the Middle Ages and into the Renaissance. Buddhism, another of the world's most influential philosophies, was founded by Siddhartha Gautama, or the Buddha, who lived during this period. In China, Confucianism arose during this era. Zoroastrianism, another of Jaspers' examples, is crucial to the development of monotheism. Jaspers also included the authors, Laozi, Homer, Socrates, Parmenides, Heraclitus, Thucydides, Archimedes, Elijah, Isaiah, Jeremiah as axial figures. Jaspers considered Socrates, Confucius and Siddhartha Gautama especially important, describing them as exemplary human beings, or as a "paradigmatic personality". Jaspers was particularly interested in the similarities in circumstance and thought of the figures during this axial age. These similarities included an engagement in the quest for human meaning and the rise of a new elite class of religious leaders and thinkers in China, India, ancient Greece and the Middle East. These four regions all gave birth to, and then institutionalized, a tradition of traveling scholars, who roamed from city to city to exchange ideas. These scholars were largely from existing religious traditions; in China, Confucianism and Taoism; in India, Hinduism, Buddhism, and Jainism; in the Middle East, the religion of Zoroaster; in Canaan, Judaism; and in Greece, sophism and other classical philosophies. Jaspers argued that these characteristics appeared under the same sociological circumstances: China, India, ancient Greece and the Middle East. Some historians argue that the Enlightenment was a "Second Axial Age", which included such leading thinkers as Isaac Newton, Sigmund Freud and Albert Einstein. In contrast, it has been suggested that the modern era is a new axial age, wherein traditional relationships between religion, secularism and traditional thought are changing.

Ayatollah, which means "sign from "in Arabic, is the title of the supreme clerical authority in Iran.

Aztecs (1325–1521), also known as Mexica, were an indigenous people of central Mexico who established an empire after 1325 around Lake Texcoco. Montezuma led the Aztecs from his capital in Tenochtitlan, where present-day Mexico City is located. Weakened by exposure to European diseases and lacking European military technology, he was defeated by Hernan Cortes and his conquistadors in the 1500s.

B-1 is a strategic bomber of the United States developed in the 1980s, which has the capacity to deliver nuclear weapons. The B-1 is capable of flying intercontinental missions without refueling.

B-29 (Superfortress) was a four-engine, propeller-driven aircraft flown by the United States during World War II and the Korean War. It was one of the largest aircrafts at the time and contained such innovations as a pressurized cabin and remote-controlled machine-gun turrets. While it was designed as a high-altitude daytime bomber, it flew more low-altitude nighttime missions. It was the primary aircraft in the U.S. firebombing campaign against Japan in the final months of World War II. B-29s carried the atomic bombs that destroyed Hiroshima and Nagasaki in August 1945.

B-36 (Peacemaker) was an intercontinental bomber with a range of 6,000 miles developed by the United States during the Cold War that was capable of delivering thermonuclear weapons. It was the largest combat aircraft ever built at that time.

B-52 is a strategic intercontinental bomber of the United States, which has the capacity to deliver nuclear weapons while being refueled in-flight. It has been one of three legs of the U.S. triad of strategic nuclear forces (the other two being submarines and intercontinental ballistic missiles) since the 1950s.

Baal was a Semitic fertility god worshipped by the Canaanites and Phoenicians, who brought his worship to other parts of the Mediterranean. His name means *Lord*. Since only priests were allowed to utter his divine name Hadad, Baal was used commonly. Although the word "Baal" can refer to any god and even to human officials, as a name it was used substantially for Hadad, who was a god of the sun, rain, thunder, fertility and agriculture, and the lord of heaven. The myths surrounding Baal are mainly of the common mythological pattern of the fertility god who is slain and resurrected, perhaps creating the change in the seasons.

Ba'ath Party was a Pan-Arab, socialist political party that was formed in Damascus, Syria in 1947

(Ba'ath is the Arabic word for renaissance). It advocated Arab nationalism and opposed imperialism and colonialism. The Ba'ath Party sought to unify all of the Arab countries into one nation. The slogan of the party was "unity, liberty and socialism". In addition to Syria, it established branches in the 1950s in Lebanon, Jordan, Yemen, Libya and Iraq. However, the Syrian branch briefly took power in 1963 and ruled until 1966 when a military coup d'état in which Hafiz al-Assad participated seized control of the government. Assad would subsequently seize control of the Syrian government in 1970 and rule until 2000, when his son, Bashar Hafez al Assad succeeded him. The Iraqi Ba'athist party took power permanently in 1968 and control over the party became gradually concentrated in Saddam Hussein. The Iraqi Ba'athist party was overthrown in 2003 as a result of the American-led Iraq War.

Babi Yar (1941–1943) is the name of a ravine located on the northern edge of Kiev in the Ukrainian region of the Soviet Union where approximately 34,000 Jews of Kiev, according to Nazi reports, were systematically murdered over a thirty-six hour period on September 29 and 30, 1941 by Nazi soldiers. The Jewish victims were marched to the ravine, forced to undress, shot by machine guns and were buried by the Nazis under thick layers of dirt. One month after the slaughter of the Jews in Babi Yar, the Nazis murdered approximately 50,000 Jews in Odessa. Even after the murder of the Jews at Babi Yar in 1941, the Nazis used Babi Yar until 1943 as a site to kill approximately 100,000 to 150,000 civilians, communists, Soviet prisoners of war and Roma. However, the exact number of people killed at Babi Yar from 1941 to 1943 and their names are unknown even today. As the Nazis retreated from the advancing Soviet troops in 1944, they attempted to hide the evidence of the killings at Babi Yar by exhuming the bodies, burning them and spreading their ashes over the surrounding farmland. The Soviet poet Yevgeny Yevtushenko wrote a poem in 1961 titled Babi Yar, which was set to music by Dmitry Shostakovich in his 13th Symphony and performed for the first time in Moscow in 1962.

Baby Boom is the term used to describe the dramatic increase in birth rate in the United States after World War II. It is estimated that approximately 75 million children were born between 1946 and 1964. Sylvia Porter, a columnist for the *New York Post* first used the term "boom" in 1951 to refer to this increase in the numbers of births.

Babylon was the largest and most important city in Mesopotamia. It was the capital of King Hammurabi in the 18th century BCE and Nebuchadnezzar in the 6th century BCE.

Babylonian Captivity of the Hebrews (587–538 BCE) is the name given by historians to the period in Jewish history when the kingdom of Judah was conquered by the Neo-Babylonians under King Nebuchadnezzar, who destroyed Solomon's Temple in Jerusalem and exiled the Jewish political, economic and cultural elite to Babylon. While in exile in Babylon, the Jewish people, who were not treated as slaves by the Neo-Babylonians, were permitted to practice their religion. During this fifty year period of exile in Babylon, the Jewish people developed a singular religious identity and the basic beliefs of Judaism. When King Cyrus the Great of Persia captured Babylon in 538 BCE, he permitted the exiled Jewish population to return to Jerusalem. King Cyrus also allowed them to rebuild their temple and practice their religion.

Babylonian Captivity of the Papacy (1309–1377) is a term used by historians to describe a period when seven consecutive popes resided in Avignon, France. During this period, those seven popes were subservient to the French kings. Living in luxury and extravagance, these popes gained a reputation for being worldly, greedy and corrupt.

Bacon, Francis (1561–1626) was an English statesman and philosopher whose advocacy of the scientific method contributed to a fundamental revision of human inquiry and knowledge. He was the Lord Chancellor during the reign of King James I. He is the author of *Utopia*, in which he advocated the benefits of science to build a peaceful society and achieve human happiness. This book would contribute to the development of the scientific method, which relies upon the development of the empirical method and the use of inductive reasoning.

Bacon, Roger (1200s) was an English philosopher, university (Oxford and University of Paris) and Franciscan friar who advocated using empirical methods to study nature. Inspired by the writings of Aristotle and Arabic scholars such as Al-hazen, he was perhaps the earliest European to advocate the use of the modern scientific method based on the collection of facts before drawing a scientific conclusion. Based on his study of Greek and Arabic works on optics, he recommended that the study of optics, which was called "perspective" in the medieval era, be included in the medieval university curriculum. He also proposed the creation of a kind of encyclopedia that would collect the expert writings of scholars in such fields as optics, astronomy, astrology, alchemy, mechanics, geography, agriculture, medicine and experimental science. In his book, *Opus Magus*, he wrote on mathematics, optics, alchemy and astronomy and offered the first description of the basic ingredients of gunpowder. Based on his study of ancient Greek and medieval Islamic astronomy, he criticized the inaccuracy of the Julian calendar then widely used in Europe. Subsequently, he proposed a reform to the Julian calendar that was similar to the changes decreed by Pope Gregory XIII in 1582 when the Gregorian calendar was adopted by the Catholic Church.

Bactria was the ancient Greek name of the country that was located in what is present-day northern Afghanistan. According to some historians Bactria was the homeland of Aryan tribes who moved southwest into Iran and into North-Western India circa 2500–2000 BCE Later it became the northern province of the Persian Empire in Central Asia. It was in these regions that the prophet Zarathustra (Zoroaster) was said to have been born and gained his first adherents. It is not known whether Bactria formed part of the Median Empire, but it was subjugated by Cyrus the Great, and from then formed one of the satrapies of the Persian Empire. After Persia had been defeated by Alexander the Great, the satrap of Bactria, tried to organize a national resistance against Alexander. After Alexander's death, his empire was eventually divided up among his generals and Bactria became a part of the Seleucid Empire.

Balance of Payments is the calculation of all of the flows of money coming into and going out of a country over a period of time that are derived, for example, from trade transactions, foreign aid, profits of businesses, sale of services and equipment to public and private entities, and tourism.

Balance of Power is a theory used in international relations to describe how security is achieved and maintained in the international system. According to this theory, when states enjoy relatively equal military power, they will form shifting and flexible alliances or make policies to counteract the acquisition of hegemonic military power by any of other states. As a result, no one state is able to dominate the other states, and hence the international system. This approach to international relations was established by the major European states at the Congress of Vienna after the defeat of Napoleon in order to prevent any one of them from becoming as politically and militarily dominant in Europe as had been the Napoleonic Empire.

Balance of Terror, which is also known as Mutual Assured Destruction, was a geopolitical concept developed after World War II when both the U.S. and the Soviet Union built large nuclear arsenals. It was argued that relative nuclear parity would prevent a nuclear war. Since both countries had the capacity to destroy each other, the threat of the use of each countries' nuclear arsenal would deter either nation from using nuclear weapons in a crisis situation.

Balance of Trade is the difference between the value of a state's exports minus the value of its imports.

Balfour Declaration (1917) was the statement issued during World War I by the British Foreign Secretary Arthur Balfour that supported the establishment of a Jewish national homeland in Palestine after the war. The Balfour Declaration also committed the British to respect Palestinian claims in Palestine.

Balkanization is a geopolitical political process by which an area of territory of a larger and more powerful state is divided into smaller and weaker states without regard to existing ethnic, cultural or political boundaries.

Balkans is a geopolitical and cultural region of southeastern Europe. The region, which is very mountainous, takes its name from the Balkan Mountains that are located in Bulgaria and Serbia. Today the Balkans is comprised of the following countries: Slovenia, Croatia, Bosnia and Herzegovina,

Serbia, Kosovo, Montenegro, Macedonia, Albania, Bulgaria, Romania, and Moldova. The Balkan region was the first area of Europe to experience the arrival of farming cultures in the Neolithic era. The practices of growing grain and raising livestock arrived in the Balkans from the Fertile Crescent by way of Anatolia and then spread to Central Europe. In classical antiquity, this region was home to Greeks, Illyrians, Thracians, and Dacians. The Roman Empire conquered most of the region and spread Roman culture and the Latin language but significant parts still remained under Greek influence. Slavs arrived in the 500s and began displacing the already Romanized and Hellenized older inhabitants of the region. During the Middle Ages, the Balkans became the stage for a series of wars between the Byzantine, Bulgarian and Serbian Empires. By the end of the 1500s, the Ottoman Empire controlled the region and began a forcible conversion of all non-Muslim peoples to Islam. Most of the Balkan nation-states emerged during the 1800s and early 1900s as they gained independence either from the Ottoman Empire or the Austro-Hungarian Empire: Serbia in 1817, Greece in 1829, Bulgaria and Montenegro in 1878, Romania in 1878, Albania in 1912, Croatia and Slovenia in 1918. In 1912–1913 the First Balkan War broke out when the nation-states of Bulgaria, Serbia, Greece and Montenegro united in an alliance against the Ottoman Empire. The defeat of the Ottoman Empire by his alliance ended five centuries of Ottoman presence in Europe. Two months after the end of the war, a Second Balkan War broke out when Bulgaria attacked its allies Serbia and Greece. The Serbs and the Greeks repelled them, after the Greek army invaded Bulgaria. World War I began in the Balkans in 1914 when a Serbian nationalist and member of the Black Hand Society assassinated Archduke Franz Ferdinand, heir to the throne of the Austro-Hungarian Empire, in Sarajevo, the capital of Bosnia and Herzegovina.

Balkan Wars (1912–1913) were two wars fought in southeastern Europe during the course of which the nations of Bulgaria, Montenegro, Greece, and Serbia formed an alliance known as to the Balkan League. These nations hoped to conquer the lands of Macedonia, Albania, and Thrace, which were controlled by the Ottoman Empire (more commonly known as the "Sick Man of Europe"). As the Ottoman Empire declined in power and influence throughout the 1800s, a number of the major European military powers such as Russia, Britain, France, and Austria-Hungary were increasingly concerned with what would happen to the Balkan provinces of a weakened and impotent Ottoman Empire. This concern would become known as the "Eastern Question." At the same time, the members of the Balkan League viewed the weakness of the Ottoman Empire as an opportune time to attack and fulfill their respective desires for expansion into the Balkan provinces of the Ottoman Empire. Even though the members of the Balkan League fought together against their common enemy, the Ottoman Empire in the two Balkan Wars, individual rivalry triumphed over unity against a common enemy. Subsequently, the Balkan League collapsed over disagreements over the distribution of the spoils resulting from the two Balkan Wars.

Ball, John (1338–1381) was an English Catholic priest who became a proponent of the ideas of John Wycliffe. He was a well-known traveling preacher who neither had a parish nor belonged to a Catholic order. As a supporter of the Lollards, he delivered radical sermons in the public marketplaces of the towns and villages throughout the English countryside, in which he emphasized the need for social equality and the creation of a classless society. Since the Catholic Church prohibited him from giving such radical sermons in any church, he, nevertheless, gave sermons in English in the courtyards outside of Catholic churches after the parishioners had attend the formal church services, which were delivered in Latin. In response to his sermons about social equality and a classless society, he was excommunicated in 1366 by the Catholic Church, which meant that any member of the Catholic Church was forbidden to listen to Ball's sermons. Nevertheless, he continued to give public sermons, even though he was imprisoned on numerous occasions, until the outbreak of the Peasant's Revolt in 1381, which he joined. He gave sermons to the participants in the Revolt and became one of its leaders. After the revolt was crushed by the English authorities, he was tried and hanged.

Ballistic Missiles are the major strategic delivery vehicles for nuclear weapons in the nuclear arsenals of the United States and Russia (previously the Soviet Union). In addition to a nuclear warhead, they can also carry conventional, chemical, or biological warheads. The Soviet Union developed the first international ballistic missiles in 1957.

Banalities were monopolies given to noble land-owners by kings during the Middle Ages in Europe that gave the nobles the right to charge serfs on a noble's land dues for the use of the noble's mill to grind the serf's grain and the use of the noble's ovens to bake the serf's bread.

Banana Republic is a term used by historians to describe corrupt dictatorial governments created by and/or supported by the U.S. policymakers and American corporations in the late 1800s, which were located primarily in the Caribbean and Central America (for example, Costa Rica, Guatemala and Honduras). These countries were dominated by a wealthy oligarchical elite who controlled the government, military and economy and were supportive of U.S. foreign policy and American business interests in their respective countries. Furthermore, these societies were largely dependent on the export of a single agricultural crop such as bananas, coffee or sugar cane which was grown on plantations owned by American multinational corporations such as the United Fruit Company (later known as Chiquita Brands International), the Standard Fruit Company (later known as Dole Food Company) and the Cuyamel Fruit Company. In addition to controlling the cultivation, harvesting and export of such agricultural products, these American corporations also controlled the transportation (road and railroads) infrastructure, the long distance communication network (telegraph and telephone) and the ports of such societies to ensure their economic and political interests. In fact, in number of these countries who were dependent on the export of a single agricultural product, American multinational corporations became the principal employer. Bananas, which were introduced into the U.S. in 1870, became very popular among American over the next sixty years. By the 1930s, United Fruit Company controlled 80–90% of the bananas imported into the U.S. The United Fruit Company became so politically influential in the U.S. that it was able to convince the U.S. in the early 1950s to support the overthrow of a democratically government in Guatemala by the Central Intelligence Agency because the president of Guatemala proposed land reform which would have confiscated unused lands owned by the United Fruit Company and redistributed that land to landless peasants. William Snyder Porter, who wrote under the pseudonym O. Henry, coined the term "banana republic" in his book *Cabbages and Kings*, which was published in 1904.

Band was a form of social organization comprised of less than fifty people that existed in hunting and gathering societies. According to anthropologists, a band did not have formal political positions.

Bandung Conference (1955) was a meeting of twenty-nine newly independent Asian and African states, which took place in Bandung, Indonesia. These twenty-nine countries represented nearly one-fourth of the Earth's land surface and a total population of 1.5 billion people. The purpose of the conference was to promote Afro-Asian economic and cultural cooperation and to oppose colonialism or neocolonialism by either the United States or the Soviet Union or any other imperialistic nations. The conference contributed to the development of the Non-Aligned Movement. This meeting reflected the growing dissatisfaction of many nations of the Third World with the reluctance by the Western powers to consult with them on decisions affecting Africa and Asia; their concern over the increasing tensions between the People's Republic of China and the United States; their desire to establish more peaceful relations between China and the West; and their opposition to colonialism, especially French influence in North Africa. A ten-point "declaration on the promotion of world peace and cooperation," incorporating the principles of the United Nations charter and Indian Prime Minister Jawaharlal Nehru's Five Principles ("mutual respect" for other nations' "territorial integrity and sovereignty," nonaggression, noninterference in "internal affairs," equality and mutual benefit, and "peaceful coexistence"), was adopted unanimously. By the early 1960s, as decolonization progressed, significant disagreements arose among the participants to the Conference.

Banner System was a form of military organization developed by the Manchu tribes of Manchuria during the 1600s that was used to conquer China. This system was developed by Nurhachi (1559–1626), who in 1601 organized his warriors into four companies of 300 men each. The companies were distinguished by banners of different colors—yellow, red, white, and blue. In 1615 four more banners were added. The yellow, white and blue banners were bordered in red and the red was bordered in white. As the Manchu expanded their conquest of China, the size of the companies was increased to 7,500 men. The Banner system also served important administrative functions. Taxation, conscription and registration of the population were carried out through this system of organization. The villages where the bannermen lived and worked in times of peace were required to contribute a certain number of men in times of war. As the Manchus expanded their conquest of the Chinese and Mongols, they organized their captives into companies modeled after the banners. In 1635 eight Mongol banners were added to the Manchu system and in 1642 eight Chinese banners were added. The new banners, which fought alongside the old, brought to 24 the total number of banner units. With these troops, the Manchus were able to conquer China and establish the Qing Dynasty (1644–1912). The bannermen were considered a form of nobility and were given preferential treatment in terms of annual pensions, land, and allotments of rice and cloth. Manchu bannermen were on the whole treated better than their Mongol and Chinese counterparts. They were prohibited from participating in trade and manual labor and those who broke the law were not tried before an ordinary civil magistrate but by a special Manchu general. During the century and a half of peace following the establishment of the Qing Dynasty, the fighting qualities of the banner forces deteriorated, and their training was neglected. During the White Lotus Rebellion (1796–1804) and then again during the Taiping Rebellion (1850–1864), the banners were unable to protect the Qing Dynasty, and the government eventually had to organize other forces. By the end of the 1800s the Banner System had become totally ineffective.

Bantustan, also known as a homeland, is the name for a rural area where black South Africans were forcibly resettled by the South African government for the purpose of permanently segregating the majority black South African population from the minority white South African population. Beginning in the late 1950s, the South African government, as part of its policy of apartheid, created 10 homelands where black South Africans were required to live. These homelands were compromised of disconnected pieces of impoverished territory that had little arable land, no economic infrastructure and few jobs, hospitals or schools. Accordingly, poverty was pervasive in the homelands. The South African government created various "tribes" based on arbitrary ethnic and linguistic categories and assigned a "tribe" to one of the 10 homelands. The 10 homelands constituted only 13% of the land of South Africa while the remaining 87% was occupied by the white South African population even though blacks made up 75% of the South African population. Under the homeland policy, the South African government attempted to create the fiction that the homelands were autonomous states even though the South African government still exercised political, military and financial control over the homelands. In addition to segregating the black population, the homeland policy deprived the black population of South African citizenship and made them citizens of one of the 10 homelands. In 1970, the South African government passed a law which formally made the black population citizens of one of the ten homelands and terminated their South African citizenship. Given the lack of jobs in the 10 homelands, millions of black South Africans were compelled to enter into annual work contracts which allowed them to be employed outside the homeland as a "guest worker" in the urban areas of South Africa. The "guest worker" program caused men and women to be away from their families for months at a time. Even if a husband and wife were permitted to work outside their homeland as "guest workers"' the could not legally visit each other in the city where they worked if their ID card restricted them to a specific neighborhood in that city. Once a "guest worker's" contract ended they were deported by the South African government to their designated homeland. Even though the South African government treated each homeland as a separate state, the 10 homelands were not recognized by any other nation in the world as an autonomous state other than by South Africa. With the end of apartheid in South Africa in 1994, the homelands were abolished and all black South Africans had their South African citizen restored.

Baptism is a form of ritual purification in which an individual is plunged or dunked in water. It was John the Baptist who baptized Jesus.

Barbarian, which is a term derived from the Greek word barbaroi, were tribes of people who were considered outsiders by both the Greeks and Romans. For the ancient Greeks, they were babblers, people who did not speak Greek. To the Romans, they were people outside the Roman Empire, who the Romans considered savages and uncivilized.

Bargaining is the process by which two or more parties communicate for the purpose of reaching an agreement.

Baroque is an ornate style in architecture intended to elicit a strong emotional response. This style was marked by an emphasis on heavy and dramatic ornamentation and curved rather than straight lines. It flourished between 1550 and 1750 and was particularly associated with the period of the Catholic Counter-Reformation.

Barracks Emperors is the term used by historians to describe the period of the Roman Empire during from 235 to 285 CE when many military commanders repeatedly usurped political power and ruled the Roman Empire. Most of these military commanders were ordinary soldiers who had risen through the ranks.

Basil II, Emperor (958–1025 CE) who was also known as the "Slayer of the Bulgars" ruled the Byzantine Empire from 976 to 1025. During his reign, the Byzantine Empire attained its greatest influence. As a result of almost constant wars, he was able to expand the Byzantine Empire by conquering Syria, Bulgaria, Armenia, Georgia, southern Italy and Sicily. He was known for his ruthlessness in war and suppressing internal strife and rebellions. After defeating the Bulgarians, it is said that he captured 15,000 prisoners and that he blinded 99 out of 100 Bulgarian soldiers, leaving 150 one-eyed soldiers to the lead the remaining prisoners home. He facilitated the conversion of Kievan Russia to Christianity.

Basileis, which means king or chief, was the title of a man who led a community in ancient Greece before the Archaic Age. Their primary function was to engage in warfare.

Bassi, Laura (1711–1778) was an Italian professor of physics at the University of Bologna from which she received her doctoral degree in 1732. She was the first woman to become a physics professor at a European university. She was the second woman

in Europe to receive a university degree; the first was Elena Cornaro who received a doctorate in philosophy from the University of Padua in 1678. Bassi introduced Newton's ideas on physics to Italy and taught courses on Newtonian physics and natural philosophy for 28 years. It would not be until the late 1800s that two other women would earn doctoral degrees from European universities: Sofia Kovalevskaya (or Sophie Kowalevski) in mathematics from the University of Gottingen and Stefania Wolicka in history from the University of Zurich.

Bastille, which was considered to be a powerful symbol of royal authority by the people of Paris, was the fortress and prison in Paris that was seized on July 14, 1789 by an armed group of about 900 Parisians, who were primarily sans-culottes. The attackers believed that the Bastille contained a large supply of weapons and ammunition. The military officer in charge of the Bastille fired into the crowd killing ninety-eight attackers. After defeating the military forces defending the Bastille, the attackers completely demolished it. This event came to symbolize popular support for the French Revolution and the beginning of the end of absolute monarchy in France.

Batavia was the name of the fort established by the Dutch East India Company in 1619 in Indonesia. Today it is the city of Jakarta.

Battle Axe Culture is a term used by archaeologists to a describe a wide range of late Neolithic and early Bronze Age cultural patterns that gradually developed in central and northern Europe between 3500 and 1800 BCE. This culture replaced the linear pottery culture. The people of the battle axe culture lived in settlements with thatched dwellings, practiced agriculture, made pottery, raised domesticated animals such as oxen and horses, and used stone and copper tools.

Bauhaus was an influential school of German art and architecture that emerged in the 1920s in response to the cultural uncertainty that followed World War I in Europe. It advocated the use of modern materials in developing new forms of architecture, design, and urban planning. The Bauhaus style, which emphasized that modern buildings and furniture should be both functional and beautiful, helped shape the idea of "modern" throughout the world during the 1900s. It influenced many leading architects and designers

Bay of Pigs (1961) was the unsuccessful invasion of Cuba from April 17–20, 1961, by Cuban exiles who were organized, trained, and supported by the CIA and the U.S. government. The rebels intended to incite an insurrection in Cuba and overthrow the communist government led by Fidel Castro.

Bayle, Pierre (1647–1706) was a French Huguenot scholar and philosopher who wrote many works on religious tolerance, superstition, and religious belief. At the Protestant Academy of Sedan, he taught philosophy and history to the persecuted Huguenots who took refuge there. He feuded with the leader of the Huguenots, Pierre Jurieu, concerning issues of political theology and was stripped of his professorship in 1693. He wrote a seminal work titled *Historical and Critical Dictionary* in 1697, which influenced such Enlightenment thinkers as Denis Diderot.

Bayonet is a short sword attached to the muzzle of a rifle. European armies first used it in the 1600s as an infantry weapon for close combat. It replaced the pikemen.

Beccaria, Cesare (1738–1794) was a Milanese nobleman who wrote *On Crimes and Punishment* in 1764. This book would become one of the most influential texts during the Enlightenment.

Beauvoir, Simone de (1908–1986) was a French writer, feminist and proponent of existentialism. While she wrote extensively on political, social and philosophical issues, she was most well-known for her book *The Second Sex* published in 1949. In this book she analyzed the impact on women of the institutions and ideas of Western European culture that had been created by men. De Beauvoir asserted that women had to develop strategies to overcome a patriarchal culture in which women were forced into social positions subordinate to men. She further contended that women had failed to create an authentic sense of self by accepting cultural norms created by men that limited a women's role in society to reproduction and motherhood. In failing to develop an authentic sense of self, she argued that women had become what de Beauvoir called the "other". She concluded that women could only develop a sense of personal fulfillment, independence and equality when they attained education, employment and economic freedom. De Beauvoir believed that such developments would eliminate the barrier that separated men from women. As a consequence, she advocated a fundamental redefinition of gender roles in European society and a reconceptualization of Western European culture. *The Second Sex* would significantly influence the women's liberation movement of the late 1960s and 1970s in France, Europe and the U.S.

Bedouins are the Arab-speaking, nomadic, pastoralist inhabitants of the Arabian Peninsula. Bedouins were divided into tribes in which each tribe was descended from one common ancestor and the head of the tribe was called a sheik. In the 600s, the Bedouins converted to Islam.

Beer is one of the world's oldest alcoholic beverages. According to archaeological evidence, the production of beer can be dated to circa 3500–3100 BCE. Such evidence was found in the Zagros Mountains in Iran. This early beer was made of barley. In Sumeria, the Code of Hammurabi included laws regulating the production and distribution of beer and beer parlors. Furthermore, the Hymn to Ninkasi", a prayer to the Mesopotamian goddess of beer, provided a recipe for the making of beer. In Egypt, reliefs on Egyptian tombs dating from 2400 BCE show beer production. The basic techniques of brewing came to Europe from the Middle East. It appears that a type of beer (did not contain hops) was spread by Germanic and Celtic tribes in Europe circa 3000 BCE. It was reported by two Roman historians Pliny (in the 1st century BCE) and Tacitus (in the 1st century CE) that Saxons, Celts and Nordic and Germanic tribes drank ale. By the 600s CE, beer was being produced and sold by European monasteries. Around 1000, hops began to be used in the production of beer in Germany. It was only in 1516 that William IV, Duke of Bavaria, adopted purity laws to ensure that the ingredients of beer were only water, hops and barley-malt.

Beer Hall Putsch (Munich Putsch) (1923) was the failed Nazi attempt to start an insurrection against the Weimar government in Germany. The insurrection began in Munich when Adolf Hitler and his small Nazi Party forced their way into a right-wing political meeting in a beer hall in Munich. Hitler obtained agreement that both groups should unite and carry the "revolution" to Berlin just as Mussolini had done a year earlier in Rome. After the failed attempt in Munich, Hitler was arrested and tried for treason. He was sentenced to five years' imprisonment, but only served eight months. While in prison, he wrote *Mein Kampf* ("My Struggle").

Beguines were Catholic lay religious communities of women established in the 1200s and 1300s in Europe who devoted themselves to prayer, good works, and caring for the poor. They were influenced by Albigensian teachings, which were condemned as heretical by the Catholic Church. A beguine was not a nun, as she took no vows and could return to the world if she wed. She neither asked for nor accepted alms, but supported herself by manual labor or by teaching the children of townspeople. She had her own dwelling and servants if she could afford them. Each community established its own rules, and was comprised of women from different social classes. Some communities only admitted women of high social status, others were exclusively reserved for women of humble background, and others accepted women from any social class. These communities spread rapidly throughout Europe and began to exercise a profound influence on the religious life of the urban populations. In 1311, Pope Clement V condemned the beguines as heretics and in many cases they were executed. The beguines were also persecuted by Popes John XXII, Urban V, and Gregory XI. Eventually, some monastic and mendicant orders absorbed these communities. Even though Pope Eugene IV rehabilitated these communities in the 1400s, the Catholic Church, during the religious conflicts of the 1500s, suppressed most of these communities.

Beijing is the capital of the Peoples Republic of China. It became the capital of China in 906.

Belisarius (505–565) was a general in the Eastern Roman Empire (Byzantine Empire) who played an important role in Emperor Justinian's attempt to reconquer the Western Roman Empire. He defeated the Vandals in North Africa and the Ostrogoths in Italy. After his defeat of the Vandals, he was granted a triumph, which was the last one ever given in the Roman Empire, when he returned to Constantinople. Despite the significant military victories of Belisarius, Justinian was unable to fulfill his plan to reunite the eastern and western parts of the Roman Empire.

Bellarmine, Saint Robert (1542–1621) was the Catholic clergyman who warned Galileo about promoting Copernicanism. He was a leader of the Catholic Counter-Reformation who wrote *Disputations on the Controversies of the Christian Faith.*

Belzec was one of the six the Nazi concentration camps established in Poland during World War II that was specifically designed to systematically murder European Jews, gypsies, socialists, communists, and other political opponents of the Nazis. Operating from 1942–1943, more than 600,000 people were killed there, nearly all of them Jews.

Benedict of Nursia, Saint (480–550 CE) was an Italian ascetic who founded a monastic community at Monte Cassino, Italy who is considered to be the father of Christian monasticism. He created the Benedictine Rule, which all Christian monks were required to follow.

Benedictine Rule refers to the rules of conduct developed by Saint Benedict that were to be followed in the monasteries under his leadership. The Benedictine Rule required poverty, sexual chastity, obedience, labor and religious devotion of all Christian monks.

Benedictines were monks and nuns who followed the code of Saint Benedict of Nursia. Saint Benedict founded twelve monasteries in the 500s CE near Rome. The Benedictines spent four to eight hours each day praying, seven or eight hours sleeping, and four to eight hours working or studying scripture. An abbot had the authority over this religious community. Many popes and cardinals came from this religious order.

Benefice was a permanent office or position in the Catholic Church, such as a bishopric, that consisted of a sacred duty and the right of the holder of that office to the income that went with such a position. Under the canon law of the Catholic Church, a benefice meant an income enjoyed from some land administered by a priest or Church official. Each benefice had a number of spiritual duties attached to it. For providing these spiritual duties, a priest would receive pay. As a result of this practice, enormous wealth became concentrated in the Catholic Church because such payments endured beyond any individual's life. Over time, the benefice system was abused throughout Europe as priests began to hold more than one benefice, which became known as "pluralism." Pluralism allowed wealthy families to buy a position (simony) in the Church for a son or relative. Furthermore, wealthy families who bought such Church offices could delegate those positions to priests who were illiterate or lacked proper training for a fraction of the benefice, while the family held the formal benefice. Growing demands for reform of this practice were one of the factors that contributed to the Protestant Reformation. As a result of the Protestant Reformation, the newly-created Christian sects rejected the benefice system. The French Revolution ended the benefice system in France by confiscating the vast wealth of the Catholic Church and making the Catholic priests employees of the state. A benefice was also the title of a grant of land by a noble to a vassal in exchange for services and an oath of loyalty by a vassal.

Bengal is a region in the northeast of India that today is divided between Bangladesh (previously East Pakistan) and the Indian state of West Bengal. Bengal was an important area for the Indian independence movement because armed revolutionary groups attempted to overthrow British colonial rule in the early 1900s. Furthermore, it was also central to the growth of political awareness of the Muslim population. The Muslim League was established in Bengal in 1906. When India gained independence in 1947, Bengal was divided (partitioned) along religious lines. The western part went to India and was named West Bengal, while the eastern part joined Pakistan as a province eventually called East Pakistan. As a result of partition, there were widespread religious riots in Bengal between Hindus and Muslims.

Beowulf is an Anglo-Saxon heroic epic poem of anonymous authorship that dates from between the 8th and the 11th centuries. The main character, Beowulf, hero of the Geats, travels great distances to prove his strength at impossible odds against supernatural demons and beasts. He fights Grendel, Grendel's mother, and a dragon. He is mortally wounded in the final battle and after his death his followers bury him in Geatland.

Bering, Vitus (1681–1741) was a Danish navigator and explorer who joined the Russian navy during the reign of Peter the Great. In 1724, he led an expedition to map Siberia and crossed into North America. The strait separating Alaska from Russia is named after him.

Beringia is the term used by geologists for the late Ice Age landmass that encompassed northeast Siberia, Alaska and the Bering Strait.

Berlin Airlift (1948) is the name used by historians for the massive effort to resupply West Berlin by air that was undertaken by the United States between June 1948 and May 1949 in response to the Soviet blockade of land routes to the city. The Soviet blockade had been instituted after the United States, Britain and France had announced the creation of a single currency for use in their zones of occupation in Germany, which the Soviets interpreted as the first step in the unification of the Allied zones of occupation. Even though the Soviets opened the land routes to Berlin in May 1949, Berlin and Germany would remain divided until 1989.

Berlin Conference (1884–1885) was the meeting of the major European powers organized by Otto von Bismarck, Chancellor of Germany, that provided the justification for and regulation of the European colonization of and trade with sub-Saharan Africa during the era described by historians as the period of "New Imperialism". This conference coincided with Germany's emergence in Europe and the world as a major economic, military and imperial power. The territorial divisions established by the European colonial powers ignored the existing geographical concentrations of indigenous cultural groups. The Berlin Conference is viewed by many historians as the formalization of the "Scramble for Africa."

Berlin Wall (1961) was the wall built in 1961 by the East German government to divide Berlin in two in order to prevent East German citizens from escaping to West Germany. It was eventually torn down in 1989.

Bernard of Clairvaux (1090–1153) was a Catholic monk and church reformer during the Middle Ages in Europe, who challenged the ideas of Peter Abelard. He stressed the mystical union with

God and argued that faith and divine inspiration were more important than reasoning and logic. His ideas influenced the Cistercian religious order.

Bicameral System is a legislative body comprised of two houses or chambers, such as the United States Congress, which is comprised of the Senate and the House of Representatives or the English Parliament which is comprised of the House of Commons and the House of Lords. In a federal system of government (U.S.), both chambers and houses are co-equal and both may initiate legislation. In a parliamentary system (England), there is a hierarchical relationship between the chambers or houses in which one is superior in the powers it my exercise. Enactment of legislation in a bicameral system typically requires the approval of a majority of the members of both chambers or houses. In a bicameral legislature, members of one chamber or house may be selected by popular vote, while the members other chamber or house may be elected or appointed. Historically, bicameral institutions first emerged in Europe in 1600s, but representation was based on social class. One chamber or house would represent the aristocracy and clergy, while the other represented the commoners, who constituted the overwhelming majority of the population.

Big Bertha was the nickname for an extremely heavy artillery piece (a howitzer) that the Germans used in World War I to bombard Belgian and French forts. The gun was built secretly before the war by Krupp, Germany's largest armaments manufacturer. The gun weighed 47 tons and was operated by 240 men. A Big Bertha fired a one-ton shell a distance of almost six miles, which could penetrate up to 40 feet of concrete and earth. Because of the weight of the shell, a crane was used to insert the shell into the gun. In order to be transported to the battlefield, the gun had to be disassembled and shipped on railway wars. At the battlefield it was reassembled and nine tractors were used to pull the gun into positon. At the Battle of Verdun (1916), the Germans used twelve Big Berthas, but they were unsuccessful in destroying the French forts, which were built with reinforced concrete.

Big Stick Diplomacy was the term coined by American newspapers to describe the foreign policy approach of President Theodore Roosevelt (1901–1909). Roosevelt advocated that in foreign affairs, especially in the Caribbean and Central America, the United States should rely on diplomacy and military strength, which he described with the aphorism "Speak softly and carry a big stick". This approach meant that Roosevelt would attempt to use peaceful negotiations to settle disputes with other nations while simultaneously threatening the use of American military force if those nations did not agree with the terms of a negotiated settlement proposed by the United States. The primary objective of Roosevelt's "Big Stick" foreign policy was to ensure the economic, military and political dominance of the United States in its sphere of influence in the Caribbean and Central and South America.

Big Three was the term used during World War II to refer to the political leaders of the United States, the Soviet Union, and Britain who planned for the defeat of Germany and Japan during World War II and negotiated postwar settlements. Until the death of President Roosevelt in April 1945, the three leaders were Josef Stalin, Winston Churchill, and Franklin Roosevelt. By the summer of 1945 after Roosevelt's death, it was comprised of Harry Truman, Clement Attlee, and Stalin.

Bigotry is an individual's conduct, opinion, belief, or attitude that is prejudiced, intolerant, and without any rational or reasonable basis.

Bikini (1946) is the name of an atoll in the Marshal Islands in the Pacific where the U.S. government tested 23 nuclear bombs on land, in the air or underwater between 1946 and 1958. The U.S. conducted it first peacetime test of a nuclear bomb at Bikini on July 1, 1946, over a fleet of 73 ships, to determine the effect of an nuclear bomb on naval vessels. In 1954, the U.S. government also tested a 15 megaton hydrogen bomb at Bikini The Bikini Atoll, which consists of 23 islands of approximately 3.4 square miles surrounding a deep central lagoon, suffered severe radioactive contamination from these tests. Prior to the first nuclear bomb test in 1946, the residents of Bikini, who expected to return to their homes in a very short time, were initially relocated by the U.S. government to an uninhabited atoll (Rongerik) that was approximately 125 miles from Bikini.

However, because of an inadequate water and food supply the Bikini inhabitants were relocated in 1948 first to the uninhabited Kwajalein Atoll (225 miles from Bikini) and finally to the uninhabited Kili Island (500 miles from Bikini). In 1969, after the U. S. government began a decontamination program to make Bikini habitable, a few residents returned to Bikini. However, in 1978, the Bikinian population was forced to return to Kili Island after the U.S. government determined that the radioactivity levels at Bikini remained too high to permit resettlement of Bikini. While the radioactivity levels at Bikini remain too high even today to permit resettlement, the U.S. government determined in 1996 that the radioactivity levels were low enough to permit first scuba diving in the lagoon and then in 1998, sport fishing. The cultural impact of the testing of nuclear weapons at Bikini has been quite significant. In 1946, Louis Réard, a French engineer, designed a two-piece bathing suit for women that he called the "bikini" and a mushroom cloud from one of Bikini tests was featured in the 1954 Japanese film *Godzilla*.

Biko, Stephen (1946–1977) was an anti-apartheid activist in South Africa. Even though he was expelled from his high school for political activism, he was able to graduate from St, Francis College, a Catholic boarding school. While a medical student at the University of Natal in 1968, he help found the South Africa Students' Organization (SASO) which espoused "black consciousness", encouraged Africans to recognize their dignity and self-worth and advocated political self–reliance for Africans. He was expelled from the University of Natal for his political activities. SASO eventually evolved into who the Black Consciousness Movement. This movement focused on the ways in which the white population had stripped Africans of their freedom and it encouraged black pride and self-reliance. In 1973, the apartheid government of South Africa prohibited him from speaking to more than one person at a time, speaking in public, publishing his writings and speaking with any media organization. The government went so far as to forbid any media organization from quoting anything Biko said in speeches or personal conversations. He played an important role in organizing the Soweto Uprising in 1976. Between 1975 and 1977, he was arrested and interrogated by the police on four separate occasions. During his fourth arrest,

he was tortured and beaten to death by the police. His death provoked outrage and protests around the world. He was considered by many people to be a martyr in the political struggle to end apartheid. After the end of apartheid, five former police officers confessed to killing Biko and applied for amnesty to the Truth and Reconciliation Commission in 1997. However, since the five police officers claimed that Biko's death was accidental, the Commission refused in 1999 to grant them amnesty. The five police officers were never prosecuted. Donald Woods, a South African journalist, wrote about Biko's life and his struggle against apartheid in his book *Biko* (1977), which was later turned into the film *Cry Freedom* (1987).

Bill of Rights is a document that is written by a legislative body in a constitutional political system specifically listing the individual rights of citizens that a government is obligated to protect. Examples of such documents include the English Bill of Rights (1689), the French Declaration of the Rights of Man and Citizen (1789) the United States Bill of Rights (1791).

Bill of Rights, English (1689) was the legislation adopted by the British Parliament that listed protections from governmental oppression that were to be enjoyed by all British citizens. It is one of the basic documents of English constitutional law, the other being the Magna Carta. The Bill of Rights guaranteed a citizen's right to petition the monarch, a citizen's right to bear arms for defense, and established circumstances under which a British monarch must obtain the consent of the governed as represented by Parliament. Furthermore, it provided the following civil and political rights: (1) freedom from royal interference with the law (the Sovereign was forbidden to establish his own courts or to act as a judge himself); (2) freedom from taxation by royal prerogative, without agreement by Parliament; (3) freedom from a peace-time standing army, without agreement by Parliament; (4) freedom for Protestants to have arms for defense; (5) freedom to elect members of Parliament without interference from the Sovereign; (6) freedom of speech in Parliament, in that proceedings in Parliament were not to be questioned in the courts or in any body outside Parliament itself (the basis of modern parliamentary privilege); (7) freedom from cruel and unusual punishments, and excessive bail; and (8) freedom from fines and forfeitures without trial.

Billeting refers to the required provision of food and lodging of soldiers in the homes of ordinary citizens.

Bin Laden, Osama is the Saudi-born radical Muslim extremist who led and funded the al Qaeda organization, which sought to end the presence of American military forces in Saudia Arabia. He was responsible for several terrorist attacks throughout the world, including the attacks on the World Trade Center and the Pentagon in 2001. He was killed by U.S. military forces in 2011.

Bipolar is a term of international relations used to describe an international system dominated by two major powers or two groups of states having relatively equal military and economic power.

Birth Control Pill is a form of oral contraceptive that women can easily take to prevent an unintended pregnancy. It became widely available in the U.S. and other countries in the mid-1960s. The "pill" gave women greater control over their fertility. As a consequence of the development of the pill, women recognized that sexual intercourse could be a means of physical pleasure divorced from reproduction and that they no longer had to choose between the traditional gender role of wife and mother and a career. The widespread use of the pill caused some religious institutions, social and political commentators and medical experts to debate the moral, social and health consequences of the use of the pill.

Bishops were originally people elected by early Christian congregations to lead them in worship and supervise their funds. Over time, they became the religious and political authorities for Christian communities within a large geographic area, called a diocese or bishopric.

Bismarck, Otto von (1815–1898) was the conservative nationalist prime minister of Prussia from 1862 to 1871 and then the first chancellor of Germany from 1871 to 1890, when he was forced to resign by Kaiser Wilhelm II. His military victories against Denmark in 1864, Austria in 1866, and France in 1870–1871 are largely responsible for the unification of Germany in 1871. He was also responsible for the economic and military dominance of Germany in Europe and the creation of the German Empire, which altered the balance of power in Europe. Although he was a conservative, he supported welfare and social reforms that would greatly influence the domestic policies of many Western European nations in the late 1800s and early 1900s.

Black Death (1348–1351) was the first of a series of bubonic plagues that struck Europe beginning in 1348. It was spread either in the bubonic form by flea bites or in the pneumonic form by the breath of one person on another. The disease, which discolored the victim's body, reappeared many times in Europe until 1701 in a less virulent form. Bubonic plague killed between 30 to 50% of the European population (about 75 million people) between 1348 and 1351 and precipitated an economic decline in Europe, from which Europe would not recover for one hundred years.

Black Hand Society (1911) was a secret Serbian nationalist society founded to achieve Pan-Slavism and Serbian independence by means of terrorism and assassination. The group sought to recruit and train Serbians for a possible war between Serbia and Austria and eventually free Serbia from Austrian control. They organized spies and saboteurs to operate within the provinces of the Austro-Hungarian Empire. Prior to World War I, Serbian military officers and members of the Black Hand Society organized and facilitated the assassination of Archduke Franz Ferdinand, heir to the throne of the Austro-Hungarian Empire, by Gavrillo Princip during the Archduke's visit to Sarajevo. This event provided the spark that ignited the outbreak of World War I in Europe that would last from 1914 until 1918.

Black Jacobins was the nickname of the rebels in the late 1700s in Saint Domingue, a French colony in the Caribbean. Included among them was Toussaint L'Ouverture, a former slave who in 1791 led the slaves of Saint Domingue in the largest and most successful slave insurrection in world history.

Blackshirts was the name of the paramilitary group organized by Mussolini. Funded by wealth landowners, the Black Shirts attacked socialist meetings and union halls and destroyed socialist newspapers and the Socialist Party headquarters during Mussolini's rise to power in Italy in the 1920s.

Black Tuesday was October 24, 1929, the day on which the U.S. stock market crashed and plunged the U.S. and international financial systems into a crisis that would take over a decade from which to recover. It contributed to the global "Great Depression", which did not end in the U.S. until World War II.

Blitzkrieg was the new military strategy of "lightning war" used by the Nazis from 1939 to 1940 when German military forces invaded Poland, Norway, Denmark, Belgium, the Netherlands, and France. This military strategy involved fast-moving and well-coordinated attacks using dive bombers, tanks, other armored vehicles, and motorized infantry to quickly penetrate and overwhelm an enemy's defenses, occupy key territory and undercut the enemies' ability will to repel an attack.

Blockwart was an individual who during the Third Reich served as a "block watch" in each neighborhood and apartment building keeping tabs on his or her neighbors. The Blockwart would determine who was loyal to the Nazi regime and who was not.

Blood Libel or **Blood Accusation** was a false accusation or claim that Jews had murdered children to use their blood in certain aspects of Jewish religious rituals, such as the baking of matzo for Passover. Such false claims as well as those of well poisoning and host desecration have a long history in Europe as the basis for the persecution of Jews. Historically, blood libel claims have been made to account for otherwise unexplained deaths of children. In some cases, an alleged victim became venerated as a martyr. One such individual who was canonized as a saint was William of Norwich. Accusations of blood libel would lead to massacres of Jews in England, Frances, Spain and Germany beginning in the 1200s.

Bloody Sunday is the term used by historians to describe the events that occurred in St. Petersburg, Russia on Sunday, January 22, 1905 when Russian soldiers fired on thousands of striking workers and their families who were peacefully marching to the Winter Palace of Tsar Nicholas II to present him with a petition of grievances requesting improved working conditions, higher wages and an eight hour work day. The soldiers killed and wounded hundreds of men women and children even though the demonstration was led by a Russian priest and the workers carried religious icons and pictures of the tsar and sang patriotic songs. In response to Bloody Sunday, workers organized strikes and demonstrations in all of Russia's major cities. This event triggered the 1905 Revolution that ended absolutist rule in Russia and created a constitutional monarchy.

Boccaccio, Giovanni (1313–1375) was a Florentine scholar and author of the *Decameron*, a series of 100 stories told over ten days from a mostly comic or cynical perspective about the human condition.

Bodin, Jean (1530–1596) was a French jurist, political philosopher, member of the Parlement of Paris and professor of Law in Toulouse. He is best known for his theory of sovereignty and absolutism which claimed the paramount responsibility of the state was to maintain order and that the monarch should have absolute power to achieve that end. Bodin lived during the Protestant Reformation when religious and civil conflict between the (Calvinist) Huguenots and the state-supported Catholic Church dominated France. His most famous work was *Six Books on the State*, which was written in 1576. In that work he stated his definition of sovereignty: "Sovereignty is that absolute and perpetual power vested in a commonwealth". Interestingly enough, he was also a strong believer in witchcraft, the virtues of numbers and the power of the stars. He claimed to have a friendly demon that touched his right ear when he considered doing something wrong and his left when he considered doing something good.

Boethius, Anicius Manlius Severinus (480–524) was a Roman philosopher who sought to preserve ancient learning. He compiled a series of handbooks, anthologies and translations of Greek philosophy which related classical Greek thought to the intellectual development of early Christianity. Even though he was an aristocrat, descended from one of Rome's oldest patrician families, he was appointed head of all government and court services by Theodoric the Great, the Ostrogothic king of Italy. Accused of treason, he was imprisoned and executed by Theodoric. Prior to his imprisonment he compiled a series of anthologies and handbooks in which he tried to explain the meaning and importance of Christian writings to Christians. He also translated the works of Aristotle on logic from Greek to Latin He is best known for his book *The Consolation of Philosophy*, which was written while he was in prison. In his book he claimed that by philosophical inquiry a person could gain a better understanding of God. He further argued that happiness could not be achieved through material possessions or fame, but that a person could gain happiness even in the worst of circumstances by understanding the value of goodness and contemplating the meaning of God. He reached this conclusion by conducting a series of imaginary conversations with "lady Philosophy", who represented wisdom. His book, *The Consolation of Philosophy*, would be one of the most widely read books during the Middle Ages after the Bible. It would influence European education for centuries.

Bohemian Revolt (1618–1620) is the name used by historians to describe the armed rebellion that arose in Bohemia (modern Czech Republic) between the Protestant Bohemian nobility and the Catholic Holy Roman Emperor Matthias and his successor Emperor Ferdinand II (1619) both of whom as ardent supporters of the Catholic Counter-Reformation wanted to recatholicize Bohemia. In 1609, the Holy Roman Emperor Rudolf II issued a Letter of Majesty which granted religious freedom to both Catholics and Protestants living in Bohemia. However Emperors Matthias and Ferdinand began to oppress the rights of Protestants in Bohemia in 1618. In the same year, Ferdinand, who was archduke of Hapsburg Austria and a Catholic, was recognized by the largely Bohemian Diet as king of Bohemia. However, in 1619, the same year that Ferdinand was elected Holy Roman Emperor, the Bohemian nobility deposed him and elected Frederick V, elector of the Palatinate, as the king of Bohemia. In response, Emperor Ferdinand, with the support of the Hapsburg dynasty in Spain, moved to crush the rebellion. Subsequently, after several battles in which the Bohemian Protestants were successful, Ferdinand achieved his first major victory over the Protestants when his army decisively defeated the

Protestant forces at the Battle of White Mountain, which was fought near Prague. Ferdinand's victory was celebrated by Catholics throughout Europe. With the revolt crushed, the leaders of the rebellion were tried and executed and their lands were confiscated, Protestants were expelled from Bohemia, constitutional rule was ended, an authoritarian government was established and Catholicism was made the state religion of Bohemia. The Bohemian Revolt marked the beginning of the Thirty Years war which would engulf the rest of Europe and devastate vast areas of Germany.

Bolivar, Simon (1783–1830) was the most important political and military leader to emerge from the various struggles for independence from Spain in South America between 1817 and 1822. He was called the "Liberator" because of his assistance in helping the military forces in Bolivia, Panama, Colombia, Ecuador, and Peru win political independence from Spain. His military victories led to the creation of the independent state of Gran Columbia. The country of Bolivia is named for him.

Bolsheviks, which means "majority" in Russian, were members of the radical Marxist faction in the Russian Socialist Democratic Party who were led by Vladimir Lenin. Dedicated to a violent revolution, they believed that a revolutionary cadre should seize power on behalf of the working class and build a socialist state. They advocated a violent revolution to destroy the capitalist political and economic institution in Russia. Under Lenin's leadership, the Bolsheviks seized power in October 1917 during the Russian Revolution from the Provisional Government and established a socialist regime in Russia. In 1918, they changed their name to the Communist Party, which would remain in power in the Soviet Union until 1991.

Bomber Gap refers to the claim by a number of U.S. officials in the 1950s that the Soviet Union had more long-range bombers capable of delivering nuclear weapons than the United States. In fact, the US had overwhelming superiority in both long-range bombers and nuclear weapons in the 1950s.

Boniface VIII, Pope was the pope from 1294 to 1303 whose claim to papal authority was threatened by the actions of King Philip IV of France. When Pope Boniface died, the papal court in Rome was moved to Avignon France by the French king, which challenged the power, influence and political legitimacy of the papacy in Europe. The papal court would remain in Avignon until 1378.

Boniface, Saint (675–754 CE) was an English Benedictine monk who was commissioned by Pope Gregory II in 719 to convert the peoples of the German territories of the Frankish Empire to Christianity.

Bonaparte, Napoleon I Emperor (1769–1821) was the Corsican-born French general who seized power in France during the later stages of the French Revolution and ruled France as a dictator from 1799–1812. He consolidated political power as first consul in 1799 and proclaimed himself emperor of France with the approval of a national election in 1804. He successfully conquered much of Europe. His military conquests exported French revolutionary ideals and political reforms to the rest of Europe. After failing to defeat the British and the Prussians during the Napoleonic War, he abdicated in 1814. He returned to power briefly in 1815, but was again defeated by a coalition of European powers (British, Russian, Prussian, and Austrian) at the Battle of Waterloo in 1815.

***Book of Common Prayer* (1549)** was a book issued during the reign of Queen Elizabeth I that expressed the theological basis for Anglicanism.

***Book of the Courtier, The* (1528)** was an etiquette manual written by Baldassare Castiglione that was designed for those within the royal courts of Italy. It described the traits and values of those who served their country, how to act at court, the roles of women at court (a beautiful entertainer), the idea of being a gentleman, and the value of love. The characteristics of a good courtier required that a man: (1) must be born of good stock; (2) must not be feminine in speech or actions; (3) must not be stubborn or loud; (4) must not lie and hope for the best of all situations; and (5) must be fluent in many languages.

***Book of the Dead* (16th century BCE)** was an Egyptian book that preserved their ideas about death and the afterlife. It explained that after

death the soul leaves the body to become part of the divine. Egyptians believed that when this book was placed in a coffin it would permit the deceased to enter paradise.

Borodino, Battle of (1812) was a costly and pointless victory for the invading French army of 130,000 soldiers led by Napoleon over a Russian army of 120,000 soldiers led by General Kutuzov. The battle was fought near the village of Borodino about 70 miles west of Moscow. Prior to Napoleon's invasion of Russia, France and Russia had been allies and Russia had supported France's economic blockade (known as the Continental System) to prevent the importation of British goods into Europe. However, a severe economic crisis in Russia caused it to begin to trade with Britain. By trading with Britain, Russia caused its alliance with France to collapse and ultimately provoked Napoleon's invasion of Russia. Both sides suffered extensive losses of men and supplies at Borodino. This one day battle was the bloodiest battle of the Napoleonic Wars with combined casualties totaling between 75,000 to 80,000 men. With the defeat of the Russian forces and their subsequent retreat from Borodino, Tsar Alexander ordered the evacuation of Moscow, leaving it undefended. Even though the French army was able to occupy Moscow without any opposition, they found Moscow deserted and on fire. When the Tsar Alexander refused to surrender after five weeks, Napoleon began his withdrawal of his army from Russia. As Napoleon's army retreated from Russia beginning in October 1812, it was constantly harassed by Russian forces. By the time the French army the crossed the Russian border into Poland, Napoleon only had approximately 30,000 soldiers remaining from his original invading force.

Bossuet, Jacques-Benigne (1627–1704) was a French bishop and theologian during the reign of Louis XIV of France who was an advocate of the theory of political absolutism. He argued that government was of divine origin and that kings received their power from God.

Bosworth Field, Battle of (1485) was a decisive battle during the War of the Roses in England in which competing noble families (Lancaster and York) fought to control the English throne. The forces of King Richard III (Lancaster) were defeated by the army led by Henry Tudor (Tudor) and Richard III was killed in the battle. As a result of Henry's victory, he assumed the throne of England and ruled as Henry VII. Henry established the Tudor dynasty (whose symbol was a white and red rose), which would rule England for over 100 years. The rulers of the Tudor dynasty included Henry's son, Henry VIII and his three children Edward VI, Mary and Elizabeth I.

Bougainville, Louis-Antoine de (1729–1811) was a French admiral, navigator and explorer who was the first Frenchmen to circumnavigate the globe. He was sent by the French government to the South Pacific to find a new route to China, new lands that might be colonized and spices that the French might export to Europe. While he did not find a new route to China, he did claim Tahiti for France in 1768, which he named New Cythera. He wrote an account of his travels in the South Pacific titled *A Voyage Round the World*, which became extremely popular in France, especially because of Bougainville's description of Tahiti as a paradise uncorrupted by civilization. He wrote of Tahiti that "I felt as if I had been transported to the Garden of Eden . . . Everywhere reigned hospitality, peace, joy and every appearance of happiness." The largest of the Solomon Islands is named for him as well the Bougainvillea plant.

Boule was the Greek name for the Council of 400 that Solon established in Athens in the 6th century BCE. Comprised only of males, it served as an advisory body to the general assembly of all male citizens in Athens.

Bourbon was the name of the dynasty that ruled France from 1589 to 1793 and from 1814 to 1830. Bourbon kings such as Louis XIV and Louis XVI would establish an absolute monarchy in France. However, Louis XVI would govern during the first stage of the French revolution from 1789 to 1792 as a constitutional monarch. The attempt by King Charles X in 1824 to reestablish an absolute monarchy in France would lead to the fall of the Bourbon dynasty, which would be replaced by the House of Orléans.

Bourbon Reforms is the term used by historians to describe a series of measures adopted by the Bourbon kings of Spain in the 1700s to modernize Spain by stimulating manufacturing and the development of new technology and to make the Spanish Empire more efficient and profitable. In the area of religion, the Bourbon kings sought to gain supremacy of the state over the Catholic Church, to abolish ecclesiastical privilege and to suppress the activities of the Society of Jesus.

Bourgeois Century is the name used by historians to describe the late 1800s in Western Europe when the expanding middle class influenced the contours of social, cultural, and political life in Europe.

Bourgeoisie is the French word for the middle class, which emerged in Europe during the late Middle Ages. They were generally a well-educated, prosperous group of townspersons (burghers) whose wealth came from manufacturing, finance, commerce, and other professions such as law and medicine. They sought greater political influence because of their wealth and individual merit. Skilled craftsmen and shopkeepers were considered to members of the "petty bourgeoisie". In the 1800s and 1900s Karl Marx and other socialist writers used the term in a different manner. It meant a capitalist social class in Europe that overthrew the feudal aristocracy and remade society according to capitalist interests and values. From the perspective of these socialist writers, the capitalist bourgeoisie established the foundation for the Industrial Revolution that emerged between 1750 and 1850.

Bouvines, Battle of the (1214) was a decisive military victory for King Philip Augustus of France over the combined military forces of the Holy Roman Empire led by Emperor Otto IV and King John of England. Pope Innocent III orchestrated the alliance of Germany and England. As a result of this victory, the power and influence of France in Europe increased. England lost most of its possessions in France and King John of England was forced by his nobles to sign the Magna Carta.

Boxer Rebellion (1898–1901) was an anti-foreign and anti-Christian peasant revolt in the rural areas of northern China led by a secret militia known as the Society of Righteous and Harmonious Fists. Foreigners and the foreign press in China called the members of this secret militia "Boxers" because the physical exercises they performed resembled boxing. The Boxers believed that their ritual physical exercises would protect them from a variety of evils, including bullets and that they were patriots acting in self-defense to protect China from foreign invaders. The objective of the Boxer revolt was to expel all "foreign devils" and their influences from China. They also claimed that droughts, famines, unemployment and other ills in China were caused by the presence of foreigners. The Boxers further claimed that foreign missionaries were telling the Chinese that their beliefs were wrong and their customs, such as ancestor worship, were primitive. As a result, the Boxers feared that the Chinese family and society were threatened by the presence of foreign influences in China. Encouraged and supported by the Qing Dynasty ruler Empress Dowager Cixi and officials in her court in Beijing, the Boxers attacked foreign merchants, Christian missionaries and Chinese converts to Christianity primarily in northern China, killing hundreds of missionaries and thousands of Chinese Christians. In 1900, the Boxers assassinated the German ambassador and began a two month siege of the foreign legations quarter in Beijing during which 76 foreigners were killed. In the midst of this siege, the Empress Dowager Cixi, the ruler of China, declared war on all foreign powers in China. In retaliation for the attack on the foreign legations and the declaration of war by the Chinese government, a heavily armed international force of 20,000 British, French, Russian, American, German and Japanese soldiers captured Beijing, ended the siege of the foreign legations and decisively defeated the Boxer revolt. In 1901, the foreign powers who comprised the international military force compelled China to apologize for the murder of foreigners by the Boxers, pay a huge financial indemnity for damages done to foreign property in China and permit the permanent stationing of foreign military forces in all the major cities in China.

Boyar was a high-level member of the medieval Russian aristocracy that emerged in Kievan Rus during the 900s and 1100s who dominated Russian society. They were a privileged class of rich landowners who held the senior positions in the government and the military, such as provincial governors and military commanders. They were drawn from about 200 families. They also formed a boyar council or duma that advised the tsar on domestic and foreign affairs. During the 1500s and 1600s, their social and political influence and power

declined. By the 1700s, Tsar Peter I the Great had abolished the rank and title of boyar.

Boyle, Robert (1627–1691) was one of the founders of modern chemistry. He was an English natural philosopher who assisted in founding the Royal Society of England. He is remembered most for Boyle's Law, which states that the volume of a gas is directly related to the pressure to which it is subjected.

Brahe, Tycho (1546–1601) was an astronomer supported by the royal Danish court who collected a huge amount of direct observational data on the planets that would be used by Johannes Kepler, Brahe's student, to develop Kepler's three laws of planetary motion.

Brandenburg Prussia refers to a group of German territories in the 1600s that were ruled by the Hohenzollern family. Relying upon the military strength of a hereditary landowning class, the Hohenzollerns would create one of the most powerful military states in Europe by the late 1800s.

Brandt, Willy (1913–1992) was the socialist chancellor of West Germany from 1969 to 1974. His policy of Ostpolitik, the opening of East Germany, made possible closer economic ties between West and East Germany and expanded opportunities for Germans to interact with one another across the east–west border.

Bread and Circuses refers to the social policy enacted by Caesar Augustus that sought to gain the support of the Roman proletariat by supplying them with essential food and entertainment.

Breech-Loading Rifle was a weapon developed in the late 1800s into which a bullet had to be individually inserted by hand. Rifles that had magazines, a compartment holding multiple bullets that could be fed rapidly into a firing chamber, would replace it.

Brest-Litovsk, Treaty of (1918) was the peace treaty signed between Germany and the Bolshevik government in Russia during World War I. By this treaty, the Bolsheviks accepted the military victory of Germany. It also required the withdrawal of Russia from World War I and the surrender of all of its western territory to Germany. After the defeat Germany in World War I by the Allies, the Bolsheviks recaptured the Ukraine and the Caucasus region of Russia.

Bretton Woods System (1944) is the name for framework established during World War II at a meeting in Bretton Woods, New Hampshire for managing the international economy. The primary components of this system are the World Bank and the International Monetary Fund (IMF). The purpose of these two institutions was to facilitate economic growth and make loans to stabilize a countries' currency. Under this international economic framework for trade and finance, the U.S. dollar would serve as the world's reserve currency, which it was hoped would facilitate international trade without extreme currency fluctuations. It was further determined that a U.S. dollar was equal to one ounce of gold, which was fixed at $35. The U.S. guaranteed that it would exchange dollars for gold at this rate. The Bretton Woods system was severely undercut by President Richard Nixon in 1971 when he determined unilaterally to cancel the direct convertibility of the United States dollar to gold. While Nixon's decision did not officially abolish the Bretton Woods system of international financial exchange, it did make that system unworkable. By 1973, the Bretton Woods system of fixed exchange rates was replaced by an international financial regime based on freely floating national currencies, which meant that the exchange rate would rise or fall as a function of market demand.

Bretwalda was the name of the early Anglo-Saxon kings. They were also known as "broad-wielders or Britain-wielders." It is an Anglo-Saxon term, the first record of which comes from the *Anglo-Saxon Chronicle* of the late 800s.

Brezhnev Doctrine (1968) was the policy developed by Leonid Brezhnev, the leader of the Soviet Union during the 1960s and 1970s, which claimed that the Soviet Union had the right to intervene and invade any socialist country if such country was faced with internal or external enemies. This doctrine was used to justify the use of Soviet troops in Czechoslovakia in August 1968 to terminate the event known as the "Prague Spring." This intervention was intended to put an end to liberalization efforts and uprisings that had

the potential to compromise Soviet hegemony inside the Eastern bloc, which was considered by the Soviets to be an essential defensive and strategic buffer in case hostilities with the West were to break out. While this doctrine permitted the limited independence of communist parties, the Soviet Union would not allow any country to leave the Warsaw Pact. The principles of the doctrine were so broad that the Soviets even used them to justify their military intervention in the non-Warsaw Pact nation of Afghanistan in 1979. The Brezhnev Doctrine stayed in effect until 1989 when Mikhail Gorbachev refused to use military force against Eastern European countries that decided to leave the Warsaw Pact.

Brezhnev, Leonid (1906–1982) was the political leader of the Soviet Union from 1964 to 1982 whose official title was General Secretary of the Communist Party. He authorized the 1968 invasion of Czechoslovakia by Soviet and Warsaw Pact troops to overthrow the Dubcek government that sought to liberalize the communist political system in Czechoslovakia. At that time, he contended that the Soviet Union had the right to interfere in the internal affairs of any nation that was a member of the Warsaw Pact in order to protect socialism. His statement would become known as the Brezhnev Doctrine. Following a disagreement that arose between China and the Soviet Union in the early 1960s, which was known as the Sino-Soviet split, relations with China continued to deteriorate during the Brezhnev era, culminating in military clashes between Soviet and Chinese troops along their border near the Ussuri River in 1969. With the establishment of new relations between the United States and China in 1971, Brezhnev initiated a series of efforts to prevent the formation of an anti-Soviet alliance between the United States and China. In 1972, he negotiated the Strategic Arms Limitation Treaty (SALT I) with the United States, which effectively established parity in nuclear weapons between the United States and the Soviet Union. This treaty represented the beginning of the era of "détente" in international relations. Furthermore, even though the Soviet Union supported the North Vietnamese government during the Vietnam War, Brezhnev supported the signing of the Paris Peace Accords by the North Vietnamese in 1973, which formally ended American involvement in the Vietnam War.

Brinkmanship was the military strategy adopted by U.S. policymakers during the Cold War of threatening to use nuclear weapons in a crisis situation involving the Soviet Union in order to achieve the most advantageous out-come for the US. In escalating dangerous events to the brink of war, U.S. policymakers wanted to convey the impression that they were willing to use extreme methods rather than concede. U.S. policymakers argued that this strategy would force the Soviet Union to back down and make concessions. Alternatively, U.S. policymakers were prepared to back-off if the Soviet Union did not concede to the demands of the US. U.S. policymakers were essentially playing a game of "chicken." Secretary of State John Forster Dulles coined this term during the Eisenhower administration. The Cuban Missile Crisis of 1962 is an example of brinksmanship in that the threat of an impending nuclear attack caused the Soviets to make concessions.

British Blockade (1914–1918) refers to the naval blockade of Germany by Britain during World War I. As a result of this policy, supplies were cut off to Germany in the hopes of impeding Germany's war effort. This policy violated several provisions of international law existing at that time.

British Commonwealth of Nations (1926) was an alliance of former British colonies and imperial territories that was formed by Britain. Under this structure, the British conferred "dominion status" on British colonies in Canada, Australia, and New Zealand. Dominion status meant that the former British colonies would continue their allegiance to Britain even after they had achieved the status of an independent nation.

British East India Company (1602–1873) was a private, joint-stock company created by the British government that was awarded a monopoly of trading rights in India in order to compete with Portuguese and Spanish traders. It was headquartered in Calcutta, which was captured by the British in 1756 during the Seven Years War. It became so powerful and influential in India between 1757 and 1857 that it not only had its own army, but also effectively ruled a large part of India. The British government abolished it in 1857 and assumed sole governmental control of India.

British Raj was the name for rule by the East India Company and then by the British government over much of South Asia between 1765 and 1947.

Broadsides were one-sided sheets of paper or brief pamphlets or leaflets printed that offered critical or satirical comments about a major social, political, economic, or cultural issue of the day. Broadsides were widely used during the American War of Independence and the French Revolution.

Broken Arrow refers to any incident in which a U.S. nuclear weapon is stolen, lost, or accidentally destroyed.

Bronze Age (circa 3500–1200 BCE) is the term used by historians to describe an era in world history when bronze was the primary metal for tools, weapons, household objects, and jewelry in southwestern Asia, Egypt and Europe. The demand for bronze, which is an alloy of tin and copper, helped create long-distance trade.

Brothers of the Common Life or Brethren of the Common Life was a religious order founded in 1376 by Dutch preacher Gerhard Groote, who translated the Bible into Dutch. He based the Brethren on the monastic teachings of Saint Augustine, who had advocated moral integrity and love. After the death of Groote, the Brethren split, forming the Augustinian Order in 1386. Brethren of the Common Life emphasized simplicity and a more personalized religious practice.

Brownshirts, known in German as the Sturmabteilung (SA), was the paramilitary arm of the Nazi Party established in 1921. In the 1920s and 1930s the Brownshirts held street marches, mass rallies and engaged in violent confrontations with Communists, Socialists, liberals, Jews and anyone who opposed the Nazis.

Bruni, Leonardo (1370–1444) was an Italian Renaissance humanist and historian who argued that the study of ancient Greece and Rome would enrich Florentine society. Believing in the importance of classical education, he translated classical Greek works by Plato, Aristotle and Plutarch into Latin. He argued that understanding the history of the Roman Republic and the causes for its decline would help Florence recreate the best qualities and values of the Roman Republic and contribute to the prosperity of Florence. He is considered to be the first historian to divide history into three secular periods: antiquity, Middle Ages and modern. He also invented the term "Middle Ages". He wrote the *History of the Florentine People*, which many historians consider to be the first modern history book. In this book, he asserted that political figures were not motivated by theology or piety, but by the quest for power, money, revenge, and glory. He further asserted that human progress is linked to human control of the earth and its resources.

Bruno, Giordano (1548–1600) was an Italian philosopher, astronomer, mathematician and Dominican friar who was an early proponent of the controversial Copernican cosmological theory of heliocentrism in which the earth revolved around the sun. Few astronomers who were contemporaries of Bruno accepted Copernican heliocentrism. During Bruno's lifetime many Roman Catholics accepted the view expressed by Aristotle that the earth was the center of the geocentric universe and that all heavenly bodies revolved around the earth in fixed circular orbits. While Bruno accepted the Copernicus's model that the sun was the center of the universe, he rejected Copernicus's belief in a finite universe with a sphere of fixed stars, all of which were a fixed distance from the earth. Bruno asserted that the sun was just one of many stars in space. He further contended that the universe contained an infinite number of worlds inhabited by intelligent beings. Based, in part, on his belief in an infinite number of worlds, the Roman Inquisition convicted him of blasphemy and heresy in 1600 after being jailed for seven years. Pope Clement VII sentenced him to death, which secular authorities enforced by burning him at the stake. While Bruno's theories influenced philosophical and scientific thinking in the 1600s, it was not until the 1700s that Bruno was recognized by many philosophers for his significant contributions to astronomy and science.

Bubonic Plague is an acute infectious bacterial disease spread from rats to humans by flea bites. The infection enters the bloodstream, producing swellings called buboes in the glands of the groin and armpit, internal bleeding, and discoloration of the body. The bubonic plague was the cause of the Black Death that killed at least one-third of the European population between 1348 and the early 1350s. In its later stages, coughing can spread the illness. It also ravaged East Asia and North Africa in the 1300s.

Buccaneer, who was also known as a corsair, was a pirate or privateer who attacked Spanish, Dutch, and French shipping in the Caribbean during the 1600s and 1700s. For Britain, whose privateers were based in Port Royal, Jamaica, buccaneering was an inexpensive and effective way to wage war on its rival, Spain, and seize the silver Spain was shipping from its colonies in the Americas to Spain. In fact, Britain licensed buccaneers as "privateers," thereby legalizing their operations in return for a share of privateer's profits. One French buccaneer destroyed so many Spanish ships and killed so many Spaniards that he was called "the Exterminator." Henry Morgan, a British buccaneer, seized so much loot from the Spanish that he was knighted by King Charles II when he returned to England. However, the British government in the 1690s withdrew its support for buccaneering or privateering because the buccaneers had become difficult to control and their operation had the potential to involve British colonies in unwanted wars with other European nations.

Buchenwald (1937–1945) was one of the first and largest concentrations camps established in Germany by the Nazis. It was established to hold primarily male prisoners who would be used as forced labor. Initially it held political prisoners, but after Kristallnacht in 1938 more male Jews aged 16 to 60 were incarcerated at Buchenwald. Most of the prisoners worked as slave laborers at work sites, such as a nearby munitions factory, the camp's stone quarry and workshops, and camp construction projects. Between 1937 and 1945, it held a total of 240,000 prisoners of which 10,000 were shipped to extermination camps. By early 1945, it held 86,000 prisoners, including more than 10,000 weak and exhausted Jewish prisoners who were forced to march to Buchenwald from Auschwitz because of the approaching Soviet troops. In April 1945, as American troops approached, the Nazis forced approximately 28,500 prisoners to march deeper into Germany during which one quarter of the prisoners died from beatings, exhaustion and execution. Buchenwald was also used by SS doctors to test the effects of viral infections, contagious diseases such as typhus and vaccines of the prisoners, hundreds of whom died. While there were no gas chambers at Buchenwald, the SS guards used beatings, executions, starvation, malnutrition, medical experiments and disease to kill 56,000 male prisoners, 11,000 of whom were Jews. In anticipation of the arrival of the advancing American soldiers, the SS guards and officers fled. When the American soldiers arrived at Buchenwald on April 11, 1945, they found that starving, weakened and emaciated prisoners had seized control of the camp. The American soldiers found more than 20,000 prisoners in the camp, 4,000 of whom were Jews.

Buddha (born between 6th & 4th century BCE), which means "enlightened," was an Indian prince named Siddhartha Gautama who renounced his wealth and social position in order to become enlightened. The principles of Buddhism that he enunciated spread throughout India, Central Asia, and Southeast and East Asia.

Buddhism is a religion that originated in India. It is based on the Four Noble Truths that are found in teachings of Siddhartha Gautama or Buddha. Its adherents desire to eliminate all distracting passions and reach nirvana.

Bull Papal is an official proclamation issued a pope in the form of a letter that is to be disseminated to the public.

Bullion is uncoined gold and silver that has been molded into bars or ingots.

Bureaucracy refers to an organization and network of government officials who regularly and routinely carry out the orders of the highest political authority of a country.

Burgher was the member of a social and economic class that emerged in the urban centers of Europe during the Middle Ages. This class was comprised of manufacturers, self-employed merchants and traders, bankers, lawyers and their political supporters.

Burke, Edmund (1729–1797) was a British writer and statesman who supported the American Revolution, but opposed the French Revolution because it disrupted the traditional social order. He expressed his conservative viewpoint in *Reflections on the Revolution in France*, in which he argued it was "natural" to support monarchies.

Bush Doctrine (2001) refers to a policy initially enunciated by President George W. Bush of the United States in the wake of the September 11, 2001 terrorist attacks in which he said that he would "make no distinction between the terrorists who committed these acts and those who harbored them." This policy implied that any nation refusing to cooperate with American efforts to attack terrorists would be considered an enemy state. The immediate application of this new foreign policy was the invasion of Afghanistan in early October 2001 after the Taliban-controlled government of Afghanistan refused to hand over to the United States Osama bin Laden, the leader of al-Qaeda, the terrorist organization responsible for the September 11th attacks. On September 20, 2001, in a televised address to a joint session of Congress, Bush summed up this policy with the words, "Every nation, in every region, now has a decision to make. Either you are with us, or you are with the terrorists." The term now generally refers to the set of policies announced by President Bush on June 1, 2002, in a speech to the graduating class of West Point. The basic elements of this policy were: (1) The presidential authorization of preemptive attacks against potential aggressors, cutting them off before they are able to launch strikes against the United States or its allies; (2) the right of the United States to pursue unilateral military action when acceptable multilateral solutions cannot be found; (3) the United States would take all military actions necessary to continue its status as the world's sole military superpower; and (4) the United States would actively promote democracy and freedom in all parts of the world.

Bushido, which means "Way of the Warrior" in Japanese, is the name for the philosophy and code of conduct that the Japanese samurai warrior was instructed in and required to observe. It is a moral code that stresses frugality, loyalty, martial arts mastery, and honor unto death. This code developed during the Tokugawa Shogunate, which ruled Japan from 1603 until 1868.

Business Cycle is the fluctuation in the aggregate economic activity of a nation. It is represented by recurrent swings from economic hard times to recovery and then growth, then back to hard times and a repetition of the cycle.

Butler, Joseph (1690–1752) was a preacher at the royal court in England and one of the foremost English moral philosophers of his age. His sermons were of great influence in shaping the discussion about nature and ethics in the 1700s in England. Increasingly concerned with the growing influence of deism, he published a very popular defense of Christianity entitled *The Analogy of Religion, Natural and Revealed, to the Constitution and Course of Nature.*

Byron, George Gordon Noel (Lord Byron) (1788–1824) was an English Romantic poet. Inheriting the title Baron and estates from his grand uncle, Lord Byron was a hereditary peer in the British House of Lords. He was a rather scandalous man, his wife left him after the birth of their daughter, his only legitimate child, amid rumors of an incestuous relationship with his sister. He left England in 1816 and never again returned to his homeland. He traveled through much of Italy, Spain, and Greece. He was close friends with Percy Shelly. Upon hearing of the Greek revolt against the Ottoman Empire, Byron went to Greece to join the fight for Greek independence. He gave large amounts of money to the cause, but died in Greece of tuberculosis. He created the Byronic hero, a tempestuous man, an outcast of society with mysterious sins in his past, a man much like Byron himself. His most famous work is the satiric *Don Juan.*

Byzantine Empire (324–1453 CE) is the name historians use to describe the eastern portion of the Roman Empire that existed for over one thousand years until 1453, when its capital Constantinople was conquered by the Ottoman Empire. The empire included present-day Libya, Egypt, Turkey, Syria, Lebanon, Israel and most of the Balkan states. Its name is derived from Byzantium, an ancient port city in Anatolia on the modern Bosphorus, which would be renamed Constantinople. The empire reached its peak of power and influence during the reign of Justinian from 527 to 565.

Byzantium was the name of the Greek colony founded in 668 BCE. In 330 CE, Constantine would rename it Constantinople. The name was also used

between the 400s and 1400s CE to refer to Eastern Roman Empire.

C

Cabot, John (1500–1550) was an Italian navigator and explorer commissioned by King Henry VII of England to find a shorter route across the North Atlantic to Asia. Henry's decision to engage Cabot was prompted by news of the discoveries by Christopher Columbus. In 1497, Cabot landed on an island off the coast of northern Canada. It is believed that he may have landed on Labrador, Cape Breton Island or Newfoundland. Regardless of where he landed, Cabot claimed the land for the king of England. He made further explorations along the northern coastline of Canada as far as New England. He is considered to be the first European to explore mainland North America since the Vikings in the 11th century. Upon his return to England, he informed King Henry that he had reached Asia somewhere north of Japan. Despite his discovery, the English did not establish any permanent colonies on the territory claimed by Cabot even though the British would later claim Canada as part of the British Empire. Today, in both Canada and England, Cabot is credited with discovering Newfoundland.

Cabral, Pedro Álvares (1467/68–1520) was a Portuguese navigator and explorer that led a Portuguese expedition of 13 ships around the Cape of Good Hope to India for the purpose of obtaining spices and establishing trade relations with India. He followed the route previously taken in 1498 by Vasco da Gama, who was the first European to reach India. In accordance with da Gama's instructions, Cabral sailed southwestward across the Atlantic which gave him the opportunity to explore the lands in the New World which belonged to Portugal as a result of the Treaty of Tordesillas (1694). These unexplored lands in the New World had previously been sighted by da Gama. After sighting land, which he initially thought was an island, he landed on the northeast coast of present-day Brazil. He made peaceful contact with the indigenous inhabitants, claimed the land for King Manuel I of Portugal and named this new land the "Island of the True Cross". After exploring the coastline, he realized that he had discovered a large land mass, which he believed was a continent. While he did not extensively explore this new territory, he sent a ship back to Portugal to inform the king of this new territory before proceeding to India. After reaching India, he established a factory (trading post) in Calicut. Despite the fact that he returned to Portugal with only four of the original 13 ships, those four ships carried enough rare spices to make extraordinary profits for the king of Portugal.

Caesar, Julius (100–44 BCE) was a Roman general who conquered the Gauls, invaded Britain and expanded Rome's territory as far as Asia Minor. He became the dictator of Rome in 46 BCE and was murdered by Brutus and Cassius in 44 BCE, which led to the rise of Octavian (Augustus), his grand-nephew and the end of the Roman Republic. Later Roman emperors were also called Caesar.

Cahiers de doléance is a French term for the list of grievances or petitions that were sent with representatives of local assemblies to the meeting of the Estates-General in 1789. These lists demonstrated the existence of widespread public discontent with the political culture of Louis XVI in France.

Cairo Conference (1943) was the meeting of President Franklin Roosevelt of the United States, Prime Minister Winston Churchill of the United Kingdom, and Generalissimo Chiang Kai-shek of the Republic of China that was held in Cairo, Egypt, in November 1943. At that meeting, these three Allied leaders discussed the Allied plans for the war against Japan and made decisions about postwar Asia such as the return to China of all Chinese territories seized by Japan since 1931.

Calendar, Gregorian (1582) was the calendar adopted by the Catholic Church that replaced the Julian calendar. It was named for Pope Gregory XIII, who decreed the reform of the Julian calendar. While the years in the Gregorian calendar continued the numbering system of the Julian calendar, which began with the birth of Jesus, the Council of Trent decided in 1563 that it was necessary to reform the Julian calendar in order to ensure that Easter was celebrated by all Christians on the same day that was first established by the Council of Nicaea in 325. This reform, it was argued, would allow for a more consistent scheduling of Easter. Initially, only Catholic countries such as Spain, Portugal, Italy, and France adopted the new calendar. During the period of the Catholic Counter-Reformation, most Protestant countries in Europe initially objected to adopting the new calendar, fearing that the new calendar was part of a plot to return them to the Catholic fold. Denmark, Norway, and the Protestant states of Germany did not adopt the new calendar until March 1700. Sweden and Finland did not adopt it until 1753. Britain and the British Empire (including their colonies in the Americas) adopted the Gregorian calendar in 1752. In Russia the Gregorian calendar was accepted after the October Revolution, in October 1917. The last European country to adopt the Gregorian calendar was Greece in March 1923. The Gregorian calendar is the most widely used calendar in the world today.

Calendar, Julian (46 BCE) was a reform of the Roman calendar that was introduced by Julius Caesar in 46 BCE. It had a regular year of 365 days divided into 12 months and a leap day added to February every four years. Hence the Julian year was on average 365.25 days long. The Julian calendar remained in use into the 1900s in some countries as a national calendar, but the modern Gregorian calendar replaced it.

Calendar, Roman (753 BCE) is believed to have been a lunar calendar. Roman tradition claimed that it was invented by Romulus, the founder of Rome, about 753 BCE. The earliest known version contained ten months, lasted 304 days, and had about 61 days of winter that did not fall within the calendar. The first reform of the Roman calendar was circa 713 BCE, when the length of the calendar was extended to 355 days.

Caligula (Gaius Caesar Germanicus) (12–41 CE) was the third emperor of the Roman Empire. He succeeded Tiberius and ruled briefly from 37 to 41. He was a member of the Julio-Claudian Dynasty that was descended from Emperor Augustus. Caligula was a nickname, meaning "little boot," which was given to him by Roman soldiers who were commanded by his father, a highly respected and revered Roman general. His father, Germanicus, was the adopted son of Emperor Tiberius. His uncle was Emperor Claudius, who succeeded Caligula, after a member of Caligula's own bodyguard assassinated him. After the murder of his father, Germanicus, on the orders of Tiberius and the banishment by Tiberius of his mother Agrippina the Elder and his brother for treason, Tiberius, his grandfather, raised Caligula.

Caliph, which means "successor to the prophet," is the title for the religious and political ruler of the Islamic community (Umma) that claims descent from Muhammad. This position was held by the sultans during the Ottoman Empire. It was abolished by Mustafa Kemal in 1924.

Caliphate is the name for the Islamic empire that emerged after the death of Muhammad. The first caliphate was the Umayyad caliphate which ruled from Damascus from 661–750. The second caliphate was the Abbassid caliphate which ruled from Baghdad from 750–1258. Historians refer to the era of the Abbassid caliphate as "the Golden Age of Islam".

Calles, Plutarco (1877–1945) was a Mexican general and politician who was president of Mexico from 1924 to 1928. He founded the National Revolutionary Party, which would eventually become the Institutional Revolutionary Party (PRI) that would govern Mexico for more than 70 years. During his presidency, a dispute arose between Mexico and the United States over whether the oil in Mexico belonged to Mexico or foreign-owned companies then operating in Mexico. When Calles came into office, he drafted a new oil law that made everything under Mexican soil the property of Mexico. His position threatened the possessions of U.S. and European oil companies in Mexico. In response, the American ambassador to Mexico branded Calles a communist. At the same time, public opinion in the United States turned particularly anti-Mexican when the first embassy of the Soviet Union in any country in the world was opened in Mexico. After this development, some officials of the U.S. government considered the Calles' government "Bolshevik" and referred to Mexico as "Soviet Mexico." Even though leading American newspapers and U.S. government officials threatened war over Mexican oil law, Calles managed to avoid war through a series of diplomatic negotiations that led to an agreement between the Mexican government and the oil companies.

Calling is the Calvinist belief that certain people known as the Elect are selected by God to perform God's will on earth. This belief gave individual Calvinists a strong sense of purpose and superiority.

Calvin, John (1509–1564) was a French-Swiss scholar, theologian, and founder of the "reformed" tradition of Christianity who helped internationalize the Protestant Reformation. He is the author of *Institutes of the Christian Religion* in 1536, which was widely disseminated and very influential in Europe during the Protestant Reformation. He stressed the absolute power of God, the need for moral reform of the Christian community, and predestination.

Campus Martius (Field of Mars) was a publicly owned area of ancient Rome. According to one legend, Campus Martius was once a field of wheat owned by Tarquinius Superbus, the last king of Rome, but was burnt down during the revolution which established the Roman Republic. Since this area was used for military training, it was dedicated to Mars and used for celebrations of successful military campaigns. In 221 BCE, a large track was built in the area for chariot racing. The area was the location for the Ara Pacis (Altar of Peace), which was built by the Senate to mark the establishment of peace by Augustus. It was intended to symbolize the successful completion of Augustus's efforts to stabilize the Roman Empire.

Canaan is an ancient term for a region approximating present-day Israel, the West Bank, and the Gaza Strip, plus parts of Lebanon and Syria. Various Canaanite sites have been excavated by archaeologists, most notably the Canaanite town of Ugarit in modern Syria, which was rediscovered in 1928. Much of the modern knowledge about the Canaanites stems from excavation in this area. Canaanites spoke a Semitic language closely related to Hebrew.

Canon is the term used to designate a collection of texts that are recognized by a specific group of experts as authoritative. In Christianity, the Old and New Testament is a collection of religious writing that Christians accept as authoritative.

Canon Law is the collection laws governing the Catholic Church. They are based on papal decrees and decisions of church councils. It was typically applied to cases involving the clergy, disputes about church property and donations to the Catholic Church. Canon law was also applied to the laity for annulling marriages, legitimating the birth of a child out of wedlock, prosecuting bigamy and protecting widows, orphans and resolving inheritance disputes. The first systematic collection of Canon laws, known as the *Decretum*, was issued in 1140

Canonical Gospels refers to the four gospels, Matthew, Mark, Luke and John, which are part of the New Testament. The Catholic Church recognized this biblical canon in the early 400s and Jerome incorporated them into the Vulgate, the Latin version of the Bible. The consensus among biblical scholars is that all four canonical gospels were originally written in Greek, the most widely used language of the Roman Empire. The majority view among biblical scholars today is that Mark is the first gospel, with Matthew and Luke borrowing passages both from that gospel and from at least one other common source, lost to history, termed by scholars as 'Q' (from German: *Quelle*, meaning "source"). Also, the majority view today among biblical scholars is that Matthew was probably written in Syria; Mark was likely written in Rome, John was probably written in Ephesus. But there is no consensus as to where Luke was written. Furthermore, the following dates represent the best understanding of the majority of biblical scholars as to when the canonical gospels were written: Mark: 68–73 or 65–70; Matthew: 70–100 or 80–85; Luke: 80–100; and John: 90–100 or 90–110.

Cannae, Battle of (216 BCE) was a major battle of the Second Punic War in which the army of Carthage under Hannibal decisively defeated a numerically superior army of the Roman Republic. Having recovered from their previous losses at Trebia (218 BCE) and Trasimene (217 BCE), the Romans decided to engage Hannibal at Cannae, with roughly 80,000 soldiers. The Carthaginians had about 50,000 soldiers Approximately 40,000 Roman soldiers were killed, 14,000 escaped and 10,000 were captured. The Carthaginians lost about 6,000 men As a result of such losses, the Roman army was effectively destroyed as a fighting force. This battle was regarded as the greatest defeat in Roman military history.

Canterbury Tales is the book written by Geoffrey Chaucer in the late 1300s that describes the various classes of people and their experiences in England during the late Middle Ages.

Canton refers to the territorial subdivisions of a country, which are typically small in terms of area and population. Switzerland is organized by cantons.

Canton System (1757–1842) was a system established by the Qing emperors to control trade with European merchants. The European merchants were limited to a few ports and were prohibited from any direct trade with Chinese civilians. Instead, the Europeans merchants, who were typically employees of trading companies such as the British East India Company, were required to trade with an association of Chinese merchants known as the Cohong. The presence of European merchants, and later American traders, was restricted to these Cohongs in Canton (Guangzhou) during the trading season. However, the foreign merchants were required to remain in Macau during the off-season. Initially, trade with China consisted of tea, silks and porcelain. This trade, especially in tea, resulted in serious financial problems for the British who began shipping opium to China from its colonies in India. The Canton System continued until the Opium Wars of 1839–1842 and 1856–1860.

Cape to Cairo Railway was the north–south railway project proposed by Cecil Rhodes in the late 1800s that would connect all of the British colonies in Africa. Cecil Rhodes argued that such a transportation system would be an important mechanism by which to unify and govern British colonial possessions, enable rapid military movement to potential hot spots, conduct a war if necessary, and foster trade. However, the British confronted a major obstacle. Germany controlled a colony in East Africa that prevented such a railway project. Even though most of the German colonial territory in Africa was taken over by the British as a result of the German defeat in World War I, the British were unable to complete the project because of economic problems. After World War II, the struggles of the African peoples for national self-determination and the end of European colonialism in Africa further prevented the completion of the Cape to Cairo railway project.

Cape to Cairo Road was a road system in Africa advocated by the British in the late 1800s that would stretch north to south across the African continent, connecting all of the existing British colonies in Africa. Proponents of the road argued that it would create cohesion among the British colonies in Africa, would give Britain the most important and dominant political and economic influence over the African continent, and would secure Britain's position in the world as a global colonial power. France had a rival strategy in the late 1890s to link its colonies from west to east across the African continent. However, the absence of French control of southern Sudan and Ethiopia prevented the completion of such a project. France subsequently sent military expeditions in 1897 to establish a protectorate in southern Sudan and to find a route across Ethiopia. The French scheme failed when British ships on the Nile confronted the French military at the point of intersection between the French and British routes. This confrontation, more commonly known as the Fashoda Incident, resulted in a diplomatic defeat for France.

Cape Verde Islands are islands off the West African coast Mauritania that served as a port for European slave ships. In 1479, Portugal signed the Treaty of Alcáçovas with Castille in Spain, which gave Portugal possession of the Azores, Madeira, and the Cape Verde islands.

Capetian Dynasty (987–1328 CE) was the ruling aristocratic family in France during the High Middle Ages (1000–1300). It was founded by Hugh Capet even though his rule was restricted to his own domain surrounding Paris. The most significant Capetian ruler was Philip II (reigned 1180–1223) who conquered much of the empire that English had built up in western France.

Capital is the cost of all of the physical assets used in production, including fixed capital, such as machinery and circulating capital, such as raw materials.

Capital Goods are the machines and tools used to produce other goods.

Capitalism is the economic system and ideology that emerged in early modern Europe which is characterized by the private or corporate ownership of the means of production. Accordingly, control over decisions concerning prices, production and the distribution of goods and services is in private or corporate hands. Human labor and commodities are bought and sold in the marketplace based on supply and demand and capital and labor move freely.

Cappadocia, which means "land of the beautiful horses" in Persian, was an area in east-central ancient Anatolia north of the Taurus Mountains, which was the home of the Hittites in the late Bronze Age. During the late 6th century BCE, it became at satrap of the Persian Empire under Darius I. After the death of Alexander the Great, it became a tributary state of the Seleucid Empire. After the Roman defeat of the Seleucid Empire in 170 BCE, it became an ally and client of the Roman Empire. It was subsequently annexed by Emperor Tiberius in 17 CE and made a province of the Roman Empire. Cappadocia would remain part of the Byzantine Empire until the 11th century.

Cappadocian Fathers were Christian theologians who made important contributions to Christian thought in their writings, refuting Arianism and elaborating on the doctrine of the Trinity. They were Basil the Great (330–379), his brother Gregory of Nyssa (330–395) and Gregory Nazianus (329–389).

Caravans were groups of men who transported and traded goods along the overland routes in North Africa and Central Asia. Large caravans consisted of 600 to 1000 camels and as many as 400 men. One of the most famous caravan routes in Eurasia was the Silk Road.

Caravels were small, highly maneuverable, three-masted vessels developed about 1450 in the Iberian peninsula that combined square sail rigging with triangular lateen sails. These ships played an important role in the development of the Portuguese trading empire in Asia. This new type of ocean-going ship could be sailed in a variety of winds, carry large cargoes of 50–70 tons, be managed by a small crew, and be defended by guns mounted on the ships. The caravel gave the Portuguese a significant advantage in global exploration and trade.

Carbonari, which means "charcoal burner" in Italian, were members of secret Italian societies of liberals and nationalists who sought to unify Italy in the 1820s. They were opposed to the conservative political order established in Europe at the Congress of Vienna in 1814–1815. The name of this secret society was derived from the practice of swearing in new members by making a mark in charcoal on the new members' forehead. The Carbonari were originally organized to oppose the armies of Napoleon, but after 1815, they advocated Italian unification.

Cárdenas, Lazaro (1895–1970) was the president of Mexico from 1934 to 1940. He created the political system that lasted in Mexico until the end of the 1980s. During his presidency, his government expropriated and redistributed millions of acres of land to peasants and initiated rural education programs. He also ensured that urban industrial workers could unionize and receive higher wages. He also sought greater control over Mexico's oil and natural gas resources and initiated economic policies that sought to nationalize Mexico's vast oil production. As the world's second-largest oil producer in 1921, Mexico also supplied approximately 20 percent of domestic demand in the United States. Subsequently, Cárdenas nationalized Mexico's oil reserves and expropriated the equipment of the foreign oil companies in Mexico in 1938. Even though he proposed compensation for the expropriated assets, he angered the international business community and foreign governments, especially the British, who severed diplomatic relations with Mexican government and boycotted Mexican oil. With the outbreak of World War II, when Mexico began to export oil to Nazi Germany, the United States and Britain settled their dispute with Mexico and ended their respective boycotts.

Cardinals were officials of the Catholic Church who emerged in late antiquity, but only achieved prominence and influence after the 1100s.

Carlowitz or Karlowitz, Treaty of (1699) was the peace treaty that ended the Austro-Ottoman War of 1683–1697 between the Ottoman Empire and the Holy League, which was comprised of Austria, Poland, Russia and Venice. After the Austrians decisively defeated the Ottoman army at the Battle of Zenta (1697), the Ottoman Empire lost control of a significant amount of its territory in east and central Europe. As a result of this treaty Austria received control of Hungary, Transylvania, Bosnia and Herzegovina, Croatia and Slovenia, which made the Austrian Empire the dominant regional political and military power in east and central Europe. The treaty also granted smaller territorial gains to Russia, Poland and Venice. This treaty marks the beginning of the decline of Ottoman political and military influence in east and central Europe.

Carlsbad Decrees (1819) were a series of repressive and reactionary resolutions adopted by representatives of the major German states to suppress liberal and nationalistic organizations and the activities of radical student organizations within their states. As part of their effort to uphold the conservative monarchical order, the various German states agreed to censor all publications, prohibit the formation of any secret and unauthorized student societies in universities, place the faculties of all schools and universities under supervisory control of a curator appointed by the government, remove any teacher or professor who propagated any ideas or doctrines hostile to or subversive of the existing government, and create an investigatory commission to root out any secret revolutionary plots or organizations directed against the existing government. While these laws were relatively successful in the short run, they were ultimately unable to stifle the growing appeal of nationalist and liberal ideas in the various German states that issued the Carlsbad Decrees.

Carnival was a traditional Catholic public celebration or parade that typically occurred in Europe during the months preceding the religious observance of Lent. People created a circus like atmosphere. They wore masks and costumes, ate and drank excessively, used satire to mock authority figures, used abusive language, engaged in rowdy spectacles, grotesquely portrayed the human body and gleefully depicted diseases and death. Carnival was a ritual atmosphere during which people would challenge existing social roles and engage in acts and behavior that would otherwise be contrary to the everyday rules, norms and religious practices without fear of retribution. Carnival would form an integral part of the Christian traditions even though elements of Carnival were derived from ancient Roman pagan festivals. The best-known examples of the tradition of Carnival originated in medieval Italy, in particular Venice. The tradition of Carnival spread from Italy to Spain, France, Portugal, and to their colonies in the North America, the Caribbean, and Latin America. In the United States, the most well-known example of the Carnival tradition is Mardi Gras, which is celebrated in New Orleans.

Carolingians were a dynasty of Frankish rulers that succeeded the Merovingian Dynasty. The most famous Carolingian king was Charlemagne (Carolus Magnus), who began his reign in 751. He ruled the territory of present-day France, a large part of Germany and a small part of Italy. The Dynasty lasted until 911 in Germany and 987 in France. The Carolingian kings had no fixed capital and moved their courts between various palaces until Aachen was made the permanent capital in the late 790s.

Carolingian Minuscule was a new form of formal, literary writing that used capital letters for the beginning of a sentence and lower case letters for the text of a sentence.

Carolingian Renaissance (700s–800s CE) refers to a revival of interest in Greek and Latin learning, literature and language that occurred during the reign of Charlemagne and his successors. The revival encompassed the founding of schools, the production of textbooks, the copying of manuscripts, and the dissemination of early Church teachings. Charlemagne specifically promoted the intensive study of Latin in order to increase governmental efficiency and propagate the Christian faith.

Carrack was a large, three or four masted ocean-going merchant vessel with both square rigged and triangular sails that was developed in the 1400s by the Genoese for use primarily in the Mediterranean. The unique sail configuration of a carrack allowed it to use any wind available to propel itself. Furthermore, as a typical carrack was very large (approximately 150 feet in length), it was more stable in the heavy seas of the Atlantic Ocean, for example. Since it could hold about 1000 tons of cargo, it was widely used by European maritime powers during the 1400s and 1500s, particularly by

the Portuguese for their long voyages of exploration and trade first along Africa's Atlantic coastline and then later to India, China and Japan. By the mid-1500s the galleon was developed and rapidly replaced the carrack among European maritime powers.

Carrhae, Battle of (53 BCE) was a battle in which a large invading Roman army of seven legions (approximately 44,000 soldiers) was decisively defeated by a numerically smaller Parthian army in Mesopotamia near the town of Carrhae. The Roman invasion force was led by Marcus Licinius Crassus, a member of the First Triumvirate and the richest man in Rome. Seeking military glory and wealth, Crassus, who had previously defeated Spartacus in 71 BCE, invaded Parthia without the consent of the Senate. During the battle, both Crassus and his son Publius, who led the Roman cavalry, were killed. While Parthian casualties were small, approximately 20,000 Romans soldiers were killed and 10,000 were captured. A surviving force of approximately 10,000 Roman soldiers retreated to Syria where the invading army had been raised by Crassus. This battle is considered by historians to be one of the most significant defeats in Roman history.

Cartels are voluntary combinations of private businesses, corporations or individuals in a specific industry who want to control the supply of a commodity or group of commodities domestically or internationally by manipulating the price, the production and the marketing of that commodity or group of commodities.

Carter Doctrine (1979) was the foreign policy announced by President Jimmy Carter that the Persian Gulf was an area of vital interest to the United States and that U.S. military forces would be used to defend the Persian Gulf in the event of an invasion by another country.

Carter, Howard (1873–1939) was the British archaeologist who discovered the intact tomb of King Tutankhamun (more commonly known as "King Tut" or "the boy king") in the Valley of the Kings in 1922. In excavating the tomb, he discovered the sarcophagus of Tutankhamun. Carter began excavations in the Valley of the Kings in

1914, but his work was halted during World War I and he would not resume any excavations until 1917. After five years of finding very little in the Valley of the Kings, Lord Carnarvon, his financial backer, told Carter in 1922 that he would fund only one more season of excavations to find the tomb of Tutankhamun. In 1902, he discovered the tombs of Queen Hatshepsut and Thutmose IV, both of which had been previously robbed of any ancient Egyptian artifacts. Archaeologists consider Tutankhamun's tomb to be the best preserved and most intact tomb to be found in the Valley of the Kings.

Cartesianism was the philosophy of René Descartes that was based on the dual existence of mind and matter and the belief that the use of skepticism could create certainty. This dualistic approach permitted scientists to view matter as something separate from themselves that could be investigated by the use of reason.

Carthaginian Empire (800–146 BCE) was a great maritime empire that rivaled Rome, which was located in present-day Tunisia. At its height of power, it stretched across the northern coast of Africa from modern-day Tunisia to the Strait of Gibraltar. It was originally founded as a Phoenician colony around 800 BCE. Carthage became a major port and commercial and naval power in the western Mediterranean until it was defeated by Rome in the Punic Wars, which began in 264 BCE and ended with the destruction of Carthage in 146 BCE.

Casablanca Conference (1943) was a meeting held in Casablanca, Morocco, during World War II at which Franklin D. Roosevelt, Winston Churchill, and Charles de Gaulle planned the European strategy of the Allies during World War II. Stalin had also been invited but declined to attend. De Gaulle had also initially refused to come but changed his mind when Churchill threatened to recognize Henri Giraud as head of the Free French in his place. Giraud was also present at Casablanca, and there was notable tension between the two men during the talks. The Allies agreed at the Conference to demand the unconditional surrender of the Axis, to aid the Soviet Union in its fight against the Nazis, to invade Sicily and Italy, and to the joint leadership of the Free French forces by De Gaulle and Giraud.

Cassiodorus, Flavius Magnus (485–585 CE) was a Roman senator, writer, historian and governmental official who served in the court of King Theodoric the Great, the Ostrogothic ruler of Italy. He wrote *History of the Goths*, which portrayed Theodoric as noble and as part of Roman history. Since Theodoric admired and respected Cassiodorus for his writing and record-keeping skills, Theodoric made him responsible his correspondence and permitted Cassiodorus to write important public documents. Cassiodorus strongly advocated studying classical Greek and Roman learning because he believed that such writings equipped a Christian to better understand the Bible and to seek salvation. He founded a monastery school on his family estate called Vivarium. While Vivarium was not governed by a set of strict monastic rules such as the Benedictines, Cassiodorus wrote a book *Institutions*, which was an annotated bibliography of classical Greek and Roman texts. He believed this bibliography should be the basic curriculum to guide a monk's course of study at Vivarium. Cassiodorus asserted that a monk should study such secular topics as grammar, rhetoric, dialectic, arithmetic, music, geometry and astronomy. He believed that these fields of study were necessary in order for a monk to thoroughly understand the Bible and God. These topics would later become the basic elements of liberal arts studies at European universities during the Middle Ages. Even though he considered reading a transformative act, he believed that the study of classical secular Greek and Roman texts should not replace the study of the Bible and other Christian texts, but augment them. At Vivarium, he also encouraged the monks to reproduce many of the ancient Greek and Roman texts, which survive to this day and are still used in western civilization classes in many universities and colleges throughout the United States.

Cassius Dio (Lucius Cassius Dio) (155–235 CE) was a Roman senator, consul and historian who wrote a history of Rome titled *Roman History*, which was comprised of 80 books and written in Greek. Today, many of these books have survived intact or in fragments. It took him 22 years of research to write *Roman History*, which covered approximately

1400 years of Roman history. His book begins with the mythological founding of Rome by the legendary Aeneas in 1200 BCE, continues with the formation of the Roman Republic in 509 BCE and the Roman Empire in 27 BCE and finally covers the period of the Roman Empire until 229 CE. He was senator under Emperor Commodus (reigned 177–192) and appointed consul by Emperors Macrinus (reigned 217–218) and Severus Alexander (reigned 222–235). As a result, *Roman History* was written from the perspective of a high government official in the Roman Empire who had direct contact with important political figures involved in key events in the empire and was thus in a unique position to observe those key events.

Caste System is a hierarchical organization of people that is based on heredity. An individual's caste is fixed at birth and will determine his or her occupation, where he or she will live, with whom he or she is permitted to eat and who he or she will be permitted to marry.

Castiglione, Baldassare (1478–1529) was the author of *The Book of the Courtier,* a popular book during the Renaissance in northern Italy that described the proper etiquette, manners, and social graces of those individuals who wanted to be considered "gentlemen."

Catal Huyuk is an important Neolithic agricultural settlement located in south-central Anatolia (present-day Turkey) that existed from 7500 to 5700 BCE. It had a large population who lived in mud-brick houses that contained a living and sleeping area and an interior hearth. The inhabitants grew edible grains and nuts and may have raised animals.

Categorical Imperative is an idea developed by the philosopher Immanuel Kant, a German philosopher, in the 1800s that every human possesses an internal sense of moral duty or awareness. He claimed that a person should act in every situation as one would have other people act in that similar situation.

Cathars were heretics who were prominent in southern France in the mid-1100s and early 1200s. As they were especially common to the Albi region of France, they were also known as Albigensians. They considered the material world evil and they

renounced wealth and marriage and promoted an ascetic existence.

Catherine the Great (1729–1796) was the German-born Russian Empress who maintained an absolutist feudal system. By the use of alliances and wars, she was able to expand the Russian borders south to the Black Sea and west into Europe. Catherine also encouraged the acceptance of Enlightenment ideas and Western cultural influences in Russia. Historians have described her as an "enlightened despot" because she furthered the westernizing reforms of Peter the Great.

Catholic Emancipation was the grant of full political rights to Roman Catholics in England by the British government in 1829.

Catholic Counter-Reformation was a series of reform efforts initiated by the Catholic Church beginning in the 1560s to respond to the Protestant Reformation. In order to win back the loyalty of those Catholics who had converted to Protestantism, the Church refuted Protestant beliefs, initiated efforts to propagandize the Catholic faith, discipline clergy and laity, reform clerical training, repress heresy and to create a new religious order, the Society of Jesus (Jesuits). The Church also established the Holy Office of the Inquisition, promulgated the Index of Forbidden Books, and implemented the decrees of the Council of Trent. The Counter-Reformation was most effective in Poland and southern Germany.

Cato, Marcus Porcius, also known as Cato the Elder or Cato the Censor (234–149 BCE) was a Roman politician, general and historian who denounced the consumption of luxury items by his fellow Romans. He was the first Roman historian to write in Latin. His only surviving work is on farming, which was written about 160 BCE.

Cavalier was the name given to a royalist supporter of King Charles I by the supporters of the Parliament during the English Civil War (1642–1646). A supporter of the Parliament was known as a "Roundhead" or a "Parliamentarian".

Cavendish, Margaret (1623–1673) was a British philosopher who based her theories on the theory of atomism–that all matter is made from small particles called atoms. The philosopher Democritus first developed this idea in ancient Greece. She saw little use in experimentation, believing it did nothing to change the outcome of the function of the observed object. She did not trust the new tools that were developing, nor human senses, as she believed that they distorted truth. Some of her books include *Elements of Philosophy* (1655) and *Observations upon Experimental Philosophy* (1666).

Cavour, Camillo Benso di (1840–1861) was an Italian nationalist who was opposed to the power and influence of the papacy in Italy and led the initial stages of revolution against Habsburg rule in Italy.

Ceausescu, Nicolae (1918–1989) was the first president of an independent Romania after the collapse of the Soviet bloc in Eastern Europe in 1989. Corruption, nepotism, and repression characterized his rule. He was overthrown in a popular uprising.

Celibacy is the doctrine that emerged in the early Christian Church that required priests and bishops to abstain from marriage. It was based, in part, on the writings of Paul, who argued that celibacy allowed a man to be in a spiritual marriage with Christ. This concept was further popularized by the early Christian theologian Origen. Clerical celibacy began to be demanded by the papacy in the 300s CE. It became obligatory for all priests in the Catholic Church in the 1100s at the First Lateran Council (1123), Second Lateran Council (1139), and the Council of Trent (1545–64).

Celts were peoples who shared a common language and culture that originated in Central Europe between 1000 and 500 BCE. After 500 BCE they spread as far as Anatolia in the east, and Spain and Britain in the west. Later the Romans and the Germanic tribes would conquer them. Their descendants survive today in Brittany, Wales, Scotland, and Ireland.

Censorate or **Board of Censors (1368– 1911/12)** was part of the Chinese governmental structure during the Ming and Qing Dynasties that was responsible for reviewing the conduct of government officials and reporting to the emperor any acts of corruption or dereliction of duty by such officials. It was considered to be the "eyes and ears" of the Chinese emperors.

Censors were powerful officials of the Roman Republic who were responsible for conducting the census and administering the government's finances for public works and preserving public morals. They also determined the economic status of citizens for voting purposes, assessed the property holdings of Roman citizens for tax purposes and determined who was eligible for military service.

Central Bank is an institution common in industrialized countries whose major tasks are to maintain the value of a state's currency and to control inflation.

Central Intelligence Agency (CIA) was created by President Truman in 1947 during the Cold War to conduct U.S. intelligence and counterintelligence operations throughout the world.

Central Powers were the nations of Germany, Austria-Hungary, Bulgaria, and the Ottoman Empire that formed a military and political alliance during World War I.

Central Treaty Organization (CENTO) (1959–1979), also known as the Baghdad Pact, was a military alliance of Turkey, Iran, Pakistan, and the United Kingdom that was formed under pressure from Britain and the United States. Its headquarters was in Baghdad. It was modeled after NATO. Promised military and economic aid by the US, the alliance's purpose was to contain the threat of Soviet expansion into the oil rich Middle East and South Asia by creating a barrier of strong states along the USSR's southwestern and southern border. Unlike NATO, it did not have a unified military command structure and not many U.S. or UK military bases were established in the member countries. After the Iraqi monarchy was overthrown in 1958 in a military coup, the new Iraqi government withdrew from CENTO. It then opened diplomatic relations with Soviet Union and adopted a non-aligned stance. After the Iraqi withdrawal, the alliance members dropped the name 'Baghdad Pact' in favor of CENTO and moved its headquarters to Ankara, Turkey. Even though the Middle East and South Asia were to be the areas of primary focus of the CENTO, it was reluctant to get involved in the Arab-Israeli War and the Indo-Pakistan Wars. Furthermore, CENTO failed to prevent the Soviet Union from establishing military, economic and political relations with Egypt, Syria, Somalia, Libya or Yemen. Following the fall of the Shah of Iran in 1979 during the Iranian

Revolution, Iran withdrew from the organization and CENTO was dissolved. It was never effective and is considered to be the least successful of the three major Cold War alliances.

Centrally Planned (Command) Economy is an economic system in which the state sets the prices for goods, decides on quotas for production and consumption of each commodity produced and controls the means of production. Under this system, all goods, services and agricultural and industrial products are strictly regulated. During the Cold War, centrally planned and controlled economies were generally associated with socialist or communities countries such as the Soviet Union and its Eastern European allies, China, Cuba and Vietnam.

Centuriate Assembly (450 BCE) was a military assembly created during the period of the Roman Republic. It included patricians and plebeians who were organized by classes and centuries (groups of 100) based on their wealth and the military equipment they could provide for military duty. It used block voting in which each group of 100 had one vote. It elected consuls, praetors and censors, passed laws, considered appeals of capital convictions and decided issues of war and peace.

Centurion was the title of an officer in the Roman army who commanded a century. A century, which was the smallest unit in a Roman legion during the Roman Empire, was comprised of 100 soldiers. Six centuries constituted a cohort and there were ten cohorts in a Roman legion of approximately 6000 soldiers. Accordingly, there were a total of 60 centurions in a legion. Typically, a centurion came from the plebeian class and was a common soldier who was promoted from the ranks based on his military skill, courage and experience. Furthermore, a centurion had to be literate in order to read the written orders sent to him by senior officers in the legion. As a centurion was responsible for training the soldiers under his command and disciplining them, he received higher pay than the common soldier and a greater share of the spoils of war. Since a centurion led his century from the front and fought alongside the soldiers he commanded, centurions suffered high casualty rates in battle. During the era of the Roman Empire, centurions gradually rose to command cohorts.

Chaeronea, Battle of (338 BCE) was a battle in central Greece in which Philip II of Macedon and his son Alexander defeated the Greeks and established the Macedonian domination of Greece.

Chalcedonians were Christians who followed the doctrines of the Council of Chalcedon established in 451 CE. Those doctrines held that Jesus' human and divine natures were equal, but entirely distinct and united in one person. Chalcedonian Christianity was generally associated with the Byzantine Empire and is called today Greek Orthodoxy.

Chaldea is the Greek name for a small, independent kingdom in southern Mesopotamia near Ur that was part of Babylonia. Its territory extended along the northern and western shores of the Persian Gulf where the Tigris and Euphrates Rivers meet to discharge their waters into the Persian Gulf. It became a Babylonian colony during the rule of Hammurabi.

Chaldeans were a Semitic speaking people who migrated from Arabia and settled in southern Mesopotamia in the early 9th century BCE about the same time as the Arameans settled Babylon. By the middle of the 8th century BCE, they had lost their political and cultural identity and were assimilated into the Babylonian civilization. During the 9th and 8th centuries BCE, the Chaldeans fought a number of losing wars against the Assyrians, but were able nonetheless to defeat the Babylonians in 721 BCE. In 626 BCE, Nabopolassar, a Chaldean leader, founded the Neo-Babylonian or Chaldean Dynasty, which would rule until 539 BCE when Cyrus the Great of Persia invaded and defeated Babylonia. Under the leadership of Nabopolassar and that of his son, Nebuchadnezzar, they were able to defeat the Assyrians and became the most powerful empire in the ancient Middle East. The Neo-Babylonian (Chaldean) armies conquered the Egyptians, the Syrians, the Phoenicians and the Kingdom of Judah, where Nebuchadnezzar destroyed Jerusalem and exiled the Jews to Babylon. When Cyrus the Great absorbed the Neo-Babylonians into the Persian Empire, the name Chaldean would only be used thereafter to refer to a class of people living in the Persian Empire who were accomplished in reading, writing, sorcery, witchcraft and magic.

Chamberlain, Houston Stewart (1855– 1927) was an English writer in the late 1800s who glorified the virtues of the Germans as a master race. In his book *The Foundations of the Nineteenth Century,* he claimed that the European conquests, colonialism, exploitation and dominance were all products of the great accomplishments of the German people. He also expressed a virulent hatred of Jews. He claimed that Jesus was not a Jew because all Jews had a moral defect that was part of their racial character. His racial views fueled anti-Semitism in Europe by manufacturing an image of Jews as an inherently inferior people. Chamberlain's views about the superiority of German society and culture were widely disseminated in Germany and avidly consumed by men such as Hitler and his colleagues in the Nazi Party. Eventually, the ideas of race and Aryanism were carried to their logical extreme by the Nazis who believed that a "superior race" had the right to eliminate an "inferior race."

Champollion, Jean Francois (1790–1832) was a French linguist, historian and Egyptologist who developed the first systematic method for deciphering Egyptian hieroglyphics in 1822. He established that Egyptian hieroglyphics represented both a written and spoken language. He also founded the field of Egyptology as an academic discipline. Champollion's work established the basis for all further developments in the field of deciphering Egyptian hieroglyphics. Even though Egyptian hieroglyphics had been known for centuries by European scholars, some scholars concluded that Egyptian hieroglyphics could not be translated into words and viewed them as mystical symbols. Other scholars considered hieroglyphics to be only ideographic symbols that did not represent a spoken language. The first advances in deciphering Egyptian were made in 1819 by Thomas Young, an English physicist, after the discovery of the Rosetta Stone by French scientists in 1799.

Chang'an is a city in eastern China that became the capital of the Han and Tang dynasties. It is located near the present-day Chinese city of Xian.

Chanson de geste, which means "song of deeds" in French, was an epic poem written between the 1100s and the 1400s which dealt primarily with events that occurred during the reigns of Charlemagne and his successor in the 700s and 800s. These poems were derived from oral traditions that had been told for centuries about heroic prowess and great battles. The length of a typical poem could range from 1500 to more than 18,000 lines in length. A chanson was generally sung or recited in the royal courts to the nobility and the performance of a chanson, depending on its length, might extend over several days. A common theme in these poems was a struggle of Christian France against a Muslim enemy. The oldest known chanson de geste is *The Song of Roland*, which is 4000 lines in length. This poem, which was composed by an anonymous poet around 1100, is set in northern Spain during the reign of Charlemagne after a battle in which a number of his soldiers are massacred by a Muslim enemy. Charlemagne is portrayed in *The Song of Roland* as a defender of Christendom. The poem praises the knightly martial values of prowess, courage and loyalty and promoted the idea that a knight's loyalty to his lord should take precedence over loyalty to a relative and even slights to the knight's honor. While *The Song of Roland* offered no understanding of Islam, it did represent Muslims as pagans who worshipped idols. Thus, the underlying religious belief expressed in *The Song of Roland* was that the defense of Christianity was a moral imperative for Christian monarchs and knights and that the killing of pagans, who were considered to be enemies of Christianity, was legitimate and just.

Charlemagne (747–814 CE), who was also known as Charles I or Charles the Great, was the Frankish king who established the Carolingian Empire, which encompassed all of Gaul, parts of Germany, and northern Italy. As king he ruled from 768 to 800 and as emperor he ruled from 800 to 814. He established the frontiers of the Frankish kingdom, and promoted cultural and institutional reform. He consolidated much of Western Europe under his rule by adding Lombardy and Saxony to the Frankish kingdoms. Imbued with a strong sense of divine purpose, he forced the Christian conversion of pagan peoples. Though illiterate, he sponsored arts and learning at his court in Aachen. He revitalized the Roman Empire by becoming the first Roman emperor in the west since the 400s. He is considered to be the first emperor of Holy Roman Empire.

Charles V (1500–1558) was the Holy Roman Emperor who reigned from1519 to 1556) and the king of Spain (Charles I) who reigned over Spain, Italy, the Low Countries (modern Belgium and the Netherlands), and Germany. He was the most powerful ruler in Europe in the 1500s. Even though he opposed the Protestant Reformation, he was forced to sign the Peace of Augsburg in 1555, which acknowledged the right of German princes to choose the religion to be practiced within their sovereign territories, either Lutheranism or Catholicism. Subsequently, he abdicated his imperial and royal titles and gave his empire to his brother Ferdinand and his Spanish possessions to his son, Philip II.

Chartered (joint-stock) Company was an association of private investors or shareholders who paid an annual fee to the Dutch, British and French governments in exchange for a monopoly over trade, exploration and colonization in Africa, India, Asia, the Caribbean and North America. They were first established by the English in the mid-1500s and later in the early 1600s by the French and the Dutch. The earliest English chartered trading company was the Company of Merchant Adventurers to New Lands(1553), which tried to establish a northern trade route to China and the Spice Islands (the Moluccas). Subsequently, the English established the Muscovy Company (1555), which had a monopoly on trade between England and Muscovy; the Spanish Company (1577), which sought to control trade between England and Spain; Eastland Company (1579), which sought to develop trade with Scandinavia and the Baltic states; the Levant Company (1581), which sought to control trade with Turkey and the countries of the Levant (Greece, Syria, Palestine and Egypt; the Venice Company (1583), which sought to monopolize trade with the Venetian colonies in the Mediterranean ; and the Turkey Company(1583), which was merged with the Venice Company in 1592. In the 1600s, the British created the East India Company (1600), the London Company(1606), the Virginia Company (1609), the Plymouth Company(1606) and the Massachusetts Bay Company (1628), the Hudson Bay Company(1670), the Royal African Company (1672). In 1889, as part of the "Scramble for Africa", the British created the British South Africa Company, which sought to promote colonization and economic exploitation in south-central Africa. All of these trading companies would contribute significantly to the growth of the English economy

and the commercial and maritime supremacy of the English by the 1700s. These trading companies would also have wide-reaching influence on the development of European imperialism and colonialism in Africa and Asia. The Dutch and the French would also establish chartered trading companies. The French established the French East India Company in 1664 and the Dutch established the Dutch East India and West India companies in 1602 and 1621 respectively. The chartered company would be supplanted by the emergence of the modern corporation.

Chartism or Chartist Movement (1838–1848) was a British working-class political movement in the 1830s and 1840s that sought democratic political reforms to benefit British workers. This movement sought universal male suffrage, the secret ballot, annual elections, equal electoral districts, annual meetings of Parliament, payment for parliamentary service, and the elimination of the property ownership requirement in order to be a member of Parliament. The movement was named for the "People's Charter," which was issued in 1838. While the movement failed, most of its proposed reforms eventually became law.

Chaucer, Geoffrey (1342/43–1400) was an English poet whose book, *The Canterbury Tales*, his greatest work, recounts the lives of thirty pilgrims on their way to the shrine of Saint Thomas a Becket.

Checkpoint Charlie was the Allied name for a border crossing between East and West Berlin that became the site of a tense military stand-off between U.S. and Soviet tanks in October 1961.

Checks and Balances refers to the structure of a central government in which the powers of the executive, legislative, and judicial branches would balance each other and the central government would be checked by the power of the individual states.

Cheka (All Russian Extraordinary Commission) was a police organization founded in December 1917 to gather information on and to arrest opponents of the Bolsheviks. Under Stalin, it evolved into the Soviet secret police.

Chelmno was a Nazi extermination camp established in Poland in 1941. It was equipped with gas chambers and five crematoriums. During its existence, the Nazis murdered 370,000 people, 365,000 of whom were Jews.

Chemical Weapons Convention (1992) is the multilateral treaty that bans the production, possession and of chemical weapons by nation-states. A chemical weapon consists of harmful toxic chemical substances that can cause death or severe harm to humans and animals. Chemical weapons can be gases, liquids or powders that can cause blistering, choking, bleeding and nerve damage. They are considered weapons of mass destruction because the effects of such weapons cannot distinguish between soldiers and civilians. The treaty includes strict verification standards and the threat of sanctions against any violations.

Chen Duxiu (1879–1942) was the intellectual leader of the May 4th Movement in China in the early 1900s, an early advocate of Marxism, and one of the founders of the Chinese Communist Party in 1921.

Chernobyl (1986) is a city in the Ukraine that was the site of the meltdown of a Soviet nuclear reactor

Chiang Kai-shek (1887–1975) was the Chinese military and political leader who succeeded Sun Yat-sen in 1925 as the head of the Chinese Nationalist Party (Kuomindang). He headed the Chinese government from 1925 to 1949 when he and his Chinese Nationalist military forces were defeated by the communists led by Mao Zedong. After 1949, he headed the Chinese Nationalist government, which had fled to Taiwan.

Chiefdom is a form of political organization in which a hereditary leader who holds power over a small collection of villages and towns exercises power.

Chinese Exclusion Act (1882) was a law passed by the U.S. Congress which prohibited all Chinese workers both skilled and unskilled from emigrating to the United States for ten years. The Act was renewed in 1892 and 1902 and continued indefinitely until 1943, when it was repealed during World War II as China was an ally of the U.S. The Chinese Exclusion Act was the first law enacted by the U.S. Congress to prevent the emigration to the U.S. of

a specific nationality or ethnic group. Beginning with the California Gold Rush (1848–1855) and the construction of the First Transcontinental Railroad (1863–1869) by the Central Pacific Railroad, thousands of Chinese men, who were primarily single males, were recruited to emigrate to the United States in order to the provide cheap labor for the gold fields and mines and railroads in the West. When gold became harder to find and the railroads were completed, the Chinese workers began to compete with American workers for other types of jobs. Many Chinese workers settled in cities such as San Francisco where they worked in low-wage restaurant and laundry jobs. Nevertheless, for many American workers in the West, the willingness of the Chinese workers to work in low wage jobs was considered a direct economic threat to the economic well-being of American workers. The Chinese workers were accused of taking jobs away from Americans and lowering the level of wages. During the economic recession of 1873–1879, anti-Chinese sentiments and hostility intensified significantly, fueled, in part, by such organizations as the American Workingman's Party (1876), which was formed to protest against any further Chinese immigration to the U.S. With over 75,000 Chinese workers in California alone and 30,000 elsewhere in the West, acts of violence against Chinese workers occurred in Wyoming and Oregon, culminating in race riots breaking out in San Francisco in 1877. In response to this increasing hostility and violence in the West against the Chinese workers, the U.S. Congress passed the Chinese Exclusion Act. Ironically, by 1902, with the supply of cheap Chinese workers cut off, employers in the West began to hire Mexican, Filipino and Japanese immigrants to work in the expanding railroad, mining construction and agricultural industries.

Chivalry, which is derived from the word for "horsemanship," was a code of conduct and an ideal of civilized behavior that emerged among a warrior-aristocracy (knights) in the 11th and 12th centuries in Europe. This code of conduct, which a knight was required to follow, emphasized courage, loyalty, honor, generosity and earning a reputation for military prowess. It originated with the knights in northern France and spread across Europe. These ideals of knighthood encouraged social graces and the pursuit of a glorious and heroic reputation. Chivalry would later evolve into an elaborate set of rules governing relations between men and women.

Cholera is a deadly infectious disease that appeared in Europe in the 1830s that caused violent vomiting and diarrhea and left the skin blue, eyes sunken, and hands and feet ice cold.

Christendom is the term used by historians to refer collectively to the various kingdoms of Europe whose populations were Christian and who used Latin as the language of worship, diplomacy, and law during the Middle Ages.

Christian Humanists were Renaissance thinkers in northern Europe in the 1400s and 1500s who sought to determine the precise meaning of the founding texts of Christianity. They were experts in Greek, Latin and Hebrew.

Christianity originally began as a sect of Judaism, but it did not emerge as a separate religion until around 200 CE. Jesus was viewed as both a savior or messiah and the son of God. It emphasized that Christ would return to create a heavenly kingdom on earth. Christianity offered salvation in the next life and a caring community in the present one. It was considered a mystery cult in the Roman Empire.

Christmas is the name of a Christian festival celebrating the birth of Jesus. The English term is of recent origin. The earlier term was Yule, which referred to the feast of the winter solstice. The early Christians distinguished between the date of Jesus' birth and the religious celebration of that event. During the first two centuries of Christianity there was strong opposition to recognizing birthdays of martyrs or Jesus. Numerous Church Fathers considered such celebrations as pagan rituals. They argued that the saints and martyrs should be honored on the day of their martyrdom. The precise origin of assigning December 25th as the birth date of Jesus is unclear. The New Testament provides no clues in this regard. December 25th was first identified as the date of Jesus' birth by Sextus Julius Africanus in 221 and later became the universally accepted date. One widespread explanation for the origin of this date is that December 25th was the Christianizing of

Sol Invictus (day of the birth of the unconquered sun), a popular holiday in the Roman Empire. Sol Invictus celebrated the winter solstice as a symbol of the resurgence of the sun, the casting away of winter and the heralding of the rebirth of spring and summer. After December 25th had become more widely accepted as the date of Jesus' birth, Christian theologians contended that there was a connection between the rebirth of the sun and the birth of the Jesus, the son of God. It was not until the 800s that Christmas began to be celebrated in the Christian Church with a specific liturgy. Prior to that time, the two major Christian holidays were Good Friday and Easter. None of the contemporary Christmas customs and traditions has any theological basis. The tradition of the Christmas tree decorated with apples first occurred in Strasbourg in 1605. The use of candles on such trees occurred in Silesia in 1611. The Advent Calendar was created in the 1800s in Munich with the first commercial calendars being printed in Germany in 1851. It is only toward the end of the 1700s that the practice of giving gifts to family members became more firmly established, even though the practice of giving gifts appears to have originated in the 1400s. The practice of sending Christmas cards began in England in the 1800s. All of these developments contributed to the view that Christmas was a secular holiday focused on gift giving and celebrations with family and friends.

Christological Controversies concerned the debate about the Christian Trinity (Father, Son, and Holy Spirit) and how Jesus can be both divine and human. This debate caused significant divisions and conflicts in the Christian Church from the 200s until the 400s.

Church Fathers were Greek and Roman Christians (for example, St. Ambrose, St. Augustine, St. Cyril, St. Jerome and John Chrysostom) who between 300 and 750 enunciated the basic doctrines of Christianity. They sought to reconcile Christianity with classical learning.

Church of England is the religious institution founded by Henry VIII in the 1530s in England after Pope Clement VII excommunicated him from the Catholic Church because of Henry's desire to have another marriage annulled by the Pope.

Churchill, Winston (1874–1965) was the British prime minister who led Britain during World War II from 1940 to 1945 and after World War II from 1951 to 1955. Many people believe that it was Churchill's courage, decisiveness, eloquence, and energy during World War II that has made him Britain's greatest political leader and statesman in the 1900s.

Cicero, Marcus Tullius (106–43 BCE) was a Roman Stoic philosopher, writer, conservative senator and politician who was one of Rome's greatest orators. He struggled for peace and social order during the civil wars that destroyed the Roman Republic after the murder of Julius Caesar. He sought to use Latin as a means by which to convey the heritage of Greek thought. He was the author of the doctrine of humanitas.

Cimon(510–450 BCE) was a conservative Athenian aristocrat, politician and general who was the son of Miltiades, the Athenian general who defeated the Persian invasion force at the Battle of Marathon. As a result of Cimon's heroic acts at the Battle of Salamis, he was promoted to general (strategos). After the formation of the Athenian led Delian League, he was appointed commander of the League's military forces. In his position of leadership in the League, he played an important role in building the Athenian Empire. Under the authority of the League, he forced a number of Greek maritime city-states located around the Aegean Sea to join the Delian League. Even though two earlier invasions of Greece in 492–490 and 480–479 BCE by the Persian Empire had been unsuccessful, King Xerxes I of Persia, nevertheless, began between 469–466 to reassemble a large army and navy to reassert control over the Greek city-states (particularly in Ionia) located along the coastline of the Aegean Sea in the western part of Anatolia (also known as Asia Minor). Xerxes assembled this invasion force at the mouth of the Eurymedon River, which was located in southern Anatolia along the Mediterranean coastline. In response to Persia's aggressive actions, Cimon was authorized by the Delian League to initiate a preemptive military attack on the Persian forces assembled at the Eurymedon River. Cimon, commanding a combined force of two hundred triremes and about 5000 soldiers, attacked and decisively defeated the combined Persian land and sea forces at the Battle

of Eurymedon in 466 BCE. (The actual date of the battle is disputed by some historians who argue that the battle occurred in 469 BCE.) Nevertheless, Cimon destroyed or captured, in only one day, approximately two hundred Persian triremes, which were manned by Phoenician sailors, and defeated the Persian ground forces. Cimon's victory at Eurymedon eliminated the Persian threat to Greece and its allies throughout the Aegean Sea. In 462 BCE, when Sparta asked Athens for help in suppressing a helot rebellion, Cimon persuaded the Athenians to consent to Sparta's request and to let him lead a military force to assist the Spartans. After the Athenian military force had been sent to Sparta, Sparta, however, changed its mind and demanded that Cimon and the Athenian soldiers return to Athens. Angered and humiliated by the Spartan behavior, Athenian political leaders ostracized Cimon for ten years beginning in 461 BCE, only to ask him five years later to return to Athens to negotiate a five year truce with Sparta.

Cincinnatus, Lucius Quinctius (519–430 BCE) was a Roman patrician who was elected consul in 460 BCE. When Rome was threatened by defeat in 458 BCE by the Aequi, a neighboring Italic tribe, the Senate requested that Cincinnatus, who was admired in the Senate for his leadership, simplicity, modesty, and lack of personal ambition, cease working his small farm and become dictator (similar to a tyrant in Greece) for a short period of time in order to defeat the Aequi. After decisively defeating the Aequi, he resigned his position as dictator and returned to farm his small plot of land. Cincinnatus was considered by members of the Roman aristocratic class to be one of the legendary heroes of early Roman history. For that powerful social class, Cincinnatus personified the ideal of civic virtue because he placed service to the common good of Rome ahead of personal interests.

Ciompi Rebellion was a revolt of workers in the woolen-cloth industry in Florence in 1378 to obtain political and economic rights. In Florence, guilds played an important political role in the governance of the city. However, the Ciompi (wool carters), who performed the hardest jobs in the woolen-cloth industry, were not permitted to form a guild by the Florentine government even though the woolen-cloth industry dominated manufacturing in Florence. Furthermore, by 1378, the woolen-cloth industry was depressed, resulting in high unemployment among the laborers in the industry. Fueled by these circumstances, the wool workers demanded tax and economic reforms and the right to form their own guild. They seized control of the city government and forced the Florentine government to recognize two guilds for laborers in the woolen-cloth industry. The Ciompi controlled the Florentine government until 1832, when mercenaries hired by the conservative Florentine political and economic elite brutally suppressed the Ciompi.

Cisalpine Gaul was the Roman name for the area in Italy between the Alps and the Rubicon River. It literally means "Gaul on this side of the Alps."

Cistercians (also known as White Monks or Bernardines) were Benedictine monks who founded a monastic religious order in Citeaux in Burgundy in 1098. They emphasized emotional devotion to Christ and Mary and sought religious purity. The Cistercians adopted an austere lifestyle and tried to separate themselves from the existing feudal political and social structures. Their influence spread rapidly in the 1100s in Europe.

City-State was a small independent state consisting of an urban center with a population in excess of 5000 inhabitants and the surrounding agricultural territory, which was ruled by a king. It was the typical form of political organization in early Mesopotamia, Archaic and Classical Greece, Phoenicia, and early Italy.

Civic Humanism was an intellectual movement advocated by Leonard Bruni and other Florentine writers and officials during the Renaissance that promoted the ethic of responsible citizenship. Followers believed that intellectuals should be more involved in governmental affairs. They also defended the republican institutions found in the cities of northern Italy during the Renaissance. They argued that moral and ethical values were necessary in public life. Many followers of civic humanism became political advisors to governments and helped establish governmental policies.

Civic Nationalism is a form of nationalism that bases its appeal on loyalty to a set of broad political ideas and institutions that are perceived as just and effective. It is an inclusionary form of nationalism that emphasizes birth or long-term residence within a nation's territory. During transitions to democracy, civic nationalism tends to emerge when elite interests are not threatened by democratization and representative and journalistic institutions are already well-established before the opinions of the population gain political power.

Civil Constitution of the Clergy (1790) was a law enacted during the French Revolution that subordinated the Catholic Church to the French government. Under this law, parishes and dioceses were redrawn, priests and bishops were elected by the laity in their parishes, and they had to swear loyalty to the state.

Civil Disobedience is a political tactic used by Mohandas Gandhi in India and suffragettes in England to protest oppression that typically involved large numbers of people peacefully breaking the law in order to obtain political reform.

Civil Rights are those basic rights of citizens in a democracy that protect an individual's freedom from unwarranted infringement by governments and private organizations. They ensure an individual's ability to participate in the civil and political life of a democratic society without discrimination or repression. Such rights include the ensuring of an individual's physical integrity and safety; protection from discrimination on grounds such as physical or mental disability, gender, religion, race, national origin, age, or sexual orientation; and individual rights such as the freedoms of thought and conscience, speech and expression, religion, the press, and movement. By contrast political rights include natural justice (procedural fairness) in law, such as the rights of the accused, including the right to a fair trial; due process; the right to seek redress or a legal remedy; and rights of participation in civil society and politics such as freedom of the speech, press and religion, freedom of association, the right to assemble, the right to petition, and the right to vote.

Civil War is a form of armed conflict in which competing political factions within an existing state try either to form a new government to govern that state or prevent the formation of new government.

Civilization is a term often used by anthropologists, archeologists, and historians to denote more complex societies. Such societies are distinguished by the development of religious and political institutions located in cities, a growing and settled population engaged in various trades and occupation, food production, a bureaucratic structure to administer the society, different levels of wealth, political power concentrated in the hands of an elite, the production of written documents, a common cultural and linguistic identity, buildings constructed for communal activities, and an educational structure for transmitting cultural and historical understanding.

Civilizing Mission was the rationale developed by European imperial powers in the late 1800s and 1900s to justify colonial expansion in Africa and Asia. Advocates of this idea argued that the Earth should be populated and governed by those races of people best equipped intellectually, technologically and morally to govern. These advocates also claimed that Europeans were a moralizing force in the world and that, as such, European nations had a duty to help the nations they viewed as backward civilize themselves. To that end, the European imperial powers sought impose western social, political, economic and cultural values and institutions on the populations they ruled. In fact, the proponents of European imperialism and colonialism went so far as to advocate the adoption of not only western culture and values, but also the adoption of western clothes, language and conversion to Christianity. Ironically, such European efforts to impose western culture, values, traditions and institutions on their colonial subjects led to the emergence of nationalist movements for independence in the 1900s, particularly after World War II, which threatened and eventually caused the demise of European colonial rule.

Cixi or Ts'u hsi), Empress Dowager (1835–1908) was the mother of Emperor Guangxi and the Empress Dowager of China. She was the consort of Emperor Xiangeng in the 1850s. She was the mother of the Tongzhi emperor who reigned from 1860–1872. After putting her son, Emperor Guangxu, under house arrest she resisted reforms of the Chinese government and armed forces. As Empress Dowager, she was the power behind the throne in the last decades of Manchu rule. She supported the anti-foreign political movement known as the Boxers and declared war on the foreign powers in China during the Boxer Rebellion.

Clan is social group comprised of relatives who are expected to defend one another and take revenge for harm done to or crimes committed against any member of the group.

Class is a large and often cohesive social group that is based on shared social, economic, and political interests. From the perspective of Marxism, a class is a social group whose identity is determined by its relationship to the means of production and the distribution of societal resources. Accordingly, the bourgeoisie, the upper class, own the means of production while the proletariat, the lower class, is comprised of the workers.

Class Consciousness refers to a sense of social separation in which individuals believe that they are distinctly different and separate from other social groups.

Class Struggle is the social, political and economic process by which a more powerful and wealthy class in a society oppresses and exploits a less politically and economically powerful group by denying that group their fair share of what they produce. In response, the oppressed class may use legal means or force to gain political and economic power in order to create a social structure that more equitably distributes the economic wealth of a society.

Classical Age (510–323 BCE) is a term used by historians to describe a period of ancient Greek history beginning with the defeat of the Persian invasions and lasting until the death of Alexander the Great. This period was marked by active involvement of the citizens in public life, the emergence of democracy, the flowering of philosophy, economic prosperity, artistic expression and literary achievement in poetry and drama. Classical Greek culture would establish the standards for the culture that would emerge in Western Europe over the centuries.

Classical Economics refers to the belief that economies grow through the free enterprise of individuals competing in a self-regulating marketplace free of government intervention.

Classical Learning is a term used by historians for the study of ancient Greek and Latin texts that emerged in the Roman Empire after Christianity became the official religion of the empire. Scholars, especially Christian monks attempted to reinterpret classical learning in order to reconcile it with a Christian way of life.

Claudius (10–54 CE) was the third emperor of the Julio-Claudian line of emperors. He was the nephew of Emperor Tiberius. Because of ill-health in his youth and an unattractive appearance, he was viewed by his family as an embarrassment and not of appropriate stature to be an emperor. Nevertheless, he became emperor after his nephew Caligula was murdered and subsequently ruled from 41 to 54. Under the influence of the historian Livy, Claudius focused his intellectual energies on historical studies. While he extended the Roman Empire to include North Africa and Britain, his rule was undercut by the strong opposition of the Senate. He was poisoned by his fourth wife Agrippina, who was also his niece, so that her son Nero could become emperor.

Cleisthenes of Athens (570–508 BCE) was an aristocratic Athenian who made major constitutional reforms circa 508 BCE and thereby facilitated the emergence of democracy in Athens. His political innovations included the Council of Five Hundred and the creation of the ten tribes.

Clergy is a term used to describe members of the Christian faith such as priests, ministers, pastors, and abbots who are officially ordained to serve the Church and its parishioners.

Client kingdoms were kingdoms still ruled by their own kings but subject to Roman rule.

Client state is a country that is politically, economically and militarily dependent on a more powerful country.

Clientage, which is also known as a patron/client relationship, was a social relationship in ancient Rome whereby a man (client) of lower social status became the supporter of a more powerful and wealthy landowner (patron) in return for the patron's legal and physical protection and financial aid. The patron would exercise such political and legal influence on behalf of the client in expectation of future political support from the client.

Clippership was a fast, streamlined sailing vessel built during the mid to late 1800s in the United States that was rigged with vast canvas sails hung from tall masts.

Clovis I (466–511 CE) was the greatest Frankish king of the Merovingian Dynasty who reigned from 486 to 511. He established the Merovingian Dynasty that would last until 751, consolidated Frankish rule in Gaul, defeated the Visigoths in 507, and accepted Roman Catholicism. Because of his conversion to Catholicism and the power of the Frankish kingdom, other barbarian groups also converted.

Clovis Culture was the term developed by anthropologists to describe the culture that was developed by the first peoples (called Paleo-Indians by anthropologists) to inhabit the Americas during the Pleistocene period, which began about 126,000 years ago. The Clovis culture existed from 12,000 to 9,000 BCE in the arid plains of present-day Texas, New Mexico and Arizona.

Cluniacs were members of a spiritual reform movement that originated at the monastery of Cluny in with Burgundy in 910. This movement emphasized strict adherence to the Benedictine Rule, the idea that the Catholic Church should pray for the world without being deeply involved in it, and the belief that their movement must be free from lay control. Cluniac abbots were especially influential in the 1100s in Europe and tried to separate its network of religious houses from lay control. There were about 1500 Cluniac monasteries in Europe modeled after Cluny. As these monasteries were independent from secular authorities, they were able to accumulate enormous wealth.

Coffee is thought to have originated in the highlands of Ethiopia and spread to the rest of the world via Egypt and Europe. In fact, the word *coffee* is derived from Arabic. In the 1400s, Muslims introduced coffee in Persia, Egypt, and Turkey. However, coffee drinking was forbidden by orthodox and conservative imams in Mecca (1511) and in Cairo (1532). Indeed, in Egypt coffeehouses and warehouses containing coffee seeds were destroyed. However, because of its growing popularity, this probation was ended in 1524 by Selim I, the Sultan of the Ottoman Empire. From the Muslim world, coffee spread to Europe, where it became popular in the 1600s, especially in English coffeehouses which were centers of intellectual and commercial activity. In 1538, a German physician who had traveled for ten years in the Middle East wrote of coffee's medicinal benefits. His remarks influenced experienced spice merchants to begin importing coffee seeds into Europe. In the 1400s, Muslims introduced coffee in Persia, Egypt, and Turkey.

Cognitive Dissonance is a psychological state in which an individual experiences an emotionally painful tension or discomfort when confronted by new information that challenges and threatens the individual's existing belief system.

Cohong System refers to the policy developed by the Chinese imperial government in the late 1700s to regulate and control trade with Western merchants. Under this system, trade was restricted to the port of Canton in Guangzhou province in southern China and Western merchants could not trade directly with Chinese merchants. They were required to work through officially licensed and strictly regulated Chinese brokers.

Colbert, Jean-Baptiste (1619–1683) was the finance minister to Louis XIV in France who advocated strong central government control over the economic life of France. He reformed France's finances and encouraged commercial and internal improvements in France.

Cold War (1945–1991) was the era in international relations between the end of World War II and 1991 that was distinguished by ideological, economic, and political tensions, differences, and conflicts between the Soviet Union and the United States. This period in world history, some contend, began after World War II when communist governments supported by the Soviet Union took control of most of the countries of East and Central Europe. Tensions were especially intensified when the Soviet Union successfully tested its first atomic bomb in 1949, beginning a nuclear arms race that would last for over forty years.

Collective Security is a doctrine under which aggression by one nation will deterred by threatening to use the combined powers of the world's most powerful states against the aggressor nation. It represented a backlash against balance of power politics that had dominated the international system in the late 1800s and 1900s. Collective security was embodied in the structure of the League of Nations and the United Nations.

Collectivization (1920s–1930s) was Stalin's plan for the nationalization of agricultural production in the Soviet Union, which began in 1929. The plan required the forced replacement of the private and village farms of the Russian peasants with large cooperative agricultural enterprises under centralized state control. One of its primary objectives of Stalin's collectivization program was to accumulate sufficient wealth so as to facilitate the independent development and financing of an industrialized society in the Soviet Union. Twenty-five million peasants were forced to give up their land and join 250,000 large collective farms. As many as fifteen million Russian peasants who resisted Stalin's plan were deported to labor camps, exiled to Siberia or sent to work in factories. It is estimated that of that number 15–20% died or were executed. Stalin also cut off food rations to those areas in the Soviet Union where resistance to collectivization was the greatest. As a result of this decision, Stalin created a man-made famine in which millions of people starved to death.

College of Cardinals is the body within the Catholic Church selected by the pope that advises the pope and elects a new pope. Cardinals emerged as officials of the Catholic Church in late antiquity and their influence in Church affairs increased significantly after the 1100s.

Collegium was a Roman legal term for any group of people organized for a common purpose or function, such as a guild, a social club, a funerary society, or a business group. The meeting hall for it was generally referred to as a curia.

Colonus (plural coloni) was the Latin name for a poor free farmer who worked on large agricultural estates known as latifundia in Italy during the late Roman Empire and early Middle Ages. These farmers, who we would call sharecroppers today, leased their farms and in exchange paid the landowners with money, service or a portion of farmer's crops. Originally the landlord-tenant relationship was contractual, which gave the tenant-farmer certain rights that could be enforced by Roman courts. However, by the 300s laws limited the freedom of the tenant-farmer, which prohibited the tenant-farmer from leaving the land he farmed or changing his occupation. Furthermore, such laws also made the debts owed the landlord inheritable by the tenant-farmer's descendants who were also legally required to farm the same piece of land as their tenant-farmer father. If the landlord decided to sell the piece of land leased by the tenant-farmer, the tenant-farmer, his family and his contract were transferred with the ownership of the land. By the 500s CE, Emperor Justinian issued a law that transformed what began as a contractual land-lord-tenant relationship into a form of slavery, permitting the landlord to chain any coloni who attempted to leave the land he farmed. The coloni were the predecessors to the serfs of Europe during the Middle Ages.

Colonialism was the policy of political, economic, and cultural expansion and exploitation, usually by force, by one national group of another group. It typically involved the extension of a nation's sovereignty, typically a European country, over the territory and people of a country located in Africa or Asia. The European nation would control the other country's resources, labor, and market for the benefit of itself. This policy was based on the belief that the values of the colonizing nation were superior to those of the colonized. Advocates of colonialism argued that colonial rule benefited the colonized by developing the economic and political infrastructure necessary for modernization.

Colons or Settlers were white planters in the French Caribbean colony of Saint Domingue (Haiti).

It was also the name for the French colonists in Algeria who administered the colonial government in Algeria from 1830–1962.

Colony is an area of land or group of people located beyond the borders of a home country over which that home country exercises political, economic, and military control.

Columbian Exchange is the name given by historians to describe the widespread exchange of peoples, plants, animals, goods, ideas, culture, technologies and microbes between the peoples of Europe and the indigenous peoples of the Americas that began after Christopher Columbus's arrival in the New World(the Americas) in 1492. The Spanish and other European colonists brought their plants, domesticated animals such as horses, donkeys, mules, pigs, cattle, sheep, goats, chickens, large dogs, cats and bees, foods such as peanuts and even diseases to the Americas. In turn, the indigenous peoples of the Americas gave the European maize (corn), manioc, tomatoes and potatoes, which subsequently transformed European diets, culture and societies. The term "Columbian Exchange" was coined by professor Alfred W. Crosby in his book *The Columbian Exchange* (1972).

Columbian Question concerns the debate among historians and epidemiologists about whether syphilis and its ancestor diseases originated in the Americas and were brought to Europe after the voyages of Columbus.

Columbus, Christopher (1451–1506) was the Genoese mariner who, in the service of the Spanish government, led expeditions across the Atlantic Ocean in the late 1400s and early 1500s that established contact between the native peoples of the Americas and the Europeans. His efforts opened the way for Spanish conquest and colonization in the Americas.

Combination Act (1799) was a law passed by the Parliament in England that outlawed the formation of unions and collective bargaining by unions on behalf of British workers for wage increases and better working conditions. A similar law was passed in 1800 because Parliament feared that if workers went on strike during a war, the

British government would be forced to accept the demands of the workers. The 1799 and 1800 acts were repealed in 1824. Nevertheless, Parliament enacted the Combinations of Workmen Act in 1825 that once again prohibited the formation of trade unions that attempted to collectively bargain on behalf of workers for wage increases and better working conditions, but also imposed criminal penalties on picketing by unions picketing and the use of any other method that might persuade workers to strike. The formation of unions was not legalized in Britain until 1871 with the passage of the Trade Union Act by Parliament.

Comintern (Communist International), which was also called the Third International (1919–1943), was an international organization of national communist parties founded in Moscow in 1919. Though its stated purpose was the promotion of world revolution, the Comintern reflected primarily Soviet national interests and served chiefly as means by which the Soviet Union exercised control over foreign communist parties. In 1943, Stalin dissolved the Comintern. In 1947, Stalin created a new organization, the Cominform, to control the international communist movements. It only lasted until 1956 when the international communist movement collapsed in the wake of the growing Sino-Soviet split over the issue of peaceful coexistence.

Committee of Public Safety (1793–1795) was the authoritarian political body of nine men established during the French Revolution that was controlled by the Jacobins. It enforced political decisions by executing thousands of people during that period of the French Revolution known as the "Reign of Terror," which lasted from September 1793 to October 1794. The Committee justified exercising absolute political power during this second phase of the French Revolution because it was confronted by political opposition in and outside France that threatened the Revolution. Under the leadership of Robespierre, its most famous leader, it raised a large conscripted army to fight those internal and external threats.

Common Land was that portion of an estate owned by the lord of the manor (a noble) in medieval England, Scotland and Wales where manorial tenants collectively had the right to pasture a tenant's cattle, horses, sheep and other animals; to fish; to mow meadows for hay; to let pigs to forage for acorns and other nuts; to extract such minerals as sand, gravel, wall stone and lime; to cut trees for wood for the tenant's house; and to cut sod for fuel. These rights attached to a specific plot of land which was leased by a tenant. A manorial tenant who had such rights was called a "commoner". However, between 1450 to 1640 and 1750 to 1860, manorial landlords in England began a process of enclosure to prevent the exercise of common grazing and other rights over common land by their tenants. The landlords claimed that by fencing in common lands with hedges, bushes, or walls, they could increase production and efficiency, achieve greater profits, and gain greater control of their land. British landlords completed this process of enclosure of common lands by the end of the 1800s.

Common Law refers to royal laws issued beginning in the 1100s in England by King Henry II that were to be applied throughout the entire country by the king's traveling justices. These laws replaced the customary law used by county and feudal courts that varied from place to place.

Common Market is a zone of economic activity in which labor and capital as well as goods flow freely across national borders. The original Common Market was established in 1957 by West German, France, Italy, Belgium, Luxembourg and the Netherlands. The political and economic leaders of these nations believed that by integrating their respective economic structures peace and prosperity could be achieved in Europe.

Common Peace was apolitical concept adopted by Greeks in the 4th century BCE in an attempt to prevent war. It was based on the idea that the city-states of Greece should live together in peace and freedom while each city state would be governed by their own laws and customs.

Commonwealth is a form of political organization in which a state is governed by agreement for the common good or well-being of all the people as opposed to an authoritarian state governed for the benefit of a specific class or group of people.

Commonwealth of Independent States (1991) was a political confederation of twelve former republics of the Soviet Union (Russia, Ukraine, Belarus, Kazakhstan, Kyrgyzstan, Tajikistan, Turkmenistan, Uzbekistan, Armenia, Azerbaijan, Georgia and Moldovia) created after the dissolution of the Soviet Union for the purpose of coordinating their foreign relations, immigration policies, economies, defense, trade, environmental protection and law enforcement. The former Soviet republics of Latvia, Lithuania and Estonia refused to join CIS. After escalation of hostilities between Russia and Georgia concerning a separatist movement in South Ossetia, Georgia withdrew from the CIS in 2009.

Communes were self-governing associations of merchants, townspeople, and workers headed by elected officials that first appeared in hundreds of cities in north-central Italy after 1070. They were organized for the purpose of obtaining basic liberties from the feudal lords. Over time, the communes evolved into city-states by seizing the control of the surrounding countryside. In the 1800s, communes were established in such cities as Paris in response to the repressive nature of the monarchical governments in Europe.

Communes, Peoples were collective farms established in rural areas in the People's Republic of China by Mao Zedong beginning in 1958 during the Great Leap Forward. The communes had governmental, political, and economic functions. Each commune was a combination of smaller farm collectives, consisting of 4000 to 5000 households, and larger ones could consist of up to 20,000 households. In a commune, everything was shared, including furniture, household items, cooking utensils and pans, animals, even stored food. Private cooking was banned and replaced by communal dining and people were not allowed to eat with their families. The commune leaders assigned all farming activities every morning. Furthermore, family life was abolished and communal nurseries and homes were established for children and the elderly.

Communism is the revolutionary form of socialism developed by Karl Marx and Friedrich Engels in the mid-1840s that promoted the violent overthrow of bourgeois or capitalist institutions and the establishment of a socialist economy and the government controlled by the dictatorship of the proletariat.

Communist Information Bureau (Cominform) (1947) was the name of the international communist information bureau that was established by Stalin to direct communist movements around the world. Khrushchev dissolved it in 1956.

Communist Manifesto **(1848)** was the document authored by Karl Marx and Friedrich Engels that described the class struggle that was occurring in Europe in the mid-1800s. It predicated the downfall of the capitalist system and the replacement of the capitalist system by an economic and political system that would be operated in the interests of the working class, the proletariat.

Comparative Advantage is an economic theory advanced by Adam Smith to explain why people in various nations or regions of the world can profit more than other people from the sale of certain goods and products. He argued that access to certain materials or skilled labor enables some people to produce specific goods more efficiently or cheaply than other people. Thus, he contended, one nation or region would have a comparative advantage in a free market system. If a country exports those goods that it produces relatively more efficiently (i.e., costs the least to produce) and imports those goods that another country produces relatively more efficiently, then there will be mutual gains that could be achieved by each country trading.

Compellence is a term used in international relations to refer to the use of force by a state to make another state, international organization or individual actor take some action or refrain from taking some action.

Comprador was the name for a class of wealthy Chinese merchants who were authorized by Chinese authorities to trade with European traders in China during the Qing Dynasty (1644 –1911/12).

Comprehensive Test Ban Treaty (1996) is a multilateral treaty that bans the testing of all nuclear weapons both above and below ground.

Compromise of 1867 was the agreement that divided the Habsburg Empire into Austria in the west and Hungary in the east. It created a dual monarchy under Emperor Franz Joseph that would be officially known as the Austro-Hungarian Empire.

Concert of Europe (also know as the Congress System) was the policy adopted by Britain, Russia, Prussia, and Austria at the Congress of Vienna (1814-1815). This policy sought to promote mutual cooperation to resolve international disputes, to preserve the balance of power in Europe, to prevent any one nation from dominating Europe as Napoleon had done between 1804 and 1815, and to suppress liberal and nationalist movements in Europe. Over time, this system fractured as a new political leader, Germany's Otto von Bismarck, emerged in Europe who increasingly used military force to secure German national interests.

Concentration Camp System (1933–1945) was a complex network of prison camps established initially in Germany after Hitler assumed power in 1933. The Nazis sought to imprison those individuals considered to be political opponents such as communists, socialists, monarchists, Jehovah's Witnesses, gypsies, homosexuals and other so-called asocials. Between 1933 and 1938, the only Jews who were imprisoned in concentration camps were those Jews who fit in one of the above-listed categories. The first three concentration camps in Germany were Dachau (near Munich in 1933), Buchenwald (near Weimar in 1937), and Sachsenhausen (near Berlin in 1938). After World War II began, the Nazis would expand the concentration camp system to the German-occupied territories.

Concession Areas were territories in China, usually port cities, established after the Opium Wars under the Treaty of Nanjing (1842) that allowed European merchants to trade in and European people to settle in those Chinese territories.

Conciliar Movement was a political and religious movement by Catholic bishops in the 1330s and 1440s in Europe that advocated ending the Great Schism by convening a general meeting or council of bishops who would exercise authority over the rival popes in Avignon and Rome, which was achieved at the Council of Constance in 1414. These Catholic bishops also wanted to reform the governance structure of the Catholic Church. They claimed that that the pope was not a supreme monarch, merely the first among equals in the Church, that final authority in spiritual matters and governance of the Catholic Church resided in a general Church council and not with the pope and that Church councils had the right and the duty to reform the Church and even correct the pope's decisions in religious matters.

Concordat is an agreement between the Catholic Church and a sovereign nation-state concerning the regulation of the Catholic Church within that nation-state. Over the centuries, a concordat has been one of the means typically used by the Papacy to influence the political decisions of governments concerning the rights and privileges of Catholic Church and its followers within the territory of that society. Concordats often included such matters as the recognition of the Catholic Church in a particular country, the creation of dioceses and parishes, the appointment of bishops and priests, the exemption of Church property from taxation and certain legal matters, issues concerning marriage and divorce and the structure and content of public education.

Concordat of 1801 was the religious settlement that Napoleon Bonaparte made with the Catholic Church that reaffirmed the Catholic Church as the established church of France. During the French Revolution, the National Assembly had confiscated Catholic Church properties and issued the Civil Constitution of the Clergy, which made the Catholic Church a department of the government and no longer subject to the authority of the pope. After successfully leading a coup d'état against the French Directory in 1799, and then declaring himself First Consul, Napoleon Bonaparte concluded that coming to terms with the Catholic Church would be crucial to the success of his political ventures. While the Concordat restored some ties with the Papacy, it largely benefited Napoleon. Although it declared that "Catholicism was the religion of the great majority of the French," it maintained religious freedom for Jews and Protestants.

Concubine was the name given to a woman of lower social status who was in a quasi-matrimonial relationship with a man of higher social status. Typically, the man had an official wife and, in addition, one or more secondary wives. Concubines had limited rights of support from the man. Their offspring were publicly acknowledged as the man's children, but were considered to be of lower social status than children born by the official wife or wives. Historically, concubinage was frequently arranged by a woman's family as a means to provide a measure of economic security for the woman involved.

Condorcet, Marquis de (1743–1794) (his full name was Marie Jean Antoine Nicolas de Caritat) was a French mathematician, writer and influential Enlightenment philosopher. Early in his life, he wrote widely-respected books and articles on mathematics. As an Enlightenment philosopher, Condorcet advocated a constitutional democracy, a liberal (free market) economy, free and equal public education, and an end to slavery. Condorcet believed, as did many Enlightenment thinkers, that a world based on rationality and the scientific method should be applied to reforming human society, solving key social, political and economic problems and achieving progress. Even though the question of women's rights in society did not concern many of the leading Enlightenment thinkers, he, nevertheless, advocated equal social and political rights for women, who he pointed out were half of the human race and exercised rationality just as men. Condorcet argued that a woman was entitled to full citizenship, including the right to vote and hold office. Unfortunately, his ideas were ignored by such Enlightenment thinkers as Hobbes, Locke, Rousseau, Montesquieu and d'Alembert. Hobbes and Locke, for example, argued that women were naturally subordinate to men. In fact, Rousseau claimed that the primary role of a woman was as housekeeper, mother, moral instructor of children and supporter of her husband. During the French Revolution, he was elected as the representative of Paris to the Legislative Assembly (1791), the newly-created national parliament of France. He presided over the Legislative Assembly, which was dominated by the Girondins, until it was replaced by the National Convention. During the trial of King Louis XVI before the National Convention, Condorcet opposed executing him and proposed, instead, that the king be imprisoned. When he criticized the draft constitution submitted by the Jacobins to the National Convention in 1793, he was branded a traitor and a warrant was issued for his arrest. In response Condorcet went in hiding. Convinced that he might be discovered, he tried to flee Paris, but was arrested and imprisoned. Two days after his arrest, he was found dead in his cell, the cause of which is unknown. Some historians have argued that a friend gave him poison, which he subsequently took, and some argue that he was murdered. While in hiding, he wrote *Sketch for a Historical Picture of the Progress of the Human Spirit* in which he expressed his belief in the inevitability of human progress and the attainment of equality and happiness. This book, published posthumously in 1795, is considered to be one of the major texts of the Enlightenment.

Condottiere is the Italian word for the mercenary military leader who sold his services and that of his private army to the highest bidder during the various wars between the Italian city-states during the Renaissance. As Machiavelli advised in his book *The Prince* any ruler who hired mercenaries to defend his territory ran the risk that the mercenaries would take over the government.

Confession of faith was an official statement of the basic beliefs and tenets of a religion that was publicly declared by a follower of that religion. During the Protestant Reformation in the 1500s, the Lutherans issued the Confessions of Augsburg; the Anglicans issued the Thirty-Nine Articles; and the Catholic Church issued the doctrinal decrees of the Council of Trent.

Conflict of the Orders (494–287 BCE), which is also known as the Struggle of the Orders, was a great social and political conflict that developed in Rome between patricians and plebeians. The plebeians wanted real political representation and safeguards against patrician domination. As a result of this struggle, the plebeians gradually won political rights and gained more political influence in the Roman Republic.

Confucianism is a philosophy based on the teachings of Confucius and Mencius that became the official ideology of the imperial Chinese state from the Han Dynasty until the end of the Qing Dynasty. Confucian doctrine emphasized order, obedience to authority, respect for tradition, the role of the gentlemen, hierarchical patterns of social relationships, duty to the society, and veneration of learning.

Confucius (Kongzi) (551–479 BCE) was a Chinese philosopher during the Warring States Period. In his book *The Analects* he expressed his ideas about the need for social order, the conduct of rituals, respect for learning, obedience to hierarchical authority, duty, and public service. His ideas would become the basis for an ideology and code of conduct known as Confucianism, which would be adopted by subsequent generations of Chinese thinkers and government officials until the 1900s.

Congo Free State was a corporate state privately controlled by King Leopold II of Belgium, through a corporation of which Leopold was the sole shareholder and chairman. The state included the entire area now known as the Democratic Republic of the Congo. Until the middle of the 1800s, the Congo was on the edge of unexplored Africa, one of the last uncolonized territories. Malaria and other diseases made it an uneconomical environment for European exploration, exploitation, or colonization. King Leopold acquired the territory in 1885, ruling it personally until its annexation by his own kingdom of Belgium in 1908. Other European imperial powers competed with Leopold for control of the territory when natural resources such as rubber, copper, and other minerals were discovered there. Leopold engaged in mass killings and maimings in order to subjugate the indigenous peoples of the region and procure slave labor. The death toll caused by Leopold's mass killings is estimated to range from five million to twenty million, depending on the source. European and U.S. press agencies exposed the conditions in the Congo Free State to the public in 1900. By 1908, public pressure and diplomatic maneuvers led to the end of Leopold's rule and to the annexation of the Congo as a colony of Belgium.

Congress of Vienna (1814–1815) was the international conference established by the great European monarchies of Britain, Russia, Prussia, and Austria that had defeated Napoleon I. This meeting established a system of international diplomacy that would affect international relations in Europe during the 1800s. Specifically, the four victorious monarchies agreed to respect each other's borders, to guard against future internal revolutions and international wars that might threaten their established governments, and to cooperate to preserve the balance of power in Europe.

Concentration Camp System (1933–1945) was a network of prison camps established initially in Germany immediately after Hitler assumed power in 1933 for those individuals the Nazis considered to be political opponents: communists, socialists, and monarchists, Jehovah's Witnesses, gypsies, homosexuals and other so-called asocials. The general roundup of Jews did not start until 1938. Before then, only Jews who fit one of the above categories were interned in concentration camps. The first three concentration camps were Dachau (near Munich in 1933), Buchenwald (near Weimar in 1937), and Sachsenhausen (near Berlin in 1938).

Conquistador, which means "conqueror" in Spanish, was a Spanish noblemen and soldier such as Cortes and Pizzaro who explored and conquered the lands of indigenous peoples in the Americas (Mexico, Central America, and Peru) in the 1500s. They conquered the indigenous peoples of the Americas based on the legal authority granted them by the king of Spain. In return for this legal privilege, the king of Spain required that the conquistadors provide him with one-fifth of all things of value found in the lands they conquered in the Americas.

Conscription is the compulsory military service of male citizens of a country of a certain age. France was the first modern state to initiate such a political program. It was known as a *levée en masse*. In fact, the use of such a military draft was a key component of the wars fought during the French Revolution and Napoleonic Empire.

Conservatism was an ideology developed by Edmund Burke that emerged in the wake of the

French Revolution in the early 1800s in Europe. Advocates of this ideology sought to prevent the spread of the revolutionary changes to other countries in Europe and supported the established social and political order as represented by the church, the monarchy, and the landed aristocracy. Historians commonly refer to such a social and political order as the Ancien Regime or Old Order. Conservatism was hostile to rapid change and it venerated traditional institutions, concepts, and beliefs. It opposed the implementation of liberal policies that would limit the absolute power of the monarch and advocated a return to the customs traditions, values and institutions associated with monarchical and authoritarian forms of government. In response to the French Revolution, the Congress of Vienna (1814–1815) built a European political order founded on the ideology of conservatism.

Constantine I the Great (280–337 CE) was Roman emperor who reigned from 312 to 337. He continued the reforms of Diocletian, restructured the Roman army, and granted toleration to the Christians, eventually becoming a Christian himself. After reuniting the Roman Empire, he moved the capital to Constantinople in the early 300s CE.

Constantinople was the former capital of the Byzantine Empire until conquered by the Ottoman Empire in 1453.

Constitutions of Clarendon (1164) were a group of sixteen laws issued by King Henry II of England that outlined the nature of the relationship between England and the Catholic Church. The purpose of these laws was to restrict papal authority in England and ecclesiastical privileges and to ensure that any Catholic clergymen convicted of serious crimes in a Church court would be subject to the jurisdiction of the royal courts for their punishment. Henry exiled Thomas Beckett, the Archbishop of Canterbury, who was opposed to the implementation of such restrictions on the Church in England.

Constitutional Monarchy is a form of government in which the king remains head of state but all lawmaking power remains in the hands of the legislature.

Constitutionalism is the theory of government that emerged in the 1600s in England which required the exercise of governmental power to be subject to the legal and legislative limitations imposed by the Parliament. It is based on the doctrine that the authority of a government depends upon the consent of the governed. Constitutionalism emphasizes a balance between the authority and power of the government on the one hand and the rights and liberties of the citizens on the other as expressed in a constitution, which may be unwritten (British and Canadian) or written (American). The movement to limit the power of the monarch was reflected in the English Civil War and the Glorious Revolution.

Consul was the official title of the two highest governmental officers in the Roman Republic. They were the supreme magistrates of the Roman state. Two consuls were elected annually for one year terms by the Senate to administer the government, lead the armies, propose legislation, and convene the various assemblies. Like the former kings of Rome, each consul exercised "imperium", which meant the power to issue commands and order punishments. The Roman Senate also imposed the principles of "annuality" and "collegiality" on all of the magistrates they appointed. Each magistrate was required to have one of more colleagues in order to prevent the rise of another king and ensure more productive magistrates and each magistrate would hold office for only one year. Napoleon was given the title of First Consul by the French Constitution of 1800.

Consulate (1799–1804) was the name for the French government established after the Directory was toppled. Napoleon Bonaparte was made First Consul, with Emmanuel Joseph Sieyès and Pierre Ducos as the two other consuls and Napoleon's advisers. While the consulate had a legislative assembly as well, its powers were limited and the First Consul was essentially a dictator. When Napoleon became emperor in 1804, the Consulate ended.

Consumer Revolution refers to a stage of economic development that began in the early 1700s in Europe in which there was an enormous increase in the consumption of goods and services.

Consumer Society is a term that was used to describe industrialized societies after World War II, particularly in Western Europe and the United States, in which the working class adopted the consumption patterns of the middle class. This societal transformation was facilitated by the development of installment plans, credit cards, and easy credit in order to purchase such consumer goods as cars, household appliances, computers, and furniture.

Consumerism is a term used to describe the purchasing of goods or consuming of materials in excess of one's needs. Consumerism is commonly associated with equating personal happiness with purchasing material possessions. It is often associated with criticisms of consumption starting with Karl Marx and Thorstein Veblen. Although consumerism is commonly associated with capitalism and industrialized societies, it is multicultural and nongeographical, as seen today in Tokyo, Singapore, Shanghai, Taipei, Tel Aviv, and Dubai, for example.

Containment was the foreign policy enunciated by U.S. policymakers in the early 1950s to prevent the expansion of the Soviet Union into Western Europe, Asia and Africa. The idea was first articulated in 1947 by George Kennan, an American diplomat stationed in Moscow, who advocated using primarily economic and political means to encircle and contain the Soviet Union. Subsequently, U.S. policy makers decided to use military means to prevent or restrict the possible attempts at military expansion by the Soviet Union through the development of collective security arrangements such as NATO. U.S. policymakers achieved their foreign policy objective of containment by supporting weaker states through political assistance, foreign aid programs, and military support. While this policy was derived from the Truman Doctrine, which was first enunciated by President Truman in 1947, it was more specifically articulated in National Security Council Memorandum 68 (NSC-68) in the early 1950s. In NSC-68, it was argued that the United States was engaged in a global struggle with the Soviet Union and that the United States should use all means available, including military force, to defeat any advance by the Soviet Union anywhere in the world.

Continental System (1806–1807) refers to the economic boycott and sanctions established by Napoleon Bonaparte in the early 1800s against Britain, under which all ships carrying British goods or trading with Britain, even those from neutral countries, were banned from European ports and were subject to seizure by French ships. Napoleon hoped that such a system of boycotts, embargoes and sanctions would weaken the British economy and its capacity to wage war. However, over time its effectiveness was undermined by smuggling.

Contract of Indenture was a voluntary agreement requiring a person to work for another person for a specific number of years in return for free passage to an overseas destination. Before 1800, most indentured servants in the United States were Europeans, and after the 1800s most indentured laborers were Asians.

Contra(s) is the name given to the U.S.-backed counterrevolutionary force formed to oppose the leftist government that came to power in Nicaragua in 1979.

Conventional Forces in Europe Treaty (1990) is a U.S.–Soviet agreement that provided for reductions in troop levels and the number of nuclear weapons in Europe.

Converso is the Spanish word used for Jews in Spain and Portugal in the 1300s and 1400s, who out of fear of death, persecution, expulsion or the Inquisition, converted to Catholicism. Even though they converted, Jews were prohibited from holding public or ecclesiastical offices and testifying against a Spanish or Portuguese Christian in a court of law. Conversos were not given legal equality by either the Spanish or the Portuguese governments. They were regarded as a subversive force within the Catholic Church by many church officials and were subject to discriminatory laws and persecution by the Spanish and Portuguese Inquisitions. Legalized prejudice against anyone of Jewish ancestry, even those who had converted to Catholicism centuries earlier, would continue in Spain and Portugal until the late 1800s and early 1900s.

Convertibility of Currency is the process by which one unit of a nation's currency is changed into the unit of currency of another nation without any restrictions being imposed by either nation. The system of fixed exchange rates established at Bretton Woods in 1944 was replaced by 1973 with an international financial regime based on freely floating national currencies. Under this new financial system the exchange rate of a nation's currency would rise or fall as a function of market demand.

Cook, James (1728–1779) was a British explorer, navigator and naval captain whose explorations in the Pacific Ocean, the last maritime frontier in the world for Europeans, would change the world maps used by European and Americans in the late 1700s and 1800s. Alongside Magellan, he is the most important explorer of the Pacific Ocean, which is so vast that it would take European explorers hundreds of years to chart it. During the Seven Years' War (1756–1763), when the British and French were fighting for control of Canada, he surveyed and mapped the entrance to the St. Lawrence River. He participated in the British assault of the French fortress at Louisbourg in Nova Scotia and the siege of Quebec City. After the end of the Seven Years' War, he spent the next four years surveying and mapping the coastline of Newfoundland. From 1768–71, 1772–75, and 1776–79, he made three expeditions to the Pacific Ocean, one of the largest expanses of water in the world. As a result of those three expeditions, he surveyed and mapped much of the Pacific Ocean for the first time. At the request of the British government and the Royal Society, which promoted scientific research, he initially sailed to Tahiti in 1768 to make astronomical observations as part of the British effort to fine a means for determining longitude. After finishing his work in Tahiti, he then attempted to locate the mythical landmass of *Terra Australis*. The idea of the existence of *Terra Australis* originated with Aristotle who believed that such a landmass had to exist to balance the landmasses of the Northern Hemisphere. During the next stage of his first expedition, he surveyed and mapped the entire coastline of New Zealand and the eastern coastline of Australia, which he claimed for Britain. Finding no trace of *Terra Australis*, he then sailed southward and became the first person to reach the rim of the Antarctic, but he was unable to explore the Antarctic because of its ice fields. During his third expedition, he tried to find the entrance to the long sought after Northwest Passage from the Pacific Ocean. He explored and mapped for the first time the northwestern coastline of North America as far as the Bering Sea, the northern limit of the Pacific Ocean. Unable to proceed any further because of the ice fields of the Bering Sea, he sailed southward into the Pacific where he discovered the Hawaiian Islands. After landing on the largest of the Hawaiian Island, he was killed, along with some of his crew, by the Hawaiians after a dispute arose between the Europeans and Hawaiians. On Cook's voyages to the Pacific, he took along a team of artists and botanists, who supplied Europeans with new information about the plants, birds, landscapes, and people of the unexplored and unknown areas of the Pacific Ocean.

Copernicus, Nicolaus (1473–1543) was the Polish monk and astronomer who advanced the idea that the earth revolved around the sun. This theory came to be known as the heliocentric theory. His theory challenged the geocentric theory of Ptolemy, who argued that the sun revolved around the earth. While he was not aware of it, his ideas contributed to the transformation of the scientific thinking in Europe.

Copper Age or Chalcolithic Period (5000–3500 BCE) is the name given by archaeologists to a transitional stage in the development of human culture after the Neolithic and before the Bronze Age in which metal tools appeared alongside stone tools. During this period, the earliest evidence of complex societies emerged such as: the location of cemeteries outside of settlements, the smelting of copper and the use of copper in tool production. The emergence of copper metallurgy appeared first in the ancient Middle East and the Caucasus and lasted for a thousand years. The Chalcolithic period in the Balkans, Eastern and Central Europe, which lasted from about 3500 to 1700 BCE, is the period of megalithic culture, the appearance of economic stratification, the presence of Indo-European speakers and the distribution of copper tools.

Coptic Orthodox Church is the Christian Church in Muslim Egypt. After the Arab conquest of Egypt in the 600s, the followers of this Greek-speaking Christian sect identified them themselves as Copts. In the 300s and 400s a theological conflict arose between the Copts and the Greek-speaking Romans in Egypt. The Council of Chalcedon of 451 rejected Monophysite doctrine—the belief that Jesus Christ had only a divine, not a human, nature—and affirmed both his divinity and his humanity. The Greek-speaking Romans in Egypt recognized the decisions of Chalcedon. The Copts however, rejected the idea about the two natures of Christ agreed upon at Chalcedon. Subsequently, the Roman Catholic and Eastern Orthodox churches denounced the Copts as heretics. In response to such a charge, the Coptic Church adopted a theological position called miaphysitism, which declared that both Christ's humanity and divinity were equally present. Although the Arab caliphs favored those who adopted Islam, they did not interfere with the religious practices of the Copts, though they did impose a tax on those non-Muslims living in an Islamic state. That tax would not be abolished until the 1700s.

Corn Laws were a series of trade laws enacted in Britain in the early 1800s to protect the domestic grain industry by imposing import tariffs on imported grain in order to keep domestic grain prices high. These laws favored the rural farmers at the expense of the urban consumers, who experienced higher prices for food. The Corn Laws were abolished in 1846 in response to a growing political movement in Britain supporting free trade.

Corporation is a form of business organization that developed in Britain in the 1800s that allowed private businesses to be owned by hundreds and even thousands of individual and institutional investors who financed the business through the purchase of stock.

Corporatism was the name for the planned economy established by Mussolini in fascist Italy beginning in 1926. He argued that the Italian people should be involved in public life not as citizens, but though their occupational roles in the economy. Mussolini sought to create a society built on grouping workers, administrators, and owners of a given enterprise into a single organization. He intended that such occupational groupings would be the basis for political representation eventually replacing the Italian parliament. He advocated the primacy of the "national community" and rejected

class-based organizations. Under this economic system, Mussolini combined private ownership of capital with government direction of Italy's economy. The state, not consumers and owners, determined what the economy would produce. All major areas of production were organized into state-controlled bodies called corporations, which were represented in a legislative body called the Chamber of Corporations that replaced the Chamber of Deputies, the traditional legislative body in Italy.

Corpus Juris Civilis (Body of Civil Law), also known as the Code of Justinian or Justinian's Code, was the massive codification of Roman law carried out by Byzantine Emperor Justinian between 529 and 532 CE in Constantinople. Tribonian headed the commission that carried out the work. The Corpus became the foundation of the legal systems among the Latin-speaking nations of Europe for the next 1000 years.

Cortés, Hernán (1485–1547) was the Spanish conquistador who conquered the Aztec Empire and its capital of Tenochtitlan (present-day Mexico City) between 1519 and 1521 on behalf of the Spanish government. While he had only 500 men, an outbreak of smallpox, the use of guns, and the support of indigenous peoples who were eager to end Aztec control of their lives aided him in his conquest.

Corvée Labor was unpaid labor service required of the peasants by nobles in France to build and maintain roads, bridges and canals. This obligation was abolished during the French Revolution in 1789.

Cosmology, which is the Greek world for "world," is a theory concerning the structure and nature of the universe, such as that proposed by Aristotle in the 4th century BCE.

Cosmopolis is a large, well-known urban center that has a culturally diverse population where a wide range of social, cultural, and political practices, traditions, and beliefs can be found.

Cosmopolitanism is a political and social theory that advocates a sophisticated, worldly international community rather than a national community.

Cossacks which is a Russian word for "freeman" or "adventurer", was the name of community of Tartar people living in the region of the Black and Caspian Seas who were famous for their self-reliance and military skills, particularly horsemanship. They were recruited by Tsar Ivan II to settle conquered lands in return for their freedom. His policy played a key role in the eastward expansion of Russia when the Cossacks conquered Siberia in the 1500s and 1600s. The Cossacks provided a southern military buffer between Poland, Lithuania and Russia and the Ottoman Empire. Cossacks served in the Russian army in various wars throughout the 1770s and 1800s. The Russian tsars often used the Cossacks to enforce pogroms against the Jewish population in Russia. During the Russian Civil War (1918–1921), they fought for both the Red Army and White Army.

Cost-Benefit Analysis is a calculation of costs incurred by a possible action and the benefits that are to be achieved.

Cottage Industries is the name used by historians for small-scale manufacturing, such as weaving, sewing, and textile production that was done at home (their cottages) by women in England during the early stages of the Industrial Revolution. These women would use raw materials supplied by capitalist entrepreneurs.

Cotton is the plant that produces fibers from which cotton textiles are woven. While native to India, the production of cotton spread throughout Asia and eventually to the New World. It was the major cash export crop of the United States in the 1800s and it was grown primarily on plantations in the South using slave labor.

Cotton Gin (1793) was the machine invented by Eli Whitney to remove seeds mechanically from cotton fiber.

Council of Chalcedon (451 CE) was the fourth ecumenical council meeting of 520 bishops of the early Christian Church that was convened by the Eastern Roman Emperor Marcian at Chalcedon, which was located near Constantinople. The meeting was held in order to resolve disputes within the Christian Church as to the nature of Jesus Christ. The Council affirmed the orthodox Christian view of Christ that was announced at the Council of Nicaea of 325 and expressed in the Nicene Creed that Christ had two natures, equally divine and human. Furthermore, it rejected monophysitism which maintained that Christ had only one nature, divine.

Council of Clermont (1095 CE) was a meeting of bishops and abbots of the Catholic Church convened by Pope Urban II at which he called for the formation of the First Crusade to rescue the Holy Land from the Muslim Turks. "God wills it," a phrase from Pope Urban's speech became the battle cry of crusaders in their religious wars against the Muslims.

Council of Constance (1414–1418) was an assembly convened by the Holy Roman Emperor Sigismund to heal deep religious and civil divisions that had emerged among Catholics in Europe because of the Great Schism. The Council deposed all existing rival popes and declared a new pope, Martin V. The Council also adopted the doctrine of conciliarism, which held that supreme authority with the Catholic Church resides in a representative general council and not with the pope. Nevertheless, Pope Martin V opposed the doctrine of conciliarism and refused to be adhere to it.

Council of the Indies (1524–1834) was the government institution created by the king of Spain that was responsible for supervising all of the legal, administrative, and commercial activities of the Spanish colonies in the Americas from 1524 to the early 1700s when it lost all of its political and economic powers while retaining only its judicial power.

Council of Ministers refers to a European Union institution in which the governmental officials of each member state meet to enact legislation and reconcile national interests.

Council for Mutual and Economic Cooperation (COMECON) (1949) was an economic community of communist states, which was formed by the

Soviet Union in 1949 as a response to the Marshall Plan. It sought coordinate economic planning and development and to increase trade between the Soviet Union and the communist states of Eastern Europe.

Council of Nicaea (325 CE) was the council of Christian bishops convened by Emperor Constantine that defined the basic doctrines of Christianity. It formulated the Nicene Creed, a statement of Christian belief that condemned Arianism in favor of the doctrine that Christ is both fully human and fully divine.

Council of Trent (1545–1563) was a series of meetings of Catholic Church officials held over eighteen years in order to respond to the challenges posed by the Protestant Reformation. These meetings were part of the Church's Counter-Reformation efforts that sought to reaffirm Catholic theological doctrine, which had been severely criticized by religious reformers such as Martin Luther, Ulrich Zwingli, and John Calvin. While it rejected many of the Protestant positions, the Council did reform the Catholic Church partly in response to the Protestant criticisms. Its decrees defined the basic tenets of Catholicism for the next 400 years.

Counterforce Targeting is the nuclear strategy developed by Secretary of Defense McNamara during the Kennedy administration by which the U.S. planned to use nuclear weapons only against Soviet conventional and nuclear military targets, not Soviet cities or industrial centers. By contrast countervalue targeting specifically planned to use nuclear weapons against Soviet cities and industrial centers.

Counterinsurgency is the name for the various military, social and political tactics developed to defeat guerrilla armies. In addition to the use of military force to defeat the guerrillas, a government may also create social programs to "win the hearts and minds" of a rural population so that they stop aiding, sheltering or supporting the guerrillas.

Counterrevolutionary Nationalism is a form of nationalism that bases its appeal on resistance to internal political groups that seek to undermine the nation's traditional institutions. This form of nationalism attempts to label as "enemies of the state" any social class, religion, cultural group or particular political ideologies that threaten existing centers of political power.

County was a territorial division of government created by the Carolingian emperors during the 700s and 800s in order to more efficiently govern their empire. Each county was administered by a count that was given land and would be sent to areas of the empire where he had no familial relationships. He would serve as a governor, judge, military commander, and representative of the emperor.

Coup d'état, which is a French phrase meaning "blow against the states," is the sudden and violent overthrow of an established state or government by a group of conspirators, usually led by military officers.

Coup of 18–19 Brumaire (1799), which is also know as the Eighteenth Brumaire, was the coup d'état in France on November 9–10, 1799 that overthrew the government of the Directory and replaced it with the Consulate. This event is considered by many historians to be the end of the French Revolution. The coup was planned by Abbé Sieyès and Talleyrand.

Courers des bois, which is a French word meaning "runners of the woods," refers to the French fur traders who lived among and often married the Native Indian populations in North America.

Courtesan was a woman who was a mistress to a wealthy and powerful man who provided luxuries and status in exchange for her companionship. During the Renaissance, courtesans played an important role in upper-class society, sometimes taking the place of wives at social functions. Typically, royal couples led separate lives, marrying simply to preserve bloodlines and to secure political alliances. In these circumstances, upper-class men would often seek sexual gratification and companionship from a courtesan. Courtesans were usually well-educated and worldly, and often held simultaneous careers as performers or artists. They were typically chosen because of their social and conversational skills, intelligence, common sense, and companionship as well as their beauty. Courtesan relationships were common in wealthy circles in Europe between the 1500s and the early 1900s.

Courtier was a person who served as an official in a royal court.

Courtly Love was a term used by historians to describe a code of romantic behavior for aristocratic men and women during the Middle Ages that portrayed the ennobling nature of love between a man and a woman. Under this code, a man viewed a woman as the paragon of beauty and virtue. In exchange for a sign of her love, a man was required to endure any hardship. Such codes were first expressed in the poems of troubadours in the late 1100s and 1200s in Europe. These codes would subsequently evolve into our present-day conception of romantic love.

Covenant is a religious agreement whereby one person or group of people promises to do some specific act or refrain from doing some specific act. Historically, the idea of a biblical covenant has played a central role in both Judaism and Christianity. In Judaism, a covenant was an agreement by Yahweh and the Hebrew people in which the Hebrew people would worship Yahweh as their only god and in turn Yahweh would consider the Hebrew people his chosen people and protect them from their enemies. The covenant is symbolized by Moses leading the Hebrews out of bondage in Egypt and receiving the Ten Commandments

Creed is a brief statement of faith that Christians are to follow devoutly.

Creole was a term used to refer to a person in a European colony in the New World who was of European and African parentage. The term was typically used to distinguish those who were born in the colonies from the indigenous population and those who came to the colonies directly from Europe or Africa. It could also refer to languages that developed in the New World out of a mixture of European and African roots.

Crimean War (1853–1856) was the conflict between the Russian and Ottoman Empires that was fought primarily in the Crimean Peninsula on the Black Sea to prevent Russian expansion into the Dardanelles. The war began as a result of Russian encroachment on Ottoman territories and the Ottoman troops were supported and aided by Britain and France. The Russians were defeated because Britain and France used advanced military technology. In response to the Russia's defeat because of its military weaknesses, Tsar Alexander initiated a number of reforms. The Crimean War was the first war covered by journalists and photographers.

Crimes Against Humanity is a category of international legal offenses created at the Nuremberg trials (1945–46) after World War II to encompass the widespread and systematic attack against the European civilian population committed by the political and military leaders of the Third Reich (Nazi Germany). The crimes included enslavement, deportation, torture, imprisonment, murder, rape, extermination and genocide.

Critical thinking is an intellectual methodology used to examine, evaluate and understand a social, political, economic, technological, scientific and cultural phenomenon by the use of reasoning and valid evidence to draw a conclusion.

Croesus, King was the last king of Lydia who reigned from 560 to 546 BCE. He was renowned for his enormous wealth and his gifts to the oracle at Delphi. He defeated the Greeks in Ionia in western Anatolia only to be defeated by the Persians in 546 under the Cyrus II the Great.

Croix de Feu (1927–1936) was a right-wing veteran's organization created in France in 1929 that denounced the "decadence" of the Third Republic. It opposed parliamentary democracy and the influence of the socialists in France.

Cro-Magnon is the name for early *Homo sapiens* who appeared about 40,000 years ago during the Late Paleolithic Age.

Cromwell, Oliver (1599–1658) was the Puritan leader of the Parliamentary Army that defeated the royalist forces during the English Civil War. After the execution of Charles I, he dissolved the Parliament and ruled as the "Lord Protector" during the Interregnum that lasted from 1653 until his death in 1658.

Crossbow was a medieval hand-held weapon that launched an arrow-like projectile, called a bolt, which could pierce the armor of knights. It consisted of a bow mounted across a wooden stock and mechanism to hold the bow in a cocked position until released by a trigger. The bolt would sit in a groove carved in the wooden stock. The military significance of this weapon was that it did not require significant strength to use it, as was the case with the long bow, and it could be fired from any position. It appears that the first recorded use of a crossbow is found in Chinese documents from the mid-4th century BCE. The second Lateran Council of 1139 outlawed use of the crossbow against Christians because its use was considered to be "odious to God."

Crucifixion was an agonizing form of executing criminals that was used by the Seleucids, Carthaginians and Romans from about the 6th century BCE until the 300s CE. This method of execution involved tying or nailing a person to a large wooden cross. As a form of punishment, crucifixion was intended to be a prolonged, painful and humiliating form of death. The length of time required for a victim to die would range from hours to days with death resulting from any combination of causes. The victim, who was nude, was crucified in public and left on display after their death as a graphic reminder to the public of what might happen if they were to commit a heinous crime. Rome had a very specific area of the city reserved for crucifixion of slaves with permanent wooden crosses. After the slave rebellion led by Spartacus was crushed in 71 BCE, the Romans crucified 6,000 of Spartacus' followers along the Appian War from Capua to Rome, a distance of about 132 miles. In 337 Emperor Constantine I abolished crucifixion in the Roman Empire.

Cruise Missile is a small winged missile that can carry either a nuclear or a conventional warhead. It can fly across thousands of miles of terrain at altitudes as low as 50 feet in order to reach a particular target.

Crusades (1096–1291 CE) were a series of eight armed expeditions ('holy wars") and pilgrimages that were initiated by the papacy between 1095 and 1291. Participants in these "holy wars" viewed a crusade as an act of Christian love and piety that compensated for and paid the penalties earned by sin. As an inducement to join a crusade, the papacy granted indulgences, which were remissions of penance and/or sin. The Crusades were designed to recover Christian property, defend the Catholic Church and Christians and to free Jerusalem and the Holy Land from the "infidels", the Muslims. However, the Crusades were also fought against Muslims in Spain, pagan Slaves in Latvia and Prussia, and heretics in southern France all of whom were viewed by the papacy as emeries or rebels against God. The First Crusade was launched by Pope Urban II at the Council of Clermont in 1095, after receiving a request from the Byzantine Emperor Alexius Comnenus for help in reconquering lost territory in Asia Minor to the Seljuk Turks. Heeding the call of Pope Urban II, French and German knights were the most prominent participants in the First Crusade. The crusaders (about 20,000 knights) of the First Crusade captured Jerusalem massacring its Muslim , Jewish and Christian inhabitants alike. During the First Crusade, the Crusaders established four feudal kingdoms in the Middle East, which were more commonly known as "crusader states". Those kingdoms were the Kingdom of Jerusalem, the County of Tripoli, the Principality of Antioch and the County of Edessa. The crusades also led to the creation of three military orders of knights, the Knights Hospitaller, the Knights Templar and Order of the Teutonic Knights, all of which combined knighthood with monasticism. The crusades ended in 1291 with the fall of the last crusade castle in the city of Acre(on the northern coast of present-day Israel.

Crystal Palace (1851) was a specially constructed exhibition hall in London that featured the greatest technological advances of the day. Made of iron and glass, similar to a gigantic greenhouse, it became well recognized as a symbol of the Industrial Age.

Cuban Missile Crisis (1962) was a crisis that occurred in October 1962 between the United States and the Soviet Union that arose when the United States discovered that the Soviet Union had installed medium-range nuclear missiles in Cuba. The United States responded with a naval blockade of Cuba. While the Soviets eventually withdrew their nuclear weapons from Cuba, the U.S. secretly promised not to invade Cuba and to withdraw its missiles stationed in Turkey. The Cuban Missile Crisis marks the moment during the Cold War when the United States and the Soviet Union came closest to nuclear war.

Cubism is a modern artistic movement that began after World War I. It was pioneered by Georges Braque and Pablo Picasso, who emphasized the fragmentation of human perception through visual experiments with geometric forms. Cubists typically used fragmented images to show several sides of an object at the same time. They rejected the existing artistic convention of three-dimensional perspective and naturalistic representation for a flat, two-dimensional perspective and abstract style.

Cuius regio, eius religio, which is a Latin phrase meaning "as the ruler, so the religion", was the principle adopted as part of the settlement of the Peace of Augsburg in 1555. Under this principle, those principalities ruled by Lutheran monarchs would have Lutheranism as their official religion and for those principalities ruled by a Catholic monarch would have Catholicism as their official religion.

Cult of Domesticity refers to a set of beliefs prevailing among many men and women in the middle class of the industrialized nations of the world beginning at the end of the 1800s and continuing throughout the 1900s. This outlook contended that women should live their lives primarily within the domestic sphere—that is, devote themselves solely to the raising of children and taking care of their home and family. It also refers to the belief that emerged during the Victorian Era in England that idealized women as nurturing wives and mothers whose primary social responsibility was taking care of the home and child rearing.

Cult of the Offensive was the strategic military doctrine that emphasized launching a rapid mobile first-strike attack against enemy forces. Advocates for this strategic doctrine, which was developed in the early 1900s, believed that launching such a constant, offensive attack would cause high enemy casualties, demoralize the enemy and prevent

any defending military force from repelling such an attack. This approach to waging a war was the prevailing military strategy among many military and political leaders in Europe before World War I. These leaders further believed that by declaring war, announcing a general mobilization of their troops and immediately launching an offensive attack on enemy would give them an overwhelming military advantage and cripple any enemies' ability to mount an effective defense. During World War I, military leaders on both sides believed that this strategic approach was the key to winning the war. Germany's Schlieffen Plan, which was implemented in World War I, is an example of the influence of the belief in the cult of the offensive. While this strategy failed to achieve a decisive victory for either side during World War I, it did cause an enormous loss of life. World War I produced approximately 38 million military and civilian casualties of which a total of 11 million soldiers were killed, about 7 million civilian were killed and 20 million civilians and soldiers were wounded. World War I is considered to be one of the deadliest wars in human history.

Cult of the Virgin Mary was a popular movement that venerated the mother of Jesus that began in the 1100s during the Middle Ages.

Cultivation refers to the preparation, use, and maintenance of soil for growing crops as well as to the growing of crops from seeds or bulbs. Cultivation can also refer to the improvement of a plant species using horticultural techniques.

Cultural Anthropology is the scientific study of the development of human cultures and alternative ways of living based on archaeological, ethnographic, linguistic, and sociological methods of analysis.

Cultural Imperialism is a term used by historians, anthropologists, sociologists and political scientists, journalists and commentators to describe the process by which the superiority of one culture is actively promoted over another culture. It involves the attempt by one society to impose forcibly its own value system and norms on another society. This process can entail the development of new political institutions, the formation of a new system of education and the required adoption of a new language. Historically, cultural imperialism has been associated primarily with the emergence of European imperialism and colonialism.

Cultural Materialism is an anthropological theory that social institutions and cultures do not emerge at random, but rather develop or evolve as a result of pressures surrounding the interaction between a population and its physical environment in order to meet their basic needs.

Cultural Nationalism is the term used by anthropologists and historians to describe the process by which a society adopts social values, customs, traditions and laws to protect that society from outside cultural influences, which are considered to be a threat the primacy of the culture of that society.

Cultural Relativism is a way of thinking that first developed in the 1500s in Europe to explain why the indigenous populations of the Americas did not appear in the Bible. It emphasized that many, but not necessarily all, standards of moral judgment are specific to particular cultures rather than the fixed truths established by natural or divine law.

Cultural Revolution (Great Proletarian Cultural Revolution) (1966–1976) was the convulsive mass political campaign ordered by Mao Zedong in China that sought to renew popular support for revolutionary communism in the younger generation and purge the Communist Party of Mao's opponents. Mao believed that the freedom of thought associated with the intellectual and cultural life of the cities threatened the communist ideology. As a result, cities and regions throughout China became battlegrounds between rival armed Red Guard factions, which were military student groups that attacked intellectuals, government and Communist Party officials, factory workers, peasants and other individuals. It is estimated that approximately 1.5 million people died during the Cultural Revolution.

Culture is the shared learned behavior, beliefs, values, customs, traditions, ideas and practices and way of life that a group of humans transmit from generation to generation through the process of socialization. Culture reflects the knowledge and adaptive behavior that communities of humans develop in response to the environment in which they live. Culture includes, for example, food preparation, politics, sculpture, architecture, painting, language, literature, philosophy, religion, drama, tools and technology.

Cuneiform was one of the earliest writing systems that developed beginning around 3500 BCE. It was a system of writing in which wedge-shaped symbols that represented words or syllables were written on clay tablets using a stylus. It originated in Mesopotamia and was used initially by the Sumerians and Akkadians, but was later adapted to represent other languages used in Mesopotamia. Because so many symbols had to be learned, literacy was confined to a relatively small group of administrators and scribes.

Curia was a town council in the Roman Empire. It would later mean the royal court of a king and then the central supervisory and administrative body of the Catholic Church.

Customs Union is a common external tariff adopted by members of a free-trade area under which participating states adopt a unified set of tariffs with regard to goods coming in from outside their borders.

Cycladic Civilization was an artistically and economically sophisticated culture which flourished on the islands of the western Aegean Sea between Greece and Anatolia during the early part of the Bronze Age between 3000 and 2000 BCE. It appears that Cycladic culture developed at the same time as the Minoan civilization on Crete. Excavations on the islands have discovered decorated pottery, marble carvings, the use of copper, agricultural production, the raising of sheep, goats and pigs, and ship building. Overtime, the Cycladic culture was absorbed by the Minoan culture.

Cynicism (Greece) was the philosophy of a group of ancient Greeks in the 4th century BCE called Cynics. The first Greek philosopher to express the ideas of cynicism was Antisthenes, a student of Socrates. Cynics ridiculed all religious observances and rejected involvement in the polis. They viewed the world as a source of evil and unhappiness and rejected all pleasures, possessions and social conventions. Cynics advocated the pursuit of virtue in a simple and non-materialistic lifestyle in order to find freedom and peace of mind. They believed virtue was the only necessity for happiness and that it was entirely sufficient for attaining happiness. The Cynics followed this philosophy to the extent of neglecting everything that did not achieve the perfection of virtue and the attainment of happiness. They neglected society, personal hygiene, family obligations, manners, dress and the pursuit money to lead an entirely virtuous and happy life. The most famous advocate of cynicism was Diogenes, who travelled throughout Greece, almost naked and without provisions, enjoying the sun, the warm weather, and the beaches while thousands of pilgrims listened to his talks. Even Alexander the Great, while en route to fight his Persian military campaigns, once went to Diogenes who advised Alexander to renounce his conquest. Alexander declined believing that his destiny had already been written.

Cynicism (modern) was a philosophy and a world view adopted by writers such as Shakespeare, Swift, and Voltaire in which they used irony, sarcasm, and satire to ridicule human conduct. In the 1900s literary and cinema figures such as Mark Twain, Dorothy Parker, H.L. Mencken, and W.C. Fields used both of these modes of perception and other, new ones in communicating their low opinions of human nature. By 1930, Bertrand Russell, in his essay *On Youthful Cynicism,* described the extent to which cynicism had penetrated Western mass consciousness, particular areas where there was much about which to be cynical: religion, country (patriotism), progress, beauty, truth. Certainly, the first half of the 1900s, with its two world wars, offered little hope to people wishing to embrace an idealism that people can be trusted, have good intentions, are caring, decent, and honorable, a view diametrically opposite from cynicism. Many social commentators argued that the second half of the 1900s was characterized by a general rejection of virtue and self-restraint and reflected a movement toward materialism. Ironically, the same communications media whose advertising bolstered consumerism and materialism also occasionally promoted entertaining conspiracy theories, thus adding a new dimension to the cynicism of some critics of contemporary society. In recent decades,

the scientific study of human nature has focused new attention on cynicism. In attempting to counter the widespread belief that competition, self-interest, and survival of the fittest are innate to the human animal, researchers have looked for a genetic basis for co-operation and altruistic behavior, and signs that human societal participation ultimately was built upon them. Today, cynicism is often used to describe a person's pessimism about the intentions of another individual.

Cyril, Saint (827–869 CE) was a Byzantine Christian monk, theologian and diplomat. He and his brother Saint Methodius were sent as missionaries by the Byzantine emperor and the Patriarch of Constantinople to convert the Slavic peoples of the Balkans and Russia to Orthodox Christianity. As a result of their missionary work they received the title "Apostles to the Slavs" by the Eastern Orthodox Church. Saint Cyril developed a Slavic form of writing known as the Cyrillic alphabet, which he used to translate the Bible into Slavic languages such as Russian.

Cyrus II (Cyrus the Great) (590/550–529 BCE) was the founder of the Achaemenid Persian Empire who reigned from 550 to 529 BCE. During his reign, he conquered Media, Lydia, Babylon, Mesopotamia and the Ionian Empire. He ruled an empire that stretched from Afghanistan in the east to the western coast of present-day Turkey. Revered by his subject peoples, he employed Persians and Medes in his administration and respected the institutions and beliefs of his subject peoples. He freed the Jews in the Persian Empire, let them return to Jerusalem and allowed them to rebuild their temple. His successors, who ruled the Persian Empire, were called "Great Kings".

Da Gama, Vasco (1460–1524) was a Portuguese explorer and navigator who was the first European to reach India by sailing around the Cape of Good Hope. Building on Bartolomeu Dias' discovery of the Cape of Good Hope in 1488, he commanded a fleet of four ships on a voyage between 1497 and 1499 that established the first sea route linking

Europe and Asia. The distance of Da Gama's round trip voyage to India exceeded the distance of a voyage around the world by the way of the Equator. Da Gama's voyage not only circumvented the monopoly of maritime trade by Venice in the Mediterranean and the Muslims along the Red Sea, but also provided the Portuguese direct access to the highly profitable spice trade in the Indian Ocean and Southeastern Asia, which the Portuguese monopolized for much of the 1500s. By the 1600s, the Netherlands, England and France began to challenge the Portuguese monopoly of maritime trade in Asia. Da Gama's discovery also facilitated the establishment of strategically located Portuguese trading posts, also known as factories, along the coastlines of countries in Africa and Asia, which formed the basis of the Portuguese Empire, the first global empire in world history. His voyage to India is widely regarded by historians as the beginning of the age of European global imperialism and colonialism.

Da Vinci, Leonardo (1452–1519) was a Florentine painter, architect, musician, sculptor, and inventor whose breadth of interest typified the ideals of the "Renaissance Man." He advocated careful study of the natural world. He is most famous for his painting *Mona Lisa.*

Dachau was the first concentration camp in Nazi Germany. It was established near Munich in 1933 after Hitler assumed power.

Dadaism was an international cultural and artistic movement, primarily in Europe and North America, which flourished in the 1920s and 1930s. This movement primarily involved the visual arts, literature, poetry, theatre and graphic design. It was comprised of artists who were revolted by the carnage, horror and senseless slaughter of World War I. The movement represented, in part, a protest against influence of nationalism, capitalism and colonialism, which many believed were the primary causes for World War I. Advocates for Dadaism were also against what they considered to be the cultural and intellectual conformity that arose because of the war. Dadaists ridiculed the meaninglessness of the modern world. They were preoccupied with the bizarre, the irrational and the chaotic. They attacked all accepted standards of art and behavior and enjoyed engaging

in outrageous conduct. This movement laid the groundwork for the emergence of surrealism and abstract expressionism.

Daimyo, which is a Japanese word that means "great names," refers to Japanese warlords and great landowners who used armed samurai to gain control of Japan between the 700s and late 1800s.

D'Alembert, Jean-Batiste le Rond (1717–1783) was a French mathematician, scientist and Enlightenment thinker who was engaged by Denis Diderot to co-edit the *Encyclopedie*. He edited the mathematics and science portion of the *Encyclopedie*, wrote numerous articles on mathematics and science for the book and wrote the introduction to the first volume of the *Encyclopedie*, which was published in 1751. As an Enlightenment thinker he believed that reason and scientific thinking were the source of true knowledge. D'Alembert argued that humans had the power to improve society if they relied upon such knowledge. He opposed religion and supported tolerance and free speech. D'Alembert claimed that the old French aristocracy should be replaced with a new enlightened intellectual aristocracy. Even though he rebelled against the old social and political order dominated by the aristocracy and the Church, he advocated a monarchical form of government for France, which would be headed by an "enlightened king".

Dance of Death was a popular belief that emerged during the 1300s and 1400s in Europe that the skeletons of the dead arose from the grave to tempt the living into dancing with them so that they both might finally meet in death. The theme of the Dance of Death appears on murals in many churches in Europe as well as in music and literature.

Danegeld refers to money paid by the Carolingian rulers to Viking raiders between 845 and 926 CE in order to maintain the peace. The payment of such money placed an enormous strain on the silver resources of the Carolingian Empire as well as undercutting the legitimacy of the Empire that based its rule on its military prowess.

Dao (Tao) means path or road, "the way of nature" or "the way of the cosmos" in Chinese culture and history. It specifically refers to the ideal of a well-ordered society, whether by human design or by natural pattern.

Daoism (Taoism) is the ancient Chinese philosophy based on the teachings of Laozi and Zhuangzi, which emphasized skeptical views about knowledge and action and promoted harmony with the natural order. It also evolved into a religious movement with a strong mystical component that focused on the quest for immortality. It originated during the Warring States Period and gained great appeal because it offered an alternative to Confucianism that emphasized hierarchy and duty. Followers of Daoism believed that the world is always changing and that there is no absolute morality or meaning in life. Daoists accepted the world as it was and believed that it was futile to try to change the world. Thus, it called for adopting a policy of inaction to deal with the complexity of the world. The *Daodejing* is the basic text of Daoism.

Daoxue, which means "Learning the Way" in Chinese, was the mystical interpretation of Confucianism that was developed during the Song Dynasty by Zhu Xi. Known as Neo-Confucianism, this outlook was more retrospective, emphasizing traditional Confucian concepts of reverence for the past.

Dardanelles, which was called the Hellespont by the ancient Greeks, is the present-day name for the narrow international waterway or strait in northwestern Turkey that connects maritime and naval shipping in the Aegean and Mediterranean Seas with the Sea of Marmara and the Black Sea via the Bosphorus. This crucial international waterway also forms the continental boundary between Europe and Asia. For nations such as Russia and the Ukraine, the Dardanelles are of strategic importance because it is the only sea access of those two countries via the Black Sea to the Aegean and Mediterranean Seas. Historically, this strait has always been considered of great economic and military importance as it is the gateway to the Black Sea from the Mediterranean. The ancient city of Troy, which was located in northwestern Anatolia near the entrance to the strait, controlled this vital sea route. During the second Persian war with ancient Greece from 480–479 BCE, King Xerxes I of Persia built a bridge across the Hellespont so that his army could invade Greece. Alexander the Great also

crossed the Hellespont (334 BCE) in order to invade and conquer the Persian Empire. Subsequently, the Dardanelles was controlled by the Ottoman Empire from the 1300s to the early 1900s. During the Crimean War (1853–1856), the Ottoman Empire, which was an ally of Britain and France, allowed their respective fleets to sail through the Dardanelles in order to attack the Russian-controlled Crimean Peninsula. In 1915, a British led invasion force attempted during World War I to capture the Gallipoli peninsula, which forms the northern side of the Ottoman-controlled Dardanelles so that Britain's ally Russia could have a sea route by which to attack the Ottoman Empire, an ally of Germany. The British force was unsuccessful in its attempt to capture the Gallipoli peninsula and was forced to withdraw its forces after suffering heavy causalities. During World War II, Turkey, which then controlled the Dardanelles, was neutral and the Dardanelles were closed to the ships of the belligerent nations involved in the war. In recent years, Turkey, which still controls this commercially important waterway, has permitted Russian oil tankers to use the Dardanelles to export oil to Europe and the U.S.

Darius I (Darius the Great) (550–446 BCE) was the third ruler of the Persian Empire and he reigned from 522 to 486 BCE. His conflict with Aristagoras, the Greek ruler of Miletus, ignited the Persian War. Darius crushed the widespread initial resistance to his rule and gave all major government posts to Persians rather than to Medes. He established a system of provinces and tribute, began construction of Persepolis, and expanded Persian control in the east (Pakistan) and west (northern Greece). Darius sent a large invasion force to Greece in 490 BCE to punish the Greeks for their intervention in the internal affairs of the Persian Empire. His numerically superior invasion force was defeated at Marathon by Athenian hoplites.

Dark Ages (Europe) (400s–700s CE) is a term that historians created to describe the period in western European history from the end of the Roman Empire to the beginning of the Renaissance, otherwise known as the Middle Ages. Traditionally, historians characterized Western Europe during this period as a place of urban decline, constant warfare, barbarity, economic deterioration, a scarcity of historical or other written records, demographic decline, limited building activity and a lack of any significant material, cultural or intellectual achievements. The idea of a "dark age" in Europe originated in Italy with Petrarch in the 1330s. Furthermore, during the Protestant Reformation of the 1500s and 1600s, Protestants characterized this era as one of Catholic dominance and corruption. Later historians generally did not question these perspectives and continued to refer to the period as the "Dark Ages." At the same time, popular culture typically portrayed the period as backward and barbaric. By the 1800s, the term "Dark Ages" was widely used by historians. It is only in the early 1900s with the emergence of modern scholarly study of the Middle Ages that historians began to challenge the pejorative image of this period as one of darkness, stagnation and decay. Instead, as a result of new knowledge and insight, historians began to recognize the significant accomplishments made during this period of almost 800 years. Today, modern historians reject the continued use of the term "Dark Ages" because it is misleading and inaccurate.

Dark Ages (Greece) (1100–800 BCE) is a term used by historians to describe a period in ancient Greek history when Greek culture declined, maritime trade stopped, food production declined, construction of large structures and public buildings declined, Linear B writing ceased, cities were depopulated and few new settlements were established. It appears that internal dissension as well as the foreign invasion by the Dorians may have contributed to these developments though the exact reasons for this catastrophic period in ancient Greek history are still uncertain.

Darwin, Charles (1809–1882) was an English naturalist who studied the plants and animals of South America and the Galapagos Islands in the Pacific Ocean. In his book *On the Origins of Species by Means of Natural Selection,* published in 1859, he enunciated his theory of natural selection to explain the evolution of plants and animals. In his *The Descent of Man,* published in 1871, he applied the concept of natural selection to the evolution of human beings.

Darwinism is the scientific theory associated with Charles Darwin that established the role of natural selection in the evolution of the human species.

In his books, *On the Origin of Species by Means of Natural Selection, or the Preservation of Favoured Races in the Struggle for Life* (1859) and *The Descent of Man, and Selection in Relation to Sex* (1871), he proposed that all forms of life develop through the process of natural selection during which those forms of life that are better adapted to their existing environment have distinct advantages and are more likely to survive and pass on their beneficial traits to their offspring.

Dauphin was the title given to the eldest son of a French king who was expected to inherit the French throne. This title was used from 1350 to 1791, when it was abolished during the French Revolution. The title was restored briefly during the reign of Charles X (1824 to 1830), but was abandoned with the end of the Bourbon dynasty in 1830.

David, King (1040–970 BCE) was king of the Hebrews who united the kingdoms of Israel and Judah and made Jerusalem his capital.

Dawes Plan (1924) was an arrangement formulated by an international committee of financial experts to facilitate Germany's ability to pay the $33 billion of reparations to France and Britain as required by the Treaty of Versailles for the damages those two nations suffered during World War I. After World War I, Germany made its first annual reparation payment in 1921, but it was unable to make any further payments because its economy was devastated by inflation and was on the verge of collapse. When Germany stopped making its reparation payments, Britain and France claimed that they could not pay their war debts to the U.S., which the U.S. was unwilling to cancel. During World War I, the U.S. had loaned England and France $10.1 billion. However, France's and Britain's ability to repay that amount was contingent upon Germany making its required annual reparation payments to France and Britain. In response to Germany's inability to make its reparation payments, France sent troops to occupy and operate the mines and factories in Germany's primary industrial center, the Ruhr region, in order to collect in-kind reparation payments. To resolve Germany's incapacity to make war reparation payments, France's occupation of the Ruhr and the unwillingness of France and Britain to pay their war debts to the U.S., the U.S. suggested the formation of an international commission of financial experts in 1924 to reevaluate the German reparation issue. This commission, headed by Charles Dawes, an American banker, produced a new and more liberal reparations plan. This plan, known as the Dawes Plan, reduced Germany's annual reparation payment to $250 million, linked the annual reparation payment to the prosperity of the German economy, rescheduled Germany's reparation payments, identified new German sources of revenue, and provided U.S. loans of $200 million to stabilize the German economy, but it did not reduce the total amount of reparations owed by Germany. Both France and Britain accepted the Dawes Plan. Germany paid approximately $1.3 billion in reparation payments under the Plan between 1924 and 1929, which, in turn, enabled France and Britain to pay their U.S. war debts. Even though the Dawes Plan contributed to stabilizing the German currency and facilitating German economic recovery, it expired in 1929 and was replaced with the Young Plan, which was formulated by Owen Young, an American businessman. The Young Plan reduced even further the amount of Germany's annual reparation payments and required Germany to make such payments until 1988. Both American and Europeans hoped that the Young Plan would provide a permanent settlement of the reparation issue. Unfortunately, when the Great Depression struck the U.S. and Europe, Germany stopped making any further reparation payments in 1933.

D-Day (June 6, 1944) was the date of the Allied amphibious landings in Normandy, France, during World War II to liberate Europe from German occupation. It marked the beginning of the second front in Europe, the first front being the Soviet effort along the eastern front in Russia and subsequently Eastern Europe. It was the largest seaborne invasion in history.

Dead Sea Scrolls are the famous ancient Jewish writing discovered in a cave above the Dead Sea that were written between 200 BCE and 100 CE. They are believed to have been produced by a group of apocalyptically oriented Essenes who lived in a monastic community from Maccabean times until the Jewish War from 66 to 70 CE.

Death Marches were the forced long-distance marches of Jewish prisoners that occurred during the last phase of World War II when the Nazis were retreating to Germany during the Soviet offensive in 1944. It is estimated that 250,000 individuals died in these death marches between the summer of 1944 and the end of the war. During these marches the Jews were starved, brutalized, and killed and the roads were littered with bodies. Very few individuals survived the Death Marches.

Debt Bondage, also known as debt peonage, was a contract in ancient Rome where a debtor pledged his person as collateral should he default on his loan. If a debtor failed to pay a debt, he became the indentured servant of the creditor. This type of contract became one of the primary political issues that would give rise to the Conflict of the Orders. It was abolished by in 326 BCE.

***Decameron, The* (1349–1353),** which was written by Giovanni Boccaccio, is a series of 100 stories told over ten days by ten travelers (three men and seven women) about the human condition. The stories are told from a comic, tragic, licentious or cynical perspective.

Decembrists (1825) were Russian army officers who had been influenced by the ideas of the Enlightenment and the French Revolution. They formed secret societies that espoused the formation of a liberal government. They attempted to take overthrow Russian government in December 1825 after the death of Tsar Alexander I and install a constitutional monarchy. Their revolt was crushed by Tsar Nicholas I and they were executed. Russian revolutionaries would later view the Decembrists as martyrs.

Decius, Gaius Messius Quintus (c. 201–251 CE), was a senator when he was appointed in 245 by Emperor Philip to command a Roman army to quell a revolt by Roman legions along the Danube who had proclaimed their leader, Pacatianus, emperor. After Decius had suppressed the rebellion in 248, his own troops declared him emperor, a title which he accepted. When he attempted to march on Rome to assume the position of emperor, he was met by an army led by Emperor Philip, who was killed in the battle. With the death of Emperor Philip, the Senate recognized Decius as emperor in 249. As emperor, Decius sought to reaffirm traditional conservative Roman religious values and practices and to suppress the growing influence of the Christian movement. In 250, Decius issued an edict that required all inhabitants of the Roman Empire (except for the Jews who were exempted) to perform a sacrifice to the ancestral Roman gods in the presence of a magistrate and to obtain a signed and witnessed certificate that they had performed such a sacrifice. Prior to Decius's reign, persecution of Christians had been sporadic and Christian communities had not been threatened with imperial persecution. Decius's edict represented the first time in the history of the Roman Empire that Christians were forced by an imperial edict to choose between their religion or death. In response to Decius's edict some Christians went into hiding, some performed the required sacrifice and obtained the necessary certificate and some refused to perform the ceremony and were executed, the exact number is unknown. While the persecutions of the Christians during the reign of Decius lasted approximately eighteen months, Decius's edict created significant long-lasting tensions within the Christian communities of the Roman Empire. Most churches considered those Christians who complied with Decius's edict as apostates, but forgave them and readmitted them back into the church. However, there were some churches who refused readmission of apostates claiming Christians should have accepted martyrdom rather than complying with Decius's edict. Approximately 50 years after "Decius's persecution" ended, a more extensive persecution of Christians in the Roman Empire was begun by Emperor Diocletian in 303.

De-Christianization was the policy adopted by the Jacobins in 1793 during the French Revolution that sought to create a more secular society by eliminating Christian practices and institutions in France. The Jacobins closed churches and eliminated religious symbols. They forced priests to give up their vocation and marry and sold buildings owned by the Catholic Church. The Jacobins established festivals of reason to compete for the allegiance of Catholic supporters.

De Gouges, Olympia (1745–1793) was a French political radical and feminist during the French Revolution who wrote the Declaration of the Rights of Women, which demanded an equal place for women in the new French Republic. Her original name was Marie Gouze.

Declaration of Independence (1776), which was drafted by Thomas Jefferson, was the list of grievances that was sent by the American colonists to George III of England in 1776 as well as a statement that the colonies would be free and independent of British rule. The principles of government expressed in this document would become some of the foundational principles of the United States, but would not be formally incorporated into the Constitution. This document, which reflected the ideas of John Locke and other Enlightenment thinkers, would influence other revolutions around the world.

Declaration of the Rights of Man and Citizen (1789), which was the preamble to the French Constitution, was the statement of fundamental political rights and liberties of French citizens that was adopted by the French National Assembly at the beginning of the French Revolution. It stated that "all men are born free and remain free and have equal rights". The Declaration also expressed such fundamental rights as freedom of speech, right to property, right to participation in governmental affairs and legal equality. The issuance of this document marked the end of absolutist aristocratic rule in France. It was influenced by the American Declaration of Independence and it in turn would influence other revolutionary movements.

Declaration of the Rights of Woman and Citizen (1891) was written during the French Revolution by Olympe de Gouges, a playwright and journalist. It challenged the dominance of male authority and demanded that French women be afforded the same rights that French men had demanded in 1789 in the Declaration of the Rights of Man and Citizen.

Declaratory Act (1766) was the legislation enacted by the British Parliament declaring that Parliament had sovereign jurisdiction over the British colonies in North America.

Decolonization was the process by which colonies in Africa and Asia gained their independence from

European colonial powers after World War II. This development was caused by rising demands for independence by colonized peoples, the declining power of European nations and the ideal of self-determination enunciated by the United States. Decolonization began with independence of Pakistan and India from Britain in 1947 and the Philippines from the United States in 1946. However, efforts to achieve independence from European colonialism began earlier in the late 1700s when American colonists revolted against British rule in the present-day United States and continued in the early 1800s when colonies of Spain and Portugal in Latin America also achieved their freedom from colonial rule.

Decurion was an official title in ancient Rome that was used in both the military and politics. In the Roman army, a decurion was a cavalry officer in the Roman army who commanded a squadron of 30 men. In order to attain such a military rank, a decurion was required to be a member of the equestrian class. In politics, a decurion was a member of a local town council, which was called a *curia*. The curia was responsible for the issuance of public contracts, the performance of religious rituals and entertainment, maintaining the water supply, feeding local troops, conducting judicial proceedings, and, most importantly, the collection of local taxes for the imperial government. In order to serve on a city council a decurion was required to be a member of the curial class, which was comprised of wealthy merchants, businessmen or landowners. As members of a wealthy and politically influential social elite, decurions often competed to display their wealth by sponsoring and even paying for the construction of public buildings such as temples, public baths, forums, triumphal arches, libraries, amphitheaters and other public activities such as festivals and games. As the primary officials who comprised the local town councils, decurions were required, most importantly, to guarantee personally the collection of taxes. If for any reason there was a deficit in the amount of taxes collected in a locality or a deficit in a town's finances, a decurion was required to make up any short fall from their own funds.

Deductive Reasoning is a method of philosophical analysis that uses general assertions of fact to explain or predict specific results. For example, "All people die. Karl Marx is a person. Karl Marx died". In short, it is a form of reasoning from the general to the particular.

DEFCON the system of categorizing defense conditions used by the U.S. military, which ranges from DEFCON 5 (the lowest state of alert) to DEFCON 1(war).

Deficit is a term used to describe the excess of government expenditures over revenues.

Deforestation is the process of rapid destruction of the world's forests. The environmental consequences of deforestation are severe. Deforestation alters the climate and destroys millions of useful plant and animal species. Because forests absorb carbon dioxide and turns it into oxygen, deforestation accelerates the greenhouse effect.

DeGaulle, Charles (1890–1970) was the youngest general in the French army at the time of the invasion of France by Nazi Germany in June 1940. After the fall of France he became the leader of the Free French forces during World War II. He sought to exercise political leadership in France after its liberation in 1944, but became disillusioned with politics. He retired in 1946, but returned to politics in 1958 when he created the Fifth Republic. He served as president of France from 1958 to 1969.

Dehumanization is the stigmatization of a people considered to be an enemy as subhuman or nonhuman. Such a stigmatization led frequently to widespread massacres or, in the worst cases, destruction of entire populations.

Deification is the process of attributing god-like qualities to human beings.

Deism was the belief influential among many writers, scientists, and politicians during the Enlightenment in Europe in the 1600s and 1700s.

Deists believed that a rational God had created the universe, but then allowed it to function without intervention according to established rational and immutable laws of nature that could be understood by human beings. However, God did not subsequently intervene in the operation of nature or human affairs. Deists, who did not belong to any particular religion, believed that freedom of religion and religious tolerance were essential to human progress.

De-Jewification was a policy established by the Nazis in Germany between 1933 and the outbreak of World War II in 1939 to force German Jews to leave Germany.

Delian League (478 BCE) was the political and military alliance of Greek city-states (poleis) originally organized in Athens by Aristides in 478 BCE to drive out the Persian invaders and to avenge the destruction caused by the Persian Wars. The Athenians gradually transformed the League into the Athenian Empire.

Demagogue is a politician who appeals to the popular fears, anxieties, prejudices, emotions of a populace in order to gain political power. A demagogue will use lies, falsehoods, distortions, myths, and half-truths, scapegoating, and emotional appeals to nationalism, xenophobia, racism, sexism and populism to manipulate a populace.

Demand is the desire of consumers to acquire goods and services and the need of producers to acquire raw materials and machinery to meet the needs of the consumers.

Demesne was the land owned by a medieval manorial lord that was under his direct control. As part of their labor services, serfs were required to work a specific number of days each week on this part of the manor.

Democracy is a form of government in which all of the citizens, however defined, have equal political and legal rights. Those citizens create their own governing structure and institutions and choose their own political leaders. In ancient Greece only a class of propertied male citizens was permitted to participate in their democratic form of governance. Women citizens without property and slaves were excluded from the political process. A democratic polis was governed by a very small percentage of the population.

Democratization is the process of adopting democratic characteristics. A country is considered to be democratized when it adopts the following features: (a) government policy is made by officials chosen through free, fair, and periodic elections in which a substantial proportion of the adult population can vote; (b) actions of officials are constrained by constitutional provisions and commitments to civil liberties; and (c) government candidates sometimes lose elections and leave office when they do; and (d) the reliance on freedom of speech and the freedom to organize to contest elections and present varied viewpoints in the media.

Democritus was a Pre-Socratic Greek philosopher of the 5th century BCE who formulated an atomic theory of the universe, which he may have derived from his teacher, Leucippus. Democritus coined the term "atom", which is the Greek word for indivisible or uncuttable. He speculated that reality consisted of these fundamental particles, which were eternal, swirled randomly in a vacuum of infinite space. With respect to the origins of religion, he argued that people who have not developed the ability or tools to understand the laws of nature create fantastical stories about gods. He sought a naturalist explanation for the origins of religion.

Demographic Transition refers to the increase in the rate of population growth that took place in Europe in the late 1800s and early 1900s, in the United States and East Asia in the mid-1900s, and most recently in Latin America and South Asia. Prior to this transition both death rates and birthrates were high, which resulted in slow population growth.

Demography is the statistical study of the size, growth, distribution, and movement of human populations. Demographers consider factors such as fertility rates, birth and death rates, population density, the impact of diseases on a population and the consequences of changes in immigration and emigration.

Demokratia was the Greek word, which means "the power of the people", that was used in Athens in the 5th century BCE to describe the city's system of direct government." Athenian society pioneered key democratic concepts such as freedom, equality, universal citizenship, and the rule of law.

Demosthenes (384–322 BCE) was an Athenian orator and statesman who warned his fellow citizens against the dangers of the Macedonians.

Denazification was an Allied policy implemented at the end of World War II to rid German and Austrian societies, culture, press, economy, judiciary, and politics of any remnants of the Nazi regime. It was carried out specifically by removing Nazi officials from positions of influence and by disbanding the organizations associated with Nazism. In practice, denazification was not limited to Germany and Austria after World War II. In every European country with a Nazi or fascist party, denazification programs were also implemented.

Deng Xiaoping (1904–1997) was the leader of the Communist Party in China who returned to political power in 1978 after the death of Mao Zedong. He initiated economic reforms in the 1980s that contributed to China's rapid economic growth. He joined the Communist Party as a student in France in the 1920s. Later, he returned to China and took part in the Long March. After rising to a leading position in the Communist Party in the 1950s, he was purged during the Cultural Revolution.

Dependency Theory offers an explanation of poverty and underdevelopment in developing countries based on their historical dependence and domination by rich countries. It argues that the lack of capital accumulation in the Third World nations is the result of the interplay between domestic class relations and the forces of foreign capital.

De Pisan, Christine (1364–1430) was a French writer who wrote about aristocratic behavior, courtly love and chivalry and the position of women in medieval society. After the death of her husband, she began to write love ballads, poems and books for wealthy French and English aristocrats in order to earn a living, which she did for 30 years. Her two most famous literary works are *The Book of the City of Ladies* and *The Treasure of the City of Ladies*, both of which she wrote in 1405. In her book *The Book of the City of Ladies*, de Pisan addressed the claim made in the 1200s by the French author Jean de Meun in his book *Romance of the Rose* that women had made the lives of men miserable. In refuting such a widely accepted world view in medieval France, she contended that such a perspective denigrated and slandered women. In *The Book of the City of Ladies*, she defended the value of women by describing the lives of a wide array of famous women throughout history and argued that women should be valued for their important contributions to the building of societies. In *The Treasure of the City of Ladies,* which was a manual for the education of women of all social classes, de Pisan emphasized the influence that a woman's language and behavior had in everyday life. As a result of such influence, she argued that women displayed a unique ability to mediate and resolve disputes among people.

Depression is a severe long-term decline in the economy of a nation. A depression is characterized by widespread unemployment, a decline in consumption, reduced industrial production, deflation of the prices of goods and services, a decline in construction, a large number of bankruptcies and bank failures, a decline in the availability of credit, volatile currency fluctuations, a reduction in international trade and defaults on sovereign debt obligations. The Great Depression that began in the United States in 1929 affected industrialized and non-industrialized economies world during the late 1920s and 1930s. In the United States, it lasted approximately 12 years. The Great Depression is considered by many economists and historians to be the most severe worldwide and long-lasting depression to occur in the 1900s. In the United States alone, approximately 25% of the population (13 million people) was unemployed. The Great Depression began with the American stock market crash on October 29, 1929 and would only end with the beginning of World War II.

Descartes, Rene (1596–1650) was a French philosopher, scientist and mathematician who is most well-known for his statement "I think, therefore I am". Descartes, who wrote and published important works in mathematics and philosophy, is considered to be the most influential philosopher in Europe in the 1600s. His system of philosophy, which became known as Cartesianism, challenged the dominant Aristotelian system of philosophical thought. In his book, the *Discourse on the Method*, he claimed that the path to knowledge could be obtained by the use of deductive reasoning. His philosophical writings influenced many prominent theologians and natural philosophers during the 1600s.

Desmoulins, Camille (1760–1794) was a French journalist who played an influential role in the storming of the Bastille on July 14, 1789. He argued that it was a crime to be a king and spoke before the French National Convention condemning King Louis XVI. He was tried and executed by the Committee of Public Safety because he was a political ally of Georges Danton.

Despotism is a form of government in which one person, a despot, rules with absolute and tyrannical power. The Pharaoh in ancient Egypt is an example of a despot since he wielded all power and authority.

De Staël, Anne Louise Germaine (1766–1817) was an influential and well-regarded Swiss writer and intellectual who lived in Paris during the French Revolution and the reign of Napoleon. Recognized for her intellectual abilities, she became one of the most well-known authors in Europe during the late 1700s and early 1800s. She was the daughter of Jacques Necker, one of the wealthiest men in Europe and the finance minister of King Louis XVI of France. She wrote plays, novels, political essays, literary criticisms, and histories. She participated in the political and intellectual debates of her times, advocated the ideas of the Enlightenment, and encouraged dissent during the reign of King Louis XVI. Throughout her life, she believed that equal rights for women in education, careers and marital relations were necessary if women were to realize their intellectual and emotional potential. While living in Paris, she organized a salon, which attracted the major European literary, political, and intellectual figures of the day. Her salon became a place where writers, artists and critics could freely express their opinions about literature and politics. She witnessed some of the important events of the French Revolution, such as the formation of a republic by the Jacobins, the violence unleashed by the "Reign of Terror", the fall of Robespierre, the emergence of the Directory and the rise to power of Napoleon. Influenced by the political views of Montesquieu, she opposed the repressive nature of absolutist monarchical rule. Rather she admired the English parliamentary model, which balanced liberty and order and prevented the outbreak of revolutionary violence. Her first publications were two plays: *Sophie*, a romantic drama (1796) and *Jeanne Grey*, a tragedy (1787). In 1788 she published *Letters on the Works and Character of J. J. Rousseau*, which made her well-known as an intellectual and a writer. During the French Revolution, she published *On the Influence of the Passions on the Happiness of Individuals and Nations* (1796). At the time of Napoleon's rise to power, she published *Literature and Its Relations with Social Institutions* (1800), in which she argued that a literary work should reflect the historical and moral circumstances of the country in which it was written. In 1802, she published one of her most influential works *Delphine*, in which she examined the social conditions of women and the limits on a women's freedom in an aristocratic society. During the reign of Napoleon, she was a persistent critic of him, who she considered to be a tyrant. In response to the controversial nature of *Delphine*, Napoleon, who was intolerant of any criticism, considered her a danger to his rule and exiled her from Paris in 1803. Napoleon said that she "teaches people to think who never thought before or who had forgotten how to think". While in exile living at her family estate, Chateau Coppet, on Lake Geneva, she organized another influential salon that became a meeting place for some of the leading European intellectuals. Ignoring Napoleon's exile, she returned to Paris in 1806, where she completed her novel *Corinne* (1807), a novel whose heroine is a brilliant women thwarted by a patriarchal system. Even though *Corinne* was widely read and extremely influential, Napoleon once again exiled her from Paris, banned *Corrine* and had all remaining copies of it destroyed. Forced to leave France, she once again returned to her family estate on Lake Geneva where she wrote one of her most important works *On Germany* (1810/1813). In *On Germany,* she introduced German history and culture to France, criticized French culture, and argued that German culture should be a model for France. When her book *On Germany* was published in France in 1810, the French police confiscated all of the already printed copies of it. After the defeat of Napoleon, she welcomed the restoration of the Bourbon monarchy and returned to France in 1814. Prior to her death she completed her last political work *Considerations on the Principle Events of the French Revolution* (1817).

De-Stalinization is the term used by historians to describe the process of social, cultural and political liberalization and reform that was launched in the Soviet Union by Nikita Khrushchev in the wake of the death of Joseph Stalin in 1953. Stalin had ruled the Soviet Union for over thirty years. In February 1956, Khrushchev delivered a four hour secret speech titled "On the Cult of Personality and Its Consequences" to a late-night closed session of the 20th Party Congress of the Communist Party of the Soviet Union in which he denounced Stalin's dictatorial rule. Khrushchev stated that Stalin's policies of mass repression, arrest and deportation, torture and execution of loyal communists without a trial all had created an atmosphere of fear and insecurity in the Soviet Union. He specifically condemned the cult of personality that had developed around Stalin, which Khrushchev stressed was inconsistent with guiding ideological principles of Marxism–Leninism. He further condemned Stalin's executions during the Great Purges of the 1930s of those loyal and dedicated members of the Communist Party who had played important historical roles in the development of communism in Russia, the Russian Revolution and the formation of the Soviet Union. Khrushchev's speech was subsequently read at Communist Party meetings throughout the Soviet Union. Khrushchev's revelations shocked those individuals involved in the communist movement throughout the world since they had been taught to admire and revere Stalin and never question

his policies. His speech facilitated the emergence of an atmosphere of intellectual openness to certain aspects of Western culture, which gave students, writers, artists and intellectuals hope for greater freedom of expression. In the years after of Khrushchev's speech, the Soviet people witnessed the adoption of new clothing trends, new musical choices such as jazz and rock and roll and the establishment of night clubs, for example. In the wake of his speech, Khrushchev attacked the icons of Stalinism. He had many cities, landmarks and other facilities that bore Stalin's name renamed. For example, Stalingrad, where the Nazis suffered their first major military defeat during World War II, was renamed Volgograd. Furthermore, Stalin's body was removed from Lenin's Mausoleum on Red Square and reburied in the Kremlin. Unfortunately, the process of liberalization and reform declined during the mid-1960s and 1970s under the rule of Leonid Brezhnev, but resurfaced in the 1980s under Mikhail Gorbachev's policies of perestroika and glasnost. Some historians today consider Khrushchev's speech to be a turning point in the history of the Soviet Union.

Détente (1969–75) was the policy to reduce tensions and improve diplomatic relations between the United States and Soviet Union that was initiated by President Nixon and Henry Kissinger between 1969 and 1975. The signing of the Strategic Arms Limitation Talks (SALT) Treaty and the Helsinki Accords highlighted this new state of affairs between the United States and the Soviet Union.

Determinism is the philosophical doctrine that argues that all actions, including human actions, are controlled by existing forces that cannot be altered by chance, fate or free will.

Deterrence is the threat to use military or economic force against another nation if that nation takes certain negative actions that threaten one's own country or one's allies. Deterrence also was the Cold War nuclear weapons policy adopted by U.S. policymakers after World War II. It relied upon the threat to use nuclear weapons in order to prevent the Soviet Union from engaging in expansionist or aggressive policies that U.S. policymakers considered contrary to the national interests of the United States.

Developing Countries is a term used in to describe those nations, typically in the Southern Hemisphere, which have the poorest economies in the world. These nations rely primarily on farming, have inadequate technology and suffer serious population and health problems. Such nations are also referred to as Third World nations, less-developed nations, and underdeveloped nations. By contrast, a developed nation, typically in the Northern Hemisphere, is a wealthy nation with well-organized industrial and agricultural institutions, advanced technologies, a sophisticated financial system and effective educational institutions.

Development is the economic process that arose in the 1800s and 1900s that led to industrialization, urbanization, the rise of a large and prosperous middle class, and substantial investment by governments in public education.

Dhow is a type of sailing vessel with lateen sails that was commonly used in the area from the Red Sea to the western coast of India.

Dialectic is a form of logical argumentation originally developed by Aristotle. In modern times, it was an idea developed by Hegel and Marx. Both Hegel and Marx were concerned with the process of historical change, which they argued resulted from the clash and reconciliation of antagonistic and conflicting ideas or forces. They claimed that history advances in stages as a result of conflict between different ideas and social groups. They also argued that this concept describes the evolution of one stage of consciousness to a superior one through a dynamic process of the fusion of the contradictions into a higher truth.

Dialectical is a term often used to describe intellectual or social processes in which opposing ideas or social forces struggle or conflict. Dialectical change in history refers to a pattern in which every concept or social force gives rise to its opposite, thereby creating conflicts that have the potential for carrying an argument, society, political structure, or culture to higher levels of development.

Dialectical Materialism is the philosophical approach to history and a method of reasoning derived from the writings of Karl Marx and Friedrich Engles claimed that political, social, and economic change occurs as the result of material forces in the world. They argued that all human knowledge is derived from the senses and is acquired by humans interacting socially in the course of their practical, day-to-day activities. Dialectical materialism is characterized by the belief that history is the product of material class struggle and obeys Hegel's philosophy of history in which the growth and development of human history (change) occurs as the result of the resolution of the tension between opposites (thesis and antithesis), which in turn produces a new stage of development (synthesis).

Dias, Bartolomeu (1450–1500) was the Portuguese sailor and explorer who led the first naval expedition in 1588 to sail around the tip of Africa from the Atlantic Ocean into the Indian Ocean.

Diaspora means the dispersal of an ethnic, religious or national group outside of their respective homeland. It is name given by historians to the period in Jewish history after the Roman destruction of the Temple in 70 CE in Jerusalem when the Jewish people were dispersed throughout the ancient world from their homeland in Israel.

Diaz, Porfirio (1830–1915) was the Mexican general who led a military coup in Mexico in 1876 that established a dictatorship that lasted until 1911. He allowed foreign business interests and investors to control much of the Mexican economy. Supported by the wealthy landowners, he did little to help the impoverished people of Mexico, who constituted the majority of the population. His dictatorial rule resulted in a period of civil war and revolution that would last until 1920.

Dickens, Charles (1812–1870) was a very popular English writer in the 1800s whose novels exposed urban crime, poverty, exploitation, and injustice in recently industrialized Britain.

Dictator was the title of an official in the Roman Republic who, during an emergency, had the authority to suspend normal government functions and was granted unlimited political power to administer the state for short period of time, typically six months. Sulla and Julius Caesar were two individuals who ignored the six month limitation.

Diderot, Denis (1713–1784), who initially went to Paris to study theology, was the leading materialistic and atheistic thinker of the 1700s. He was the guiding force behind the publication of the *Encyclopedie,* which was the first compendium of all human knowledge. Diderot believed that the *Encyclopedie* would demonstrate how reason could be applied to nearly all forms of human thought. He worked on the *Encyclopedie* from 1745 to 1772. He was also a prolific author, writing novels, art criticism, plays, and essays on natural philosophy, science and political theory. In 1773, he sold his library to Catherine the Great, Empress of Russia, who appointed him her librarian with an annual salary for life.

Diem, Ngo Dinh (1901–1963) was the president of the Republic of Vietnam from 1954 to 1963. He became president in 1954 after defeating Emperor Bao Dai in a controversial election. Staunchly anti-communist, he was financially and militarily supported by the United States in in his efforts to institute a counterinsurgency program. In 1959, he passed a series of laws that made it legal to arrest and jail any person without any form charges if they were suspected of being a communist. As his regime became known for brutality and corruption, Diem faced stiff opposition to his authoritarian rule from Buddhists, intellectuals and students. On a number of occasions those opposition forces were attacked by Diem's military and secret police. Diem claimed that such opposition forces were helping the military forces of the Democratic Republic of Vietnam (North Vietnam) occupy South Vietnam. While he promised land reform, he did not effectively institute enough social and economic reforms to win the support of the population. By 1961, the United States had increased its level of economic, technological and military assistance to Vietnam. As part of Diem's counterinsurgency effort, he launched the Strategic Hamlet Program which rounded up villagers and placed them in hamlets constructed and guarded by South Vietnamese soldiers. The villagers resented being forced off their land that had belonged to their ancestors and some even joined the National Liberation Front (NLF or Viet Cong). In 1963, because of the failure of the Strategic Hamlet Program and reports of increasing success of the NLF in the countryside, Diem's soldiers and secret police raided Buddhist pagodas throughout Vietnam claiming that they harbored Communists.

In response to such repressive actions, massive demonstrations led by Buddhists monks were held in Saigon. During the Buddhist led demonstrations, one Buddhist monk engaged in self-immolation and pictures of the monk engulfed in flames were seen in newspapers and TVs around the world. Even though President Kennedy provided 16,000 military advisers to assist Diem is his military effort against the guerrilla activities of NLF in South Vietnam, the Buddhist protests convinced Kennedy and his advisors that Diem could not maintain stability and was no longer a viable leader for South Vietnam. Subsequently, the Kennedy administration supported a coup d'état by Diem's generals in November 1963 during which Diem and his brother, the head of the secret police, were assassinated.

Dien Bien Phu, Battle of (1954) was a military confrontation during in the First Indochina War (1946–1954) in which the Viet Minh, under the leadership of General Vo Nguyen Giáp, decisively defeated the French forces. In an attempt to defeat the Viet Minh in the north of Vietnam, French military forces occupied and fortified the village of Dien Bien Phu, which was located in a valley in northwestern Vietnam near the Laotian border. From this base, the French attempted to cut the Viet Minh's supply lines into Laos and draw the Viet Minh into a major battle in which the French would defeat them with superior firepower. Contrary to the expectations of the French forces, the Viet Minh quickly cut all roads into Dien Bien Phu and surrounded the French base with forty thousand men, forcing the French to be resupplied only by air. With the Viet Minh's emplacement of heavy artillery and anti-aircraft guns in the hills surrounding Dien Bien Phu, the Viet Minh was able to continually bombard the French positions. After a two month siege and despite substantial U.S. military assistance, the French positions were overrun by the Viet Minh and the French forces surrendered. The decisive Viet Minh victory at Dien Bien Phu convinced the French that they could no longer maintain their colony in Vietnam. Within two months of the Viet Minh victory, France withdrew all of its military forces from Vietnam, effectively ending French colonial rule in Vietnam.

Diet was the name of the legislature of the Holy Roman Empire and many German states. It included representatives of German princes, independent cities and the Catholic Church.

Diet of Worms (1521) was the meeting of representatives of the Holy Roman Empire in the German city of Worms at which Martin Luther was ordered to recant the books he published that challenged 1500 years of Christian theology. After Luther refused to recant his writings, the Diet issued an edict that declared Luther to be an outlaw and ordered his books to be burned. Even though Luther was an outlaw, he was secretly hidden by Frederick the Elector of Saxony for almost one year in his castle at Wartburg.

Digital Divide refers to the limited access by poorer nations of the world, commonly referred to as the "have-nots", to the computing and Internet technologies that are essential to compete in the global economy of the 21st century. Since the 1980s, dramatic changes in mass communication have occurred around the world. As a result of the developments of computers, cell phones, the Internet, and other means of information storage, many people primarily in advanced industrialized nations around the world have had unprecedented and rapid access to vast amounts of information.

Diktat, which means "dictated peace" in German, was a word used by Germans after World War I to describe the nature of the Treaty of Versailles, which many Germans believed imposed a humiliating peace on Germany.

Diocese was an administrative district in the Roman Empire that was governed by a prefect responsible to the Emperor. The Christian church subsequently adopted the term "diocese" to mean territory under the authority of a bishop.

Diocletian (245–316 CE) was a Roman emperor who ruled from 284 to 305 CE. He was elevated to the position of emperor by the army and transformed the empire into an autocratic state. Diocletian restored the frontiers of the Roman Empire after their collapse in the 200s CE, reformed the Roman administration, and supported paganism. Recognizing that the Roman Empire had become too big to be governed by one person from one place, he initiated the tetrarchy, which divided the Roman Empire into two parts, each with its own

emperor and co-emperor. However, he remained the dominant ruler. At the end of his reign, he initiated the last and most severe persecution of Christians in the Roman Empire, many of whom died as martyrs to their faith.

Diocletian's Persecution or the "Great Persecution", are the terms used by historians to describe Emperor Diocletian's severe and brutal government authorized persecution of Christians throughout the Roman Empire. The Great Persecution was the longest and most destructive government sponsored persecution waged against Christians in the history of the Roman Empire. During most of his reign Diocletian ignored the presence of Christians in the Roman Empire. In the wake of the "Crisis of the Third century" (235-284) during which Roman Empire was confronted with Germanic invasions, severe economic problems, urban decline, political assassinations and the plague, Diocletian concluded that these crises represented punishment by the Roman gods for Romans abandoning traditional Roman religion practices and accepting Christian beliefs. Believing that Christians should pay the price for waning devotion to the Roman gods, Diocletian issued four empire-wide edicts in 303 that ordered the destruction of Christian churches, the burning of Christian holy books, the arrest of members of the clergy, and the prohibition of Christians assembling for worship. He also required all Christians to comply with traditional Roman religious practices by making a public sacrifice to the Roman gods. Any Christian who refused to comply with Diocletian's edicts suffered torture, imprisonment, death and seizure of their property. Diocletian's violent program against the Christians would be called by historians the "Great Persecution". However, those Christians who complied with Diocletian's edicts and made a public sacrifice to the Roman gods were granted amnesty. The persecutions began with the destruction of a Christian church in Nicomedia in Anatolia, the capital of the eastern part of the Roman Empire. Until the Great Persecution, persecutions of Christians had been intermittent over the previous two hundred years. Prior to 64, the Roman government had not officially sanctioned any persecutions of Christians. However, after the "Great Fire" of Rome, Emperor Nero authorized the first persecution of Christians organized by the Roman government. Furthermore, in 250 CE, Decius issued an edict that required all inhabitants of the Roman Empire (except for the Jews who were exempted) to perform a sacrifice to the Roman gods in the presence of a magistrate and to obtain a signed and witnessed certificate that they had performed such a sacrifice. Prior to Decius's reign, persecution of Christians had been sporadic and Christian communities had not been threatened with imperial persecution. While Decius's edict did not call for the persecution of Christians, it, nevertheless, forced Christians to choose between their religion or death. Diocletian enforced his edicts in the eastern part of the Roman Empire while his co-emperor Maximian enforced the edicts in the west. The persecution of Christians was worse in the east than the west and worse in cities than the countryside. Christians in Gaul and Britain experienced little if any persecution. When Diocletian and Maximian abdicated in 305, the persecutions temporarily ended. However, Emperor Galerius, Diocletian's successor, continued the persecutions in the east until 311 when he issued an edict of toleration, which permitted Christians to practice their faith without fear of persecution. Nevertheless, Galerius's successor, Emperor Maximinus II, continued to enforce the Diocletian's edicts in the east until 313, when he was succeeded by co-Emperors Constantine and Licinius who jointly issued the Edict of Milan which legalized the practice of Christianity throughout the Roman Empire. While the exact number of Christians killed during the Great Persecution is unknown, the early Christian church claimed that 17,000 Christians were killed during the Great Persecution. Contemporary historians contend that 3,000 to 3,500 Christians were killed.

Diogenes (412–324 BCE) was an ancient Greek philosopher whose thinking was greatly influenced by the Cynics, a school of philosophy that arose in ancient Greece during the 500s BCE. The Cynics emphasized living a moral life through self-sufficiency, rejection of luxury (asceticism), disregard for existing institutions, customs, laws, values and social conventions of Greek society and exposing folly, vanity, artificiality and hypocrisy of the Greeks. Diogenes lived his philosophy. He lived in poverty, slept on the streets or in public buildings of Athens, begged for his food and performed bodily functions in public. He is supposed to have walked throughout Athens in the daytime with a lighted lantern looking for an honest man.

Dionysus (Bacchus in Rome) was the ancient Greek god of wine and ecstasy who was worshipped widely, especially among women, in ancient Rome. Because of his supposed power to inspire, worship of Dionysus was particularly influential among many ancient Greek artists and writers. In fact, plays, be they tragedies or comedies, were performed in Athens as part of two festivals honoring Dionysus. The bull, serpent, ivy and wine were symbols associated with the cult of Dionysus that developed in ancient Greece. Lavish ritual rites called Dionysia, later Bacchanalia in Rome, were held in ancient Greece, especially among women, to honor him. As a result of the presence of Greek cultural influences in southern Italy, the worship of Dionysus began to influence Roman culture circa 200 BCE. Festivals honoring Dionysus (Bacchanalia) became such a source of social and political tension in Rome that the Senate banned them in 186 BCE.

Diplomacy is the practice of countries whereby they try to influence the behavior of other countries by bargaining, negotiating, taking non-coercive actions or refraining from such or appealing to the public for support of a specific position the country has adopted.

Directory (1795–1799) was the name of the five-member group that ruled France from October 1795 until the coup d'état by Napoleon Bonaparte in November 1799. The Directory ended the "Reign of Terror", replaced the National Convention, refused to restore the monarchy and continued to wage successfully the on-going war against France's enemies. This period of the French Revolution was characterized by a weak executive, political polarization and social and political instability. The Directory consolidated many of the political gains made during the first years of the French Revolution, but it proved incapable of maintaining a republican form of government.

Dirty War (1976–1983) was the name of the internal conflict waged by the Argentine military against leftist groups that was characterized by illegal imprisonment, torture, and executions by the military.

Disarmament is the policy adopted by a nation or a group of nations to eliminate all military weapons or a specific class of weapons. This policy is based on the belief that the elimination of all or some weapons would achieve greater security.

Discourse on Method (1637) is the book of philosophy written by Rene Descartes in which he argued that knowledge would only occur through logical speculation that began with one's own self. He is famous for the statement: "I think, therefore I am".

Discrimination is the act of seeing, noting, or recognizing a difference or distinction in favor or against a person or a group based on that person's or group's ethnicity, gender, religion, political beliefs, nationality, cultural practices, or sexual orientation.

Disputation was the model of teaching, examination and argument that dominated medieval and early modern universities in Europe. It was based upon logical deduction from received authorities.

Divination is the practice of foretelling future events by interpreting the actions of the gods, which could appear in dreams, in the entrails of animals, patterns of smoke or other messages found in nature. In ancient China, for example, divination was used to determine the will of the gods by interpreting cracks in oracle bones.

Divine Right of Kings was the political doctrine influential in the 1500s and 1600s in Europe which claimed that a monarch derived his authority to rule from God, that he functioned as God's representative on earth, and that he was only answerable to God for his actions. Any acts of resistance to the actions of the monarch were considered to be acts of both treason and blasphemy.

Division of Labor is a technique that developed in the beginning of industrialization in Britain in the mid-1700s by which the manufacture of a product was broken down into simple and repetitive tasks that could be performed by an unskilled worker or group of workers. The objective was to increase the efficiency and productivity of the workers and lower the cost of the manufactured goods. This technique was first developed by Josiah Wedgwood in his pottery works in Britain.

Djoser was an Egyptian pharaoh who ruled from Memphis during the 3rd Dynasty (2650–2575 BCE), which was in the Early Dynastic period. During his reign, his minister, Imhotep, built a new form of burial structure for the king, a six-stepped pyramid. Furthermore, Imhotep constructed this new shape of pyramid entirely of stone. The tombs and other structures he designed and built expressed the power of the Egyptian pharaohs. The stepped pyramid became the basic shape of pyramids during the Old Kingdom. Imhotep is often considered to be the first architect.

DMZ refers to the demilitarized zone between North and South Korea that was established in 1953 when the Korean War ended. It is one of the most heavily fortified borders in the world.

DNA is the genetic material that forms the basis of each cell. The discovery of the structure of DNA in 1952 has had a revolutionary effect on genetics, molecular biology, and other scientific and medical fields.

Doge was name for the government leader of the Venetian Republic during the Renaissance.

Dollar Diplomacy was the term used by President Taft to describe his foreign policy approach in Latin American and East Asia between 1909 and 1913. Rather than using military force to impose American dominance in Latin America and East Asia, President Taft and Secretary of State Knox emphasized the use of economic and financial power to open foreign markets in Latin America and East Asia to American business interests and investments. Through investments and loans to foreign governments for projects such as railroad building, they hoped to achieve greater political and economic stability and to preserve American political and military supremacy in Latin America and East Asia. Despite their efforts, they continued to use military intervention to oppose revolutionary movements and to safeguard American business and financial interests in such countries as Mexico, Nicaragua, the Dominican Republic, and China.

Domestication is the process of manipulating the breeding of animals and plants over many generations in order to make them more useful to humans as sources of transportation, food, wool, energy, and other by-products. This process began about 10,000 years ago.

Dominate (285–476 CE), which is derived from the Latin word dominus ("master" or "lord") was the name of the authoritarian style of rule that characterized the Roman Empire from the reign of Diocletian (285–305) onward. It replaced the Principate that was established by Caesar Augustus (Octavian) during his reign from 27 BCE to 14 CE.

Dominic, Saint (Dominic de Guzman) (1170–1221) was a Spanish nobleman and priest who opposed the heretical ideas of Manicheanism preached by the Albigensians (Cathars) in the south of France in late 11th century. In response to the growing influence of the Albigensians, he founded a religious order, the Dominicans, to fight against such heresies.

Dominican Order (Order of the Preachers) (1215 CE) was a mendicant religious order founded by Dominic de Guzman, a Spanish priest, in 1215. The order, which was approved by Pope Innocent III in 1216, was dedicated to combating heresy, preaching and education, hearing confessions, converting Jews and Muslims and living exemplary lives. Dominicans sought to emulate the apostolic life of the early Church leaders through poverty and preaching. Many Dominicans, who became teachers in European universities, contributed to the development of philosophy and theology during the Middle Ages. Dominicans played an influential role in the Spanish Inquisition. Four popes and over sixty cardinals have come from the Dominican Order.

Domino Theory was the geopolitical belief expressed by American policymakers during the Vietnam War that the loss of influence over one state to communists would lead to a subsequent loss of control over neighboring states, just as dominos fall one after another. This theory was used by the United States to justify support for South Vietnam and intervention in the Vietnam War. American policymakers feared that if South Vietnam became communist, neighboring countries in Southeast and East Asia would also fall under communist influence and control.

Don Quixote (1605–1615) was written by Miguel de Cervantes in two parts. In this book, a nobleman wanders the Spanish countryside hoping to recreate deeds and restore the glory and grandeur of Spain. The book was written in the wake of the defeat of the Spanish Armada by the English in 1588. At that time, Spain had the most powerful navy in the world and extensive and wealthy colonies in the Americas.

Donation of Constantine (1439–1440) is the title of a book that was written by Lorenz Valla in the 1400s during the Renaissance that proved that a book entitled *Donation of Constantine* was not written at the time of the reign of Emperor Constantine. The *Donation of Constantine* purported to record Constantine's transfer to the pope of jurisdiction over Rome and the western half of the Roman Empire. Valla's book undermined the claim of the papacy to exercise legitimate political authority and rule in central Italy.

Donatism was a heretical religious movement that emerged in North Africa during the 300s and 400s that was named for Donatus, a Catholic bishop. Donatists contended that Christian priests who collaborated with Roman persecutors of Christians were false and immoral that the sacraments administered to Christians by such priests were not valid.

Doomsday Book was a detailed survey of the royal landholdings of England undertaken by William the Conqueror between 1080 and 1086 CE. Historians consider it to be an important source of economic and social information about England during the Middle Ages.

Dorians were Greek speakers who migrated from Thessaly to the Peloponnese after about 1200 BCE and settled around Sparta. In Greek legend they were considered to be barbaric invaders of Mycenaean Greece.

Dowry was the property that a bride brought to her marriage, the size of which depended on the wealth or status of the bridegroom.

Draco (7th century BCE) was an Athenian aristocrat who was authorized in 620 BCE by the Areopagus, the council of elders who governed Athens, to write Athens's first comprehensive law code, which was first published in 621 BCE. Even though Draco's law code required severe punishments for such minor crimes as idleness, petty theft, and vagrancy, it embodied the belief that the law belonged to all Athenian citizens and did not serve exclusively the interests of the wealthy aristocratic families who controlled Athens. Draco's law code, which was administered and enforced by Athenian government officials and courts, replaced the traditional private system of oral laws manipulated by wealthy Athenian aristocratic families and enforced by them through blood feuds, personal vendettas and private wars. In 594 BCE, Solon, an aristocratic political and legal reformer and chief magistrate (archon) of Athens, replaced Draco's law code with a new code of laws, whose purpose was to limit the powers of the Athenian aristocracy. The adjective "draconian", which is used today to mean harsh, arbitrary and severe, is derived from the harsh punishments that Draco imposed on Athenians.

Dreadnought was the name for the newly designed class of British battleships developed in the late 1890s that many believed would revolutionize naval warfare and make existing fleets obsolete because of its heavy armaments. Germany's desire to build a fleet of Dreadnoughts led to a naval arms race with Britain and heightened tensions between the two countries in the years before World War I.

Dreyfus Affair (1894–1906) was the name of the political scandal that arose in France in 1894 when a Jewish captain, Alfred Dreyfus, was falsely accused of selling military secrets to Germany. He was convicted of treason and sentenced to life imprisonment. As a result of public protest, it was disclosed that the documents upon which his conviction was based were forgeries and he was released from prison. After a second trial in 1899, he was pardoned. In 1906, he was exonerated and reinstated in the French army. Because he was Jewish, many people, including Emile Zola, a noted French writer, contended that the accusations, the trial, and his conviction revealed a strong popular undercurrent of anti-Semitism in France.

Druids were a group of religious followers who conducted rituals and preserved sacred lore among some ancient Celtic peoples. They provided education, mediated disputes between kinship groups and eventually were suppressed by the Romans who viewed them as a potential source of opposition to Roman rule.

Drumont, Edouard Adolphe (1844–1917) was an influential French anti-Semitic writer and journalist. In 1886, he published a book titled *Jewish France,* which attacked the role of Jews in French society and argued for their expulsion from France. Drumont's book was well-received and 100,000 copies of it were sold during its first year of publication. During the first two years after the publication of *Jewish France,* 140 editions were printed. Having attracted many supporters of his ideas expressed in *Jewish France*, he founded and edited a newspaper in 1892 titled *The Free Word,* which became the primary French publication for expressing virulent anti-Semitism. Inspired by the success of his book *Jewish France,* Drumont founded the Anti-Semitic League in 1889, which supported the false accusation that Alfred Dreyfus, a Jewish captain in the French army, had sold military secrets to Germany. The League also organized anti-Semitic demonstrations, some of which provoked riots. Nevertheless, Drumont's anti-Semitic ideas would later influence the political program adopted by the Nazis in Germany.

Dual Alliance (1879) was a defensive military alliance between Germany and Austria-Hungary created by Bismarck as part of his system of alliances to prevent and limit war in Europe. Their common fear of Russia caused them to enter into this alliance. In 1878, Russia defeated the Ottoman Empire in the Russo-Turkish War, which gave Russia considerable influence in the Balkans. This development outraged Austria-Hungary, who was Russia's chief competitor for influence in the Balkan region. Bismarck, who wanted to portray his nation as a peacemaker and preserver of the European status quo, viewed the alliance as a means to gain more power for the German Empire and unify Germany even though it was an ally of Russia in the Three Emperors' League. Despite Bismarck's attempts to play the role of an "honest broker" at the Congress of Berlin in 1878 which reversed Russian gains in the Russo-Turkish War, Russo-German relations deteriorated. Subsequently, the Three Emperors' League was ended in 1887.

Dual Monarchy (1867) was the shared power arrangement that was established by the Habsburg

Empire and Hungary after the Prussian defeat of the Austrian Empire in 1866–1867.

Dualism is the philosophy that reality and the human being are divided into two distinct and irreconcilable substances: material (the body) and immaterial (the soul). It is also expresses a belief that the universe is dominated by two opposing forces, one good and one evil.

Dubcek, Alexander (1921–1992) was the elected Communist leader of the Czechoslovakian government. Beginning in January 1968, he sought to put a "human face" to socialism by encouraging debate within the Communist Party, less censorship and academic and artistic freedom. Fearful that his efforts to democratize the Communist Party in Czechoslovakia would create demands for political reforms in other nations in the Warsaw Pact, the Soviet Union and other members of the Warsaw Pact invaded Czechoslovakia in August 1968 with 500,000 soldiers and tanks. As a result of its occupation of Czechoslovakia, the Soviet Union was able to oust Dubcek and his allies and crush the reform movement. This period of political liberalization and reform begun by Dubcek in early 1968 is known as the "Prague Spring".

Duce is the Italian word for leader, which Benito Mussolini adopted as the head of the Fascist Party in Italy in the 1920s and 1930s.

Duma was the name for the lower house of the Russian parliament that was created by Tsar Nicholas II in 1905. The upper house was called the State Council. While representatives to the Duma were elected by universal male suffrage, the representatives of the upper house were appointed by the Tsar. The Duma could debate and pass laws, but the Tsar could veto any law passed by the Duma. The Duma met on only five occasions between May 1906 and March 1917, when the Russian Revolution began. All five meetings of the Duma were dominated by middle–class liberal reformers and socialists who demanded the creation of a constitutional monarchy, a representative legislature, civil liberties and the right to vote. After Russia's defeat by Japan in the Russo–Japanese War (1904–05), widespread discontent and increasing demands for political reform arose throughout the country, culminating in the Revolution of 1905. During the Revolution of 1905, demonstrations were held in all the major Russian cities In support of the 1905 Revolution, workers organized strikes, university students and prominent intellectuals protested, merchants closed their stores, factory owners closed their plants, lawyers refused to proceed with pending court cases, peasants revolted, and soldiers and sailors mutinied. In response to these developments, which virtually paralyzed the country, the Tsar issued the October Manifesto of 1905. The Manifesto granted Russian citizens full civil rights and promised the creation of a constitutional government and the formation of a popularly elected Duma. In May 1906, when the Duma first convened, Tsar Nichols II issued the Fundamental Laws which permitted him to retain extensive autocratic political powers. Under these laws, the Tsar controlled all ministerial appointments, financial policy and military and foreign affairs. The Fundamental Laws also allowed him to dismiss the Duma and announce new elections whenever he so desired. Despite the concessions by the Tsar in the October Manifesto, political unrest and disorder and violence continued to erupt throughout Russia between 1905 and 1907. In response, Tsar Nicholas II revoked his promises made in the October Manifesto. He limited the major powers of the Duma and decreed that representatives to the Duma would be elected indirectly based on their social class. As a consequence of the Tsar's actions, the constitutional monarchy he created was short-lived.

Dumbarton Oaks Conference (Washington Conversations on International Peace and Security Organization) was a meeting held in August 1944 in Washington, D.C. during which the treaty establishing the United Nations was negotiated. Representatives of the United States, the Soviet Union, the United Kingdom, and the Republic of China attended the conference.

Dunkirk (1940) is the French port on the English Channel from which the British Navy with the assistance of commercial and pleasure boats evacuated over three hundred thousand British and French troops who had retreated there after being defeated by the German forces during the invasion of France in May and June 1940.

Dutch East India Company (1602–1799) was a joint-stock trading company established by the

Dutch government to monopolize trade of a limited number of products from Asia, particularly the spice trade. It was an innovative business organization in that it combined government management of trade with both public and private investment. By creating a permanent pool of capital, the Dutch East India Company facilitated international trade and the growth of Dutch colonies, fortified towns and trading posts (factories), especially in Indonesia, China, and Japan, where it acted as an independent government.

Dutch Revolt, which is also known as the Eighty Years' War (1568–1648), was the approximately eighty-year rebellion against Spanish rule by seven of the northern provinces of the Netherlands, which were largely Protestant. After winning their independence from Spain, the seven provinces formed a new state known as the Dutch Republic, which was also known as the Republic of the Seven United Provinces or the Republic of the Netherlands. The remaining ten southern provinces, which were largely Catholic, remained under Spanish rule. Between 1500 and the 1700, the Dutch Republic built a vast colonial empire in which Dutch merchants traded throughout the world, operated the largest merchant fleet in the world and became a center for international finance. It also gave refuge to Portuguese and Spanish Jews and Huguenots, who contributed significantly to the prosperity of the country. Unfortunately, the Dutch Republic collapsed after it was invaded by France in 1974–1795 during the French Revolution. The Dutch Republic gained its independence from France in 1813, but it was renamed the United Provinces of the Netherlands. In 1815, the remaining ten southern provinces called the Austrian Netherlands, which were largely Catholic, joined the United Provinces of the Netherlands to form the Kingdom of the Netherlands.

Dutch West India Company (1621–1794) was an international trading company established by the Dutch government to conduct the trade of Dutch merchants in the Americas and Africa.

Dyarchy is a form of government in which two individuals jointly govern with each having the power to veto any decision by the other. This system of government was designed to prevent the exercise of absolute power by anyone person. The governments of Sparta and the Roman Republic were both dyarchies. Sparta was ruled by two hereditary kings from two aristocratic families, who served as heads of the state religion and generals in the Spartan army. One king was required to remain in Sparta while the other king commanded the Spartan soldiers in battle. Both kings were considered to be descendants of Hercules, the greatest hero in Greek mythology. During the Roman Republic (509–31 BCE), two chief magistrates called consuls were elected annually by an assembly of all male citizens to serve a term of only one year. They were specifically prohibited from succeeding themselves. As chief executives of the Republic, consuls exercised supreme civil and military authority. They administered the government, supervised its financial affairs and commanded the Roman army in battle. As each consul was endowed with *imperium,* they had the authority to issue commands and order punishments, including executions. Members of the patrician class monopolized the office of consul until 367 BCE when a law was passed which required that one of the consuls be a member of the plebian class.

Dynasty is a period of time during which a single family of rulers maintains its authority from generation to generation by the process of hereditary succession.

Eastern Bloc is the name used during the Cold War for those communist countries in Central and Eastern which were aligned with the Soviet Union. The Eastern Bloc was composed of East Germany, Poland, Czechoslovakia, Hungary, Romania and Bulgaria. These countries were also members of the Warsaw Pact, a collective defense alliance created by the Soviet Union in 1955.

Eastern Front was the battlefront between Germany and Russia that was located primarily in Russia during both World Wars I and II. Germany's defeat of ill-prepared and poorly led and equipped Russian soldiers on the Eastern Front during World War I led to the downfall of the tsarist government and the Russian Revolution of 1917.

Eastern Orthodox Church is one of the branches of Christianity that emerged between the 4th and 11th century in the Eastern Roman (Byzantine) Empire. The center for this branch of Christianity was Constantinople (also called "New Rome") where the patriarch, the head of the Eastern Orthodox Church, resided. As a result of missionary activities over the centuries, its influence spread throughout the Balkans, Middle East, the Caucasus and Russia. The doctrines and practices of the Eastern Orthodox Church were defined by the first seven ecumenical councils held by the early Christian Church between 325 and 787. The political rivalry that arose between the Eastern and Western portions of the Roman Empire after the barbarian invasions of Italy contributed significantly to emerging differences over religious doctrine and Church authority between the Roman Catholic Church centered in Rome and the Eastern Orthodox Catholic Church. These political and theological tensions as well as linguistic and cultural differences resulted in a schism between the two branches of Christianity in 1054 that continues until today.

Eastern Roman Empire was the part of the Roman Empire that arose after the founding of Constantinople in the early 300s by Emperor Constantine. As its population grew and it became more prosperous, its Greek-speaking inhabitants considered themselves to be the heirs to the Roman Empire and they believed that their Orthodox Church to be the true manifestation of Christianity. Historians would later name it the Byzantine Empire.

Eastern Question was the name given by the Great Powers in Europe to the political issue that arose prior to and during World War I concerning the future of the territories of the weakening Ottoman Empire.

Ebla Tablets (circa 2350 BCE) is the name for the 17,000 clay cuneiform tablets found in a palace archive in Syria that record economic transactions, inventories, royal correspondence, commercial and political relations of Ebla with other cities and its import and export activities. The Ebla Tablets contain the world's first dictionary. These tablets also suggest that Ebla was a prosperous, Semitic-speaking kingdom which was at the height of its power between 2600–2240 BCE. It was located in northwestern Syria and exercised political and military dominance over northern Syria, Lebanon and parts of northern Mesopotamia. Ebla was known as a center of international trade and commerce, scholarship, metalworking and the manufacture of olive oil, linen, wool and beer. It traded with Egypt, Anatolia, Sumer, Cyprus and Iran. Ebla was conquered by the Amorites around 2000 BCE.

Economic Development refers to the effect of capital accumulation, rising per capita incomes, the increasing skills and education of a population, and the adoption of new technology on the standard of living and the quality of life of a society.

Economic Imperialism refers to the process by which banks, corporations, and businesses from developed nations establish a presence in underdeveloped nations and invest in the economies of those underdeveloped nations for the purpose of making high profits.

Economic Liberalism is the theory that a peaceful and prosperous world can be created when governments adopt policies that support free markets, free trade and economic cooperation, the major elements of a capitalist economy. This theory, which is also known as neo-liberalism, is based on the belief that the role of the state in the economy should minimized. The idea of economic liberalism is derived from the writings of Adam Smith, who argued that the "invisible hand" of the market place and free competition would benefit all individuals, rich and poor.

Economic Nationalism is the idea that a country should protect and foster their own businesses by imposing high protective tariffs on imported goods as well as eliminating tariffs within a country.

Economic Sanctions are domestic penalties applied by one country (or group of countries) on another for a variety of reasons. Economic sanctions include tariffs, trade barriers, import duties, and import or export quotas. Economic sanctions are retaliatory in nature and may be imposed for political purposes.

Economics is a social science that attempts to explain the behavior and interaction of economic actors in a society in terms of the value that they exchange.

Ecumenical Council or **General Council** is a meeting of the bishops of the whole Christian Church convened to discuss and settle matters of Church doctrine and practice. From the 300s–800s, seven councils were held before the East West Schism divided the Roman Catholic Church and the Eastern Orthodox Church. The first Seven Ecumenical Councils were: First Council of Nicaea (325) which repudiated Arianism and adopted the Nicene Creed; First Council of Constantinople (381) which repudiated Arianism and revised the Nicene Creed; Council of Ephesus (431) which repudiated Nestorianism, proclaimed the Virgin Mary as the Mother of God and reaffirmed the Nicene Creed; Second Council of Ephesus (449); Council of Chalcedon (451) which repudiated the doctrine of Monophysitism; Second Council of Constantinople (553) which further repudiated Nestorianism; Third Council of Constantinople and Second Council of Nicaea (787) which restored the veneration of icons previously condemned in 754. Between 869 and 1965, there were fourteen other general council meetings of the Roman Catholic Church. For example, the First Council of the Lateran (1123) addressed investiture of bishops and the Holy Roman Emperor's role in the investiture process; the Second Council of the Lateran (1139) addressed clerical discipline such as dress and marriage; the Third Council of the Lateran (1179) restricted papal election of the cardinals and condemned simony; the Fourth Council of the Lateran (1215) defined transubstantiation; the Second Council of Lyon (1274) which attempted a reunion with the Eastern churches, approved Franciscan and Dominican orders and a tithe to support crusades; the Council of Constance (1414–1418) which resolved the Great Western Schism and condemned John Hus; the Council of Trent (1545–1563) which addressed Church reform and repudiated Protestantism; and First Council of the Vatican (1870–1960) which defined the pope's primacy in Church governance and his infallibility and repudiated rationalism, materialism and atheism.

Edict of Milan (313 CE) was the decree issued by Roman co-emperors Constantine and Licinius which made Christianity a legal religion in the Roman Empire. This decree permitted Christians to practice their religion openly without fear of persecution and to have returned to them the properties seized by the Roman state. The decree also promoted and supported the Christian church by granting it tax immunities and relieving the clergy of military service.

Edict of Nantes (1598) was the decree issued by King Henry IV of France to end religious violence. While the decree declared France a Catholic country, it permitted some forms of Protestant worship. Specifically, the decree granted Huguenots the right to practice their faith. It also gave them the right to have their own army, church organization, and political autonomy within the walled cities that they occupied. The Huguenots were also guaranteed access to schools, hospitals, royal appointments, and their own separate judicial institutions. However, they were banned from the royal court and the city of Paris. Louis XIV revoked this law in 1685.

Egalitarianism is a political theory and ideology that argues for social, political and economic equality. The belief that the best kind of society is one that tries to equalize wealth, political influence, social and economic opportunities for all of its citizens is the foundation upon which this ideology is based. Advocates for this ideology claim that that equality reflects the natural state of humanity, that all people should be treated as equals regardless of religion, ethnicity, political affiliation, economic status, social status, and cultural heritage, and that all humans are equal in worth or social status.

Ego is one of the three elements of the model of the human psyche developed by Sigmund Freud. According to him, the ego mediates between the id and the superego and allows the personality to cope with the internal and external demands of a person's existence.

Eichmann, Adolf (1906–1962) was the Nazi military officer who was responsible implementing the "final solution to the Jewish question" by organizing the transportation of Jews from all over Europe to the death and concentration camps. He was a participant at the Wannsee Conference on January 20, 1942, during which the program for the killing of all Jews in German-occupied territories was organized. Eichmann was arrested at the end of World War II in the American zone, but escaped, went underground, and disappeared. On May 11, 1960, members of the Israeli Secret Service discovered him living in Argentina, captured him, and smuggled him to Israel. He was tried in Jerusalem (between April and December 1961), convicted, and sentenced to death. He was executed on May 31, 1962.

Eiffel Tower (1889) is a steel monument completed in 1889 for the Paris Exposition. At the time that it was built, it was twice the height of any other building in the world.

Einhard (770–840 CE) was the author of many books, the best known of which was the biography of Charlemagne, which was modeled on Suetonius's *Lives of the Twelve Caesars*.

Einsatzgruppen, which is a German word for "strike force" or "task force," was the name given to the four special Security Police and SS commando units that followed the German armies into the Soviet Union in June 1941 for "special missions in occupied territory". They were directed to kill all Polish and Russian resistance fighters, Russian civilians, Jews, and Communist Party members in the areas of Poland and the Soviet Union occupied by German military forces during World War II. They used local Ukrainian, Latvian and Estonian volunteers to shoot the victims and bury them in mass graves. During the summer of 1941, this "special strike force" killed at least 1.3 million Jews in Poland and the Soviet Union.

Einstein, Albert (1879–1955) was a German-born theoretical physicist. He is best known for his theory of relativity and mass–energy equivalence, $E + mc^2$. Einstein received the 1921 Nobel Prize in Physics "for his services to Theoretical Physics, and especially for his discovery of the law of the photoelectric effect." Einstein's many contributions to physics include his special theory of relativity, which reconciled mechanics with electromagnetism, and his general theory of relativity, which extended the principle of relativity to non-uniform motion, creating a new theory of gravitation. In 1999 Time magazine named him the "Person of the Century". In popular culture the name "Einstein" has become synonymous with genius.

Eisenhower Doctrine (1957) was the policy adopted by the Eisenhower administration to provide military and economic aid to any Middle Eastern countries fighting communism.

El Alamein, Battle of (1942–1943) refers to two extended battles that took place in North Africa in 1942 and 1943 that played a major role in the outcome of World War II. The Allied victory at El Alamein ended Axis hopes of occupying Egypt, controlling access to the Suez Canal, and gaining access to the Middle Eastern oil fields. The defeat at El Alamein marked the end of Axis power in North Africa.

Elect was a concept developed by John Calvin to describe those predestined by God for salvation. It is another way of referring to a group of people as "chosen." The use of the term is derived from Paul's phrase in Romans 11:5 "the election of grace," that is, literally, God's "choice of favorites".

Elector or Prince-Elector was the title used by the seven German princes who comprised the electoral college, which was created by the Golden Bull of 1356 issued by Emperor Charles IV. With the issuance of the Golden Bull, Charles created a constitution that sought to ensure the importance of German princes in the selection of the Holy Roman Emperor and to prevent papal interference in German politics. The electoral college created by the Golden Bull was comprised of three ecclesiastical leaders and four secular German princes. Between 1623 and 1803 three additional princes were added to the electoral college. The princes who comprised the electoral college continued to exercise their sovereign powers within the respective territories each governed. Between 1493 and 1711, the House of Hapsburg was able to monopolize the position of Holy Roman Emperor. Even though the Hapsburg dynasty had only one vote in the electoral college, the size and wealth of the land they controlled permitted them to impose their candidate for the position of the Holy Roman Emperor on the other electors. As a result the dominance of Hapsburgs in the electoral college, they effectively became hereditary holders of the title of Holy Roman Emperor. The Holy Roman Empire was abolished in 1806 after Francis II, the last Holy Roman Emperor, was decisively defeated by Napoleon at the Battle of Austerlitz.

Electric Telegraph was a new technological means for rapid, long-distance transmission of information that was first introduced in Britain and the United States in the 1830s and 1840s. It replaced slower communication systems that relied upon visual signals such as semaphores.

Electricity was a form of energy that was used for lighting, industrial motors, and railroads beginning in the 1880s. However, as early as the 1830s and 1840s, electricity was used for a new technological means for rapid, long-distance transmission of information—the telegraph system that connected Britain and the United States.

Elite Theory seeks to explain the power relationships in contemporary democratic society. It contends that a small minority of influential individuals holds the most political and economic power in society outside of the democratic elections process. Through positions in corporations or on corporate boards and through financial support of foundations or positions with think tanks, members of such an "elite" are able to exert significant power over the decision-making process of corporations and governments.

Elizabeth I (1533–1603) was the first woman to occupy the British throne successfully. After the political turmoil of previous reigns, she brought stability to Britain. She strengthened Protestantism in Britain, encouraged the expansion of British overseas commerce, defeated the Spanish Armada, and encouraged a renaissance in poetry, literature, and drama.

Elizabethan Religious Settlement (The Revolution of 1559) were two laws that were promulgated by the English parliament to resolve the religious divisions created by the reigns of Henry VIII and Mary I. The Act of Supremacy of 1559 re-established the Church of England's independence from Rome, with Parliament conferring on Elizabeth the title Supreme Governor of the Church of England. The Act of Uniformity of 1559 set out the form the English church would now take, including the re-establishment of the *Book of Common Prayer*. Under these two laws, the Church of England would retain a hierarchy of bishops and the Catholic liturgy, but in English and the monarch, in this case Queen Elizabeth, would be responsible for appointing all bishops of the Church of England. By these two laws Queen Elizabeth, in essence, simply replaced the pope as ultimate religious authority in England.

Emancipation of Serfs (1861) refers to Tsar Alexander II's abolition of serfdom in Russia. The abolition of serfdom was part of Alexander's program of reform and modernization in Russia, but his program produced a limited amount of change. Under the Tsar's program approximately 22 million former serfs had legal rights and were given title to a portion of the land they had worked. However, the land was not granted to them individually, but collectively to the village commune where they were required to live until they had paid for the land. The serfs were also required to pay for the land in installments to the village commune, who in turn paid the government for the loans it issued to pay for the land. As the interest rates on the loans from the government were high, most peasants agreed to fifty-year mortgages. Also, under this system of land ownership, each peasant village was collectively responsible for the installment payments of all of the families in the village. While the former owners of the serfs were compensated by the government, many landowners inflated their claims for compensation and kept the best land themselves. As a result, the freed serfs were given land that was of such poor quality that it could not support the freed serf and his family. The effects of the Tsar's reforms were limited. Collective ownership of land and the system of payments to the government made it extremely difficult for the freed serfs to simply sell their land and leave their villages. While officially free, they were still essentially bound to work the land for the benefit of the landowner. Rather than being an independent farmer, they were remained essentially agricultural laborers.

Embargo is a trade policy adopted by a nation to reduce imports or exports to zero.

Émigré is the French word for those nobles, clergy and commoners (over 150,000) who fled France during the French Revolution and Napoleon's reign (1789–1814). With British, Austrian and Russian support, the emigres established a center of political and military opposition across the German border in Koblenz. The property of the emigres was seized and sold during the French Revolution. During the period of the Directory a large number of emigres returned to France and Napoleon granted them partial amnesty in 1800. Under the Bourbon Restoration, King Louis XVIII paid the emigres compensation for the property they had lost. The term is used today more broadly to refer to any person who leaves his or her country for political reasons.

Empire is a form of political organization comprised of various territories, countries, or states that are controlled and exploited by a foreign country that is located either on the same continent or overseas. An empire may be comprised by numerous multi-ethnic regions locally ruled by governors or client kings who govern in the name of an emperor. Throughout world history, empires have been created and maintained by the use of force.

Empiricism is the philosophical theory of inductive reasoning that was developed by Francis Bacon and John Locke which claimed that all knowledge is based on experience, direct observation of events, and experimentation. They contended that the use of experimentation and observable material evidence should be used to construct a scientific theory or philosophy of knowledge. This philosophical approach was first developed by Aristotle, who argued that a theory must be built on specific data derived from observation and explanation.

Enabling Act (1933) was the emergency legislation passed by the German parliament (Reichstag) that allowed Hitler, Germany's chancellor or prime minister, to suspend constitutional government for four years in order to deal with the economic crisis in Germany resulting from the Depression. As a result of this law, Hitler was authorized to exercise dictatorial powers and suspend civil liberties in Germany. This law was passed after a suspicious fire destroyed the Reichstag, which Hitler claimed had been started by his political opponents.

Enclosure (of the commons) was the process of consolidating and privatizing strips of land, common fields, public lands, and reclaimed waste lands into one large block of land. This movement, which was begun in Britain between 1750 and 1860, sought to make farming more productive, efficient, and profitable and to stimulate commercial agricultural production. As a consequence of the enclosure process, British farmers, who relied on common fields for farming and pasturing their animals, were forced to leave the rural areas of Britain to seek work in the emerging factories in the cities.

Encomienda was a form of economic and social organization established by the king of Spain that gave Spanish settlers (encomenderos) a royal grant of land in the Americas. This royal grant gave Spanish settlers the right to collect tribute from Native Americans living on the lands granted to the settlers, to compel them to work as laborers in the mines or as agricultural workers on farms, and to convert the them to Catholicism. In return for receiving such a royal grant, the settlers were required to provide military or other services to the king of Spain.

Encyclical is a letter from the pope to all of the members of the Catholic Church.

Encyclopedia (1751–1765) which was also known as the Systematic *Dictionary of the Sciences, Arts, and Crafts,* was the multi-volume, illustrated compilation of all modern knowledge that was co-edited by Denis Diderot and Jean d'Alembert. It contained over 70,000 articles.

Endlösung is the German word used by the Nazis in 1941 for the "final solution to Jewish question", which came to mean the killing of all Jews in Europe.

Engels, Friedrich (1820–1895) was a German social and political philosopher who collaborated with Karl Marx in writing numerous publications critiquing capitalism and advocating socialism and communism.

English Civil War (1642–1651) was the armed conflict that arose between King Charles I, an advocate of royal absolutism, and the Parliament, which sought to limit the powers of the king. Supporters of the king were known as "Cavaliers" and supporters of Parliament were known as "Roundheads". The conflict was precipitated by King Charles I's arrest of his critics. As a result of the defeat of the royalist forces and the execution of King Charles I on charges of treason, royal absolutism was eliminated in England. Subsequently, the hereditary House of Lords was abolished and England was declared a commonwealth. With the emergence of the Glorious Revolution of 1688 and the English Bill of Rights of 1689, a constitutional monarchy was firmly established in England.

English Navigation Acts were a series of laws passed by the British Parliament between 1651 and

1673 that required that only English ships could carry goods between Britain and its colonies. The objective of these laws was to prevent foreign merchant ships competing with English ships. These laws also prohibited English colonies from trading with the Netherlands, Spain and France or any of their colonies. Reflecting the British policy of mercantilism, the laws sought to limit the loss of gold and silver to foreign merchants and to limit the ability of British colonies to trade with other countries. These laws were widely resented in the American colonies, which manufactured goods that competed with British products. These laws established the basic contours of British trade policy for nearly 200 years. The laws were repealed in 1849 because of the growing acceptance of the free trade philosophy.

English Peasants' Revolt (1381) was the revolt by English peasants in 1381 in response to the attempt by King Richard II to impose a poll tax on them. The rebellion, the first popular one in English history, was led by Wat Tyler. Under his leadership his peasant army of approximately 50,000 men marched to London, occupied the London Bridge and the Tower of London, and captured the King Richard's chancellor and the treasurer. Blaming the poll tax on the chancellor and the treasurer, the peasants killed both of them. The peasant army then destroyed the palace of King Richard's uncle, who they also killed. In response to these developments, King Richard agreed to meet with the leader of the rebels, Wat Tyler. However, during that meeting the mayor of London, who was a member of the king's entourage, killed Wat Tyler in the presence of King Richard. Subsequently, King Richard met with the leaderless rebel army promised them reforms and persuaded them to disperse, which they did. The rebellion, which lasted only a month, was over. Subsequently, the nobles rapidly reestablished political control with the assistance of a militia 7,000, which the nobles had quickly created. After the collapse of the revolt, King Richard failed to implement the reforms that he had promised the rebels and had the remaining leaders of the rebellion captured and executed.

ENIAC is the acronym for Electronic Numerical Integrator and Computer, the first modern digital computer. It was designed for the U.S. Army during World War II to calculate cannon trajectories and other military computations. ENIAC was a 30-ton, 1,500-square-foot piece of hardware that contained 18,000 vacuum tube processors and required 150,000 watts of power. It was able to multiply, divide and calculate square roots as well as perform 5,000 additions or subtractions per second. ENIAC was the forerunner of commercial computers.

Enkidu is the friend of Gilgamesh whose numerous adventures together are described in the *Epic of Gilgamesh*. According to Sumerian mythology, he was a wild-savage created by the god Anu who was civilized in order to curb the harsh rule of the king of Uruk, Gilgamesh. After being defeated in a wrestling match with Gilgamesh, Enkidu swore an oath of friendship to Gilgamesh.

Enlightened Despots were benevolent absolutist European monarchs in Central and Eastern Europe in the late 1700s who initiated a series of economic, legal, and political reforms based on the ideas of the Enlightenment. Such reforms encouraged greater freedom of speech and the press, permitted religious toleration, expanded education, and improved agricultural production by permitting some peasants to own the land they worked. However, these monarchs did not relinquish their absolute political authority. Catherine the Great of Russia, Frederick the Great of Prussia, and Joseph II of Austria were examples of enlightened despots.

Enlightenment (1600–1800) was a social, political, and cultural movement in the 1700s in Europe that argued that change and reform through the application of reason and science was necessary to achieve human progress. Enlightenment thinkers claimed that human reason could overcome oppression, tyranny and superstition, which was perceived as a threat to religion and religious thought. As a worldview, it played a significant role in spreading the ideas of the Scientific Revolution. The Enlightenment fostered the belief that a person could reform a society by discovering the rational laws that govern social behavior, that those laws were just as scientific as the laws of physics and that those laws could be applied to the human society. The central concepts of the Enlightenment were the use of reason, the use of scientific method, secularism, progress, knowledge and freedom. Immanuel Kant captured the spirit of the Enlightenment in his statement "Have courage to know".

Enlil is the ancient Sumerian god of air, wind and agriculture. In Sumerian mythology, Enlil caused storms and hurricanes as well as the spring winds. There were two other important gods in the Sumerian pantheon of gods: Anu, god of the sky and Ea, god of water. In the Babylonian pantheon of gods, Marduk replaced Enlil.

Enrichez-Vous is a French phrase that means "Get Rich!" that was used during the July Monarchy of 1830–1848 in France. The phrase is attributed to Francois Guizot, who was Louis-Phillipe's chief minister. He is supposed to have said it in response to the demands to reform the suffrage laws that favored the wealthy in France. Regardless of whether he actually said it, the phrase reflected the insensitivity of the reign of Louis-Philippe to the concerns of the average French citizen.

Entente Cordiale (1904) was a defensive political alliance established by Britain, France and Russia that was designed to respect the colonial holdings of each nation and to restrain German territorial ambitions in Europe and overseas. This alliance, which sought to improve Anglo-Franco relations, marked the end of hundreds of years of conflict between the two nations. With British participation in this alliance, Britain ended a century of isolation from conflicts in continental Europe.

Entjudung, which means "De-Jewification", is the German word used by the Nazis to describe their policy of forcing Jews to leave Germany between 1933 and the outbreak of World War II in 1939.

Entrepot was a port, trading house, warehouse, or a city where goods and commodities were brought for storage before being exchanged or shipped overseas to sellers and consumers. The Dutch originated this commercial institution.

Entrepreneur is a French word for a person who assumes the risk of organizing and operating a new business venture in the hopes of making a profit. Technological inventions by British entrepreneurs contributed significantly to the industrialization of Britain between 1750 and 1850.

Epic is a long narrative poem that deals with myths, legends and heroic deeds. Traditionally, such poems were first transmitted orally over generations before they were written down.

Epic of Gilgamesh is one of the earliest known works of literature. It originated in Sumer as part of an oral tradition, but it was first recorded by Babylonian scribes. The *Epic of Gilgamesh* recounts the adventures of a semi-mythical king named Gilgamesh who battles gods and monsters in pursuit of immortality.

Epicureanism was a Hellenistic philosophy founded by Epicurus (341–270 BCE), a Greek philosopher who argued that the world was composed of a random collection of atoms, which had no underlying purpose. Epicurus claimed that while the soul was made up of atoms, the soul did not exist after death. His philosophy emphasized the individual, the avoidance of pain, the pursuit of happiness (freedom from emotional turmoil) or pleasures (intellectual rather than sensual), and denied the existence of spiritual forces. This philosophy originated among the Hellenistic Greeks and was later popularized by the Romans.

Epicycles was the idea expressed by some astronomers during the Scientific Revolution that some planets made small circular orbits while revolving around the main circular orbit of another planet.

Epigraphy is the study of inscriptions and writings recorded on any hard or durable surface or material, such as stone, marble, metal, clay, pottery, tablets, papyrus, parchment, terracotta, wood, and wax, that have been found by archaeologists among the earliest human civilizations. Such first-hand accounts of ancient civilizations are one of the primary sources used by historians in constructing their understanding of ancient civilizations.

Epistemology is a branch of philosophy that is concerned with the study of the fundamental structures and categories of human knowledge. The central question in epistemology is: How do we know what we know?

Equestrians were a class of extremely wealthy men in the late Roman Republic who were barred from high political office. They were called equestrians because many of them had begun as cavalry officers (equites). This class was comprised of wealthy aristocrats, businessmen, landowners and middle-ranking government officials who were just below the senators in terms of status in

Roman society. Some Roman emperors sought to form alliances with this socially influential group in order to counter the influence of the old aristocracy and would use the equestrians to serve in the imperial civil service.

Erasistratus (c 304 – c 250 BCE) was a Greek physician who established a hospital in Alexandria named after him where he trained many highly-regarded physicians. As a result of his study of human anatomy, he was able to determine the function of the valves of the heart and that the heart, rather than being a center of sensations, was in fact simply a pump. His research of the human circulatory and nervous systems led him to distinguish between veins and arteries and sensory and motor nerves. He is regarded as the founder of the field of physiology.

Erasmus, Desiderius (1469–1536) was a Dutch Christian humanist monk, theologian and religious reformer during the Renaissance. He argued that Christians should follow the practices of the original followers of Jesus. He considered the hierarchy of the Catholic Church, its rituals and sacraments, its worship of saints, the performance of pilgrimages and the purchase of indulgences as barriers to true faith. In his *Handbook of the Christian Soldier* (1503), he claimed that a person who imitated Jesus could achieve oneness with God and thereby eliminate the need for saints, pilgrimages and priests. In *The Praise of Folly* (1514), a satire, Erasmus attacked the corruption of the papacy, mocked corrupt priests and ridiculed those Christians who engaged in pilgrimages to buy relics. He reinterpreted Greek and Roman writings and emphasized tolerance, reason, faith in goodness and the educability of a person. He edited the Greek *New Testament*, called for reform of the Catholic Church, but eventually broke with the Protestants over the issue of free will. He translated the Bible and the writings of the early Church fathers into Latin. His translation of the *Bible* influenced the theology of Martin Luther.

Eratosthenes of Cyrene (276–194 BCE) was a Greek astronomer and mathematician who calculated the circumference of the earth.

Ersatz is a German word meaning synthetic. During World War II, various governments encouraged their chemical industries to develop synthetic equivalents of normally traded goods and resources that were in scarce supply because of the war.

Eschatology is a concept in philosophy and theology relating to be the final events of history, the ultimate destiny of humanity, and the end of ordinary reality and reunion with a divinity. This concept is more commonly referred to as the "end of the world," "end of days" or "end time". Christian and Jewish eschatologies claim a future event, such as the emergence of a messiah or messianic age, is prophesied the *Bible*. According to this apocalyptic belief, there will be, in the future, a violent disruption or destruction of the world of, which results in the consummation or perfection of God's creation of the world. This historical perspective claims that life follows a linear path which God has created and that the world is inevitably headed toward God's final goal for creation, which is the world to come.

Essenes were a Jewish sect that hoped for the arrival of a savior. They stressed the need to maintain their own ritual purity in the face of the coming apocalypse. Their beliefs were similar to some of the core beliefs of the early Christians.

Established Religion was any religion approved as the official religion of a state. For example, in France before the French Revolution, it was Catholicism, and in England, it was the Church of England.

Estate or Social Order refers to the three classes or orders—the clergy, the nobility, and the commoners—into which French society was legally divided.

Estates General (1614) was the national French representative assembly that was established in 1614. It consisted of three groups or estates: clergy (First Estate), nobility (Second Estate), and commoners (Third Estate). In 1789, Louis XVI ordered it to meet for the first time since 1614 in order to deal with a severe economic and financial crisis in France. However, disputes about voting procedures among the three estates led to the Third Estate abandoning the Estates General and forming the National Assembly in 1789.

Ethnic Cleansing is a euphemism for a government policy of systematically using intimidation, persecution, mass killings, rape, torture, and forced deportations against members of an ethnic group in order to eliminate the presence or existence of that ethnic group and to establish an ethnically homogenous society. Once an unwanted ethnic group was either massacred or deported by the "victorious" ethnic group, the land and personal property of the massacred or deported ethnic group was seized. Beginning in 1991, this tactic, which constituted gross violations of a people's human rights, was employed by Slobodan Milosevic in Yugoslavia against Bosnian Muslims in order to unite all Serbs, many of whom lived in neighboring Croatia, Bosnia-Herzegovina, and Kosovo.

Ethnic Group is a group of people with a distinctive collective identity based on a common language, culture, and history.

Ethnic Nationalism is an exclusionary form of nationalism that emphasizes the existence of a common culture, language, religion, shared history, and the myth of shared kinship among a people and uses those criteria as a basis to exclude a specific people from a nation. This form of nationalism has emerged in nations where political institutions were weak and elite interests were tied to a specific cultural identity.

Ethnocentrism is the practice of regarding one's own civilization, culture, or ethnic group as superior to another's.

Ethnography is the process of studying a person or group of people in their own natural environment.

Etruscans were a people living in central Italy who established a league of twelve independent city-states north of Rome in Etruria in the seventh and sixth centuries BCE. Etruscan kings, who grew rich from war and trade, supported well-organized armies. They significantly influenced ancient Roman culture and the formation of the Roman state. Etruscan kings ruled Rome until 509 BCE when they were expelled by the Romans.

Eucharist, which is also known as Holy Communion or the Lord's Supper, is the religious service that celebrates Jesus' last meal with his apostles. During this ritual the priest and the parishioner consume consecrated wafers of bread and wine in celebration of the last supper of Jesus. The religious doctrine of transubstantiation, which was adopted by the Catholic Church at the Fourth Lateran Council in 1215, explains how the substance of the consecrated wafers of bread and wine is changed into the body and blood of Jesus during the Eucharist. The Eucharist is considered by Catholics and some Protestant groups to be the central sacrament and act of worship of Christianity.

Euclid (circa 300 BCE) was an ancient Hellenistic mathematician who formulated the rules of geometry in the 3rd century BCE. His book *Elements of Geometry* became the basis for modern geometry.

Eugenics was a pseudoscientific movement that emerged in Europe and the United States in the late 1800s and early 1900s to control and improve the human physical and intellectual capacities of a population by encouraging individuals with certain "desirable" traits to reproduce. This movement also sought to discourage individuals with certain "undesirable" traits from reproducing. Proponents of eugenics attempted to apply the same principles of selective breeding of plants and animals to human procreation. By adopting such techniques, scientists, politicians, and social critics in Europe and the United States argued that healthier, more intelligent, and superior children could be created. Francis Galton, a highly-regard British scientist, is considered to have founded the field of eugenics in 1883 and to have coined the term" eugenics." In Germany, eugenics was the policy pursued by the Nazis to achieve "Aryan purity" in Germany.

Eunuch was a castrated man who served Chinese emperors as reliable and trustworthy guardians of the emperor's wives and concubines. Eunuchs, who came primarily from families of low social status, were brought to the Chinese imperial court as boys where they were castrated and made personal servants to the emperor. Aware of the development of possible factions within the imperial family, the eunuch system was created by Emperor Qin Shi Huang Di during the Qin Dynasty (221–207 BCE). The eunuch system was a standard feature of Chinese imperial rule until the Qing Dynasty (1644–1911/12 CE). Eunuchs were a significant political force in the imperial courts throughout Chinese history because various emperors believed that they would not seek imperial power since they could not have a family. Some eunuchs did, however, become advisers and confidants to Chinese emperors who used them as counterweights to powerful court officials. During the Tang Dynasty (618–907 CE), the imperial court created armies led by eunuchs and during the Ming Dynasty (1368–1644 CE) Emperor Hong Wu (reigned 1368–1398) attempted to limit the power of eunuchs by forbidding them to be involved in politics. Some historians consider the court intrigues initiated by powerful eunuchs to be a factor in the decline of the Ming Dynasty.

Euphemism is a word or a phrase that is less offensive, disturbing, challenging, threatening or troubling to the listener than the word or phrase it replaces. A euphemism is typically used to hide what a culture, a society, a group, an organization or a person might find as an unpleasant, disturbing, offensive or threatening idea, even if the literal meaning of a word or phrase is not necessarily offensive. The use of euphemisms is also referred to sometimes as "doublespeak." An example of a euphemism is concentration camp, a phrase used by the Nazis during World War II instead of death or extermination camp.

Eurasia is the combined geographic area of Europe and Asia.

Euripides (485–406 BCE) was one of three great classical Athenian playwrights whose wrote tragedies. He wrote 92 plays, but only 19 exist today. Deeply influenced by Sophists such as Protagoras and Anaxagoras, his plays reflected his questioning of traditional Greek religion, legends and myths. His plays focused on the basic flaws, uncontrolled passions, vulnerabilities and moral confusion of human beings and on the immorality of the gods who caused or participated in human tragedies. In his plays, Euripides emphasized that the gods acted unjustly and were oblivious or uncaring as to the harm that they caused humans. Some of his existing plays include *Alcestis, Medea, Children of Heracles, Hippolytus, Iphigenia Among the Taurians, Iphigenia at Aulis, Hecuba, Trojan Women, Madness of Heracles, Electra, Helen, Suppliants, Ion, Phoenician Women, Andromache, Bacchants,* and *Orestes.*

Euro is name of the common European currency adopted by of nineteen member states of the European Union in 1999. It replaced the national currencies of those nineteen EU member states in 2002.

Eurocommunism was a political program espoused by many Europeans that became influential in Europe after the invasion of Czechoslovakia by Soviet troops in 1968. While it was a form of communism, it deemphasized Marxist ideology.

European Court of Justice (1952) is the judicial arm of the European Union based in Luxembourg. The Court has actively established its jurisdiction and its right to overrule national law when it conflicts with law of the European Union.

European Economic Community (EEC or Common Market) (1957–1967) was the name of an international organization established after World War II by six founding members, Belgium, France, West Germany, Italy, Luxembourg, and the Netherlands, to promote economic growth and prosperity, free trade, economic cooperation and integration, and international peace among its members. Between 1973 and 1990, the EEC expanded to include Denmark, Ireland, the United Kingdom, Greece, Portugal, Spain, East Germany, Cyprus and Malta. The European Economic Community was renamed the European Community (EC) in 1967.

European Union (EU) is a political and economic union of twenty eight European nations that was established by the Maastricht Treaty in 1993. By creating a standardized system of laws that apply to all the member states, the EU has adopted policies to ensure the free movement of people, goods and services within a single integrated market. The EU represents an effort to integrate European political, economic, cultural and military structures and policies. The origins of the EU can be traced to the creation in 1951 of the European Coal and Steel Community, the European Economic Community established in 1957 and the European Community created in 1967.

Euthanasia Program (T4 Program) (1939–1945) was the Nazi program of killing those Germans who were socially and genetically inferior, incurably ill, physically or mentally disabled, permanently disabled or deformed and the elderly. The Nazis claimed that such people were superfluous or threatening to German racial health and considered the program's victims as "burdensome lives" and "useless eaters." Initially, the program's victims were killed by starvation and lethal injection. Subsequently, asphyxiation by poison gas became the preferred killing technique.

This program was part of the Nazi effort to improve the quality of the German race. During the first two years of the program 70,000 people were killed. It is estimated that another 200,000 were killed between 1941 and 1945. The code name "T4" was derived from the address for the headquarters of the Euthanasia Program, "4 Tiergartenstrasse".

Evans, Sir Arthur (1851–1941) was the British archaeologist who excavated Knossos. At Knossos he discovered the remains of a palace complex which he named the Palace of Minos after a mythical Cretan king. He argued that Mycenaean people from mainland Greece subsequently colonized the Minoan/Cretan civilization on Crete.

Evil Empire was a phrase first used by President Reagan in a speech in 1983 to describe the Soviet Union. The use of this phrase by Reagan, who viewed the Cold War as a struggle between good and evil, contributed to escalating tensions between the United States and the Soviet Union. Nevertheless, Reagan and the Soviet leader Mikhail Gorbachev negotiated, in 1987, a reduction in their respective nuclear arsenals and the elimination of intermediate range nuclear missiles. In 1988, after Gorbachev began his program of reforms known as perestroika and glasnost, Reagan stated publicly that he no longer considered the Soviet Union an "evil empire" even though it still lacked democratic institutions.

Evolution is the biological theory developed by Charles Darwin in the mid-1800s that genetic changes in plants, animals, and humans occur over millions of years as a result of natural selection, which is the process by which traits that enhance survival and reproduction become more common in successive generations of a population resulting in a new species. Natural selection is the framework used by most scientists today to understand the process of evolution and to account for the diversity and complexity of life on earth.

Evolutionary Socialism was a political doctrine enunciated by Edouard Bernstein that argued that socialists in Europe should stress cooperation with the existing political and economic structures of a nation in order to attain political power. He emphasized a democratic process of evolution rather than conflict or revolution.

Exchange Rate is an economic term that describes the rate at which one state's currency can be exchanged for the currency of another state. Since 1973, the international monetary system has depended mainly on flexible (or floating) rather than fixed exchange rates. Floating exchange rates are determined by global currency markets in which private investors and governments alike buy and sell currencies.

Excommunication is the process by which a pope or bishop in the Catholic Church issues a decree formally prohibiting a member of the Church from participating in the sacraments of the Church. The ex-member of the Church is also forbidden to have any social contacts with the community in which he or she lives.

Existentialism is a philosophical and cultural movement that emerged in Europe after World War I and influenced many intellectuals, writers and artists after World War II. Influential existentialist writers such as Jean Paul Sartre and Albert Camus explored life in a world which they considered to be cast adrift from it cultural moorings. They emphasized the need for individual freedom in a world which they considered to be devoid of meaning or coherence. Existentialists argued that individual human beings have full responsibility for their own decisions and dilemmas and creating meaning for their own lives. Some ideas associated with existentialism include dread, boredom, alienation, and absurdity. Existentialism developed as a reaction against more traditional philosophies, such as rationalism and empiricism, which sought to discover an ultimate order in the structure of the observed world. While the existentialist movement had its origins in the philosophical ideas of Kierkegaard and Nietzsche in the 1800s, it was the sense of despair and desperation born of the experiences of World Wars I and II that attracted more adherents to this ideology in the post-World War II period.

Experiment or Experimental Method is a method, procedure, or process designed to test and validate a specific principle or hypothesis by subjecting that principle or hypothesis to carefully defined and repeated tests. The experimental method was pioneered by Galileo. Rather than speculate about what might or should happen in an experiment, he conducted controlled experiments to find out what actually happened.

Exports refer to the outflow of goods and services of a country that must be paid for in foreign currencies.

Expressionism was a modernist artistic movement in painting that emerged in the early 1900s in Germany and Austria in which the artist distorted reality in order to achieve a certain emotional effect. In many cases the artist used bold colors and experimental forms in order to express the emotional fears and anxieties of the artist.

Expulsion of the Jews (1200s–1800s) was the policy adopted by some European Christian rulers to expel Jews from their kingdoms, which reflected the increasing anti-Judaic hatred and persecution to which Jews were subject throughout the Middle Ages. While these rulers claimed that the Jews, who refused to abandon their faith, were a threat to Christian society, some rulers exploited these anti-Judaic sentiments because of monetary considerations. Some rulers were motivated, in part, to expel the Jews because of the inability or unwillingness of those rulers to repay the monies that they had extorted or borrowed from Jews living in their kingdoms. While anti-Judaic sentiments had been articulated by Christian clerics and theologians and secular leaders for centuries prior to the Middle Ages, persecution of European Jews had escalated dramatically in the wake of the Crusades, which had begun in 1196. From the 300s onward as Christianity became the dominant religion in Europe, Jews were subjected to increasing hatred and persecution as a result of the wide-spread acceptance of certain falsehoods about the Jews articulated by Christian clerics, theologians, secular political leaders and Christian parishioners. Jews were continually accused of:

- being responsible for the death of Christ (Decide),
- stealing consecrated communions wafers and desecrating them (Host Desecration),
- moneylending, usury and profiteering (Usury),
- kidnapping and ritually murdering Christian boys and using their blood in the baking of matzos for the Jewish holiday of Passover (Blood Libel),
- poisoning wells to cause epidemics such as the Black Death (Well-Poisoning),

- attempting to destroy Christianity, and
- engaging in obscene, inhuman and satanic behavior with unclean animals such as pigs and owls (Impurity).

It was within this centuries-old virulent anti-Judaic context that King Edward I issued an edict in 1290 expelling all Jews from England. Jews would not be permitted to return to England until 1657, 350 years later. It is estimated that approximately 16,000 Jews were expelled from England pursuant to Edward's edict. Jews were also subsequently expelled from:

- France (1309, 1322, 1394 and 1453),
- Hungary 1349, 1360 and 1582),
- Belgium (1370),
- Austria (1421, 1559, 1593, 1669 and 1670),
- the Netherlands (1442, 1444 and 1582),
- Italy (1485, 1492, 1496, 1515, 1533, 1541,1555 and 1597),
- Spain and Portugal (1492 and 1496),
- the Papal States (1569), and
- Russia (1619, 1648, 1654, 1727, 1740, 1772, 1804, 1808, 1843 and 1880s).

It is estimated that over 100,000 Jews were expelled from Spain and Portugal. Relying upon the same pervasive anti-Judaic falsehoods, numerous kingdoms, principalities, regions and cities in the Holy Roman Empire also frequently expelled Jews between the mid-1300s and early 1800s. Those entities were:

- Hielbronn (1349),
- Saxony (1349),
- Strasbourg (1388),
- Fribourg (1424),
- Zurich, (1424),
- Cologne (1424),
- Mainz (1438, 1462 and 1483),
- Augsburg (1439),
- Bavaria (1453 and 1815),
- Breslau (1453),
- Nuremberg (1498),
- Prussia (1510),
- Regensburg (1519),
- Bohemia (1542),
- Prague (1542, 1557,1561 and 1744),
- Wurzburg (1567),
- Brandenburg (1571 and 1593),
- Frankfurt (1614),
- Worms (1615),

- Hamburg (1649),
- Wurttemberg (1738),
- Bohemia (1744),
- Franconia (1815),
- Swabia (1815),
- Lubeck (1815) and
- Bremen (1815 and 1820).

Extended Deterrence is the strategic nuclear policy of the United States to threaten to use or use nuclear weapons to deter a conventional or nuclear attack on its allies in Western Europe as well.

Extermination Camp was a type of Nazi concentration camp that specialized in the mass murder of Jews, Roma (Gypsies), Slavs, homosexuals, alleged mental and physically handicapped individuals, Soviet prisoners of war and others in the Third Reich and Nazi occupied territories. The major camps were in German-occupied Poland and included Auschwitz, Belzec, Chelmno, Majdanek, Sobibor, and Treblinka. Auschwitz was the most notorious of the camps. Typically, able-bodied male prisoners were initially used in forced-labor battalions until they were virtually worked to death. The creation of these death camps represented a fundamental change in Nazi policy. With the invasion of the Soviet Union in June 1941, Jews were initially rounded up and taken to nearby sites, such as Babi Yar in the Ukraine and were executed by mobile killing units such as the Einsatzgruppen. This process proved difficult to hide from the local populations. Furthermore, the killing of so many people posed severe morale problems for the soldiers in the mobile killing units. The creation of extermination camps sought to alleviate those two problems. Subsequently, it was decided by the Nazis that individuals were to be transported by rail to the six permanent extermination camps in Poland where large numbers of victims could be murdered more quickly by a greatly reduced number of personnel. For example, the staff of Treblinka was comprised of only 120 soldiers. Killing at each of the extermination camps was done by poison gas. Chelmno, the first of the extermination camps, where gassing began on December 8, 1941, employed gas vans whose carbon-monoxide exhaust asphyxiated passengers. Auschwitz, the largest and most lethal of the camps, used Zyklon B. Majdanek and Auschwitz were also slave-labor

centers, while Treblinka, Belzec, and Sobibor were devoted solely to killing. The Nazis murdered between 1.1 million and 1.5 million people at Auschwitz, 750,000–900,000 at Treblinka, and at least 600,000 at Belzec during its 10 months of operation. The overwhelming majority of the victims were Jews. At Chelmno, which was established in 1941, 370,000 people were murdered there, 365,000 of whom were Jews. At Sobibor, which was established in 1942, between 225,000 and 250,000 Jews were murdered. Sobibor was closed in 1943 after an inmate uprising in which 300 prisoners escaped. Treblinka and Belzec were closed in 1943, their task completed as the ghettos of Poland were emptied and their Jews killed. Auschwitz continued to receive victims from throughout Europe until Soviet troops occupied it in 1945.

Extraterritoriality is the legal right that foreign residents in a country live under the laws of their native country and not the laws of the country in which they are currently living. In the 1800s and 1900s, European and American nationals living in certain cities in China were granted this legal right by the Chinese government. This concept, which was applied within all foreign "spheres of influence" in China, exempted all foreigners living in China from Chinese legal jurisdiction.

Fabian Society was a political organization founded in 1884 which sought to establish a democratic socialist economy in Britain. Fabians, who considered capitalism as inefficient and unjust, considered socialism to be the economic counterpart to democracy. They advocated collective ownership of the means of production by the state in order to bring about a more just society. This objective was to be achieved peacefully through gradual reform rather than through revolution and class warfare as advocated by proponents of Marxism. George Bernard Shaw, H. G. Wells and Emmeline Pankhurst as well as other prominent British intellectuals were members of the Fabian Society.

Factory was a centralized workplace where a large number of people worked together to mass produce goods. The first factories in Europe were built in Britain in the 1700s and were made possible by the development of the steam engine, which provided a central source of power. The mechanized production of goods in factories during the 1700s responded to the growing demands for goods by an increasing population.

Factory Act (1833) was legislation passed by the British Parliament that prohibited factory work by children under the age of nine, provided two hours of daily education for children working in factories, and limited adults to twelve hours of work each day.

Fair Deal (1945) was a liberal domestic reform program promised by President Truman. Truman had called for expanded social security, new wage-and-hour reforms and public-housing legislation, and a permanent Fair Employment Practices Act that would prevent racial or religious discrimination in hiring. Congress, which was preoccupied with problems of inflation and of converting the country to a peacetime economy, paid little attention to Truman's proposals. Subsequently, after Truman's surprise victory in the 1948 presidential elections, Congress agreed to accept a few of the president's recommendations. It raised the minimum wage, promoted slum clearance, and extended old-age benefits to an additional 10,000,000 people.

Faisal I (also Faysal) (1885–1933) was the Arab prince who became the leader of the Arab Revolt against the Ottoman Empire during World War I. The British made him king of a new state that they created in the Middle East in 1921 called Iraq. He reigned under British protection until 1933.

Faith is the questioned acceptance of the validity, credibility, and trustworthiness of an unproven idea. In religion, it refers to a trusting belief in a supreme being and some transcendent reality such as immortality.

Fallout Shelter is an underground concrete structure that is often stocked with food and water supplies and designed to withstand fallout from a nuclear attack. They were popular in the United States in the 1950s and 1960s during the nuclear arms race between the United States and the Soviet Union.

Fallow means to allow a land that otherwise would be cultivated to remain idle during a growing season so as to prevent exhaustion of the nutrients in the soil.

Fanatic is a person who expresses extreme enthusiasm in religious and political matters, often using violent means to achieve his or her objective. In some cases, a religious fanatic will claim that he or she is pursuing a divinely inspired mission.

Farben, I.G. was a German chemical conglomerate that played an important role in Hitler's rearming of Germany and the Nazi war effort during World War II. During World War II, Farben made extensive use of slave labor in its factory IG Auschwitz that it established near the Auschwitz extermination camp. The IG Auschwitz factory, which was larger than all of the Auschwitz concentrations camps together, manufactured synthetic gasoline and rubber contributing significantly to the Nazi's ability to wage war. Farben also owned the company that produced Zyklon B, the poison gas used in Nazi exterminations camps. In 1947, 24 individuals, who had been board members, executives or mangers of Farben, were tried by U.S. military authorities in Germany. The IG Farben trial was the sixth of twelve subsequent Nuremberg war crimes trials conducted by U.S. military authorities after World War II. It was also the second of three trials of leading German industrialists (Krupp and Flick KG) for their conduct during World War II. The 24 defendants at the Farben trial were charged with: planning, preparing and waging a war of aggression; war crimes and crimes against humanity through the plundering of Nazi occupied territory; war crimes and crimes against humanity through participation in the enslavement and deportation to slave labor of concentrations camp inmates, civilians and prisoners of war and their mistreatment, torture and murder; membership in a criminal organization (SS) and conspiracy to commit the four previously enumerated crimes. All of the defendants were acquitted of waging a war of aggression and conspiracy to do so. Three defendants were acquitted of membership in a criminal organization. Nine defendants were found guilty of war crimes and crimes against humanity through plundering. Five defendants were found guilty of war crimes and crimes against humanity through the deportation and enslavement of concentration camp inmates, civilians and prisoners of war. Ten defendants were acquitted of all charges. The thirteen defendants who were found guilty served prison terms ranging from one and one half years to eight years in prison. By 1951 all of the incarcerated defendants were released.

Fasces was a symbol of authority in ancient Rome carried by officials (lictors) in public to symbolize the authority of a magistrate. It had an ax head projecting from a bundle of elm or birch rods tied together with a red strap. The Romans adopted the fasces from the Etruscans. It would be lowered as a form of salute to a higher ranking official. The number of fasces carried in a public by lictors reflected the power and authority of official in the procession. For example, Emperor Augustus had twelve fasces. However, after the reign of Emperor Domitian emperors and dictators had twenty-four fasces, a consul would have twelve and a praetor six. The Fascist Party that was established by Benito Mussolini in the 1920s in Italy was named after the fasces.

Fascism is the political ideology and mass movement that was prominent in many European nations between 1919 and 1945. It was founded by Benito Mussolini in Italy in the 1920s. Mussolini glorified the authoritarian power of the state, nationalism, militarism and the use violence to achieve political ends. He argued that the needs of the individual should be subordinated to the needs of the state. He said that there is "nothing above the state, nothing outside the state and nothing against the state". Fascism was anti-democratic and rejected the existing political ideologies of liberalism, conservatism, socialism, and communism. Fascism reached its peak of influence and power with the Nazis in Germany from 1933 to 1945. In both Germany and Italy, fascism had some of its strongest support from the middle class.

Fascist Party (1919) was the Italian rightwing political party founded by Benito Mussolini in 1919 whose political program favored aggressive nationalism and corporatism. Under the dictatorship of Mussolini, the Fascist Party would rule Italy from 1922 to 1943.

Fashoda Incident (1898) refers to a conflict between the British and the French in 1898 in the Sudanese town of Fashoda over colonial claims that almost resulted in a war between both

imperialist nations. During the late 1800s, the British were attempting to create a solid block of influence from southern Africa through East Africa to Egypt, which was already under British control. The British wanted to link their possessions in southern Africa (modern South Africa, Botswana, Zimbabwe, and Zambia), with their territories in East Africa (modern Kenya), and these two areas with the Nile basin. Sudan (which in those days included modern-day Uganda) was the key to the fulfillment of these ambitions. At the same time, the French were attempting to expand from West Africa along the southern border of the Sahara Desert in order to control all of the trade in that area of Africa. The French thrust into the African interior was mainly from the continent's Atlantic coast (modern-day Senegal) eastward along the southern border of the Sahara, a territory covering modern-day Senegal, Mali, Niger, and Chad. Their ultimate goal was to have an uninterrupted link between the Niger River and the Nile, hence controlling all trade to and from that region, by virtue of their existing control over the caravan routes through the Sahara. In short, Britain sought to extend its East African empire from Cairo to the Cape of Good Hope, while France at the same time sought to extend its own holdings from Dakar to the Sudan, which would enable its empire to span the entire African continent from the Atlantic Ocean to the Red Sea. These competing claims of British and French colonial control intersected in Fashoda. Subsequently, a military standoff between British and French forces led the two countries to the brink of war, but the crisis was finally solved diplomatically. In March 1889, the French and British agreed that the source of the Nile and the Congo rivers should mark the frontier between their respective spheres of influence and France ceded southern Sudan to Britain in exchange for the British halting any further expansion. The resolution of the competing British and French colonial claims would be the last serious colonial dispute between Britain and France and would lead to the eventual end of the "Scramble for Africa".

Fashoda Syndrome refers to the French foreign policy in Africa that emerged in the late 1800s and early 1900s, by which the French sought to assert their influence in areas that were becoming more susceptible to British influence. Because of the Fashoda Incident, French policymakers became increasingly concerned about British encroachment into areas of Africa that the French considered to be within their sphere of influence.

Fatalism is the philosophical belief that all events are predetermined, that humans are powerless to alter those events, that any resistance to the inevitable would be futile and that humans should simply resign themselves to future inevitable events.

Fatimid Dynasty (909–1171 CE) was a Shi'ite Muslim empire that emerged in North Africa and Egypt between 909 and 1171 that sought to build, unsuccessfully, a universal Islamic state. They claimed descent from Muhammad through his daughter Fatima, from whom they got their name. They attempted to overthrow the Sunni Muslim Abbasid Dynasty centered in Baghdad who then dominated the Islamic world. At its peak, the Fatimid Empire included North Africa, Sicily, the Red Sea coast of Africa, Syria, Palestine, Yemen and Egypt, which was the center of their empire. They built Cairo, which would become the capital of their empire. During their reign, their empire was threatened by the Byzantines, the Seljuk Turks of Anatolia and the Christian crusaders of Europe. The Fatimid Dynasty ended, in part, because of internal dissension in the army over the role of the caliph in political affairs and because the majority of Muslims in the world who were Sunnis rejected the Fatimid's religious doctrines.

Favorable Balance of Trade is an economic condition in which a nation seeks to maximize the export of its own goods and limit imports of foreign goods, so as to remain a creditor in international trade. Britain's mercantile system introduced by the Navigation Acts in the 1700s was designed to guarantee Britain a favorable balance of trade.

Fealty was an oath of loyalty, faithfulness, subservience, and duty that a vassal made to his lord. The vassal also promised to perform military and other services for the lord he serves.

February Patent (1861) was the law enacted by the Austrian Emperor Franz Joseph that established a constitutional monarchy in the Austrian Empire. The law guaranteed civil liberties and provided for local self-government and an elected parliament.

February Revolution (1917) was the spontaneous popular uprising that began in March 1917 (under the old Russian calendar February) in Petrograd, Russia. The uprising led to the Russian Revolution, the abdication of Tsar Nicolas II, the end of the Romanov Dynasty in Russia and the establishment of a provisional government to rule Russia.

Federal Republic of Germany (West Germany) (1949–1990) was the country formed from the areas occupied by the Allies after World War II. The Federal Republic was rapidly democratized by the United States and integrated into the world economy.

Federalism is the term used to describe the structure of a government in which the authority to make laws is divided, according to a written constitution, between a national or central government and regional or state governments.

Feminism is a political ideology that developed in the late 1700s and early 1800s in Europe, which held that women are not inferior to men and that the social, political, and economic subordination of women was unjust. Proponents of feminism argued that women should have equal access to education, the right to vote and participate in politics, economic independence and greater cultural involvement in society. Today, feminism tends to be a diverse collection of social theories, political movements, and moral philosophies, largely motivated by or concerning the experiences of women, especially in terms of their social, political, and economic situation. As a social movement, feminism largely focuses on limiting or eradicating gender inequality and promoting women's rights, interests, and issues in society.

Ferdinand, Archduke Franz (1863–1914) was the Archduke of Austria and heir to the Austro-Hungarian Empire who was assassinated by a Serbian nationalist in Sarajevo in 1914. His assassination led to the beginning of the First World War.

Ferry, Jules (1832–1893) was a French statesman and politician in the late 1800s who, after the French defeat in the Franco-Prussian War, advocated that France acquire a great colonial empire in order to economically exploit those colonies. In 1883, he declared that "the superior races" have a right and a duty "to civilize the inferior races" in the world.

Under Ferry's leadership, France established a protectorate in Tunis (1881), occupied Madagascar (1885), explored the Congo and Niger regions in Africa, and conquered Annam and Tonkin (1885). The conquest of Annam and Tonkin, which would be known as Indochina, led to a war with China, who claimed sovereignty over Annam and Tonkin. As a result of the war with China, China would sign a peace treaty by which it gave up sovereignty over Annam, Cochinchina and Tonkin to the French.

Fertile Crescent is the term that was created by James Henry Breasted, an American archaeologist, in 1900 to describe the crescent-shaped geographic area of rich arable land that stretches from the modern day Iraq/Iran border along the Persian Gulf northward along the Tigris-Euphrates River Valley to southern Turkey and then turns southward along the eastern Mediterranean coast of present day Syria, Lebanon and Israel. Archaeologists have determined the earliest complex societies arose in the Fertile Crescent. Agricultural production, the domestication of plants and animals, the building of irrigation canals, the invention of pottery, the growth of permanent farming villages and the building of urban centers first emerged along the Tigris-Euphrates River Valley sometime between 9000 and 3000 BCE. The Sumerian, Akkadian, Babylonian, Assyrian, Hittite, Phoenician and Hebrew civilizations would all develop in the Fertile Crescent.

Feudalism is a term used by historians to describe a form of economic, political and social, organization that emerged in the 11th and 12th centuries in Europe in which a knight would become a vassal to a noble by taking an oath of allegiance and loyalty to a noble and making a promise to provide a noble some personal or military service. In turn, a noble would grant a knight a tract of land (a fief) or some other form of income. While there was no uniform system of feudalism in medieval Europe, this system describes a society governed through personal ties of dependency and subservience to a person of superior social status.

Feuillants (1791–1792) was the name of a French political club established during the initial stages of the French Revolution by former members of the Jacobins who supported a constitutional monarchy.

Fichte, Johann Gottlieb (1764–1814) was a German philosopher who contributed to the intellectual underpinnings of German nationalism and anti-Semitism. In his *Addresses to the German Nation* (1808), he urged the German people to find their Germanness in the German language and the German virtues celebrated by Tacitus (56–117) in his *Germania* (98). He further claimed that inherent in the idea of Germanness was anti-Semitism. He argued that "making Jews free German citizens would hurt the German nation." Fichte considered Jews in Germany to be "a state within a state" that would "undermine the German nation." With respect to Jews obtaining civil rights, he stated that that would only be possible if one were "to cut off all of their heads in one night, and set new ones on their shoulders, which should contain not a single Jewish idea."

Ficino, Marsilio (1433–1499) was an Italian Renaissance philosopher, theologian, and member of the Platonic Academy who translated the complete works of Plato.

Fideism was a religious form of skepticism that viewed the uncertainty and weakness of natural human knowledge as an indication of the necessity of faith.

Fief was the grant of land or some other form of income by a lord to a vassal during the Middle Ages. In exchange, the vassal would take an oath of loyalty and provide military and other services to the lord.

Fifth Column is a group of people who secretly try to undermine the war efforts of a nation in which they live and to which they are presumed loyal. The term originated with a radio address in 1936 by a nationalist general during the Spanish Civil War. As four of his army columns moved on Madrid, the general referred to his supporters within the city as his "fifth column," who would clandestinely undermine the Republican government from within. During World War II, the term was used extensively to describe those nationalist resistance forces in Europe that were fighting against the Nazis. The fear of a fifth column in the United States was the justification for the internment of Japanese-Americans along the West Coast and the internment of Japanese-Canadians in British Columbia. This was not the first time that claims of the existence of a fifth column were expressed in the United States. During World War I, President

Woodrow Wilson blamed Irish-Americans in the Democratic Party for blocking attempts for the United States to ally with Britain. He also blamed German-Americans for their loyalty to Germany and denounced "hyphenated Americans" as potentially traitorous.

Filmer, Robert (1588–1653) was an English political theorist who was a leading advocate for absolutism. His political theory was founded upon the belief that the governance of a family by the father is the original model for all governments. In the beginning of the world, according to him, God gave authority to Adam, who had complete control over his descendants, and from Adam this authority was inherited by Noah. Filmer argued that Noah sailed up the Mediterranean and allotted the three continents of the Old World to the rule of his three sons, Shem, Ham, and Japheth, who inherited the absolute power of Noah, which they exercised over their families and servants. Furthermore, according to Filmer, all subsequent kings derive their authority in this manner, which is absolute and founded upon the idea of divine right. Thus, from his perspective, a king is free from all human control. John Locke viewed Filmer as an example of an advocate for the theory of divine right of kings. Locke attacked Filmer's ideas in the first part of the *Two Treatises of Government*. Filmer was also a critic of democracy, which he considered to be simply the rule of a mob.

Final Solution to the Jewish Question was the termed developed by the Nazis for their plan to systematically murder all the Jews of German-occupied Europe. This plan was based on Nazi theories of racial inferiority. Beginning in 1941–42, Jews were rounded up and sent to extermination camps in Poland such as Auschwitz. However, the Nazis informed the Jews that they were simply being "resettled" in the East. As a result of this program by the Third Reich, six million Jewish men, women, and children were executed by the Nazis. This massacre of European Jews by the Nazis from 1941–1945 is known as the Holocaust of the Shoah.

First Consul, a governmental title that was taken from the Roman Empire, was the title of the most important consul established by the French Constitution of 1800. It was the title given to Napoleon Bonaparte.

First Crusade (1096–1099) was initiated when the Byzantine Emperor Alexis Comenius requested help from Pope Urban II to reconquer Byzantine territory in Anatolia that was seized by the Seljuk Turks. In response to Comenius' request, Pope Urban convened the Council of Clermont in 1095 at which he called upon European knights to form an armed "pilgrimage" to recover Jerusalem from the Muslims. He also sought to use this military expedition to strengthen the papacy by bringing the Greek Orthodox Church under papal authority. Prior to their departure from Europe for Jerusalem, groups of crusaders massacred Jews in the Rhineland towns of Speyer, Worms, Mainz and Cologne. In 1099 about 20,000 crusaders captured Jerusalem and massacred its inhabitants (Muslims, Jews and Christians alike). As a result of the First Crusade, the crusaders also established four feudal Christian states along the eastern Mediterranean coastline: the County of Edessa, the Principality of Antioch, the County of Tripoli and the Kingdom of Jerusalem.

First International (1864–1876), also known as the International Working Men's Association, was an organization that attempted to unite the various European socialist, communist, and anarchist political groups and trade unions that were opposed to capitalism. With local federations in a number of European countries, it is estimated that it had between 5–8 million members. Karl Marx played an important leadership role in the organization. By 1872, the organization had become deeply divided ideologically between those who supported socialism and those who supported anarchism. In 1876, the organization was disbanded.

First Italo–Ethiopian War (1895–1896), fought between Italy and Ethiopia, was one of the very few instances of a successful armed African resistance to European colonialism. In March 1889, King Menelik II of Ethiopia (Abyssinia) signed a treaty of friendship with Italy, which, allegedly unbeknownst to Menelik, established an Italian protectorate over Ethiopia. When this fact became known, Menelik repudiated the treaty. In response, the Italians initiated a military campaign against Ethiopia in 1895 expecting disaffected ethnic groups in Ethiopia to join them in their fight against Menelik. Instead, all of those ethnic groups flocked to the side of King Menelik. At the Battle of Adowa on

March 1, 1896, the Ethiopians decisively defeated the Italian forces.

First Servile War (135–132 BCE) was the first of three unsuccessful slave rebellions during the Roman Republic It took place in Sicily and involved about 200,000 abused and poorly fed men and women. After some minor victories by the slaves, the slaves were defeated by a much larger Roman army.

First-Strike Capability is the ability of the United States to preemptively launch a nuclear attack and destroy most of or almost all of an enemy's nuclear missile forces resulting in an enemy's inability to retaliate effectively with its remaining nuclear missile forces. First-strike weapons include ICBMs, which are highly accurate, fast and provide little warning time. However, in their fixed silos ICBMs would be vulnerable to an enemy attack. The United States enjoyed a first-strike capability over the Soviet Union until the late 1950s when the Soviet Union first developed inter-continental ballistic missiles.

First Temple (957 BCE) was a monumental sanctuary built in Jerusalem by King Solomon in the 10th century BCE to be the religious center for the Israelite god Yahweh. The Temple priesthood conducted sacrifices, received a tithe or percentage of agricultural revenues, and became economically and politically powerful. The First Temple was destroyed by the Babylonians in 587 BCE, rebuilt on a modest scale in the late 6th century BCE, and replaced by King Herod's Second Temple in the late 1st century BCE, which was subsequently destroyed by the Romans in 70 CE.

First Triumvirate (59–53 BCE), which is a Latin word for "group of three," was an informal political alliance between Julius Caesar, Licinius Crassus, and Gnaeus Pompey in 60 BCE in which they agreed to share political power in the Roman Republic and to advance one another's interests. This alliance led to the collapse of the Republic.

First World is a term used in international relations that describes the industrialized democratic and capitalist nations of Western Europe, North America, Australia, New Zealand and Japan who were aligned with the United States against the Soviet Union during the Cold War. With the end of the Cold war, the term has taken on a new meaning. It now refers to those nations who are highly developed or advanced politically and economically. The rise of multinational corporations, the problem of outsourcing, the growth and influence of information technology and social, cultural, economic integration that transcends the boundaries of the traditional nation-state are all developments typically associated with the First World.

Fiscal Policy is a government's decisions about spending and taxation.

Five Good Emperors was the name for the five extremely competent and successful emperors who ruled the Roman Empire wisely, fairly, and humanely from 96 to 180. They created an unparalled period of peace and prosperity. The five emperors were Nerva, Trajan, Hadrian, Antoninus Pius, and Marcus Aurelieus.

Five Pillars of Islam refers to the basic teachings of Islam, which are: the profession of faith that there is no God but Allah and Muhammad is his prophet; individual prayer five times daily; fasting from sunrise to sunset during the month of Ramadan; giving charity or alms to the poor; and a pilgrimage to Mecca at least once in a person's life.

Five-Year Plans (1928–1937) were the two economic programs introduced by Joseph Stalin in the Soviet Union beginning in 1928. The purpose of the plans was to rapidly industrialize the Soviet Union by replacing the existing market-based economy with a state-owned and state-managed economy. Under the two Five-Year Plans, every aspect of economic production and distribution was to be determined in advance by the central government for a period of five years. By promoting rapid economic development, Stalin hoped to "catch and overtake" the leading capitalist economies. The First Five-Year Plan went from 1928 to 1933, and the Second Five-Year Plan went from 1933 to 1937. As a result of those two plans, the Soviet Union succeeded in becoming a major industrial power in the world within only ten years.

Fixed Exchange Rate was the official rate of exchange for currencies set by governments, which ended in 1973.

Flagellants were a group of Christians in the 1400s in Europe who believed that the plague was God's punishment for human sins. To do penance for the commission of such sins and to appease what they believed to be the anger of God, flagellants publicly whipped themselves.

Flat Earth Theory was a perspective held by many ancient civilizations that the Earth's shape was a flat plane or disk. It is believed that the Greek philosophers Pythagoras, in the 6th century BCE, and Parmenides, in the 5th century BCE, both concluded that the Earth was spherical. Around 330 BCE, Aristotle maintained on the basis of observational evidence that the Earth was spherical. Early Egyptian and Mesopotamian thought viewed the world as a flat disk floating in the ocean. Homer and Hesiod offered a similar perspective. The Hebrew Bible described a circular earth with a solid roof, surrounded by water above and below. The pre-Socratic philosophers such as Thales, Anaximander, Anaximenes, Democritus, Anaxagoras, Hecataeus and Xenophanes all considered that the earth was flat. Even Herodotus expressed such a perspective. Furthermore, in ancient China, the idea that the earth was flat was the generally accepted belief until the introduction of European astronomy in the 1600s. However as early as 240 BCE, Eratosthenes of Cyrene determined the circumference of the Earth. In fact, in the 2nd century BCE, Crates of Mallus created a sphere that divided the Earth into four continents with people presumed to be living in each of the four regions. By the 1st century CE, Pliny the Elder claimed that the idea of a spherical Earth was widely accepted. Subsequently, in the 100s CE Ptolemy based his maps on a spherical Earth and developed a system of latitude and longitude. His thinking would influence European astronomy throughout the Middle Ages. By the 300s CE, Augustine accepted the view of his contemporaries that the Earth was spherical. By Late Antiquity and the Early Middle Ages (476–900), the concept of a spherical Earth had become wide-spread. Even early Christian scholars such as Boethius (480–524), Bishop Isidore of Seville (560–636), Saint Bede (c.672–735) accepted the idea that the earth was round. By the High Middle Ages (1000–1300), Saint Thomas Aquinas (1225–1274), the most important theologian of the Middle Ages, expressed his belief that the Earth was round in his *Summa Theologica*. The book *On the Sphere of the World*, the most influential astronomy textbook of the 1200s and required reading by students in all Western European universities, described the world

as a sphere. The Portuguese exploration of Africa and Asia, Columbus's voyage to the Americas and finally Ferdinand Magellan's circumnavigation of the Earth provided the final proof for the spherical shape of the Earth. Despite this body of historical evidence, a myth arose that during the Middle Ages people believed that the Earth was flat. This myth became so widespread in the United States in the 1900s that in 1945 the *Members of the Historical Association* officially stated that: "The idea that educated men at the time of Columbus believed that the earth was flat, and that this belief was one of the obstacles to be overcome by Columbus before he could get his project sanctioned, remains one of the hardiest errors in teaching." It appears that this myth has its origins in a biography of Columbus that was published by Washington Irving in 1828. In *A History of the Life and Voyages of Christopher Columbus*, Irving popularized the idea that Columbus had difficulty obtaining financial support for his plan because many Catholic theologians insisted that the Earth was flat. Even though there have been numerous books and articles written since the 1920s devoted to debunking Irving's historically inaccurate representation, the flat earth error has persisted in popular culture and in teaching American secondary schools.

Flavians (69–96 CE) was a dynasty of Roman emperors beginning with Vespasian, who reigned from 69 to 79, Titus, who reigned from 79 to 81, and Domitian, who reigned from 81 to 96. Unlike the Julio-Claudians, the Flavians were descended from Italian landowners, not old Roman nobility. All three emperors ruled during a period of relative peace in the Roman Empire.

Flavius, Josephus (37/38–100 CE), whose original name was Joseph Ben Matthias, was a Jewish historian who wrote about the Jewish Revolt of 66–70. While he was a Pharisee who willingly submitted to Roman rule and thought resistance to rule futile, he, nevertheless, reluctantly joined the Revolt and was appointed military commander of Galilee. After his capture by the Romans who were led by the future emperor Vespasian, he was released and joined the Roman forces under Titus, Vespasian's son. In that capacity, he attempted to mediate the conflict between the Jewish rebels and the Romans, but was unsuccessful. After the fall of Jerusalem and the destruction of the Temple, he went to Rome where he became a Roman citizen. He was highly regarded by emperors Vespasian, Titus and Domitian. While in Rome he wrote his *History of the Jewish War* between 75 and 79, which was extremely critical of the Jewish Revolt of 66–70. Nevertheless, the *History of the Jewish War* is valuable because it is our principal source for understanding the Jewish Revolt.

Flexible Response (1961) was a military strategy adopted by President John F. Kennedy to address the weakness of the strategic nuclear doctrine of massive retaliation. With the introduction of intercontinental ballistic missiles in the late 1950s by the Soviet Union, the U.S. policymakers claimed that they could no longer rely on nuclear threats to provide security for the United States and its allies in Europe and that the credibility of massive retaliation as an effective deterrent had been undermined. They further contended that massive retaliation left U.S. policymakers with only two choices in the face of Soviet aggression: defeat on the ground or the resort to the use of nuclear weapons. Rather than engaging in immediate massive retaliation to a Soviet attack on Western Europe, U.S. policymakers claimed that the doctrine of flexible response would give U.S. policymakers a wide-range of military options (strategic, tactical or conventional) to deter to Soviet aggression in Western Europe other than with nuclear weapons. Flexible response, it was argued, would permit the U.S. to prevail in response to any potential Soviet threat by employing gradual and controlled escalation of military force. With the adoption of the doctrine of flexible response, U.S. policymakers subsequently emphasized the survivability of nuclear retaliatory capability, which, in turn, led to the diversification of the American strategic nuclear force and development of the strategic nuclear triad. As part of the flexible response strategy, U.S. policymakers also stressed the importance of counterinsurgency operations and the development of unconventional military forces, unconventional tactics, and "civic action" programs, all tactics that were used by American forces in the Vietnam War.

Floating Exchange Rate is the system by which the actual value of a currency as compared to other currencies is determined by supply and demand. Under this system global currency markets composed of private investors and governments buy and sell currencies. This system for determining the value of a currency was established in 1973.

Fodder Crops were crops such as turnips that were grown in Europe during the Middle Ages not for human consumption, but to feed animals and to improve the nutrients in the soil.

Folklore is a term used to describe stories, ideas, beliefs, traditions, and sayings that have been transmitted orally or in writing from generation to generation. Witchcraft and magic are examples of folk beliefs. Little Red Riding Hood is an example of a fairy or folk tale. "A bird in hand is better than two in the bush" is an example of a folk saying.

Food Production is the practice of growing crops and raising livestock as opposed to hunting and gathering. Food production made civilizations possible.

Foragers were people who support themselves by hunting wild animals and gathering wild edible plants.

Forbidden City is the name for the walled section of Beijing where the Chinese emperor lived from 1121 to 1924.

Fordism was the term developed by American social critics in the 1930s to describe an industrialized economic system based on the mass production of standardized goods affordable for a mass society, especially the workers who produced such goods. This system, which breaks down complex tasks into its component parts, depends on an assembly line composed of highly specialized machinery operated by unskilled workers. Fordism is based on the methods of improved productivity introduced by Henry Ford's application of mass production to the manufacture of automobiles.

Foreign Assistance is money or other forms of aid made available by governments or international organizations to Third-World states to help them speed up economic development or meet humanitarian needs.

Foreign Direct Investment is the acquisition by residents of one country of control over a new or existing business in another country.

Foreign Policy is a set of political goals that informs how a particular country will interact with the other countries of the world. Foreign policies generally are designed to help protect a country's national interests, national security, ideological goals, and economic prosperity, all of which can be achieved and result in peaceful cooperation, aggression, war, or exploitation.

Forms are the eternal and unchanging absolutes such as truth, justice, goodness, and beauty that were taught by Plato. According to Plato, these forms represent true reality as opposed to the approximations of reality that humans encounter in their everyday lives. They are the perfect models of all things that underlie all worldly objects. Plato argued that any object humans see in daily life is only an imperfect imitation of an object's true form, which cannot be seen but reflects a person's recollections from a previous life.

Fortune's Wheel or Wheel of Fortune was a concept in Roman mythology that referred to the arbitrary and capricious role of fate and destiny in human affairs. In Roman mythology, Fortuna, the Roman goddess of chance and controller of destinies, would spin the wheel at random, causing some humans great misfortune and others great success. This theme would be reflected in the works of such Renaissance writers as Dante, Chaucer, Shakespeare, and Machiavelli.

Forum was a public meeting place in Rome. It was the political and religious center of Rome throughout the Republic and the Empire. All cities in the Roman Empire had a forum imitating the one in Rome.

Four Noble Truths are the foundational ideas of Buddhism, which are: life is pain; pain is caused by desire; elimination of desire will bring an end to pain; and living life based on the Noble Eightfold Path will eliminate desire.

Four Policemen was the name given by President Franklin Roosevelt to the four major allies during World War II (United States, Great Britain, the Soviet Union and the Republic of China, who he argued should work together after World War II to prevent any future wars, guarantee the peace in the international system and maintain stability and order within their respective spheres of influence. Roosevelt's plan required that the United States' sphere of influence would be the Western Hemisphere, Great Britain's would be the Western Europe and its empire, the Soviet Union's would be Eastern Europe and central Asia, and China's would be East Asia and the Western Pacific. In order to prevent future wars and ensure stability in the international system, Roosevelt proposed that all countries in the world would be disarmed except for the Four Policemen. Subsequently, Roosevelt's Four Policemen would become the permanent members of the United Nations Security Council. The fifth member, France, would be added later.

Four Tigers or Four Dragons is the name given to the most successful newly industrialized areas of East Asia: South Korea, Taiwan, Hong Kong, and Singapore.

Fourier, Charles (1772–1837) was a French socialist and philosopher who tried and failed to establish many utopian communities. He created a social system, Fourierism, which was rooted in the idea of harmony of the universe, which was comprised of four parts: the material universe, the animal life, the organic life, and the human society.

Fourteen Points (1918) were the political principles enunciated by President Wilson that he believed should guide the creation of a new international order after World War I. The primary objectives of this new structure for international relations were to prevent another war similar to World War I and to create a lasting peace in the world. This new international order proposed by Wilson was to be based on open diplomacy, free trade, reduced armaments, self-determination for nationalities, and an association of nations to guarantee the peace and territorial integrity of nations, which was to be named the League of Nations.

Fourth Lateran Council (1215) was an ecumenical council ordered by Pope Innocent III to strengthen papal authority over the Church and the clergy, to strengthen the standards governing the Church and the qualifications of the priesthood, to address the issue of the establishment of religious orders without the approval of the Church, and to address the causes and penalties for heresy and dissent. The Council was attended by over 1300 officials of the Church as well as representatives of various European monarchs. It affirmed that the Church was a papal monarchy over which no secular state had power and that kings did not have the right to tax or exercise any judicial authority over the clergy. The Council established stricter qualifications for the priesthood and specifically identified certain behavior by the priesthood that was forbidden, such as hunting, frequenting of pubs, drunkenness, officiating at ordeals or trials by combat or engaging in surgery. The Council also endorsed the doctrine of transubstantiation as the explanation for the Eucharist, defined the sacraments, imposed a yearly obligation of confession and communion on all Christians over eight years old, confirmed marriage as a sacrament, and imposed restrictions on who could be married and under what conditions. The Council imposed stricter standards for the election of bishops and prohibited simony by priests and bishops. Reflecting the increased persecution of the Jews in the Middle Ages, the Council also required that Jews wear special forms of dress to distinguish them from Christians in order to prevent Christian men having relations with Jewish women, prohibited Jews from appearing in public three days before Easter, and encouraged the development of Jewish ghettos to isolate Jews from Christians.

Franchise is the right to vote, which is also known as suffrage.

Francia was the area around Paris that was ruled by the Franks from the 200s to the 900s CE. The name France is derived from it.

Francis of Assisi, Saint (1181–1226) was a Roman Catholic monk and the founder of the Order of Friar Minors, more commonly known as the Franciscans. Supposedly, after hearing a sermon in which Christ tells his followers that they should go forth and proclaim that the Kingdom of Heaven was upon them, that they should take no money with them, Francis was inspired to devote himself wholly to a life of poverty. He renounced his wealth and decided to found a religious community dedicated to engaging in charitable works.

Franciscans, who were also known as the Order of Friars Minor, were a mendicant order of monks founded by Saint Francis of Assisi in 1209 CE who were dedicated to living lives of simplicity, humility, poverty, and imitating the life and example of Jesus. They preached particularly to the poor in the towns and cities of medieval Europe. This order was founded by Pope Innocent III in 1209.

Franco-Prussian War or Franco-German War (1870–1871) was a conflict between France and Prussia that marked the downfall of Napoleon III and the end of the French Second Empire, which was replaced by the Third Republic. This conflict was the culmination of years of tension between the two powers. This war is also known as the Franco-German War or in France as the 1870 War. The German victory in this war facilitated the final unification of the German Empire under King William I of Prussia. As part of the settlement of this war, the territory of Alsace-Lorraine was taken by Germany, which would retain it until World War I. The German forces proved successful because of their efficient use of railroads and artillery. A series of swift German victories in eastern France culminated in the Battle of Sedan, at which Napoleon III was captured with his whole army. Yet this defeat did not end the war, as the Third Republic was declared in Paris and French resistance continued. After a five-month campaign, the German armies defeated the newly recruited French armies in a series of battles fought across northern France. Following a prolonged siege, the French capital Paris fell in January 1871. The final peace Treaty of Frankfurt was signed May 10, 1871, during the time of the bloody Paris Commune of 1871.

Franco-Spanish War (1635–1659) was a military conflict between France and Spain that began with French intervention in 1635 into the Thirty Years' War, in which Spain was already a participant. Warfare between the two kingdoms continued until 1659, when the Treaty of the Pyrenees was signed. For years, France had been a major rival of the House of Habsburg, whose two branches ruled Spain and the Holy Roman Empire, respectively. For much of the 1500s and 1600s, France faced Habsburg territory on three sides—the Spanish Netherlands to the north, the Franche-Comté on its eastern border, and Spain to the south. The Habsburgs thus stood in the way of French territorial expansion, and during a time of conflict, faced the possibility of invasion from multiple fronts. France thus sought to weaken the Habsburg control over these border possessions. During the Thirty Years' War, in which various Protestant forces battled the armies of the

Holy Roman Empire, France provided subsidies to the enemies of the Holy Roman Empire. France supported a Swedish invasion of the Holy Roman Empire after 1630. After some early successes, the Swedish army was decisively defeated in 1634 by a combined Spanish–Holy Roman Empire army, leading to a peace treaty favorable to the Holy Roman Emperor. Unhappy with this outcome, France's First Minister, Cardinal Richelieu, decided in 1635 to actively involve his kingdom in the fighting and declared war on Spain. The French army now tied up Spanish forces in the southern Netherlands. During the last decade of the Thirty Years' War, the Spanish forces in the southern Netherlands were sandwiched between French and Dutch forces. When the Peace of Westphalia was negotiated in 1648 ending the Thirty Years War, France gained the Spanish territory in Alsace.

Frank, Hans (1900–1946) was the legal expert of the Nazi party and Hitler's personal lawyer. Frank was an early supporter of Hitler and participated in the beer hall putsch in 1923. He served as the head of the Government General in Poland from 1939–45. In that official capacity, he controlled Europe's largest Jewish population and oversaw the Nazis' major killing centers in Poland, such as Auschwitz. He was tried at International Military Tribunal at Nuremberg, where he was convicted of crimes against humanity and war crimes. Frank was sentenced to death and hanged in 1946.

Frankfurt National Assembly or Frankfurt Parliament (1848–1849) was a meeting of popularly elected delegates from all of the German states that attempted to create a unified German state under a new liberal constitution and a single monarch. The Assembly drafted a constitution and offered the German throne to Friedrich Wilhelm IV, King of Prussia. He declined that offer, in part, because representatives of the people had offered the office to him. The Assembly was dissolved in 1849.

Franks were Germanic peoples who gradually moved south from the mouth of the Rhine toward Paris. They built a powerful kingdom under the Merovingian and Carolingian families of kings.

Frederick I or Frederick Barbarossa ("Red Bread") (1123–1190) was the king of Germany and Holy Roman Emperor who reigned from 1152 to 1190. During his reign, he resisted papal authority and tried to make Germany the dominant power in Europe. He along with Philip Augustus of France and Richard the Lion-heart of England led the Third Crusade, but he drowned before reaching Palestine. He considered himself heir to the emperors Constantine, Justinian and Charlemagne and viewed the Holy Roman Empire as e successor to the Roman Empire. In order to provide greater finanin cial support for his empire, he invaded the wealthy city states of northern Italy such as Milan, which, while part of his empire, acted independently. In order to resist his claims to rule in northern Italy, the city-states of northern Italy formed an alliance called the Lombard League that was supported by the papacy. He was decisively defeated by the Lombard League at the Battle of Legnano in 1176 and forced to recognize the autonomy of the city-states of northern Italy.

Frederick II (1194–1250) was a German king who reigned from 1212 to 1250 and the Holy Roman Emperor who reigned from 1220 to 1250. He was the grandson of Frederick I. While on a crusade to Palestine from 1227 to 1229, he was able to reconquer Jerusalem, Bethlehem and Nazareth. Believing himself to be the new messiah, he issued a manifesto upon entering Jerusalem that compared himself to Jesus Christ.

Frederick the Great (1740–1786) was the autocratic Prussian ruler who developed a strong military and an efficient governmental bureaucracy in Prussia. He transformed Prussia into a major military power and led the Prussian army to victory in three wars against Austria. He encouraged Enlightenment thinking, artistic efforts, and the study of philosophy, history, poetry, and French literature in Prussia in the 1700s.

Free Economic Zones were established in the southern coastal provinces of China in the 1980s and 1990s that were opened to foreign investment and run on capitalist principles with export-oriented industries.

Free Market is an economic system where goods and services are exchanged in between producers and consumers without government interference or regulations and in quantities and at prices solely dictated by the factors of supply and demand.

Free Trade is the flow of goods, services and investments across national boundaries unimpeded by tariffs or other governmental restrictions. Under this system, market forces determine the prices of goods and services exchanged between countries. It is an essential element of capitalism. Free trade has been a central element of the economic policies of Britain and the United States for the past 200 years. This economic theory, which was developed in Britain in the late 1700s and early 1800s, was influenced by the ideas of Adam Smith. Advocates for free trade argued for the abolition of all tariffs on imports and exports. This economic doctrine was especially popular among industrialists who believed that lowering or ending tariffs would ensure foreign markets for their manufactured goods.

Free Trade Imperialism was the name given to trade policies of the United States and Britain in the late 1800s and early 1900s by various critics of such policies. Those critics argued that the trade policies of the United States and Britain economically dominated the weaker economies of nations in Latin America even though those Latin American nations were sovereign and independent republics.

Free Trade Zone is a geographic area of a county where two or more states have agreed that goods can move freely cross the border of those states without being subject to tariffs, taxes, trade restrictions or any other restrictions that might protect the domestic producers of those goods. It is claimed that a free trade zone would attract foreign corporations who will provide more jobs for the populations of the participating countries.

Freedmsent an was the legal status of slaves in ancient Rome who had been granted their freedom by their owners.

Freemasons is a secret society of men and women that developed during the Enlightenment. This society, which was based on the rituals of stonemason' guilds, provided a place where middle class professionals, nobles, and even artisans could meet to discuss shared interest in the ideas of the Enlightenment and social and political reform. This movement began in Britain and subsequently spread across Europe. It was and still is dedicated to the creation of a society based on reason, virtue, and the principles of liberty and equality.

Freikorps, which means "volunteer troops" in German, was the name for the right-wing paramilitary groups consisting primarily of veterans that existed in Germany after World War I. They fought communist uprisings throughout Germany. The Nazis used the Freikorps as their vanguard in their political struggles in Germany during the 1920s.

French and Indian War (1756–1763), which is also known as the Great War for the Empire or the Seven Years' War, was a conflict between Britain and France for control of North America. With help from the American colonists, the British won this war and eliminated France as a political and military threat in North America.

French Revolution of 1830 was a popular rebellion against King Charles X who had issued the July Ordinances of 1830. These laws denied the right to vote to everyone except the nobility and dissolved the Chamber of Deputies. In response to several days of violence against the July Ordinances, Charles X abdicated and he was replaced by King Louis Philippe I, a constitutional monarch.

French Revolution of 1848 was a revolt that sought to overthrow the reign of King Louis Philippe I, This revolution led to the formation of the Second Republic (1848–1852). Initially, the revolution was supported by the middle class, Parisian workers and the peasantry, who had participated for the first time in an election. After the newly elected government adopted conservative policies, the workers of Paris revolted in June and December 1848. Subsequently, Louis-Napoleon Bonaparte, the nephew of Napoleon Bonaparte, was elected president of the Second Republic. However, the Second Republic was abolished in 1852 by Louis-Na, Germanypoleon when he declared him.r.

French Wars of Religion (1562–1598) were a series of political assassinations, massacres, and military engagements between French Catholics and Calvinist (Huguenots).

Fresco is a technique of painting on walls covered with moist plaster. It was used extensively to decorate Minoan and Mycenaean palaces and Roman villas.

Freud, Sigmund (1856–1939) was an Austrian physician who was the founder of psychoanalysis, a method of treating psychological problems by exploring the unconscious. He argued that people were motivated in part by their unconscious feelings and drives. By emphasizing the role of the unconscious, Freud drew attention to the irrational forces in the human psyche that plays a significant role in human behavior. Freud also argued that psychological problems were caused by traumas in early childhood that were repressed in later life, especially sexual experiences. This idea caused a great deal of controversy among psychologists as well as the general public. While his views on repressed sexuality are no longer widely accepted today, his psychoanalytic methods are still widely accepted.

Friars were "brothers" of mendicant religious orders such as the Franciscans and the Dominicans, who begged for alms in the countryside and in cities during the Middle Ages. They also preached to laypeople and helped the sick, the poor and the outcast.

Friendly Societies were voluntary mutual-aid associations formed by skilled industrial workers in the 1800s in Europe in response to industrialization. The workers, who were members of these societies, pooled their resources to provide financial assistance to any member of the association who faced the possibility of indebtedness resulting from unemployment, job-related accidents, disease, old age or death. These societies represented a growing feeling of group solidarity among skilled industrial workers and contributed to an emerging sense of working class identity.

Fronde (1648–1653), which means sling in French, was a series of aristocratic rebellions against royal absolutism in France. These rebellions challenged royal authority, especially the tax policies of King Louis XIV and Cardinal Mazarin. This civil war in France occurred in the midst of the Franco-Spanish War, which had begun in 1635. The Fronde was divided into two campaigns, the Fronde of the parlements and the Fronde of the nobles. The outbreak of the Fronde of the parlements occurred after the Peace of Westphalia, which ended the Thirty Years War. The primary objective of the rebellions was to protect ancient "liberties" from encroachment by the royal power and to defend the right of the parlements to limit the king's power. The pressure to erode these liberties arose from the king's need to pay for recent wars by increasing taxation. The costs

of the Thirty Years War constrained the ability of Mazarin's government to raise funds by traditional means. The nobility refused to be taxed, based on their conception of "liberties" or privileges, and so the burden of the taxes fell primarily on the bourgeoisie. The movement soon degenerated into factions, some of which attempted to overthrow Mazarin's government, but the revolt failed.

Fuhrer, which is the German word for "leader," was the title taken by Adolf Hitler as head of the Nazi Party after his release from prison in 1925. It would become his formal state title in 1934, after the death of Paul von Hindenburg, president of the Weimar Republic.

Fusion Weapons are extremely destructive, expensive, and technologically sophisticated weapons in which two small atoms fuse together into a larger atom, releasing energy. They are also referred to as "thermonuclear weapons" or "hydrogen bombs."

Futurism was a movement of artists and intellectuals in the late 1800s and early 1900s in Europe who wished to create a new culture free from traditional western civilization. They admired technology, the masses, violence, and upheaval. The Italian fascist movement under Mussolini embraced this movement.

G

Galen of Pergamum (129–216 CE) was an influential Greek physician. He was the court physician during the era of Pax Romana to three Roman emperors: Marcus Aurelius, Commodus and Septimius Severus. His encyclopedic writings on medicine, his dissection and experimentation of animals, his conclusions about the human anatomy and his demonstration that the arteries carried blood not air would influence the theory, teaching and practice of medicine in the Byzantine world, the Muslim world and Europe until the 1800s. In fact, his use of bloodletting as a remedy for many ailments remained an influential medical practice well into the 1800s.

Galileo Galilei (1564–1642) was an Italian mathematician, astronomer, inventor, and physicist who provided evidence supporting Copernicus' heliocentric view of the universe. In 1609, he built a refracting astronomical telescope, which had been invented one year earlier in the Netherlands by a spectacle maker and master lens grinder, to observe the planets. In 1610, he published *Starry Messenger,* which described his observations of Venus and the moons of Jupiter. His observations supported the heliocentric view of the universe first expressed by Nicholas Copernicus. As a result of the publication of his astronomical observations, the Catholic Inquisition charged him with heresy and thesological error in 1633. Condemned by the Catholic Church, he was forced to recant his support for Copernicus and the heliocentric theory of the universe and was placed under house arrest for the rest of his life, during which time he was forbidden from writing. His condemnation by the Catholic Church spurred great popular debate about his ideas. Nevertheless, he completed and smuggled out his writings about the heliocentric theory, which became the foundational work of an emerging new understanding of physics. His astronomical observations and his subsequent scientific discoveries significantly influenced the development of the scientific revolution.

Gallipoli, Battle of (1915) was the decisive victory by the Ottoman Turks during World War I of the Allied invasion of the Gallipoli Peninsula. The Allied invasion force was composed of soldiers from Britain, Australia, New Zealand and France. The Allied invasion of the Gallipoli Peninsula was the first large scale amphibious invasion in history. The Gallipoli Peninsula was of strategic importance to the Allies becaof use it bordered the Dardanelles which connected the Mediterranean Sea with the Black Sea. Two hundred thousand Allied soldiers were killed after seven months of fighting. The plan for the invasion was developed by Winston Churchill, First Lord of the British Admiralty.

Galleon was a large, fast, heavily armed, wind-powered and highly maneuverable sailing ship used primarily for military purposes by European nations between the 1400s–1600s. It was first developed by the Venetians. A galleon had three or four masts which carried square-rigged and lateen sails. As it was multi-decked and heavily armed, it carried two tiers of cannons on both sides of the ship. The

Spanish used galleons as part of their convoys of ships to carry silver from its colonies in the New World to Spain. Galleons were the primary type of warship used by the English and Spanish fleets in 1588 when Spain attempted to invade England.

Galley was a type of ship that was powered by one to three rows of oarsman. The galley was used extensively in the Mediterranean from 8th century BCE to the 1600s CE in both the merchant and naval fleets of the ancient empires of the Egyptians, Assyrians, Phoenicians, Persians, Greeks, Romans, Carthaginians, Byzantines, Muslims and the maritime republics of Venice, Genoa and Pisa. The Phoenicians introduced the bireme with two rows of oarsmen in the 7th century BCE and the Greeks developed the trireme with three rows of oarsmen in the 5th century BCE. The trireme was used by the ancient The Habsburgsks at Battle of Salamis against the Persians and the Romans used it at the Battle of Actium against the combined fleets of Mark Antony and Cleopatra. The decisive defeat of the Ottoman fleet by an allied Christian naval force led by Spain, Venice and Genoa at the Battle of Lepanto in 1571 represented the climax of the age of galleys in the Mediterranean.

Game Theory is a mathematical theory developed by John von Neumann, a mathematician, and Oskar Morgenstern, an economist, which was used extensively by U.S. policymakers and military strategists during the Cold War to evaluate the range of choices made in a decision-making situations, where a choice by one state affects the actions of another state. They argued that each party in a decision-making situation knows its respective range of options and payoffs associated with each specific decision.

Gandhi, Mohandas K. (Mahatma) (1869–1948) was an Indian nationalist political leader who advocated aggressive mass nonviolent resistance to British colonial rule in India. His tactics helped India gain independence in 1947. After being educated as a lawyer in Britain, he returned to India to become leader of the Indian National Congress in the 1920s. He appealed to the poor of India, led large nonviolent demonstrations against British colonial rule, and was jailed many times for his political activities. He was assassinated soon after India gained independence from the British because he attempted to stop the rioting and killing between Hindus and Muslims.

Gang of Four refers to the radical followers of Mao Zedong in China who in the 1970s advocated an anti-bureaucratic vision for the Chinese Communist Party and sought to seize control of the Chinese government. Mao's wife Jiang Qing led the Gang of Four. Following the death of Mao Zedong, the Gang of Four was arrested and sentenced to life **1807–1882)** was an Italian nationalist political leader who led the revolutionary fight to free Sicily and Naples from the Habsburg Empire. Those lands along with Sardinia would be combined in 1860 to form a unified Italy.

Gas Chambers were buildings constructed by the Nazis at six extermination camps (Auschwitz, Belzec, Chełmno, Majdanek, Sobibor and Treblinka) which were comprised of an anteroom, a gas chamber that could hold approximately 2,000 individuals and a crematorium. The six extermination camps were responsible for the mass murder of approximately three million European Jews. All prisoners arrived by train at the six extermination camps. Except for those prisoners who were selected to work at slave labor camps, the majority of prisoners were taken directly to a reception area where their possessions were seized by the Nazis and they were informed that they were required to take a shower. In the anteroom to the gas chamber the prisoners were forced to undress and enter a large room with shower heads. The door to the "shower room" was sealed and poisonous Zyklon B gas was released from the shower heads. When all the victims were dead, the corpses were wheeled to the crematorium and burned. This method of mass, industrialized extermination was considered by the Nazis to be the most efficient and inexpensive means to achieve their objective of the "final solution to the Jewish question".

Gaul was a region of the Roman Empire today comprised of modern France, Belgium and western Germany. This region of the Roman Empire was the home of the Celtic people, who defeated a Roman army and sacked Rome in 390 CE. Gauls was the Roman name for the Celts.

Gaugamela, Battle of (331 BCE) was the second decisive defeat of King Darius III, the last king of the Achaemenid dynasty of Persia, by Alexander the Great.

Gdansk Shipyard (1980) was the site of a mass strike by shipyard workers in Poland that led to the formation of the first independent trade union, Solidarity, among the nations of the communist bloc in Europe.

Gender implies those aspects of one's sexual identity that are biological in nature.

General Agreement on Tariffs and Trade (GATT) (1947) was a group of multilateral trade agreements entered into by 23 nations that sought to increase international trade by reducing tariff barriers and restrictions and subsidies on trade. GATT was initially considered a temporary arrangement until a more permanent international trade organization could be established. Between 1947 and 1993, seven subsequent trade conferences were held by the signatory states to negotiate further tariff reductions and to resolve issues affecting certain commodities and the trade practices of certain states. As a result of these subsequent negotiations, GATT played a central role in the dramatic increase in international trade in the post-World War II period. GATT was subsequently replaced by thecWorld Tlade Organization in 1995.

General Strike is a coordinated refusal to work by all of or most of ton workers in a society. Georges Sorel espoused this idea in the 1800s as a political action that could be used by the workers to destroy capitalist society.

General War is a conflict designed to conquer and occupy enemy territory by using all available weapons of warfare. In a general war both military targets and civilian facilities are targeted.

General Will was Jean Jacque Rousseau's concept of popular consensus under which individual interests are subordinated to the public good.

Generation Gap refers to the difference between the more liberal social, political, and cultural values of a generation of people who came of age in the 1960s and the more conservative or traditional values of their parents.

Geneva Accords (1988) was the agreement by the Soviet Union, United States, Afghanistan, and

Pakistan that required the Soviets to withdraw their troops from Afghanistan by February 1989.

Geneva Conference (1954) was an international conference held in Geneva, Switzerland to negotiate an end to the Korean War and the First Indochina War between the French and the Viet Minh and to determine the future of Vietnam. This conference followed the decisive defeat of French colonial forces at Dien Bien Phu by the Viet Minh. Representatives of Cambodia, the People's Republic of China, France, Laos, the United Kingdom, the United States, the Soviet Union, the State of Vietnam (South Vietnam) and the Democratic Republic of Vietnam (North Vietnam) attended the conference. The conference resulted in an armistice agreement known as the Geneva Accords by which Vietnam was temporarily divided along the 17th parallel into North and South Vietnam until free elections could be held throughout the country in 1956 to reunify the country. The Accords further mandated that northern part of Vietnam would become the Democratic Republic of Vietnam under Ho Chi Minh and the southern part would become the State of Vietnam under Emperor Bao Dai. The United States did not support the accords and worked to undercut them. Believing that the Accords gave too much power to the Vietnamese communists, the United States supported the creation of an anti-communist alternative in the south. Subsequently, Ngo Dinh Diem, who had been Foreign Minister under Emperor Bao Dai and was staunchly anti-communist, defeated Bao Dai in a controversial election. He ousted Emperor Bao Dai and made himself the president of the Republic of Vietnam, which was the successor to the French-created State of Vietnam. Diem, who was financially and militarily supported by the United States in its efforts to oppose the Communist government of North Vietnam, refused to hold the elections in 1956 to establish a national government as required by the Accords. Diem's refusal to implement the national elections required by the Accords is one of the major factors that led to the Second Indochina War, which would be waged by the U.S. from 1963 to 1973.

Genghis Khan (Temujin) (1162–1227), which means "universal ruler," was the founder of the Mongol Empire and ruled the Mongols from 1206 to 1227. The Mongol Empire was the largest land empire in world history. By the time of his death, it stretched from the Pacific Ocean to the Black Sea and from Siberia to Southeast Asia.

Genocide is the intentional and systematic, and in certain cases state-sponsored, extermination of an ethnic, religious, racial, or national group, in whole or in part. The term was first coined by Raphael Lemkin in 1944 to describe the Nazis' extermination of the Jews of Europe. Lemkin, a Polish Jew, lost 72 of the 74 members of his family in the Holocaust. Genocide was made a crime under international law by the United Nations General Assembly when it adopted the Convention on the Prevention and Punishment of the Crime of Genocide (Genocide Convention) in 1948. The Genocide Convention was passed in response to the Armenian Genocide by the Ottoman Empire during World War I and the Holocaust by Nazi Germany during World War II. The first time the Genocide Convention was enforced occurred in 1998 when the International Criminal Court found the former mayor of a Rwandan town guilty of genocide. In 2007, the International Criminal Court subsequently found that Serbia had breached the Genocide Convention for failing to prevent genocide in Srebrenica in 1995 during the Bosnian War. While the United States played a major role in drafting the Genocide Convention and was one of the original signatories of it, the United States Senate did not ratify the Genocide Convention until 1988. Since 1948, the Genocide Convention has been ratified by more than 130 countries.

Gens was a clan or group of families in ancient Rome who shared a common name derived from a common male ancestor. The relationship of various gens was a major factor in ancient Roman politics with members of the same genes generally being political allies. In ancient Rome, names had three parts, the second name referred to the gens to which an individual belonged.

Gentlemen's Agreement (1907) was an agreement between the United States and Japan negotiated by President Theodore Roosevelt that sought to reduce growing tensions between the two countries concerning the increasing immigration of Japanese workers to the United States. In the late 1800s, Japanese workers were first recruited by American businessmen to emigrate to the United States. As a result of this development, the United States entered into a treaty with Japan in 1894 that assured Japan of the continued free immigration of Japanese workers to the United States. Nevertheless, Japanese workers were met with widespread hostility, bias and discrimination by Californians who believed that the Japanese workers would depress wages and buy good farmland. Racial tensions in California significantly intensified after the formation of the Japanese and Korean Exclusion League, which claimed that Japanese workers were a "menace" who should be excluded from emigrating to the United States and the decision by the San Francisco Board of Education that required children of Japanese parents to be segregated in schools from white students. The relations between the United States and Japan were further strained by Japan's decisive military victory in 1905 of Russia in the Russo-Japanese War, which was viewed by American policymakers as a threat to American economic and military interests in the Pacific. Under the terms of the Gentlemen's Agreement, Japan would cease issuing passports to Japanese workers who sought to emigrate to the United States. In turn, President Roosevelt persuaded the San Francisco Board of Education to rescind its order segregating Japanese students from white students in its schools. While the U.S. Congress did not transform the Gentlemen's Agreement into a law, the agreement was nullified by the passage of the Immigration Act of 1924, which specifically excluded, in part, any further Japanese immigration to the United States.

Gentile is a Jewish term for non-Jews. Paul helped spread Christianity by not distinguishing between Jews and Gentiles. The crucial question facing Paul in the New Testament was whether Gentiles could be allowed to become Christians without first converting to Judaism.

Gentry is the name of a class of wealthy, educated, and socially ambitious rural land-owning families in England who formed a unique social group. Their status was just below that of the nobility. They adopted the traditional values and customs of the nobility and supported the monarchy. The gentry played an important role in the English Civil Wars (1642–1651).

Geocentric Theory is a system of astronomy in which the earth is the center of the universe and the sun and other celestial objects revolve around the earth. This conception of the universe was first developed in the 6th century BCE by Anaximander, a Pre-Socratic Greek philosopher who lived in Miletus in Ionia. In the 4th century BCE, both Plato and Aristotle advocated the geocentric model of the universe. Ptolemy of Alexandria (85–165 BCE), an ancient Greek astronomer, mathematician, and geographer, articulated the most highly developed version of the geocentric theory in the 100s CE. The geocentric model of the universe dominated European thinking until the 1500s when the heliocentric theory of the universe was first articulated by Nicolaus Copernicus, a polish monk and astronomer.

Geopolitics is the study of the geographical distribution of economic and military power among states in the international system. This approach focuses on the rivalry among the major economic and military powers in the world. Geopolitics is based on the assumption that certain areas of the world are more valuable because of their strategic political, economic, and military importance. Any disputes among the great economic and military powers over territorial expansion may lead to the use of military force to resolve such disputes.

Germ Theory was the scientific theory advanced by Louis Pasteur in the mid-1800s in France that microscopic organisms, such as bacteria and viruses caused the spread of many diseases. He also developed the process of pasteurization and the anthrax and rabies vaccines.

German Confederation (1815–1866) was the alliance of German states established at the Congress of Vienna that replaced the Holy Roman Empire.

German Democratic Republic (GDR) (1949–1990) was the nation created after World War II from the Soviet zone of occupation in Germany, which was also known as East Germany.

German-Soviet Non-Aggression Pact (1939) was the agreement Stalin and Hitler signed in August 1939 after Stalin decided he needed to buy time against a possible Nazi invasion. Under this agreement, each side would remain neutral if either nation got into a war with another nation. This pact allowed Germany and the Soviet Union to divide Poland between themselves and the Soviet Union to attack the Baltic states. Shortly after the signing of this agreement, the German invaded Poland on September 1, 1939, which was the beginning of World War II in Europe.

Gestapo (German name Geheime Staats Polizei) was the Nazi Secret State Police that was established in 1933 by Herman Goring. Its primary purpose was to enforce Nazi totalitarian rule. It did so by arresting and persecuting the Jews and political opponents in Germany and Nazi occupied Europe. Under the direction of Heinrich Himmler, the Gestapo played a significant role in the "Final Solution".

Ghetto was a segregated section within a community in Europe where Jews were legally required to live. The rulers of Venice established the first European ghetto in 1516 in Venice on the site of an iron foundry. The Nazis revived the term "ghetto" to designate a walled community in the poor sections of eastern European cities such as Lodz, Warsaw, Vilna, Riga, and Minsk, where all the Jews living in the surrounding areas were transported and forced to live. Non-Jews had previously been evicted from these areas. The ghettos were surrounded by barbed wire or walls and were sealed so that no one could legally leave. The ghettos were vastly overcrowded; food was scarce and sanitation poor; disease and starvation killed hundreds daily. These ghettos served as collection centers and facilitated the subsequent deportations of the Jews to the death camps. Today, the term is used more broadly to indicate an area of an American city where specific low-income groups, such as African-Americans and Hispanics, are segregated.

Giap, Vo Nguyen (General) (1912–2013) is the Vietnamese political and military leader whose use of guerrilla and conventional military tactics led the Viet Minh and later the National Liberation Front and North Vietnam to victory over the French in the First Indochina War (1946–1954) and US in the Second Indochina War (1955–1973).

Gilgamesh of Uruk is the main character and hero in a Sumerian epic poem, *The Epic of Gilgamesh*, which had been transmitted orally for over 1000 years and was first written down around 2000 BCE This epic poem included the story of the "Great Flood". Gilgamesh was the legendary Sumerian king of the Mesopotamian city-state of Uruk, which existed circa 2700 BCE. He was a powerful ruler who, along with his friend Enkidu, battled monsters and gods and searched for immortality.

Girondins were the more moderate faction of French revolutionaries in the National Legislative Assembly and the National Convention during the French Revolution, many of whom came from the Gironde district in Bordeaux region of France. While many Girondins supported liberal economics and representative democracy, they were opposed to direct democracy. They were members of the Jacobin Club who dominated the National Legislative Assembly when it began to meet in 1791. They advocated a constitutional monarchy, greater economic freedom, and opposed any further centralization of state power during the Revolution. Their support for a more moderate course for the French Revolution put them in conflict with the more politically radical Jacobins. They were purged from the National Convention in 1793 and many were executed during the Reign of Terror.

Gladiators were criminals, convicts, slaves, and sometimes freemen from throughout the Roman Empire who were sentenced to fight each other or wild animals to the death in Roman arenas as public entertainment.

Glasnost, which is the Russian term for "openness," was the policy initiated by Mikhail Gorbachev in the Soviet in the late 1980s that provided increased opportunities for freedom of speech, association, and the press in the Soviet Union. By introducing this policy, Gorbachev called for greater transparency in the operation of the Soviet governmental institutions, a reduction of censorship in the mass media in the Soviet Union and a dramatic reduction of exiting bans on the political, intellectual and cultural lives of Soviet citizens. As a result of Gorbachev's policy of "Glasnost", public social and political criticism of Soviet society became more pervasive and freer dissemination of news and information emerged.

Global Commons is a term used in international relations to describe those areas of the world and resources that are governed by no sovereign nation and are considered to be the responsibility of the entire world. The Global Commons includes the oceans beyond the 200 mile limit, outer space and Antarctica.

Global Warming is the process by which the increased emission of greenhouse gases produced by burning fossil fuels, such as oil, coal and natural, prevents solar heat from escaping the earth's lower atmosphere, which in turn leads to the gradual rise in the surface temperatures of the earth. The increasing concentration of greenhouse gases, such as carbon dioxide, chlorofluorocarbons methane gas and nitrous oxide, in the atmosphere is known as the greenhouse effect. There currently exists a consensus among climate scientists that global warming is caused by human activities.

Globalization is the term used to describe the political, social, economic, and cultural processes and networks that have emerged in the late 1990s as a result of the growing interdependence and interconnectedness of the world. Global exchanges within these networks are not limited by nation-states and often rely upon new information technologies, international laws and organizations, and economic forces. As a result of globalization, the traditional boundaries of the nation-states have been broken down by global cultural trends as well as global financial transactions. Nevertheless, since the development of the first civilizations in ancient Mesopotamia and Egypt, human societies have interacted culturally and economically and adopted new ideas and technologies as a result of trade with one another overtime.

Glorious Revolution (1688–1689) was the coup by the Tories and the Whigs that overthrew the Catholic King James II of England. He was peacefully replaced by Parliament with Mary, who was the Protestant daughter of King James II, and her husband, the popular Dutch ruler William of Orange. Parliament imposed on the new sovereigns a Bill of Rights that confirmed Parliament's power and protected freedom of speech. The Glorious Revolution marked the beginning of constitutional monarchy in Britain in which Parliament had sovereign authority over the king. It was called "glorious" because the overthrow of the king was achieved without violence. The political changes brought about by the Glorious Revolution contributed significantly to the economic and commercial growth in Britain during the late 1600s and 1700s.

Gnostics were early Christians who claimed that they had secret knowledge of God and the universe. They believed that elements of the divine had become entrapped in the evil material world. They argued that these divine elements could be released only by acquiring the secret gnosis or hidden truth, which was a way of releasing spiritual reality from the prison of the evil material world. The bishops of the early Christian Church opposed the Gnostics.

Goa was an island on the west coast of India on the Arabian Sea that was captured by Admiral Alfonso de Albuquerque in the early 1500s in order to control the lucrative spice trade in Asia. Goa was the first territorial acquisition of the Portuguese in Asia, where they subsequently established a colonial settlement and a naval base. Goa would later become the capital of the Portuguese Empire in Asia.

Gobineau, Joseph-Arthur (1816–1882) was a French writer whose pseudoscientific, racist Ideology provided a rationale for European imperialism in Africa and Asia in the late 1800s. He claimed that the white race was superior to all other races in the world and that the German people, who he designated as "Aryans", represented the highest level of civilization.

Goebbels, Joseph (1897–1945) joined the Nazi party in 1924 and became the party's chief of propaganda in 1930. He was responsible for building support for the Nazis among the general population. After Hitler's rise to power in 1933, Goebbels became the minister of propaganda and public information. He controlled the media and oversaw the "Nazification" of public discourse and written materials. He supervised the publication of *Der Stürmer* and conducted the propaganda campaign against the Jews. He was responsible for the book burning of May 10, 1933. On the day following Hitler's death, Goebbels and his wife committed suicide in Hitler's bunker, after first ordering the murder of their six children, all under the age of thirteen.

Gobekli Tepe is a Neolithic archaeological site in southeastern Turkey that consists of a series of circular structures built on top of a hill. Archaeologists believe that these structures were used for ritual or religious purposes and were probably built by hunter/gathers in the 9th and 10th millennium BCE, 6000 years before the construction of Stonehenge in England. While archaeologists have found twenty round structures, they have excavated only four. Each of those four structures contains T-shaped limestone pillars, some of which are up to 16 feet in height and weigh between 7 and 10 tons. Two of the pillars are in the middle of the structures and up to eight pillars are placed evenly around the walls of the structures. Each circular structure has roughly the same layout. Carved on the surface of the pillars are animals and abstract symbols. Once one of the circular structures was completed, it was covered with dirt and the hunter/gathers built a new circular structure on top of the old one. In order to build these structures, the hunter/gathers used stone hammers and blades and flint tools. Archaeologists found no evidence of a settlement at Gobekli Tete.

Goering, Herman (1893–1946) joined the Nazi party in 1922 and took part in the Beer Hall Putsch of 1923. He was one of the men responsible for creating the Gestapo and was the commander of the German Luftwaffe (air force). Göring also supervised the confiscation and administration of Jewish wealth. He was tried and sentenced to death at the Nuremberg trials, but he poisoned himself in his cell before the sentence could be carried out.

Gold Coast was the name given by European merchants, slave traders and government officials to that part of Western Africa on the coast of the Gulf of Guinea from which gold and slaves were exported between the 1400s and 1800s. While this area was originally controlled by the Portuguese, it was subject to intense competition by the Dutch and the British. The Gold Coast was acquired by the British from the Dutch in 1871. In 1957, the Gold Coast declared its independence from the United Kingdom and established the nation of Ghana.

Gold Standard was a monetary system that was introduced by Great Britain in 1821. Under this system, the value of a national currency was pegged to the value of gold and the central bank of a country was required to exchange gold for its currency. In the wake of the Great Depression, the gold standard was abandoned by most countries.

Golden Bull (1356) was the edict of the Holy Roman Emperor Charles IV that established the method for electing a new emperor of the Holy Roman Empire. It acknowledged the political autonomy of Germany's seven regional princes and created a seven-member body of German princes that would select the Holy Roman Emperor.

Golden Horde was the name of one of the four Mongol tribes that ruled a territory much of which today constitutes south central Russia. This part of the Mongol Empire, which was established after the death of Genghis Khan, was ruled by his grandson, Batu.

Goliard was a wandering student or cleric in the 1100s and 1200s in England, France and Germany who drank, gambled and wrote satirical poems about the Catholic Church, the papacy and political leaders. They also wrote graphic love poems and songs about drinking wine, sexual love, debauchery and hedonism.

Gorbachev, Mikhail (1931–present) was the General Secretary of the Communist Party in the Soviet Union who, beginning in 1985, attempted to reform the communist system in the Soviet Union through arms reduction, liberalization in the states of Eastern Europe, glasnost or openness to discussion and criticism, and perestroika or economic restructuring. These measures subsequently failed and Gorbachev presided over the end of communism in the Soviet Union.

Gosplan (1921) was the agency established in the Soviet Union to administer the Five-Year Plans developed by Stalin. It determined production schedules, prices, and the allocation of resources.

Gothic is a style of architecture dominant in Europe from the 1200s to the early 1500s that was characterized by pointed arches, ribbed vaults, and large, stained-glass windows that tended to draw the eyes of worshippers in churches upward toward God. The Cathedral of Notre Dame in Paris is an example of Gothic architecture.

Goths were Germanic tribes that originated in Scandinavia and began to attack the frontier of the Roman Empire along the Danube during the reign of Marcus Aurelius in the mid-200s CE. After 395, they split into two groups: the Visigoths who settled in southern Gaul and Spain and the Ostrogoths who settled in Italy. The Goths converted to Arian Christianity between 340 and 350 and passed their Arian faith to other Germanic tribes, such as the Vandals. After defeating an Eastern Roman army at the Battle of Adrianople in 378, Theodosius I, the emperor of the Eastern Roman Empire hired them as a mercenary army to protect the borders of the Eastern Roman Empire.

Government is a form of social organization that has the power to make and enforce laws for a certain territory. Governments concern themselves with overseeing and administering many areas of human activity, such as economics, education, health, science, and war. Governments use a variety of methods to maintain support and legitimacy for the established political order. Governments will organize and control police and military forces, make agreements with other states, provide a justice system, administer social welfare programs, and hold elections to name a few of its functions.

Goya, Francisco (1746–1828) was a Spanish artist who painted for three Spanish kings. He is considered to be the first modern painters because of his use of abstract concepts. His works subsequently influenced such later artists as Pablo Picasso and Edouard Manet.

Gracchi Brothers refers to Tiberius and Gaius Gracchus, who were tribunes in Rome and were popular political leaders. They led a political faction in Rome named after them. Both brothers challenged the conservative Senate on behalf of the poor. Their patrician political enemies murdered them both.

Grace is a key term used in Christian theology by Paul meaning both divine mercy and divine favor. Augustine interpreted this term to mean the inner help of God in healing the disease of sin and strengthening the soul to do good. The doctrine of grace is crucial for Aquinas, Luther, and Calvin.

Graffiti refers to writings, inscriptions, drawings or paintings on public buildings and monuments or the walls of homes and businesses that express some form of social criticism. Graffiti was commonly used in ancient Rome to express in very explicit and graphic terms social, political and cultural dissatisfaction, to attack public figures or to make fun of well-known individuals. The first known example of "modern style" graffiti survives in the ancient Greek city of Ephesus (in modern-day Turkey) and appears to advertise prostitution, according to the tour guides of the city. The Romans carved graffiti into their own walls and monuments. The eruption of Vesuvius preserved graffiti carved on the walls of Pompeii.

Grand Canal (581–618 CE) was the 1,104-mile waterway in China that linked the Chinese population in the north along the Huang He (Yellow River) with the Chinese population in the south along the Yangzi River. It went from Beijing to Hangzhou. The Grand Canal was begun during the 5th century BCE and completed during the Sui Dynasty in the 7th century BCE.

Grand Jury was created in medieval England as a result of the judicial reforms initiated by Henry II. When a circuit judged arrived in a village, the local sheriff would assemble a group of men familiar with local affairs who would constitute the grand jury and report to the judge the major crimes that had been committed since the judge's last visit.

Granicus, Battle of (334 BCE) was the first major battle fought by Alexander the Great as part of his invasion of the Persian Empire. He decisively defeated the Persian forces. He would go on to fight two other major battles at Issus and Gaugamela before he defeated the Persian arm at Persepolis, the capital of the Persian Empire. After the battle, Alexander looted and destroyed Persepolis.

Gravitation, Universal Law of (1687) is the law of physics that was developed by Sir Isaac Newton in 1687 holding that everybody in the universe attracts every other body in the universe in a precise mathematical relationship. Thus, according to Newton, the force of attraction of any two bodies is directly proportional to product of their masses and inversely proportional to the square of the distance between them.

Great Chain of Being was a hierarchical form of social organization that was first developed by the Roman philosopher Plotinus in the 3rd century CE. In developing this form of social organization, he drew upon concepts from Plato and Aristotle. This view of an ordered universe in which everything has its appropriate place was influential on Western European thought until the early 1800s, but it was especially influential among Neoplatonist thinkers during the Renaissance. According to this view, the universe was divinely inspired, complete, immutable, and hierarchical, with every animate and inanimate object in the universe ranked according in its proper place. The ranking of an object in this universal order depended on the relative proportion of "spirit" and "matter" it contained. If an object has less "spirit" and more "matter", it ranked toward the lower end of the hierarchy. Thus, at the bottom of the hierarchy were such inanimate objects as dirt, rocks, minerals, and stones, for example. Above these objects were plants, trees, animals, humans, and angels, which had more "spirit" and less "matter." At the very top of the hierarchy was a supreme being. The specific rankings were described by St. Aquinas in the following descending order: God; Angels; Kings/Queens/Popes; Archbishops; Dukes/ Duchesses; Bishops Marquises/Marchionesses; Earls/Countesses; Viscounts/Vis-countesses; Barons/Baronesses; Abbots/Deacons/ Knights; Ladies-in-Waiting; Priests/Monks; Squires; Pages; Messengers; Merchants/Shopkeepers; Tradesmen; Yeoman Farmers; Soldiers; Household Servants; Tenant Farmers; Shepherds/Herders; Beggars; Actors; Thieves/Pirates; Gypsies; Animals; Birds; Worms; Plants; and Minerals/Rocks/Dirt.

Great Depression (1929–1941) was a prolonged period of worldwide economic crisis that began with the collapse of the New York Stock Exchange in October 29, 1929 (Black Tuesday). It witnessed a calamitous drop in prices and production and high unemployment. It devastated the global economy for over a decade during the 1930s until the beginning of World War II. Today, it is widely accepted that over production and under consumption as well as speculation were the primary causes for the Great Depression

Great Depression in Trade and Agriculture was the serious downturn in prices and profits, particularly in the agricultural sector, in Europe from 1873 through the 1880s.

Great Famine (1315–1322) was an extensive famine that affected northern Europe after a period of uncommonly heavy rain that killed the crops (wheat, barley and rye) on which peasants, urban dwellers and the poor depended. The effect of the famine was compounded by a disease that killed farm animals, which were an important source of meat, fleece and labor. As a result of the scarcity of food caused by the famine, the prices of ordinary food rose dramatically. Some merchants, nobility and wealthy peasants profited greatly from the high prices they could charge for food.

Great Fear (1789) is a term used by historians to describe the panic in the French countryside that arose among the peasants following the outbreak of the French Revolution. The peasants believed that an aristocratic plot existed to pay beggars and vagrants to burn the peasant's crops and barns. In response, the peasants formed local militias, attacked the local aristocrats and burned records of the feudal dues owed by the peasants to the local nobility.

Great Game (1813–1917) was a term used by Europeans to describe the geopolitical rivalry and strategic conflict between the British Empire and the Russian Empire during the 1800s for domination and control of Central Asia. This concept was created by Rudyard Kipling in his novel *Kim*, published in 1901.

Great Ice Age or Pleistocene Epoch was the geological era that occurred between 2.5 million years ago and 11,700 years ago. As a result of climate shifts, large numbers of new species evolved during this period.

Great Leap Forward (1958–1959) was the economic plan launched by Mao Zedong in China that sought to dramatically increase agricultural and industrial production. This plan required each town to build its own factories and establish People's Communes in which tens of thousands of farming households were joined into a single production unit. However, widespread food shortages and famine occurred in China due to inadequate planning and bad weather.

Great Man Theory of History refers to the belief among some historians that certain great figures in history have been the most important forces in the evolution of human societies. Historians who follow this approach primarily study those few exceptional persons who they believe have had the greatest influence in changing the world.

Great Migration (1835–1840) was the migration of Boer settlers (Voortrekkers) in the British Cape Colony (present day South Africa and Namibia) to escape the influence of British colonial rule. They left the British dominated areas in the south in order to establish their own independent settlements in the Orange River and Natal regions in the north. One of the factors that contributed to this migration was the British emancipation of the slaves owned by the Boers. The Boers believed that the British were too liberal in their treatment of blacks in the Cape Colony and viewed the freeing of the slaves as meddling in private affairs of the Boers.

Great Patriotic War, The (1941–1945) was the term used by Josef Stalin during World War II to unite Soviet citizens against the German invasion. He appealed to the sense of Russian nationalism and past heroic efforts by the Russian people to resist foreign invasion rather than communist ideology.

Great Powers were the most powerful economic and military states in the world from the 1700s until at least 1918 that had the ability to shape world affairs. As a result of their economic and military power, they dominated international politics and contributed to defining the rules and customs of the international system. During the 1700s and early 1800s, the Great Powers were comprised of Britain, France, Austria-Hungary, Russia, Germany, but the United States and Japan were included among the "Great Powers" by the late 1800s.

Great Purges (also known as the Great Terror) (1934–1939) refers to a series of mass arrests, imprisonments, and executions of millions of Soviet citizens, particularly Communist Party members, by Stalin between 1934 and 1939. During the purges, approximately a million and a half people were deported to labor camps (gulags). The purges enabled Stalin to consolidate his dictatorial rule over the Soviet Union by removing from positions of political influence all of his enemies.

Great Reform Bill or Reform Act (1832) was legislation passed by the British Parliament that expanded the electorate to include a wider number of property owners, that is, men of the middle class. It resulted in a 50 percent increase in those eligible to vote and thus laid the groundwork for other reforms of the British constitutional system. It provided parliamentary seats for new urban areas that had not been previously represented in Parliament. This law was viewed by the middle class as major political victory over the aristocracy.

Great Schism or East-West Schism (1054) refers to the division of the Christian Church into the Latin Catholic Church and the Greek Orthodox Church.

Great Schism (1378–1417) refers to the period in the history of the Catholic Church when it was divided between rival Italian and French claimants to the papal throne. One pope was located in Rome and the other in Avignon, France. The schism was ended by the Council of Constance (1414–1418), which elected Pope Martin V as the new pope. The schism damaged the image of the pope and weakened the legitimacy of the Catholic Church among many Christians across Europe.

Great Society was the phrase used to describe the domestic U.S. social programs initiated by President Lyndon Johnson in the 1960s that included civil rights legislation, improved health care, and a general "war on poverty".

Great War, The (1914–1918) was the original name given by the Allies to World War I.

Great White Fleet (1907–1909) was the name for the sixteen U.S. battleships and their escorts that made a circumnavigation of the world (43,000 miles) from December 16, 1907, to February 22, 1909, by order of President Theodore Roosevelt. He wanted to demonstrate to his country and the world that the U.S. Navy was capable of operating in a global theater, particularly in the Pacific. This display of military power was important at a time because tensions were growing between the United States and Japan, which had recently defeated the Russian navy in the Russo-Japanese War.

Greater East Asia Co-Prosperity Sphere (1940–1945) was a concept created by the Japanese government and military during the 1930s to justify their occupation of Asian countries and exploitation of the economies of those nations for the benefit of the Japanese Empire.

Greek War of Independence or Greek Revolution (1821–1829) was the nationalist rebellion for independence in Ottoman Empire. After Egypt came to the aid of the Ottoman Empire in order to crush the revolt, widespread sympathy for the Greek war of independence grew throughout Europe. The Greek revolutionaries were subsequently aided by British, French and Russian troops in their successful war against the Ottoman Empire.

Greek Fire was a mixture of petroleum, sulfur, saltpeter, and lime that ignited on contact with water. It was invented by Callimachus and was first used by the Byzantines in their defense of Constantinople in 678.

Green Movement is a political environmentalist movement that began in West Germany in the 1970s and has subsequently spread to a number of industrialized nations in Europe as well as the United States.

Green Revolution is a term used to describe the international effort that emerged in the late 1960s to reduce world hunger by increasing agricultural productivity, primarily in Third World countries. This global initiative involved the use of high-yielding varieties of wheat and rice seeds, chemical fertilizers, plant disease and pest control, plant breeding, and the use of tractors.

Gregorian Reform was the movement for the Catholic Church reform that included clerical celibacy and an end to lay investiture that was initiated by Pope Gregory VII in the 11th century.

Gregory I, Pope (540–604), who was also known as Gregory the Great, was the pope who, as the first bishop of Rome, facilitated a more universal role for the papacy. He used his political influence and theological teachings to widen the rift between the western Latin (Catholic) Church and the eastern Greek Orthodox Church. Pope Gregory sent missionaries to Anglo-Saxon England and wrote influential books. He ruled Rome as a temporary ruler in the absence of effective secular Roman political rule. Pope Gregory articulated the Church's official position on Jews. He also supported the development of the Benedictine monastic movement and encouraged missionary expeditions.

Gregory VII, Pope (1073–1085) initiated a new conception of the Catholic Church and the role of the papacy within it. He initiated a movement to reform the Catholic Church that would become known as the "Gregorian reforms". Gregory asserted that the Church was required to create "right order in the world" rather than withdraw from it. To that end, he issued papal bulls that urged Christian princes in Europe to recover the lands in Spain controlled by Muslims. Gregory also claimed the right to create a "papal monarchy" with moral authority over the secular state. These claims and others were articulated in his *Dictates of the Pope*. In that document he further asserted the supremacy of the pope over the entire Church including the eastern branch; the right to organize a diocese; the right to be the final judge in all ecclesiastical cases; the claim to be exempt from human judgment; the power to issue canon law; and papal supremacy over all secular political leaders. In essence, Gregory claimed that the papacy was the final judge in all matters that arose in the feudal system in Europe during the Middle Ages. Finally, as part of his reform efforts, Pope Gregory also ended three controversial practices: the purchase of church offices, clerical marriages and lay investiture.

Gross Domestic Product (GDP) is the total value of a nation's annual production of goods and services, excluding exports and imports

Gross National Income-Per Capita (GDI) is derived by dividing a nation's income by its total population.

Gross National Product (GNP) is the total value of a nation's annual production of goods and services, including exports and imports

Grossdeutschland was the German word for the political position adopted by certain liberal German nationalists meeting in Frankfurt, Germany during the Revolution of 1848. They contended that the German-speaking portions of the Habsburg Empire should be included in a greater, united Germany.

Group of 8 (G-8) (1975) was an informal association of the world's eight largest economies (United States, Japan, Russia, Germany, France, Britain, Italy, and Canada) in the world that began to meet in the 1970s for the purpose of coordinating economic policies. Excluded were China and Brazil, whose economies, in terms of gross domestic product, would rank them today as the 2nd and 6th largest economies in the world. Although these eight countries represented about 60 percent of the world economy, the majority of global military power and almost all active nuclear weapons, they only represented about 14 percent of the world population. In 2007, the combined G-8 military spending was $850 billion, which was 72 percent of the world's total military expenditures. Four of the G-8 members—the United Kingdom, the United States, France, and Russia—together account for 96 to 99 percent of the world's nuclear weapons. With the exclusion of China and Brazil, the G-8 no longer represents the concentration of economic power it once did when the G-8 was created in 1975. The lack of representation by the China and Brazil has caused many critics to label the G-8 as an institution that continued Western economic domination of the international economic and financial system. In 2009, the Group of 8 was replaced by the G-20 as the primary economic council of the world's wealthiest nations. In 2014, the G-8 became the G-7 when Russia was suspended from the group. Russia formally withdrew from the G-8 in 2017.

Group of Twenty (G-20) is an economic council composed of the finance ministers and central bank governors from the 20 largest national economies in the world (19 countries and the European Union) that meets semi-annually to consider major policy issues concerning the effective functioning of the global economy and the international financial system. Switzerland, Iran, Taiwan, Norway and Thailand are not members of the G-20 even though their economies are among the top 25 economies in the world. The G-20 was inaugurated in 2009. The economies of members of the G-20, which represents two-thirds of the world's population, account for more than 85% of the gross world product and 80% of world trade. Furthermore, the G-20 accounted for over 80% of the world's economic growth between 2010 and 2016. The members of the G-20 are: Argentina, Australia, Brazil, Canada, China, France, Germany, India, Indonesia, Italy, Japan, South Korea, Mexico, Russia, Saudi Arabia, South Africa, Turkey, the United Kingdom, the United States and the European Union.

Guanxu (1871–1908) was the next-to-last emperor of the Qing Dynasty. Dominated by his great aunt, the Empress Dowager Cixi, he began to rule in his own right in the mid-1890s. His support for reform in the summer of 1898 led to his house arrest in September. He died in 1908 on the eve of Cixi's death, leading to speculation that he was poisoned.

Guernica (1937) was the town in the Basque region of Spain that was bombed in April 1937 by the German planes during the Spanish Civil War. The brutal destruction of Guernica became the subject of a famous painting by Pablo Picasso.

Guerrilla, which is a Spanish word for "little war," is the name that was used to describe the Portuguese and Spanish peasants who organized to fight against Napoleon's efforts to conquer Portugal and Spain in the early 1800s. Today, a guerrilla war is referred to as an unconventional war in which irregular military forces attempt to seize state power. A guerrilla war is waged without front lines, supported and protected by large segments of the civilian population of a society and fought with lightly armed, non-regular forces against a larger and more conventionally equipped army. Guerrillas typically use such methods of warfare as sabotage, ambushes, roadside bombs and sniper fire.

Guild was an association of craftsmen, tradesmen, merchants, and professors that was organized in European cities and towns beginning in the 1200s to protect their economic and political interests. It provided protection to its members and set the rules and standards for their work, professional practices, their training, the manufacture of their products as well as the pricing and sale of the products that guild members produced. They also provided economic benefits to their members, fostered a sense of community, and served as mutual assistance societies. Guilds came to control much of the production process and to restrict entry into various trades in the centuries prior to the Industrial Revolution.

Gulag, which is an acronym in Russian for "main camp administration," refers to a network of 476 forced labor and prison camps that were created by Stalin throughout the Soviet Union in the 1930s for both ordinary criminals and Stalin's political opponents, who he claimed were engaged in anti-Soviet agitation or counter-revolutionary activities. Gulags were first used by Lenin in 1918, but were extensively expanded by Stalin. Even though the exact figure is unknown, some historians have estimated that tens of millions of Soviet citizens were sent to the Gulags between 1928 and 1953. The gulag system was made famous by the writer Aleksandr Solzhenitsyn.

Gunboat Diplomacy is a term that refers to a foreign policy based on the threat or use of military force. During the late 1800s and early 1900s, European powers and the United States typically used the presence of naval warships as part of their negotiating strategy in a dispute over trade issues with nations in South America, Africa, and Asia. The mere presence of naval forces off the coast of a less powerful nation allowed the European powers or the United States to wring concessions from or take over another country.

Gunpowder is a mixture of saltpeter, sulfur, and charcoal that was first developed in China in the 400s or 500s CE. At first, it was used to make fumigators to repel insects and evil spirits. Subsequently, it was used to make explosives and grenades and to propel cannonballs and bullets. Between 1000 and 1200 CE, gunpowder began to spread from China to the Islamic world and then medieval Europe.

Gutenberg, Johannes (1398–1468) was the German inventor of movable metal type. His invention made possible the publication of the first printed book in Europe, the *Gutenberg Bible*, in the 1450s. Furthermore, printed books and broadsides would play a critical role in the dissemination of the ideas of the Renaissance and the Protestant Reformation.

Gymnasium was a social and cultural institution that emerged in Greek city-states during the classical era of Greece between the 5th and 4th centuries BCE. It offered various activities including recreation, exercise, education and cultural exchange. The gymnasium combined athletic training, poetic performances, and philosophy lectures during the period of classical Greece. During the Hellenistic era, it was a secondary school with a curriculum centered on music, physical exercise, and literature.

Habiru or Apiru, which is also spelled Hapiru, was the name used by Sumerians, Akkadians, Egyptians and the Hittites for a nomadic or semi-nomadic people who lived a marginal existence on the fringes of settled Mesopotamian and Egyptian societies between 1800 and 1100 BCE. The Habiru were considered by these societies to be an inferior social class. According to ancient Sumerian, Akkadian, Egyptian and Hittite texts, the Habiru were described as invaders, mercenaries, robbers, vagrants, slaves or laborers. Some scholars contend that the term Hebrew is derived from Habiru or Hapiru.

Habsburg was the name of a royal Austrian dynasty whose members were kings in the Holy Roman Empire from the 1000 until 1918. The head of the family was customarily the emperor of the Holy Roman Empire. The Habsburgs founded the Austrian, later the Austro-Hungarian Empire. They ruled Spain, the Netherlands and Central Europe in the 1600s and 1700s. By the late 1600s, the Austrian Hapsburg Empire was comprised of approximately 300 kingdoms and principalities. The Habsburgs would play a dominant role in European affairs for centuries. They waged a series of wars against the French Revolution and the Napoleonic Empire between 1792 and 1815. Marie Antoinette was a member of the Hapsburg family, who became queen of France when she married King Louis XVI. In 1867, the Hapsburg Empire was reorganized into the Austro-Hungarian Dual Monarchy. The Habsburg Empire collapsed in 1918 as a result of its defeat in World War I.

Hacienda was a large landed estate first established in the Spanish colonies in the Americas in the late 1600s. They eventually replaced the encomiendas throughout much of the Spanish colonies in the Americas.

Hadith are the sayings of the prophet Muhammad that have been collected, written down, and are studied in the Islamic world as a source of religious guidance, but are not considered to be of the same import as the Quran. Next to the Quran, they are the most important basis for Islamic law.

Hadrian (76–138 CE), who was the adopted son of Emperor Trajan, was a Roman emperor who reigned from 117–138. During his reign he united the Roman Empire and ended its expansion. He traveled widely throughout the Roman Empire strengthening its frontier defenses. He built a wall (Hadrian's Wall) in the northern part of England in 122 as a defense against an invasion of Roman-controlled England by the northern barbarian tribes from what is present-day Scotland. The wall was 73 miles long and 20 feet high and was connected by watchtowers and forts. It remained in use until the Romans left England during the 400s.

Hagia Sophia is the church of "Holy Wisdom" built in Constantinople between 532 and 537 CE by Emperor Justinian. At the time of its construction, it was the largest Christian church in the world. It is famous for its dome that rests on four great arches. When the Ottoman Turks captured Constantinople in 1453, it was converted into a mosque.

Hajj is the annual pilgrimage of Muslims to Mecca to worship Allah at the Ka'ba. As one of the Five Pillars of Islam, Muslims are encouraged to undertake this pilgrimage at least once in their lifetime, if they are physically and financially able to do so.

Hallstatt culture is the name given by archaeologists to the early Iron Age society that emerged in western and central Europe from the 12th to the 5th centuries BCE. Archaeologists commonly associate the Hallstatt culture with the emerging Celtic populations of Western Europe. The Hallstatt culture was named for the Austrian village of Hallstatt where a large ancient cemetery containing approximately 2000 graves of individuals of various social classes

was discovered by Johann Ramsauer in 1846. Excavation of the site, which continued until 1899, established that cremation was used extensively. The Hallstatt culture was based on farming, metal-working, salt mining and long-distance trade with ancient Greece and some Mediterranean cities such as present-day Marseilles. Hallstatt society was organized into tribes, lived in fortified settlements built on hilltops and was comprised of elite classes of chieftains and warriors. Material characteristics of Hallstatt culture include elaborate jewelry made of gold, silver, bronze and amber, iron swords, daggers, axeheads and tools, bronze containers, vessels, armor and helmets, backpacks made of wood and leather and well-made pottery. While archaeologists have speculated for some time about the causes for the collapse of the Hallstatt culture, the actual causes for its demise remain uncertain.

Hamoukar (circa 4000 BCE) was a walled city-state located in what is now northeastern Syria. It developed independent of and likely before southern Mesopotamian city-states, which have long been considered the birthplace of urban society. Hamoukar emerged as an urban center of trade and manufacturing before 4000 BCE. As it was located on a key trade route from Anatolia across northern Syria and the Tigris River into southern Mesopotamia, it became a center for the manufacture of obsidian tools, which it exported to other city states in southern Mesopotamia. The obsidian, which was not native to Hamoukar, was brought from a source in Anatolia about 70 miles away. The trade and manufacture of obsidian contributed to the emergence of a specialized class of urban craftsman. Hamoukar was destroyed as a result of a war in 3500 BCE.

Hammurabi of Babylon was the king who ruled the Babylonians from 1792 to 1750 BCE. He issued his famous and influential code of laws circa 1790 BCE, which was inscribed on stone slabs erected throughout his empire. His code of laws was comprised of 282 legal decisions by him and past Babylonian rulers on a wide range of civil, criminal, and commercial cases. The Code of Hammurabi developed an important legal principle that would influence Western legal thought to this day, that is, the idea that a punishment must fit the crime. The Code of Hammurabi is the world's oldest surviving law code.

Han is the name of a dynasty of emperors that ruled China from 202 BCE to 220 CE. It is also a term used to refer to those ethnic Chinese who originated in the Yellow River valley and spread throughout regions of China that were suitable for agriculture.

Han Fei 2i (280–233 BCE) was a Chinese philosopher during the Qin Dynasty. He developed a sophisticated paradigm for the Legalist doctrines of rewards and punishments. Han Fei argued that human nature was a blank slate and that by the use of rewards and punishments people could be shaped to be obedient citizens.

Han Yu (768–824 CE) was a Chinese scholar and official in the late Tang Dynasty who promoted a Confucian revival, criticized what he saw as the negative influence of Buddhism on Chinese culture, and called for a return to the values of the early Han Dynasty.

Hannibal (247–182 BCE) was a Carthaginian general who invaded Italy in 218 BCE during the Second Punic War. He led a Carthaginian army, compose of 40,000 soldiers accompanied by elephants, from Spain across the Alps to invade Italy. While his army was in Italy, he scored three decisive military victories over the Roman forces, the most significant of which was the Battle of Cannae. He was eventually defeated in 202 BCE by the Romans during the Battle of Zama in North Africa. For the next twenty years, the Romans constantly pursued him until he committed suicide in 182 BCE.

Hanseatic League (1200s–1600s) was a commercial and political alliance of over 100 northern German trading cities. It was centered in the German city of Lubeck and was established in 1241 in order to provide mutual protection and security. The members of the League dominated the coastal trade of wool, grain, fish, and furs in northern Europe from the 1300s until the 1400s.

Harem was a secluded quarter of a palace or a Muslim household where the wives, concubines, female relatives, and servants would be confined.

Harvey, William (1578–1657) was an English physician whose greatest achievement was discovering the function of the heart and its part in circulating blood. He was the court physician to King James I and King Charles I of England.

Hasidim was the name of a sect of Judaism that emerged in the mid-1700s in Poland and Lithuania. Hasidim challenged the formalism of synagogue worship. Instead, this sect emphasized ardent spiritual devotion, exceptional respect for the Talmud and strict observance of the Ten Commandments and the Sabbath (Judaic law) in daily life.

Haskalah was the name for the Jewish enlightenment that emerged in the late 1800s in Europe, and was led by Moses Mendelssohn, a Prussian philosopher.

Hasmoneans is an alternative name for the Maccabeans, the family of Jewish priests that began the revolt against Syria in 167 BCE and ruled Israel before the Roman conquest in 63 BCE.

Hatshepsut (1508–1432 BCE) was the Pharaoh of Egypt who reigned during the New Kingdom from 1473–1478 BCE. During her reign, she launched several successful military campaigns and sent a naval expedition down the Red Sea to Punt (possibly northeast Sudan or Eretria), which was the source of myrrh. She is believed to have constructed the first tomb in the Valley of the Kings. Though she never pretended to be a man, she was routinely portrayed as a masculine figure. There is evidence of opposition to a woman as ruler of Egypt for after her death her name and image were frequently defaced. She is one of the few women in antiquity to hold sovereign political power.

Hattusha was the name of the capital of the Hittite Empire during the late Bronze Age and was located in Anatolia. From Hattusha, the Hittites played an important role in the network of communication and trade that developed in the ancient Middle East during the late Bronze Age and established diplomatic relations with the rulers in Syria, Egypt, Mesopotamia and the Mycenaean lands in the Aegean.

Havel, Vaclav (1936–2011) was the Czech playwright and politician who became a leading advocate for human rights and democracy in

Czechoslovakia during the 1970s. Following the peaceful overthrow of communism in Czechoslovakia in 1989, more popularly known as the Velvet Revolution, he became the president of an independent Czechoslovakia.

Heavy-Wheeled Plow was a farming implement that cut more deeply into the heavy, wet soil of northern Europe and created furrows that drained excess water. It permitted cultivation of the thicker soils of river valleys.

Hebrew Bible (1200–100 BCE) is a collection of sacred books containing diverse materials concerning the origins, experiences, beliefs, and practices of the Israelites. Most of the existing text today was compiled by members of the priestly class in the 2nd and 1st centuries BCE and reflects the concerns and views of this group.

Hebrews were a Semitic-speaking nomadic tribe who developed a monotheistic belief in Yahweh. They entered Palestine circa 1200 BCE, with Joshua capturing Jericho.

Hecataeus of Miletus (550–476 BCE) was a Greek historian who traveled extensively around the Mediterranean Sea. He is considered by some scholars to be the first Greek historian. In his book *Tour Round the World,* he described the peoples and societies around the Mediterranean and the Black Sea (the then-known world) that he encountered. His works were used by Herodotus.

Hegel, G. W. F. (1770–1831) was an influential philosopher in the late 1700s and early 1800s. Greek philosophy and the writings of Jean-Jacques Rousseau, Immanuel Kant, and Baruch Spinoza influenced his thinking. Hegel's goal was to create a system that could encompass all philosophies from the past as well as could include all future philosophical thoughts. In developing this system, Hegel hoped to define all of reality. For Hegel, the "Absolute" was manifested in three ways: art, religion, and philosophy. Art was the material form, religion was the symbolic form, and philosophy was the abstract rational form. In his *Introductory Lectures on Aesthetics,* he wrote of poetry being "the universal realization of the art of the human mind." At his death, he was the foremost German philosopher. His students and admirers split into two groups: right-wing Hegelians who tended to be more conservative and orthodox in their philosophical approach, and left-wing Hegelians whose approach was focused more on atheistic and revolutionary concerns. Karl Marx was part of the left-Hegelians.

Hegelianism was a philosophical movement in Europe in the 1830s and 1840s that debated the social implications of the ideas of Georg Hegel, a prominent and influential German philosopher. This movement was divided between one group known as the left-Hegelians, who claimed that the ideas of Hegel showed the need for radical social change based on reason and freedom. By contrast, right-Hegelians argued that existing institutions were already generally based on reason and freedom.

Hegemonic state arises when a state that has an overwhelming preponderance of economic and military power tries to control and dominate the activities of another state or states. Such a state can often single-handedly establish and enforce the rules, norms and arrangements by which the political, economic, and military activities of other states in the international system are conducted. A war fought by a hegemonic state is fought for control of the entire world, which is also known as a world war, global war, general war, or systemic war.

Hegemonic power is a term used in international relations to describe the role of the United States in the international system after the end of the Cold War, when it possessed unchallenged economic and military power. After the end of the Cold War, the military power of the former Soviet Union was greatly diminished and Communist China was considered a regional power with limited ability to project its military power beyond its borders.

Hegira or Hijra (622 CE) is the name given in the Islamic religion to the "flight" or pilgrimage of the prophet Muhammad and his followers from Mecca, where his life was in danger, to Medina in 622. At Medina he was welcomed as the political leader of the community. The Hegira marks the beginning of the Islamic calendar. It is considered to be the beginning of the Islamic faith.

Heliocentric theory is a system of astronomy in which the sun is the center of the cosmos and the earth revolves around the sun. This theory was articulated by Nicholas Copernicus in the 1500s and was supported by the scientific and mathematical discoveries of Johannes Kepler. Galileo was condemned by the Catholic Church for supporting the heliocentric theory. However, by the 1600s the heliocentric theory had gained wide acceptance. This theory was first proposed by Aristarchus of Samos sometime between 316-330 BCE.

Hellas is the name which the ancient Greeks called the land where they lived.

Hellenes is the name which the ancient Greeks called themselves.

Hellenistic Age (323–30 BCE) was the name for the period in Greek history between the death of Alexander the Great and conquest of Ptolemaic Egypt by the Roman Empire. During this era, after the conquests of Alexander the Great, Greek culture spread across western Asia and northeastern Africa. The period ended when the last major Hellenistic kingdom of the Ptolemies in Egypt fell to Rome. However, Greek cultural influence persisted until the spread of Islam in the 600s CE. After Alexander overthrew the Persian Empire, he began spreading Hellenism, i.e. Greek culture, language, thought and way of life, as far as India. The Hellenistic age was an era in which Greek cultural influences were pervasive.

Hellenistic Kingdoms were, following the death of Alexander the Great, the three independent states created by Alexander's generals from the vast empire that Alexander had conquered. Those generals were Ptolemy, who, along with his heirs, ruled Ptolemaic Egypt; Seleucus, who, along with his heirs, ruled Seleucid Asia; and Antigonus I of Macedonia, who, along with his heirs, ruled Antigonid Greece. While each state maintained its independence, they were influenced by Greek culture and heritage.

Hellenization is the term used by historians to describe the process by which Greek language and culture spread throughout the Mediterranean and the Middle East. This process began with the conquests of Alexander the Great. One of the ancient cultures and civilizations deeply influenced by Greek culture was Rome. This influence began as early as the 6th century BCE.

Heloise (1090–1164) was a pupil and the wife of the philosopher Peter Abelard. She was one of the foremost scholars of her time and she founded a new religious order for women.

Helot was the name for the people from Messenia who were conquered by the Spartans in 750 BCE and made state-owned, hereditary slaves. They were tied to the land that they farmed and were treated brutally by the Spartans.

Helsinki Accords (1975) were a series of political and human rights agreements that were entered into in Helsinki, Finland, by thirty-five countries, including the United States, the Soviet Union, Canada, and every European nation, except Albania. The Accords recognized the existing postwar European borders as permanent, increased economic and environmental cooperation, advocated arms control, and promoted freedom of expression, religion, and travel. Political movements that advocated greater freedom in the Soviet bloc relied on the human rights provisions of the Helsinki Accords to discredit existing communist governments in Eastern Europe. These developments are considered today by historians to be the apex of the era of détente.

Henry of Navarre or Henry of Bourbon (1553–1610) renounced his Protestant faith when he was crowned King Henry IV of France. However, he issued the Edict of Nantes in 1598 that granted limited tolerance to the Huguenots.

Henry, te Navigator, Prince (1394–1460) was the Portuguese nobleman who encouraged the study of navigation and the exploration, conquest and colonization of the western coast of Africa. The Portuguese established trading posts along the western coast of Africa from which they traded in gold and slaves. These trading posts, which were also known as factories, would become the foundation for the Portuguese Empire.

Henry VIII (1491–1547) was the English king who broke with the Catholic Church when the pope refused to grant him an annulment even though he supported Catholicism in Britain. He argued that he needed an anullment in order to marry a younger woman who might be able to produce a male heir to the British throne. He decided to form his own church with himself as the head of it. That church would become known as the Church of England, which practiced a form of Christianity known as Anglicanism. While Henry VIII did not intend it, his dispute with the Catholic Church supported efforts by Protestant reformers in Britain.

Heraclius, Emperor (575–641 CE) was a Byzantine emperor from 610 to 641 who defeated the Persians only to lose to the Arabs. He failed to achieve religious unity and he began to promote a more Greek culture in the eastern part of the Roman Empire. He initiated the theme system as a new form of administration.

Heraclitus of Ephesus (535–475 BCE) was a pre-Socratic philosopher from Ionia, which was part of the Persian Empire, who claimed fire was the basic element of the universe, that change was the fundamental nature of the universe and that change results from the clash of opposites. He contended that even though things were constantly changing, there was an underlying coherence to the universe known as Logos. While the term Logos has various interpretations, he defined Logos as "reason", which is the interpretation that a Greek philosopher of his time would have used. He summed up his ideas about change in the following-well-known statement: "All things flow" and "You cannot step into the same river twice". His philosophy influenced the development of Stoicism, the predominant philosophy of the Roman Empire. Stoics believed that the basic elements of their philosophy were derived from the ideas expressed by Heraclitus.

Heresy is any belief or teaching that is contrary to generally accepted orthodox political or religious thinking. A heretic was a person who publicly dissented from officially accepted political or religious dogma.

Hermeticism was an intellectual movement beginning in the 1400s in Europe that taught that divinity is embodied in all aspects of nature. Supporters of this movement wrote on alchemy and magic as well as theology and philosophy. This movement would continue into the 1600s and influence leading thinkers during the Scientific Revolution.

Hero Cults involved important ancient Greek families who would claim that an impressive Mycenaean tomb belonged to one of their famous ancestors. The Greek families would then practice sacrifices and other observances at the tomb to strengthen their claim. The practice of this devotion could also extend to include the families their followers as well as later whole communities, in which the family was influential, would adopt such supposed ancestors as local heroes.

Herodotus (485–425 BCE) was an ancient Greek historian who, along with Thucydides, originated the western tradition of historical writing. The word "history" comes from the Greek word "historia," which means learning or knowing by inquiry. Herodotus came from Anatolia and traveled extensively, collecting information in western Asia and the lands along the eastern Mediterranean. He traced the origins of and chronicled the Persian Wars between the Greek city-states and the Persian Empire. He considered the fall of the Persian Empire to be part of a perpetual historical cycle of the rise and fall of empires.

Herzl, Theodore (1860–1904) was an Austrian journalist and playwright who founded Zionism, a worldwide political movement that advocated the establishment of a Jewish homeland in Palestine. In 1897, he organized the first meeting of the World Zionist Organization and became its first president.

Hesiod (700s BCE) was a Greek poet who lived circa 700 BCE. Historians have debated the priority of Hesiod or of Homer. Modern scholars disagree as to which was earlier. Many scholars argue that their lives very likely overlapped. Hesiod serves as a major source for knowledge of Greek mythology, farming techniques, archaic Greek astronomy and ancient time-keeping. In his epic poem, *Theogony* he recounts the creation and origins of the Greek gods. In his other book *Works and Days* he emphasized the goodness of hard work and claimed that labor is the universal lot of humans. He also attacked idleness, unjust judges and the practice of usury. He regarded labor as the source of all good, in that both gods and men hated the idle, who he argued resembled drones in a hive.

Hess, Rudolf (1894–1987) was one of the first individuals to join the Nazi party in 1920. He was arrested and imprisoned along with Hitler after the November 1923 beer hall putsch. He helped Hitler compose *Mein Kampf* while they were both in prison. In May 1941 Hess flew to Britain in the hope of persuading the British to make peace with Germany. Hess was arrested upon landing and spent the rest of his life in prison. He committed suicide in 1987.

Hetairai were elite ancient Greek courtesans who were sophisticated, witty and attractive woman. They charged fees to entertain men and provide companionship at the symposia. Hetairai typically offered intellectual and musical entertainment as well as sexual companionship.

Heuristic is a technique used in philosophy for problem solving. According to this approach, in the event that an exhaustive search to solve a problem proves impractical, heuristic methods can be used to find a satisfactory solution by the use of mental shortcuts, which include using a rule of thumb, an educated guess, an intuitive judgment, stereotyping, or common sense. Some commonly used heuristic approaches include the following: 1) If one is having difficulty understanding a problem, try drawing a picture; 2) If one cannot find a solution, try assuming that there is a solution and seeing what can be derived from that solution by working backward; 3) If the problem is abstract, try examining a concrete example; and 4) Try solving a more general problem first.

Heydrich, Reinhard (1904–1942) was the primary planner and executor of the anti-Jewish policies of the Nazis. In June 1942 he was attacked by Czech resistance fighters and died of his wounds. In retaliation the Germans destroyed the Czech town of Lidice and killed all its male inhabitants.

Hidden Imam was the last in the series of twelve descendants of Muhammad's son-in-law Ali, the 1st of whom the Shi'ites considered divinely appointed leaders of the Muslim community. He is expected to return as a messiah at the end of time.

Hierarchy is a system of social differentiation that ranks certain people as more important and more dominant than other people.

Hieroglyphics, which means "sacred carvings," was the name of the complex writing system of ancient Egypt. This writing system was comprised of over 700 signs, including pictographic, phonographic (syllables) and ideographic elements. It was used primarily for official inscriptions on monuments in ancient Egypt. Because of the long period of study required to master this system, literacy in hieroglyphics was confined to a relatively small group of scribes and administrators. The use of hieroglyphs fell out of use when Egypt was absorbed into the Roman Empire. As a result of the French discovery of the Rosetta Stone in the early 1800s, Jean-Francois Champollion (a French historian and linguist) was able to decipher hieroglyphic texts and render them legible for the first time after thousands of years. Champollion is considered to be one of the founding figures in the field of Egyptology.

High Culture refers to those aspects of culture that are most highly valued and esteemed by a society's political, social, economic, and intellectual elite. This elite has the social, political, and economic power to define the elements of high culture.

High Priest was the highest-ranking religious official in Judaism. The High Priest was responsible for the operation of the Temple in Jerusalem and its priests.

High seas is an international legal term used to describe that portion of the oceans of the world that are considered the common territory of humanity and are not under the jurisdiction of any one state.

Himmler, Heinrich (1900–1945) was leader of the SS, Gestapo and German minister of the interior from 1943–45. He was the most powerful man in Germany after Hitler. Himmler was instrumental in establishing the concentration camp system and overseeing the implementation of the Final Solution. After Germany's surrender he tried to escape but was captured by the British. He committed suicide in May 1945 before he could be brought to trial for war crimes.

Hiroshima (1945) is the Japanese port city in the southern part of Japan where the United States dropped the first atomic bomb on August 6, 1945. The bombing contributed to ending World War II in the Pacific.

Hitler, Adolf (1889–1945) was the author of *Mein Kampf* and the leader of the Nazi Party in Germany from the 1920s until 1945 when he committed suicide in a bunker in Berlin. While born in Austria, he served in the German Army during World War I. After World War I, he became a radical German nationalist. He led the National Socialist German Workers Party (Nazis) in the 1920s and became dictator of Germany in 1933. His aggressive policies in Europe resulted in World War II, during which he orchestrated the systematic murder of over eleven million people, approximately six million of whom were Jews.

Hittites (2000–710 BCE) were an IndoEuropean speaking people from central Anatolia who established an empire in Anatolia and Syria in the third millennium BCE. With wealth from the trade in metals and military power based on chariot forces, the Hittites and New Kingdom Egypt battled to a standstill at the Battle of Kadesh, for fighting control of the trade routes in Palestine and Syria. The stalemate at Kadesh led the Egyptians and Hittites to enter into the world's first peace treaty. Hittite is the oldest recorded Indo-European language group to which English belongs.

Ho Chi Minh (Nguyen Sinh Cung) (1890–1969) was the Vietnamese nationalist and communist political leader who led the armed resistance struggle against French colonial rule throughout most of the 1900s. He led North Vietnam after the Geneva Accords were signed in 1954 and during the first years of the American war in Vietnam. He was also known as Nguyen Tat Thanh or Nguyen Ai Quoc.

Ho Chi Minh Trail was the name given to a network of dirt roads and trails that carried supplies from North Vietnam through Laos, Cambodia, and South Vietnam to National Liberation Front and North Vietnamese forces fighting to topple the Saigon government during the American war in Vietnam.

Hobbes, Thomas (1588–1679) was the author of *Leviathan*, which endorsed realism rather than idealism in politics. In that book, he contended that humans live in a "state of nature" in which there was a "war of all against all." His ideas followed in the tradition of the ideas expressed by Machiavelli in *The Prince*. He, like Plato and Machiavelli, wrote at a time of massive political crisis and, similar to both of them, his remedy was based on a diagnosis of human nature and a prescription of strong leadership. Born at the time of the threatened invasion by the Spanish Armada in 1588, he said that his mother unknowingly gave birth to twins: himself and fear. He elaborated a complex, controversial, and widely influential system of philosophy that embraced epistemology, physics, human nature, politics, and the state. He translated *History of the Peloponnesian* War by Thucydides into English and recommended that his contemporaries follow the lessons drawn by Thucydides.

Hobson, John Atkinson (1858–1940) was a British economist and critic of British imperialism. During his journalistic coverage of the Second Boer War in South Africa on behalf of the *Manchester Guardian*, Hobson began to form the idea that imperialism was the direct result of the expanding forces of modern capitalism. Upon his return to Britain he condemned the conflict and began to explore the links between imperialism and international conflict. In *Imperialism* (1902), he argued that imperial expansion is driven by a search for new markets and investment opportunities overseas. *Imperialism* gained Hobson an international reputation, and influenced such notable thinkers as Lenin and Trotsky and Hannah Arendt (who wrote *The Origins of Totalitarianism* in 1951).

Hohenzollern Dynasty was the name of a noble family and royal dynasty of kings and emperors of Prussia, Germany, and Romania, which originated circa the 11th century. This dynastic family would rule Germany until the early 1900s.

Hollywood Blacklist was a group of mainly film actors, directors, and screenwriters in the late 1940s and early 1950s in the United States that were unable to work openly after having been targeted by the House Committee on Un-American Activities for alleged communist activities. In October of 1947, alleged communists, deemed "subversives," working in the Hollywood film industry were summoned to appear before the House Committee on Un-American Activities, which was investigating communist influence in the Hollywood labor unions. This group of American screenwriters, actors, and directors were either alleged or admitted members of the American Communist Party. Ten of those subpoenaed refused to give evidence, citing their First Amendment rights. The U.S. House of Representatives voted 346 to 17 on November 24, 1947, to approve citations for contempt of Congress. These men, soon dubbed the "Hollywood Ten," were convicted in 1948 and, following unsuccessful appeals and denial of review by the Supreme Court, they served prison terms in the 1950s.

Holocaust, which is Shoah in Hebrew, is the Greek term meaning "whole burning" that was used after World War II to describe the systematic program by Adolf Hitler and the Nazis during World War II to murder all of those people considered undesirable by the Nazis. Some six million European Jews were murdered by the Nazis between 1940 and 1945, along with five million Russians, Poles, socialists, communists, Gypsies, and others. The Nazis referred to the mass killing of the European Jewish population as "the final solution to the Jewish problem."

Holocene Epoch is the geological era when temperatures warmed up following the end of the Great Ice Age about 11,700 years ago. During this period, there was much more forest cover and the summers were relatively dry. At the same time, plant cover became more diverse and wild cereal grasses emerged, which could be later harvested.

Holy Alliance (1815) was the coalition formed by the monarchies of Prussia, Austria, and Russia after the defeat of Napoleon and at the recommendation of Tsar Alexander I of Russia. The Alliance had a number of objectives. Fearing the influence that the French Revolution might have on European society, the members of the Alliance sought to suppress the revolutionary movements that were based on the ideals of liberalism and nationalism. Furthermore, in response to the growing influence of Enlightenment ideas and secularism, the Alliance also sought to promote the importance of the divine right of kings to legitimate monarchical rule and to restore the influence of Christian values and beliefs. Even though the Alliance represented an important symbol of traditional conservative monarchical values, it had little impact on political and diplomatic relations among the major European powers in the 1800s, which were influenced more significantly by the idea of Realpolitik (political realism). In fact, the leaders of Great Britain, the Papal States and the Ottoman Empire refused to join the Alliance. The Holy Alliance collapsed after the death of Tsar Alexander in 1825.

Holy League (1571) was a naval alliance of the European Catholic states in the western Mediterranean that was organized by Pope Pius V to halt the western advance of Ottoman naval forces in the Mediterranean, which was considered a threat to European maritime trade in the Mediterranean. The members of this coalition included Spain, the Republics of Venice and Genoa, and the Duchies of Savoy, Urbino and Tuscany. France, Portugal and the Holy Roman Empire were not members of the alliance. In response to the Ottoman attempt to conquer Cyprus, which was controlled by Venice, the League employed a fleet of 206 war galleys to win a decisive victory against the Ottoman fleet of 222 war galleys at the Battle of Lepanto, which was fought in the Gulf of Patras near the southwestern coast of Greece. Venice subsequently signed a peace treaty with the Ottoman Turks and surrendered Cyrus to them in 1573. The Battle of Lepanto represented not only the first naval victory of Christian forces against the Ottoman Empire, but also the last major naval engagement to be fought entirely by galleys. Furthermore, the battle created a division of the Mediterranean, with the Ottoman Empire controlling the eastern Mediterranean and the Spanish Empire and its Italian allies controlling the western Mediterranean. After the death of Pope Pius V, the Holy League was disbanded.

Holy of Holies was the inner part of the Jewish Temple in which God's presence on earth was believed to dwell. No one could enter this room except the High Priest on the Day of Atonement to make a sacrifice for the sins of the Jewish people.

Holy Office of the Inquisition (1542) was created by Pope Paul III to respond to the spread of Protestantism. It was not concerned about heresy within the general Catholic lay population, but was focused on whether the academic writings of the clergy and theologians complied with the accepted doctrines and orthodoxy of the Catholic Church. The Holy Office issued the Index of Forbidden Books in 1559. The Index was a list of books that were morally wrong according to the Catholic Church or were offensive to the Catholic faith. The Holy Office condemned Galileo in 1633 for his support of the heliocentric theory. The Holy Office lasted until 1965 when Pope Paul VI restructured the office; and it is now known as the Congregation for the Doctrine of the Faith.

Holy Roman Empire (800–1806 CE) was a loose federation of mostly German states and principalities in central and Western Europe ruled by an emperor elected by nine German princes. It was based primarily in Germany and northern Italy. It represented an attempt by the Catholic Church to revive the Roman Empire. Voltaire said that the Holy Roman Empire was "neither holy, nor Roman, nor an empire." The head of the Habsburg family was customarily the emperor of the Holy Roman Empire. The origins of the Holy Roman Empire are identified with the Frankish Empire of Charlemagne, who was crowned emperor of Rome by the pope in 800 CE.

Holy Russia was the name applied to Muscovy, and then to the Russian Empire, by Slavic Eastern Orthodox clerics who, after the end of the Byzantine Empire, hoped that Russia would become the new home to and protector of the Eastern Orthodox faith.

Homage was an oath of loyalty and allegiance that a vassal, in Europe during the Middle Ages, swore publicly to his lord.

Home Front was a term made popular during World War I and World War II to describe the civilian population of mostly women and men ineligible for military service that actively supported the war effort by assuming the primary role of producing the goods that were considered indispensable to the national war effort. In the 1900s, a modern industrial nation depended on the civilian population to produce the supplies, equipment, and services necessary to support the military war effort. Traditionally, until the 1900s, civilian populations were typically not involved in combat. However, the rapid increase of military technology and the expanded destructive capabilities of modern warfare increased the direct military threat to civilian populations. As a result, a nation's military effort has come to include the "home front" because of its capacity to produce weapons as well as its vulnerability to direct attack. Accordingly, if factories and workers producing war material are part of the war effort, they become legitimate targets for attack.

Homer is the ancient Greek poet considered to be the author of the *Iliad* and the *Odyssey,* which were written sometime between 750 and 700 BCE. Homer may have come from Asia Minor. The *Iliad* is an epic poem about the last year of a ten-year war with Troy. The *Odyssey* is another epic poem which tells of the ten year wandering of Odysseus after the Trojan War. The Greeks believed that Homer composed these poems, but he may have done no more than put in writing oral folk tales that had been already in existence for hundreds of years.

Hominid is the biological family of primates, including modern humans, characterized by bipedalism. Primates evolved after the evolutionary spilt with the great apes. Apes are a subset of anthropoids that tended to be large-bodied and are the closest living relatives of modern humans.

Homo erectus is the first hominid to live in both Asia and Africa. It is thought of as a turning point in human evolution because it walked upright. Homo erectus appeared in Africa about 1.7 million years ago and became extinct, though still hotly debated, about 200,000 years ago. Homo erectus used cleavers and hand axes and learned how to control fire. It is the most widespread of the prehistoric hominids and most similar to the modern human species of *Homo sapiens*.

Homo habilis is the first human species (now extinct) that appeared in Africa from about 2.0 to 1.5 million years ago. It is famous for being the first to manufacture stone tools.

Homo naledi is a recently discovered, unknown species of hominids that some paleontologists believe may be the transitional species between the ape-like australopithecines, such as Australopithecus afarensis, and early humans such as Homo habilis. The remains of this species were found in the Rising Star cave system in South Africa in 1915. Homo naledi has mix of primitive and modern features. They have a tiny head with a brain the size of an orange, but their skull is human-like in shape. Their hands were adapted for manipulating objects and their feet for walking upright. However, their shoulders and fingers were built for climbing. While some paleontologists believe that Homo naledi may be among the earliest members of the genus Homo, which would mean that they most likely existed around 2.5 million years ago, they have been unable so far to accurately date the remains.

Homo Neanderthalensis (Neanderthal) is a hominid that is likely a separate species from modern humans, but overlapped with them in time and place. The Neanderthals lived in Asia and Europe from about 300,000 to between 35,000 and 24,000 years ago.

Homo sapiens, which means "thinking human," is a hominid who first appeared between 400,000–500,000 years ago. Anatomically modern humans, homo sapien sapiens, evolved from homo sapiens.

Homo Sapien Sapiens, which means "wise man" or "most intelligent people", is an intellectually and physically modern human being. They first appeared in Africa between 200,000 to 150,000 years ago. Cro-Magnon and Neanderthals, both now extinct, fall into this category.

Hong Xiuquan (1814–1864) was the founder and leader of the Taiping Heavenly Kingdom, which was formed in China during the mid-1800s. He was a failed examination candidate from Guandong Province who believed that he was the younger brother of Jesus Christ. His movement almost toppled the Qing Dynasty, and its suppression caused between 20–30 million deaths.

Honestiores was the name for the senatorial and equestrian classes, municipal officials, and army veterans who were entitled to immunity from torture, criminal fines and exemption from crucifixion in capital cases.

Hooke, Robert (1635–1703) was an English biologist who demonstrated the potential of the recently developed compound microscope to study the cellular structure of plants.

Horn of Africa is the geographic term for the northeastern corner of the African continent that includes the present day states of Somalia, Ethiopia, Eritrea and Djibouti. Drought, famine and ethnic warfare in the 1980s and 1990s resulted in political turmoil and civil war in these states.

Hoss, Rudolf (1901–1947) was a member of the SS and became the first commandant of Auschwitz in 1940. As commandant, he directed the killing of more than one million people. He was convicted of crimes against humanity at Nuremberg in 1946 and was hanged in Auschwitz in 1947.

Hoplite (late 8th century BCE) was a heavily armored Greek infantryman of the Archaic and Classical periods of ancient Greece that fought in a close-packed phalanx formation. They would be armed with a long spear for thrusting and short iron sword and a large round bronze shield. In battle, hoplites stood should-to-shoulder and shield-to-shield in a close formation, eight ranks deep, called a phalanx. Hoplite armies were composed of middle and upper class citizens who could afford to supply their own equipment. The hoplite tactics made soldiers dependent on one another and thereby contributed to the internal cohesion of the Greek city state and eventually the rise of democracy. The hoplite phalanx was the dominant military formation used throughout the Middle East and the Mediterranean until 197 BCE.

Horse Collar (1100s) was the harnessing method that developed in Europe in the Middle Ages that increased the efficiency of horses by shifting the point of traction from the animal's neck to its shoulders. With the development of this farming technology, the use of horse-drawn plows and vehicles contributed to increasing agricultural production in Europe.

Hortensian Law (287 BCE) was the Roman law that made the decisions of the plebeian assembly binding on all Romans.

Horus was the falcon-headed Egyptian god whose earthly form was the reigning pharaoh in ancient Egypt.

Hot Line Agreement (1963) was the direct communications link between the U.S. and the Soviet Union that, in the wake of the Cuban Missile Crisis, was implemented to minimize the danger of an accidental war. It has been upgraded several times since then and similar hot lines have been established between other nations.

House of Wisdom was a public library and an academic center for research and learning that was founded in Baghdad by the Caliph Al-Rashid, who ruled from 786–809 CE. The library included books and manuscripts written in different languages and on various subjects in the arts and sciences. The books and manuscripts were initially collected by al-Rashid's grandfather, Caliph Al Mansour, who ruled from 754–775 CE and by Al-Rashid's father, Caliph Al-Mahdi, who ruled from 775–785 CE. Caliph Al-Ma'mun, the son of Al-Rashid, who ruled from (813–833 CE), further expanded the library's collection of books and manuscripts and constructed the first astronomical observatory in the Islamic world in 828. All four caliphs were members of the Abbasid dynasty. Scholars, writers, philosophers and scientists of many faiths and ethnicities from throughout the Islamic world came to the House of Wisdom to read, discuss, debate and build on the various books and manuscripts in the humanities, mathematics, physics, astronomy, geography, medicine, alchemy, astrology, chemistry, zoology, cartography and philosophy. Many of the books and manuscripts, which were written in Aramaic, Hebrew, Syriac, Persian, Chinese, Sanskrit, Latin and Greek, were translated into Arabic. As a result, scholars associated with the House of Wisdom were able to make significant original contributions in their various respective fields. The House of Wisdom was destroyed in 1258 with the Mongol invasion of Baghdad. The House of Wisdom was one of the great intellectual academies in world history.

Household gods were Roman deities who supposedly watched over a family's farmland and household possessions. The daily worship by the household was the responsibility of the paterfamilias

Humiliores was everyone in Roman society, apart from Honestiores and slaves, that were counted as property. The Humiliores were expected to obey the law, pay their taxes, participate in public religious rituals, and conform to the ethical duties of public service and care for the family.

Humanitarian Intervention is the United Nations' authorized armed intervention by a state or group of states into a sovereign state, without its consent, to prevent or alleviate widespread threats to the health, safety, security and well-being of a group of people in that country, each of which could, individually or collectively.

Hubris is a Greek word for exaggerated arrogance or excessive pride brought on by great wealth or good fortune that results in moral blindness.

Huguenots were French Calvinists, many of whom were middle class merchants and members of the lower nobility in France. They constituted 10% of the French population and were led by Henry of Navarre during the French Wars of Religion. They endured severe persecution in the 1500s and 1600s, including the St. Bartholomew's Day Massacre in Paris in 1572 when thousands of Parisian Protestants were slaughtered. Many Huguenots emigrated to other Western European countries and the American colonies after the Edict of Nantes was revoked. Huguenots would not gain full religious freedom in France until the 1800s.

***Human Comedy, The* (1829–1847)** is a series of 90 novels and novellas written by Honoree de Balzac in the 1800s that criticized materialist values.

Humanism was an intellectual movement that arose during the Renaissance (1350–1600 CE) which emphasized the importance of having the ability to read and understand the writings of the ancient world. It was characterized by a belief in the superiority of ancient Greek and Roman history, politics, and literature, a concern for human beings, an interest in the secular rather than theological issues, and a focus on the individual. Even though humanists were religious, they, nevertheless, sought to replace the emphasis on logic and philosophy, which was associated with scholasticism, with the study of ancient languages, literature and ethics. Humanists were writers and scholars who studied Latin and Greek texts on grammar, rhetoric, poetry, history, and ethics and focused on realizing human potential. Ludovico Ariosto, a Renaissance Italian poet coined the term "humanism". His epic poem *Orlando furioso* is considered to be the finest expression of humanism during the Renaissance. Eventually, humanism became a program of study in European universities built around seven core liberal arts: grammar, rhetoric, mathematics, music, geometry, and astronomy.

Humanitarian Intervention is the United Nations' authorized armed intervention by a state or group states into a sovereign state, without its consent, to prevent or alleviate widespread threats to the health, safety, security and well-being of a group of people in that country, all of which constitute severe human rights violations.

Humanitarianism is an ideology that expressed the philosophical belief in the need to improve the human race. As an ethical and philosophical doctrine, it contends that it is the duty of each human to help relieve the suffering of others. This concept emerged in the late 1800s in Europe when social and political reformers such as Cesare Beccaria in Italy and Jeremy Bentham in Britain questioned the cruelty of the criminal justice and prison systems. As an ideology, it emphasized the equal dignity, rationality, and responsibility of the individual, the welfare of human beings, and the need for ethical conduct in human relations. Advocates of humanitarianism argued that it was a person's duty to alleviate human suffering and promote human welfare through social, political, and legal reforms.

Humanitas refers to Cicero's idea of "humanness," which for him meant generous and honest treatment of others based on natural law. It was also the Roman name for a liberal arts education.

Hume, David (1711–1776) was one of Europe's most respected and influential philosophers during the 1700s. He believed that Newton's method of scientific inquiry, skepticism and empiricism could be applied to the study of morality, the mind and government.

Hundred Days of Reform (1898) refers to the period of Chinese history when Kang Youwei and Liang Qichao attempted to meet the challenge posed by western nations to China. They advocated western-style social and political reforms to Chinese society that would transform China into a modern industrial nation.

Hundred Flowers Campaign (1956), which is also known as the Hundred Flowers Movement, was a political movement initiated by Mao Zedong and the Chinese Communist Party to grant greater freedom of thought and speech. This movement was inspired, in part, by the denunciation of the policies of Joseph Stalin by Premier Nikita Khrushchev in 1956. Mao wanted to initiate criticism of the policies of the Chinese Communist Party. He said "let a hundred flowers bloom, and a hundred schools of thought contend." Within a year, the Communist Party became subject to extensive criticisms by the Chinese people. Wall posters denounced the government, students and professors, and criticized party members of economic corruption. People demonstrated in the streets against the privileges of the Communist Party leadership demanded the right to express their ideas freely and openly. Magazine articles were written criticizing Mao and his policies and the low standard of living. Recognizing that the criticism had gone too far, Mao and the Communist Party leadership quickly suppressed the dissent and punished the critics by firing them from jobs, imprisoning them or forcing them to do manual labor in the countryside. As a result of the Hundred Flowers Campaign future criticism of Mao and his policies was discouraged and intellectuals, especially those educated in Western universities, government officials, students, artists and dissidents, were persecuted.

Hundred Years' War (1337–1453) was a series of conflicts between the ruling families of France and England prompted by English claims to land in France as well as English claims to the French throne. This long conflict was fought mostly in France, which devastated the countryside and limited population growth. The leadership of Joan of Arc contributed to France's eventual success in expelling the British from the disputed land. Ironically, the English won most of the battles, but the French won the war.

Hungarian Revolution (1956) was the mass uprising that began with reformist efforts by Hungarian Communist Party leader Imre Nagy. It was eventually crushed by Soviet troops.

Huns were fierce nomadic warriors from the frontiers of China who began to threaten the Western Roman Empire from 370 until their defeat in 451.

Hunting and Gathering was an economic and social system in which groups of humans who did not live in permanent settlements survived by collecting food such as nuts and fruits from uncultivated plants, hunting of wild animals, and fishing. During the Neolithic Revolution, some hunting-gathering societies began to raise crops or livestock for food.

Hurrians were a people who lived in northern Mesopotamia and Syria beginning approximately 2500 BCE. Like most aspects of Hurrian society, their origins are still a mystery. Archaeological knowledge of the Hurrians is still fairly scanty, relying mostly on cuneiform tablets from the capital of the Hittites, whose civilization was greatly influenced by the Hurrians. However, by about 2400 BCE the Hurrians had expanded southward from the Zagros Mountains or from Anatolia and entered the Babylonian Empire circa 1750 BCE. By 1725 BCE they had also moved into northern Syria. Between 1650 BCE and 1590 BCE, Hurrians expanded into areas controlled by the Hittites. While there was no Hurrian Empire, a number of Hurrian-dominated states had been established in northern Mesopotamia between 1540 and 1520 BCE. By 1530 BCE the state of Mitanni, with a mostly-Hurrian population, was founded and it rapidly became the center of Hurrian power and culture. This kingdom was conquered by Assyria circa 1270 BCE.

Hus, Jan (1370–1415) was a Bohemian priest and religious reformer who attacked the power and privileges of the clergy of the Catholic Church. He strongly advocated reform of Church practices. Hus adopted many of the ideas of the English theologian John Wycliffe and demanded that the laity be permitted to receive both the consecrated bread and wine of the Eucharist. The Council of Constance burned him at the stake for heresy. In response to the execution of Hus, his supporters, the Hussites unsuccessfully revolted against the Catholic Church.

Hussein, Saddam (1937–2006) was the former dictator of Iraq who invaded Iran in 1980 and started the eight-year-long Iraq-Iran War. Hussein also invaded Kuwait in 1991, which led to the Gulf War. He was the president of Iraq from 1979 until he was overthrown by the American invasion of Iraq in 2003.

Hussites were followers of Jan Hus, who, in the early 1400s questioned, the teachings of the Catholic Church about the Eucharist, rejected the sale of indulgences by the Catholic Church, and opposed German political dominance in Bohemia. They attempted to break down the distinction between priests and worshippers in the Catholic Church. In 1420 Pope Martin V issued a Papal Bull announcing a crusade against the Hussites. A subsequent crusade was organized by Pope Martin V in 1427 that decisively defeated the Hussites.

Hu Yaobang (1915–1989) was a Chinese Communist Party official who rose to be general secretary during the reform period of the 1980s. His death in April 1989 triggered the student movement that culminated in military suppression in June in Tiananmen Square.

Hydrogen Bomb, which was first tested in 1952 by the United States and in 1953 by the Soviets, is a nuclear weapon hundreds of times more powerful than the atomic bombs dropped on Hiroshima and Nagasaki. A hydrogen bomb is created by the fusion process during which atoms are smashed together to create a thermonuclear exploision.

Hyksos were Semitic-speaking peoples from Palestine who conquered Egypt beginning in 1630 BCE and ruled the Nile Delta area of Egypt for approximately

150 years. The Egyptians called them "Rulers of the Uplands." Their invasion of Egypt ended the Middle Kingdom.

Hypatia (350/370–415 CE) was a Greek female mathematician, philosopher, writer and astronomer who lived in Alexandria, Egypt. She was head of the Platonist school at Alexandria where she taught the works of Plato and Aristotle. She was the last librarian of the Library of Alexandria. She was influenced by Plotinus, who encouraged logical and mathematical studies. After being accused of witchcraft, godlessness and of causing religious turmoil, a mob of Christian monks attacked her, stripped her naked and dragged her through the streets of Alexandria and then killed her.

Hyperinflation is an extreme, rapid and uncontrolled rise in prices and decline in the value of the currency of a society. In 1923, post-World War I Germany experienced catastrophic price increases and currency devaluation.

Hypothesis is a tentative assumption or proposition about causal relations in the natural and social sciences put forward to explore and test its logical and usually empirical consequences. It is either supported or falsified by experimentation or other data.

I

Ibn Battuta (1304–1369 or 1377) was a Muslim scholar from Morocco who was considered to be one of the most well-traveled men of his times. He wrote a detailed account of his visits to Islamic countries from Spain to China.

Ibn Khaldun (1332–1406) was an Arab historian who developed a theory concerning the rise and fall of nations.

Ice Age is a period of long-term reduction in the temperature of Earth's climate, resulting in an expansion of the continental ice sheets, polar ice sheets, and mountain glaciers over the North American and Eurasian continents. There have been at least four major ice ages in the Earth's

past. The earliest hypothesized ice age occurred approximately 2.7 to 2.3 billion years ago. The earliest well-documented and most severe ice age occurred from 850 to 630 million years ago. The most recent ice age began 40 million years ago, but it intensified about 3 million years ago with the spread of ice sheets in the Northern Hemisphere. Since then, the world has seen cycles of ice sheets advancing and retreating on 40,000 and 100,000-year time intervals. The most recent ice age ended about 10,000 years ago.

Icon is a symbolic representation of a religious person, theme or event in the form of a mosaic or fresco, a painting on wood, paper or canvas or sculptures in stone or metal. The Iconoclastic Controversy, which emerged in the Byzantine Empire during the 700s and 800s, involved a dispute about the religious purpose, function and role of icons in the religious practices of the Eastern Orthodox Church.

Iconoclastic Controversy was a religious movement initiated by Emperor Leo III in the Byzantine Empire in the 700s and 800s against the veneration of icons (images) of sacred religious figures such as Jesus, Mary, and the saints in Byzantine art. According to Emperor Leo III, veneration of icons was considered to be idolatry and sinful. As a result of this movement, numbers of religious images were destroyed. Byzantine emperors banned icons from 726 to 787 and a modified ban was revived in 815 that lasted until 843. The papacy in Rome, however, refused to ban the veneration of icons. The papacy claimed that icons manifested the physical form of those who were considered holy.

Id is one of the three elements of the model of the human psyche developed by Sigmund Freud. According to him, the id consists of the amoral, irrational instincts for self-gratification. The two other elements of Freud's model are the ego and the superego.

Idealism is a term used in international relations to describe a worldview that rejects power politics (realism or realpolitik). Idealists argue that a nation's foreign policy should be based on morality, international law, international cooperation, participation in international organizations and humanitarianism. Proponents of idealism contend that war can be prevented when states cooperate to solve problems and that the establishment of international processes and institutions will improve the existing world order.

Identity is a person's sense of self that is shaped such factors as individual self-reflection, ideas, national history, gender, sexual orientation, language, class, ethnicity, recognition of being part of specific cultural group and a strong sense of the differences with other cultural groups.

Ideologues were a group of liberal writers and philosophers in France who opposed the religious policies of Napoleon. They contended that Napoleon's policies would initiate a return to religious superstition.

Ideology is a systematic body of concepts, beliefs, values, theories, and ideas about human life and culture that guides an individual, social movement, institution, class, or large group of people and offers some political and social plan along with the means for putting such a plan into operation. This body of ideas typically reflects the social needs and aspirations of an individual, group, class, or culture and will form the basis of a political, economic, social, or religious system, such as capitalism, fascism, communism, or socialism. An ideology is the body of basic ideas, beliefs, and goals of a social, cultural, religious, economic, or political movement or organization. In short, it is a comprehensive worldview or picture of reality.

Idols of the Mind is a term used by Francis Bacon to refer to the fictions of the tribe, the cave, the marketplace, and the theater created by humans through language and custom.

Ilkhanate was the name of the Mongol state that ruled Persia after the defeat of the Abbasid Empire in the 1200s.

Iman is a Muslim religious leader and also a political-religious descendant of Ali, believed by some Muslims to have a special relationship with Allah.

Imhotep was the chief minister to the Egyptian King Djoser, who ruled in the 3rd Dynasty. He is often considered to be the first architect. He designed tombs and other structures to express the power of the Egyptian pharaohs.

Imperator was the title of a victorious military commander in the Roman Republic who was given temporary dictatorial powers by the Senate. Under Augustus and his successors, imperator became the title of the ruler of the Roman Empire, that is, emperor.

Imperial Period (27 BCE–476 CE) is a term used by historians for the period of ancient Roman history from the time of Augustus until the collapse of the Roman Empire.

Imperialism is the policy and practice of extending the political domination of one nation over another through territorial conquest and/or economic exploitation. In communism, it is considered to be the final stage of expansion of the capitalist system. This term is typically associated with the expansion of European powers and their conquest and colonization of African and Asian nations from the 1500s until the late 1800s. The term was first developed in the mid-1800s.

Imperium, which is a Latin word meaning "right to command", was the authority that chief executive officers such as consuls and praetors possessed in the Roman Republic to issue commands and to enforce them by fines, arrests, and even corporal and capital punishment.

Impressionism was a style of painting that was developed in the late 1800s by French artists such as Degas, Monet, and Renoir. It was influenced by new theories about how images were transmitted to the brain as small light particles, which the brain then reconstructed. Impressionists sought not only to capture what things looked like before they were distorted by the brain, but also to capture their subjective impressions of the changing effects of light on color and objects in nature.

In Vitro Fertilization is a process developed by scientists in the 1970s by which the eggs of a woman are fertilized by sperm outside of the woman's body and then implanted in the woman's uterus.

Inanna is the ancient Sumerian goddess of sexual love, fertility and warfare. She is considered the most prominent female deity in ancient Mesopotamia and was associated with the city of Uruk. Inanna is always depicted as a young woman, never as a mother or faithful wife, who is fully aware of her feminine power. She confronts life without fear of how she will be perceived by others, especially by men. She is often shown in the company of a lion, which denotes courage. In her role as goddess of war, Inanna is depicted in the battle armor of a man armed with a quiver and bow. There were many temples dedicated to Inanna in Mesopotamia. The Temple of Eanna, ("house of heaven") in Uruk was the most important one, where sacred prostitution was a common practice. She became identified with the Akkadian goddess Ishtar, the Phoenician Astarte, the Greek Aphrodite, the Roman Venus. Inanna appeared in many ancient legends and myths, the most notable was *The Epic of Gilgamesh* in which she appeared as Ishtar.

Incas were the South American Indians who ruled an extensive and highly organized empire that stretched along the Pacific coast of South America from present day Ecuador to Chile. The Spanish conquistador Francisco Pizarro conquered the Incas in 1532.

Indentured Laborer was an immigrant to the British colonies in North America who worked without wages for a contracted period of time in exchange for the price of a ship passage to the British colonies and food, lodging, and clothing during the period of his or her indenture. Wealthy planters would pay the poor in England to sell a portion of their working lives, typically for four to seven years, in exchange for passage to the colonies. Indentured laborers were an important source of labor in the American colonies.

Index of Forbidden Books (1559) was a list of books that the Catholic Church banned because of moral or doctrinal errors or heretical viewpoints. While it was continually revised, the Index was enforced intermittently by the Catholic Church and had little impact on the writing habits of educated Europeans. It was abolished by the Church in 1966.

Indian Civil Service was the governmental bureaucracy established during the British colonial rule of India and was comprised primarily of British-educated Indians who eventually constituted an elite political group in India.

Indian Mutiny (1857), also called the Sepoy Mutiny or the Great Rebellion, was the revolt in India by Indian soldiers in the British army against certain British military practices that violated their religious customs. The Sepoys, who were both Hindu and Muslim, were mercenary soldiers recruited by the British from the warrior and peasant castes in India to serve in the British colonial army, especially the infantry. The Indian troops wanted to bring religious purification, an egalitarian society and local and communal solidarity to India without the interference of British colonial rule.

Indian National Congress (1885) was a nationalist political party and movement formed in India that advocated greater Indian participation in government. Its membership was primarily middle class and its demands were very modest until World War I. Under the leadership of Mohandas Gandhi in the 1920s, it appealed increasingly to the poor of India and organized mass protests demanding self-government, independence, cultural nationalism, and industrialization.

Individualism is a philosophy that emphasizes the unique traits of each person. It was a basic element of the Italian Renaissance stressing personality, uniqueness, genius, and selfconsciousness.

Indo-European is the name given to an extensive language family, the survivors of which today include Hindi, Persian, Russian, Polish, Armenian, Albanian, Greek, Italian, Spanish, French, German, English, Portuguese, Dutch, and the Scandinavian languages.

Indochina was an area of Southeast Asia that became part of the French Empire between 1858 and 1893. It was comprised of three countries, Vietnam, Laos, and Cambodia. After gaining control of Vietnam, the French divided Vietnam into three administrative units: Tonkin in the north, Annam in the middle and Cochinchina in the south.

Inductive Reasoning is a method of logical analysis and reasoning that systematically accumulates specific empirical evidence to make general assertions about past or future events in nature or history. It is a form of reasoning that proceeds from the particular to the general or from a number of common facts to a general conclusion.

Indulgence was an official letter authorized by the pope promising remission of sins and release from time to be served in Purgatory. Typically, they were issued by the Catholic Church for going on a pilgrimage or performing a pious act. However, during the Babylonian Captivity of the Church (105-1378), the popes began to sell indulgences, in part, to pay for Saint Peter's Basilica in Rome. Indulgences were sold in the public squares of towns and cities throughout Germany in the early 1500s. Martin Luther's Ninety-Five Theses presented a critique and denunciation of the sale of indulgences. The sale of indulgences was one of the factors that contributed to the emergence of the Protestant Reformation.

Industrial Revolution is the term used by historians to describe the period of sustained transformation of the economy, environment, and living conditions that first began in Britain in the mid-1700s and subsequently spread to other European nations. This stage of economic development was represented by the mechanization of manufacturing, mass production, division of labor, the development of new technologies such as the steam engine, and the development of extensive networks of transportation and communication. New technologies developed during this stage of economic production led to the emergence of the factory system. The Industrial Revolution represents the transition in modern societies from economies based on hand tools, agricultural production, and the use of animal or human power to economies based on machine tools, machine power, and mass production.

Infanticide is the practice of intentionally murdering newborn children or infants. While infanticide was not practiced in ancient Greece, exposure of newborns to the elements was widely practiced. Typically, the father made the decision. In Sparta, however, it was a council of elders. The Greeks did not consider exposure to be equal to infanticide because the exposed child would die

of natural causes, such as hunger, asphyxiation or exposure to the elements.

Infidel is a derogatory term applied to a person who does not believe in a particular religion. During thee Middle Ages in Europe, Muslims were considered by Christians to be infidels because they did not believe in Christianity.

Information Revolution refers to the most recent stage in technological development that has fundamentally transformed the availability of information and facilitated more rapid global communication. This dramatic change has resulted from the development of personal computers, cell phones and the Internet.

Inquisition was the religious court established by the papacy in the 1230s in medieval Europe that had the authority to investigate, try and condemn individuals for heresy and other religious crimes. The Inquisition was used by the Catholic Church to enforce religious orthodoxy and conformity. Those individuals accused of heresy who refused to admit their errors were treated brutally.

Inquisition, Spanish (1480–1834) was the religious court that was established by King Ferdinand and Queen Isabella of Spain to uncover and combat heresy. It used torture to obtain confessions. By papal authority Ferdinand and Isabella were able to control the grand inquisitor and thereby expand state power. The Spanish Inquisition investigated and condemned many former Jews and Muslims who were believed to have insincerely converted to Christianity.

Institutes of the Christian Religion (1536) was the title of the book written by John Calvin on Christian doctrine, which became the systematic theology for Protestantism The book is based on the Ten Commandments, the Lord's Prayer, and the Apostle's Creed.

Intellectuals or Intelligentsia are individuals who teach or write about ideas, the creative arts, or social, political, cultural and scientific ideas. Historically, they have played two important societal roles: they produce new knowledge and new critiques of society. The term emerged in France in the late 1800s.

Intendants were royal officials, who were not nobles, appointed by the kings in France during the 1600s and 1700s to administer a province or part of a province. They oversaw all aspects of royal authority. Intendants were a critical component in the effort by Louis XIV to centralize political control in his hands. Intendants were regarded by the French monarchs as more reliable than the hereditary nobility and were viewed as direct representatives of the king, who were to execute his orders. At the time of the French Revolution in 1789 there were thirty-four of them.

Intercontinental Ballistic Missile (ICBM) is a land-based missile that typically carries a nuclear warhead that can reach targets of over 5000 miles away. With the development of MIRV technology (multiple independently targeted re-entry vehicles) in the 1960s, ICBMs could carry a number of warheads aimed at separate targets. Minuteman was the name for the ICBMs developed by the United States in the 1960s that were deployed in silos. They were developed in order to replace the dependency on long-range bombers. ICBMs were first developed by the Soviet Union in the late 1950s.

Interdependence is a close political and economic relationship of mutual dependence in which two or more states are mutually dependent on each other for the well-being of the respective societies.

Interdict was a papal decree issued by the Catholic Church prohibiting the celebration of the sacraments in an entire city of kingdom in order to pressure the local rulers of that city or kingdom to comply with teachings of the Catholic Church.

Intergovernmental Organizations (IGOs) are organizations, such as the United Nations, whose members are state governments.

Intermediate-Range Ballistic Missiles (IRBM) are missiles that typically carry a nuclear warhead that can reach targets between 600 and 3500 miles away.

Intermediate-Range Nuclear Forces (INF) Treaty (1988) was the first nuclear arms control agreement that banned an entire class of missiles that both the Soviet Union and the United States had deployed in Europe. Those banned missiles included medium and shortrange nuclear missiles that had a range of 300 to 3,400 miles. This treaty signed by President Reagan of the United States and Premier Gorbachev of the Soviet Union represented a significant advance in U.S.-Soviet relations during the Cold War. The United States and the Soviet Union collectively dismantled more than 2600 missiles.

International Committee of the Red Cross (ICRC) (1875) is a nongovernmental organization (NGO) that provides medical care and food to civilians caught in wars and to prisoners of war (POWs). Exchanges of POWs are usually negotiated through the ICRC.

International human rights law consists of civil, political, economic, social and cultural rights to which every human being is entitled regardless of his or her identity or status. These rights are created by treaties or customary international law, i.e., wide acceptance of the rights by nations because of a sense of legal duty. Human rights include many different protections such as the prohibition of slavery, the prohibition of genocide, the prohibition of torture, the right to a fair trial, freedom from unlawful imprisonment, freedom of speech and religion, and the right to education. The political demand for human rights emerged in response to the war crimes committed during World War II and the genocidal atrocities of the Holocaust. These efforts culminated in the adoption of the United Nations Charter in 1945 and Universal Declaration of Human in 1948, signaling the beginning of the human rights movement.

International Law is the body of rules and principles governing the relations or conduct of nations, intergovernmental organizations, non-governmental organizations, and individuals. It has increased in use and importance vastly over the 1900s primarily because of the increase in global trade, armed conflict, and environmental deterioration on a worldwide scale, human rights violations, rapid and vast increases in international transportation, and a boom in global communications. It further includes the important functions of the maintenance of international peace and security, arms control, the pacific settlement of disputes, and the regulation of the use of force in international relations. Even when the law is not able to stop the outbreak of war, it has developed principles to govern the conduct of hostilities and the treatment of military combatants and non-combatants and civilians. Modern international law developed significantly beginning in the mid1800s. World Wars I and II, the League of Nations, the United Nations, the Nuremberg Trials, the Genocide Convention, the Geneva Conventions, the Universal Declaration of Human Rights, the International Labor Organization, the World Health Organization, and the World Trade Organization, to name a few developments, have all contributed the evolution and development of the modern international legal system. Thus, during the 1900s, international law has come to play a greater role in the conduct of international relations than in previous centuries.

International Military Tribunal for the Far East (1946–1948), which is also known as the Tokyo War Crimes Tribunal, was organized by the United States to try the leaders of Japan accused of war crimes. The charter establishing these trials followed closely the Charter that established the Nuremberg Trials. Twenty-five Japanese senior military and political leaders were tried and convicted, of whom, seven were sentenced to hang, 16 were given life imprisonment, and two were sentenced to lesser terms. The Japanese Emperor Hirohito and all members of the imperial family were not prosecuted for involvement in war crimes because U.S. policy-makers were concerned that the political reforms they wished to implement would need the approval of Emperor Hirohito if such reforms were to be accepted by the Japanese people. Some critics have dismissed these trials as "victors' justice."

International Monetary Fund (IMF) (1944) is an intergovernmental organization (IGO) that coordinates international currency exchange, the balance of international payments, and national accounts. Along with the World Bank, it is one of the pillars of the international financial system.

International Relations is the study of the interactions among various actors (states, international organizations, nongovernmental organizations, and other entities such as bureaucracies, corporations, local governments, and individuals) that participate in international politics. It involves a diverse range of issues, such as the environment, nuclear proliferation, foreign aid, economic development, and human rights.

International Settlements were special areas of Chinese cities that were established for foreigners in the 1800s as a result of the Opium Wars. No Chinese were permitted to live within these areas and the activities of the foreigners were governed by the laws of their respective home countries.

International System refers to the structure of the rules, norms, and patterns of interaction that govern states and other international actors.

Interregnum (1649–1660), which means between the reigns, was a period in English history from the execution of Charles I to the restoration of Charles II. During the years of the Interregnum, England was a commonwealth ruled by Oliver Cromwell.

Intervention was the principle established after the Congress of Vienna by the great powers of Europe (England, France, Russia, Prussia and Austria) that those five nations had the collective right to invade any European monarchy experiencing revolutions in order to restore legitimate monarchs to their thrones.

Intolerable or Coercive Acts (1774) were laws passed by the British Parliament to punish the British colony in Massachusetts and to strengthen British authority in their colonies in the Americas. The laws provoked opposition that led to the American War of Independence.

Investiture Conflict (Controversy) (11th and early 12th century CE) was the name given to the institutional and ideological battle between Pope Gregory VII and the Holy Roman Emperor Henry IV of Germany that tested the power of kings over Church matters. Specifically, it concerned the issue of who held ultimate authority over bishops and abbots in the Holy Roman Empire—that is, who had the right to appoint bishops and invest them with the spiritual symbols of their office, the ring and staff. After years of diplomatic and military hostility, Pope Calixtus II and Holy Roman Emperor Henry V reached a compromise in 1122 in the Concordat of Worms, which established the idea of the separation of secular and religious authority. The compromise stipulated that only the pope could appoint bishops and invest them with the religious symbols of spiritual power (a ring and pastoral staff), that bishops were part of the Church hierarchy headed by the pope and that bishops were to be loyal to the Church and not to the secular ruler of the region in which the bishop lived. In turn, a ruler or emperor could invest the bishops who lived in the region each governed with the symbol of secular authority (a scepter). The Investiture Conflict contributed to the emerging distinction in Europe between church and state.

Invisible Hand is the idea expressed by Adam Smith in his book *The Wealth of Nations* that when governments leave trade and financial sectors of an economy unregulated, the forces of supply and demand in free markets will produce greater economic efficiency and growth to meet the economic demands of a society.

Ionian Revolt (499–494 BCE) was a rebellion by Greek city-states in Ionia against the Persian Empire who ruled them. When the rebellion spread quickly to other Ionian Greek city-states who desired independence from the Persian Empire, the Persians sent a military force to reclaim their cities. Subsequently, Athens and Eretria sent troops to aid the rebelling Ionian city-states. The Athenian and Eretrian troops attacked Sardis, the capital of Lydia, another province of the Persian Empire. The Greeks also pillaged Sardis and burned it down. Even though Persian soldiers were able to force the Greek troops to return to Greece, the Ionian Revolt spread to the Greek cities in Cyprus as well as those surrounding the Hellespont. Because of their geographic isolation from city-states of Greece, the Ionian city-states were not able to maintain their independence for long in the face of the overwhelming military power of the Persian Empire. By 494 BCE, the Ionian Revolt had been crushed.

Iran Hostage Crisis (1979) refers to the seizure by Iranian students of 52 American hostages for 444 days before releasing them unharmed. This crisis occurred after the U.S.-backed leader, Shah Mohammed Reza Pahlavi, was forced to flee Iran by the Islamic Revolution led by the Ayatollah Ruhollah Khomeini.

Iran-Contra Affair (1984–1986) was a political scandal that arose during President Ronald Reagan's administration when it was discovered that the United States was secretly selling military weapons to Iran, an avowed enemy. At the time, Americans were being held hostage by Islamic terrorists in Lebanon, and it was hoped that Iran would influence the terrorists to release the hostages. At the same time, Iran, which was in the midst of the Iran-Iraq War, could find few nations willing to supply it with weapons. The United States diverted proceeds from the sale of military weapons to Iran in order to illegally fund the Contras, an anti-Communist guerrilla group engaged in an insurgency against the Marxist Sandinista government of Nicaragua. Both the sale of weapons and the funding of the Contras violated the stated administration policy as well as legislation passed by the U.S. Congress, which had prohibited further Contra funding.

Irish Home Rule was the political program and movement led by Sinn Fein that advocated self-rule for Ireland within the British Empire between the 1880s and 1914.

Irish Potato Famine (Great Famine (1845–1849) was the prolonged, severe and devastating famine in Ireland that led to extensive starvation, disease and the emigration of over one million people to the United States. It is estimated that approximately one million people died during the famine. The famine caused Ireland's population to decline between 20% and 25%. The cause of the famine was a disease commonly known as potato blight. Although potato crops of other European nations were ravaged by the potato blight during the 1840s, the human cost of the potato blight was greatest in Ireland where one-third of the population was entirely dependent on the potato for food. The famine dramatically changed the political, cultural and demographic nature of Ireland. Some contemporary historians regard the famine as a watershed event in Irish history.

Iron Age (1200 BCE) is the term typically used by archeologists and historians for the period during which iron replaced bronze in the manufacture of weapons, tools, utensils and agricultural implements. The advent of iron technology began at different times in different parts of the world, but it appears to have begun in Anatolia about 1200 BCE. The use of iron would take place in China about 600 BCE. Between 1200 BCE and 1000 BCE, knowledge of iron metallurgy would spread to the Middle East and Europe. It represented a dramatic technological shift that would have enormous cultural consequences.

Iron Curtain was a metaphor used by Winston Churchill in a speech on March 5, 1946 at Westminster College in Fulton, Missouri to warn of a growing political and ideological divide between communist and democratic nations in postwar Europe. In his speech, Churchill blamed the Soviet Union for this emerging divide. Churchill's speech significantly influenced American public opinion. Many American policymakers feared at the time that the United States might revert to pre–World War II isolationism.

Iron Law of Wages was an economic theory promoted by Ferdinand Lassalle, an English economist in the early 1800s. He argued that the wages of workers should never rise above a subsistence level, because higher wages caused a growth in the population of a society, food shortages, and an oversupply of labor, which would result in lower wages.

Irredentism is the national policy of a country to reclaim lost territory inhabited by a people who have linguistic, ethnic, historical and cultural links to that country, but who are living in a neighboring country. Irredentism is a form of nationalism whose goal is to regain territory lost to another state that in many cases can result in violent conflicts.

Isagoras (6th century BCE) was one of the leaders of the factional strife that affected Athens from 510 to 508 BCE. He was supported by the Spartans, but was eventually defeated by Cleisthenes.

Ishtar gate is a massive brick gate built over the main entrance to the city of Babylon around 575 BCE. Its bricks were painted blue with gold representations of the god Marduk decorating many of the bricks. It has been reconstructed and can be found in the Pergamon Museum in Berlin, Germany.

Islam, which is an Arabic word for "the surrender," is the monotheistic religion influenced by Judaism and Christianity that was founded by Muhammad in the mid-600s in Arabian peninsula. Islam calls on all people to recognize one god—Allah—who rewards or punishes believers after death according to how they led their lives. It involves a complete surrender of an individual to will of Allah. A follower of Islam is known as a Muslim, meaning "one who submits." Muslims believe that God revealed the Qur'an to Muhammad, God's final prophet, and regard the Qur'an and the Sunnah (words and deeds of Muhammad) as the fundamental sources of Islam. Muslims do not regard Muhammad as the founder of a new religion, but as the restorer of the original monotheistic faith of Abraham, Moses, Jesus, and other prophets. Islamic tradition holds that Judaism and Christianity distorted the messages of these prophets. Thus, Muhammad is considered to be the final prophet. Followers of Islam are required to observe the Five Pillars of Islam, which are five duties that unite Muslims into a community. In addition to the Five Pillars, Islamic law (sharia) has developed a tradition of rulings that touch on virtually all aspects of life and society. This tradition encompasses everything from practical matters such as dietary laws and banking to warfare. Today, Muslims belong to one of two major denominations, the Sunni or Shi'a. The schism developed in the late 600s following a disagreement over the religious and political leadership of the Muslim community. Roughly 85% of Muslims are Sunni and 15 percent are Shi'a. There are between 1.1 billion and 1.8 billion Muslims, making Islam the second-largest religion in the world, after Christianity, with about 20 percent of all Muslims living in Arab countries in the Middle East.

Isocrates (436–338 BCE) was a Greek orator and statesman who argued for the union of all Greeks.

Isolationism was the worldview expressed by many Americans that the United States should not become embroiled in foreign conflicts and world politics. This worldview has continually been an element in American politics, but was especially strong in the years following World War I. American entry into World War II temporarily suppressed isolationist sentiments, but they returned in the postwar years in response to America's new international role, particularly as a reaction to the new United Nations and its affiliated international organizations. Some feared the loss of American sovereignty to these new transnational organizations. The United States, China, and Japan have all adopted this policy at one point in their history. Japan had a policy of isolation for hundreds of years before making an alliance with Great Britain in 1902. In the United States, George Washington himself encouraged the practice in his Farewell Address in 1796, warned against involvement in the "affairs of Europe." While Thomas Jefferson, James Monroe, and other early presidents rhetorically supported the ideas of isolationism, in actuality, the United States expanded westward in the 1800s, purchasing land from France, Russia, and Mexico. This myth of isolationism was further undercut when the United States occupied the Philippines, Guam, Puerto Rico, and Cuba during the Spanish-American War, entered World Wars I and II, and became a founding member of the United Nations and NATO after World War II.

Israel is the name in antiquity for land between the eastern shore of the Mediterranean and the Jordan River that was occupied by the Hebrews (Israelites) around 1200 BCE or earlier. The name also refers to the northernmost of the two kingdoms that emerged in Palestine after the death of Solomon with its capital at Samaria. The Assyrians conquered Israel in 722 BCE.

Italia Irrendenta is the Italian term used by Italian nationalists after World War I to refer to those "unredeemed" Italian-speaking lands to the north of Italy and across the Adriatic from Italy that had been left under Austrian rule at the time of the unification of Italy in the mid-1800s.

Issus, Battle of (333 BCE) was the second major battle fought by Alexander the Great during his invasion of the Persian Empire. Once again, he decisively defeated the Persian army, which was led by Darius III, the last king of the Persian Empire. However, recognizing that the Persian forces were outnumbered, Darius fled the battlefield even before the battle began.

Ivan the Great (Ivan III) (1440–1505) was the Russian emperor who responsible for freeing Russia from Mongol rule after 1462. He annexed neighboring territories and began the emergence of Russia as a European political and military power.

Ivan IV ("the Terrible") (1530–1584) was the first Russian ruler to routinely use the title "tsar." He presided over the expansion and the centralization of the Russian state. During his reign, Russia expanded into Siberia. He also circumvented the power of the local nobles by creating a body of officials who were personally loyal to him.

Jacobins was the leading and most radical faction among the French revolutionaries at the time of the French Revolution in 1789. The Jacobins formed a national network of political clubs throughout France. They advocated a republic rather than a constitutional monarchy. They dominated the National Convention from 1792 until 1794 and were supported by the sansculottes. They replaced the Girondins and lead the wars against European powers who threatened the French Revolution. The Jacobins were led by Maximillien Robespierre, who organized the Reign of Terror, which lasted from 1793 to 1794. The name was derived from the Church of Saint-Jacques, a Dominican convent in Paris, where they originally met.

Jacquerie (1358) was the peasant revolt in northern France against the aristocracy and the king that was part of the struggle for rights caused by labor shortage after the Black Death. It was also a reaction to the monarchical demands to increases in taxes in order to pay for French wars.

James I (1566–1625) was the king of both Scotland and England from 1603 to 1625. He encouraged the translation of the Bible into English, which is known today as the King James version of the Bible. He was also known as James VI of Scotland

Janissaries were enslaved groups of soldiers recruited as children from the Christian provinces of the Ottoman Empire to serve the Ottoman state and the sultan as his personal bodyguards. Armed with firearms, they constituted the elite of the Ottoman army from the 1400s until 1826, when they were abolished. As a result of their intense loyalty, the sultan often used them to repress efforts at local autonomy in the Ottoman Empire.

Jansenism was a movement within the Catholic Church in the 1600s in Europe that taught that human beings were so corrupted by original sin that they could do nothing good nor could they secure their own salvation without divine grace. They emphasized that the texts of Saint Augustine stressed predestination and the need for personal and unmerited grace. The Jesuits opposed them.

Jerome, Saint (347–420) was a Roman who became a Christian ascetic. He wrote many letters and translated the Bible into Latin. He is considered one of the fathers of the Catholic Church.

Jesuits (1540) were members of the Society of Jesus, founded by Ignatius Loyola and approved by the papacy in 1540. Their goal was to spread the Roman Catholic faith through humanistic schools and missionary activity. The Society stressed "modern" methods in its works and by 1600 numbered over 8,500 members.

Jesus of Nazareth (circa 4 BCE–30–36 CE) was a Jew from Galilee in northern Israel who sought to reform Jewish beliefs and practices. The Romans executed him as a revolutionary. Hailed by his followers as the "anointed one" as foretold by the Hebrew Bible, he became the central figure in Christianity, a belief system that developed in the centuries after his death. The popularity of his teachings led to a clash with Jewish and Roman authorities in Jerusalem and his crucifixion by the Romans.

Jewish Deicide is a belief that Jewish people as a whole were responsible for the death of Jesus. This accusation was typically expressed in the slur "Christ-killer." As a part of Second Vatican Council (1962–1965), the Roman Catholic Church under Pope Paul VI issued a declaration which, in part, repudiated the belief in the collective Jewish guilt for the crucifixion of Jesus. In 1998, the Church Council of Evangelical Lutheran Church in America adopted a resolution stating that "the New Testament . . . must not be used as justification for hostility towards present-day Jews," and that "blame for the death of Jesus should not be attributed to Judaism or the Jewish people."

Jewish-Roman Wars were three major rebellions by the Jews of Judaea against Roman rule. The first, the Great Revolt was from 66–73. The second, the Kitos War, was from 115–117. The third, Bar Kokhba's Revolt, was from 132–135 CE. The Great Revolt arose because of Greek and Jewish religious tensions. However, it escalated into protests against Roman taxes. After the Roman military garrison in Judaea was initially overrun by the rebels, Emperor Nero gave command of the Roman legions to Vespasian and his son Titus. The Great Revolt ended when legions under Titus destroyed rebel resistance in Jerusalem in 70 CE.

Jiang Qing (1914–1991) was the wife of Mao Zedong. During the Cultural Revolution, she was responsible for the reform of the performing arts. She became the leader of the so-called Gang of Four, who sought to promote a radical vision of egalitarian revolution.

Jiang Zemin (1926–2002) was the Communist Party official and former mayor of Shanghai who became general secretary of the Chinese Communist Party after the suppression of the Tiananmen student movement in June 1989. He restored order and returned to the path of reform and openness to the outside world inaugurated by Deng Xiaoping.

Jiangxi Soviet (1931–1934) was an independent government established by Mao Zedong and his comrade Zhu De in Jiangxi province in southeastern China, even though the majority of China was still under the control of the nationalist government of the Republic of China. It was during this Jiangxi Soviet period that Mao gained the experience in guerrilla warfare and peasant organization that he later used to accomplish the conquest of China in 1949. Under the leadership of Mao Zedong, the Jiangxi Soviet gradually had a population of more than three million people and an army of more than 140,000 soldiers. After repeated successful attacks and encirclement by the Kuomindang forces led by Chiang Kai-shek, the almost annihilated Chinese Red Army was forced to abandon the Jiangxi Soviet in 1934 and begin what would be later known as the Long March.

Jihad is an Arabic word meaning "struggle," including violent struggle against unbelievers. The doctrine is based on the section of Koran that justified the use of military force against non-Muslims. The doctrine was more fully developed after 750. According to a Muslim scholar at that time, Muslims were obligated to establish a single Islamic world state called the House of Islam, which would observe Islamic law. For those scholars jihad meant political and legal unity rather than religious unity, for Christians and Jews were permitted to practice their respective religions within the House of Islam.

Jingoism refers to an attitude or belief of extreme and belligerent patriotism that is often used to gain popular support for a war and other political causes. It involves the use of public opinion by politicians and governmental leaders to build nationalist support for a person's country and hatred of the people of another nation. Jingoism was used extensively to justify imperial expansion and colonization around the world in the 1800s and 1900s by European nations and the United States.

Jinnah, Muhammad Ali (1876–1948) was an Indian Muslim lawyer and politician who joined the All-India Muslim League in 1913. He eventually became the leader of the League and negotiated with the British and the Indian National Congress for Muslim participation in Indian politics. After 1940, he led the movement for independence of India's Muslims and the creation of separate state, Pakistan.

Joan of Arc, Saint (1412–1431) was the French female teenager who claimed that she was divinely inspired to lead the French forces against the English during the Hundred Years' War. She was burned at the stake by the English for heresy and later made a Catholic saint.

Joint-Stock Company was a form of business organization that was organized by a group of English merchants in the 1600s in order to raise capital for investment purposes. It raised capital by selling shares to individuals who hoped to receive a dividend/profit on their investment and who wished to spread their risk among a number of investors. The shareholders in a joint-stock company could be held responsible for the company's debt only up to the amount they had invested in the company. The London Company was a joint-stock company chartered by the English in 1606 that, after renaming itself the Virginia Company, was responsible for founding the first permanent English settlement in America, Jamestown, Virginia, in 1607.

Josephus, Flavius (37–100 CE) was a Jewish court historian who was appointed by the Roman emperor Vespasian. His books, *The Jewish War* and *The Antiquities of the Jews* are the principal sources for information about Palestine during the 1st century CE.

Juarez, Benito (1806–1872) led Mexico's resistance to the French invasion in 1863 and the installation of Maximillian as emperor. Born in poverty, he was educated as a lawyer and rose to become chief justice of the Mexican Supreme Court and then president of Mexico from 1858 to 1872.

Judah or Judaea was the southernmost of the two Israelite kingdoms that were established after the death of Solomon in the 10th century BCE. Its capital was in Jerusalem. It was conquered by the Neo-Babylonians in 586 BCE.

Julia Agrippina (15–59 CE), also known as Agrippina the younger, was a Roman patrician woman who was the great granddaughter of Emperor Augustus, the sister of Emperor Caligula, the wife of emperor Claudius (her uncle), and the mother of emperor Nero. Suspected of poisoning Caligula, she was exiled, but was allowed to return to Rome when Claudius, her uncle, became emperor. Subsequently, she married Claudius and convinced him to adopt Nero as his son and make Nero the heir to the throne instead of Claudius's own son. When Nero succeeded Claudius to the throne, he was only sixteen, so Agrippina initially acted as regent and controlled the Roman Empire until Nero, in a power struggle with her, took control of the government and expelled her from the imperial palace.

Julian the Apostate (331/332–363 CE) was the last pagan ruler of the Roman Empire who reigned from 361 to 363. He attempted a revival of paganism throughout the Roman Empire in order to reverse the gains made by Christianity since Constantine.

Julio-Claudians was a dynasty of Roman emperors founded by Augustus. The members of this dynasty would provide the emperors of Rome from 14 CE to 68 CE. The succession consisted of Augustus stepson Tiberius, great-grandson Caligula, grand-nephew Claudius, and great-great-grandson Nero. The reign of the Julio-Claudians was considered a time of stability and peace by the lower classes, but the elite Romans considered it a time of decadence and scandal.

Julius Caesar (100–44 BCE) was a brilliant, ambitious, and enigmatic Roman politician who held high offices in Rome, won military glory and individual riches in Gaul, and became dictator in Rome. He was eventually murdered in the Senate as the result of a conspiracy among the senators of Rome.

July Revolution (1830) was a liberal democratic revolt in France by the upper and middle classes against the reactionary and absolutist policies of King Charles X. Charles opposed the liberal reforms that had been instituted in France since 1814. He wanted to strengthen the power of the nobility and the Catholic Church and wanted to restore the divine right monarchy of the Bourbons in France. In order to achieve his goals, Charles issued ordinances dissolved the newly formed legislative body known as the Chamber of Deputies He ordered a new election based on an extremely limited franchise, suspended freedom of the press, permitted him to rule by decree. After five days of protests, demonstrations, and street fighting, Charles X was forced to abdicate. This Revolution represented a significant political victory for the supporters of a constitutional monarchy. It brought Louis Phillipe to the throne as the French king whose constitutional monarchy lasted until 1848. This revolt against the absolutist government of Charles X also inspired similar uprisings in Belgium, Germany, Italy, and Russian Poland.

June Days (1848) was a political uprising in Paris by workers and radicals that was brutally suppressed by the government forces of the new French Republic. This event represented the growing political conflict between supporters of liberal democracy and advocates of workingclass militancy.

Junk was the named used to describe the very large sailing ships that were built and used during the Tang, Song, and Ming dynasties in China.

Junkers were the traditional nobility and landlords of eastern Prussia whose large estates and tradition of military and bureaucratic service ensured their political dominance in the Prussian state. They were a class of aristocratic, authoritarian, and militaristic landholders from which many German military officers would be drawn.

Jupiter refers to a class of U.S. intermediaterange ballistic missiles developed in the 1950s by a team of scientists led by Wernher Von Braun, who had previously developed V-1 and V-2 rockets for Nazi Germany.

Just War Doctrine is a doctrine of international law and political theory that defines when wars can be justly started (jus *ad bellum*) and how they can be justly fought (jus *in bello*). Saint Augustine developed the standards for a Christian "just war" around 400 CE. He argued that there five standard that had to be met in order for a war by Christians to be considered just. First, there had to be a "rightful intention" on the part of the participants in war, which should always be expressed in terms of the love of God and one's neighbor. Second, there must be a just cause. Third, there must be a proclamation by a legitimate and qualified authority that a war is just. Fourth, in a just war the use of violence and its consequences, death and injury, are morally neutral rather than intrinsically evil and whether violence is good or bad is a matter of intention. Fifth, Christ, who is concerned with the political order of humans, has endowed his agents on earth, kings, popes and bishops, with the authority to establish a Christian republic, which has the moral imperative to use force to defend that Christian republic from God's enemies, whether they be foreign infidels or domestic heretics.

Justification by Faith refers to Luther's central theological tenet that humanity is incapable of performing enough religious good works to earn eternal salvation. Luther's idea challenged the authority and the fundamental practices of the Catholic Church. Specifically, he argued that salvation is an unmerited gift from God called grace, and those who receive grace are called the Elect. In Christianity, justification is the process through which an individual, who has been alienated from God because of sin, is reconciled to God and becomes righteous once again through faith in Christ.

Justin Martyr, Saint (100–165 CE) was a Greek philosopher and Christian apologist who formulated the early version of the doctrine of the Trinity. He wrote *Dialogue with Trypho the Jew* in order to differentiate between Christianity and Judaism. In that book, he tried to prove the truth of Christianity to Trypho, a learned Jew. Justin argued that a new covenant had superseded the old covenant that God had with the Jewish people. Furthermore, he contended that Jesus was the messiah announced in the Old Testament and that the gentiles had been chosen by God to replace Israel as God's chosen people. As an apologist for Christianity, he wrote the *First Apology* which he addressed to emperors Antoninus Pius and Marcus Aurelius. In that book, he defended Christianity against the charges of atheism and hostility to the Roman state and explained the central ideas of Christian philosophy. In his book *Second Apology*, he argued that the Christians were being unjustly persecuted by Rome.

Justinian I (483–565 CE) was the emperor of the Byzantine Empire who ruled from 529–565. He reconquered some of the western provinces of the Roman Empire, including North Africa, Italy, and part of Spain; overhauled the administration of his portion of the Byzantine Empire; codified Roman law and issued the *Corpus Juris Civilis* (also know as Justinian's Code or the Code of Justinian): and built the Hagia Sophia in Constantinople, which for a time was the largest church in the world. His efforts to rebuild the Roman Empire overtaxed the Byzantine Empire.

Juvenal (55/60–127 CE) was a Roman poet who focused on the more unpleasant aspects of Roman imperial culture. He wrote social commentary about the crowded, noisy, and unsafe streets of Rome as well as its thieves and murders. His most famous book is entitled *The Satires*, in which he wrote: "A man's word is believed just to the extent of the wealth in his coffers. Though he may swear on all the altars from here to Samothrace, a poor man isn't believed."

Ka'ba is the religious shrine in the city of Mecca that became the holiest shrine of Islam. For those Muslims embarking on a hajj, the goal is to go to the Ka'ba.

Kadesh, Battle of (1274 BCE) was a battle between Egyptian and Hittite armies in Syria that set the territorial limits of both empires in Canaan and the Middle East for a century during the International Bronze Age.

Kamikaze, which means "divine wind" in Japanese, refers to the suicide attacks by Japanese pilots against U.S. ships in the Pacific beginning in 1944. Originally, it was used by the Japanese to describe the storms that destroyed the attempted Mongol invasions in 1274 and 1281. Kamikaze pilots would attempt to intentionally crash their aircraft (usually laden with explosives, bombs, torpedoes, and full fuel tanks) into U.S. ships with a goal of causing greater damage than a conventional attack such as dropping bombs, torpedoing, or using machine guns. The objective of such attacks was to stop or slow the U.S. advance toward Japan by causing as much damage and destruction as possible to the American fleet.

Kang Youwei (1858–1927) was one of the leaders of the Hundred Days of Reform in China in 1898, but he later became an advocate for a constitutional monarchy for China.

Kangxi (1654–1722) was the second emperor of the Qing Dynasty. He presided over the suppression of the rebellion of Wu Sangui and launched campaigns to bring the Mongol tribes in Xinjiang into the Qing Empire. He ruled from 1661–1722.

Kant, Immanuel (1724–1804) was a German philosopher who wrote *Critique of Pure Reason,* in which Kant examined human knowledge and designed his own individual epistemology. He was unorthodox in his religious teachings and was banned from teaching or writing about religion by Frederick William II, the King of Prussia. Kant did not teach any religious philosophy until after the death of King Frederick William II, believing that he was free of his obligation. In *Metaphysics of Ethics*, Kant explained that ethics based on reason was the highest moral power. In his *Critique of Practical Reason*, Kant expressed his views concerning freedom, the freedom of self-government, and the freedom to obey the laws of the universe as understood by reason.

Kassites (1600–1100 BCE) was the name of a mountain tribe who migrated to the Zagros Mountains and Mesopotamia between 1600 and 1200 BCE. They conquered Mesopotamia, bringing the Old Babylonian era to an end and for, the first time, welding together the network of independent, feuding city-states into a territory that would be called "Babylonia." Kassite hegemony in Babylon, Nippur and other urban centers lasted from about 1595 to 1155 BCE. The circumstances of their rise to power are unknown, due to a lack of documentation from this so-called "Dark Age" period of widespread dislocation.

Keats, John (1795–1821) was an English poet whose inspiration was the beauty of the natural world. His most famous poem is *The Grecian Urn,* which contains the notable line that "truth is beauty". However, Keats's career was cut short when he died of tuberculosis at the age of 25.

Kellogg-Briand Pact (1928) was an international agreement signed by 54 nations after World War I condemning aggressive war as illegal and promising not to use war to resolve any disputes or conflicts that may arise among them. The U.S. Senate ratified the treaty by a vote of 85–1. The treaty did not live up to expectations. Within a few years the U.S. militarily intervened in Central America, the Japanese invaded Manchuria in 1931, Italy invaded Abyssinia in 1935 and Germany and the Soviet Union invaded Poland in 1939.

Kent State (1970) refers to the incident on May 4, 1970, at Kent State University in Ohio, when four students protesting the Vietnam War were shot to death by Ohio National Guard troops. This incident galvanized popular opposition to the Vietnam War.

Kepler, Johannes (1571–1630) was an astronomer and mathematician whose thinking altered science. After studying astronomy with Tycho Brahe and as a result of Brahe's astronomical data, he became convinced that the sun must be at the center of the universe and he deduced his three laws of planetary motion. He mathematically confirmed the heliocentric theory of Copernicus. His work was essential to the work of Newton. His ideas, known as Kepler's Laws, are still accepted today.

Kerensky, Alexander (1881–1970) was a moderate socialist revolutionary who supported Russia's participation in World War I. When the Russian Revolution took place in March 1917, he advocated the dissolution of the monarchy. He served as the leader of the Provisional Government in Russia from July to October 1917. During that period, he instituted such reforms as freedom of speech, press, assembly, and religion; universal suffrage; and equal rights for women. However, he failed to gain the support of the Russian population. Specifically, he refused to redistribute land from the aristocracy to the peasants until after World War I, and he promised the Allies that Russia would continue fighting against the Germans in World War I even though the war was highly unpopular among most Russians. In October 1917, the Bolsheviks staged an uprising in St. Petersburg that caused the Provisional Government led by Kerensky to fall.

Keynes, John Maynard (1883–1946) was a British economist whose views on a planned economy influenced the New Deal policies of President Franklin Roosevelt. The unemployment crisis in Britain in the 1920s and 1930s inspired his two famous books: *A Treatise on Money* and *The General Theory of Employment, Interest and Money* in 1936. Perhaps his most significant contribution to economic thought concerns the nature of value. Since the development of economics in the 1700s, economists had endeavored to develop a precise and objective definition of value. Both Adam Smith and Karl Marx argued that value was primarily determined by the cost of production, especially the cost of labor. By contrast Keynes argued that the primary force that determines the value of an object is the relationship of the consumer to the object—that is, value is determined by consumer demand in the marketplace.

Keynesian Economics is the economic theory of John Maynard Keynes that became influential in Britain and the United States in the 1930s. His theory opposed classical laissez-faire economics and emphasized government spending to encourage investment and increase employment. He contended that free market economies cannot always be relied upon to self-correct and therefore must sometimes be actively managed by a central government. He urged government to minimize the effects of the boom-and-bust cycles inherent in laissez-faire economies by manipulating interest rates and employment through the development of public works projects. He specifically argued that governments could spend their economies out of a depression by running deficits to encourage employment and stimulate the production and consumption of goods.

KGB was the name of the secret Soviet police and spy agency that was formed first as the Cheka not long after the Bolshevik Revolution in October 1917. At its height in the 1980s, it had 750,000 operatives who held military ranks.

Khanate was a major political unit of the vast Mongol Empire. There were four khanates, including the Yuan Empire in China, that were forged by Chingiz Khan's grandson Kublai in the 1200s.

Khedive was the title of the Turkish ruler of Egypt from 1867–1914.

Khomeini, Ayatollah Rudollah (1900– 1989) was the Iranian Shi'ite philosopher and religious leader who led the revolt and overthrow of the Shah of Iran in 1979 and created an Islamic Republic in Iran.

Khrushchev, Nikita (1894–1971) was the leader of the Soviet Union during the Cuban Missile Crisis.

He came to power after the death of Stalin in 1953, but his criticisms of Stalin's policies and his political reforms led to his fall from power in 1964.

Khublai Khan (1215–1294) was the last of the Great Khans of the Mongol Empire. After conquering the Song Dynasty in China, he founded the Yuan Dynasty that lasted only about 100 years. He was the grandson of Temujin. As the first emperor of the Yuan Dynasty, he established the Mongol capital at Dadu, presentday Beijing.

Kibbutz is the Hebrew word for a collective farm that was established by European Jews who immigrated to Palestine in the late 1800s and early 1900s. On these collective farms, the Jewish immigrants wanted to establish a socialist society in which the wealth of the kibbutz was shared among all of its members.

Kiloton is the equivalent 1000 tons of TNT. The atomic bomb dropped on Hiroshima was equal to more than 15 kilotons.

Kipling, Rudyard (1865–1936) was an English author and poet, born in Bombay, India, and best known for his works *The Jungle Book* (1894), *The Second Jungle Book* (1895), *Just So Stories* (1902), and *Puck of Pook's Hill* (1906), his novel, *Kim* (1901), and his poems, including "Mandalay" (1890), "Gunga Din" (1890), "The White Man's Burden" (1899), and "If _____" (1910). Kipling was one of the most popular writers in Britain in the late 1800s and early 1900s. However, Kipling was viewed as an advocate of British imperialism, racial prejudice, and militarism. His poem "The White Man's Burden" was originally published in 1899 in *McClure's,* a popular American magazine, with the subtitle "The United States and the Philippine Islands." It was written in response to the U.S. conquest of the Philippines and other former Spanish colonies during the Spanish-American War. Although Kipling's poem combined encouragement to build an empire with warnings of the costs of empire, imperialists within the United States latched onto the phrase "white man's burden" as a characterization for imperialism that justified the policy as a noble enterprise. The poem has been viewed by many as a command to white men to colonize and rule people of other nations for their own benefit.

Because of this theme and its title, it became a symbol both of European and American racism and of Western aspirations to dominate the developing world.

Knight was a soldier who fought on horseback during the Middle Ages. He was a vassal of a lord who usually financed the knight's expenses for armor, weapons, and raising and feeding a horse. For his military service to the lord, he was typically given a grant of land known as a fief.

Knossos is the site of a huge palace complex built by the Minoan kings on Crete.

Koine was a "common" or "shared" form of Greek that became the international language in the Hellenistic period.

Korean War (1950–1953) was the conflict that began with North Korea's invasion of South Korea. This invasion led to the involvement of the United Nations and its authorization of the UN-sponsored military forces led by the United States to force the North Koreans to withdraw from South Korea. During this war, the United States was the ally of South Korea and the People's Republic of China supported the North Koreans.

Kosovo, Battle of (1488) was the decisive military victory in Kosovo, Serbia by the Ottoman Empire over the Christian Crusaders led by the king of Hungary who had sought to free the Balkans and Constantinople from the threat of the Ottoman Empire.

Kremlin was used during the Cold War to refer to the Soviet government. It is the walled fortress in the center of Moscow where much of the Soviet government was located.

Kristallnacht (The Night of the Broken Glass) was the name for the pogroms carried out on November 9–10, 1938 in Germany. Hundreds of synagogues and Jewish-owned stores were burned and looted. Many Jews were beaten and killed, and about 30,000 were rounded up and sent to concentration camps. The name was derived from the glass fragments from broken windows that littered the streets after this nationwide pogrom. This event marked the first nationally coordinated and government supported campaign of violence against Jews in Germany.

Krypteia was the Spartan secret police who spied on the helots and other Spartans.

Kulaks were a class of relatively prosperous and wealthy Russian peasant farmers who benefited under Lenin's New Economic Policy (NEO), but who subsequently resisted the agricultural collectivization programs of Stalin in the Soviet Union in the 1920s and 1930s. Many of the kulaks were killed or deported to the gulags by Stalin.

Kulturkamp, which means the "battle for culture" or "struggle for civilization" in German, was the conflict between the Catholic Church and the government of the German Empire in the 1870s.

Kuomindang was the Chinese name for the Chinese Nationalist Party that was founded on democratic principles by Sun Yat-sen in 1912. After 1925, Chiang Kai-shek, who turned it into an authoritarian political movement, headed the Kuomindang. It has been centered in Taiwan since the end of the Chinese civil war in 1949

Kush, which was an Egyptian name for Nubia, was the region along the Nile River south of Egypt where an indigenous kingdom with its own distinctive institutions and cultural traditions arose beginning in the early second millennium BCE. It was deeply influenced by Egyptian culture and at times under the control of Egypt, which coveted its rich deposits of gold and luxury products from sub-Saharan Africa carried up the Nile corridor.

$\mathcal{L}$

Laissez-faire is a French term ("Let it do as it wants to do or allow to do") used in the 1700s for an economic policy that argued that government should allow free markets for the sale of grain. This economic doctrine was eventually adopted by English economists to describe economies that were free from government regulations, controls, and intervention. Adam Smith and the physiocrats in France were the leading proponents of this idea. The removal of governmental barriers to free trade became a central feature of the liberal political agenda in Europe in the 1800s. Laissez-faire is also known as the theory of classical liberal economics.

Land Mines are concealed explosive devices that are often left behind by regular and irregular armies, which kill or maim civilians after a war has ended. Today, there are more than 100 million such mines, primarily in Angola, Bosnia, Afghanistan, and Cambodia. A movement to ban land mines is under way, and nearly 100 states have agreed to do so.

Land Reform refers to the political and economic policy adopted by the Chinese Communist Party between 1948 and 1952 that led to the seizure and redistribution of land in China. The program was designed to eliminate the old system of land tenure in China in which a small elite held a substantial majority of the arable land, renting it to farming families. Land was distributed to all peasants, male and female alike. As a result of this program, the power of the landlord class over rural farming society was broken and agricultural production increased.

Laozi (6th century BCE) is the name of the legendary philosopher of the Warring States Period (6th century BCE) whose ideas became the foundation for Daoism. He rejected the positivism of Confucian thought and encouraged a skeptical approach to knowledge and action. He also advocated seeking harmony with nature.

Lapis Lazuli is a precious deep-blue gemstone found in the Middle East that was traded widely for jewelry during the Bronze Age.

Las Casas, Bartolome de (1474–1566) was the first bishop of Chiapas in southern Mexico. He devoted his life to protecting the people of Mexico from exploitation by the Spanish. He was able to have passed the New Laws of 1542, which limited the ability of Spanish settlers to compel the native population to work for them.

Lascaux is the setting of a complex of caves in southwestern France famous for its cave paintings.

They contain some of the most well-known Paleolithic art, dating back to somewhere between 15,000 and 13,000 BCE. The paintings consist mostly of realistic images of large animals, most of which are known from fossil evidence to have lived in the area at the time. The cave contains nearly 2000 figures.

Late Antiquity (200–800) is the term used by historians to describe the period between the end of the ancient world and the beginning of the Middle Ages.

Lateen Sail is a triangular sail attached to a long yardarm commonly used by dhows.

Lateran Treaty (1929) was the treaty between the Italian government led by Benito Mussolini and the papacy by which the papacy recognized the state of Italy and in turn Italy recognized papal authority over Vatican City. Under this treaty Italy only recognized the validity of a Catholic marriage, that those marriages were governed by canon law and ecclesiastical courts and that divorce was prohibited. Furthermore, the treaty permitted religious instruction in Italian public schools and that bishops had the authority to appoint and dismiss teachers in all schools and approve the textbooks used in all public schools.

Latifundia were large agricultural estates for growing cash crops owned by wealthy Romans, including the emperor, that were worked by mainly slaves, but also by free tenant farmers, who were called coloni.

Latin is the Indo-European language of ancient Rome and its empire from which today's Romance languages such as Italian, French, Spanish, and Rumanian developed.

Latin Right was a legal status of half-citizenship that was conferred on loyal allies and colonists of the Roman Empire. Individuals having this status would have all the rights and privileges of an ancient Roman citizen except the right to vote or to hold office.

Latin Christendom or Latin West is the term used by some historians for the territories of Europe that adhered to the Latin rite of the Catholic

Church and used the Latin language for intellectual exchange between 1000–1500 CE.

Latitudinarinism was a movement within the early modern Church of England that accepted the appropriateness of wide differences of belief, ritual, and interpretation of the Scriptures within Christianity.

Latium was the name for the region in Italy where Rome is located. Its inhabitants were known as Latins.

Lausanne, Treaty of (1923) was part of the Versailles peace settlement ending World War I. This treaty recognized the boundaries of modern Turkey, the possession of Cyprus by Britain and made the straits connecting the Black Sea and the Aegean Sea open to all shipping. It also partitioned the Arab territories of the Ottoman Empire among the victorious European nations. Specifically, Palestine, Transjordan and Iraq became mandates of Britain and Syria and Lebanon became mandates of France.

Law of the Twelve Tables (450 BCE) was the first codification of Roman law and was posted in the forum on twelve bronze tablets. As part of the Conflict of the Orders, the plebeians demanded that unwritten law enforced by the patrician-controlled courts be written down. The plebeians argued that in order to defend their legal rights from patrician abuse they had to know the law.

League of Augsburg (1686), which was also known as the Grand Alliance, was a European coalition of nations, consisting at various times of Austria, Bavaria, Brandenburg, Britain, the Holy Roman Empire, the Palatinate of the Rhine, Portugal, Savoy, Saxony, Spain, Sweden, and the United Provinces. The primary reason for the League's creation was to defend the Palatinate from France. This organization fought the War of the Grand Alliance against France from 1688 to 1697. Between 1689 and 1698 it fought the Nine Years' War against France. In 1701, it became the Alliance of the War of Spanish Succession. The Grand Alliance gained enormous cultural and political importance as an example of a possible European union supported by most of the German territories, Britain, and the Netherlands as

well as by many French intellectuals dissatisfied with the absolutist rule of Louis XIV and the eviction of the Huguenots from France in 1685. The end of the Great Alliance was due primarily to a growing dissatisfaction among the British populace concerning the financial costs of the wars. The Great Alliance and wars fought by the Alliance also contributed to a new sense of how wars would be fought in the future in Europe. While the death toll of the wars fought by the Alliance was enormous, none of the three wars fought from 1689 to 1721 led to a repeat of the atrocities of the Thirty Years' War. Instead, the generals of the Great Alliance became heroes of a Europe who were "civilized even when at war." This illusion of civilized war would last until the beginning of the 1900s.

League of Nations (1919–1946) was the international organization created after World War I to promote world peace and cooperation and to resolve international disputes and conflict through open and peaceful negotiations. While its constitution was drafted by Woodrow Wilson at the Paris Peace Conference in 1919, the League was greatly weakened in terms of its effectiveness by the refusal of the U.S. Senate to approve joining it. The League would prove ineffectual in preventing the aggression by Italy, Japan, and Germany in the 1930s that culminated in World War II. It was the forerunner of the United Nations.

Lebensraum, which means "living space" in German, was a policy first articulated in Germany in the late 1800s by which German leaders claimed the need to expand German territory into Eastern and Central Europe and Russia in order to accommodate the growing German population. The Nazis during World War II implemented this policy of colonization.

Legalism was a philosophy developed in China that was closely associated with the Qin Dynasty during the Warring States period. It emphasized the unruliness of human nature, justified coercion by the state in order to control the population, and was based on a system of rewards and punishments. Laws and regulations were established by the state, and anyone who violated those laws or regulations, whether high government official or lowly peasant, would be punished equally. The rulers of the Qin Dynasty used this philosophy to justify the authoritarian nature of their social and political policies.

Legion was the main unit of the Roman army that was comprised of approximately 6000 men organized into 60 centuries. The smallest unit of a Roman legion was a century, which was comprised of 100 soldiers commanded by a centurion. Six centuries constituted a cohort and there were ten cohorts in a Roman legion. The legion was a highly innovative and successful military formation. The legion included many flexible, adaptable, and semi-independent groups that weakened the Roman enemies first with the use of long-range javelins before charging with sword and shield.

Legitimacy is the claim of the moral and legal authority to wield power. Such authority may be justified, for example, on the basis of religious beliefs, law, custom, heredity, or the consent of the governed. All forms of social organization develop a form of authority in which an individual or a group of individuals (decision-makers) wield power over the majority. In order for these decision-makers to wield power, they must convince the majority that they, the decision-makers, deserve the authority that they wield. In fact, all forms of government are built on political theories that address two fundamental questions: who should have the authority to make political decisions, and why? Whenever a justification for authority is rejected by a powerful group in a society or the majority of the people in a society, a crisis of legitimacy occurs. In such a situation, a change in the form of government may occur, sometimes by force, such as a revolution, in order to reflect a different basis for the authoritative exercise of political power. The American, French, Russian, and Chinese revolutions are examples of the social and political results of a crisis of legitimacy.

Legitimacy, Principle of was the idea that was enunciated by the victorious European powers at the Congress of Vienna after the Napoleonic Wars that peace could be best reestablished by restoring legitimate monarchs to power and preserving traditional institutions.

Lend-Lease Act (1941) was the law passed by the U.S. Congress in March 1941 that gave Britain access to American industrial products and military supplies during the early stages of World War II before U.S. involvement. President Roosevelt was authorized to lend or to lease weapons or any other aid to countries that he designated. Any payment for such goods would be postponed until after World War II.

Lenin, Vladimir or Vladimir Ilyich Ulyanov (1870–1924) was the leader of the Bolsheviks beginning in 1903 and during the Russian Revolution of 1917. He lived in exile in Switzerland until 1917 and then returned to Russia with the assistance of Germany to lead the Bolsheviks during the Russian Revolution in October 1917 against the Provisional Government led by Alexander Kerensky. He concluded the Treaty of Brest-Litovsk with Germany that ended Russian participation in World War I. He led the Soviet Union during the civil war that followed the Revolution and began the establishment of communism in the Soviet Union. Leninism refers to the ideological revisions to Marxism made by Lenin in which he argued that Russia did not have to experience a bourgeois revolution before it could move toward socialism.

Leo III was the Byzantine emperor who reigned from 717–741 CE. He repelled the Arabic siege of Constantinople in 717–718 and issued the edict against the veneration of icons in 726 which began the Iconoclasm Controversy.

Leonidas (died 480 BCE) was the Spartan king at the time of the Persian invasions who died at the Battle of Thermopylae in 480 BCE.

Leopold II, King (1835–1909) was the monarch of Belgium who actively encouraged the exploration and colonization of Central Africa. He brutally ruled the Congo Free State until 1908.

Lepanto, Battle of (1571) was the decisive naval victory by the Spanish led forces over the larger Ottoman fleet in the eastern part of the Mediterranean. The battle was part of Spain's self-appointed role as defender of Christendom against the Islamic Ottoman Empire.

Lepidus, Marcus Aemilius (died 13/12 BCE) was a supporter of Julius Caesar when he became dictator of Rome. However, after Caesar was assassinated by Brutus, Lepidus became an ally of Mark Antony. He formed the Second Triumvirate with Octavian and Mark Antony in 43 BCE, but was politically outmaneuvered by Octavian in 36 BCE and stripped of his political and military powers.

Less-Developed Countries are the world's poorest regions located in the global south where most people live. They are also called underdeveloped countries or developing countries.

Levée en masse (1793) is the French phrase for the universal conscription or drafting of all unmarried males between the ages of 18 and 25 (300,000 soldiers) into the French army in 1793 during the French Revolution.

Levant, which is derived from a French word meaning "to rise," is a geographical term used by historians and archaeologists that historically has encompassed the ancient societies along the eastern Mediterranean shores of Syria, Phoenicia and Palestine.

Li is a basic concept in neo-Confucianism in China arguing that by observing natural patterns, one could understand the underlying principles of the universe, and that a person could only be in harmony with the natural patterns by doing good or proper acts.

Li Dazhao (1889–1927) was an influential educator and intellectual who was involved in the May 4th Movement and was one of the founders of the Chinese Communist Party.

Li Shimin (598–649) was the second emperor of the Tang Dynasty who expanded the Tang Empire into central Asia. His imperial name was Taizong.

Li Zicheng (1605–1645) was the leader of a peasant rebellion against the Ming Dynasty in the 1640s who succeeded in capturing Beijing in April 1644. He established a short-lived dynasty, but was defeated by the Mongols in June 1644.

Liang Qichao (1873–1929) was an influential political and social reformer and writer in China in the late 1800s and early 1900s who participated with Kang Youwei in the Hundred Days of Reform in 1898. He later became a publisher of radical newspapers in Shanghai and Japan.

Liberal Arts were the seven areas of study that formed the basis of university education in medieval and early modern Europe. They consisted of grammar, rhetoric, dialectic or logic, mathematics, geometry, astronomy, and music.

Liberalism is a political theory and ideology that emerged in the early 1800s founded on the belief that individual freedom is of supreme importance and that the primary responsibility of government is to protect that freedom. It argued that political authority is inherently corruptible. Liberalism advocated individual rights, representative constitutional government, legal reforms, religious tolerance, and a free-market economy. It generally opposed revolutionary change, but favored institutional reforms that would protect or enhance civil rights and personal freedom. This ideology was greatly influenced by the Enlightenment and was especially popular among the property-owning middle class in Europe and the United States.

Libertarianism is a political philosophy that emphasizes the minimization or the elimination of government in society and the economy in order to maximize individual liberty and freedom. Libertarians differ over the degree to which government should be reduced. Some advocate that the government should only provide protection from aggression, theft, breach of contract, and fraud, while others advocate complete elimination of the state.

Liberty is a concept in political philosophy that articulates the relationship of individuals to a society. Specifically, this concept identifies the condition under which human beings are able to govern themselves and exercise freedoms and rights that are essential to liberty. Traditional conceptions of liberty as expressed in the U.S. Constitution consist of the freedom of individuals from outside compulsion or coercion, also known as negative liberty.

Library of Alexandria (3rd century BCE–48 BCE) is considered to be the largest and most important library of the ancient world. It was established and supported by the Ptolemaic rulers of Egypt. It became the foremost intellectual, cultural and scientific center for scholarship and research in the ancient world. The purpose of the Library was to collect all of the world's knowledge that was written on papyrus scrolls. In fact, the Library had a large collection of Greek authors, including poems by Homer, histories by Herodotus and Thucydides and philosophical works by Plato and Aristotle. Eratosthenes of Cyrene became one of its head librarians. It is claimed that the Library had 700,000 papyrus scrolls. According to some ancient accounts, it is claimed that Julius Caesar accidently burned the library down in 48 BCE.

Library of Ashurbanipal is a large collection of writings drawn from the ancient literary, religious, and scientific traditions of Mesopotamia. The Assyrian ruler Ashurbanipal assembled it in the 500s BCE. The many tablets unearthed by archaeologists constitute one of the most important sources of present-day knowledge of the long literary tradition of Mesopotamia.

Licinian-Sexton Law (367 BCE) was the Roman law that stipulated that of the two consuls elected each year to administer the Roman government and lead its armies, one was required be a plebeian. Until this law, only patricians could serve as consuls.

Limited Test Ban Treaty (1963) was a multilateral arms control agreement among the United States, Great Britain, and the Soviet Union that prohibited the testing of nuclear weapons in the atmosphere, space, and underwater.

Lin Biao (1908–1971) was a communist military leader and minister of defense who became Mao's designated successor in 1969. He is reported to have attempted to assassinate Mao before fleeing in an airplane, which was shot down over Mongolia.

Lin Zexu (1785–1850) was a Qing Dynasty official who was put in charge of opium suppression in Guangzhou in 1838. His strong efforts to eliminate the drug trade led the British to launch the Opium War (1839–1842).

Linear A is the name given to the writing found on Minoan Crete, but it has not yet been deciphered.

Linear B is the name given to the writing found on Minoan Crete that was deciphered by Michael Ventris in the early 1950s. It was used in the Mycenaean palaces of the Late Bronze Age to write an early form of Greek. It was used primarily for palace records. The surviving Linear B tablets provide substantial information about the economic organization of Mycenaean society and some clues about political, social, and religious institutions.

Linear Perspective was a revolutionary technique in painting developed by Florentine artists during the Renaissance to give a flat surface the appearance of depth and dimension. It uses geometrical principles to depict three-dimensional space on a flat, two-dimensional surface. Linear perspective is based on the observation that as two parallel lines recede, they appear to converge. Historians credit Filippo Brunelleschi, a Florentine architect, with formulating the principles of linear perspective even though the first paintings exhibiting linear perspective were produced by Ambrogio Lorenzetti, a Florentine painter, in the mid-1300s. Leon Battista Alberti, another Italian Renaissance architect, would document the basic principles of linear perspective in his book *On Painting* published in 1435. The use of this revolutionary artistic tool would be adopted not only in Italy during the Renaissance, but throughout Europe and remains today a standard artistic technique.

Lingua Franca refers to any language widely used beyond the population of its native speakers. Any language normally becomes a *lingua franca* primarily by being used for international commerce, but can be accepted in other cultural exchanges, especially diplomacy. For example, French was the *lingua franca* of diplomacy and English the *lingua franca* of international commerce.

Linkage refers to the U.S. negotiating policy developed by Henry Kissinger during the Nixon administration to offer concessions to the Soviet Union on technology and trade in exchange for a more responsible Soviet foreign policy.

Literati were the educated elite of a society, many of whom typically would fill the official bureaucratic positions in a government. Membership in this group was generally based on educational accomplishment. However, since an education required economic resources, the literati tended to come from the economic elite.

Lithograph was a mass-produced print, which played a key role in transmitting social and political commentary during the 1830s to 1850s in Europe.

Little Ice Age was a period of general climatic cooling in Europe and North America that occurred between the 1500s and 1800s that affected agricultural production, according to some climatologists and historians. However, climatologists and historians disagree on when it began or ended. The Little Ice Age brought bitterly cold winters to many parts of the world, but it is most thoroughly documented in Europe and North America. For example, beginning in the 1600s and for the next few centuries, glaciers in the Swiss Alps gradually advanced, destroying farms and villages; the Thames River in England froze over, causing the development of winter fairs that took place on the frozen river; canals and rivers in the Netherlands often froze; an area of the Bosphorus near Istanbul froze; and during the winters of 1658 and 1780, the harbor in New York froze over, permitting people from Manhattan to walk to Staten Island. In some locations snowfall was much heavier than recorded before or since, and the snow remained on the ground for many months longer than it does today. Scientists have identified two possible causes for the Little Ice Age: decreased sunlight and increased volcanic activity. For example, in 1815 the eruption of a volcano in Indonesia blanketed the atmosphere with so much ash that the following year, 1816, came to be known as the "Year Without Summer" when frost and snow were reported in June and July in both New England and Northern Europe. Beginning circa 1850, the climate began warming and the Little Ice Age ended.

Liturgy is the form of Christian worship including the prayers, chants, and rituals said, sung, or performed during religious services.

Liu Bang (247–195 BCE) was a minor official of the Qin state who rebelled and raised an army that allowed him to establish a new dynasty, the Han, in 202 BCE. He reigned as first emperor of the Han Dynasty.

Liu Shaoqi (1898–1969) was a Communist Party leader and president of the People's Republic of China in the 1950s and early 1960s. Because he was a political opponent of Mao's policies, he was denounced as a "capitalist roader" during the Cultural Revolution and was purged from office and imprisoned.

Livia Drusilla (58 BCE–29 CE) was the wife of Augustus and the mother of Tiberius. She is noted for the intrigues that she initiated to secure the position of emperor for Tiberius, the successor to Augustus. She was suspected of poisoning several family members, including Augustus himself.

Livy (Titus Livisus Patavinus) (59 BCE–17 CE) was a Roman historian who wrote *History of Rome* that covered the period from Rome's legendary founding until 9 BCE. He wrote celebratory history the glorified Rome's greatness and encouraged patriotism. His narrative was based on myths and earlier accounts with no original research. Livy's book is an important source, even today, for understanding the Roman monarchy and the early Roman Republic.

Locarno, Treaty of (1925) was an agreement by which France and Germany both accepted the post-World War I border between them. Germany was also accepted as a diplomatic equal and was allowed to enter the League of Nations. For many political leaders at the time, this treaty represented a more cooperative spirit in international affairs.

Locke, John (1632–1704) was a British philosopher whose writings contributed to the modern theories of epistemology and political philosophy. He is best known for his *Essay Concerning Human Understanding* and the *Second Treatise of Government*. In his *Two Treatises of Government*, he offered a revolutionary vision of government based on the idea of a social contract and human rights. He argued that the state arises from a contract that individuals freely accept. He argued that as a result of the consent of the governed, political sovereignty of a state resides with the people who have the right to rebel against the government if that government abuses its political power.

Loess is the fine, light silt that constitutes the soil of the Yellow River valley in northern China.

Because it is not compacted, it can be worked with very simple tools.

Logos, which means "divine reason or fire", was, according to the Stoics of ancient Greece, the guiding principle in nature. Every human being had a spark of this divinity, which returned to the eternal divine spirit upon death.

Lollards or Idlers were the rural followers of John Wycliffe in the 1300s in Europe who questioned the supremacy and privileges of the pope and the hierarchy of the Catholic Church.

Lombards were Germanic people who entered Italy in 568 and gradually built a strong kingdom with a rich culture, especially in law, only to fall to the more powerful Franks in 773–774.

Long March (1934–1936) was the 6000-mile flight of the Chinese Communist Party and the Red Army from Jiangxi province in the southeast of China to Shanxi province in the northwest between October 1934 and October 1935. Mao Zedong led the communists and Chiang Kai-shek, who led the Chinese nationalist army (the Kuomindang), pursued the communists. Of the approximately 100,000 communists swho began this trek, only about 6,000–8,000 survived. Those survivors of the Long March would form the nucleus of the rebuilt Communist Party that would defeat the Kuomindang after World War II and would be venerated as heroes of the Chinese Revolution.

Long Parliament (1640–1653) was the English parliament that met from 1640 until 1653. It forced political reforms by Charles I, defeated the royal armies during the English Civil War, and tried and executed Charles I.

Lord was the title of a privileged landowner during the Middle Ages in Europe who exercised authority over the people who lived on his land. Typically, he offered protection to the people who lived on his land in return for service and/or payment of rents.

Los Alamos was the U.S. nuclear research and testing facility in the New Mexico desert where the world's first atomic bomb was developed during World War II.

Lost Generation refers to the 17 million former members of the Red Guard and other Chinese youth who were denied an education from the late 1960s to the mid-1970s as a result of the Cultural Revolution in China.

Louis XIV (1638–1715) was the longest-reigning ruler in European history. He imposed absolutist rule on France and he waged several wars in order to dominate Europe. Known as the "Sun King," he encouraged the development of French society and culture. He reigned from 1643 to 1715.

Lower Egypt is the area of the Nile Delta.

L'Ouverture, Francois Dominique Toussaint (1743–1803) was the ex-slave leader of the Haitian revolt against French colonial rule. He freed the slaves and gained independence for Haiti despite the military intervention by the British and the French to stop the Haitian revolt. He governed the Island of Saint Domingue (Haiti) as an independent state from 1791 until 1802, when French forces captured him. He died in prison.

Loyalists were individuals in England who remained loyal to the English Crown during the English Civil War. The term is also used to refer to those English colonists in North America who supported the British during the American Revolution.

Loyola, Ignatius (Saint Ignatius of Loyola) (1491–1556) was a Spanish nobleman who studied in Paris and founded the Society of Jesus (Jesuits), which became part of the Catholic effort of reform in the wake of the Protestant Reformation. After approval of the new religious order by the papacy, the Jesuits focused primarily on educating Catholics and trying to bring Protestants back to the Catholic faith.

Lucknow Pact (1916) was an agreement to establish unity between the Indian National Congress and the All-India Muslim League, the leading nationalist forces in India at that time. Specifically, this agreement dealt with the structure of the Indian government and the relations between Hindus and Muslims. It also contributed to the emergence a few years later of the Noncooperation Movement led by Mohandas Gandhi.

Lucretius (1ˢᵗ century BCE) wrote poem *On the Nature of Things* in which he argued that religious beliefs develop because of ignorance about the natural causes of phenomena and people motivated by religious conviction will commit horrific pain and suffering. He wrote that "such is the terrible evil that religion is able to induce." He speculated that that every phenomena has a natural, as opposed to a supernatural, explanation.

Luddites were organized groups of British artisans and workers formed in 1811 to 1812 who were opposed to the new machinery and technology associated with industrialization. They smashed new machinery and protested against industrialization, which they believed threatened their economic livelihoods. Their name is derived from the name of their leader, Ned Ludd, an English farmer who, in the beginning of the Industrial Revolution, led riots to destroy machinery.

Lusitania was the British ocean liner sunk by a German submarine in May 1915. Germany claimed at the time that the *Lusitania* was carrying munitions, a claim that was later proved to be correct. The attack caused 1195 deaths of which 128 were American. After protest by the United States, Germany ceased its campaign of unrestricted attacks against neutral shipping in the Atlantic Ocean. The United States entered World War I two years later in 1917, only after Germany resumed unrestricted submarine warfare.

Luther, Martin (1483–1536) was a German Augustinian priest and religious scholar who became alienated from the Catholic Church over the issue of the sale of indulgences, free will, good works, and faith. He initiated the reform of the Catholic Church in Germany. He began the Protestant Reformation in 1517 when he published his 95 theses requesting the Catholic Church to debate the issue of indulgences and salvation. With his translation of the *Bible* into German in 1522, he standardized the modern German language.

Lyceum was a school that was established by Aristotle in Athens.

Lycurgus (7th century BCE) is the legendary figure to whom the Spartans attributed the founding of their governmental institutions and laws.

Lydia was the name for the Roman province in western Anatolia whose traditional capital was Sardis. Lydia arose following the collapse of the Hittite Empire in the 12th century BCE. According to Herodotus, the Lydians were the first people to introduce the use of gold and silver coins circa 650–660 BCE and the first to establish retail shops in permanent locations.

Lysander (4th century BCE) was the general who commanded the Spartan fleet during the Peloponnesian War that defeated the Athenian fleet in the Hellespont in 405 BCE. This defeat cut-off food supply of Athens and starved Athenians into submission. As a consequence, he was able in 404 BCE to force the Athenians to surrender and end the Peloponnesian War. After Athens surrender, Lysander established the oligarchy of the Thirty Tyrants to govern Athens. As a result of the Peloponnesian War, the Athenian Empire came to an end.

Maastricht Treaty (1991) is the treaty by the twelve European Community (EC) countries that created the European Union. Under this treaty, each member state agreed to cooperate on social, foreign, judicial, and security issues. They also adopted a specific timetable for implementing a common policy on workers' rights, a common currency (the euro), and a common banking structure.

Macartney Mission (1792–1793) was the name for the unsuccessful attempt by the British Empire to negotiate trading rights with the Qing Empire in China. Claiming that their empire was self-sufficient, the Chinese rejected the British efforts.

Maccabean Revolt was the Jewish uprising led the Maccabees against the Syrian monarch Antiochus beginning in 167 BCE. The Maccabees objected to the forced imposition of Hellenistic religion, laws, and culture on the Jews and the prohibition of Jewish practices such as circumcision.

Macedon is a northern region of Greece that is comprised of Thessaly and Thrace and was the birthplace of Alexander the Great. The first Macedonian state was created in the 8th or early 7th century BCE by people who allegedly migrated to the region from the southern Greek city-state of Argos. A unified Macedonian state was eventually established by the late 4th century BCE. The first king of a united Macedonian state had three sons. The first two, Alexander II and Perdiccas III reigned only briefly. Perdiccas III's infant heir was deposed by the king's' third son, Philip II (359–336 BCE) of Macedon, who made himself king and ushered in a period of Macedonian dominance of Greece. Philip II 359–336 BCE Macedon expanded into and conquered a number of territories. This governing structure contrasted sharply with the political cultures of other Greek city-states that were typically ruled by an aristocratic elite. Philip's son, Alexander the Great (356–323 BCE), conquered the city-states in central Greece, the Persian Empire, and Egypt. Alexander adopted some of the styles of government of the conquered territories. He facilitated the spread of Greek culture and learning throughout his vast empire. Although Alexander's empire fractured into multiple regimes shortly after his death, his conquests created numerous Greek-speaking cities in Persia. Under Philip V of Macedon (221–179 BCE) and his son Perseus of Macedon (179–168 BCE), the Macedonian kingdom clashed with the rising power of the Roman Republic. During the 2nd and 1st centuries BCE, Macedon fought a series of wars with Rome. Macedon was defeated by the Romans in 197 BCE and 168 BCE.

Macedonian Renaissance (867–1056) was the period during the Macedonian rule of Byzantium when the aristocratic families, the Catholic Church, and monasteries devoted their immense riches to enhancing Constantinople with new buildings, new mosaics and icons, and sponsoring new historical, philosophical and religious writings.

Machiavelli, Niccolo (1469–1527) was a major political philosopher of the Renaissance who wrote *The Prince*. He was a member of a distinguished family who, as a diplomat for Florence, learned about power politics and met many of the major political figures of the day, such as Cesare Borgia, Pope Julius II, and Maximilian I, the Holy Roman Emperor. When the Medicis took political power in Florence in 1512, he was dismissed from his governmental position and was briefly imprisoned

for his alleged role in a conspiracy against the Medicis. In *The Prince,* he describes the methods to acquire and maintain power. He argues that a successful political leader must be able to anticipate and consider the consequences of his decisions. Because of this book, Machiavelli has often been interpreted as an advocate for despotism.

Madrassa is a Muslim school devoted to the study of the Quran and Islam.

Mafia is the name of the organization of armed men that took control of local politics and the economy in Sicily in the late 1800s.

Magellan, Ferdinand (1480–1521) was a Portuguese sea captain and navigator who led a Spanish expedition from 1519 to 1522 that was the first to sail around the world. He was killed in the Philippines in 1519, but one of his ships returned in 1522.

Magic involves the manipulation of supposed supernatural and occult forces and evil spirits believed to exist in nature that supposedly influence events in one's life. Europeans relied upon two types of magic. Natural magic used words and drawings to manipulate occult forces without calling on supernatural beings for assistance. Demonic magic invoked evil spirits for the purpose of using their supernatural powers to change the course of nature or alter behavior.

Maginot Line was a 200-mile network of permanent fortifications built along France's eastern border in the 1930s primarily as a defense against a German frontal invasion of France. When Germany invaded France in 1940, its soldiers simply outflanked the Maginot Line.

Magna Carta (1215) was the "Great Charter" that the English nobles forced King John to sign in 1215. The nobles forced John to cease abusing royal and feudal prerogatives and to accept the superiority of the law. Pursuant to the Magna Carta, the king pledged to respect the traditional feudal privileges of the nobility, townspeople, and clergy. Subsequent English kings swore to uphold the Magna Carta, thereby accepting the fundamental principle that even the king was obligated to respect the law.

Magna Graecia, which means "Great Greece" in Latin, was the name given by the Romans to southern Italy and Sicily because there were so many Greek colonies in those regions.

Magyars were the Hungarian-speaking people of the Habsburg Empire who began to push for Hungarian independence in the 1840s.

Mahayana Buddhism (Great Vehicle) is the branch of Buddhism that became influential in China, Japan, and Central Asia. It revered those enlightened people who postponed Nirvana to help others attain enlightenment.

Majoritarianism is a concept in political philosophy that contends that a majority of the population is entitled to make decisions that affect the whole society. Under a democratic majoritarian political structure, it is possible the majority could violate the rights of the minority population of a society, which has been referred to as "tyranny of the majority".

Malacca is the port city in modern Malaysia that was founded by the Portuguese circa 1400 as a trading center on the Strait of Malacca, which connected the South China Sea with the Indian Ocean.

Mali was the empire created by indigenous Muslims in West Africa that existed from the 1200s to the 1400s. It was famous for its role in the trans-Saharan gold trade with North Africa and Europe.

Malta is an island in the Mediterranean where a meeting between Bush and Gorbachev was held on warships in December 1989 weeks after the fall of the Berlin Wall. At that meeting, both leaders agreed to pursue further conventional and nuclear weapons cuts.

Malthus, Thomas (1766–1834) was the British economist who published the Essay *on the Principle of Population that* warned that population growth threatened future generations because population growth would always outstrip increases in agricultural production. Since population has the natural tendency to increase faster than the means of subsistence, he argued that efforts should be made to cut the birth rate, either by self-restraint or birth control.

Manchu is the name of a group of people from northwest Asia that defeated the Ming Dynasty and founded the Qing Dynasty in China in 1644.

Mandate of Heaven is the central concept of political legitimacy in traditional Chinese culture. It was developed during the Zhou Dynasty. According to this concept, Heaven bestows the Mandate on a particular individual and his descendants so long as they rule in the general interest of Chinese society. If the rulers become cruel and abusive, Heaven will withdraw the Mandate, the dynasty will be overthrown, and a new dynasty will be established by whoever receives the Mandate.

Mandate System was the name given to the administration of former German colonies and Ottoman possessions in Africa and the Middle East by Britain, France, Japan, Belgium, Australia, and South Africa after World War I. These nations claimed that under their tutelage the mandated territories would someday advance to independence. Many considered this system to be an attempt by the victors in World War I to continue imperialism. In the Middle East, for example, France administered Lebanon and Syria and Britain administered Palestine and Iraq as mandates.

Mandela, Nelson (1918–2013) is the South Africa opponent of apartheid who led the African National Congress. He was imprisoned from 1962 to 1990. After his release from prison he worked to establish majority rule in South Africa and became the first black president of South Africa in 1994.

Manhattan Project (1942–1945) was the code name given by the U.S. government, during World War II, to the secret Anglo-American project in Los Alamos, New Mexico, to build an atomic bomb. The first atomic bomb was successfully tested on July 16, 1945.

Manichaeanism was a religion established in Persia by the prophet Mani in the 200s CE that was an amalgamation of Christian and Zoroastrian themes. It taught that good and evil were equally powerful in the world, that they were in an eternal struggle, and that neither could ultimately triumph over the other. Manichaeanism was regarded as heresy by the Catholic Church, as it spread throughout the Roman Empire. Manichaeanism influenced Augustine when he was a young man. It also maintained that the soul was a fragment of pure divine light trapped in the filth of the body and could be liberated only through asceticism. Manichaeanism would be an important component of many medieval heresies.

Manifest Destiny is a phrase first used in 1845 that expressed the belief that the United States had a divinely inspired mission to expand throughout the world, and spread its form of democracy and freedom. Originally a political catch phrase in the 1800s, Manifest Destiny eventually became a standard historical term, often used as a synonym for the territorial expansion of the United States across North America towards the Pacific Ocean. Manifest Destiny was always a general idea rather than a specific governmental policy. In addition to expansionism, the term also encompassed notions of American Exceptionalism, and a belief in the natural superiority of what was then called the "Anglo-Saxon race". While many writers focused primarily upon American expansionism when discussing Manifest Destiny, others saw in the term a broader expression of a belief in America's "mission" in the world, a belief that has meant different things to different people over the years. The phrase "Manifest Destiny" was first used primarily by Jackson Democrats in the 1840s to promote the annexation of much of what is now the western United States (the Oregon Territory, the Texas Annexation, and the Mexican Cession). The term was revived in the 1890s, this time with Republican supporters, as a theoretical justification for U.S. intervention outside of North America. The term fell out of common usage by politicians, but some commentators believe that aspects of Manifest Destiny continued to have an influence on American political ideology in the 1900s.

Mannerism was a style of painting, sculpture, architecture, and decorative arts that was influential during the Renaissance between 1520 and 1600 that permitted artists to express their own "manner" or feelings. It used a distorted perspective, which created bizarre effects that contrasted with the emphasis on precision and harmony of Renaissance art. German art historians popularized mannerism in the early 1900s in order to categorize a type of art that no longer exhibited the harmonious and rational approaches associated with Renaissance art. Some mannerists were notable for elongated forms, exaggerated, out-of-balance poses, manipulated irrational space, and unnatural lighting. Mannerism reflected a growing cultural trend in which it was argued that purpose of art was to inspire awe and devotion and to entertain and educate.

Manor is the English name for a self-sufficient medieval landholding (estate) consisting of a lord's residence (manor house), outbuildings, arable fields, vineyards, meadows, woodland, peasant village, and surrounding land. Some portion of the land was reserved to support the lord and some part was reserved to the peasants themselves, for which they paid rent to the lord. A noble ordinarily owned a manor, but a monastery or a church could also own a manor. Under this system, the peasants and serfs performed labor services and paid various rents and dues to the noble lord in exchange for the protection of the lord. This form of economic organization was common in England, northern France, and Germany in the Middle Ages.

Manumission is the formal written grant of freedom to a slave by the slave owner.

Manzikert, Battle of (1071) was the armed conflict between the Byzantine Empire and the Seljuk Turks that resulted in the defeat of the Byzantine Empire. This defeat allowed the Seljuk Turks to conquer most of Anatolia.

Mao Zedong (1893–1976) was one of the founders of the Communist Party and the leader of the Chinese Communist Party from 1927 to 1976. During the 1920s, he advocated organizing the peasants rather than the industrial proletariat. He led the communists on the Long March to Yanan in 1934 to 1935. He rebuilt the Communist Party and the Red Army between 1937 and 1945 during the occupation of China by Japan. He defeated the nationalist forces led by Chiang Kai-shek in 1949. He was responsible for the Great Leap Forward in the 1950s and the Cultural Revolution that began in 1966.

Maoism was the official ideology of China under the rule of Mao Zedong (1949–1976), it emphasized anti-imperialism and export of revolution.

Marathon, Battle of (490 BCE) occurred during the first Persian invasion of Greece that was led by Darius I. This invasion was in response to Athenian military support for the Ionian Revolt that sought to overthrow Persian rule. After the Athenian military captured and burned Sardis, Darius decided to invade Greece, burn down Athens and subjugate the Greeks. Once the Ionian Revolt was finally crushed by the Persians, Darius sent a naval task force to attack Athens that landed in the bay near the town of Marathon. Despite the numerical advantage of the Persians, the Athenian hoplites under the command of Miltiades defeated the Persian force. The defeat at Marathon marked the end of the first Persian invasion of Greece. After Darius died, his son Xerxes I began preparations for a second invasion of Greece that began in 480 BCE. Although the legend of the Greek messenger Pheidippides running to Athens with news of the victory is historically inaccurate, the legend did become the inspiration for the marathon race, which was introduced at the 1896 Athens Olympics and was originally run between Marathon and Athens. Herodotus, however, wrote that Pheidippides was sent from Athens to Sparta before the battle in order to request assistance from the Spartans and that he covered about 150 miles in about two days.

March on Rome (1922) refers to the threat by Benito Mussolini and his fascist followers to take over the Italian government by having the Italian military forces march on Rome. As a result of this march, King Victor Emmanuel II made Mussolini his prime minister.

Marcus Aurelius (121–180) was the last of the "good emperors" of Rome and the author of an important Stoic work entitled *Meditations.*

Marius, Gaius (157–86 BCE) was Roman general and politician elected consul seven times, which was contrary to Roman law and tradition. He gained prominence because of his military victory during the Jugurthine War in North Africa against Jugurtha and the Numidians in 111BCE. He also defeated the Celts (Gauls) that had annihilated a Roman army and threatened an invasion of Italy. He was considered a "New Man" because he was not a member of the old Roman aristocracy, the group from which a consul had been traditionally selected. As a member of the equestrian class, he was the first in his family to achieve the position of consul. He also initiated important reforms of the Roman army making it into a professional army. He recruited volunteers mostly from the landless peasants and urban poor who swore an oath of loyalty to Marius and not the Senate. These two groups, who enlisted for a long term of service, began to see the army as an opportunity for a career in which they were ensured food, clothing, shelter, rewards from military victories and, when they retired, land or a bonus. His new system of military recruitment placed more power in the hands of an individual general. Marius' innovations would give future military leaders enough power to challenge the civilian authority of the Senate.

Market Leninism was the policy adopted after the Beijing Massacre in 1989 by the Chinese Communist government that asserted greater power over society and fostered an even stronger market orientation of the economy than had existed under market socialism.

Market Socialism was the economic policy adopted by the Chinese Communist government from 1978 to 1989 that mixed free enterprise, economic liberalization and state controls over the economy. These policies produced enormous economic growth in China.

Marshall Plan (1948) was the economic and financial aid program established after World War II by the U.S. government to help rebuild the war-torn economies in Europe and to prevent communist takeover of European governments. It was originally named the European Recovery Program. Under this program, nearly $13 billion of economic and financial assistance was provided from 1948 to 1952 to all European nations that suffered from World War II. By 1961, almost $20 billion in economic aid had been dispersed. The Marshall Plan program played an important role in facilitating European prosperity in the 1950s and 1960s. The plan was named for U.S. Secretary of State George C. Marshall, who conceived of the program.

Martel, Charles (688–741) was the Carolingian ruler of the Frankish territory of Austrasia. He was the son of Pepin, who defeated a Muslim army at Lyon.

Martyr, which is a Greek word for "witness", is someone who dies for his or her religious beliefs. In a Roman legal proceeding, it was typically a Christian who refused to make a public sacrifice to the Roman emperor, the Roman gods and to renounce Christianity

Marx, Karl (1818–1883) was a German philosopher, social scientist, and economist who was the founder of the Marxist branch of socialism. He believed that a revolution of the working class would overthrow the capitalist order and create a classless society. He is the author of *The Communist Manifesto* in 1848 and three volumes of *Das Kapital*. Although he considered capitalism to be the most efficient and dynamic economic system that had ever been developed, he claimed that capitalism was doomed because severe bouts of inflation and depression were inherent in the structure of capitalism. He contended that socialism was both inevitable and the only viable alternative to capitalism.

Marxian Dialectic is the mechanism conceived of by Karl Marx to explain how historical change occurs. He argued that it involved the tension between a socioeconomic structure (thesis) with its opposite (antithesis). A synthesis or merging of the two opposites will ultimately resolve the supposed tension. This synthesis then constitutes a new superior "thesis," thus permitting the process to begin over again.

Marxism is the economic and political theory of Karl Marx and Friedrich Engels that history is the result of class conflict or struggle between opposing economic classes. According to Marx and Engels, this struggle would end in the inevitable triumph of the industrial proletariat over the bourgeoisie and the abolition of private property, social classes, and the state.

Mass Deportation is the forcible removal and relocation of large numbers of people or entire populations.

Mass Education refers to a state-run educational system, the objective of which is to ensure that all children in a society have at least a basic education. Typically, such state-run educational systems were free and compulsory. By the late 1800s, such education systems were found primarily in industrialized societies.

Mass Leisure refers to forms of leisure-time or amusement activities that developed in industrialized societies in the late 1800s. Leisure-time activities, that took place after work and on weekends appealed to a large number of people in that society, especially the working class.

Mass Media refers to electronic systems of communication that reach a large nation-wide audience on a daily basis through the use of broadcasting technologies such as radio, television, films, videos, recorded music, cable transmissions and the Internet. Despite the proliferation of electronic media, print media such as newspapers, magazines, comics, pamphlets and books continue to play an important role in mass communication. Five corporations own or have controlling interests in the organizations that provide most of the electronic and print mass media content available to Americans.

Mass Politics refers to the political order found in industrialized societies in the late 1800s that was characterized by large, national political parties and universal male and, eventually, female suffrage.

Mass Production is a system in which large numbers of people work in highly mechanized factories in order to produce large quantities of goods more efficiently and cheaply. The manufacture of identical products is accomplished by dividing production into many small, repetitive tasks. This method was first introduced in Britain in the manufacturing of pottery by Josiah Wedgwood and in the spinning of cotton thread by Richard Arkwright. Technological advances such as the steam engine facilitated mass production.

Mass Society is an industrialized society in which the social, political, economic, and cultural concerns of the majority of the population, the middle class, and the working class play a prominent role. Such a society is characterized by increasing urbanization, the development of new technologies for mass communication and transportation, an improved standard of living of the middle and working classes, mass leisure-time activities, mass politics, and mass compulsory primary and secondary education.

Massive Retaliation was the U.S. nuclear weapons strategy developed during the Eisenhower administration that pledged a massive, all-out U.S. nuclear attack in response to Soviet expansion. The term was coined by Secretary of John Foster Dulles in a speech on January 12, 1954. President Kennedy abandoned this policy during the Cuban Missile Crisis (1962) and replaced it with the military strategy of flexible response.

Master Eckhart (1260–1327) was a Dominican monk and mystic who preached an introspective and charismatic version of Christian piety during the High Middle Ages.

Materialism is the philosophical doctrine that physical matter is the only knowable reality in the universe. Given that only things made of matter truly exist, a materialist denies the existence of the soul or any nonmaterial phenomena. This doctrine contends that everything mental or spiritual in the world is an outgrowth of physical forces and that truth is found only in concrete material existence and not through feeling or intuition.

Maternalism concerns the belief that a woman's most proper and powerful role in a society is in the family. It emphasizes that the mother who bears, nurtures, instructs, and raises a child is the true creator of human society.

Matrilineal Kinship refers to a pattern of kinship that traces descent through the female line. It involves the attribution of the name and the inheritance line.

Matteotti Murder (1924) was the killing of a moderate socialist, Giacomo Matteotti, in Italy in 1924 by fascist sympathizers after he had condemned the fascist violence that had accompanied a national election. In the wake of his murder, Benito Mussolini created a fascist state in Italy.

Maurras, Charles (1868–1952) was a French writer, philosopher, and journalist who was a strong proponent of nationalism, Catholicism, and monarchy in France in the late 1800s and early 1900s. He was a director of the pro-monarchy newspaper *L'Action Française*. His writings criticized the French Revolution, foreigners living in France, and Jews. He was condemned to life in prison for working with the Vichy government during World War II However, he was released in 1952 due to his health and died soon after.

Maxentius, Marcus Aurelius Valerius (278–312) was the Roman emperor who ruled from 306 to 312. He was defeated and killed at the Battle of the Milvian Bridge by Constantine in 312.

Maxim Machine Gun (1884) was the first portable machine gun. It was invented in the United States by Hiram Maxim. It was capable of firing 500 rounds per minute. It was widely adopted by the majority of the European armies and played a major role in the imperial conquest by the European nations in the late 1800s.

May 4th Movement (1919) was the name for the student demonstrations that took place in Beijing in 1919 to protest the perceived betrayal of China at the Versailles Peace Conference after World War I. The Conference allowed Japan to keep the former German territorial concessions in Shandong province. The movement involved anti-Japanese boycotts and strikes throughout China and helped to inspire opposition to imperialist influences in China. The May 4th Movement also promoted a growing sense of national unity.

Mazarin, Cardinal Jules (1602–1661) was an Italian diplomat that was a protégé of Cardinal Richelieu. Mazarin succeeded Richelieu and served as the chief minister of France from 1642 until his death. Mazarin functioned essentially as the king of France during the period when the King Louis VIV, who inherited the throne at the age of five, was still a boy and while his mother, Ann of Austria, served as Louis's regent. Mazarin functioned essentially as the ruler of France. However, he was unable to prevent a civil revolt from occurring in 1648, when the French government was challenged by the Fronde, a political movement initiated by powerful nobles who resented the centralization policies begun by Richelieu and continued by Mazarin.

Mazzini, Giuseppe (1805–1872) was the founder of Young Italy and a leader of the Italian nationalist movement in the 1800s.

McCarthyism is the name given by historians to the U.S. campaign to root out alleged communists in government and American society during the late 1940s and 1950s. This "witch-hunt", which was based on rumors and lies, was led by Senator Joseph McCarthy.

Mecca was a major commercial center on the Arabian peninsula in the 500s where the founder of Islam, Muhammad, was born and achieved prominence. From the earliest days of the spread of Islam, Mecca was the destination for the traditional religious pilgrimage required for Muslims.

Mechanization is the process by which machinery is applied to manufacturing and other processes of production. Among the first manufacturing processes that were mechanized were the spinning of cotton thread and the weaving of cotton cloth in Britain in the late 1700s and early 1800s.

Medes were people who lived in the Zagros Mountains north of Mesopotamia that allied with the Persians to defeat the Assyrians.

Medici, Cosimo de' (1389–1464) was an influential Florentine banker, statesman, and the founder of the Platonic Academy. He was a great patron of the arts, supporting artists, architects, and scholars. He was exiled from Florence for a year in 1433, but returned and gained most of the political power in the city through his economic influence.

Medici, Lorenzo de' (1449–1492), also known as Lorenzo the Magnificent, was a Florentine statesman, banker, and great patron of the arts during the Renaissance. While an able statesman, he poorly managed the family finances. Lorenzo

became popular when he ended a war with Naples through diplomacy in 1478. As a patron of the arts, he supported the great Renaissance artists Michelangelo and Botticelli as well as philosophers Marsilio Ficino and Pico Della Mirandola.

Medieval, literally meaning "middle age," is a term used by historians to describe the period from 500 to 1500. The term is typically used to signify an intermediate period between Greco-Roman antiquity and the Renaissance. Italian historians first used this term in the 1400s.

Megaliths are structures of very large stones constructed in Europe for ceremonial and religious purposes during the Neolithic period of history.

Megalomania is a mental disorder marked by delusions of grandeur and great personal power, importance, or wealth.

Megaton is the equivalent of one million tons of TNT. It has been estimated that one U.S. B-52 bomber alone carries 25 megatons of nuclear weapons or 12.5 times the destructive power of all the bombs dropped during World War II.

Mehmed II was the sultan of the Ottoman Empire that completed the conquest of the Byzantine Empire by capturing Constantinople in 1453.

Meiji Restoration (1868–1912) was a fundamental change in the Japanese government that reinstalled the emperor as the legitimate ruler of Japan in place of the military leaders, known as shoguns. The shoguns had dominated Japanese politics for many years. The Meiji Restoration also represented the political program begun by a new generation of political leaders that set Japan on the path to political centralization, industrialization, and imperialism. As part of the Meiji reforms, a new constitution was adopted that created the Diet, parliament that could pass laws, approve budgets, advise the government, but could not control the government. Under the leadership of Emperor Mutsuhito, Japan became, between 1868 and 1902, a world industrial and naval power.

Mein Kampf (My Struggle) is the title of the book that Hitler wrote while he was imprisoned in 1924 for his role in the Beer Hall Putsch of 1923.

All his ideas, beliefs, and plans for Germany were outlined in the book. He specifically outlined his racial ideology. He argued that since Germans, belonged to the "superior" Aryan race, they had the right to living space (Lebensraum) in the East (Poland and the Soviet Union) that was inhabited by "inferior" Slavs. Throughout the book, Hitler accused the Jews of being the source of all evil and compares them to the communists. However, at the same time he claimed the Jews controlled international capitalism. Except for Hitler's admirers, most of the people that read Mein Kampf at the time it was published did not take it seriously and believed it to be the ravings of a maniac.

Memphis was the capital of Old Kingdom in ancient Egypt located near the Nile Delta. Early Egyptian rulers were buried in the nearby pyramids.

Menander (342–292 BCE) was a popular Hellenistic author and playwright in ancient Greece whose "new comedies" blended romance, comedy, and domestic situations. He wrote over 100 plays, many of which were standards for hundreds of years. His only complete surviving play, *The Grouch,* was rediscovered in 1957.

Mencius (Mengzi) (371–289 BCE) was an ancient Chinese philosopher and interpreter of Confucius. Mencius emphasized the reciprocal nature of social relationships, especially the right of people to overthrow unjust rulers. He also stressed the natural division of society into those who labor with their backs and those who work with their minds.

Mendicant Friars were members of religious orders, such as the Dominicans or Franciscans, who wandered from city to city and throughout the countryside of Europe during the Middle Ages, begging for alms rather than residing in a monastery. Mendicant friars tended to help ordinary people by preaching and administering to the sick and poor.

Menes, King (2925 BCE), also known as Narmer, was considered to be the person who united Upper and Lower Egypt and founded Memphis, the capital of ancient Egypt.

Mengele, Josef (1911–1979) was the SS physician at Auschwitz, notorious for his pseudo-medical experiments on camp inmates and especially on twins and Gypsies. Inmates called him the "Angel of Death" because he was the one who determined if new arrivals would live or die immediately in the gas chambers. A simple gesture of his hand pointing to the left or right would seal an arrival's fate. Those considered too weak or too old were sent to the gas chambers; those who he considered able to work were sent to the concentration or labor camps. After the war Mengele spent some time in a British internment hospital, but he escaped. With the assistance of governmental authorities in Brazil and Portugal, Mengele succeeded in avoiding arrest and trial for his crimes. He is reported to have died in Brazil in 1985.

Mensheviks, which is a Russian term meaning "minority persons," was the term used by Lenin to describe the larger and more moderate faction of the Russian Social Democrats that opposed Lenin's efforts in 1903 to develop a centrally controlled party organization comprised of professional revolutionaries. The Mensheviks opposed Lenin and the Bolsheviks during the Russian Revolution. The argued for a less-rigid and tightly controlled association of socialists.

Mercantilism was the prevailing political and economic theory of European nations in the 1500s and 1600s. It contended that a nation's power and wealth Such precious metals were determined by its supply of precious metals. were to be acquired by increasing exports (paid for with gold) and reducing imports to achieve domestic self-sufficiency. This theory was held predominantly by European merchants in the 1500s and 1600s that maintained that a country should maximize its wealth by regulating trade so as to create a trade surplus and thus an inflow of money into a country. Proponents of mercantilism claimed that, the wealth of a nation depended on its ability to export more than it imported. This economic theory encouraged government intervention in the economy and regulation of trade.

Meroë was the capital of a flourishing kingdom in southern Nubia from the 4th century BCE to the 4th century CE. During this period, Nubian culture exerted more independence from Egypt.

Merovingian Dynasty (476–750) was a Frankish dynasty that provided the first kings of France. The most significant Merovingian monarch was Clovis I who united nearly all of Gaul except for Burgundy and what is now present-day Provence. He was converted to Christianity in either 496 or 506. At his death in 511, he divided his realm among his four sons, who frequently fought among themselves. The last Merovingian king was deposed in 750 by Pippin III (the Short), who established the Carolingian Dynasty.

Mesmerism was the pseudoscience adopted by Franz Anton Mesmer in the 1700s that treated sickness by massaging or hypnotizing the patient to produce a crisis that restored the patient's health.

Mesolithic Era, which is also known as the Middle Stone Age, began about 15,000 years ago when the glaciers that remained from the final Ice Age began to recede.

Mesopotamia, which means "between the rivers," is a Greek word used by historians today to describe the land between the Tigris and Euphrates rivers where the first civilizations appeared about 3000 BCE. Sumer and Akkad were two of the earliest societies to be found in this area.

Messenian War was the conflict between Sparta and Messenia circa 600 BCE that resulted in the conquest of Messenia and the enslavement of its people by the Spartans.

Messiah the Hebrew word for the "anointed one." The messiah was the supposed redeemer that the Jews believed would establish the kingdom of God on earth. The Hebrews believed that the messiah was the legitimate successor of King David and the savior of Israel. Messiah means "Christos in Greek", the title given to Jesus of Nazareth by the early Christians.

Mestizo was the term used by the Spanish authorities in their colonies in the Americas to describe someone of mixed Native Indian and European descent.

Metaphysics is a branch of philosophy concerned with ultimate universal principles such as the existence and purpose of human life. By studying ideas that transcend the physical world, metaphysics seeks to show the higher meaning of material existence or being.

Methodism was an English evangelical religious movement begun by John Wesley in the 1700s that stressed inward, heartfelt religion and the possibility of attaining Christian perfection in this life. Wesley broke away from the Anglican Church in England, he insisted on strict self-discipline and a "methodical" approach to religious study and observance. Wesley emphasized an intense personal experience of salvation and a life of thrift, abstinence, and hard work, values that appealed to a middle class audience. Followers of this branch of Christianity are known today as Methodists.

Metropole was a term used by imperialist European nations in the 1800s and 1900s for the homeland of a European colonial empire.

Metropolis was the mother city or parent of an ancient Greek overseas colony.

Metropolitan was a religious leader in the Orthodox Church that was the equivalent of an archbishop in the Roman Catholic Church

Metternich, Prince Klemens Von (1773–1859) was an Austrian diplomat and statesman who, for over three decades, was the central political figure in Europe. In his service to the Habsburgs, he was an envoy at the Congress of Rastadt in 1797, then ambassador to Saxony in 1801, Prussia in 1803, and to France in 1806 when it was ruled by Napoleon. After Napoleon's defeat, Metternich prevented Russia, at the Congress of Vienna, from taking Poland. He created a German Confederacy with Austria, but failed at making an Italian Confederation. Trying to prevent further revolutions within Europe, Metternich tried to use the Quadruple Alliance (Britain, Russia, Prussia, and Austria) as a means to suppress liberal and nationalist revolutions in Europe, but his efforts failed. He became chancellor of the Habsburg Empire in 1821 until a revolution in 1848 forced him out of power. Metternich used secret police to spy for him, hoping to undercut the growing influence of liberalism. Metternich feared revolutions, and tried to prevent them at any cost. Reflecting his fear of the spread of revolutions in Europe, in France, Metternich stated that "When Paris sneezes, Europe catches cold."

Mexican-American War (1846–1848) was a conflict fought between the United States and Mexico the U.S. annexation of Texas in 1845 and border disputes along the Texas–Mexico border. After decisively defeating Mexico, the United States compelled Mexico to enter into the Treaty of Guadalupe Hidlago. In accordance with the terms of the Treaty, the United States annexed the Mexican territory that today comprises the states of Texas, New Mexico, Colorado, Arizona, Nevada, Utah and California.

Michelangelo, Buonoratti (1475–1564 CE) was a Florentine artist who mastered the techniques, styles, and influences of his time to produce breathtakingly original works of art, such as the statute of David and the Pieta and the ceiling of the Sistine Chapel.

Midway, Battle of (1942) was the United States naval victory over the Japanese during World War II in which the Japanese lost four of their best aircraft carriers. The Japanese defeat at Midway is is considered to be a turning point of the war in the Pacific.

Middle Ages is the term used by historians to describe the period in Western European history from approximately 500 to 1500 CE.

Middle Kingdom was the period in Egyptian history from 2050 to 1650 BCE. It was followed the Second Intermediate Period (1650–1550 BCE).

Middle Passage was the name for that very harsh part of the Atlantic trade circuit between Britain, Africa, and the Americas involving the transportation of enslaved Africans across the Atlantic to the Americas.

Militarism was a policy of aggressive military preparedness that was pursued by most of the European nations prior to World War I. The basic elements of this policy included maintaining large armies based on mass conscription, the development of advanced military technology, and complex and inflexible plans for mass mobilization of the military.

Military-Industrial Complex was the phrase used by President Dwight Eisenhower in 1958 to describe to a huge interlocking network of governmental agencies, industrial corporations, and research institutes, all working together to promote and benefit from increased military spending during the Cold War.

Mill, John Stuart (1806–1873) was a British philosopher who wrote *On Liberty*. He was the leader of the utilitarian movement in Britain in the 1800s. He tried to promote social policies that would lead to more equal division of profits. He also advocated a cooperative system of agriculture and increased rights for women.

Millenarianism is a belief expressed by religious, social or political group or movement that a society will be totally transformed by an anticipated supernatural force, based on a one-thousand-year cycle. Millenarian groups typically claim that their current society and its rulers are corrupt, unjust and oppressive. They believe their society will be destroyed by a great disaster or battle and some supernatural power will create a new and purified world in which the true believers will be rewarded.

Milosevic, Slobodan (1941–2006) was the Serbian nationalist politician that took control of the Serbian government and orchestrated the genocide of thousands of Croatians, Bosnian Muslims, Albanians, and Kosovars. He was eventually ousted in a popular revolt in 2000.

Milvian Bridge, Battle of (312) was the conflict on the bridge over the Tiber where Constantine militarily defeated Maxentius after supposedly having a vision sent by the Christian god.

Ming Dynasty (1368–1644) was the dynasty established in China by Zhu Yuanzhang after the overthrow of the Yuan Dynasty. Yongle, one of the Ming emperors, sponsored the building of the Forbidden City in Beijing and the voyages of Zheng He.

Minoan is the name for the culture and prosperous civilization that developed in the Aegean on the island of Crete between 2700 and 1500 BCE. As a sea empire, the Minoans engaged in far flung commerce around the Mediterranean and exerted powerful cultural influences on the early Greeks. The symbol of their culture was the palace and its surrounding buildings, the most important one being at Knossos.

Mir was a Russian farm community that was developed in the 1800s after the emancipation of the serfs in 1861. The mir provided for holding the land in common and regulating the movements of any individual who was a member of the mir. As a result, the mir hindered the free movement of labor, individual agricultural enterprise, and efforts at modernization of the Russian economy.

Mishnah was the oral interpretation of the Torah that was developed by the Pharisees. It was later developed into a written body of legal interpretations.

Missi Dominici were royal envoys of the Carolingian kings that ensured that local officials throughout the Carolingian Empire implemented royal decisions.

Missile Gap was President Kennedy's deceptive 1960 election campaign claim that helped him get elected. He claimed that the Soviet Union had surpassed the United States in nuclear weaponry when, if fact, the U.S. maintained nuclear superiority.

Mitanni was a kingdom of Hurrian tribes in northern Mesopotamia circa 1500 BCE that occupied a territory that encompassed present-day southeastern Turkey, northern Syria and northern Iraq It is believed that the Hurrians lived east of the river Tigris on the northern rim of Mesopotamia. The Mitanni gradually moved south into Mesopotamia sometime before the 17th century BCE. The Mitanni kingdom is thought to have been a feudal state led by a warrior nobility of Indo-Aryan descent. The military superiority of Mitanni was probably based on the use of two-wheeled war-chariots. No sources for the history of the Mitanni have been found so far. Their history is mainly based on Assyrian, Hittite and Egyptian sources. It is believed that the warring Hurrian tribes and city-states became united under one dynasty after the collapse of Babylon due to Hittite attacks and a Kassite invasion. The Hittite conquest of Aleppo, weak Assyrian kings, and internal strife of the Hittites are all factors that helped create a power vacuum in upper Mesopotamia. This power vaccum led to the formation of the kingdom of Mitanni. The

legendary founder of the Mitannian Dynasty was a King Kirta, who was followed by King Shuttarna. Nothing is known about these early kings. After a few clashes with the Egyptians over the control of Syria, the Mitanni sought peace with Egypt and an alliance was formed. In the early 14th century BCE the relationship was very amicable and King Shuttarna sent his daughter to Egypt to be married to Pharaoh Amenhotep III. At this juncture in the 14th century BCE, the Mitanni kingdom was at the peak of its power. However, under the rule of Thutmose III, Egyptian troops crossed the Euphrates and entered the lands of the Mitanni. At Megiddo, Thutmose III fought an alliance of 330 Mitanni princes and tribal leaders under the ruler of Kadesh. Whether this was done because of existing treaties or only in reaction to a common threat, remains open to debate. Thutmose III again waged a victorious war against the Mitanni. Egyptian victories by Thutmose III did not lead to permanent rule over the Mitanni. The Egyptians only exercised control over Phoenicia. By the 13th century BCE a new political and military power arose in Mesopotamia, the Assyrians that conquered the Mitanni and made it a vassal state of the Assyrian Empire.

Mithraism was a mystery religion practiced in the Roman Empire between the 1st and the 4th centuries CE that focused on the power of light over darkness. It was not based on a supernaturally-revealed body of scripture, and hence very little written documentary evidence survives. Soldiers and the lower nobility appeared to be the primary followers of Mithraism. No Mithraic scripture or first-hand account of its highly secret rituals survives. Religious practice was centered on either a natural cave or cavern or an artificial building imitating a cavern that were typically dark and windowless. Mithraism began to attract attention in Rome near the end of the 1st century CE. By the year 200, Mithraism had spread widely throughout the Roman army and among traders and slaves. During festivals, all participants were equal including slaves. By the 200s Mithraism was officially sanctioned by Roman emperors. Mithraic ruins have been found in the city of Ostia, and in Rome, where as many as seven hundred Mithraic temples may have existed. There is very little information about the decline of the religion. The Edict of Theodosius I in 394 made paganism, such as Mithraism, illegal. Official recognition of Mithra in the army stopped at this time, but we have no information on what other effect the edict had.

Mitteleuropa, which means "central Europe" in German, was a termed used by influential military leaders in Germany before World War I to refer to the land in both Central and Eastern Europe that they hoped to acquire as a substitute for a vast colonial empire in Africa and Asia. The occupation of this territory in Central and Eastern Europe became an important military objective in World War I and under Hitler in World War II.

Mocha was a port city on the Red Sea coast of Yemen and the principal port of Yemen until the 1800s. From the 1400s until the 1600s, Mocha was famous for being the major marketplace for coffee seeds, also known as mocha beans, that were prized for their strong, chocolate flavor. When the Ottoman Turks assumed political power in Arabia, they required all ships entering the Red Sea to put in at Mocha and pay duty on their cargoes. The brewing of coffee from roasted beans spread initially to Egypt and Anatolia and only later on to the Roman Empire.

Modern Devotion Movement (Devotio moderna) was the religious movement in the 1400s in Europe led by the Brother of the Common Life, an influential religious order, that stressed individual piety, ethical behavior, and intense religious education.

Modernism is the term used to describe the nontraditional literary and artistic movement of cultural styles and outlook that emerged in the late 1800s through the 1950s, Modernists sought to create new aesthetic forms and values and to elevate the aesthetic experience of a work of art above the attempt to portray reality as accurately as possible. Manifestations of this artistic movement would include Impressionism and Cubism.

Modernity is the belief, attitude, outlook, or worldview that social, political, economic, intellectual, scientific, technological, and cultural developments have changed the nature of life in the present that are fundamentally different from those of the past. Modernity is typically experienced by the individual in terms of a proliferation of social, political, economic, and cultural alternatives, choices, and possibilities. In many cultures, this proliferation of alternatives, choices, and possibilities has often caused great anxiety, resulting in efforts by critics of modernity to oppose it. Many times the term is used to specifically to refer to the social, political, economic, scientific, technological, and cultural changes—such as the accelerated pace of life, the mass politics, and the growth of urban life—that have resulted from the spread of industrialization among many of the nations of the world beginning in the late 1800s. Today, many people view the behavior patterns and the social and cultural rituals in which they engage as new and innovative. Yet, the fact much of modern culture is built on traditional ways of thinking repeated relatively unchanged even though those ways of thinking are regarded as innovative. Thus, traditional rituals such as sports, for example, play a significant role in modern cultures even though the origin and meaning of those rituals have been erased, ignored, or misunderstood. What has changed is our historical understanding of the continuing influence of traditional ways of thinking, behavior, and rituals on modern cultures.

Modernization is the process of reforming the political, economic, social, military, and cultural traditions of a non-Western society by imitating Western societies without accommodating the local cultural traditions of those non-Western societies.

Modus Vivendi, which means "way of living" in Latin, means a temporary or provisional agreement between parties to a political dispute that they intend to be replaced by a more detailed and permanent agreement. An armistice is an example of such an agreement.

Moirea, which means the "apportioners" in Greek, was often called "The Fates" in Greek mythology. The "Fates" were considered by the Greeks to be agents of destiny that controlled the life of every mortal and immortal from birth to death. Even the gods, supposedly, feared Moirae. It was claimed that even Zeus was subject to their power. Moirae may have originated as birth-goddesses. The three Moirae were: Clotho ("spinner") who spun the thread of life; Lachesis (allotter" or "drawer of lots") who measured the thread of life with her rod; and Atropos ("inexorable" or "inevitable", literally") who was the cutter of the thread of life and chose the manner of a person's death. The Moirae were supposed to appear three nights after a child's birth to determine the course of its life. The Moirae were usually described as cold, remorseless and unfeeling, and depicted as hags. Despite their forbidding reputation, Moirae were worshipped as goddesses. Brides in Athens offered them locks of hair and women swore by them.

Moism or Mohism was the name of the teachings of the thinker Mozi, who lived during the Warring States Period of Chinese history. He emphasized a doctrine of "universal love" in contrast to what he saw as the family-centered teachings of Confucius. Mozi contended that the use of aggressive warfare was unprofitable, and so he began to develop new techniques of defense.

Moldboard Plow was a heavy, wheeled plow introduced during the Middle Ages that could cut deep into the thick, moist soil of northern Europe and could form furrows that drained the excess water.

Monarchy is the rule by a single individual for life who is descended from a hereditary line of monarchs. The term is derived from the Greek word meaning "the rule of one man,".

Monasticism was a movement in the Christian Church that arose first in the eastern Roman Empire in the 200s and 300s. Individual hermits were organized into religious communities of men and women (monks and nuns). These men and women would separate themselves from the world to lead lives in imitation of Jesus. They would pursue a life of spirituality through work, prayer, and asceticism. They would also adhere to a strict rule of chastity, obedience, and poverty.

Monetary Policy is the government control of the money supply and credit of a nation by the manipulation of short-term interest rates or bank reserves in order to affect the economy.

Mongols is the name of a nomadic people living in northeastern Asia that established an enormous empire beginning in 1206 under the leadership of Genghis Khan, The Mongol Empire linked China with Europe.

Monism is philosophical belief that the universe is made of one substance.

Monophysitism was the Christian heresy prominent in the eastern Mediterranean in the 400s CE that taught that Jesus had only one nature, divine. The Council of Chalcedon condemned this view in 451 and declared that Jesus had two authentic natures equally divine and human.

Monopoly is an economic structure in which there is exclusive economic control of a market or an industry by one or a small group of companies.

Monotheism is the belief in the existence of a single divine entity (one God). The Hebrew Bible places this belief as originating about 2000 to 1500 BCE when God commanded Abraham to give up polytheism for the belief in one god. Some scholars cite the devotion of the Egyptian pharaoh Akhenaten to Aten (sun-disk) and his suppression of traditional gods as the earliest instance of monotheism. The exclusive belief in one god is the foundation of Judaism, Christianity, Islam, and Zoroastrianism.

Monroe Doctrine (1823) was a U.S. foreign policy doctrine created by President James Monroe that warned European powers that they should no longer colonize or interfere with the affairs of the newly independent nations of Latin America. The United States had planned to stay neutral in wars between the European powers and their colonies. However, if these wars for national independence were to occur in Latin America, the United States would view such actions as hostile. The Monroe Doctrine not only represented the growing strength of the United States, but also expressed the growing imperialistic views of the United States toward the nations of Latin America.

Montagnards (The Mountain) were members of a radical political faction within the Jacobins that sat on the left side of the meeting hall of the National Convention during the second stage of the French Revolution They advocated the death of King Louis XVI, opposed the Girondins, who advocated the centralization of state power, and supported the Reign of Terror.

Montesquieu (Charles-Louis de Secondat), Baron de La Brede et de (1689–1755) was one of the most influential and widely read political theorists in Europe in the 1700s. He came to prominence with the publication of his satiric *Persian Letters* in 1721. His *The Spirit of the Laws* is considered by many to be the foundation for sociological thinking. In that book, he argued that individual freedom is most secure when the political power of government is divided into three branches, legislative, executive and judicial.

Montezuma II (1466–1520) was the last Aztec emperor conquered by the Spanish conquistador Hernan Cortes.

Moors was the name for a Muslim people from North Africa (Algeria and Morocco) that invaded and conquered Spain in the 700s. They were driven out of Spain in 1492.

More, Thomas (1478–1535) was an English lawyer, politician, and Christian humanist who was the author of *Utopia,* a book that was highly critical of contemporary European monarchies. *Utopia* describes a fictional land of peace and harmony that had outlawed private property and all forms of wealth. He was a diplomat in the court of Henry VIII and was appointed Lord Chancellor in 1529. More challenged the authority of Henry as the head of the Church of England, when he refused to swear allegiance to Henry as required by the Act of Supremacy. He was executed by Henry VIII for opposing Henry's divorce and was, as a consequence, celebrated as a martyr by the Roman Catholic Church.

Morelos, José Mariá (1765–1814) was the Mexican priest who led the Mexican people that were fighting for Mexican independence from Spain.

Morgenthau Plan (1944) was a plan for the occupation of Germany after World War II that advocated harsh measures to permanently weaken Germany as an industrial power. It was proposed by American Treasury Secretary Henry Morgenthau, Jr., but it was rejected by President Franklin D. Roosevelt.

Moscow, Battle of (1941–1942) was the largest and bloodiest battle in human history. It was the first major defeat for the Nazis and it destroyed the myth that the Nazis were invincible. The battle, which lasted from September 30, 1941 to April 20, 1942, occurred as part of the German blitzkrieg invasion of Russia. Over seven million soldiers were involved in this battle, twice the number that would later fight at Stalingrad. At the Battle of Moscow over 2.5 million soldiers were killed, missing, taken prisoner or severely wounded with 1.9 million casualties on the Soviet side alone. The human losses at Moscow were twice those at Stalingrad.

Mossadegh, Mohammed (1880–1967) was the premier of Iran from 1951 to 1953. He was removed from power by Mohammad Reza Pahlavi, the Shah of Iran in a coup led by British and U.S. intelligence agencies after Mossadegh had enforced the Oil Nationalization Act. This law, which was passed by the Iranian Parliament in 1951, nationalized Iran's oil industry and authorized the Iranian government to seize control of the British-owned and British-operated Anglo-Iranian Oil Company.

Most Favored Nation Status is a clause in a commercial treaty between nations that awards to one of the nations special privileges to trade in another nation free from the tariffs imposed by that nation.

Movable Type refers to a printing process by which individual letters, each cast on a separate piece of metal, were arranged to form words, sentences, and paragraphs on a page. Movable type replaced woodblock printing that required the carving of an entire page at one time. The first known movable type system using ceramic type was developed by the Chinese circa 1041. Metal movable type was first invented in Korea circa 1230.

Muhammad (570–632 CE) was a merchant from Mecca and the founder of Islam. He claimed to be the prophet that God (Allah) had chosen for God's final revelation to humanity. After moving from Mecca to Medina in 622, he became the ruler of that city and subsequently defeated Mecca in 630. After his death in 632, the Arabs expanded throughout the Arabian Peninsula and, in less than one hundred years, created a vast empire.

Muhammad Ali (1769–1849) was the leader of modernization efforts in Egypt in the early 1800s. He ruled Egypt as a governor of the Ottoman Empire. His descendants would rule Egypt until 1952.

Mujahedeen, which means "soldiers of god," is the name of U.S.-supported Islamic rebels who fought against the Soviet-backed regime established in Afghanistan in 1979.

Mulatto was a term used by the Spanish authorities, in their colonies in the Americas, to describe someone of mixed African and European descent.

Mullahs were Iranian religious leaders that led the opposition movement against the Shah of Iran in the late 1970s. They created a theocratic government in Iran beginning in 1979. They were vehemently opposed to American materialist and secularist culture.

Multiculturalism is a term often used to describe societies or nations that have many distinct cultural groups, usually as the result of immigration. It has also been used to describe governmental policies that emphasize the unique cultural characteristics of different immigrant groups and that the different cultures of the immigrant groups should be preserved. These governmental policies have been used by some politicians and political groups in Europe and the United States to raise fears and anxieties that the national cultural identity of a nation was being threatened.

Multilateralism is a term in international relations that refers to multiple countries working cooperatively on a specific issue. International organizations are multilateral by their very nature. The UN and NATO are examples of contemporary multilateral international organizations. In the modern era, one of the first instances of multilateralism was the Concert of Europe system established at the Congress of Vienna at the end of the Napoleonic Wars. Since the end of World War II, a wide array of multilateral organizations have been created.

Multinational Corporations (MNCs) are businesses that operate production facilities, sales, finance, or other business activities in several foreign countries.

Multipolar refers to an international system in which there are three or more states of roughly equal military strength.

Mummy was a body preserved by chemical processes. In ancient Egypt, the bodies of people who could afford mummification underwent a complex process of removing organs, filling body cavities, dehydrating the corpse with natron, and then wrapping the body with linen bandages and enclosing it in a wooden sarcophagus.

Munich Agreement (1938) was the agreement between Britain and Germany that allowed Nazi Germany to occupy the Sudetenland, the German-speaking part of Czechoslovakia.

Muscovy was the Russian principality that emerged gradually during the period of Mongol domination. The Muscovite Dynasty would rule without interruption from 1276 to 1598.

Music Hall was the most popular venue for entertainment in Britain from the 1830s to 1900. It featured singing, dancing, comedy, and other forms of entertainment.

Musket was a large-caliber, smooth-bore firearm that fired a lead ball. It was aimed and fired from the shoulder and it first appeared in Spain in the 1500s.

Muslim Brotherhood (1928) was the Egyptian organization founded by Hassan al-Banna that attacked liberal democracy as a façade for middle class, business, and landowning interests. It fought for a return to a purified form of Islam.

Mussolini, Benito (1883–1945) was the fascist dictator of Italy from 1922 to 1943. He was called Il Duce, which means "the leader". Mussolini founded the Italian fascist movement in 1919 and took political power in Italy in 1922. He replaced Italy's parliamentary democracy with a corporatist state. Mussolini pursued an expansionist foreign policy, invading Ethiopia in 1935. He concluded the Pact of Steel with Germany in 1939 and entered World War II on the side of Germany in 1940. Mussolini was overthrown in 1943 when the Allies invaded Italy and was killed by partisans in 1945.

Mutual Assured Destruction (MAD) is a U.S. nuclear weapons doctrine developed during the Cold War based on the theory of deterrence, in which the threat of full-scale use of nuclear weapons and the potential total destruction of both sides would prevent the use of nuclear weapons. This doctrine reflected a belief that nuclear war could best be prevented or deterred if both the United States and the Soviet Union had sufficient nuclear weapons that, even if one launched a preemptive first strike, the other could respond and devastate the attacker.

MX is the name of a U.S. intercontinental ballistic missile (ICBM) that has a range of 5,000 miles and carries ten nuclear warheads, each with an explosive yield of 300 kilotons.

Mycenae was the site of a fortified palace complex in southern Greece that controlled a Late Bronze Age kingdom that flourished from 1400 to 1100 BCE. In Homer's epic poems, Mycenae was the home of King Agamemnon, who commanded the Greeks when they attacked Troy. The Myceneans settled in the Peloponnese in Greece circa 1600 BCE and organized their society around powerful citadels, and developed the Linear B script. The Myceneans conquered the Minoans between 1550 and 1375 BCE.

Mystery Religions were the popular Hellenistic cults of Isis, Mithra, and Osiris, that promised salvation to those initiated into the secret or mystery of their rites. Those rites were not to be divulged to anyone not initiated into the cult. These mystery religions incorporated aspects of both Greek and Eastern religions and had broad appeal for both Greeks and Easterners that yearned for personal immortality.

Mysticism is a term developed by modern scholars to describe people having or claiming to have direct experiences with a god, gods or supernatural forces. The term was used by medieval scholars, religious thinkers and writers to refer to a tradition of thought concerned with the ultimate union of the soul with God.

Mythology is a body of stories which have become traditional for a given human society. Very frequently, mythologies are associated with religious beliefs, and thus the word "mythology" often has distinct religious connotations. The stories which make up a mythology can vary dramatically. Myths typically attempt to offer an explanation of a natural phenomenon, a learned behavior, a system of social organization, or a particular value or belief. Other types of stories that can be a component of mythology include legends and folktales. A legend is a story that purports to be based, at least, in part on historical fact, but that is interpreted and retold in an imaginative way by the storyteller. Folktales, by contrast, usually include much more fiction than fact, though even folktales sometimes have their origin in an actual occurrence. In American culture. The ride of Paul Revere is an example of a story which, though based on an historical event, has become legendary.

Myths are invented stories and legends of unknown origin that narrate in imaginative and symbolic ways the basic customs, practices, traditions, and beliefs upon which a culture, society, or religion is built. Typically, they attempt to explain the causes for something that arises in nature.

Nabonidus was the last king of the Neo-Babylonian Empire (626-539 BCE) before it was defeated by Cyrus the Great, the king of Persia. During the reign of Nabonidus (556-539 BCE), he ruled over ancient Iraq and Syria. He is considered to be the first archaeologist in history. Nabonidus excavated ancient buildings and built a museum to house the objects that he discovered. The history of his reign is found on a single clay tablet inscribed in cuneiform, which is known as the Nabonidus Chronicle. The Nabonidus Chronicle is part of a larger series of clay tablets inscribed in cuneiform known as the Babylonian Chronicles. The Nabonidus Chronicle covers the conquest of Babylon by Cyrus the Great of Persia and the rule of Babylon by Cambyses, Cyrus's son.

Nag Hammadi is the village in southern Egypt near the place where a collection of Gnostic writings was discovered in 1945, including the Gospel of Thomas.

Nagasaki was the second Japanese city on which the United States dropped an atomic bomb. It was attacked on August 9, 1945. The Japanese surrendered shortly thereafter, ending World War II.

Nanjing, Treaty of (1842) was the treaty between China and Britain that ended the Opium War. As result of the British victory in the Opium War, China was required to pay a large indemnity to Britain, open new Chinese ports to trade with British merchants, and cede the island of Hong Kong to Britain.

Napoleonic Code or Civil Code (1801) was the legal code established by Napoleon Bonaparte that included some of the ideas of the French Revolution, such as equality before the law and taxation of all social classes. The Code codified existing French law and included modern forms of property ownership and contract law. At the same time, it strengthened paternal control of families, outlawed divorce in most circumstances, and placed women under the legal control and domination of their fathers and husbands.

Nara Period (710–784 CE) was a period of Japanese history during which Chinese cultural influences dominated around the city of Nara.

Naram-Sin, who was the grandson of King Sargon the Great, ruled the Akkadian Empire from 2254 to 2218 BCE. He claimed to be a living divinity and adopted the title of "God of Akkad". He is considered to be the first ruler in Mesopotamia to represent himself as a living god. By approximately 2154 BCE, the Gutians, a nomadic tribe from the Zagros had conquered the Akkadian Empire and destroyed Akkad.

Nation is a large community of people that possess a sense of unity based on the belief that they have a common homeland and share a common language and culture.

Nation-State is the political organization formed when people sharing the same historical, cultural, or linguistic roots form their own state with borders, a government, and international recognition.

National Legislative Assembly (1789–1791) was the governing body of France that succeeded the Estates General during the French Revolution. It ruled France from 1789 to 1791. National Assembly was organized by and largely composed of delegates of the Third Estate. It passed *The Declaration of the Rights of Man and Citizen* in 1789 as well as a constitution that called for a constitutional monarchy. National Assembly was later reorganized as the Legislative Assembly, which governed France from 1791 to 1792. The Legislative Assembly was replaced in 17922 by the National Convention, which marked the formal beginning of a republic in France.

National Convention (1792–1795) was the legislative body that was established during the second stage of the French Revolution.

National Defense Education Act (1958) was the legislation passed by the U.S. Congress after the Soviet Union launched *Sputnik* by which the United States began spending $2 billion a year on higher education in an effort to win the "brain race" with the Soviets.

National Front for the Liberation of Angola (FNLA) (1954) was a nationalist organization that fought a war for independence from Portugal that lasted until 1975. Beginning in the early 1960s, many governments such as France, Germany, Romania, Israel, South Africa and the United States provided military aid and advisers to the FNLA. After a lengthy war, Angola gained its independence in 1975. Unfortunately, even after independences, Angola witnessed an intense civil war that lasted from 1975 to 2002. The FNLA became a political party in 1992.

National Guard (1789) was the militia of citizen-soldiers that was organized initially in Paris during the French Revolution to resist the army of King Louis XVI. It was commanded by the Marquis de Lafayette. Subsequently, other cities and towns throughout France would establish their own separate National Guard units.

National Liberation Front of South Vietnam (NLF) (1960) was the name of the communist-led revolutionary political movement that was established in South Vietnam in 1960. It sought to overthrow the American-supported South Vietnamese government, to reunite North and South Vietnam, and to resist American intervention in Vietnam. The NLF established a provisional government in South Vietnam in 1969.

National Security Council Memorandum (NSC-68) (1950) predicted the Soviets could launch a nuclear attack on the United States by 1954 and recommended an increase in U.S. defense spending for nuclear and conventional arms.

National Self-Determination is the doctrine advocated by nationalists that any group that considers itself a nation has the right to be governed only by members of its own nation and to have all members of that nation governed by the same political authority.

National Socialist German Workers Party (NSDAP) (1919), more commonly known as the Nazi Party, was the official name of the political party that Adolf Hitler joined in 1920. Its political program emphasized nationalism, racism, anti-Semitism, and militarism. When Hitler became chancellor of Germany in 1933, the Nazi Party became the only legal political party in Germany, and Nazism was the dominant political ideology until 1945, when Germany was defeated in World War II.

Nationalism is a political ideology that emphasizes a sense of unity among a people living in a particular area, based on a common language, shared customs, history, religion, and culture, often accompanied by hostility to outsiders (xenophobia), and a strong desire to create an autonomous political community or nation. In the late 1700s and early 1800s, nationalism was a powerful force for creating unity among many of the nations of Western Europe. By the late 1800s, it became a powerful force that contributed to the disintegration of the Austro-Hungarian and Ottoman Empires. By the 1900s, nationalism would provide the ideological foundation for European colonies in Asia and Africa to demand their political independence.

Nationalities Problem refers to the political, social, and cultural problems faced by the Austro-Hungarian Empire in the late 1800s and early 1900s when it tried to unite a wide variety of ethnic groups, including Austrians, Serbs, Croats, Hungarians, Poles, Czechs, Slovaks, and Slovenes in a united multiethnic empire.

Nationalization is the economic policy adopted by a government to take control and ownership of the assets of a privately held business or industry. Nationalization may occur with or without compensation to the former owners of the business or industry. Historically, this process arose in the 1900s. One of the primary motives for assuming state ownership of a business or industry has been resentment over foreign control of a natural resource upon which a nation is dependent. For example, the oil industries of Mexico and Iran were nationalized in 1938 and 1951, respectively, and Egypt nationalized the Suez Canal in 1956. Nationalization of all businesses and industries occurred in Russia in 1917 and in Cuba in 1960. However, nationalization of certain businesses or industries has occurred in contexts other than a communist or socialist revolution. Between 1945 and 1955, the British and French governments nationalized their respective coal, electric, gas, and transportation industries.

Nations, Battle of the (Battle of Leipzig) (1813) was the battle at Leipzig, Germany, in which the French army of approximately 185,000 soldiers led by Napoleon was defeated by the combined armies of approximately 320,000 soldiers of Austria, Prussia, Russia, and Sweden. This defeat combined with Napoleon's disastrous withdrawal from Russia represented the end of the French Empire in Eastern Europe.

Natufian Culture (13,000–11,000 BCE) is the term used by archaeologists and anthropologists for a semi-sedentary community of hunters and gathers that emerged in the ancient Levant (Syria, Lebanon and Israel) before the development of agriculture.

Natural Selection is the biological process identified by Charles Darwin by which organisms evolve through a struggle for existence and those that have a marginal advantage over other organisms live long enough to propagate their kind. Darwin contended that within any population of plants, humans and animals, there will be some organisms better adapted to their environment than others, that, in turn, leads to greater reproductive success for that specific organism.

Naturalism was the worldview expressed by a group of writers and artists in the late 1800s and early 1900s that advocated portraying nature and human reality without sentimentality. They believed that the details of nature and human reality should be described realistically.

Navigation Acts were laws passed by the British Parliament in the 1700s that required all goods produced in British colonies in North America to be shipped on British ships.

Neanderthals is a hominid that is considered to be a separate species from modern humans that overlapped with humans in terms of time and place. Modern humans and Neanderthals share a common ancestor in Africa between 300,000 and 100,000 years ago. Neanderthals were the closest known relative to modern humans and they disappeared between 35,000 and 24,000 years ago. Neanderthal was barrel-chested, with a heavy jaw and brow, used primitive tools, and buried their dead. However, they seem to have lacked the capacity of modern humans for abstract thought. While they presumably were able to breed with Homo sapiens, there is no clear evidence that they ever did. They lived in Europe for some 200,000 years, but they failed to survive contact with modern humans who began spreading into Europe about 60,000 to 50,000 years ago.

Nebuchadnezzar II (630–561 BCE), who reigned from 605 to 562 BCE, is considered to be the greatest king of the Neo-Babylonians. He conquered Judah and deported thousands of Jews to Babylon. He ruled the shortlived Chaldean Empire from Babylon, which he built into a magnificent city.

Nehru, Jawaharial (1889–1964) was a prominent Indian nationalist in the 1930s and 1940s. He was an early supporter of Gandhi's program of resistance to British colonialism. Nehru spent more than nine years in British jails for his anti-colonialist political activities. As one of the leaders of the Indian National Congress, he played a major role in negotiating independence for India. Nehru was

the first prime minister of an independent India and would remain in office from 1948 to 1964. While prime minister, he advocated democracy and socialism as two important components of his domestic policies. During the early years of the Cold War, he emerged as one of the leaders of the movement of nonaligned nations.

Neo-Assyrian Empire (746–609 BCE) was an empire extending from western Iran to Syria-Palestine conquered by the Assyrians of northern Mesopotamia between the 10th and 7th centuries BCE. They used force and terror and exploited the wealth and labor of their subjects. They also preserved and continued the cultural and scientific developments of Mesopotamian civilization. Its capital was in Nineveh.

Neo-Babylonian Empire was ruled by the Chaldeans, a nomadic group that settled in southern Mesopotamia in the early 1st millennium BCE. Under their leadership, Babylon again became a major political and cultural center in the 7th and 6th centuries BCE. They created the famous Hanging Gardens of Babylon.

Neo-colonialism refers to the continuation of colonial exploitation in a former colony without direct formal political control. It is typically used to describe an international economic arrangement by which an ex-colonial power or private businesses supported by such an ex-colonial power effectively control the economy of a former colony even though the former colony has achieved political independence.

Neo-Confucianism refers to the ideas of Daoxue, who emphasized a return to the traditional Confucian concepts of reverence for the past and obedience to hierarchy. This approach to understanding classic Confucianism became the basic ruling philosophy from the Song Dynasty until the collapse of the Qing Dynasty in the early 1900s. Neo-Confucianism sought to merge certain basic elements of Confucianism with Buddhism. One of the most important Neo-Confucianist thinkers was Zhu Xi.

Neo-Conservativism is the political philosophy that emerged in the United States in the 1970s in reaction to what some Americans considered to be the harmful consequences of the social policies of the Johnson administration and the social, political, and cultural upheaval caused by the civil rights and anti-war movements of the 1960s. Neo-conservatives typically opposed the values represented by the counter-culture movement of the 1960s and what they felt was a growing anti-Americanism among many baby boomers as exemplified by the emergence of the movement against the Vietnam War. As American politics became more radicalized during the Vietnam War, some Americans that identified themselves as politically liberal moved farther to the right politically and culturally. They supported a more aggressive U.S. foreign policy, were strongly anti-communist and became more disillusioned with the social programs of the Johnson administration. While the outlines of this new political philosophy were first formulated in the 1950s, the movement achieved its first political victory in 1964 with the nomination of Senator Barry Goldwater as the Republican presidential candidate. Neo-conservatives significantly influenced the presidential administrations of Ronald Reagan, George H. W. Bush, and George W. Bush and represented a fundamental realignment in American politics. Neo-conservatives claimed that the federal government had grown too large and powerful and should be reduced in size. They argued for greater states' rights policies and the cutting of tax rates in order to stimulate steady economic growth. Neo-Conservatives were more concerned about balancing the federal budget than using deficits as a means to achieve social justice and economic growth. They further contended that as there had been a decline in our democratic culture and our traditional values, government should play a greater role in enforcing moral standards. Finally, Neo-Conservatives believed that the United States should continue to play an aggressive leadership role in world affairs and be prepared to actively defend democratic nations that might be under attack from nondemocratic forces in those areas of the world where American national interests were involved.

Neo-Liberalism is a political theory that emerged in the United States and Britain beginning in the late 1970s that advocated a return to the principles of classical liberalism of the 1800s, including a reduction in welfare-state programs and cutting taxes for the wealthy in order to stimulate economic growth. The term has also been used by nations in Latin America and other developing regions of the world to describe free-market policies such as reducing tariff protections, the sale of public-sector industries such as national airlines and public utilities to private investors or foreign corporations, and the reduction of social welfare policies and public-sector employment.

Neo-Platonism was a philosophical movement that attempted to revive and reinterpret Plato's doctrine of essential, preexisting "forms." It began as early as the 3rd century BCE with the writings of Plotinus. The neo-Platonic tradition subscribes to Plato's theory that reason can reveal an understandable order in the universe. This tradition has influenced many movements during the past two thousand years, including the Romantic movement in Britain and the United States in the 1800s. Neo-Platonism rejects the possibility that there could be more than one interpretation of such concepts as goodness, truth, and justice, for example.

Neo-Stoicism was a school of philosophical thought that emerged in Europe in the 1500s and 1600s dedicated to the revival of moral values of the Stoics of ancient Greece such as calmness, self-discipline, and steadfastness.

Neolithic Revolution, also known as the "New Stone Age," refers to the transition that began circa 11,000 to 10,000 BCE from hunter-gather societies to settled communities of farmers and artisans. Agricultural production, domestication of plants and animals, and the development of new technologies such as pottery and weaving characterized this period. The earliest Neolithic societies appeared about 8000 to 7000 BCE in the area of the world we know today as the Middle East.

Nepotism is the appointment of family members to important political or economic positions regardless of merit or qualifications. Nepotism gained its name during the Middle Ages, when some Catholic popes and bishops, who had no children because they had taken vows of chastity, appointed their nephews to important positions in the Catholic Church, such as cardinal or bishop. This practice was ended by Pope Innocent XII in 1692.

Nerchinsk, Treaty of (1869) was a treaty between China and Russia that established the boundaries and rules of trade between the two countries.

Nero, Claudius (37–68 CE) was the Roman emperor from 52 to 68. He was the adopted son of Claudius and began his rule at 16. As emperor, he devoted most of his time to poetry and the arts finding little time for the administration of the Roman Empire. Anyone he perceived to be a potential rival or threat to his position as emperor, he murdered including his mother Agrippina. Because he was a disaster as an emperor, the army revolted against him in 68. He was declared a "public enemy" and he committed suicide while running away from the Roman army that was pursuing him.

Nestorianism is the religious doctrine that Jesus exists as two persons, the man Jesus and the divine Son of God, rather than as a unified person. This doctrine is identified with Nestorius, Archbishop of Constantinople. This view of Christ was condemned at the Council of Ephesus in 431. Nestorius contended that Mary, even though she was the mother of Jesus, was not the mother of God. The Catholic Church condemned such teachings because Mary was considered by Church doctrine to be "Mary, the Mother of God."

Nestorius (386–451 CE) was archbishop of Constantinople from 428 to 431. He developed the religious doctrine position known as Nestorianism, which was declared a heresy by the Catholic Church. Nestorius contended that Mary, even though she was the mother of Jesus, was not the mother of God. The Catholic Church condemned such teachings because Mary was considered by Church doctrine to be "Mary, the Mother of God." Emperor Theodosius II issued an imperial edict that exiled Nestorius to a monastery in Egypt. His writings were burnt wherever they could be found.

New Culture Movement was the name given to the cultural movement that arose in China in the 1910s and 1920s that rejected traditional Chinese culture, especially Confucianism and the imperial state. Followers of this movement advocated the use of simplified Chinese characters and vernacular language in writing.

New Deal (1933–1939) refers to the program of government reforms initiated by President Franklin Roosevelt during the 1930s to combat the social and economic effects of the Great Depression. These programs sought to provide jobs for the unemployed, social welfare programs for the poor, and regulations for the financial and securities markets in the United States. These programs were heavily influenced by Keynesian economic ideas. The New Deal established such federal governmental agencies as the Securities and Exchange Commission (SEC), the Federal Deposit Insurance Corporation (FDIC), the Works Projects Administration (WPA), the Civilian Conversation Corps (CCC), and the Social Security system.

New Economic Policy (NEP) (1921–1928) was the economic liberalization program formulated by Lenin in 1921 that allowed limited capitalism in the areas of light industry and agriculture in order to repair the damage caused to the Russian economy by the Russian Revolution and the subsequent civil war. In an effort to revive the economy, this program permitted private enterprise and allowed peasants to sell some of their harvest. After some initial economic success, Stalin considered this program a threat to the socialist state. He ended the NEP in 1928 and replaced it with state-controlled central planning.

New France was the colony established in 1608 by the French in North America with its capital in Quebec. The British conquered New France in 1763 during the Seven Years' War.

New Imperialism was the named used by historians to describe the wave of conquests and colonizations by various European nations and the United States of countries in Africa, Asia, the Pacific, and the Middle East during the late 1800s and early 1900s. New Imperialism took a variety of forms, including territorial occupation, colonization, exploitation of labor and raw materials, and development of economic spheres of influence. As a result of New Imperialism, the European nations of Britain, France, Belgium, and Germany would eventually control over 500 million people in Africa and Asia—that is, one-half of the world's non-European population. In essence, this form of imperialism was simply the domination by the industrial powers of the world over the non-industrial nations.

New International Economic Order (NIEO) was a program advocated by nations of the Third World in the mid-1970s to restructure the world economy so as to make economic transactions between the industrialized nations and the Third World nations more favorable to the nations of the Third World.

New Kingdom was the period in Egyptian history from 1500 to 1000 BCE. It followed the Second Intermediate Period. It was a time that saw the emergence of the Egyptian Empire.

New Look Doctrine was the name given to the national security policy of the United States during the administration of President Dwight D. Eisenhower. It reflected Eisenhower's concern for balancing the Cold War military commitments of the United States with the nation's financial resources and emphasized reliance on strategic nuclear weapons to deter potential threats posed by the nations of the Soviet Bloc. Eisenhower was particularly concerned that U.S. resources would be drained by Soviet-inspired regional conflicts.

New Order was the Nazi plan for their conquered territories that included the killing of all Jews and other people considered to be inferior, the exploitation of the resources of the conquered territories, the German colonization of Eastern Europe and Russia and the use of Poles, Russians and Ukrainians as slaver labor.

New Woman was a term used to describe women, often from the middle class, who at the beginning of the 1900s lived apart from their families, supported themselves, and dressed practically.

New World Order (1991) was a concept announced by President George H. W. Bush during the Iraq-Kuwait crisis that included four principles: peaceful settlement of disputes, solidarity against aggression, reduced military arsenals, and just treatment of all peoples.

Newton, Isaac (1642–1727) was an English scientist and mathematician who made revolutionary discoveries in gravitation, calculus, and the composition of light. He published his theories regarding gravitation and other subjects in his famous *The Mathematical Principles of Natural Philosophy*, which was published in 1687. His mathematical calculations concerning the laws of gravity, planetary motion, and the theory of inertia confirmed the theories of Copernicus. Although a professor of mathematics at Cambridge University, he was a deeply pious man. He was extremely interested in alchemy and numerology. In fact, he wrote more on those subjects than in the area of science and mathematics. He developed the modern theory of light. He is also famous for his intellectual quarrel with Leibniz over which of them had been the first to invent calculus.

Nicene Creed (325 CE) was the declaration made at the Council of Nicaea that condemned Arianism in favor of the doctrine that Christ is both fully human and fully divine. It is a Christian statement of faith that is viewed as authoritative by the Roman Catholic, Eastern Orthodox, Anglican, and major Protestant churches.

Nicholas II (1868–1918) was the last Russian Tsar who abdicated his throne in 1917 during the Russian Revolution. The Bolsheviks executed him and his family on July 17, 1918.

Nietzsche, Friedrich (1844–1900) was the German philosopher that denied the possibility of knowing absolute "truth" or "reality" because he argued that all knowledge is filtered through linguistic, scientific, or artistic systems of representation. He also criticized Judeo-Christian morality for instilling a repressive conformity that he believed drained civilization of its vitality.

Nihilism is a philosophy that rejects all established norms, laws, and institutions as meaningless and contends that absolute truths can never be established.

Nika Riots was a rebellion that nearly resulted in the overthrow of Emperor Justinian. The rebellion was brutally suppressed by Belisarius. Some historians have claimed that Belisarius was responsible for killing 30,000 rebels were in the Hippodrome during the Nika Riots.

No-Man's Land was the area between the trenches of combatants on the Western Front during World War I.

Nobiles was a small group of wealthy aristocrats and plebeians that were elected to office in the late Roman Republic.

Nobility or Nobles were members of the aristocracy that received official recognition of their hereditary status, including their titles of honor and legal privileges. It was a small fraction of the total population that strongly influenced all aspects of the political, economic, religious, social, and cultural areas of an aristocratic society.

Nomadism is an economic way of life, caused by a scarcity of resources, in which groups of people continually migrate to find food, pastures, and water. Some nomads are pastoral in that they engage in the breeding, rearing, and harvesting of livestock such as horses, goats, and sheep.

Nominalism was the philosophical school of thinking beginning with Plato that held that abstract concepts, general terms, or universals have no independent existence, but exist only as names. Nominalism contends that various objects labeled by the same term have nothing in common but their name. In this view, it is only actual physical particulars that can be said to be real. This doctrine was associated primarily with William of Ockham.

Nonaligned Movement was an international political movement of Third World nations, led by India and Yugoslavia, that attempted, beginning in the 1950s, to remain neutral during the Cold War.

Non-Governmental Organization (NGOs) is a transnational group such as the Catholic Church, Greenpeace, and the International Olympic Committee that interacts with states, multinational corporations (MNCs), other NGOs, and intergovernmental organizations (IGOs). NGOs today influence the development and conduct of international relations among nations of the world.

Non-Proliferation of Nuclear Weapons Treaty (NPT) (1968) was the multilateral arms control agreement that created a framework for controlling the spread of nuclear materials. It established the United Nations International Atomic Energy Agency (IAEA) that is responsible for inspecting the nuclear power industry in NPT member states to ensure that nuclear materials designed for peaceful purposes are not being diverted to military use.

Noriega, Manuel (1938–present) was the former dictator of Panama and an ally of the United States. He was removed from power by U.S. military forces who invaded Panama in 1990. He was subsequently arrested by U.S. military forces and convicted in a U.S. federal court of smuggling narcotics into the United States.

Norm is a standard, model, type, or pattern regarded as typical for a certain group. A process is said to be "normative" when it results in bringing atypical patterns in line with typical ones. Socialization, for example, is often considered to be a normative process, as it involves bringing social pressures to bear on behavior that is considered by a certain group as unusual or atypical.

North is a term traditionally used in international relations to refer to the industrialized nations of the world primarily located in North America and Europe. However, with the emergence of Japan and China as industrial powers, this does not accurately describe the distribution of economic power in the international system.

North American Free Trade Agreement (NAFTA) (1992) is a regional free-trade zone established by the United States, Canada, and Mexico. It is the second largest free-trade zone in the world.

North Atlantic Treaty Organization (NATO) (1949) is a regional military and political alliance between the nations of Western Europe and the United States that was established for the purpose of defending Europe from aggression and expansion by the then Soviet Union and its allies. Under the NATO agreement between the United States, Canada, Britain, and eight other European nations, an armed attack against any one of the NATO members by the then Soviet Union or any of its Eastern European allies would be regarded as an attack against all of the NATO members. The corresponding alliance of the then Soviet Union and its allies was known as the Warsaw Pact.

North-South Gap refers to the disparity in resources (income, wealth, and power) between the industrialized nations of North America and Europe and the poorer countries of Africa, the Middle East, Asia, and Latin America.

Northern Renaissance was an intellectual movement in northern Europe in the late 1400s and early 1500s that combined an interest in the classics of the Italian Renaissance with an interest in the sources of early Christianity, including the New Testament and the writings of the Church Fathers.

Notables were prominent wealthy individuals that supported Napoleon. He award them with noble titles and state honors.

Nubia was the area south of Egypt where the kingdom of Kush was located. The Kingdom of Kush invaded and dominated Egypt from 750 to 664 BCE.

Nuclear Club refers to a group of nations that possess nuclear weapons. It originally consisted only of the United States and the Soviet Union, but it has expanded over the years to include Britain, France, the People's Republic of China, India, Pakistan, and Israel.

Nuclear Triad is the U.S. nuclear force structure built on three legs, ICBMs, SLBMs and supersonic nuclear bombers that gives the U.S. the ability to launch nuclear weapons from sea, land and air.

Nuclear Utilization Target Selection (NUTS) is a nuclear weapons strategy that contends that it is possible to fight and win a limited nuclear war. It relies upon the development of highly accurate first strike weapons and a survivable second-strike capacity. It views nuclear weapons as simply one more rung on the ladder of military escalation, an idea developed by Herman Kahn in the 1950s. Since this strategy considers a limited nuclear war as a viable option, the ability to launch such attacks holds a great deal of appeal among some strategic military planners and theorists. Advocates for this approach contend that a mutually assured destruction type deterrent is not credible in cases of a suicide attack carried out on a single city and that the NUTS strategy would give a nation the ability respond to such an initial small attack with a limited attack on one or more enemy cities. NUTS theorists believe that a missile defense system would be an important component in this strategy

since it would protect against a limited nuclear attack. During the late 1970s and the 1980s, U.S. policy-makers began to adopt strategies to make it possible to control escalation and reduce the risk of an all-out nuclear attack even though they doubted that a limited nuclear war could remain limited for very long.

Nuclear Winter is the theoretical effect of a 5,000 megaton nuclear exchange that would cause so much ash to ascend into the atmosphere that most of the sun's rays would be blocked from the earth and temperatures would plunge as much as 36 degrees Fahrenheit in the northern hemisphere where 90% of the world's populations lives, wiping out crops and causing mass starvation. The radiation would also destroy the earth's ozone layer, without which virtually all life on earth would become extinct.

Nuremberg Code is a set of research ethics and principles for human experimentation that were established in 1947 as a result of the "Doctors Trial," one of subsequent Nuremberg Trials. The Code includes such principles as informed consent, absence of coercion, a properly formulated scientific experiment, and compensation for experiment participants.

Nuremberg Laws (1935) were laws promulgated in Nazi Germany that prohibited marriages and extramarital intercourse between Jews and "citizens of German or related blood"; employment in Jewish households of female citizens of "German or related blood" under the age of 45; and the raising of the Reich flag by Jews. Another law passed in 1935 stated that only persons of "German or related blood" could be citizens. Jews from that point on were regarded as "subjects," not citizens, of Germany.

Nuremberg Trials (1945–1949) were a series of thirteen trials of the prominent members of the political, military, and economic leadership of Nazi Germany. The trials were held in the city of Nuremberg, Germany, from 1945 to 1949. The first and best known of these trials was the Trial of the Major War Criminals Before the International Military Tribunal that tried twenty-four of the most important captured leaders of Nazi Germany. The

Nuremberg Trials was held from November 20, 1945, to October 1, 1946. The Nazi leaders were tried for participating in a common plan or conspiracy to commit crimes against peace; for planning, initiating, and waging wars of aggression and other crimes against peace; for committing war crimes; and for committing crimes against humanity. The second series of twelve trials of lesser Nazi war criminals included doctors, judges, economic, and military leaders, as well as corporations and Nazi organizations.

Nurhaci (1559–1626) was the founder and leader of the Manchus that sought to revive the former Jin Dynasty of the Jurchen people and overthrow the Ming Dynasty.

O

Obelisk is a tall, four-sided, tapered shaft of stone topped with a pyramid. In ancient Egypt, they were typically placed in pairs at the entrance to a temple.

Obsidian is hard glassy rock formed by volcanos. Typically, it is black in color, but the presence of such impurities as iron oxide or magnesium may produce reddish-brown or dark green varieties. Since obsidian is hard and brittle, it easily fractures producing sharp edges that were used as early as the Stone Age as cutting and piercing tools and arrowheads. Obsidian was imported by the ancient Egyptians from the eastern Mediterranean and southern Red Sea regions for use as a semiprecious stone or as a cutting tool in ritual circumcisions.

Octavian (Caesar Augustus) (63BCE–14CE) was the honorific name of Gaius Julius Caesar Octavianus, founder of the Roman Principate, the military dictatorship that ended the rule of the Roman Republic. He was the grandnephew and adopted heir of Julius Caesar and the first emperor of the Roman Empire. He was a member of the Second Triumvirate in 43 BCE along with Mark Antony and Lepidus. After defeating Mark Antony and Cleopatra at the Battle of Actium in 31BCE, he ruled the Roman Empire for forty years.

He established the institutional and administrative framework for the stability and prosperity in the Roman Empire for over two centuries. The month of August is named after him.

October Days (1789) was the period during the French Revolution when approximately 10,000 Parisian women accompanied by Marquis de Lafayette and the National Guard marched from Paris to the Versailles Palace to protest the high cost of bread. This group forced King Louis XVI and his family to return to Paris with them.

October Manifesto (1905) was the declaretion issued by Czar Nicholas II of Russia that provided Russia with a written constitution and guaranteed freedom of speech and assembly.

Officium was the Roman word for a sense of "duty", which meant that it was the responsibility of a Roman citizen to perform to the best of his ability. The primary duty a Roman citizen owed was to the state and the most important aspect of this sense of duty was to obey and respect authority (pietas). This sense of duty was perhaps the single most important idea the ancient Romans incorporated into their culture. This sense of duty was derived from the Stoics. For the Stoics, the universe was ordered by the gods and this order was the *logos,* "meaning" or "rational order" of the universe. Each and every event, physical and historical, had a place within this larger rational order. Since the order was rational, nothing happenned which was not part of some larger reason or good. For the ancient Romans, this larger good translated into the spread of law through Roman imperial conquest. Therefore, each and every function a Roman undertook for the state, whether as a farmer or foot-soldier, a philosopher or emperor, became part of this larger purpose or good.

Oil Embargo is the term used to describe the decisions in 1973 and 1979 by the Arab leaders of the Organization of Petroleum Exporting Countries (OPEC) to increase the price oil that was exported to Western nations that had supported Israel during the 1972 Arab-Israeli war. As a result of these two embargoes, Western countries experienced severe economic problems, including high inflation and a prolonged recession, which lasted nearly ten years.

Old Kingdom was the period of Egyptian history from 3100 to 2200 BCE.

Oligarchy is a form government in which a few people or a small minority holds all social, political, and economic power that they exercise in order to favor their own interests. Typically, military dictatorships and political machines that run urban governments in democracies are oligarchic.

Omdurman, Battle of (1898) was the British victory over the Mahdi in the Sudan in 1898 during which General Kitchener led a military force of British and Egyptian soldiers armed with rapid-firing rifles and machine guns. The battle was a demonstration of the superiority of a highly disciplined European army equipped with modern rifles and artillery over tribesmen with older weapons. While the Sudanese forces suffered approximately 10,000 deaths, the British had only 48 soldiers killed.

Open Door Policy (1899–1900) was the U.S. foreign policy concerning China that was adopted after the United States became a major power in East Asia as a result of its acquisition of the Philippines in 1898. In the late 1800s, when it appeared to U.S. policymakers that European nations and Japan intended to partition China into spheres of influence excluding the United States, U.S. policymakers concluded that such efforts would be contrary to the commercial national interests of the United States. In response to this potential development, Secretary of State Hay asked Britain, France, Germany, Italy, Russia, and Japan to permit the free use of their respective ports in China by U.S. commercial interests. Even though those nations agreed to such an "open door policy," vigorous competition among these various powers for economic concessions in China continued unabated.

Open-Field System refers to the division of the agricultural land of the medieval European manor into three large fields. The noble lord held land for his direct profit in all of these three fields, as well as the serfs who had strips of land leased to them by the lord at the same time, in all of the three fields. As a result, the land for the direct profit of the lord and the land worked by the serfs for themselves individually under their respective leases was mixed with and open to neighboring plots of land. This confusing and complex system

of agriculture would last in England and France long after the end of serfdom in those countries.

Open Skies was the proposal made by President Eisenhower in the mid-1950s to let the United States and the Soviet Union see each other's military blueprints and installations and place reconnaissance units in each other's territory. Khrushchev's rejection led to the U.S. deployment of the U-2 spy plane.

Operation Ivy (1952) was the code name for the U.S. detonation of the first hydrogen bomb, which had a force that was equivalent to more than 10 million tons of TNT, about 1,000 times the power of the Hiroshima bomb. The test of the first hydrogen bomb took place at Enewetak atoll in the Marshall Islands, which are located in the western Pacific ocean.

Operation PBSuccess was the code name for a 1950s CIA operation that used exiles and peasants to overthrow the government of Guatemalan President Jacobo Arbenz after his land reform program threatened the holdings of the U.S.-based United Fruit Company.

Operation Rolling Thunder was the name of the U.S. bombing campaign against North Vietnam launched by President Johnson in response to a Viet Cong attack on an air base at Pleiku in 1965 that killed eight Americans and wounded hundreds more.

Opitamtes, which means "best men," were the aristocratic leaders in the late Roman Republic. They generally came from senatorial families and wished to retain their oligarchical privileges. The Optimates comprised the traditionalist Roman political faction that succeeded the Gracchi that sought to preserve the senatorial oligarchy against the Populares.

Opium is an addictive drug that is derived from the heads of poppy plants. It was imported into China contrary to Chinese law by the British from India in the late 1700s and 1800s.

Opium Wars (1839–1842 and 1856–1860) were two wars between Britain and China over the issue of the British claim that it had the right to import and trade opium in Hong Kong contrary to the law of China. As a result of its defeat of China in the Opium War, the victorious British imposed the Treaty of Nanking on China. The Treaty of Nanking required China to cede Hong Kong to the British and to open other Chinese ports to the importation and trading of opium.

Oracle at Delphi was the most important religious shrine in ancient Greece. A priestess of Apollo, who cared for the shrine, was believed to be able to predict the future. The shrine dated from 1400 BCE, but ceased to function in the 300s CE.

Oracle Bones were means to foretell the future in ancient China used during the Shang Dynasty (1766–1122 BCE).

Oral Tradition refers to those songs, myths, legends, and stories passed on orally from one generation to another that become the core of a traditional culture of a society.

Organization of African Unity (OAU) (1963) was established by thirty-two newly independent African nations to promote unity and solidarity among the nations of Africa. The OAU was a collective voice for the continent, to secure Africa's long-term economic and political future, and to eradicate colonialism. It was disbanded in 2002 and replaced by the African Union.

Organization of Petroleum Exporting Countries (OPEC) (1960) is an international organization made up of the oil-producing nations of Iraq, Indonesia, Iran, Kuwait, Libya, Angola, Algeria, Nigeria, Qatar, Saudi Arabia, the United Arab Emirates, and Venezuela that was established to regulate the production and pricing of crude oil. It has become the most prominent economic cartel in the international economy today. OPEC exercises enormous political influence, as its members control about half the world's total oil exports.

Orthodoxy, which means "holding the right opinions," is a term used in Christianity to indicate doctrinally correct or right beliefs. However, definitions of orthodoxy have changed on numerous occasions in the history of Christianity.

Osiris was the ancient Egyptian god who was considered to be the ruler of the underworld.

Ostpolitik (Eastern Policy) refers to the policy of West German Chancellor Willy Brandt during the Cold War that sought to improve ties with Soviet Bloc nations. This policy led to treaties with Poland, the Soviet Union, and East Germany and won Brandt the Nobel Peace Prize in 1971.

Ostracism was the annual democratic procedure in ancient Athens by which anyone deemed to threaten the political order could be banished from the city for ten years without the loss of property. Ostracism required the vote of six thousand male citizens and it derived its name from the pottery shards on which the candidates' names were written.

Ostrogoths were a Germanic people who built a kingdom in Italy under their king, Theodoric (493–526), only to be defeated by the armies of Justinian, the Roman emperor.

Ottoman Empire (1300–1918) was the Islamic state founded by Osman in northwestern Anatolia circa 1300. After the fall of the Byzantine Empire in 1453, the capital of the Ottoman Empire became Istanbul (formerly Constantinople). At its height the Ottoman Empire encompassed parts of the Balkans, the Caucasus, North Africa, and the Middle East until 1918, when it was defeated during World War I.

Ottonian Renaissance refers to a period in English history during the reign of the Saxon Emperor Otto 1st (936–973) when he and his brother Bruno brought learned monks, Greek philosophers and Italian scholars to their imperial court. Their efforts stimulated a cultural revival in literature and the arts.

Ovid (43 BCE–17 CE) was a Roman poet who wrote about romance, humor, love, and sensual themes. His writings focused on the lighter side of Roman imperial culture and the Roman world. His most famous work, *Ars Amatoria* (*Art of Love*), which is a poem about the art of seduction, was written when he was fifty years old.

Owen, Robert (1771–1858) was a British textile manufacturer and utopian socialist. While working in the textile industry, he noticed that when he improved working conditions, production improved. Based on his experiences, he concluded that humanity could advance under better working and living conditions and that an individual's character was based on the environment in which an individual lived and worked. Having found some success with this philosophy, he established a utopian community in New Lanark, Scotland. Owen also bought 20,000 acres in Indiana and Illinois, where he started an experimental utopian society, New Harmony, but it quickly failed.

Owen, Wilfred (1893–1918) was a British soldier and poet who fought in World War I. He died one week before the war ended. His poem "Dulce et Decorum est", which describes a poison gas attack, captured the horror and inhumanity of modern warfare.

P

Pacific Century is a term that has been recently used to predict that the 21st century will be dominated, especially economically, by the Pacific Rim states surrounding the Pacific Ocean, in particular China, Japan, and the United States.

Pacific Rim refers to the countries and cities located around the edge of the Pacific Ocean. There are many economic centers around the Pacific Rim, such as Hong Kong, Singapore, Seoul, Tokyo, Manila, Los Angeles, Shanghai, Taipei, Sydney, Melbourne, Brisbane, Auckland, Santiago, San Francisco, Seattle, San Diego, Portland, and Vancouver. Some writers argue that the established centers of industrialism and the world's economic center of gravity in Europe and North America are stagnating and that the center of world economic activity may shift to the Pacific Rim, with a consequent decline in the Western countries surrounding the Atlantic Ocean. This idea arose in the late 1980s and 1990s, when previously underdeveloped Asian economies such as Thailand, Malaysia, and South Korea began to rapidly modernize and grow at phenomenal rates. Before this time the only major industrialized economy in the region had been Japan, somewhat isolated from the major developed areas of the world, and at least partly dependent on export trade with Europe and North America to maintain its changing living standards. The recent appearance of the "Asian Tigers" or "Dragons" as the newly developing countries became known, drew the attention of the West to the region, and opened the possibility that the old economic world order might be under threat from these dynamic young economies. The Pacific Rim concept was based on the belief that these growing Asian economies might be drawn into more extensive economic relationships with other nations bordering the Pacific, such as Australia, California, and the Pacific Northwest.

Paganism was the Christian term for polytheistic worship. During Late Antiquity the Catholic Church suppressed paganism, the traditional religion of the Roman Empire.

Pahlavi, Muhammad Reza Shah (1878–1944) was the shah of Iran and the founder of the Pahlavi royal dynasty that would rule Iran until 1979. After World War I, Persia, which is the former name of Iran, was a protectorate of Britain. The then-ruling royal family was corrupt and ineffective. Reza Pahlavi, who was a general in the Persian army, staged a coup in 1921 and overthrew the monarchical government with the support of the British. Initially, he established a military dictatorship. But, in 1925, he declared himself king ("shah" in Persian) and established the Pahlavi Dynasty. After restoring the royal government, he renamed the country *Iran* and initiated efforts to modernize the country. He established a national army; modernized the bureaucracy and the legal and educational systems; built roads and railroads; established government factories to produce textiles, steel, sugar, and cement; and took control of the oil industry. As an admirer of Kemal Ataturk of Turkey, he adopted a Western-influenced law code, outlawed the veiling of women, and encouraged men to wear Western-style clothes. Because of his support for Nazi Germany during World War II, his country was invaded and occupied by British and Russian forces and he was forced to abdicate in 1941 in favor of his son, Muhammad Reza Shah Pahlavi, who would rule Iran until 1979.

Pahlavi, Reza Shah (1919–1980) was the Shah of Iran from 1941 until 1979, when he was overthrown and an Islamic theocracy was established under the leadership of the Ayatollah Ruhollah Khomeini. He succeeded his father Reza Shah Pahlavi, who was forced to abdicate in 1941 after Britain and the Soviet Union invaded and occupied Iran during World War II to prevent Reza Shah Pahlavi's cooperation with Nazi Germany. In the early 1950s, a political power struggle arose between the Shah of Iran and the Nationalist Front Party, a nationalist-oriented political party headed by Mohammed Mossadegh, the premier of Iran. In 1951, the Iranian parliament passed a law to nationalize the British-owned Anglo-Iranian Oil Company. This nationalization effort had severe economic and political consequences for Iran. When the Shah attempted to remove Mossadegh from office in 1953, public demonstrations forced the Shah to leave Iran. Subsequently, pro-monarchy forces that were political opponents of Mossadegh overthrew his regime and, with the support and assistance of the U.S. government, restored the Shah to power. After the removal of Mossadegh, the Shah initiated a policy of economic development, land redistribution, and social reform called the "White Revolution." However, opposition to the autocratic, corrupt and repressive rule of the Shah became more widespread after 1973. By 1978, a revolt by a coalition of students, merchants, and Shi'ite clergy forced the Shah to leave Iran. While he did not abdicate, a national referendum declared Iran an Islamic republic in April 1979.

Paleolithic (2,500,000–10,000 BCE) was the period of human history known as the Old Stone Age in which the tools used by humans were made of stone. It predates the Neolithic period.

Paleontology is the study of prehistoric fossilized animals and plants in order to determine the interactions with each other and the environments in which they lived. It draws from a wide range of sciences including biology, geology, archaeology engineering, biochemistry and mathematics. Paleontology has played an important role in reconstructing Earth's history and has provided the evidence to support the theory of evolution.

Palestine Liberation Organization (PLO) (1964) is a multiparty confederation founded to struggle for Palestinian rights. Since 1974, it has been recognized as the sole legitimate representative of the Palestinian people. It was originally founded by the Arab League and was initially controlled primarily by the Egyptian government. The original PLO Charter outlined goals that included the destruction of the State of Israel by armed struggle and a right of return and self-determination for Palestinian Arabs. Palestinian statehood was not mentioned in its original charter, but the PLO adopted the idea of an independent state between the Jordan River and Mediterranean Sea in 1974. More recently, the PLO officially adopted a two-state solution, with Israel and Palestine living side by side. This policy requires making East Jerusalem the capital of the Palestinian state and giving Palestinians right of return, even though some Palestinian leaders have declared their goal is still "liberation" of all of Palestine. Yasser Arafat was the Chairman of the PLO Executive Committee from 1969 until his death in 2004. Arafat was succeeded by Mahmoud Abbas (also known as Abu Mazen).

Palimpsests were reused sheets of parchment, which often contained layers of valuable texts that were later recovered by scientists. Because parchment sheets used for copying were expensive, monks during the Middle Ages often scrubbed off an old text and copied another in its place.

Pan-African Congress was a series of seven meetings held between 1919 and 1994 that sought to address the consequences of European colonization of Africa. These conferences demanded an end to colonial rule, racial discrimination and imperialism and sought human rights and political and economic equality.

Pan-Africanism was a political movement that sought to overcome the divisions between rival ethnic groups in the newly emergent independent African states. This movement did not view the national boundaries established by European colonial powers in Africa as the basis for creating unity among the disparate groups in Africa. Advocates of Pan-Africanism, such as Jomo Kenyatta and Kwame Nkrumah, hoped that all Africans would cooperate to form a "united states" of nations on the African continent.

Pan-Arabism was a secular form of Arab nationalism that emerged in the Middle East in the era of decolonization after World War II. It was especially influential in Egypt, Syria and Iraq.

Pan-Hellenic was the nationalist ideology and movement that arose in the late 1800s and early 1900s that stressed the identity that all Greeks felt in common with each other. It applied especially to athletic games, such as the Olympic Games, the Nemean Games and the Isthmian games in which competitors came from all over the Greek world.

Pan-Slavism was the nationalist ideology and movement that arose in the late 1800s and early 1900s that stressed the unity and shared interests of various Slavic peoples—Russian, Serbians, and Ukrainians—in the Russian and Habsburg empires. This ideology and movement originated in the 1830s as Slavic peoples in the Balkans struggled for independence from the Ottoman and Austrian Empires.

Panama Canal (1880–1914) is the ship canal that was built by the United States across the Isthmus of Panama. When it opened in 1914, it greatly shortened the sea voyage between the east and west Coasts of North America. The United States relinquished control of the Panama Canal and turned it over to Panama in 2000.

Pandemic is a global outbreak of an infectious disease that affects people or animals over an extensive geographical area.

Pantheism is the belief that God exists in all things, living and inanimate.

Papacy is the name for the institution ruled by the bishop of Rome, who in the Roman Catholic tradition is the successor to Peter, the most prominent of Jesus' apostles. Since Peter was believed to be the leader of the original followers of Christ, his successors, the popes, were considered to be the leaders of the Catholic Church.

Papal Bull is a document issued by a pope closed with a lead seal known as a bulla. Papal bulls were originally issued by the pope for many kinds of formal public communications.

Papal Curia is the bureaucracy that serves as the central financial and judicial administration of the Catholic Church.

Papal Infallibility (1869–1870) is the doctrine of the Catholic Church enumerated at the First Vatican Council in 1870 that the pope is infallible when making official pronouncements in his capacity as head of the Catholic Church on matters of faith and morals.

Papal Monarchy refers to the period during the 1100s and 1200s when the power of the Catholic Church was increasingly expanded and centralized in the hands of the popes that focused on recovering lost lands and property rights in central Italy.

Papal States was the territory in central Italy ruled by the pope from the 700s until 1870. Over the centuries the Papal States would encompass an extensive strip of mountainous territory that extended diagonally across Italy from the Tyrrhenian Sea to the Adriatic Sea. An important development in the creation of the Papal States was what has been called the "Donation of Pepin". Between 754 and 756, the first Carolingian king, Pepin the Short, conquered the territories of the Lombards in central Italy. Subsequently, Pepin granted Pope Stephen II rights over that land in central Italy. As the papacy was still subject to the authority of the Byzantine emperor in Constantinople, the Donation of Pepin made the papacy, for the first time, a temporal ruler over civil authorities on Byzantine imperial lands in Italy. The Donation of Pepin was confirmed by his successors Charlemagne in 778 and Louis the Pious in 817. Charlemagne was the son of Pepin and Louis the Pious was the son of Charlemagne.

Papyrus is a reed that grows along the banks of the Nile River in Egypt. From it was produced a flexible, durable, and paper-like writing medium used by the Egyptians, Greeks, and Romans.

Paradigm is a conceptual model or intellectual framework within which scientists conduct their research and experimentation.

Paris Commune (1871) refers to the revolt of workers in Paris that sought to establish a workers' government. Discontented workers organized it in the aftermath of the siege of Paris during the Franco-Prussian War. The French national army crushed it after a brief struggle. The Paris commune became the symbol of revolution for radical politicians, especially the Marxists, in the late 1800s in Europe.

Paris Peace Accords (1973) was the agreement that ended U.S. involvement in the Vietnam War.

Paris Peace Conference (1919–1920) was the meeting of the victors of the Britain, France, the United States and Italy following the end of World War I to establish peace terms for the defeated nations of Germany, Austro-Hungary, Ottoman Empire, and Bulgaria. The victors reshaped the map of Europe with new borders and countries in Eastern Europe and imposed military restrictions and stringent financial penalties on Germany, held Germany responsible for starting the war and divided the colonies of Germany and the Ottoman Empire in Africa, the Middle East, and Asia among the British and French. Germany and the Soviet Union were not invited to the meeting. The meeting also created the League of Nations.

Paris, Treaty of (1858) ended the Crimean war and denied the Russians, who had been defeated, access to the Black Sea.

Parlements were the thirteen regional provincial law courts in France dominated by the hereditary nobility that functioned as a supreme court of appeals. They were established in the 1400s. The Parlement of Paris was the largest and most powerful Parlement, covering about one-third of the country and two-thirds of France's population of 25 million. The judges owned their offices. While the judges could not make laws, they did have the power to approve or overturn the registration of royal edicts in their regions. In the 1600s and 1700s some of the parlements often tried to obstruct the absolutist policies of the French kings. The National Assembly abolished the parlements in 1789.

Parliament is an English governmental institution that grew from the royal court and the consultative function of the nobles. It emerged in the 1200s, but took hundreds of years to reach the height of its powers after the Glorious Revolution of 1688. Parliaments were meetings of the royal courts in the Middle Ages that were used to secure the consensus of the nobles for the policies of the king. However, over time prosperous merchants and farmers that lacked noble title were represented in Parliament because a king needed to raise money to fight foreign wars.

Parthenon is the temple built in honor of Athena on the Acropolis in Athens. Its sculptures were completed in 432 BCE. The chief architects were Ictinus and Callicrates and the chief sculptor was Pheidias. It was built as part of a building program during the time of Pericles and was financed by the treasury of the Delian League.

Pastoralists were nomadic communities that moved from place to place to find pastures/ grazing lands for their herds of domesticated animals.

Patent of Toleration (1871) was an edict issued by King Joseph II of Austria that granted freedom of worship to Protestants and members of the Greek Orthodox Church.

Paterfamilias was a doctrine in ancient Rome pursuant to which the oldest male of the family held supreme legal power over the lives of the women and children in his family as long as he lived. Only the paterfamilias could own property.

Patriarch is the name for the head of the Greek Orthodox Church, which officially split with the pope and the Roman Catholic Church in 1054.

Patriarchy is a form of social organization marked by the supremacy of the father, the legal dependence of wives and children to the father, and the inheritance of property only by males. In a patriarchy, the father, as the head of the family, also exercises complete social authority over the activities of the members of the family.

Patrician, which means "the well-fathered ones" in Latin, were the ruling class of ancient Rome. They were hereditary aristocracy and wealthy landowners that held political power during the Roman Republic.

Patrilineal Kinship refers to a pattern of kinship that traces descent through the male line. It involves the attribution of the name and the inheritance to children through the male line.

Patristic Era (100–451 CE) is the period of the early Christian Church when a group of theologians known as the Church Fathers significantly influenced the development of the Church. The Church Fathers included Justin Martyr, Irenaeus of Lyons, Clement of Alexandria, Tertullian, Origen, Cyprian of Carthage, Athanasius, Gregory of Nazianzus, Basil of Caesarea, Gregory of Nyssa, Theodore of Mopsuestia, Augustine of Hippo, Pelagius, Vincent of Lérins, Cyril of Alexandria, and Nestorius. The Church Fathers wrote on the following subjects: Christianity's relationship with Judaism, the development of the New Testament, the defense and explanation of Christianity, the development of Christian creeds, the nature of Christ, the doctrine of the Trinity and the doctrine of divine grace.

Patronage refers to corrupt use of state resources to advance the interests of certain political groups, families, ethnic groups, or religious groups in exchange for electoral support. Typically, a government official would give jobs, award business contracts, or do favors as a means for rewarding or enforcing political loyalty. Political leaders often have at their disposal a great deal of patronage, in the sense that they make decisions concerning the appointment of government officials and contracts. Patronage is therefore a recognized power of the executive branch of a government to make many governmental appointments to its loyal followers or fellow party members.

Paul of Tarsus (Saint Paul, the Apostle) (5/4 BCE-62/64 CE), also known as Saul, was a Greek-speaking Jew who preached the teachings of Jesus to the gentile and Jewish communities across the Roman Empire. Of the twenty seven books that comprise the New Testament, thirteen are attributed to Paul. Before his conversion, he persecuted the early disciples of Jesus in Jerusalem. While traveling from Jerusalem to Damascus, he claimed that Jesus appeared to him and he was struck blind. However, after three days he regained his sight. As a result of that experience, he began to preach that Jesus of Nazareth was the Jewish Messiah and the Son of God.

Pax Americana is a Latin phrase meaning "American Peace." It denotes the period of relative peace in the world since the end of World War II and coincides with the dominant military and economic position of the United States. It places the United States in the military and diplomatic role of a modern-day Roman Empire or British Empire (based on *Pax Romana* and *Pax Britannica*, respectively). During this period, no armed conflict has emerged among major industrialized nations of Europe and Japan and no nuclear weapons have been used. However, the United States and its allies have been involved in various regional wars, such as the Korean War, the Vietnam War, the Persian Gulf War, and the Iraq War.

Pax Romana (27 BCE–180 CE), which means "Roman Peace" in Latin, refers to the period of peace, stability, cultural brilliance, and economic prosperity that Roman rule begun under Emperor Augustus brought to the lands of the Roman Empire during the 1st and 2nd centuries CE. During this period, which ended with Emperor Marcus Aurelius, the movement of people and trade goods along Roman-protected roads and seas allowed for the spread of goods, cultural practices, technologies, and religious ideas throughout the Roman Empire.

Peace Corps (1961) was started by President John Kennedy in 1961 to provide U.S. volunteers for technical development assistance to Third World nations.

Peace of Augsburg (1555) was a treaty signed between Charles V, Holy Roman Emperor, and a league of Protestant German princes on September 25, 1555 at the city of Augsburg in Germany. The effect of the treaty was to officially recognize the existence of the Lutheran faith in the Holy Roman Empire. According to the doctrine of "in the Prince's land, the Prince's religion", the ruler of a specific region would determine the religion of his people, Catholic or Protestant. Although the Peace of Augsburg was moderately successful in relieving tension in the Holy Roman Empire and increasing tolerance, it left important things undone. Neither the Anabaptists nor the Calvinists were protected under the peace, so many Protestant groups living under the rule of a Lutheran prince still found themselves in danger of the charge of heresy. In fact, tolerance was not officially extended to Calvinists until the Treaty of Westphalia in 1648.

Peace of Paris (1763) is the treaty that ended the French and Indian War. Britain and Spain acquired French territories in North America, and Britain acquired Spanish Florida. Britain also acquired French colonies in India.

Peace of Westphalia (1648) is the name of a series of treaties that ended the Thirty Years' War. It recognized the autonomy and sovereign authority of over 300 German principalities in the Holy Roman Empire. It acknowledged the independence of the United Provinces of the Netherlands. The treaty also made Calvinism a permissible religion along with Lutheranism and Catholicism within the Holy Roman Empire. The effect of this treaty was to severely weaken the power of the Holy Roman Emperor and reduce the role of the Catholic Church in European politics.

Peaceful Coexistence was the term used by Premier Khrushchev in 1963 to describe a situation in which the United States and Soviet Union would continue to compete economically and politically without launching a thermonuclear war.

Pearl Harbor is the U.S. naval base in Hawaii that was attacked by Japanese aircraft on December 7, 1941. The sinking of much of the U.S. Pacific fleet caused the United States to enter World War II.

Peisistratus or Pisistratus (6th century–527 BCE) was the Athenian politician who was responsible for unifying the Athenians and encouraging prosperity. He instituted a tyranny in Athens in 560 BCE that was continued by his sons for generations.

Pelagianism was a religious doctrine associated with a British monk named Pelgaius who lived during the late 300s and early 400s CE. This doctrine maintained that human beings did not need grace to fulfill God's moral commands, thus they could achieve salvation through their own efforts. Furthermore, it denied the effects of original sin

on the human will. The Catholic Church councils in the early 400s CE declared Pelagianism to be a heresy.

Peloponnesian War (431–404 BCE) was a protracted and costly conflict between the Athenian and Spartan alliance systems that convulsed most of the Greek world beginning in 431 BCE. The war was largely a consequence of Athenian imperialism. Possession of a naval empire allowed Athens to fight a war of attrition. Ultimately, Sparta prevailed because of Athenian errors and Persian financial support. The war ended with the destruction of the Athenian fleet in 404 BCE.

Peloponnesus or Peloponnese is the name applied to the large portion of southern Greece where Sparta was located.

Peng Dehuai (1898–1974) was a Chinese military leader and veteran of the Long March who led Chinese forces in the Korean War and served as minister of the defense in the 1950s. He was purged in 1959 for criticizing Mao Zedong over the Great Leap Forward.

Pentagon Papers (1971) is a 7,000-page, top-secret U.S. Department of Defense history of the U.S. involvement in the Vietnam War from 1945 to 1971. The Pentagon Papers were leaked in 1971 by Department of Defense worker Daniel Ellsberg. Excerpts were published as a series of articles in *The New York Times* beginning June 13, 1971. The document revealed, among other things, that the government had planned to expand its role in Vietnam even when President Lyndon Johnson was promising not to, that the Gulf of Tonkin incident had been largely fabricated to this end, and that there was no plan to end the war. The document increased belief that the Johnson administration had lied to the American people about the Vietnam War. Shortly after *The New York Times* began publishing the series, President Nixon became incensed. His words to Secretary of State Henry Kissinger that day included "people have gotta be put to the torch for this sort of thing . . ." and "let's get the son-of-a-bitch in jail." The next day, Attorney General John Mitchell talked Nixon into getting a federal court injunction to cease publication of the documents. This was the first time in U.S. history that any executive successfully obtained a judicial prior restraint against publication for national security reasons.

Pentateuch, which literally means "the five scrolls," designates the first five books of the Hebrew Bible (Genesis, Exodus, Leviticus, Numbers, and Deuteronomy). It is also known as the Torah or the Law of Moses.

Pentecost is a Greek word for "fifty," which was used to designate the Jewish agricultural festival celebrated fifty days after the feast of Passover.

Peons were poor agricultural workers in Latin America. Typically, they were indebted to their employers and were therefore unable to sell their labor in the marketplace freely or seek other employment. The system of peonage dated from the arrival of the Spanish in the Americas in the 1500s.

People's Charter (1839) was a document issued by the Chartist movement in Britain calling for universal suffrage for all male adults, the secret ballot, electoral districts, and annual parliamentary elections. Over three million British citizens signed this document.

People's Liberation Army is the name of the Chinese army that defeated the Kuomindang during the Chinese civil war that ended in 1949.

People's War was a military-political strategy developed by Mao Zedong in which he argued that it was necessary during a revolution to maintain the support of the population and to use mobile warfare and guerrilla warfare to defeat the enemy. After the Sino-Vietnamese War in 1979, Deng Xiaoping abandoned people's war for "people's war under modern conditions," which moved away from reliance on large numbers of troops to greater reliance on technology. In its original formulation by Mao, a people's war relied upon broad-based popular support. A people's war strategically avoids decisive battles, since a tiny force of a few dozen soldiers would easily be routed in an all-out confrontation with the state. Instead, it favors the strategy of protracted warfare, with carefully chosen battles that can realistically be won. A revolutionary force conducting people's war starts in a remote area with mountainous or otherwise difficult terrain in which its enemy is weak. It attempts to establish a local stronghold known as a revolutionary base area. As it grows in power, it establishes other revolutionary base areas and spreads its influence through the surrounding countryside, where it may become the governing power and gain popular support through such programs as land reform. Eventually it may have enough strength to encircle and capture small cities, then larger ones, until finally it seizes power in the entire country. The concept of a people's war was the basis for the military strategy used against the Japanese during World War II.

Pepper is a spice from the Malabar region of India that was imported by ancient Greece as early as the 4th century BCE, though it so expensive that only the rich could afford it. By circa 30 BCE during the early Roman Empire, the trade of pepper along the land and sea routes of the Arabian Peninsula had become commonplace. It became so valued in trade throughout the Mediterranean that it was referred to as "black gold." During the Middle Ages, virtually all of the black pepper found in Europe, the Middle East, and North Africa was imported from the Malabar region of India. According to the Roman geographer Strabo, the Roman Empire sent a fleet of approximately 120 ships annually to India. The Roman fleet traveled through the Arabian Sea and across the Indian Ocean. Returning from India, the Roman ships traveled up the Red Sea and then carried the cargo overland and by barge to Alexandria where the pepper was shipped to Rome. This same trade route would dominate the pepper trade into Europe for about 1500 years. After the collapse of the Roman Empire, the portion of the spice trade between India and Egypt came under Islamic control. The portion of the trade route between India and Europe was dominated by Venice and Genoa.

Percussion Caps are gunpowder-filled capsules that, when struck by the hammer of a gun, ignite the explosive charge in a gun. The development of percussion caps meant that guns no longer had to be loaded by hand and thereby could be fired more rapidly.

Perestroika, which means "restructuring" in Russian, was the name given to the economic and political reforms introduced in the Soviet Union by Mikhail Gorbachev in June 1987. Under this program, the state bureaucracies were restructured, privileges of the political elite were reduced, and a shift from a centrally planned economy to a mixed economy based on markets forces was begun.

Pericles (495–429 BCE) was a leading aristocratic political and military leader who guided the Athenian state from 460 to 429 BCE through the transformation to full participatory democracy for all male citizens. His reforms gave every male Athenian citizen the right to propose and amend legislation and to participate in the public assembly. Pericles also reformed the great appeals court of Athens by paying an average day's wage for attendance. He established Athens as a center for art and literature. He supervised construction of the Acropolis and pursued a policy of imperial expansion that led to the Peloponnesian War.

Periodization is the attempt by historians to categorize or divide history into discrete named blocks of time. All of such periods are retrospectively defined and useful to the extent that they merely provide a convenient description for historical events that occurred within limited temporal and geographical boundaries. To the extent that history is continuous, all systems of periodization are more or less arbitrary. Nevertheless, historians contend that it is useful to divide up history into periods in order to make sense of the past and to articulate changes over time. Different nations and cultures that experience different histories, require different models of periodization. Periodizing labels are continually challenged and redefined. However, in most cases people living through a period are unable to identify themselves as belonging to the period that historians may later assign to them. This is partly because they are unable to predict the future, and so will not be able to tell whether they are at the beginning, middle, or end of a period. Another reason may be that their own sense of historical development may be determined by religions or ideologies that differ from those used by later historians.

Permissive Society was a term used especially after World War II to describe a Western society in which new attitudes emerged about sexual freedom and the use of drugs.

Perry, Commodore Matthew (1794–1858) was the American naval officer that, on July 8, 1853, became the first foreigner to break down the barrier of isolation established by Japanese rulers for 250 years.

Persepolis was a complex of palaces, reception halls, and buildings erected by the Persian kings Darius I and Xerxes in Persia. It was destroyed by Alexander the Great when he conquered Persia.

Pershing Missiles were a class of U.S. nuclear missiles deployed in West Germany in the 1970s and 1980s that had a limited range but a large explosive yield.

Pershing, General John J. (1860–1948) was the U.S. Army general who led U.S. military forces against Pancho Villa in Mexico in 1916 and the American Expeditionary Forces in Europe during World War I.

Persian Empire (550–330 BCE) was established by Cyrus the Great. It was the largest empire of the ancient world and is considered by some historians today to be the world's first superpower. Its borders stretched from the Indus Valley to the Mediterranean encompassing today's Iran, Iraq, Pakistan, Afghanistan, Turkmenistan, Uzbekistan, Tajikstan, Turkey, Jordan, Cyprus, Syria, Lebanon, Israel, Egypt, and the Caucasus region. Thus, it was strategically located between the civilizations of the East and West. Under the leadership of such kings as Cyrus the Great, it became a religiously and culturally tolerant empire comprised of 23 different peoples. The state religion of the Persian Empire was Zoroastrianism. Its teachings, such as good and evil, free will, heaven and hell, final judgment, and one powerful god, influenced the three main faiths that would develop in the ancient Middle East, Judaism, Christianity and Islam.

Persian Wars were a series of conflicts between Greek city-states and the Persian Empire ranging from the Ionian Revolt (499–494 BCE) through Darius's punitive expedition that failed at Marathon (490 BCE) and the defeat of Xerxes' massive invasion of Greece by the Spartan-led Hellenic League (480–479 BCE). The wars took place when the Persians invaded mainland Greece to avenge the military assistance provided by mainland Greek city-states, primarily Athens, to Greek city-states in Ionia that had rebelled against Persian rule. Herodotus chronicled these events in his writings.

Persians were the people that allied with the Medes and built a large and prosperous empire known for its form of government and its culture. The Persian Empire lasted from circa 550 BCE to 330 BCE, when Alexander the Great conquered it. The Persians built the first great navy.

Personalist Leaders is a term used by historians to describe certain political leaders that rely on a combination of charisma and their ability to mobilize and direct the masses of citizens of a country outside the authority of a constitution and laws.

Peso was a widely circulated coin minted from gold that was mined in the Spanish colonies in the New World. It was also known as a "piece of eight" as it was worth eight reales. *Real* is a Spanish word for "royal."

Peter I (Peter the Great) (1672–1725) was the Russian tsar from 1689 to 1725 who revolutionized Russian society, politics, and culture by introducing Western languages and technologies to the Russian elite. He hoped to make Russian society and social customs resemble those of France, Britain, and the Dutch Republic. He centralized the government, modernized the army, created a navy, and reformed education and the economy. He moved the capital of Russia from Moscow to a new city that he created, St. Petersburg, in order to have a Russian "window" on the West. In essence, he began the process of modernizing Russia and making it a great world power.

Peter the Hermit (1050–1115 CE) was a knight, an ascetic and an itinerant preacher who traveled throughout France and Germany preaching support for the First Crusade. He was also one of the leaders of the People's Crusade.

Peterloo Massacre (1819) refers to the killing of 11 workers and the wounding of another 460 workers in Manchester, England by British troops following a peaceful demonstration by workers protesting against the Corn Laws and demanding political reform.

Petrarch, Francesco (1304–1374) is considered to be the greatest figure of the early Renaissance. He was a Florentine humanist scholar, poet, biographer, and traveler. He advocated imitating the practices, values, and culture of the ancient Romans in order to reform society.

Petrine Succession is the doctrine advocated by early Roman bishops that Jesus had endowed Peter, traditionally considered to be the first bishop of Rome, with supreme responsibility for the Church and that the successor to Peter, the pope, is the leader of the Catholic Church.

Petrograd Soviet of Workers' and Soldiers' Deputies (1917) was a council of leaders that was elected in Russia during World War I when workers in the city of Petrograd protested against the severe wartime food and coal shortages. This council was central to the Bolshevik Revolution and eventually became the temporary ruling political power in Moscow.

Phalanx was a rectangular military formation of heavily armed infantrymen equipped with pikes that formed the core of Greek and Hellenistic hoplite armies. Standing shoulder to shoulder in ranks often eight men deep, hoplites moved in unison and depended on one another for protection.

Pharaoh, which means "great house," is the central figure in the ancient Egyptian state. Believed to be an earthly manifestation of the gods, he used his absolute power to maintain the safety and prosperity of Egypt. He was the leader of religious and political life in the Old Kingdom and he commanded the wealth, resources, and people of Egypt. It was believed that the pharaoh represented the ancestors of the Egyptians and guaranteed the fertility of the soil.

Pharisees refers to a Jewish sect of teachers and preachers that emerged during the Maccabean period. They emphasized strict adherence to the purity of the laws of the Torah and developed special oral laws known as the Mishnah to help them to do so. They also insisted that all of God's (Yahweh's) commandments were binding on all Jews.

Philip II (1527–1598) was the Catholic king of Spain from 1556 to 1598. He was the son of

Charles V, the Holy Roman Emperor. He ruled Spain at the height of its influence and power. He sent the Armada to invade England and restore Catholicism there. He also attempted, unsuccessfully, to suppress the revolt in the Netherlands.

Philip II (382–336 BCE) was the King of Macedon from 359 to 336 BCE that was responsible for the unification of Macedon and its expansion and conquest of Greece. He developed a full-time, well-trained professional army and mastered the art of siege warfare. He was the father of Alexander the Great.

Philippine–American War (Philippine War of Independence or the Philippine Insurrection) (1899–1902) was an armed military conflict between the US and Filipino nationalists that sought their independence after the US had annexed the Philippines. As a result of the Spanish-American War (1898), the Treaty of Paris transferred Philippine sovereignty from Spain to the United States. However, Filipino leaders that had fought for independence from Spain during the Spanish-American War and whose troops actually controlled the majority of the Philippines refused to recognize American sovereignty. Prior to the Spanish-American War, the Filipinos had already fought the Philippine Revolution (1896–1898) against Spanish colonial rule. With the outbreak of the Spanish-American War, the Filipino forces occupied nearly all the Spanish-held territory in the Philippines except Manila. As a result, the Filipinos declared independence from Spain and the First Philippine Republic was established that declared war against the US in 1899. After the capture of Emilio Aguinaldo, the leader of the Filipino resistance forces, the end of the war was declared in 1902, even though some groups continued to fight until 1913. During the war, there were between 34,000 and 1,000,000 causalities. The US would occupy the Philippines until 1946 when the US granted the Philippines independence.

Philistines were an ancient people who inhabited the southern coast of Canaan. Their origin has been debated, but modern archaeology has suggested early cultural links with the Mycenaean world. The Philistines occupied the five cities of Gaza, Ashkelon, Ashdod, Ekron, and Gath, along the coastal strip of southwestern Canaan that was

part of the Egyptian Empire. The biblical stories of Samson, Samuel, Saul, and David include accounts of Philistine-Israelite conflicts. The Philistines long held a monopoly on iron smithing. They frequently attacked the Hebrews causing almost perpetual war between the two peoples. The Philistines lost their independence to Tiglath-Pileser III of Assyria circa 732 BCE. Later, Nebuchadnezzar II of Babylon conquered all of Syria and the Kingdom of Judah and the former Philistine cities became part of the Neo-Babylonian Empire. Eventually all traces of the Philistines as a people disappeared. Subsequently the Philistine cities came under the control of Persian Empire, the Seleucid Empire, Romans and subsequent empires.

Philosophe is the French term for writers, critics, and public intellectuals in France in the 1700s who proclaimed that they were bringing Enlightenment knowledge to their fellow citizens. They believed in applying rational criticism to all things, including religion and politics. They wrote and spoke on a range of topics with the primary objective of reforming society. They advocated intellectual and religious freedom as well as a variety of practical political reforms. They sought to apply reason and common sense to understanding the nature of the institutions and societies of their time. They were greatly influenced by the ideas of Newton and other scientific thinkers. Voltaire, Diderot, and Condorcet are examples of leading French philosophes.

Philosophy, which means "love of wisdom" in Greek, concerns the systematic and critical examination of the fundamental values, beliefs, principles, and ideas that influence human conduct. Historically, philosophical speculation has played a central role in the development of virtually all of the world's civilizations. The main branches of philosophy are metaphysics (investigation of the nature of existence and the world); epistemology (investigation of the nature and scope of knowledge); ethics (investigation of how a person should act); logic (investigation of patterns of thinking); philosophy of the mind (investigation of the nature of the mind and its relationship to the human body); aesthetics (investigation of beauty, art, and perception); and political philosophy (investigation of the nature of government and relationship of the individual to the state). Many subjects, such as physics, psychology, and science, have had their historical origins in philosophy.

Phoenicians were Semitic-speaking Canaanites living on the coast of modern Lebanon circa 1200 to 800 BCE. From major cities such as Tyre and Sidon, Phoenician merchants and sailors explored the Mediterranean, engaged in widespread commerce, and founded Carthage and other trading colonies in the western Mediterranean after circa 900 BCE. The Phoenicians exported their alphabet that they derived from Ugarit to the Mediterranean world.

Phony War (1939–1940) refers to the lull in the fighting during World War II between the German defeat of Poland in 1939 and the German attack on the nations of Western Europe in the spring of 1940. In German, it was known as Sitzkrieg.

Physiocrats were French economists in the 1700s that attacked the mercantilist regulation of the economy and advocated a limited role for the government in the economy. They advocated a deregulation of the grain trade and a more equitable tax system to encourage agricultural productivity. They believed that all economic production depended on a sound agricultural base. Physiocrats advanced the idea that land was wealth and thus improvements in agriculture should take first priority in any political or economic reforms initiated by the state.

Pico Della Mirandola, Giovanni (1463–1494) was a Florentine humanist philosopher influenced by the discovery of the works of Plato who became an advocate of Neoplatonism, a school of thought that sought to blend the thinking of Plato with elements of ancient mysticism and Christianity. He was a member of the Platonic Academy that was founded by Cosimo de' Medici. The Academy was an organization of scholars who met to hear readings and lectures on the works of Plato. Influenced by the writings of Plato, he wrote *Oration on the Dignity of Man,* in which he argued that humans could perfect their existence since God had endowed humans with the capacity to determine their fate. While he contended that "nothing is more wonderful than man," he did not advocate the involvement of humans in public affairs.

Pictograms were the earliest form of writing in Mesopotamia, circa 3500 BCE, in which pictures represented particular objects such as animals.

Pidgin English is a term used to refer to any of the languages derived from English. From the 1600s to the 1800s, there was a "Chinese Pidgin English" spoken in Cantonese-speaking portions of China. Historically, it was a modified form of English developed in the 1600s for use as a trade language or *lingua franca* between the British and the Chinese. Chinese Pidgin got its start in Guangzhou (Canton), China, after the British established their first trading post there in 1664. Because the British found Chinese an extremely difficult language to learn and because the Chinese held the English in low esteem and therefore disdained to learn their language, Pidgin English was developed by the English and adapted by the Chinese for business purposes. It continued in use until the end of the 1800s, when Pidgin came to be looked upon by the Chinese as humiliating, and so they preferred to learn standard English instead. "Japanese Pidgin English" was spoken in Japanese ports, such as Yokohama, in the 1800s.

Pietas is the Latin word one of the principal cultural values of ancient Rome, which means "respect for authority."

Pietism was a revivalist movement within the Lutheran Church beginning in the 1600s that emphasized deeply emotional religious experience over formality and orthodoxy.

Pilgrimage is a religious journey made to holy sites in order to show piety, fulfill vows, encounter relics, or gain absolution for sins.

Ping-Pong Diplomacy (1971) refers to the U.S. table-tennis team visit to China that helped improve ties between the two countries and led in part to President Nixon's historic 1972 visit to China.

Pinochet, Augusto (1915–2006) was the Chilean general who led a military coup in 1973 with the support of the United States that overthrew the democratically elected socialist government of President Salvador Allende. As the president of Chile from 1974 to 1990, he established a repressive dictatorial regime that sought to eliminate liberal and leftist political influences in Chile and to re-establish a free-market economy. His regime was characterized by massive human rights abuses such as arbitrary arrests, kidnapping and disappearance of political opponents, the extensive use of torture, and the murder of over 3,000 political opponents of his regime.

Pizzaro, Francisco (1475–1541) was the Spanish explorer and conquistador who conquered the Incan Empire in Peru between 1531 and 1533.

Plantations were large tracts of land owned by a colonial settler that had emigrated from Western Europe that produced basic staple crops such as sugar, coffee, cotton, rice, and tobacco that were farmed with slave labor. A plantation economy was the economic system that produced crops, especially tobacco, cotton, sugar, and rice, using slave labor on large estates that in the colonies in the Americas stretched from the Chesapeake Bay to Brazil.

Plantation Colonies were first established by Portuguese settlers in the Cape Verde Islands in the Atlantic Ocean off the western coast of Africa in order to cultivate cash crops such as sugar, indigo, cotton, coffee, and tobacco with African slave labor. This form of economic production was later exported by the Portuguese to the Americas. The plantation system was the agricultural system that the Portuguese developed on their island colonies in the Atlantic Ocean in the 1400s and 1500s to produce sugar using slaves brought forcibly from the west coast of Africa. The basic elements of this system included a wealthy absentee landlord that owned a vast tract of lands, the production of a cash crop for export, and the use of forced farm labor. This model would be adopted by the French and English in the 1600s and 1700s in their colonies in the Caribbean.

Plataea was an ancient Greek city located south of Thebes. It was the location of the Battle of Plataea in 479 BCE, in which an alliance of Greek city-states decisively defeated the Persians and ended the Persian Wars. Plataea was destroyed in the Peloponnesian War in 427 BCE by Thebes and Sparta and rebuilt in 386 BCE. With Athens as its ally, the Plataeans were able to avoid subjugation by Thebes and Corinth. Because of this alliance, they would be the only Greek city-state to fight on the side of Athens at the Battle of Marathon.

Plato (328/27–348/347 BCE) was a student of Socrates and teacher of Aristotle. Some consider him to be the most influential of the Greek philosophers. He was an advocate for idealism. Plato believed that the senses are misleading and that truth can only be attained by training the mind to overcome commonsense evidence. He was the founder of the Academy and a prolific writer of dialogues and treatises. He is particularly known for his theory of ideal forms and his writing of the *Republic*. For Plato, ideal forms were the eternal absolutes such as truth, justice and beauty. He claimed that any object humans see in daily life is only an imperfect imitation of the object's ideal form. He claimed that while humans have a dualistic nature composed of an eternal soul temporally housed in a mortal human body, humans, could, nevertheless, aspire to perfection. His contend that that particular things in the observable reality were merely reflections of universal truths. This idea was formulated by Plato in his "Allegory of the Cave". In the *Republic*, he describes an ideal state ruled by philosopher-kings that would be trained to act benevolently and unselfishly. The works of Plato would not be fully known in Western Europe until the Renaissance.

Platonic Academy was an organization of scholars founded by Cosimo de Medici in Florence to honor and study the works of Plato.

Plebeians were a hereditary social class of Roman citizens that were economically, politically and legally inferior to the patricians. They were comprised of peasants, farmers, artisans, merchants and the urban poor. As a result of the Conflict of Orders, they would gain political and legal equality with the patricians.

Plebiscita, which means "it is the opinion of the plebs", was a law passed by the Council of the Plebs during the Roman Republic. It was binding only on the plebeians, not the patricians. Today, a plebiscite, also known as a referendum, is a vote by an electorate in a democratic society concerning candidates running for political office, a particular government policy or proposal, the adoption of a new constitution, a constitutional amendment or law or the recall of an elected official.

Pleistocene is a geological era from approximately 1.8 million years ago to 11,500 years ago. During this geological era, the modern continents were essentially at their present position and the climate was characterized by repeated glacial cycles. It is estimated that 30 percent of the Earth's surface was covered with ice. Each glacial advance tied up huge volumes of water, resulting in a temporary sea level drop of one hundred meters or more over the entire Earth. Scientific evidence indicates that humans evolved into their present form during this period, there were major extinctions of large mammals such as mammoths and mastodons, horses and camels became extinct in North America, and Neanderthals also became extinct. The end of the Pleistocene era corresponds with the end of the Paleolithic Age used in archeology.

Plotinus (204–270 CE) was a Roman philosopher who taught that everything that exists is derived from the divine and that the highest goal of life should be the mystic reunion of the soul with the divine, which can only be achieved through contemplation and asceticism.

Pluralism is the political theory of modern democracy that a multitude of interest groups, not the people as a whole, governs the United States. These organizations, which include among others unions, trade and professional associations, environmentalists, civil rights activists, business and financial lobbies, and formal and informal coalitions of like-minded people influence the making and administration of laws and policy. One of the earliest arguments for pluralism came from James Madison in The Federalist Papers #10. Madison feared that factionalism would lead to in-fighting in the new American republic and devotes this paper to questioning how best to avoid such an occurrence. He argued that to avoid factionalism, it is best to allow many competing factions to prevent any one dominating the political system. Since the participants in this competitive political process constitute only a tiny fraction of the populace, the public acts mainly as bystanders. Indeed, some pluralists believe that direct democracy is not only unworkable; it is not even necessarily desirable. Besides the logistical problems of having every citizen meet at one time to decide policies, pluralists argue that political issues require continuous and expert attention, which the average citizen does not have. Some advocates of pluralism further argue that most people concentrate their time and energies on activities involving work, family, health, friendship, recreation, and other nonpolitical activities. Other pluralists go even further arguing that the common person lacks the virtues, reason, intelligence, and patience necessary for self-government and that direct democracy leads to anarchy and the loss of freedom.

Plutarch (50–120 CE) was a scholar and philosopher who was born and lived in Greece, but viewed himself as a Roman. He traveled widely throughout the Roman Empire and wrote about the Greco-Roman culture that evolved during the Roman Empire.

Plutocracy is a form of government in which the wealthy rule society. Political power and economic and social opportunity are centralized within this affluent social class. In a plutocracy, economic inequality is high and the level of social mobility is low.

Pogrom, which comes from the Yiddish word for "devastation," was a violent attack against Jewish populations in Europe, especially Russia, in the 1800s and 1900s. While usually spontaneous, governments typically did not intervene to stop. Often rumors, such as blood libels (in which the Jews are accused of stealing a Christian child for sacrifice in their rituals) were circulated to justify the attacks.

Polaris is the name of the first submarinelaunched ballistic missiles (SLBMs) that were developed by the United States. The more advanced Poseidon missiles soon replaced them.

Polis is the Greek term for a city-state, an urban center and the agricultural territory under its control farmed by citizens of the polis. It was the characteristic form of political organization in southern and central Greece in the Archaic and Classical periods. It was a self-governing community. A city-state would typically control a limited amount of territory. The urban center would typically contain markets, meeting places, a temple, and an assembly place for men to discuss community affairs.

Politburo was the name of the executive committee of the Communist Party of the Soviet Union.

Political Parties are a form of social organization comprised of people that identify with it based on shared political, social, cultural and economic interests. They initially developed in Britain in the 1700s and 1800s.

Political Power is an attribute of a government that implies a capacity to make laws and the authority to use force or violence to enforce those laws enacted by that government.

Politics is the process of making decisions for social groups. Although it is generally applied to governments, politics is also observed in all human group interactions. Politics is essentially "who gets what, when, and how." The word "politics" is derived from the Greek word for city-state, "polis."

Politiques were French Catholics that joined with the Huguenots during the French Wars of Religion in the 1500s to demand a settlement to the religious wars. They placed politics above religion, believing that no religious truth was worth the destruction to society caused by a civil war. They argued that limited toleration of the Calvinists in France would strengthen the French monarchy.

Polo, Marco (1254–1324) was a Venetian merchant traveler who traveled to and lived in China between 1275 and 1290. He served as an official under Khublai Khan and left a memoir of his travels, which was criticized in Europe at the time as wildly exaggerated.

Polybius (200–118 BCE) was a Greek historian captured by the Romans. He lived in exile in Rome, where he wrote a history of the Hellenistic world that emphasized Rome's rise to political and military greatness and the unique features of the Roman constitution. His book *The Histories* or *The Rise of the Roman Empire* describes the rise of Rome to a dominant power in the Mediterranean in the period from 220 to 146 BCE. He is the first historian to attempt to present history as a sequence of causes and effects and thereby provided a unified view of history rather than a chronology. Polybius also argued the cyclical nature of governments in which the first stage is monarchy (rule by a tyrant), the second is oligarchy (rule by aristocracy), the third is democracy (rule by the mob), and, finally, the fourth stage is a return to monarchy.

Polytheism is the belief in and worship of many gods or deities simultaneously.

Pompey (106–48 BCE) was a Roman politician during the late Roman Republic who was a political ally of Julius Caesar. Having militarily defeated the pirates who threatened Rome in 66 BCE, he became a popular military hero. He joined Julius Caesar and Crassus in the First Triumvirate that ruled Rome from 61–54 BCE. However, when a civil war erupted in Rome in 49 BCE, he opposed the tyrannical rule of Caesar. His army was defeated in 48 BCE and he fled to Egypt where he was later murdered.

Pontifex Maximus was the title of the chief priest of ancient Rome. The popes later assumed this title.

Pop Art refers to a style in the visual arts that mimicked advertising and consumerism. It used ordinary objects as part of paintings and other compositions.

Pop Culture or Popular Culture refers to the cultural meaning systems and cultural practices employed by the majority classes in a society. The movie with the biggest week-end gross box office total, the number one song on the Billboard charts, the most widely read books and the highest ranking television show in the Nielsen ratings are important elements of U.S. popular culture. Popular culture is often discussed in contrast to high culture.

Pope is the bishop of Rome who, because of the Petrine theory of succession and the central location of Rome in the Roman Empire, achieved a leading position among all of the bishops in the early Christian Church.

Pope Saint Gregory I or Gregory the Great (540–604 CE) was pope from 590–604. He is also known as **Gregory Dialogus** (*the Dialogist*) in Eastern Orthodoxy because of the *Dialogues,* which he wrote. He was the first of the Popes from a monastic background. Gregory is a Doctor of the Church and one of the four great Latin Fathers of the Church (the others being Ambrose, Augustine, and Jerome). Of all popes, Gregory I had the most influence on the early medieval Church.

Popular Front refers to the anti-fascist electoral alliances and governing coalitions that communists promoted in Europe from 1934 to 1939 to resist the spread of fascism. Popular front coalition governments won control in both Spain and France in 1936.

Popular Movement for the Liberation of Angola (MPLA) was one of three groups that vied for power during the civil war in Angola (1975–2002) after Portugal withdrew in 1975. Members of the MPLA received military training in Cuba and arms from Moscow.

Popular Sovereignty is the doctrine that political power is derived from the consent of the will of the people who are the highest political power in the state.

Populares, which means "favoring the people," were the aristocratic Roman politicians in the late Roman Republic that sought to pursue a political career based on the support of the people rather than just the aristocracy. They used the people's assemblies in an effort to break the stranglehold of the nobles on political offices. They emerged as an important political faction in Roman politics after the rule of the Gracchi brothers.

Portolanos were books or charts of sailing directions and distances that first appeared in Europe in the 1300s.

Positivism is the philosophy developed by August Comte (1798-1857), a French philosopher, in the 1800s arguing that human societies passed through a series of stages, leading to a final positive stage in which the accumulation of scientific data would enable the scientists to discover the laws that guide human behavior and thereby improve the nature of society. Positivists argued that social and economic problems could be solved by the application of the scientific method, which would lead from their perspective to continuous societal progress.

Post-industrialism is a concept that has been used since the end of the Cold War by some historians, economists, commentators, reporters, social critics, and political scientists to describe a new stage in the evolution of industrialism. It is argued that in many areas of commerce, computers have radically transformed the nature of work and the workplace. As computers now operate machines and robots, the manual work traditionally required by industry is disappearing and new areas of the economy have emerged, such as telecommunications that are more knowledge and service oriented. It is further argued that this economic evolution has significant implications for home and the workplace. As a result of inexpensive computers and rapid data transmission, more people are able to work from home or other nontraditional locations, rather than going to a place of work. Since information and knowledge are more important in this era than capital equipment, it is also argued that more people will have wider access to controlling the productive resources of society, which will supposedly translate into new, more democratic political forms and processes.

Post-modernism refers to a philosophy that developed in the late 1900s that criticized beliefs in precise knowledge and rationality that were the basis for the Scientific Revolution and the Enlightenment.

Potosi was the site in Bolivia where one of the richest silver mining operations was located in colonial Spanish America (New Spain).

Potsdam Conference (1945) was a meeting of the heads of the governments of the victorious Allies (the United States, the Soviet Union, and Great Britain) during World War II outside Berlin from July 17 to August 2, 1945. The participants, Joseph Stalin, Prime Minister Clement Attlee, and President Harry S. Truman, met to decide how to administer the defeated Nazi Germany, which had agreed to unconditional surrender on May 8, 1945. The goals of the conference also included the establishment of postwar order, negotiation of peace treaties, the terms of surrender for Japan, and plans to counter the effects of war. The three Allied leaders specifically decided that all German annexations in Europe after 1937 and separation of Austria from Germany should be reversed; that the objective of the occupation of Germany by the Allies would be demilitarization, denazification, democratization, and decartelization; that Germany and Austria would each be divided into four occupation zones as well as Berlin and Vienna; that Nazi war criminals would be prosecuted; that the Oder-Neisse line should be the border of Poland; and the amount of war reparations owed by Germany.

Power is a relationship between two or more individuals, groups, or states in which one party has the ability by the possession of certain tangible and intangible characteristics both to influence the other and to force outcomes that the other party may not want.

Power Politics is a state of international relations in which nations protect their own interests by threatening one another with military and/or economic aggression. Power politics represents a type of international relations in which nations compete for the world's resources. According to this theory of international relations, the pursuit of a country's national self-interest is considered paramount to that of the nation interest of any other nation in the international system. Techniques of power politics could include, for example, development of new types of weaponry; the massing of military units on a border of a nation; the imposition of tariffs, economic sanctions, boycotts, or blockades; and pre-emptive military strikes; covert operations, and counterinsurgency warfare. Power politics describes the foreign policy of pursued by Otto von Bismarck of Prussia between 1862 and 1871 to achieve the unification of the German territories and the creation of the German Empire.

Power Projection is the ability to use military force in areas far from a country or its sphere of influence.

Praetorian Guard was the elite military unit in the Roman Empire that served as the personal bodyguard to the Roman emperors. Augustus first formed this group of soldiers.

Praetor was the chief judicial officer of the Roman Republic. This was a new office created in Rome in 366 BCE. These people would act in place of consuls when they were away, although they primarily dealt with the administration of justice. They were elected annually. Initially, there were only two, then as many as eight.

Pragmatic Sanction was the document negotiated by Emperor Charles V, who reigned from 1711 to 1740, that established the legal basis for the succession of his daughter Maria Theresa to the Habsburg throne. As a result of this document, she would rule the Habsburg possessions in Europe from 1740 to 1780.

Pragmatic Sanction of Bourges (1438) was the decree issued by King Charles V of France that declared that the pope was subject to the decisions of a general meeting of the leaders of the Catholic Church and that the power of the pope was limited by the power and will of the king. As a result of this decree, Charles exercised virtual control of the Catholic Church in France, giving him the ability to use revenues from the Church for government purposes. King Louis XI of France revoked this decree in 1491.

Prague Spring (1968) was a brief period of political reform and liberalization in Czechoslovakia that occurred between January and August 1968 under the leadership of Alexander Dubcek. This period of expanding freedom and cultural openness in the Communist Bloc ended on August 20, 1968, when 200,000 Soviet and Warsaw Pact troops invaded along with 5,000 tanks and Dubcek was arrested.

Predestination is the doctrine advanced by John Calvin that since God is all-knowing and all-powerful and knows everything in advance, then the salvation or damnation of any individual was already predetermined or preordained by God for each person before creation and nothing could be done to reverse this fate. Those chosen for salvation were considered to be the "elect." The doctrine of predestination is considered to be a fundamental principle of Calvinist theology.

Preemptive War is a military strategy by which one nation launches an initial attack against another with the objective of preventing that other nation from launching its own attack.

Prefect was the title of the chief administrator in a department of the French government that had been appointed by the central government. This position was established by Napoleon as part of his effort to centralize governmental decision-making.

Pre-history is a term used by historians to describe that period of human history that occurred before the advent of written records.

Prejudice means a personal opinion, attitude, judgment, or belief that is formed unfairly or unjustly without any rational or reasonable basis.

Prerogative was the set of powers exercised by the English monarch alone, rather than in conjunction with Parliament.

Presbyter, which means "elder," was a person that directed the affairs of the early Christian congregations. Presbyters were subordinate to the bishops as the hierarchy developed in the early Christian Church.

Presbyterians were Scottish Calvinist and English Protestants that advocated a national church composed of semi-autonomous congregations governed by "presbyteries."

Pre-Socratic Philosophers were a group of intellectuals from Ionia including Thales, Anaximander and Anaximenes and Hecataeus who raised questions about the relationship between the natural world, the gods and humans. They attempted to formulate rational theories to explain the physical universe.

Prestor John (also Presbyter John) was the name for a legend popular in Europe from the Middle Ages through the Renaissance. The legend of Prestor John directly and indirectly influenced and encouraged the imagination of generations of European explorers, missionaries, scholars, and treasure hunters to quest for the land of Prestor John in Asia. The legend told of a Christian priest and king that was said to rule over a lost Christian nation in central Asia. According to the legend, he was a descendant of one of the Three Magi and the King of India and was a virtuous and generous ruler whose realm was full of riches, strange creatures, and the Fountain of Youth. Eventually, Portuguese explorers in the 1400s and 1500s convinced themselves that they had found him in Ethiopia. In fact, for many years Europeans associated the name Prestor John with the King of Ethiopia.

Price Revolution was the dramatic increase in prices of goods (inflation) during the 1500s and 1600s in Europe caused by population growth and the influx of gold and silver from Spain's colonies in the New World. After a long period of falling or stable prices that stretched back to the 1300s, Europe sustained steady price increases between 1540 and 1640 that caused widespread economic and social turmoil. As a result of this Price Revolution, people sought new means of employment, protested the rise in taxes, looked for scapegoats, and concentrated the wealth in a smaller group of people that would become a new class known as the gentry.

Priesthood of All Believers is Martin Luther's doctrine that all those of pure faith were themselves priests. This doctrine undermined the authority of the Catholic clergy over the laity.

Primates are a division of mammals that includes prosimians, monkeys, apes, extinct human ancestors, and modern humans.

Primogeniture, which means "first born," is the legal process by which the lands, offices, and titles of a noble were inherited by the noble's first male heir and that heir's descendants. It was practiced throughout Europe in order to keep estates intact and to maintain property within a family.

***Prince, The* (1532)** is the extremely influential book written by Niccolo Machiavelli between 1513 and 1514 that attempts to establish the means and methods by which to secure and maintain political power.

Princeps was a title used by Augustus in Rome meaning "first citizen." He adopted this title to reassure the Roman public that he was preserving the traditional constitutional forms of government even though he was acting as a military dictator and emperor. It later came to mean "prince" in the sense of a sovereign ruler.

Principate (27BCE-284CE) was the name for the period during the early years of the Roman Empire when Rome was ruled by autocratic emperors. During this period of the Roman history, the emperors sought to create the illusion of the continuance of the Roman Republic.

Principle of Intervention was the policy adopted after the Napoleonic Wars at the Congress of Vienna in 1815 that the Great Powers (Britain, France, Russia, Prussia and Austria) had the right to use military force in any country in Europe where the traditional monarchical system was threatened by revolution or to restore to power a legitimate monarch that had been overthrown.

Printing Press was a mechanical device that was developed to transfer text or graphics from a woodblock or type to paper using ink. Presses with movable type first appeared in Europe circa1450.

Prisoners of War (POWs) are soldiers that receive a special protective status under the laws of war because they have surrendered or have been captured.

Proclamation of the German Reich (1871) was the document that created the nation-state of Germany by uniting the thirty-eight German states into a single national entity.

Professionalization refers to the process that arose in the 1800s in Europe and the United States by which common standards and requirements were adopted, either by governmental regulation of self-regulation, in such professions as medicine, law, architecture, and engineering as well as other professions whose prestige relied upon a claim of exclusive expertise.

Progress refers to the belief that each generation has more knowledge and more advanced technologies than all previous generations and that by using reason and rationality it is possible for humans to create better societies and better people. While many times the idea of progress is used to refer to scientific and technological knowledge, it also is used to suggest that political, social, and economic institutions are also advancing or becoming more rational.

Progressivism is the political theory that advocates social, political and economic reforms through governmental action. The term first emerged in the late 1800s and early 1900s in the United States to describe those individuals that sought a political alternative to both the conservative and radical responses to the social and economic changes brought about by industrialization. Progressives supported, for example, laws regulating tenement housing, child labor and better working conditions for women. Progressive social, political and economic reforms were achieved by presidents Theodore Roosevelt, Woodrow Wilson, Franklin Delano Roosevelt, and Lyndon Baines Johnson.

Proletarian was a derogatory term used to during the Roman Republic to refer to those people that were so poor that males in this class were not eligible to serve in the army.

Proletariat is the urban industrial working class. It is the word used by Karl Marx and Friedrich Engles to identify a class of workers that must sell their labor power to capitalists in order to survive and whose labor is needed to produce surplus value. More specifically for them, the proletariat consisted of industrial factory workers who received their income from wages. Marx and Engles argued that the proletariat would be the class that would spearhead the socialist revolution.

Proliferation is the spread of weapons of mass destruction (nuclear, chemical, or biological weapons) into the hands of more states, organizations, or individuals.

Protectionism is a governmental policy of protecting, supporting and aiding domestic industries and producers from foreign competition by the use of high trade tariffs on cheaper imported goods of another country and other barriers.

Protestant, which is a Latin term meaning "they protest," first appeared in a document in 1529 written by German princes that protested Emperor Charles V's edict to repress religious dissent. The word *Protestant* became the catchall name for members of the religious sect that formed when Martin Luther and his followers broke away from the Catholic Church in 1517.

Protestant Reformation (circa 1500s) was the religious reform movement within the Catholic Church that began in 1517. It resulted in the "protesters" forming several new Christian denominations, including Lutherans, Calvinists, Anglicans, Baptists, Quakers, and Presbyterians, to name a few of the new religious sects.

Protestant Work Ethic is the theory advanced by Max Weber in 1904 that the qualities of religious confidence and self-disciplined activism that were supposedly uniquely associated with Protestantism produced an ethic that stimulated the spirit that was necessary for emerging capitalism in Europe and the United States.

Protestantism was the division of Christianity that emerged in the 1500s in Western Europe. It focused on individual spiritual needs and rejected the social, political, and cultural authority of the papacy and the Catholic clergy.

Provisional Government refers to the political body that ruled Russia from March to November 1917 in the wake of the Russian Revolution that overthrew the tsarist government of Russia. It was intended to be temporary until a constituent assembly was elected. The Bolsheviks overthrew it.

Proxy Wars were civil wars that took place in the Third World during the Cold War in which the United States and the Soviet Union jockeyed for political power and influence by arming, training, financing, supplying, and advising opposing political factions.

Prussia, Kingdom of was a nation that controlled much of modern northeast Germany and Poland beginning in the early 1800s. Under the leadership of Frederick the Great, Prussia became an important military power in Europe in the 1800s. After the victory of Kaiser Wilhelm I in the Franco-Prussian War of 1870 to 1871. Prussia became the core of a newly unified Germany and the German Empire under the leadership of Otto von Bismarck.

Ptolemaic Dynasty (305–30 BCE) was the name of the Macedonian Greek royal family that ruled the Ptolemaic Empire in Egypt during the Hellenistic period. The dynasty was descended from Ptolemy I, one of Alexander the Great's officers. This dynasty ruled Egypt for 300 years. Ptolemy and his descendants created a kingdom that stretched from Syria in the north to modern Libya in the west to Nubia in the south. In order to gain the support of the Egyptian populace, the Ptolemies named themselves the successors to the pharaohs. The Ptolemaic Dynasty was the most sophisticated and longest-lasting of the Hellenistic kingdoms created after Alexander's death. Cleopatra was the last ruler of this Dynasty.

Public Sphere refers to any forum outside a royal court, such as newspapers, salons, and academies, in which the educated could participate in debates about the social, political, economic and cultural issues of the day.

Punic Wars (264–241 BCE, 218–201 BCE, and 149–146 BCE) were three wars between the Romans and the Carthaginians. The Roman victories in these wars brought about Roman domination and control of the western Mediterranean. The Romans later adopted the plantation system that had been used by the Carthaginians, which used large numbers of slaves.

Punt, Land of was the name of a fabled land in eastern Africa that was the source of many exotic and precious products sought by ancient Egyptians, such as gold, incense, frankincense, myrrh, African blackwood, ebony, ivory, slaves, and wild animals. The ancient Egyptians also referred to it as "God's Land." This designation did not mean that Punt was considered a holy land by the Egyptians, but rather it was used to refer to region of the Sun God, that is, region located in the direction of the sunrise. Modern academic consensus places Punt in the area of northern Ethiopia, Eritrea, or the southeastern Beja lands of Sudan.

Puppet States are governments that have little power in international affairs and follow the polices of their more powerful neighbors or patrons.

Purgatory is the place where, according to Catholic belief, after death the soul is purged of past sins and becomes fit for Heaven.

Purges, Great (also known as the Great Terror) were a series of mass arrests, imprisonments, and executions of millions of Soviet citizens, particularly Communist Party members, by Stalin between 1934 and 1939. Stalin accused the victims of the purges of being "wreckers" of communism or saboteurs. The hysterical fear among the public caused by the purges enabled Stalin to consolidate his dictatorial rule over the Soviet Union by removing from positions of political influence all of his enemies.

Puritans were devout English Calvinists whose members led a reform movement in the 1600s within the Church of England that advocated "purifying" the Church of England of all vestiges and traces of Catholicism, such as bishops, ceremonies, rituals, and organizational structure. They also believed that God had already predetermined before birth which individual would go to heaven or hell. They followed a strict moral code that emphasized Bible-reading, preaching, and private scrutiny of one's conscience, and de-emphasized institutional rituals and clerical authority. They became the majority in Parliament during the reign of Charles I and led the revolt against the king during the

English Civil War. They were also influential in founding the Massachusetts Bay Colony in 1629.

Putin, Vladimir (1952–present) was elected president of Russia in 2000. He was the successor to Boris Yeltsin. He had been director of the KGB, the Soviet secret police, before becoming prime minister in 1999. He was responsible for repressing the insurgency in Chechnya.

Putsch, which means "thrust" in German, is typically used to describe any secretly planned attempt to overthrow a government. The Beer Hall Putsch of 1923 in Germany is an example.

Putting-Out System was a manufacturing system that developed in Britain in the 1700s for producing thread and cloth by spinners and weavers using their own equipment in their homes in the country. It was a largely an informal system that linked merchant/employers with female rural laborers and craftpersons for the production of large quantities of manufactured goods. This system allowed the merchants to circumvent the control of the guilds in the cities over the production of manufactured goods. Specifically, the merchants would purchase raw materials and then "put them out" to be finished by individual female workers in rural areas. The rural workers would return the finished goods made at home on their own equipment to the merchant. This system expanded in the 1700s, as female rural workers needed more income from nonfarm work in the off seasons to supplement their earnings from agricultural work.

Puyi, Henry (1906–1967) was the last emperor of the Qing Dynasty. He was put on the throne in 1908 at the age of three and abdicated in 1912. He was later the puppet emperor of Manchukuo under the Japanese from 1934 to 1945.

Pyramid is a large, triangular stone monument, used in Egypt and Nubia as a burial place for the king. The largest pyramids, erected during the Old Kingdom near Memphis with stone tools and compulsory labor, reflect the Egyptian belief that the proper and spectacular burial of the divine ruler would guarantee the continued prosperity of the land.

Pyrrhic War was the war between the Romans and King Pyrrhus of Epirus from 280 to 276 BCE in which King Pyrrhus won battles, but so depleted

his resources that he eventually lost the war. The war was caused by Roman expansion into southern Italy and resulted in growing Roman involvement in the Balkans. Today, a pyrrhic victory is a phrase used to describe a military victory despite extremely high casualties.

Pyrrhonism is an extreme form of philosophical skepticism named after the Greek skeptic Pyrrho. It is best known for its doubt that "Nothing can be known with certainty."

Pythagoras (570–500/490 BCE) was a Greek philosopher and mathematician who taught in southern Italy in the late 6th century BCE. He stressed pure contemplation as the only path to true knowledge. He developed the "Pythagorean theorem."

Pythagorean Theorem is mathematical proof in Euclidean geometry concerning the relation among the three sides of a right triangle. The theorem is that in a right triangle, the square of the hypotenuse is equal to the sum of the squares of the other two sides. This equation provides a simple relation among the three sides of a right triangle so that if the lengths of any two sides are known, the length of the third side can be found.

Q

Q Source is the source used by both the Gospel of Matthew and the Gospel of Luke for the stories and sayings they have in common that are not found in Mark. The document no longer exists but has been reconstructed on the basis of the Gospels of Matthew and Luke. This title comes from the German word "quelle," which means source.

Qianlong (1711–1799) was the fourth emperor of the Qing Dynasty and reigned for sixty years, from 1736 to 1795. He retired in order not to exceed the reign of his grandfather, Kangxi. Qianlong's reign is considered by many historians to be the high point of the Qing era.

Qin Dynasty (221–207 BCE) was the first dynasty in China. It was located in the Wei valley in eastern China. Its ruler, Shi Huangdi, ruthlessly conquered rival states, standardized many aspects of Chinese society, and used force to mobilize his subjects for military and construction projects, such as building defensive walls. Because of the hostility that his rule engendered, his dynasty collapsed quickly after his death. Nevertheless, the social and political framework of the Qin Dynasty was adopted by the Han Dynasty. The Qin Dynasty marked the first efforts at unification in China.

Qing Dynasty (1644–1911/12) was the dynastic name adopted by the Manchus who overthrew the Ming Dynasty in 1644. During the rule of the kings of the Qing Dynasty, they controlled Manchuria, Mongolia, Turkestan, and Tibet. The last Qing emperor, Pu Yi, was overthrown in 1911.

Quadrivium was one part of the basic curriculum that became the standard program of study at medieval universities. It was comprised of mathematics, astronomy, geometry and music. The other part was known as trivium and it was comprised of the verbal arts of grammar, logic and rhetoric.

Quadruple Alliance (1813–1815) was the pact signed by the four nations that had defeated Napoleon—Britain, Austria, Russia, and Prussia—for the purpose of protecting Europe against any future French aggression.

Quaestors were the chief financial officers of the Roman Republic. Initially, there were two of them and they were elected annually.

Quakers (Religious Society of Friends) was a Christian sect founded during the Protestant Reformation whose members had no formal clergy or church hierarchy and based their faith upon an individual relationship with God. Believing in finding "Christ within," truth and sincerity were considered as important as literally following the "Word of God". Quakers, in imitation of Christ, dressed, lived, and spoke in plain and simple ways. In fact, it was not until the 1800s that Quakers stopped using the word "thee" and began using the more formal "you." Quakerism also considered both sexes equal in that men or women could lead or take part in any service or organization within the Society of Friends. George Fox was the first to preach the concept of "Christ within" and is considered the first leader of the Quakers. However, he never meant to create a separate religious sect.

Querelles des Femmes, which means "arguments about women" in French, refers to a debate about the nature of women that arose during the Scientific Revolution in which it was argued that new anatomical and medical evidence developed during the Scientific Revolution supported the long-held belief in the inferiority of women.

Quinine was an important medical advance in the 1800s used for treating malaria. In so doing, it permitted a large number of Europeans to travel to areas of the world where malaria was present without risking death and disease. It is obtained from the bark of the Andean cinchona tree.

Quisling is the name of a Norwegian fascist politician who assisted Nazi Germany in conquering Norway during World War II. During World War II, his name was commonly used to describe those fascist political parties and military and paramilitary forces in Nazi-occupied countries in Europe that collaborated with the Nazis. Thus, the term "quisling" was used to describe a person who was a traitor or a collaborator.

Qumran is the place near the Dead Sea where the Dead Sea Scrolls were discovered in 1945. During the 1st century CE, Qumran was the home to a group of Essenes. Many scholars consider the Essenes to be the Jewish sect that wrote and hide the Dead Sea Scrolls.

Quran (Koran) is Islam's sacred holy book that contains Allah's divine revelations to Muhammad.

Quriltai is the grand assembly of the Mongol tribes that elected the Great Khan. Temujin convened it in 1206, at which time he had himself proclaimed Chinggis (Genghis) Khan. Genghis Khan means "Oceanic or Universal Ruler."

R

Rabbinic Judaism was the main form of Judaism that emerged in the 1st century CE under the leadership of the rabbis. Rabbinic Judaism interpreted the Hebrew Bible in order to clarify Jewish practice, to elevate oral law to equal authority with the written Torah, and to bring greater flexibility to Judaism.

Rabelais, Francois (1494–1553) was a French humanist writer who is best known for his satires, in which he espoused his lifestyle of "eat, drink, and be merry." He had previously been a novice in the Franciscan order and also a Benedictine monk.

Race is a term that has been used to suggest that moral and behavioral attributes of a specific population of humans can be determined by arbitrarily selecting certain visible genetic traits, such as skin color, hair type, blood type, the shape of the body and head, and facial features. Scientists agree today that such a term has no biological validity and that there is only one race in existence, the human race.

Racism is the pseudoscientific belief that biological features are the main determinant of human traits, intellectual abilities, moral character, and worth and that racial differences produce inherently superior and inferior peoples.

Radical was a term widely used in the 1800s in Europe to describe those individuals and political organizations that favored a total reconstruction of the traditional European state system.

Radio Free Europe/Radio Liberty (1949– 1995) were radio stations started by the United States in the early 1950s in an effort to reach the people of Eastern Europe and the Soviet Union.

Raiders of the Lands and Seas is the name given by Egyptians to the diverse groups of peoples who used naval and land forces to destroy many cities and kingdoms in the eastern Mediterranean and Anatolia by the late Bronze Age.

Raison d'état, which is a French phrase meaning "reason of state," is the political theory articulated Cardinal Richelieu, a French statesmen, that claims that the interests and needs of the state override any moral or legal principles governing the conduct and behavior of the state.

Ramadan is the Muslim holiday that requires all Muslims to abstain for thirty days from eating, drinking and having sex during the daylight hours. Such fasting demonstrates sacrifice for their faith and an understanding of the hunger suffered by the poor.

Ramesses II, The Great (also known as Ozymandias in Greek) (1303–1213 BCE) was the ruler of New Kingdom in Egypt who reigned from 1297–1213 BCE. He extended the power of Egypt into Palestine and reached peace treaty with the Hittites after a standoff in the battle of Kadesh in Syria.

Rape of Nanjing (1937), which is also known as the Nanjing Massacre, was an infamous war crime committed by the Japanese military in Nanjing, the capital of China, after it fell to the Imperial Japanese Army on December 13, 1937. The duration of the massacre lasted for six weeks, until early February 1938. During the occupation of Nanjing, the Japanese army committed numerous atrocities, such as rape, looting, arson and the execution of prisoners of war and civilians. Although the executions began under the pretext of eliminating Chinese soldiers disguised as civilians, a large number of innocent men were intentionally identified as enemy combatants and executed. A large number of women and children were also killed, as rape and murder became more wide-spread. The commanding general of the Japanese troops who captured Nanjing and another senior military commanders who had personally participated in acts of murder and rape were tried, convicted and executed for the commission of war crimes by the International Military Tribunal for the Far East (Tokyo War Crimes Tribunal) in 1946. It is estimated that between 100,000 and 300,000 Chinese died.

Rationalism is the philosophical doctrine that all fundamental knowledge is based on reason and that truth can only be attained by the rational analysis of ideas and empirical evidence rather than relying upon emotions or prior received authority or traditions.

Realism is a style of artistic and literary expression that seeks to depict the physical world and human life with objectivity and detached observation. Proponents of realism seek to portray common situations as they would appear in reality.

Realism is a theory of international relations that emphasizes that a state's primary interest is to accumulate power in order to ensure security in an anarchic world. This theory is based on the belief that individuals are power seeking and that states act in pursuit of their own national interest. Realism is associated with such thinkers as Thucydides, Niccolo Machiavelli and Thomas Hobbes.

Realpolitik is a German word for "political realism" or "practical politics." It is also often referred to as "power politics." The term *realpolitik* is often used negatively to imply politics that are coercive, illegal, unethical, and immoral. This political strategy argued that politics must be based on operating within limits defined by practical reality, rather than ideological notions that tend to favor principles and ideals over all other considerations. Realpolitik is distinct from ideological politics in that it is not dictated by a fixed set of rules, but instead tends to be goal-oriented. It focuses on the most practical means of securing national interests. The term was coined by Ludwig August von Rochau, a German writer and politician in the early 1800s. After the Congress of Vienna in 1815, the term *realpolitik* became associated with efforts by the European monarchies to find ways to balance the power of existing European empires—that is, to maintain peace in Europe by preventing any one nation from becoming dominant. Otto von Bismarck used realpolitik to achieve Prussian dominance in Germany in the mid-1800s. In that regard, he would manipulate political issues with little care for ethics, morals, or legalities.

Recession is a prolonged downturn in the business activity of a nation that is usually associated with slower economic growth and rising unemployment.

Reconquista (418–1400) is the Spanish word for the military campaigns initiated by various Christian states on the Iberian Peninsula that began in the 11th century. These military campaigns sought to recapture territory taken by the Muslims or Moors. By 1492, the last Muslim ruler was defeated and Spain and Portugal emerged as united kingdoms.

Red Army or Workers'-Peasants' Red Army was the name of the armed forces of the Soviet Union that were formed in 1918 after the Bolshevik Revolution. Leon Trotsky played a central role in creating it. After World War II, its name was changed to the Soviet Army.

Red Guards (1966–1976) was the name of the student battalions organized in China during the Cultural Revolution. Mao Zedong encouraged them to carry his "little red book" and rebel against "the remnants of capitalism in China."

Redstone is the name of the ballistic missile developed by a team of scientists led by Wernher Von Braun. It was successfully tested in August 1953 and had a range of 500 miles. It was used to lift the first U.S. astronaut into space.

Refusniks was the name given to those Soviet Jews and others who were denied exit visas and were persecuted for trying to leave the Soviet Union during the Cold War.

Regal Period (753–509 BCE) is term used by historians to describe a period of Roman history when kings ruled Rome.

Regent was a person appointed to govern during the absence, childhood, or incapacity of a monarch.

Reich is the German word for realm or kingdom. The First Reich lasted from the 800s to 1806. The Second Reich lasted from 1871 to 1919. The Third Reich of Nazi Germany lasted from 1933 to 1945.

Reichstag was the national legislative body of the German Empire whose representatives were elected by universal male suffrage. It existed in various forms until 1945.

Reign of Terror (1793–1794) was the name for the period during the French Revolution governed by the Committee of Public Safety that was led by Maximillien Robespierre. The Committee of Public Safety wanted to establish a republic of virtue, but it arrested hundreds of thousands of people suspected of being enemies of the French Revolution. The Reign of Terror is considered to be the most radical period of the French Revolution because opponents of the Revolution were tried and executed for political crimes. It is estimated that as few as 17,000 and as many as 40,000 "enemies" of the state were executed, including aristocrats, Girondins, and sans-culottes. The Reign of Terror ended in July 1794 when Robespierre was arrested and executed.

Reinsurance Treaty (1887) was an attempt by Otto von Bismarck to form an alliance with Russia in order to isolate France politically. Bismarck believed that such an alliance was essential to German security. This secret treaty had two parts. First, Germany and Russia both agreed to observe neutrality should the other be involved in a war with a third nation. However, neutrality would not apply should Germany attack France or Russia attack Austria-Hungary. Second, Germany would declare itself neutral in the event of a Russian intervention in the Bosporus and the Dardanelles. In 1890 Russia wanted to renew this treaty, but Kaiser Wilhelm II refused, believing that his own personal relationship with the Russian tsar would be sufficient to ensure further diplomatic ties. He also believed that maintaining a close relation with Russia would act to the detriment of his aims to attract Britain into the German sphere of influence. Kaiser Wilhelm II believed that Anglo-Russian relations were strained because of the growing influence of Russia in the Balkans and Russia's desire to gain access to up the Dardanelles, which would threaten British colonial interests in the Middle East. However, having become alarmed at its growing isolation, Russia entered into an alliance with France in 1892, thus bringing to an end the isolation of France. In 1896 this secret treaty was exposed by a German newspaper, which caused an outcry in Germany and Austria-Hungary. The failure of this treaty is seen as one of the factors contributing to World War I.

Relics were sacred objects in Christian beliefs that were supposed to have miraculous powers. They were typically the bones of saints and biblical figures or some object associated with them that many people considered worthy of veneration. They served as a contact between the the profane and the divine and were verified by miracles.

Remarque, Erich Maria (1898–1970) wrote *All Quiet on the Western Front,* a powerful indictment of World War I based on his experiences in trench warfare in World War I.

Remilitarization of the Rhineland (1936) was the reoccupation of German territory by German troops in violation of the Treaty of Versailles. When the French and the British did not resist the presence of the German troops in the Rhineland, Adolf Hitler became more emboldened to commit additional acts of aggression in Europe.

Renaissance (1400s–1500s) is a French word translated from Italian and first used by the art historian and critic Giorgio Vasari, which means "rebirth". It was a cultural movement that emphasized the importance of the culture of classical Greco-Roman antiquity. The term has been traditionally applied by historians to events in northern Italy during the period from 1300 to 1550. However, this period of intense artistic and intellectual activity in Italy spread to other parts of Europe. Thus, there was also a Northern Renaissance from about the early 1400s to the early 1600s. As a result of the Renaissance, traditional religious values began to be supplanted by new secular and scientific values.

Reparations were money payments imposed by the Treaty of Versailles on Germany to cover the costs incurred by the Allies in fighting World War I.

Repartimiento was a labor system established by the Spanish in their colonies in the Americas that replaced the encomienda system. Under this new system, native communities were forced to provide laborers for the farms or mines owned by the Spanish employers, who were expected to pay fair wages.

Repatriation is the policy of voluntarily or forcibly returning refugees, immigrants, or other groups or persons, considered to be foreign because of their legal status, religion, or ethnicity, to their country of origin.

Reproduction refers to the anthropological process by which certain aspects of a culture are passed on from person to person or from society to society. The most common form of cultural reproduction is "enculturation" by which an older generation induces and/or compels a younger generation to adopt the ways of thinking and behaving of the older generation. Parents and educators are two of the most influential forces for enculturation. Diffusion is another form of cultural reproduction, which occurs when patterns of cultural behavior or meaning are passed from one society to another. Diffusion explains why many Americans enjoy sushi, a Japanese delicacy, and make common use of French words like "boutique" or "salon,"

Republic Period (509–31 BCE) is term used by historians to describe the period when the last king was expelled to when Octavian established the Roman Empire. During the Republic, Rome was a militaristic oligarchy largely governed by the aristocratic Roman Senate and magistrates.

***Republic, The* (380 BCE)** is a book written by Plato that is considered to be the first systematic treatment of political philosophy ever written. It argued for an oligarchical state in which the people would be governed by intellectually superior "philosopher-kings".

Republicanism is a political theory first developed by the ancient Greeks, especially the philosopher Plato, but elaborated upon by the ancient Romans. Its fundamental principle was that the people or a portion of the people should elect government officials. Representatives elected on a broad basis of suffrage traditionally govern a republican government that serves the interests of all the citizens.

Requeriemiento was a document read by the conquistadors to the indigenous peoples in the Americas before making war on them. It briefly explained the principles of Christianity and commanded the native populations to accept those religious principles immediately along with the authority of the pope and the sovereignty of the King of Spain. If the native peoples refused to accept those terms, they were warned that they would be forced to accept conversion to Christianity and be subjected to the sovereignty of Spain anyway.

Res Publica is a Latin phrase that means "public thing" or "public matter." It is the basis for the word *republic Res Publica.* refers to a thing that is not considered to be private property or a private matter, but that which is held in common by many people. It could also be used to refer to "public affairs" and/or the general system of government of a state.

Resistance, The is the name for the underground groups during World War II in Nazi-held territory that engaged in sabotage, intelligence gathering, publishing, and any other anti-Nazi political or military activity.

Restoration Period (1815–1848) was the period after the defeat of Napoleon when political movements arose in Europe that sought to restore the dynasties and monarchical institutions that had been disrupted by the French Revolution and the Napoleonic era. These movements also sought to prevent radical political movements from threatening the traditional monarchical political order.

Revolution is a fundamental change in the political, social, and economic organization of a nation. Typically, it involves the forcible, often violent, change in nature of a government and the structure of the society and its economy.

Revolutionary Nationalism is the term used for a political revolution that brings to power a new regime to govern and to exclude those who are viewed as trying to undo such revolutionary change. This exclusionary form of nationalism has historically emerged during moves toward democracy when state institutions have collapsed and opportunistic and politically powerful elites have mobilized mass support for themselves as the leaders of the nation.

Revolutions of 1848 were the democratic and nationalist revolutions that swept Europe. As a result of these revolutions, the French monarchy was overthrown, while in Germany, Austria, Italy, and Hungary, the revolutions failed.

Reykjavik Summit (1986) was the meeting held in Iceland between Gorbachev and Reagan at which Gorbachev offered two surprise proposals: cut strategic nuclear forces in half and eliminate all nuclear weapons in 10 years. His plan, which was designed to halt the "Star Wars" program begun by the United States, failed.

Rhetoric is the art of persuasive or emotive speaking and writing, which the ancient Greeks and Romans practiced. In the Middle Ages, it became one of the seven liberal arts.

Rhodes, Cecil (1853–1902) was a British businessman and politician who was involved in expanding the British Empire from South Africa into Central Africa. The colonies of Southern Rhodesia (now Zimbabwe) and Northern Rhodesia (now Zambia) were named after him as well as the Rhodes Scholarship program.

Ricardo, David (1772–1823) was a British economist who acquired a self-made fortune in business. He wrote *Principles of Political Economy and Taxation*. He was an influential advocate for free trade in Britain.

Richelieu, Armand Cardinal (1585–1642) was the chief minister to King Louis XIII of France. He centralized political power and deprived the Huguenots of many of the religious and political rights they had obtained previously.

Rights is a concept in political philosophy that refers to the fundamental political, legal, social, economic or ethical principles or rules of a democratic society that are granted, endowed or owed to a people according to a written or unwritten constitution. Thus, rights are considered a fundamental pillar of a democratic society. However, in the development of rights, rights have not been granted or endowed as much as they have been claimed as a result of political conflict and social struggles.

Risorgimento, which is an Italian word for resurgence, was the term used to describe the liberal nationalist political movement that led to the unification of Italy by 1870.

Robespierre, Maximillien (1758–1794) was a lawyer who led the most radical phase of the French Revolution known as the Reign of Terror. His execution ended the Reign of Terror.

Roman Catholicism, which means, "universal" is the Christian Church headed by the pope.

Roman Names typically had three elements. The first identified the individual, the second the gens or clan of the individual and the third, the name of a family within a clan. Extra names could be added by adoption as an honorific title or as nicknames.

Roman Republic (509–31 BCE) was a system of government based on shared decision-making and the election of male officials by assemblies organized on the basis of social hierarchies. During the Republic, Rome was a militaristic oligarchy largely governed by the aristocratic Roman Senate.

Roman Senate was a council whose members were the heads of wealthy, landowning families. It was originally an advisory body to the early kings. In the era of the Roman Republic, the Senate governed the Roman state and the growing empire. Under Senate leadership, Rome conquered an empire of unprecedented extent in the lands surrounding the Mediterranean Sea. In the 1st century BCE, quarrels among powerful and ambitious senators and failure to address social and economic problems led to civil wars and the emergence of the rule of the emperors.

Romance Languages are a branch of the Indo-European language family comprising all the languages that have descended from Latin, such as French, Spanish, Italian, Portuguese and Romanian. Romance languages have their roots in the Latin spoken by soldiers, settlers, peasants and merchants of the Roman Empire, as distinguished from the classical form of the Latin used by Roman intellectuals.

Romanesque, which means "in the Roman style," was a style of monumental architecture that dominated construction in Europe from circa 900 to 1150. Arched stone roofs supported by rounded arches, massive stone pillars, thick walls, and relatively simple ornamentation characterized Romanesque churches.

Romanization is the process by which the Latin language and Roman law and culture became dominant in the western provinces of the Roman Empire. The Roman government did not actively seek to Romanize its subjects, but indigenous peoples in the provinces often chose to Romanize because of the political and economic advantages that it brought as well as the allure of Roman success.

Romanov was the name of a Russian monarchical dynasty that lasted from 1613 to 1917. It was founded by Mikhail Romanov and ended with Tsar Nicholas II.

Romanticism was an artistic, philosophical, musical, and literary movement that began in Germany and Britain in the late 1700s and early 1800s, which involved a reaction against what many considered to be the excessive rationality and scientific narrowness of the Enlightenment. Romanticism glorified personal experience, imagination, and an emotional response to the power of beauty and nature. It was often associated with nationalism.

Rome, Treaty of (1957) is the founding document of the European Economic Community (EEC) or Common Market, now known as the European Union.

Rome-Berlin Axis (1936) was the alliance formed between Mussolini's fascist Italy and Hitler's Nazi Germany. This alliance began as an informal understanding, but became more formal with the signing of the anti-Comintern Pact. It eventually became a military alliance with the signing of the Pact of Steel in 1939.

Romulus Augustulus, Emperor was the last emperor of the Western Roman Empire. He was defeated by Odoacer in 476. For many historians, his over-throw marks the date for the "fall" of the Roman Empire.

Roosevelt, Franklin Delano (1882–1945) was president of the United States from 1933 to 1945 during the Great Depression of the 1930s and during World War II. His New Deal programs were innovative responses to the economic and social dislocations caused by the Great Depression.

Rousseau, Jean-Jacques (1712–1778) was a French philosopher and radical political theorist whose book *The Social Contract* attacked the inequality caused by the existing elite social system based on status, patronage, and feudal and noble privileges. In *The Social Contract*, he wrote about a hypothetical state that had direct democracy and its citizens who enjoyed a wide range of rights and liberties. While he moved in Enlightenment circles in Paris, he criticized the belief of the philosophes in progress and their reliance on reason. One of the primary principles of his political philosophy is that politics and morality should not be separated.

After the publication of his influential work *Emile,* in which he criticized Christianity, he was banished from Paris. He subsequently fled to Switzerland, where he was subject to Protestant persecution for his views about Christianity.

Royal African Company (1660–1667) was a company chartered by the King Charles II, the English king, to engage in trading of gold, silver and slaves with African tribes along the Atlantic coast. It was led by the Duke of York, the brother of the king. Between 1688 and 1722, it provided gold to the English Mint to make coins. Between 1672 and 1689 it transported approximately 90,000–100,000 slaves, some branded with the letters DY for the Duke of York and some branded with the company's initials RAC. It continued to trade in slaves until 1731 when it began trading in ivory and gold dust. It was dissolved in 1752.

Royal Road was an ancient highway built by King Darius I of Achaemenid Empire in the 5th century BCE. Darius built the road to facilitate rapid communication by his couriers throughout his very large empire. These messengers could travel 1,677 miles in seven days. The Greek historian Herodotus wrote, "There is nothing in the world that travels faster than these Persian couriers." Herodotus praised these couriers: "neither snow, nor rain, nor heat, nor darkness of night prevents these couriers from completing their designated stages with utmost speed", which became the inspiration for the unofficial motto of the United States Postal Service. The Road began in the west in Sardis traveled east to the old Assyrian capital of Nineveh, then traveled south to Babylon. From Babylon, it is believed to have split into two routes, one traveling northwest then west along the Silk Road, the other continuing east through Susa and then southeast to Persepolis. The road also helped Persia increase long distance trade, which reached its peak during the time of Alexander the Great. Because the road did not follow the shortest or the easiest route between the important cities of the Persian Empire, archeologists believe the western-most sections of the road may have originally been built by the Assyrian kings, as the road goes through the heart of the old Assyrian Empire. However, Darius I improved the Royal Road and made it into a unified whole. The road was of such quality that it continued to be used by the Romans.

Royal Society (1660) is the name of an organization formed by a group of British intellectuals in 1660 to discuss natural philosophy and observe each other's scientific experimentation. The Society's official publication, *Philosophical Transactions,* was first published in 1665, and is the oldest continuously published scientific journal in the world.

Russian Revolution (1905) was a revolt against the autocratic government of Tsar Nicholas II. Angered by the burden of heavy taxation and the defeat in the Russo-Japanese War, peasants, workers, and the military demanded political reforms such as the creation of a legislature. Tsar Nicholas met peaceful demonstrations for democratic reforms with brutal reprisals.

Russification was the program designed by Russian tsars in the late 1800s to assimilate the people of over 146 dialects into the Russian Empire.

Russo-Japanese War (1904–1905) was a conflict that grew out of the rival imperialist ambitions of the Russian Empire and the Japanese Empire over Manchuria and Korea. The Russians were in constant pursuit of a warm-water port on the Pacific for their navy as well as maritime trade. The recently established Pacific seaport of Vladivostok was the only active Russian port that was operational during the summer season. The Russians wanted to establish a port at Port Arthur, which was located in an area of China that had been controlled by the Japanese since Japan's victory over China in the First Sino-Japanese War (1894–1895). Japanese negotiations with the Russian government about Port Arthur proved futile, and the Japanese chose war to maintain exclusive dominance in Manchuria and Korea. During this brief war, the Japanese military consistently achieved victory over the Russian forces, which was unexpected by the European powers. These Japanese victories dramatically transformed the balance of power in East Asia and signaled the emergence of Japan as a world military power. The embarrassing string of defeats during this war increased dissatisfaction of the Russian populace with the Tsar's inefficient and autocratic rule and was a major cause of the Russian Revolution of 1905.

Russo-Turkish War (1877–1878) was a conflict between Russia and Turkey over Ottoman rule in the Balkans. The origins of this war can be found during the early 1800s when the Turks were forced to cede Balkan territories to European powers as a result of nationalist revolts by Christians. Before 1829, the entire Balkan peninsula was controlled by the Ottoman Empire. However, in 1829, at the conclusion of a war between Turkey and Russia, the Sultan of the Ottoman Empire granted independence to Greece and autonomy to Serbia and another province that would later become Romania. As a result of this war in 1829, resentment in the Balkans against Ottoman rule spread because the once-powerful Ottoman Empire had become known as the "sick man of Europe." By 1875 and 1876, there were nationalist uprisings in Bosnia, Bulgaria, and Herzegovina, which were brutally repressed by the Turks. Reports of atrocities by the Turks against Christians gave Russia the excuse to renew its struggle for dominance in the Balkans and gain access to the Mediterranean. With the Russians achieving an overwhelming victory in the Russo-Turkish war, the Ottoman Empire was forced to surrender nearly all of its territory in Europe. However, fearing that Russia would use its dominance in the Balkans to gain the long-desired access to the Mediterranean, the Great Powers, led by Britain and Austria, opposed Russian influence over so large an amount of European territory. In a meeting of the Great Powers in Berlin in 1878, they decided that control of Bosnia and Herzegovina should be assigned to Austria and that Serbia, Montenegro, and Romania should become independent states.

Rwanda is a former Belgian colony in central Africa that has been torn by ethnic violence between the Hutus and the Tutsis since before the country's independence in 1962.

S

Sacraments are the religious rites that were considered imperative for the salvation of an individual in the Catholic Church. By the 1200s, they consisted of the Eucharist, baptism, marriage, penance, extreme unction, hold orders, and confirmation of children.

Sacred Union (1914) was an agreement to co-operate between the leaders of different French political groups during World War I. When World War I began, the leaders of the French government feared that the socialists in France might sabotage the war effort. Yet, in fact, the socialists enthusiastically joined the French government in supporting the war effort.

Sacrifice is a gift given to a deity for the purpose of creating a relationship, gaining favor, of obligating the god to provide some benefit such as a good harvest, or of protecting a society or an individual from natural disasters. The gift given to the deity could be as simple as a cup of wine poured on the ground, a live animal slain on the altar, or, in the most extreme case, the ritual killing of a human being.

Sadducees was a conservative Jewish sect that did not believe in angels or resurrection because such teachings were not found in the five books of the Old Testament. They were supportive of the Temple cult and the Jewish priests who administered the Temple. This group was comprised primarily of the Jewish aristocracy in Judea, whose leader, the High Priest, served as the highest-ranking official and chief liaison with the Roman governor.

Sahelanthropus tchadensis is the best current candidate for the oldest hominid at about 7 million years ago. It was found in Chad in central Africa in 2002.

Saint Anthony (251–356) was a Christian from Alexandria who led an ascetic life as a hermit in the Egyptian desert. His conduct inspired many Christians to follow an ascetic life and became the basis for the ideals of upon which monasticism was built.

Saint Bartholomew's Day Massacre (1752) was the killing of thousands of French Protestants (Huguenots) by Catholic crowds in Paris on August 24, 1752. The killing of Protestants spread throughout France and continued until October, resulting in more than 70,000 Huguenots being killed in France because of their religion.

Saint Domingue was the former French colony in the Caribbean on which the first successful slave rebellion took place in 1791. The rebellion lasted until 1804, when it was declared the independent nation of Haiti.

Saladin (1137–1193) was the Sultan of Syria and Egypt who during the Second Crusade invaded the Holy Land and reconquered Jerusalem in 1187. After the Third Crusade collapsed, he negotiated a settlement with Richard the Lion-heart allowing Christian pilgrims free access to Jerusalem. Except during the 1200s, Jerusalem would remain under Islamic control until the 1900s.

Salamis, Battle of (480 BCE) was a decisive naval battle in which the Athenian fleet led by Themistocles defeated a Persian naval force led by Xerxes.

Salon, which is a French word for "living room," was the name given to the informal social gatherings in private homes of philosophers, writers, artists, and other prominent supporters of the Enlightenment. The salons were frequently organized by middle class or aristocratic women. At these informal gatherings prominent intellectuals would discuss and debate a wide-range of literary, artistic, social, political, and philosophical developments.

Samaritans were inhabitants of Samaria, located between Galilee and Judea that were considered by some Jews to be apostates because their lineage could be traced to intermarriages between Jews and pagans. Today, a samaritan is compassionate person who is willing to help someone who is injured. This term is derived from the parable of the Good Samaritan in the New Testament in which Jesus tells the story of a Samaritan woman who helped an injured man who had been ignored by others.

Samnite Wars were a series of three wars between 343 and 290 BCE in which the Romans defeated the Samnites, a people who lived south of Latium. These wars brought the Romans directly into contact with the Greeks of southern Italy.

Samurai, which means "those who serve" in Japanese, was the hereditary military elite that developed during the Tokugawa Shogunate who lived according to the code of bushido.

Sand, George (1804–1876) was a French female Romantic novelist whose real name was Amandine Aurore Lucile Baronne Dudevant. She is best known for her feminist ideology and romantic affairs. Her most famous novel, *Indiana*, is about the restrictions placed on women in Europe during the 1800s. Amandine was an unconventional woman for her time. She left her husband out of boredom and joined a group of artists in Paris. There she had romances with the French poet alfred de Musset and composer Frédéric Chopin. Her writing was often humanitarian in nature, showing great empathy for human troubles.

Sandinistas were members of a leftist coalition in Nicaragua that overthrew the dictatorship of Anastasia Somoza in 1979. When they attempted to establish a socialist economy, the United States financed the arming of the opposition known as the Contras.

Sans Culottes is a French word meaning "those without knee breeches." It is a term that was used during the French revolution to describe the poor, the workers, and the artisans of Paris who initiated the radical stage of the French Revolution in 1792. They were the people who worked with their hands and wore the long trousers of the workingman rather than the knee breeches of the upper classes.

Sappho (610–550 BCE) was one of the most famous Greek lyric poets. She was from the island of Lesbos. She wrote odes, wedding songs, hymns, and poetry about romantic longing and sexual lust, sometimes about men, but more often about women. She wrote about female sexuality in a society and culture that was dominated by men.

Sargon I of Akkad (2334–2279 BCE) ruled over the Akkadians, conquered the Sumerian cities, and built the first known empire in Mesopotamia.

Sassanid Empire (224–651) was the Iranian Empire that was overthrown by Islamic Arab armies circa 651. The Sassanid emperors established Zoroastrianism as the state religion.

Satire is the use of wit, in the form of irony, mockery, sarcasm, and innuendo, to reveal human foolishness and vice. Often in literature, satire is used to make a social commentary. During the 1600s and 1700s, noted satirists included Alexander Pope, Jane Austen, Voltaire, and Jonathan Swift. Swift wrote *Gulliver's Travels,* a popular attack on politics of the time.

Satrap was a governor of a province (a satrapy) and had both civil and military duties in the Persian Empire. Usually, this person, who was directly responsible to the emperor, was a relative of the king. He was responsible for protection of the province and for forwarding tribute to the king. Some satraps that were distant from the capital enjoyed considerable autonomy.

Saturnalia was a popular Roman festival that took place on December 17th each year. It commemorated the dedication of the temple of the god Saturn. Saturnalia was originally celebrated in Rome for only a day, but it was so popular it soon lasted a week, despite efforts to reduce it to its original length. It was marked by eating, drinking, games, conventional sacrifices, and reversal of social roles, in which slaves and masters ostensibly switched places.

Scapegoating is the act or practice of assigning blame or failure to another so as to deflect attention or responsibility away from oneself.

Schlieffen Plan (1905) was the German military's strategy at the beginning of World War I for achieving a quick victory in Western Europe by invading France through Belgium, the Netherlands, and Luxembourg even though these were neutral countries. The plan required that France was attacked first through Belgium and a quick victory secured so that the German army could then fight Russia on the Eastern Front. The objective of this plan was to avoid fighting a two-front war in Europe. It was devised by Count Alfred von Schlieffen in 1905 and put into operation on August 2, 1914.

Schliemann, Heinrich (1822–1890) was a German archeologist whose work at Troy and Mycenae constituted the first major excavations of Bronze Age civilizations.

Scholasticism was a philosophical and theological system of thought that fused Aristotelian philosophy and Christian theology. It was closely associated with Thomas Aquinas. It dominated the schools of Europe in the late 1300s until the end of the 1600s. Scholasticism assumed that truth already existed and that students only had to organize and defend knowledge that they learned from authoritative texts, especially those of Aristotle and the Church Fathers.

Scientific Racism was the pseudo-scientific attempt in the late 1800s to develop a typology of different "human races" based on a biological conception of race. Such theories provided popular ideological justifications for racism, slavery and colonialism during the European imperialist expansion into Africa and Asia in the second half of the 1800s. Such theories, which often postulated a "master race", usually "Nordic" and "Aryan", had a significant effect on Nazi racial policies. A leading proponent of this theory was Arthur de Gobineau who wrote *The Inequality of the Human Races* in 1853, a book which greatly influenced Nazism.

Scientific Revolution is a term used by historians to describe the sweeping changes in human understanding of the natural world that occurred in Europe in the 1500s and 1600s and that laid the foundation for modern science. It represented a new method or framework by which humans could evaluate the validity of knowledge. This period of new scientific inquiry, experimentation, and discovery resulted in a new understanding of the universe based on mathematical principles and led to the development of modern sciences such as astronomy and physics. Historians typically date the Scientific Revolution from the publication of *On the Revolution of the Celestial Spheres* by Copernicus in 1543 to the publication of *Mathematical Principles of Natural Philosophy* by Newton in 1687.

Scots Confession of 1560 was a document written by six religious leaders in Scotland that established a new church in Scotland. This new church emphasized individual faith and conscience. Instead of the hierarchical structure of the Church of England which gave bishops authority over religious doctrine, the new Scottish church was to have a presbyterian structure in which doctrinal and organizational authority was given to the pastors and elders of the various congregations. The pastors and the elders of each congregation were to be considered of equal status.

Scramble for Africa (1870–1914) is the term used by historians to describe the rapid and sudden wave of European conquests and colonizations in Africa between 1870 while 1914. Britain obtained most of eastern Africa and France obtained most of northwestern Africa. Other countries such as Germany, Belgium, Portugal, Italy, and Spain acquired lesser amounts.

Scribe was an official position in the governments of many ancient societies held by men who were trained to read and write using cuneiform, hieroglyphics, or other early writing systems.

Scutage was the payment of money or something else of value during the Middle Ages by a knight to his lord. Scutage replaced the military service obligation that the knight owed his lord. Scutage existed in various countries, including France and Germany, but was most highly developed in England beginning in the 1100s. However, By the 1300s, the practice of scutage had become obsolete.

Scythians were horse-riding nomadic pastoralists who dominated throughout antiquity the vast area covering present-day Ukraine, southern Russia and Central Asia. Scholars generally classify the Scythian language as a member of the Iranian language and the Scythians as a branch of the ancient Iranian peoples who expand into Iran from the steppe region north of Iran circa 1000 BCE. Much of the surviving information about the Scythians comes from the Greek historian Herodotus in his *Histories* and from the exquisite gold work found in Scythian burial mounds. Around 770 BCE, the Scythians attacked Assyria, but were defeated. The Scythians apparently obtained their wealth from their control of the slave-trade in the Greek Black Sea colonies. The expansion of Scythian tribes westward brought them into conflict with Philip II of Macedon who defeated them in 339 BCE.

Sea Peoples is the term used for a confederation of seafaring raiders who sailed into the eastern shores of the Mediterranean. They caused political unrest and attempted to conquer Egyptian territory during the reign of Ramesses III.

Secession is the formal withdrawal by a smaller political entity from a larger political entity, such as the withdrawal of several southern states from the United States during 1860 to 1861.

Second Front was the name of an Allied military offensive, during World War II, in France against the Nazis so as to match the efforts of the Russians in the East. The Russian had been fighting against about one-half of the Nazi army since Russia was invaded in 1941. After several delays, which caused tension among the allies, American troops, in cooperation with British and Canadian troops, launched a second front with the D-Day invasion of Normandy on June 6, 1944.

Second Industrial Revolution is a term used by historians to refer to the new phase in the process of industrialization and consumption in Europe, the United States, and Japan which is considered by scholars to have begun the 1870s. This period of economic growth would witness the emergence of new industries; new technological developments, such as new techniques for producing steel; increased availability of electricity for commercial, industrial, and residential use; advances in chemical manufacturing; and the creation of the internal combustion engine.

Second International (1889–1916) was a federation of socialist and labor political parties from 20 countries formed in Paris in 1889. It continued the work of the dissolved First International. The Second International rejected the gradual achievement of socialism and accepted the Marxist doctrine of class struggle and the inevitability of revolution. It significantly influenced the European labor movement before World War I. It sought to make May 1st "International Workers' Day," March 8th "International Women's Day" and it initiated the international campaign for the eight hour working day. The Second International was dissolved during World War I when the separate national socialist parties that comprised the Second International decided to support their respective nations' role

in World War I. An attempt to reconstruct the Second International failed in 1920 when only a few of the pre-World War I membership supported such an effort.

Second Italo–Abyssinian War (1935–1936) was a brief war between Italy and the Ethiopian Empire (also called Abyssinia). The war is best remembered for the Italian use of illegal mustard gas. The war resulted in the annexation of Ethiopia into Italian East Africa. Politically, the war is best remembered for exposing the inherent weakness of the League of Nations because the League was unable to control Italy or to protect Ethiopia. Italian dictator Benito Mussolini had long held a desire for a new Italian Empire that would rule over the Mediterranean and North Africa and would be reminiscent of the Roman Empire. He hoped that this new empire would also avenge past Italian defeats such as the Italian defeat at the Battle of Adwa during the First Italo–Ethiopian War (1895–1896). Mussolini promised the Italian people "a place in the sun," matching the extensive colonial empires of the United Kingdom and France. Ethiopia was a prime candidate of Italy's expansionist policies for several reasons: It was one of the few remaining independent African nations, it was militarily weak, and was rich in resources.

Second Reform Bill (1867) was a British law that extended the right to vote by lowering the property qualification. It also established equal population requirements for all parliamentary districts. As a result of this new law, people who previously did not have the right to vote, such as clerks, artisans, and other skilled workers, now became enfranchised.

Second Servile War (104–100 BCE) was the second unsuccessful slave rebellion against the Roman Republic in Sicily. It was caused by the same factors as the First Servile War: abuse by slave masters and inadequate food. However, during this war, the slaves were able to build an army of trained and equipped slaves, including 2,000 cavalry and 20,000 infantry. While the slaves were once again defeated by a much larger Roman army, this war was more difficult for the Roman army than was the First Servile War.

Second-Strike Capability is the ability of a state to absorb an enemy's first-strike, retaliate and inflict unacceptable damage on the enemy. In 1964, Secretary of Defense McNamara defined it as the ability to destroy half of the Soviet industry and a quarter of its population.

Second-Strike Weapons are those weapons that can either drop nuclear bombs directly or fire from a distance. Second-strike weapons included air launched cruise missiles (ALCM), surface-to-surface ballistic missiles (SSBMs), or submarine launched ballistic missiles (SLBMs). Nuclear bombs launched from a bomber or submarines are slower and less accurate than those dropped directly, but less vulnerable to enemy attack. Second-strike weapons are better targeted against an enemy's cities and armies. There is some overlap between first and second-strike weapons. An ICBM in a hardened missile silo could survive an enemy attack and be used to retaliate, whereas SLBMs are as fast and accurate as ICBMs, and thus have some first-strike capabilities.

Second Triumvirate (43–33 BCE) was an informal political alliance in 43 BCE between Octavian, Mark Antony, and Marcus Lepidus to rule Rome and to destroy the political leaders who had assassinated Julius Caesar. As a result of his participation in this triumvirate, Octavian would consolidate his political power and defeat Antony and Cleopatra at the Battle of Actium in 31 BCE.

Second Vatican Council (1962-1965) was a Catholic Council called by Pope John XXIII, which met between 1962 and 1965, to modernize Church teachings such as the condemnation of the Jews for the supposed killing of Jesus. The Council decided that the Mass was to be conducted in the vernacular instead of Latin. The Council also sought to draw attention to the concerns of developing nations and to promote cooperation among the various faiths in the world.

Second World is a term invented during the Cold War to refer to the Communist countries in the world, as opposed to the democratic/ capitalist countries (First World) and the former European colonies in Africa and Asia (Third World).

Sect is a dissenting faction within a religion or political group that many times is regarded as heretical, unorthodox, or even blasphemous by the larger body of believers and followers.

Secular means worldly or temporal. A secular state is a state created apart from religious influences and in which there is a high degree of separation between religious and political organizations.

Secularization is the process by which a nation or a people become more concerned with material, worldly, or temporal things and less with spiritual and religious matters. During this process, politics, economics, society, and culture are separated from religious influence, control, and domination. This process reflects an emerging belief that explanations for social, political, economic, and other problems can be understood by using reason rather than through revelation or spiritual belief.

See was a territory under the authority of a bishop in the early Christian Church. There were five sees initially founded by Peter: Rome, Constantinople, Alexandria, Antioch and Jerusalem.

Seigneur was the lord of a French estate in medieval France who received payments from the peasants who lived on his land. He was also responsible for maintaining order, administering justice, and arbitrating disputes among the tenants on his land. Seigneurialism was a system by which peasants owed various fees and dues to the local lord even if the peasants owned their own land.

Seleucid Dynasty (312–64 BCE) was a dynasty of rulers in Syria, Palestine, and Mesopotamia who were descended from one of Alexander's generals, Seleucus. They founded the city of Antioch. The Romans eventually conquered them in the 1st century BCE.

Self-Determination is the name for the political belief, which became popular after World War I, that all people in the world have the right to determine their own political future, that every nation is entitled to a sovereign territorial state, and that every identifiable population should choose to which state it belongs. Today, the term is commonly used to justify the aspirations of an ethnic group that identifies itself as a nation to form an independent sovereign state. The principle of self-determination formally expresses a central claim of nationalism—namely, the entitlement of each nation to be its own nation state. In the 1900s the principle was central to the demands of national movements in Africa and Asia for decolonization.

Self-Strengthening Movement (1861–1895) was the name of the attempt by various Chinese thinkers to blend traditional Chinese thought and cultural traditions with European industrial technology.

Seljuk Turks were a Sunni Muslim Turkic group whose migrations into areas that had once been controlled by the Byzantine Empire contributed to causing the First Crusade.

Semiotics is the study of how signs and symbols relate to the things they represent. In discussions about culture, the meaning of a sign or symbol is not fixed; it varies over time depending on the context and the intent of the user of it. The relationship between a symbol or sign and what it represents can also be contested, with different individuals or groups of individuals expressing different views concerning the content of a sign or symbol.

Semitic is the name for a family of related languages long spoken across parts of western Asia and northern Africa. In antiquity these languages included Akkadian, Hebrew, Aramaic, and Phoenician. The most widespread modern member of the Semitic family is Arabic.

Senators were the highest-ranking members of the Roman aristocracy. This group of about 300 was comprised of the wealthiest men in Rome. They served for life in the Roman Senate and were responsible for governing the vast Roman bureaucracy during the Republic. They were still visible and active during the Empire, but their political power had been diminished substantially with the ascension of the emperor.

Separate Spheres was the idea that emerged in the 1800s in Europe and the United States, especially among the middle class, that men and women should have clearly differentiated roles in society. Women were to be wives, mothers, and homemakers. Men were to be the breadwinners and participants in business and politics.

Separation of Powers is the idea that despotism could be avoided when political power was divided and shared by a variety of classes and legal estates holding unequal rights and privileges.

Separatists were Puritans who separated from the Church of England in the 1600s and settled in North America in order to practice their form of Christian worship.

Septimus Severus, Emperor (145–211) was the Roman Emperor who reigned from 193 to 211. He was a Roman senator from North Africa who seized the imperial throne during a civil war. He established the Severan Dynasty, the last imperial dynasty of the Principate.

Septuagint was the Greek version of the Hebrew Bible, allegedly prepared by seventy translators in seventy days in Alexandria. It was seven books longer than the Hebrew version and it is still authoritative in Orthodox churches.

Serbia was a province of the Ottoman Empire in the Balkans that revolted against Ottoman political control in the early 1800s. After World War I, it became the central province of Yugoslavia. Serbian leaders struggled to maintain dominance as the Yugoslav state dissolved in the 1990s.

Serf or Villein was an agricultural laborer in Europe during the Middle Ages who was legally bound to a lord's property and obligated to perform labor services and pay rents to that lord. Typically, serfs worked and lived on a plot of land granted to them by a lord to whom they would owe a portion of their crops in payment of rent. They could not leave the land, but they had certain rights that were denied to slaves. They had the right to marry, to keep part of their produce, and to remain on the land that they worked. Serfdom was essentially a slavery-like system whereby peasants were kept poor and stationary by their lords.

Settler Colonies were created when a private person obtained authorization (a license) from a European king to seize an island or parcel of land that was either inhabited or uninhabited and to populate the island or land with people from Europe who would export their culture to those lands. Such colonies first appeared in the islands in the Atlantic Ocean off the southwestern coast of Europe near Africa and in portions of the Americas.

Seven Years' War (1756–1763) was the first major war fought between Britain and France in their overseas empires for control of those overseas possessions. At the same time, France was involved in a conflict in Europe in which it and Austria tried to contain Prussia. While the war ended when Prussia defeated Austria, establishing itself as a European political and military power, Britain emerged as the decisive global winner. It gained control of India and many French colonies, including Canada, by the Treaty of Paris. In the United States, it was known as the French and Indian War.

Sextant is an optical instrument used in maritime navigation to measure the angles of celestial bodies above the horizon.

Shaft Graves is a term used for the burial sites of elite members of Mycenaean Greek society in the mid-2nd millennium BCE. At the bottom of deep shafts lined with stone slabs, the bodies were laid out along with gold and bronze jewelry, implements, weapons, and masks.

Shamanism is a religion based on the belief that certain individuals in a society, shamans, have magical powers to control spirits and call them back to this world and heal diseases.

Shang Dynasty (1766–1122 BCE) is the name given by historians to the earliest Chinese dynasty for which written records exist. Characteristics of Shang culture include ancestor worship, divination by means of oracle bones, and the use of bronze vessels for ritual purposes.

Shell Shock was a new psychological diagnosis that was developed during World War I to describe the psychic distress of soldiers in the trenches who had been subjected to near constant shelling. During World War II, it would be known as battle fatigue, and after the Vietnam War, post-traumatic stress disorder.

Shihuangdi (259–210 BCE) was the king of the state of Qin at the end of the Warring States. He proclaimed himself First Emperor in 221 BCE when Qin's last rival was defeated. His mausoleum near Xian contains the famous terra cotta warriors.

Shiites is the second-largest denomination of Muslims. They believe that Muhammad had appointed his cousin and son-in-law Ali ibn Abi Talib, Muhammad's only living descendent, as his successor. They believe that Ali, as the male head of Muhammad's family, had a dynastic right to religious authority over all Muslims. After Muhammad's death, Ali claimed succession to Muhammad in terms of religious and political authority. Thereafter Ali's family and its supporters claimed that Muhammad's family, including Ali, was both the best source of knowledge regarding Islam and the Quran and the best qualified to be protectors of Islam. Shiites reject the rule of the initial three caliphs who proclaimed leadership of the Muslim community after Muhammad's death and believe them to be illegitimate rulers and inferior to Muhammad's family in all respects. Ali was the fourth caliph. Today, Shiites govern Iran and are the majority of the population in Iraq. Shiites constitute only ten per cent of the worldwide population of Muslims.

Shintoism is the indigenous Japanese religion that emphasizes purity, clan loyalty, and the divinity of the emperor.

Shogun was the name for the Japanese military leader who ruled in the place of the emperor. The Meiji Restoration in 1868 ended the official role of the shogun in Japanese society.

Show Trials (1937–1938) refers to the trials of major communist leaders on trumped-up charges that were staged for ideological and propaganda reasons by Josef Stalin in the Soviet Union from 1936 to 1938. Stalin used the trials to persuade Soviet citizens that a high-level conspiracy was responsible for the economic problems in the Soviet Union, not his Five-Year Plans.

Shun (23rd–22nd century BCE) was the legendary sage king of antiquity. He was named as successor to Emperor Yao, who set aside his own son because of Shun's moral uprightness.

Sicilian Expedition was the Athenian naval expedition to Sicily from 415 to 413 BCE. It ended with the capture and the destruction of the Athenian military forces.

Siddhartha Gautama Buddha (563–486/ 483 BCE) was an Indian prince who founded Buddhism. He rejected the material luxury of his life and sought to understand the origins of suffering and how to transcend it.

Silk Road was an interconnected series of routes through Central Asia traversed by caravans and ocean vessels and connecting Chang'an (today's Xi'an), China, with Antioch, Syria. Its influence carried over into Korea and Japan. These exchanges were critical not only for the development of the great civilizations of ancient Egypt, China, India and Rome, but it also laid the foundations of our modern world. The continental Silk Road separated into northern and southern routes as it extended from China. The northern route led to Eastern Europe and the Crimean peninsula and from there across the Black Sea and the Balkans to Venice. The southern route went through Turkestan into Mesopotamia and Anatolia and then through Antioch in Southern Anatolia into the Mediterranean Sea or through the Levant into Egypt and North Africa. The phrase "Silk Road" was first used by a German geographer in the 1800s.

Sima Qian (145–87 BCE) was the chief astrologer of the Han Dynasty Emperor Wu. He wrote a monumental history of China from its legendary beginnings to his own time. He is considered to be the Chinese "father of history."

Simony was the sale or purchase of sacraments, holy offices or positions or promotions in the hierarchy of the Catholic Church. Simony was widespread in Europe in the 800s and 900s. While Pope Gregory VII (1073–1085) attacked the problem of simony, it only disappeared after the 1500s. It was an important issue during the Investiture Controversy in the 1100s. It was named for Simon Magus, a figure in the New Testament, who attempted to purchase from Apostles Peter and John the power to confer gifts of the Holy Spirit.

Single Integrated Operational Plan (1961– 2003) (SIOP) is a blueprint that tells how American nuclear weapons would be used in the event of war. The plan integrates the nuclear capabilities of manned bombers, longrange intercontinental missiles, and ballisticmissile-firing nuclear submarines. The SIOP is implemented in case the United States is under nuclear attack or if a nuclear attack on the United States is imminent. Only the president of the United States, in collaboration with the secretary of defense, may order that the SIOP be implemented. These two individuals must confer through secure communications with the chairman of the Joint Chiefs of Staff and agree that a nuclear strike must be ordered.

Single Whip Reforms (1581) was the set of changes to the fiscal and revenue policies during the Ming Dynasty in the 1580s. As a result of these reforms, taxes were paid in silver rather than in grain or cloth as had previously been done. This change especially benefited the commercially advanced coastal and river provinces, but posed problems for the provinces in the arid northwest and mountainous provinces in the southwest.

Sinn Fein (1905), which means "ourselves alone", was an Irish nationalist political movement that was founded in 1905. It advocated complete independence for Ireland from Britain.

Sino-Japanese War (1894–1895) was the conflict between China and Japan over the control of Korea. As a result of China's defeat, it was forced to relinquish control of Taiwan to Japan.

Sino-Soviet Split (1960–1989) was a political disagreement that developed between the Soviet Union and China in the 1960s. It concerned China's opposition to Soviet efforts at peaceful coexistence with the United States.

Six-Day War (1967) refers to Israel's surprise offensive, launched on June 5, 1967, to preempt a planned Arab invasion. This brief war destroyed Egypt's air force on the first day and left Israel with the Sinai, the Golan Heights, eastern Jerusalem, and the West Bank.

Skepticism is a philosophical belief that nothing can ever be known beyond all doubt and that humanity's best hope is the suspension of judgment.

Slash-and-Burn Agriculture involves the clearing of forests and then the burning of the felled trees and undergrowth. The resulting ash from the trees is used as fertilizer when the field is planted.

Slave Trade refers to the trade by European nations with Africa in which Africans were bought and forcibly shipped to the Americas to be sold to plantation owners. The trade reached its peak in the 1700s, when approximately seven million Africans were shipped to the Americas. The trade in human beings was an integral part of the Atlantic triangular trade system that connected Europe, Africa, and the Americas.

Smith, Adam (1723–1790) was a Scottish economist and philosopher who proposed that the pursuit of individual self-interest led to order and progress. He also argued that labor, not land or money, was both the source and final measure of value. He suggested that the individual economic activities of people were often guided by an "invisible hand" that would ultimately benefit the society as well as its members individually. He contended that free trade and a self-regulating economy would result in social progress. He became famous for his book *The Wealth of Nations*, written in 1776, which enunciated the theory of free-market capitalism or laissez-faire economics.

Social Contract Theory is a political theory which argued that political authority is derived from agreements by people, not divine authority, to form a government. This theory contended that people give up some rights in order to receive social order. This theory provided the rationale behind the doctrine that legitimate state authority must be derived from the consent of the governed. This theory assumes a human condition without any social order, which is called the "state of nature" or "natural state". In this state of nature, an individual's actions are limited only by his or her conscience. Based on this assumption various proponents of social contract theory attempted to explain, in different ways, why it is in an individual's rational self-interest to voluntarily relinquish the absolute freedom of action an individual had under the natural state (their so called "natural rights") in order to obtain the benefits provided by the formation of social structures. Common to all of these proponents is the idea of a sovereign will, which requires all members to accept the limitations on individual behavior imposed by the social contract. The various social contract theories that have developed are largely differentiated by their definition of the sovereign will, be it a king (monarchy), a council (oligarchy) or a majority of the population (republic or democracy). Thomas Hobbes (1651), John Locke (1689), and Jean-Jacques Rousseau (1762) are the most famous philosophers associated with this theory. Social contract theory established the theoretical groundwork for democracy. Hobbes conceived of the state of nature as a brutal struggle of all against all, a conception that may have been influenced by his experience during the English Civil War. Locke saw humanity as inherently social and his state of nature was similar to a society in which tribal peoples lived in accordance with the existing social structure. For Locke, the social contract and the civil rights it provided were neither "natural" nor permanently fixed. Rather, the idea of a social contract was a means to an end. It was only legitimate to the extent that it fulfilled the needs of the population. Therefore, when the requirements of the contract were no longer acceptable, citizens could renegotiate the terms of the contract using methods such as elections and even rebellion. Locke thought that the reason why man leave the state of nature, however harmonious, is because its lacks a common and recognized judge/authority to resolve conflicts between parties.

Social Darwinism is an ideology that developed in the second half of the 1800s that attempted to apply Darwin's idea of "survival of the fittest" to explain the evolution of human societies and social relationships. It attempted to account for why one social group is more politically and economically powerful than another group. This pseudo-scientific theory was used by many European imperialist nations in the late 1800s to justify their conquest, colonization, and domination of nations in Africa and Asia.

Social Democracy was the political movement and political ideology that was developed in Germany by August Bebel and Wilhelm Liebknecht when they formed the German Social Democratic Labor Party in 1869. Supporters of social democracy advocated a peaceful and evolutionary transition from capitalism to socialism within the existing political and legal framework rather than by violent revolutionary change. In 1875, the Social Democratic Labor Party merged with another German political party to form the Social Democratic Party of Germany (SDP). The SDP played a central role in the formation of the Weimar Republic, was part of several coalitions that governed Germany between 1919 and 1933, and opposed the rise of Adolf Hitler and the Nazi Party. When the Nazis came to power in 1933, they banned the SDP. It was revived in 1945 after the fall of the Third Reich. The SDP influenced the development of other social democratic parties in Europe. After World War II, social democratic parties came to power in West Germany, Sweden, and Britain and became known for their advocacy of social welfare programs.

Social War (Italic War or Marsic War) (91–88 BCE) was a rebellion in central and Southern Italy, by Rome's twelve Italian allies who had voluntarily allied with Rome or been militarily defeated during Rome's expansion in Italy between 343 and 282 BCE. Over the centuries these Italian allies had provided tribute money and soldiers to Rome. By the 2nd century BCE, these Italian allies contributed between one half to two-thirds of the soldiers in the Roman armies. In return, the Italian allies were to receive a portion of the treasure and land seized by Rome during its conquests of other lands. But, when Rome keep more of the profits for itself despite objections from their Italian allies, the allies decided that they wanted to be independent nations, free from the yoke of Rome's autocratic rule. In 91 BCE, the tribune Marcus Livius Drusus tried to solve the allies' grievances by proposing legislation that would have given all Italian allies Roman citizenship and more political influence in the affairs of the Roman Republic. But, unfortunately, Drusus was assassinated and his legislation was declared invalid by the Senate. Angered and frustrated, the Italian allies revolted. In response to the revolt, a law was passed granting Roman citizenship to all Italian allies who had not participated in the revolt. This law satisfied many of the Italian allies. By 88 BCE, with the remaining rebels defeated, the revolt was essentially over.

Socialism is the political and economic ideology that developed in Europe in the 1830s. It is an economic and social system that relies on government intervention in the economy and public ownership of the means of production. Socialists sought the more equitable distribution of wealth among the population, the protection of workers from exploitation, the ownership of industries by government, and the achievement of a classless society with the collective ownership of all property. The emergence of this ideology led to the founding of socialist or labor political parties throughout Europe in the second half of the 1800s.

Socialist Market Economy is a form of economic organization that is practiced in the People's Republic of China, where it is called socialism with Chinese characteristics. Under the Chinese system, major industries are owned by state entities, but compete with each other within a pricing system set by the market. In contrast with market socialism, the state does not routinely intervene in the setting of prices nor does it attempt to favor state-owned enterprises over private ones.

Socialist Realism was an art form that arose in the Soviet Union after the Russian Revolution. It glorified proletarian values and served as pro-communist propaganda. Socialist Realism was the only type of artistic expression officially accepted by the Soviet government in the 1930s.

Socialist Revisionism was the belief, which arose in the 1800 samong those German socialists that followed Edouard Bernstein. Proponents of social revisionism claimed that a humane socialist society based on equality could be built through evolutionary participation in democratic politics rather than through violent revolution. Socialist revisionists rejected Marx's emphasis on class struggle and they argued that workers should work through political parties to bring about gradual change.

Socialist Revolutionary Party (SR) (1901) was one of three revolutionary political parties in Russia at the beginning of the 1900s. While its political support came primarily from the peasantry who wanted socialization of the land, it relied upon terrorist tactics such as assassinating Russian government officials in the hopes of toppling the tsarist government. Alexander Kerensky, who was the head of the Provisional Government after the abdication of the tsar in February 1917, was a member of the SR. After the Bolshevik victory in the Civil War (1918–1921), Lenin repressed the SR and its leaders.

Society is any group of people that has shared customs, laws, institutions and organizations and lives together as an interdependent community in a country or region. The term can also be used to refer to smaller groups of people, such as a "rural society" or "academic society."

Society of Revolutionary Republican Women (1793) was a powerful political club in France during the French Revolution that represented the interests of female sans-culottes. The society was included in a general ban of political participation of women in the French Revolution by the Committee of Public Safety in October 1793.

Sociology is the formal study of how humans behave in groups. Sociology tends to focus on how human groups originate, how they are organized, and how they relate to one another.

Socrates (470–399 BCE) was an Athenian philosopher who shifted the emphasis of philosophical investigation from questions of natural science to ethics and human behavior. He argued that one who truly understood goodness would never chose to do evil. He attracted young disciples from elite families but made enemies by revealing the ignorance and pretensions of others, culminating in his trial and execution by the Athenian state. He developed a rigorous method for dissecting the arguments of others. He was put to death in 399 BCE for allegedly corrupting the youth of Athens and for alleged impiety.

Socratic Method is a method of intellectual and philosophical inquiry and teaching primarily applied to the examination of key moral and ethical concepts. It was first described by Plato in the *Socratic Dialogues*. The method is credited to Socrates, who began to engage in such discussion with his fellow Athenians after a visit to the Oracle of Delphi. The Socratic method uses a question-answer format to enable students to reach conclusions by their own reasoning. The central technique of the Socratic method is cross-examination for the purpose of refutation.

Sol Invictus, which means "the unconquered sun god," was a sun festival that was celebrated in Rome when the amount of daylight first began to increase after the winter solstice. The Romans held this festival annually on December 25th, "the birthday of the unconquered sun." December 25th was also considered to be the date of the winter solstice. Sol Invictus was the official sun god during the later Roman Empire. In 274, Emperor Aurelian made Sol Invictus an official cult and therefore part of state religious practice. The cult of Sol Invictus continued until paganism was abolished by Theodosius I in 390.

Solidarism was a political movement by conservative and liberal political parties in the late 1800s in Europe to blunt the growing appeal of socialism. It emphasized the mutual responsibility of classes and individuals for one another's well-being. This movement led to the passage of laws to improve the lives of the working class.

Solidarity (1976) was the first independent non-communist trade union established in the Communist Bloc. It emerged out of the mass protests at the Lenin shipyards in Gdansk, Poland, in the summer of 1980. Its leader, Lech Walesa, was later elected president of Poland. Solidarity became the nucleus for widespread political change in Poland. While it was forced underground in 1981, it significantly contributed to the collapse of communism in Poland. It was victorious in the first democratic elections in Poland after the collapse of communism there.

Solipsism is a highly skeptical philosophical approach that believes that a one's own mind is the only thing that exists. It argues that knowledge of anything outside the mind is unjustified and that the external material world cannot be known and might not exist. In other words, solipsism expressed a worldview that denied the existence of a material world independent from the mind of the individual. The most controversial feature of the solipsistic world view is the denial of the existence of other minds. Since humans can never directly know another's mental state, solipsism contends that another person's experiences can be known only by analogy to one's own experiences. Solipsism was first articulated by the Pre-Socratic Greek Sophist, Gorgas (483–375 BCE) who stated that nothing exists and that even if something exists, nothing can be known about it and that even if something could be known about it, knowledge about it cannot be communicated to others.

Solon (630–560 BCE) was an aristocratic Athenian statesman who was entrusted by his fellow citizens in 594 BCE with revising the laws of Athens in order to prevent civil strife. He attempted to transform Athenian society through mediation, moderation, and respect for the laws. He initiated a number of wide-ranging political and economic reforms that helped spark a commercial expansion.

Son of God was a term used in Greco-Roman communities to designate a person born from the union of God and a mortal. This person was thought to be able to perform miraculous deeds or convey divine teachings. In the Jewish communities, the term was used to designate a person chosen to stand in a special relationship with the God of Israel.

Song Dynasty (960–1279), which was located in central and southern China, was characterized by significant advances in technology, medicine, astronomy, and mathematics. It was a highly urbanized and cosmopolitan era in Chinese history. The Lao people controlled the northern part of the Song Empire, while the Jinn people controlled the southern part of the empire.

Sophists were popular but controversial wandering professional teachers and philosophers who came to Athens circa 450 BCE. They stressed the importance of rhetoric and tended toward skepticism and relativism. They received a very large fee for teaching and they lectured on a variety of topics, including linguistics, metaphysics, and especially rhetoric and the study of argumentation. Protagoras was the most well-known sophist.

Sophocles (497/6–406/5 BCE) was an Athenian author and playwright well known for his tragedies, such as *Antigone,* which deals with the conflicting obligations of a person to the family and the state.

His *Oedipus Rex* is considered by many to be one of the finest plays ever written.

South refers to the developing countries of Africa, Latin America, and southern Asia.

South African War or the Boer War (1899–1902) was the conflict between the British and the Dutch colonists in South Africa that resulted in bringing Afrikaners under the control of the British.

Southeast Asia Treaty Organization (SEATO) (1954) was an alliance among Thailand, Malaysia, Singapore, Indonesia, and the Philippines which was established by the United States after the Korean War in order to contain communism and promote economic progress and social stability in the countries of Southeast Asia. It lacked British and French support and proved ineffective during the Vietnam War. It was disbanded after the victory of communist North Vietnam over the South Vietnamese forces in 1975.

Sovereignty is the exclusive political and legal right to exercise supreme authority over a geographic region and a group of people. Sovereignty over a nation is generally vested in a government. In international law, the concept of sovereignty refers to the exercise of lawful political power by a state. A modern state is said to be sovereign when it makes the laws governing a society, controls the judicial system of a society, and uses military force and police powers within a specific geo graphic area.

Soviet Bloc was the international political and military alliance that included the Eastern European countries of the Warsaw Pact as well as the Soviet Union and Cuba.

Soviets were elected councils of workers, soldiers, and peasant representatives that were formed as strike committees in St. Petersburg beginning in 1905. They initially represented a form of local self-government. They became an important center of political power for Lenin and the Bolsheviks during the Russian Revolution.

Spanish-American War (1898) was the conflict between the United States and Spain in Cuba, Puerto Rico, and the Philippines. As a result of the defeat of Spain, the United States gained the colonial possessions of the Philippines, Guam, and Puerto Rico and gave Cuba partial independence.

Spanish Flu Pandemic (Great Influenza Pandemic) (1918–1920) was an unusually deadly strain of avian influenza that killed some 25 million to 50 million people worldwide in 1918 and 1919. It is thought to have been one of the most deadly pandemics in human history. The nations of the Allied side of World War I frequently called it the "Spanish Flu," primarily because Spain had one of the worst early outbreaks of the disease.

Species is a grouping of organisms whose members can all interbreed with one another and produce fertile offspring.

Speer, Albert (1905–1981) was Hitler's architect and the German minister of armaments from 1942–45. In this position, Speer dramatically increased armaments production through the use of millions of slave laborers. After the war, Speer was tried at Nuremberg, found guilty of war crimes and crimes against humanity and sentenced to twenty years in prison. At his trial Speer admitted his guilt and took responsibility for the actions of the Nazi regime.

Spencer, Herbert (1820–1903) was an English philosopher who is best known for developing the term "survival of the fittest" after reading Charles Darwin's *The Origin of Species*. Spencer is now primarily remembered for his political theory, Social Darwinism, by which he applied the law of the survival of the fittest to societies. Under his theory, he argued that humanitarian impulses must be resisted, as nothing should be allowed to interfere with the severity of the social struggle for existence, the entire point of which was to produce winners and losers.

Spheres of Influence is a term used in international relations to describe the political, economic, and military influence or control of a group of weaker nations by a more powerful hegemonic nation. The term was first used in the 1800s to describe a form of imperial control over foreign markets and territory exercised by the European nations in Africa and Asia. It was later used to describe American influence over the nations of Latin America and Japanese influence over China in the late 1800s and the first part of the 1900s.

Spice Islands was the name for the Molucca Islands in Indonesia, which, from as early as the Roman Empire, became known for its production of spices, including cloves, nutmeg, and mace. The spices of the Moluccas reached the Roman Empire and in later centuries Europe only after passing through the hands of many Javanese, Chinese, Indian, and Arab traders along the India Ocean and Silk Road trade routes. The primary western terminus for these two trade networks was Alexandria, Egypt. Between 1200 and 1500, Venice came to monopolize the spice trade in the Mediterranean. However, with the emergence of the Ottoman Empire in the Middle East, Venice's dominance of the extremely lucrative spice trade declined significantly. It was this decline in power and influence by Venice over the spice trade that precipitated efforts by other European nations during the 1400s and 1500s to discover an alternate trade route to Asia in order to obtain the spices upon which many Europeans had become dependent. Portugal played an important initial role in charting the sea route around Africa to India, Indonesia, and China, establishing a network of trading posts in the process. Portugal's initial success and dominance was subsequently challenged and overcome by the efforts of the Spanish, French, British, and the Dutch, who for centuries would compete for control of the lucrative emerging global market in spices.

Spice Trade is the name that has been given by historians to describe the international commercial trade in spices that developed over the centuries between India, China, Southeast Asia, Africa, and Europe on account of the growing use by Europeans of spices in food preservation, cooking, and medicine. As far back as two thousand years ago, the ancient Egyptians, Greeks, and Romans traded by land (the Silk Road) and sea (Indian Ocean, Red Sea, and the Mediterranean) with India, China, Indonesia, and Africa. From those countries, they obtained such luxury goods as incense; ebony; aromatics such as musk, camphor, ambergris, and sandalwood, fine textiles such as cotton and silk, ivory, gold, and spices such as cinnamon, mace, pepper, cloves, and nutmeg. As a result of increasing demand of the nobility and the wealthy in Europe during the high and late Middle Ages (1100–1500) for such luxury goods, economic and military competition among the then-major European naval powers such as Portugal, Spain, Holland, and England for control of the global spice trade intensified.

Spinning Jenny (1764) was the invention by James Hargreaves in the 1700s that revolutionized the British textile industry by massproducing thread.

Spinoza, Baruch (1632–1677) was one of the preeminent philosophers of the 1600s. He was educated at a rabbinical school where he studied Hebrew, the Talmud, and the Old Testament. In 1656, he was excommunicated from the Jewish community in Amsterdam for expressing doubts about orthodox Judaism. Even though he was offered a chair in philosophy at the University of Heidelberg, he refused it, preferring to spend the rest of his life in Holland grinding lenses and developing his philosophy.

Spiritualism is the belief that the physical world is permeated by a deeper soul or spirit and that the spirits of the dead can be accessed by the living with the assistance of a medium.

Spiritualists were radical Protestant sects, such as the Mennonites, Moravians, and Quakers, that in the 1500s and 1600s in Europe tended to emphasize the power of personal spiritual illumination, called the "inner word," which they considered to be a living form of the Scriptures written directly on the believer's soul by the hand of God. Such sects exalted the divine within the human and deliberately abstained from the demands of worldly existence.

Splendid Isolation was the term used to describe Britain's foreign policy during the late 1800s. During the late 1800s, Britain's primary goal in foreign policy was to maintain the balance of power in Europe and to intervene should that balance be upset. Its secondary goal was to protect its overseas interest in the colonies and dominions, as free trade was what kept the British Empire alive. The sea routes to the colonies, especially those linking Britain to India via Gibraltar and the Suez Canal, were vital. The policy of Splendid

Isolation was characterized by a reluctance to enter into permanent European alliances or commitments with the other great European powers and by an increase in the importance given by British policymakers to British colonies, protectorates, and dependencies overseas. However, circumstances in Europe began to change after the unification of Germany. Bismarck began to establish alliances with other European powers in order to prevent France's revenge for its defeat in the Franco-Prussian War. Furthermore, the rise of Germany in both industrial and military terms alarmed Britain, especially the german's naval aspirations, and contributed to a growing sense of isolation in Britain. Britain's sense of isolation ended with the signing of the Anglo-Japanese Treaty in 1902.

SPQR means "The Senate and People of Rome".

Spring and Autumn Period was the period in Chinese history from the mid-7th century through the early 5th century BCE when the central authority of the Zhou kings began to decline. This period is named after the historical records of the state of Lu, which are believed to have been edited by Confucius.

Sputnik **(1957)** was the name of the first artificial Earth satellite that was launched by the Soviet Union. The successful launching of *Sputnik* sparked fears in the United States of Soviet dominance in technology and outer space. It subsequently led to the creation of NASA and the space race.

SS (Schutzstaffel) (Protective Squad) were the elite Nazi black-shirted soldiers led by Heinrich Himmler during World War II. They were responsible for some of the worst atrocities of the Nazi regime. It was formed in 1925 to serve as Hitler's personal security force and to guard the Nazi Party (NDSAP) meetings. It was built into a powerful organization by Heinrich Himmler. It became the most powerful organization of the Nazi party, virtually a state within a state. They were notorious for their participation in carrying out Nazi policies such as the "Final Solution to the Jewish Problem".

SS-4 was a type of Soviet ballistic missile positioned in Cuba that set off the Cuban Missile Crisis.

SS-20 was a type of Soviet missile with a limited range of 5,000 miles that was capable of attacking China and countries in the Middle East, South Asia, and Western Europe. The INF Treaty eliminated it in 1987.

Stab-in-the-Back Myth refers to the belief, which was widely held among Germans after World War II about their unexpected loss in World War I. Many Germans from all political perspectives and social and economic classes believed that political intrigue and revolution at home had sabotaged the German war effort. This myth contributed to the alienation of Germans from and their dissatisfaction with the new liberal democratic Weimar government.

Stagflation refers to the simultaneous combination of high employment and high inflation, which occurred in the United States in the 1970s as a result of the OPEC oil embargo.

Stalin, Joseph (1878–1953) was the Bolshevik revolutionary and head of the Soviet Communist Party from 1924 to 1953. He succeeded Lenin as the leader of the Soviet Union in 1924. Under his dictatorial and brutal rule, he initiated the agricultural collectivization of the Soviet Union and developed his two Five Year Plans (1928–1938) to rapidly industrialize the Soviet Union. He concluded the German-Soviet Non-Aggression Pact in 1939, but joined the Allies against Nazi Germany in World War II after the German invasion of the Soviet Union in 1941. After World War II, he supported the communist takeover of governments in Eastern Europe. He was the leader of the Soviet Union during the early years of the Cold War.

Stalingrad, Battle of (1942–1943) was the city in the Soviet Union named for Joseph Stalin. It was where the Soviet army first defeated Germany in World War II. The Battle of Stalingrad is considered by many people to be the turning point of the war in Europe. At Stalingrad, the Soviet army suffered an enormous number of casualties in their effort to halt the advance of the German Sixth Army, which eventually surrendered.

Stalinism was the system that prevailed during Stalin's rule in the Soviet Union from 1924 to 1953, which was marked by totalitarian state control under the Communist Party and the ruthless elimination of the regime's opponents on a massive scale.

Stanley, Henry Morton (1841–1904) was a British-American explorer of Africa who became famous for his expeditions in search of Dr. David Livingston. He also helped King Leopold II establish the Congo Free State.

Star of David is a long-standing symbol of Judaism. It was used by the Nazis on badges to identify Jews. After September 1, 1941, all Jews in Germany over the age of six had to wear this badge whenever they appeared in public. Being caught without it could mean death. The Nazis required Jews to wear badges in all the countries occupied by the German army.

Stasi was the name for the East German secret police that kept files on 5 million East Germans (a third of the population) and infiltrated the West German military and government.

State is an organized political community occupying a definite territory, having an organized government, and possessing internal and external sovereignty. Recognition of the state's claim to independence by other states, enabling it to enter into international agreements, is often important to the establishment of its sovereignty.

State of Nature is the term used in social contract theory to describe the supposed human condition before the establishment of any governmental authority.

State-Sponsored Terrorism refers to the use of terrorist groups by states, usually under the control of a state's intelligence agency, to achieve political aims.

Status Quo is a Latin term meaning the present, current state of affairs. To maintain the status quo is to keep things the way they currently are. Arguing to preserve the status quo is usually done in the context of opposing a large, often radical change. The term frequently refers to the status of a large issue, such as the current culture or social climate of an entire society or nation. Status quo can also refer to social status in the workplace or peer groups at school. Politicians sometimes refer to a status quo. Sometimes specific institutions are founded to actively maintain the status quo. The United Nations, for example, was intended to help solidify the peaceful international status quo that immediately followed World War II.

Steam Engine was a machine that converted steam into mechanical energy that was used to power manufacturing machinery, ships and locomotives. The steam engine made the development of factories and mass production possible. By providing a new source of power, it allowed factories to be established anywhere. Thomas Newcomen built the first workable steam engine in 1712. James Watt improved the Newcomen device in the 1760s and 1770s.

Steel is a form of iron that is both durable and flexible. It was first mass-produced in the 1860s. It became the most widely used metal in construction, machinery production, and railroad equipment.

Stele or stela was a large stone commemorative monument onto which was carved a king's important military victories, the record of a king's reign or a king's laws or decrees. Steles were used extensively in ancient Mesopotamia and Egypt. The most well-known steles are the Code of Hammurabi (Babylon) and the victory stele of King Naram Sin (Akkad), and the Rosetta Stone.

Steppes are the vast, flat expanses of treeless and semi-arid grasslands that stretch across northern Eurasia. These plains of coarse grass supported nomads who bred horses and developed military skills that would be essential to the rise of the Mongol Empire.

Stereotyping is a process by which a person assigns a false or simplified attribute or image thought to be definitive of a specific group and possessed by all of the members of that group.

Stirrup (4500 BCE) is device for securing the feet of a rider of a horse. Historically, it enabled a rider to wield weapons more effectively. The first evidence of the use of stirrups was found among the Kushan people of northern Afghanistan in the 1st century CE.

Stock Exchange/Stock Market is a place where brokers and dealers buy and sell the shares of a company. Stock exchanges facilitate the financing of businesses and government activity by bringing together those seeking capital and those seeking to invest.

Stoicism was the most popular of Hellenistic philosophies that taught that happiness or inner peace could be obtained only by accepting one's lot in life and living in harmony with the will of the gods. It stressed calm obedience to natural law, adherence to moral duty and equality of all. It argued that human misery was caused by passion, which was a disease of the soul. Accordingly, the wise person sought freedom from passion and lived a life of moderation, unmoved by grief or joy. It considered nature an expression of divine will and that people could be happy only when living in accordance with nature. It was founded by Zeno of Citium (334–262 BCE) who taught in Athens.

Stone Age is the term used by historians to characterize a period in history when tools were produced from stone and other nonmetallic substances. It was followed in some places by the Bronze Age and then by the Iron Age.

Strait of Malacca is a narrow, 550-mile channel of water separating the Indonesian island of Sumatra and the Malay Peninsula, on which is the port city of Singapore located. Historically, the Strait has been one of the most important economic and strategic shipping lanes in the world, equivalent in economic and strategic importance to the Suez and Panama canals, which were built in the mid-1800s and early 1900s, respectively. Before arriving at Guangzhou in southern China traders from Egypt, Rome, Arabia, Africa, Turkey, Persia, and India used to reach the Malay Peninsula by relying upon the monsoon trade winds of the Indian Ocean. Traditionally, it has been the main shipping lane between the Indian Ocean and the Pacific Ocean, linking the major exporting countries of China, India, and Indonesia. Since the end of World War II, the Strait has also grown in importance for the powerful exporting economies that emerged in Japan, Korea, and Taiwan. Today, approximately one-fifth of the world's seaborne trade goes through the Strait and about one-third of the world's crude oil shipments.

Strategic Arms Limitation Treaties (SALT) SALT I (1972) and SALT II (1979) are two bilateral nuclear arms control agreements that put formal ceilings on the growth of U.S. and Soviet strategic nuclear weapons. SALT I, which was signed by President Nixon and Premier Brezhnev in 1972, specifically limited each country's ballistic missile defense and froze the deployment of intercontinental ballistic missile (ICBM) launchers. SALT II, which was signed by President Carter and Premier Brezhnev in 1979, set limits on the number of strategic missile launchers and other systems each country could deploy. Both countries largely followed SALT II even though the U.S. Senate never ratified it because of the Soviet invasion of Afghanistan.

Strategic Arms Reduction Treaty (START) START I (1991) is a bilateral nuclear arms control agreement that called for reduction of the strategic nuclear arsenals of the United States and the Soviet Union by about 30 percent.

Strategic Bombing refers to the military doctrine of aerial bombardment of populated and industrial areas, which was initiated by Germany during World War II. It was intended to destroy the morale and willingness to fight of the civilian population as well as destroy a nation's industrial capacity. As a result of this doctrine, civilian targets became the objects of attacks during wartime. Allied forces used this strategy extensively in the bombing of Germany and Japan.

Strategic Defense Initiative (SDI) (1983) refers to a U.S. effort, also known as "Star Wars," initiated by President Ronald Reagan, to develop defenses' satellites and space-based missiles that could shoot down incoming ballistic nuclear missiles aimed at the United States. Although SDI was criticized as expensive, unfeasible, and in violation of the Antiballistic Missile (ABM) Treaty, Congress approved billions of dollars for its development.

Strategic Offensive Reductions Treaty (SORT) (2003–2011), which is also known as the Moscow Treaty, is a bilateral arms control agreement between the United States and Russia to reduce the number of operationally deployed nuclear warheads on each side to between 1,700 and 2,200 by the end of 2012.

Stratification is the degree to which there is an uneven distribution of resources and wealth among different groups of individuals and states.

Strike is the collective work stoppage initiated by workers individually or through unions to protest the conduct of their employer and their general working conditions. By causing the employer some economic pain, strikers seek to gain such improvements as increased pay, safety improvement, and other benefits.

Subinfeudation was the practice in medieval Europe by which a lord's most important vassals subdivided their land or fiefs and had vassals of their own. Those vassals, in turn, subdivided their land or fiefs and so on down to the knights, whose fiefs were too small to subdivide.

Subjectivism was the belief especially associated the Protagoras, a sophist, that there is no absolute realty behind and independent of appearances.

Submarine Telegraph Cables (1851) were copper-insulated cables laid along the ocean floor that transmitted telegraphic communications. The first cable was laid across the English Channel in 1851. The first successful transatlantic cable was laid in 1866.

Sub-Saharan Africa is that portion of the African continent that lies south of the Sahara Desert.

Suez Canal (1859–1869) was the 101-mile shippingcanal that was built across the Isthmus of Suez in Egypt in order to connect the Mediterranean Sea with the Red Sea. Upon its completion in 1869, it shortened the sea voyage between Europe and Asia and thereby reduced the cost of international trade. Ferdinand de Lesseps designed it. The Suez Canal became strategically important to the British when they conquered Egypt in 1882.

Suez Crisis (1956–1957) refers to the British, French, and Israeli attack on Egypt to regain control of the Suez Canal after the Egyptian government, led by Egyptian President Gamal Abdel Nasser, nationalized it in 1956. This seizure of the Suez Canal produced strong opposition throughout the world, forcing the three nations to withdraw. Subsequently, UN and U.S. opposition and Soviet threats of intervention ended the assault.

Suffrage is the right to vote for candidates for public office or to vote on specific legislation. During the 1800s and 1900s in Europe and the United States, the right to vote was gradually expanded to include wider groups of people who had previously been disenfranchised.

Suffragettes were militant members of the British feminist political movement that fought for women's right to vote in the early 1900s. They were led by Emmeline Parkhurst and they engaged in acts of violence against private property in order to obtain the right to vote.

Sui Dynasty (589–618) was the name of the Chinese dynasty that constructed the Grand Canal, reunified China, and established the foundation upon which the Tang Dynasty would be built.

Sulla (138–78 BCE) was a Roman general and politically conservative politician from a distinguished family, he was appointed dictator in 82 BCE. He represented the conservative reaction to the growing influence of the plebeians in Roman political life. He brutally eliminated his opponents, expanded the power of the Roman Senate, and limited the power of the tribunes, which represented the plebeians. After ruling for three years, he retired.

Sultan was the Islamic political leader in the Ottoman Empire. He was supposed to symbolize both a warrior and a devout follower of Islam.

Sumerians (4500/4000–2270 BCE) were a people who dominated southern Mesopotamia through the end of the 3rd millennium BCE. They established thirty city-states and were responsible for the creation of many fundamental elements of a common Mesopotamian culture, such elements as irrigation technology, cuneiform writing, and religious practices.

Summa is a Latin term that emerged in the Middles Ages for a systematic work that purported to survey and summarize a whole field of knowledge on a particular subject. Thomas Aquinas wrote the best known summas.

Sumptuary Laws were laws enacted in Europe against luxury and extravagance. Such laws prohibited extravagance in dress and conduct and were designed to maintain moral standards and distinctions between social classes. Often, such laws targeted women.

Sun Yat-sen (1866–1925) was a Chinese nationalist revolutionary and the founder and leader of the Chinese Nationalist Party (Kuomindang). He attempted to create a democratic political movement in China after the collapse of the Manchu Dynasty, but was hindered by the emergence of numerous warlords throughout China in the early part of the 1900s. The political philosophy of Kuomindang as articulated by Sun Yat-sen emphasized nationalism, democracy, and the livelihood of the Chinese people.

Sunnis are the largest Islamic denomination. After Muhammad's death in 632 a dispute arose over who was to lead the Muslim community and how the leader was to be chosen. Subsequently, a group of Muslims gave their allegiance to Abu Bakr, Muhammad's father-in-law, who then became the first caliph. Sunnis today accept Abu Bakr as the rightful caliph. Shiite Muslims believe that Muhammad had appointed his son-in-law Ali ibn Abi Talib as his successor and that in following Abu Bakr, the Muslim community had strayed from the true path of Islam. Thirty years after Muhammad's death, the Islamic community plunged into an Islamic civil war. This civil war led to the emergence of two major Islamic groups: the Sunnis and the Shiites. The Sunnis regard the first four caliphs (Abu Bakr, Umar ibn al-Khattab, Uthman, and Ali) as "Rightly Guided Caliphs", who ruled in accordance with the Quran and the teachings of Muhammad.

Sunzi or Sun Tzu (5th century BCE) was a general and military strategist during the early Warring States period of Chinese history (476–221 BCE). He is considered to be the author of *The Art of War*, the earliest known treatise on military strategy and tactics for rulers and military leaders. In that book, he emphasized deception, speed, attacking the enemy's weakness, careful preparation, the gathering of accurate information, knowledge of the terrain, the use of flexible strategies and tactics and the unpredictability of war. He claimed that "If you know the enemy and know yourself, you need not fear the result of a hundred battles. If you know yourself but not the enemy, for every victory gained you will suffer a defeat. If you know neither the enemy nor yourself, you will succumb in every battle." The *Art of War* influenced Mao Zedong in his civil war with Chiang Kai-shek and the Kuomintang and General Vo Nguyen Giap, the military strategist who led the Vietnamese to victories over French and American forces in Vietnam.

Superego is one of the three elements in the model of the human psyche developed by Sigmund Freud. According to him, the superego embodies the external morality imposed on one's personality by society.

Superpower refers to the most powerful state(s) among a group of other powerful states. The term was coined during the Cold War to refer to the United States and Soviet Union.

Suppiluliumas I, King (14th century BCE) was the Hittite ruler who extended the boundaries of the Hittite Empire between 1380 and 1346 BCE. He is considered to be the greatest of the Hittite kings.

Surplus Value is an idea developed by Karl Marx that measures the difference between a product's real value and the wages a worker receives for producing that product.

Surrealism was a movement in literature and the visual arts that emerged in Paris in the early 1920s after World War I. While it mocked existing social conventions, it did so by exploring the realm of the subconscious by following some of the psychological insights of Freud.

Swastika is a holy symbol in Hinduism, Jainism, and Buddhism. Today, it is most widely known and used as a symbol of Nazism. The motif seems to have first been used in Neolithic Eurasia. It was also adopted in Native American cultures, seemingly independently. The swastika is used universally in religious and civil ceremonies in India. Most Indian temples, weddings, festivals, and celebrations are decorated with swastikas. The symbol was introduced to Southeast Asia by Hindu kings and remains an integral part of Balinese Hinduism to this day, and it is a common sight in Indonesia. By the early 1900s it was widely used worldwide and was regarded as a symbol of good luck. Since its adoption by the Nazi Party of Adolf Hitler in the 1920s, the swastika has been associated in much of the world with fascism, racism, white supremacy, World War II, and the Holocaust. Heinrich Schliemann discovered the symbol in the site of ancient Troy and associated it with the ancient migrations of Indo-European ("Aryan") peoples, and also connected it with similar shapes found on ancient pots in Germany. He theorized that the swastika was a "significant religious symbol of our remote ancestors." Nazi use of the swastika arose from this idea, that it was a symbol of "Aryan" identity, a concept which came to be equated by Nazi theorists with a Nordic master race originating in northern Europe.

Sweatshop was another name for factories with poor working conditions and poor pay that existed in the United States and Britain in the late 1800s. Industries in which sweatshops existed were marked by especially oppressive and exploitative working conditions, including lack of safety features, low pay, restrictions on personal conduct, long working hours, and denial of basic legal rights.

Sykes-Picot Agreement (1916) was the secret treaty made during World War I by Britain and France to take over parts of the Ottoman Empire. This treaty provided that France would acquire coastal Syria, Lebanon, and Mosul in Iraq. Britain was to control Baghdad and Basra in Iraq and northern Palestine. The southern part of Palestine was to be administered by an international regime. Britain and France also agreed to permit Russia to control certain Armenian and Kurdish-dominated areas of Turkey. In 1917, when the Bolsheviks came to power and withdrew Russia from the war, they disclosed the terms of the treaty, which contradicted wartime promises made by the British and the French to their Arab allies and to Zionists in the Balfour Declaration. The treaty also undercut the efforts by President Wilson to have the Allies use his Fourteen Points as the basis for negotiations to end World War I.

Symbol is anything that is taken to mean something beyond that which it is physically. For example, depending on the culture of an ancient society, a storm could symbolize troubled times or the blessing of the gods. The sound or written appearance of a word is a symbol when someone hears or reads it and understands its meaning. For instance, the three letters in the word "dog" symbolize a dog.

Symposium was a drinking party for aristocratic Greek men that featured games, songs, poetry, hired female companions, and philosophical discussions.

Synagogue is the name for the place for Jewish worship, prayer, and reading of the Torah. It is derived from a Greek word meaning "being brought together."

Syncretism, which is derived from a Latin word meaning "a union of communities," is a process by which the ideas, customs, practices and cultural traditions of one society are, willingly or unwillingly adopted, in whole or in part, by another society in order to unify diverse peoples and cultures. Since syncretism tends to facilitate coexistence and constructive interaction between different cultures, it is especially useful for rulers of multi-ethnic empires. For example, this process helped to unify the diverse peoples and religions under Sumerian, Akkadian, Babylonian, Persian, and Roman rule.

Syndicalism was a French labor movement in the late 1800s and early 1900s that sought to improve the working conditions for workers through direct political and economic protest, especially mass general strikes, sabotage, and violence.

Synoptic Gospels are the Gospels of Matthew, Mark, and Luke, which narrate so many of the same stories that they can be placed next to each other and be seen together, which is the literal meaning of *synoptic.* The Synoptic Problem refers to the textual relationships among the synoptic Gospels of Matthew, Mark, and Luke.

Synthesis is one of the concepts used by Hegel to explain how ideas develop. According to him, a synthesis emerges as a result of the tension and clash between the thesis and antithesis which results in a new, superior thesis.

Syracuse was the largest and the wealthiest of the Greek city-states in Sicily. It was invaded by the Athenians during the Peloponnesian War.

Tabula Rasa, which means "blank slate," was a term used by John Locke to argue that all concepts and ways of thinking are derived from human experience. According to Locke, the human mind at birth is like a blank slate on which the environment writes the individual's understanding and beliefs. Thus, humans enter the world with unformed minds that are wholly constituted by experience.

Tacitus, Cornelius (56–117) was a historian of the early imperial Rome. He praised the simple virtues of the Germanic tribes and expressed nostalgia for the era of the Roman Republic. His greatest written works were *The Histories,* which discussed the civil wars of Rome, and *The Annals,* which chronicled the reigns of Roman emperors from Tiberius to Nero.

Taille was a direct tax on the French peasantry by the monarchy.

Taiping is a Chinese word that means "Great Peace." It was used as shorthand for the Taiping Tianguo, which means the "Heavenly Kingdom of Great Peace." Taiping was the name adopted by the rebellious state created by Hong Xiuquan between 1850 and 1864 that controlled much of central and south China and ruled over perhaps as many as 100 million people.

Taiping Rebellion (1850–1864) was a civil war in China that threatened to topple the Qing Empire. The rebels that revolted against the Qing emperor were greatly influenced by Christianity. It was the most destructive civil war in the world before the 1900s.

Taliban is the name for the extremist Sunni Muslim movement that ruled most of Afghanistan from 1995 until 2001, when their leaders were removed from power by the United States, United Kingdom, and the Northern Alliance. The movement is headed by Mullah Mohammed Omar. The overwhelming majority of the members of the Taliban are Pashtuns from southern Afghanistan and western Pakistan, along with a small number of volunteers from Eurasia to China. The Taliban received valuable training, supplies, and arms from the Pakistani government, particularly the Inter-Services Intelligence (ISI). Although in control of Afghanistan's capital (Kabul) and much or most of the country for five years, the Taliban regime, or "Islamic Emirate of Afghanistan," gained diplomatic recognition from only three states: Pakistan, Saudi Arabia, and the United Arab Emirates. While in power, the Taliban implemented the "strictest interpretation of Sharia law ever seen in the Muslim world," and became notorious internationally for their treatment of women. Under the Taliban, women were forced to wear the burqa in public. They were allowed neither to work nor to be educated after the age of eight, and until then were permitted only to study the Qur'an. Women seeking an education were forced to attend underground schools, where they and their teachers risked execution if caught. Male doctors could not treat them unless accompanied by a female chaperon, which led to illnesses remaining untreated. They faced public flogging in the street and public execution for violations of the Taliban's laws.

Talleyrand-Périgord, Charles Maurice de (1754–1838) was French statesman during the French Revolution, and the Napoleonic Wars, and was a key player at the Congress of Vienna. He was the foreign minister for both the Directory and Napoleon. Talleyrand distrusted Napoleon and plotted his overthrow with Louis XVIII. He represented France at the Congress of Vienna, successfully negotiating a return to the pre-Revolution borders of France. In 1815, royalists forced him out of French politics because of his past support of Napoleon. However, he convinced Louis Philippe to take the throne during the July Revolution (1830) and served as an ambassador to Britain in the 1830s.

Talmud is a religious work that records civil and ceremonial law and Jewish legend. It is a collection of commentaries on Jewish law. This collection of ancient Jewish traditions contains both the Mishnah and the later commentaries on the Mishnah called the Gemarah. There are two collections of the Talmud. One was made in Palestine during the early 400s CE and the other was made in Babylon, perhaps a century later. The Babylonian Talmud is usually considered to be the more authoritative of the two.

Tang Dynasty (618–907 CE) was the Chinese dynasty that unified China and established a magnificent court at Chang'an. Tang Taizong, who ruled from 627 to 649, established the Tang Dynasty.

Tariff is a tax on imported goods imposed by a state. Typically, tariffs are imposed to raise revenues, to discourage imports, and to protect domestic industries. Tariff protection is a government's way of supporting and aiding its own economy by establishing high tariffs on the cheaper, imported goods of another country.

Tehran Conference (1943) refers to the meeting between Stalin, Churchill, and Roosevelt that took place in Tehran, Iran, where the Allies agreed to open a western front against Nazi Germany in order to take pressure off the Soviets and pledged to recognize Iran's independence. It was the first war conference among the Allied Powers in which Stalin was present.

Telescope is a device used for seeing distant objects by means of shaped lenses. It was invented in 1608 in the Netherlands by Hans Lippershey, a spectacle maker and master lens grinder. He found that using a brass tube with both convex and concave lens made distant objects appear closer. Before their use in scientific research, telescopes were used for military purposes. Based on the work in the Netherlands, Galileo built his own refracting telescope in 1609. When Galileo used his telescope to observe the moon, he discovered that the moon's surface was not smooth. Galileo subsequently discovered the existence of four moons revolving around Jupiter.

Temperance Movement was a political movement to discourage the consumption of alcohol, which began in the early 1800s in Europe and the United States.

Ten Lost Tribes of Israel were ten of the original twelve Hebrew tribes of Canaan who were assimilated by other societies and were lost to history when the Kingdom of Israel was conquered by the Assyrians in 721 BCE. In 930 BCE Canaan had been divided, with ten tribes forming the independent Kingdom of Israel in the north and the two other tribes establishing the Kingdom of Judah in the south.

Tenement is the name for an overcrowded and, many times, dilapidated apartment buildings in urban areas.

Tennis Court Oath (1789) was the pledge signed by 576 out of the 577 deputies of the Third Estate, and a by few members of the Second Estate, on June 20, 1789. The deputies pledged that they would continue to meet until a constitution was drafted for France. This pledge was signed at an indoor tennis court near the Palace of Versailles. The oath was a revolutionary act, for the deputies were claiming that political authority derived from the people and their representatives rather than from the monarch himself. Their solidarity forced Louis XVI to order the clergy and the nobility to join with the Third Estate in the newly formed National Assembly.

Terrorism is the use of violence by groups or states to intimidate, cause fear, or punish their victims, primarily civilians, to achieve certain political goals. Terrorists many times believe that extreme and what might appear to be random violence will destabilize a government and demoralize a people. Though an old political tactic used by various groups throughout history, it came to prominence in the late 1900s and early 2000s as a result of the development of worldwide news coverages that intensified public fears of political violence.

Tet Offensive (1968) refers to the series of North Vietnamese and Viet Cong attacks launched in South Vietnam in January and February of 1968. This event has been seen by many as the turning point in the Vietnam War.

Tetrarchy, which means "rule by four," was the system of governance established by Diocletian, who reigned from 306–337. Under this system of governance, the Roman Empire was ruled by four men with their power divided territorially. Diocletian established this form of governance to deal with the Empire's growing political instability, huge size and complexity, to promote experienced men to govern, and to provide for an orderly succession of power. Under his system of succession, two Augustuses and two Caesars would jointly rule the Roman Empire and provide for orderly succession upon the death of the emperor.

Thales of Miletus (6th century BCE) was one of the pre-Socratic philosophers from Miletus in Ionia. While none of his writings survive, he is believed to have significantly influenced the development of Greek geometry and astronomy. According to Aristotle, Thales developed the first systematic theory about the nature of the universe. He claimed the universe was a living organism, that the Earth was a flat disk floating on water, that water was the basic element from which all of nature was created, that water can take the form of a gas, solid or liquid and that water nourished life. The significance of Thales lies in his effort to use reason to understand the natural phenomena rather than seeking explanations in supernatural, anthropomorphic gods. By assuming that the world was knowable and understandable, Thales provided the first intellectual bridge between the worlds of myth, religion, and reason.

Thatcher, Margaret (1925–2013) was the conservative prime minister of Britain from 1979 to 1990, during which time she promoted privatization and free enterprise in Britain at the expense of the welfare system and British labor unions. Some have called the social, political, and economic changes that resulted from her policies "Thatcher's conservative revolution."

Thebes was the capital city of Egypt and home of the ruling dynasties during the Middle and New Kingdoms. Amon, patron deity of Thebes, became one of the chief gods of Egypt. Monarchs were buried across the Nile River in the Valley of the Kings.

Themes were military districts in the Eastern Roman Empire that were organized by local generals in which soldiers settled on the land. Themes developed gradually after 600 and partially replaced the standing professional army.

Themistocles (524–460 BCE) was an Athenian political and military leader during and after the Persian Wars. He fought at the Battle of Marathon. He is remembered for convincing the Athenians to leave Athens and fight the Persians at Salamis, where he was victorious. As a political leader, he brought about the passage of legislation that gave the lowest classes virtually full political participation. Despite his victory at the Battle of Salamis, he was, nevertheless, ostracized by the Athenians. Cimon, a conservative Athenian politician, was probably responsible for the ostracism of Themistocles.

Theocracy is a form of government ruled by a religious order.

Theocratic Kingship is a form of royal rule that emerged in Mesopotamia and then appeared subsequently in a number of Western European societies. Under this form of royal rule, it was claimed that the kings ruled as specially designated agents of the gods, to whom the kings were answerable.

Theodoric I (454–526 CE) was the king of the Ostrogoths who controlled Italy from 493 to 526. Influenced by his service in the Roman army, he attempted to preserve Roman culture and urban life during his reign.

Theodosian Code was a compilation of the laws of the Roman Empire and was promulgated by Christian Roman emperors since 312. The Code was the first attempt by a Roman emperor since the Twelve Tables (450 BCE) to collect and publish all the laws of the Roman Empire.

Theodosius I, Emperor Flavius (347–395 CE), also known as Theodosius the Great, was the Roman emperor who restored the Roman army after its disastrous defeat at Adrianople. He did so by integrating barbarian tribes into the army. He convened the Second Ecumenical Council in 381 and outlawed pagan cults in 391–392.

Theodosius II, (401–450) was the Eastern Roman emperor who built the enormous defensive wall to protect Constantinople from invasion by land. He also issued the Theodosian Code, which was a compilation of Roman law issued by the Christian Roman emperors after 312.

Theory is an explanation or generalization based on observation, evidence, and reason that has been tested and confirmed as a general principle explaining a large number of related facts.

Thermidorean Reaction (1794) was a period during the French Revolution. It began in July 1794 (the month of Thermidor) when there was revolt against the radicalism associated with the Reign of Terror. During this period the instruments of the Terror were dismantled and supporters of the Jacobins were harassed or even murdered. This revolt led to the downfall and execution of Robespierre, the overthrow of the Committee of Public Safety, the end of the Reign of Terror, and the beginning of the more politically moderate Directory.

Thermonuclear Device, which is also known as a hydrogen bomb, or H-bomb, is hundreds of thousands of times more powerful than an atomic bomb and can cause death and destruction for miles around. Radioactive contamination resulting from the detonation of such a device could last for years and be carried around the world.

Thermopylae, Battle of (480 BCE) was a battle in which a vastly outnumbered alliance of Greek city-states (10,000 Athenians and Spartans) held back an invading Persian army of Xerxes I at the narrow pass of Thermopylae, which was six miles long and approximately fifty feet wide. King Leonidas of Sparta, leading a small force of 300 Spartans and 1,100 Boeotians (all of whom died in the battle), blocked the pass for three days. However, a local resident named Ephialtes betrayed the Greeks to the Persians by revealing to the Persians a mountain path that led behind the Greek lines. By holding their position for three days, King Leonidas and his small force allowed the retreat of the other Greek forces.

Thesis is a claim or assertion about what something is.

Third-Century Crisis is the term used by historians for the political, military, and economic turmoil that beset the Roman Empire during much of the 200s CE. Specifically, the Empire suffered frequent changes of rulers, civil wars, barbarian invasions, plague, assassinations, massive inflation, decline of urban centers, and near-total destruction of long-distance commerce and of the monetary economy. After 284, Diocletian restored order by making fundamental changes.

Third Estate was the lowest class among the three classes in France before the French Revolution. The First Estate was comprised of the clergy, the Second Estate the nobility, and the Third Estate the peasants and the bourgeoisie. Representatives of the Third Estate were amongst the delegates to the meeting of the Estates General, the French legislature, which was called into session by Louis XVI in 1789. He presumed that the votes of the First and Second Estates would overrule those of the Third Estate even though the members of the Third Estate vastly outnumbered the clergy and the nobles. The refusal by the Third Estate to capitulate to the demands of the nobility and the clergy led to the formation of the National Assembly and the Tennis Court Oath, the two events that essentially began the French Revolution.

Third Reich (1933–1945) was the name of the German government under Adolf Hitler and the Nazi Party. The Third Reich began in 1933 and remained in power until 1945.

Third Servile War (73–71 BCE), which was also called the Gladiator War or the War of Spartacus, was the last of the unsuccessful slave rebellions against the Roman Republic. This revolt was fought in the Campania region of Italy. The revolt began when about 78 gladiators, led by a Thracian slave named Spartacus, escaped from a gladiatorial school near Capua. After their escape, the slaves recruited other slaves in the region to join them and they rapidly grew into a rebel group of over 120,000 men, women and children. The freed slaves chose three leaders, one of whom was Spartacus. Initially, the armed rebels were successful in withstanding the repeated attacks by Roman military, in part because Roman legions were suppressing a revolt in Spain and fighting the Third Mithridatic War. Alarmed by such unexpected military success by unorganized and untrained slaves, the Senate created an army of eight legions (approximately 40,000–50,000 soldiers) to crush the rebellion. The Senate placed Marcus Licinius Crassus, the wealthiest man in Rome, in command of that army. By late 71 BCE,

the rebel army led by Spartacus had retreated to the south of Italy near the Strait of Messina. Pursued by Crassus' legions and cut off from supplies, the rebellion was finally crushed. While most of the rebel slaves were killed in the final battle, some 6,000 survivors were captured and all were crucified along the Appian Way from Rome to Capua. It is believed that Spartacus was killed in the battle, but his body was never found.

Third World is a term that developed after World War II to describe those nations primarily in Asia, Latin America, and Africa that were emerging from imperial domination. Those nations were economically and politically underdeveloped because of decades of colonial rule. Typically, many of these nations considered themselves "nonaligned" during the Cold War.

Thirty Years' War (1618–1648) was an extremely destructive religious conflict between Protestants and Catholics that began in Germany. It escalated into a general European war and was fought primarily in Germany by Sweden, France, and the Holy Roman Empire. The Peace of Westphalia ended the war.

Thirty-Eighth Parallel (38th Parallel) is the dividing line between North and South Korea that was first established to separate Soviet and U.S. occupation zones after Japan's defeat in 1945. The Korean War began in 1950 after North Korean forces crossed the 38th parallel into South Korea.

Thrace occupied a geographic area during ancient times that included present day Bulgaria, European Turkey, north-eastern Greece and parts of eastern Serbia and eastern Macedonia. Its boundaries were between the Danube River to the north and the Aegean Sea to the south, and between the Black Seaand the Sea of Marmara to the east and to the Vardar and Great Morava rivers to the west. Thracian troops accompanied Alexander the Great when he crossed the Hellespont and conquered the Persian Empire. Divided into separate tribes, the Thracians did not manage to form a lasting political organization or any form of political unity until the 4th century BCE. The Thracians were considered barbarians by their more urbanized Greek neighbors. The first Greek colonies in Thrace were founded in the 6th century BCE.

Throughout that period, Thracian infantry was heavily recruited by Greek city-states and large deposits of gold and silver were mined in Thrace. The region was conquered by Philip II of Macedon in the 4th century BCE. As a result of the conflict between Rome and Macedon during the Macedonian Wars, Roman authority was extended to Thrace in 168 BCE. However, neither the Thracians nor the Macedonians accepted Roman control and several revolts took place between 168 and 149 BCE. The next 150 years saw the slow development of Thrace into a permanent Roman client state. Thracians gave assistance to both Pompey and Caesar, and later supported the Roman armies against Antonius and Octavian in the final days of the Republic. In 279 BCE, Celtic Gauls advanced into Macedonia, southern Greece and Thrace. They were soon forced out of Macedonia and southern Greece, but they remained in Thrace until the end of the century. From Thrace, three Celtic tribes advanced into Anatolia and formed a new kingdom called Galatia. Following the Third Macedonian War, Thrace acknowledged Roman authority and became a Roman province in 46 BCE. The lack of large urban centers made Thrace a difficult place to manage, but eventually the province flourished under Roman rule. Roman authority in Thrace relied on the legions stationed there. Over the next few centuries, the province was periodically and increasingly attacked by migrating Germanic tribes. The reign of Justinian saw the construction of over 100 fortresses. Owing to their reputation as fierce fighters, Thracians had been used as mercenaries by the Greek kings of Syria, Pergamum, and other regions. By the mid-400s CE, as the Roman Empire began to crumble, Thrace turned into a battleground. The successor of the Roman Empire in the Balkans, the Byzantine Empire, controlled Thrace until the beginning of the 800s when most of the region was incorporated into Bulgaria. The Byzantine Empire regained Thrace in 972 only to lose it again to the Bulgarians at the end of the 1100s.

Three Emperors League (1872) was a political and military alliance created by the emperors of Germany, Austria-Hungary, and Russia, the three largest powers in Eastern and Central Europe at the time. It was created to oppose liberal forms of government in Western Europe. The monarchical leaders of all three countries were wary of the growing appeal of liberalism, so they created an alliance that would protect their conservative governments. The League was also part of Otto von Bismarck's foreign policy plan to keep France isolated and keep both Austria-Hungary and Russia on his side. The League disintegrated as a result of Russia's dissatisfaction with the Congress of Berlin of 1878. The League was resurrected in 1881 after Bismarck secretly persuaded Russia to rejoin the League. Under pressure from Emperor Wilhelm II, Bismarck was forced to resign as the German foreign minister in 1890. The resignation was a result of Germany's shift away from Bismarck's conservative foreign policy. In the same year, Germany rejected Russia's proposal to renew the League. Russia, now isolated, sought an alliance with France to counter the threat of the alliance of Germany and Austria-Hungary. The collapse of the League is widely considered as one of the long-term causes of World War I.

Three-Field System was the agricultural system developed in Europe during the Middle Ages. One-third of the land was planted in autumn with wheat or rye, one-third remained fallow, and one-third was planted in the spring with a crop that added nutrients to the soil.

Three Principles of the People was the political philosophy of Sun Yat-sen and the Kuomindang. Sun Yat-sen's Three Principles emphasized nationalism, democracy, and people's livelihood.

Thucydides (455–397 BCE) was an ancient Greek historian who, along with Herodotus, founded the writing of history in the West. As a result of his military background as a general, he was able to make an accurate and careful study of the Peloponnesian War.

Thutmose III (reigned from 1479–1426) was the New Kingdom pharaoh who defeated the Canaanites in 1457 BCE and established the Egyptian Empire.

Tiananmen Square (1989) is the largest public square in the world. It is located in Beijing and was the site of a Chinese pro-democracy demonstration, which was crushed by the Chinese military, killing as many as 1,000 of the student protesters. Tian is the Chinese word for "heaven".

Tibet is a country located on the mountainous plateau north of India. Between the 600s and 1200s, Tibetan political power extended north into China. Today, the Chinese government considers Tibet to be a province of China and not a separate independent nation.

Time of Troubles was the period from 1604 to 1613 when Russia fell into chaos following the death of Ivan the Terrible. It ended when the national assembly elected Tsar Michael Romanov. The Romanov Dynasty would rule Russia until 1917 when it was deposed during the Russian Revolution.

Titan is a type of U.S. intercontinental ballistic missile that became part of the U.S. strategic nuclear arsenal in 1963. They were dismantled in 1987 under the SALT I treaty. Titan missiles had a 7,500-mile range and carried 9-megaton warheads.

Tithe was a tax levied by the Catholic Church, which was equivalent to one-tenth of the earnings of its parishioners.

Tocqueville, Alex de (1805–1859) was a French statesman and political writer who is most well-known for his *Democracy in America,* one of the earliest studies of American life. He was a member of the French Chamber of Deputies for a time and the vice president of the National Assembly in 1849.

Tokugawa Shogunate (1600–1867) was the last of the three shogunates of Japan. Tokugawa Ieyasu, who unified Japan, was the founder of it.

Tonkin Gulf Incident (1964) refers to the alleged attack on the USS Maddox by North Vietnamese patrol boats in the Gulf of Tonkin on August 2, 1964. Five days later, the U.S. Congress approved the Gulf of Tonkin Resolution, giving President Johnson authority to conventional military force against North Vietnam.

Torah, which is a Hebrew word meaning teaching doctrine or instruction contains the first five books of the Hebrew Bible. The Torah describes God's covenant or agreement with the Hebrews. The Torah was accepted by the Hebrews as sacred circa 425 BCE. Moses is thought to have written Genesis, Exodus, Leviticus, Numbers, and Deuteronomy.

Treaty of Tordesillas (1494) was the agreement negotiated between Spain and Portugal in 1494. The Treaty established the rights of each nation to the lands in the New World, which had been discovered by Christopher Columbus on behalf of Spain in 1492. Fearful that Spain would be prevented from exploring and claiming any lands in the New World, King Ferdinand of Aragon and Isabelle of Castille requested that Pope Alexander VI determine the rights of each nation to those newly discovered lands. In 1493, Pope Alexander VI issued a papal bull dividing the western and eastern hemispheres of the world along a north-south demarcation line located west of the Azores. According to his bull, Spain had the exclusive right to the lands west of that demarcation line and Portugal had similar rights to the east of that demarcation line. By the Treaty of Tordesillas, Spain and Portugal agreed that the demarcation line should be moved to west of the Cape Verde islands off the west coast of Africa, which permitted Portugal the exclusive rights to present-day Brazil. The papal bull and the treaty were never recognized by any other European nation.

Tories were members of a British political party in the 1600s that defended the system of hereditary succession to the British throne. They sought to preserve the traditional political structure and the authority of the Anglican Church. The Whigs opposed them.

Total War was a military strategy first adopted beginning in World War I that required the total mobilization of all elements of a society to fight a war, extensive centralized governmental regulation of economic production, distribution, consumption, and civil rights. As a result of this total mobilization of society, civilian targets became the objects of attacks during wartime, making a total war to be a highly destructive type of war.

Totalitarian State is a society in which a government controls all aspects of the economic, political, cultural and intellectual life of its citizens. Totalitarian governments typically demand the subordination of the needs and interest of the individual to the interest of the state and require the active participation of citizens in achieving the political objectives of the state.

Totalitarianism is an ideology that advocated government control of all aspects of the economic, political, cultural and intellectual life of a society. This idea exalted the authority of the state and claimed the right to direct all facets of a state's culture, law, art, education, economy, and religion in the interests of the state. A dictator, such as Hitler in Germany and Stalin in the Soviet Union, defined those interests. Totalitarian governments typically demand the subordination of the needs and interest of the individual to the interest of the state and require the active participation of citizens in achieving the political objectives of the state.

Trade Unions are organizations of workers whose objective is to represent the interest of their members in negotiations with their employer over salaries, benefits, and working conditions.

Trading Posts were built by European traders along the coasts of countries in Africa and Asia between 1400 and 1800. Also known as factories, these trading posts were islands of European culture, law, and sovereignty in foreign lands. The Portuguese trading post dominated the Indian Ocean trade in the 1500s through fortified and strategically located naval bases.

Trafalgar, Battle of (1805) was a British naval victory over French forces during the Napoleonic Wars. The decisive defeat of French naval forces at the battle of Trafalgar would result in British naval supremacy in the world for the next 100 years.

Tragedy is a dramatic work meant to evoke fear and/or pity and whose major character, perhaps owing to a fatal character flaw, suffers deeply and may be brought to ruin. The character may also earn the reader's respect through a heroic struggle against his or her fate. This dramatic form was prevalent in ancient Greece and it usually treated a mythological theme and led to a catastrophe for some of the characters.

Trail of Tears (1837–1838) was the forced relocation of the Cherokees from the East to Oklahoma.

It became symbolic of western expansionism in the United States in the 1800s and the destruction of indigenous Indian societies.

Trajan (53–117 CE) was a Roman emperor who reigned from 98 to 117. He was the second of the "Five Good Emperors." As a result of his conquests, the Roman Empire was at its greatest territorial extent. He is considered by many historians to be the greatest Roman emperor after Augustus.

Transnational refers to actions by various nonstate actors, such as private individuals and nongovernmental organizations whose sphere of effective activity transcends the traditional boundaries of the nation-state.

Transubstantiation is a religious doctrine of the Catholic Church that was promulgated at the Fourth Lateran Council in 1215. It explains how the substance of the bread and wine is changed into the body and blood of Jesus during the Eucharist.

Treaty Ports were ports in China opened to almost exclusively for European residents as a result of treaties that the Qing Empire was forced to sign with various European nations. The activities of Europeans residing in China were governed by the laws of their home country, not Chinese law. This legal right was known as extraterritoriality.

Trench Warfare is a type of static warfare in which the opposing forces attack and counterattack from a relatively permanent system of trenches and underground bunkers. It also describes the nature of war on the Western Front during World War I. Both the Germans and the Allies built a series of three lines of virtually continuous trenches on either side of a "No Man's Land." These trenches stretched from the Belgian coast along the English Channel in the north to the Swiss border in the south. almost 440 miles.

Triangular Trade is the name used by historians to describe a series of Atlantic trade routes that developed between the American colonies and Britain in the 1700s. Shippers took rum from New England to Africa, traded the rum for slaves, took the slaves to the Caribbean islands, and brought back sugar to New England to be made into rum. The trade would also deliver raw materials to Britain from the British colonies and, in turn, British manufactured goods would be sent to their colonies.

Tribe was a form of social organization comprised of a confederation of clans that trace their descent from a common ancestor. Typically, a headman or chief was the primary form of political authority. He was constantly required to reaffirm his right to lead the tribe by his deeds. In ancient Rome a tribe was a grouping of Roman citizens based on where they lived. Originally, there were only three tribes, but as the Roman Empire expanded, the number of tribes increased to total of thirty-five (four urban and thirty-one rural).

Tribune was a Roman official who was the primary representative of the plebeians. A tribune was elected by the plebeian assembly to protect plebeians from the arbitrary power of the patrician magistrates. There were ten tribunes that were elected annually. Some of whom became powerful in Roman politics.

Trident is a type of U.S. submarine-launched ballistic missile that is armed with multiple warheads. Trident II missiles have a range of more than 4,000 miles and carry ten to fifteen warheads each.

Tripartite Pact (1940) was an alliance between Germany, Italy, and Japan requiring that they would cooperate together in all future military ventures.

Triple Alliance (1882) was a defensive military alliance formed before World War I by Germany Austria-Hungary, and Italy. It was formed to counter the FrancoRussian Alliance that would later become the Triple Entente. This emerging system of competing alliances undercut the peace achieved in Europe by the Concert of Europe during the 1800s and contributed to the escalation of tensions among the European great powers in Europe, which unexpectedly culminated in the outbreak of World War I.

Triple Entente (1907) was a defensive military alliance formed before World War I that linked France, Britain, and Russia. It was organized to counter the Triple Alliance. With the defection of Russia from the Three Emperor's League, this alliance hemmed in Germany on both its eastern and western borders. During World War I, it was expanded to include Belgium, Italy, Romania, Greece and the United States.

Trireme was a Greek and Phoenician warship of the 5th and 4th centuries BCE. It was sleek and light, powered by 170 oars arranged in three vertical tiers or by sail. Manned by skilled sailors, it was capable of short bursts of speed and complex maneuvers. The Phoenicians introduced the bireme with two decks of oars about 700 BCE.

Trojan War (13th century BCE) was the conflict between the Greeks (Myceneans) and the Trojans that was immortalized in Homer's *Iliad*. Allegedly, the Greeks were avenging the abduction of Helen, the wife of King Menelaus of Sparta. More probably, the war was the result of a commercial dispute or economic rivalry.

Trotsky, Leon (1879–1940) was a Russian revolutionary and one of the members of the Bolshevik party. He played, along with Lenin, a leading role in organizing the October Revolution in 1917. During the Civil War from 1918 to 1921, he built and commanded the Red Army, which eventually defeated the White Russian military forces. After Lenin's death, he was involved in a power struggle with Stalin over the future of socialism in the Soviet Union. Trotsky argued that true socialism could not occur in the Soviet Union until revolutions had occurred throughout the world. By contrast, Stalin contended that socialism could exist in one country. Defeated in this ideological struggle by Stalin, Trotsky was expelled from the Communist Party in 1927 and exiled in 1929. He was murdered in Mexico in 1940, supposedly by a Stalinist agent.

Troubadour was a wandering poet whose poems focused on love, themes especially those having to do with courtly love. They wrote romantic lyrics or tales in the common vernacular and enjoyed the patronage of nobles around Europe beginning in the 1100s.

Troy is the site in northwest Anatolia, overlooking the Hellespont strait, where archaeologists have excavated a series of Bronze Age cities. As reported in Homer's epic poems, the Greeks may have destroyed one of those cities circa 1260 to 1240 BCE. Troy prospered from trade, but its influence in the area had already ended because of an earthquake by the time Homer's Trojan War would have taken place.

Truman Doctrine (1947) was the policy announced, by President Truman, that the United States would provide military and economic aid to any nation in Europe threatened by communist subversion. It was established after Britain announced that it could no longer afford to provide aid to Greece and Turkey in their respective civil wars. This policy would become more commonly known as the "containment" doctrine, which U.S. policymakers would use during the Cold War to support any country whose policymakers were considered to be threatened by communism.

Tsar (Czar) was the title of the Russian emperor. Ivan III, who ruled from 1462 to 1505, first used it. It is similar to the German "Kaiser" and both are derived from the Roman title "Caesar"(emperor).

TU-95, which was also known as the "Bison bomber," was a Soviet jet bomber capable of delivering a nuclear device to the United States. It was was first displayed at the 1955 Moscow Air Show. While there were only ten at the time, Western military strategists believed that the Soviets possessed hundreds of such bombers. With the development of this long-range bomber, the United States lost its monopoly on long-range strategic bombers.

Tudor Dynasty was the name of the royal English dynasty that included Henry VII, his son Henry VIII, Edward VI, Mary I, and Elizabeth I.

Tudor, Mary I (1516–1558) was the Catholic daughter of Henry VII. She reinstated Catholicism in Britain when she took the throne. She was called "Bloody Mary" because of her brutal suppression of Protestants during her five-year reign.

Twelfth Century Renaissance was a period, in the 1100s and 1200s in medieval Europe, in which there was a revival of interest in ancient Greek philosophy and science, Roman law, vernacular literature, and Romanesque and Gothic styles of architecture.

Twenty-One Demands (1915) were a set of demands made by the Japanese government during World War I for special privileges in China that were already allowed to the major European powers. The demands called for confirmation of Japan's railway and mining claims in Shandong province; granting of special concessions in Manchuria; Sino-Japanese control of the Han-Ye-Ping mining base in central China; access to harbors, bays and islands along China's coast; and Japanese control, through advisers, of Chinese financial, political, and police affairs. After China rejected the demands, the Japanese government reduced the demands to thirteen, but gave the Chinese government only two days to decide. Since the Chinese government, led by President Yuan Shikai, was already fighting various local warlords for control of China and he was not in a position to risk war with Japan if he refused to agree to the Japanese demands, Yuan capitulated and entered into a series of agreements with Japan on May 25, 1915. The immediate political reaction to Japan's actions among the Chinese was the emergence of the antiJapanese May Fourth Movement.

Two Treatises on Government (1690) is the title of the book written by John Locke in which he attacked the legitimacy of the rule of absolutist monarchs. His ideas concerning "consent of the governed" would influence the thinking of the authors of the U.S. Constitution.

Tyranny is a form of absolutist government in which the ruler is cruel, unjust, and despotic. A tyrant is someone who seizes and holds political power in violation of the normal laws, procedures, and traditions of a community. Historically, many tyrants were popular leaders welcomed by their subjects.

Tyrant is the term the Greeks used to describe someone who seized and held power in violation of the normal procedures and traditions of the community. They were neither elected nor bound by existing law. Tyrants appeared in many Greek city-states between 700 and 500 BCE, often taking advantage of the disaffection of the emerging middle class. The term did not have the negative connotation that it has today, as many tyrants were popular leaders who were welcomed by the populace.

U-2 was a high altitude U.S. reconnaissance aircraft operated by the Central Intelligence Agency that was shot down over the Soviet Union in May 1960 by a Soviet surface-to-air missile. Its pilot, Gary Powers, was taken prisoner by the Soviet Union. The U-2 was capable of taking pictures from as high as 70,000 feet. Before the development of satellite reconnaissance in the 1970s, the U-2 was used extensively to gather photographic intelligence over the Soviet Union, Vietnam and Cuba. In 1961, after the election of President Kennedy, Premier Khrushchev released Gary Powers, the U-2 pilot.

Ubaid was the culture that flourished in Mesopotamia between 5500 and 4000 BCE that was characterized by large village settlements and temples.

U-Boat is the abbreviation for "Unterseeboot," the German word used to describe a submarine, especially the type that was first used during World War I.

Ugarit was a thriving cosmopolitan port and trading center that emerged along the Mediterranean coast of northern Syria circa 1400 to 1200 BCE. The alphabet invented by scribes from Ugarit is the source of today's widely used Roman alphabet. Ugarit possessed important natural resources and a natural harbor that made it an important international trading center. The elite of Ugarit were known for their literacy, knowledge of other languages and diplomatic skills.

Uighurs were a group of Turkic-speaking people that controlled their own centralized empire in Mongolia and Central Asia from 744 to 840 CE.

Ulama, which means "persons with correct knowledge," refers to Muslim religious scholars who from the 800s onward became the primary interpreters of Islamic law.

Umayyad Caliphate (661–750 CE) was the first hereditary dynasty of caliphs who were not closely related to Muhammad himself, though they traced their ancestry to Umayyah, a member of Muhammad's tribe in Mecca. From their capital in Damascus, they ruled an empire that extended from Spain to India.

Umma is the name for the community of all those individuals who are believers in Islam.

Unconditional Surrender refers to complete and unqualified surrender of the military forces of a nation. During World War II, the Allies demanded the unconditional surrender of Germany and Japan.

Unconscious is a term developed by Sigmund Freud to describe that aspect of the human mind from which he argued humans derive instinctual ideas and impulses of which the conscious mind is not aware. Freud's theory of psychoanalysis describes a complex interaction among three parts of the human psyche: the "id" (the instinctual unconscious), the "ego" (the conscious self) and the "superego" (internalized social and cultural norms).

Underdevelopment refers to a stage of economic development that has been experienced primarily in the post–World War II period by nations that were once colonies of the European imperialist nations. Even though these nations have experienced political independence and self-determination, they depend on the export of natural resources and agricultural crops. Industrialization, if any, is limited and there is low investment of capital, domestic or foreign.

Union is an organization of workers in a particular industry, trade, or profession that has been created to defend the interests of its members through collective bargaining with employers, and strikes, if necessary.

Unipolar is an international system where there is only one dominant military and economic power.

Unitarians were a religious reform movement that began during the Protestant Reformation. They rejected the Christian doctrine of the Holy Trinity. Unitarians also believed in a rationalist interpretation of the Scriptures and argued that Jesus was a divinely inspired man, not God-become man

United Kingdom of Great Britain is a political entity that today comprises the countries of England, Scotland, Wales, and Northern Ireland. The union of England with Wales took place in 1536, with Scotland in 1701, and with Ireland in 1801.

United Nations (UN) (1945) is an international organization of nearly all states in the world that was created after World War II to promote collective security, peace, cooperation, and recognition of human rights. At the time of the formation of the UN, the major powers—the United States, the USSR, France, Great Britain, and China—were afforded the privileged position under the UN Charter of being permanent members of the Security Council, which gives each of them the right of veto.

United Nations Charter is the founding document of the United Nations. It is based on the principles that states are equal, exercise sovereignty over their own affairs, enjoy independence and territorial integrity, and must fulfill international obligations. The Charter also lays out the structure and operations of the United Nations.

United Nations Convention on the Law of the Sea (UNCLOS) (1982) is a multilateral treaty governing use of the oceans. The UNCLOS treaty established rules governing the territorial waters of countries in the wold.

United Nations General Assembly is comprised of the representatives of all states. It allocates UN funds, passes nonbinding resolutions, coordinates third world development programs, and oversees various autonomous agencies through the Economic and Social Council.

United Nations Security Council is a body of five major powers (the United States, Russia, England, France and the Peoples republic of China) and ten rotating member states that make decisions about international peace and security, including the deployment of UN peacekeeping forces.

United States–Japanese Security Treaty (1951) is a bilateral alliance between the United States and Japan, created during the Cold War to respond to the potential Soviet threat to Japan.

The United States maintains troops in Japan and is committed to defend Japan if it is attacked. Japan pays the United States to offset about half the cost of maintaining U.S. troops in Japan.

Universal Declaration of Human Rights (1948) was the declaration issued by the United Nations that enumerated the social, political and economic rights to which all humans are entitled.

Universalism refers to a belief that certain values express truths that transcend all national and cultural boundaries.

University was a degree-granting institution of higher learning created by either a guild of master teachers or by students that first appeared in medieval Europe between the 1100s and 1200s. These universities only offered degrees in the arts, theology, law and medicine. The first universities were in Bologna and Paris.

Upper Egypt is that part of Egypt that runs from the Nile Delta to the border with Sudan.

Urban II, Pope (1035–1099) advocated the formation of the First Crusade at the Council of Clermont in 1095. After receiving a request from Emperor Alexius I for assistance against the Seljuk Turks who had taken over Palestine, Pope Urban appealed to the Christian knights in Europe to stop fighting among themselves and unite to fight a holy war against the true enemy of Christianity, the Muslims. He promised remission of sins to those who would fight and liberate Jerusalem and the Holy Land from the infidels. He said that "All who die by the way, whether by land or sea, or in battle against the pagans, shall have immediate remission of sins." By 1096, four large armies of approximately 100,000 men had been formed.

Ursulines (1535) was a religious order for women organized by Angela Merici (1474–1540). The Ursulines began in Italy and spread to France. They was composed of young, unmarried women who lived with their families, but lived chaste lives. While these unmarried women were subject to the discipline of the Ursulines, they rejected living a cloistered monastic life. They devoted their lives to educating women in moral values.

Ussher Chronology (1642–1644) was the name of a chronology of the history of the world created by James Ussher, the Anglican Archbishop of Armagh. Ussher is one of the first people in the modern period to look back at the broad stretch of human history. He went through the Bible and added up the various dates for such biblical figures as Noah, Joshua, Abraham and others. Based on a literal reading of the Bible, Ussher concluded that the first day of creation began at nightfall on Sunday, October 23, 4004 BCE. Prior to Ussher, there were other Biblically based estimates, such as those of Saint Bede (3952 BCE), Johannes Kepler (3992 BCE) and Sir Isaac Newton (4000 BCE).

Utilitarianism is the liberal philosophy developed by Jeremy Bentham, a British philosopher, in the early 1800s that sought to ensure social harmony through the measurement of pain and pleasure. He argued that the principle of utility, defined as the greatest good for the greatest number of people, should be applied to governmental policymaking as well as economic and judicial decision-making. Democracy was implicit in this theory in that the greatest number of people could ensure their own well-being only by voting for their rulers. Accordingly, the test of any government was its usefulness in meeting the needs of the greatest number of its people.

Utopia is a Latin word for "no-place." It is the name for Thomas More's fictional island kingdom and has become synonymous with the notion of an ideal society that is unattainable.

Utopian Socialism was the ideology that was developed by Charles Fourier in the early 1800s that sought to create humane alternatives to the capitalist system by building self-sustaining communities whose inhabitants would work co-operatively. Fourier dreamt of transforming states, workplaces, and human relations and proposed plans to do so.

Utrecht, Treaty of (1713) was the treaty that ended the War of Spanish Succession. It redistributed territory among the warring nations of Europe and encouraged Britain's colonial conquests in North America.

V

Vandals were a Germanic people who crossed the Rhine in 406. They raided Spain for twenty-five years, crossed into North Africa, and practiced piracy in the Mediterranean. Emperor Justinian defeated them in 532 to 534.

Vassal was a free man (knight) who voluntarily submitted himself to a king or lord by taking an oath of fealty, homage, and loyalty. Vassals owed the king or noble certain services, usually military, and sometimes received in exchange a grant of land known as a fief. Eventually, leading nobles and their vassals formed the social and political elite of Europe.

Velvet Revolution (1989–1990) was the name of the nonviolent mass protests in Czechoslovakia that were led by playwright Vaclev Havel and that culminated in the fall of communism in that country in November 1989.

Verdun, Treaty of (843) divided the Carolingian Empire among Charles the Bald, Louis the German and Lothar I, the three surviving sons of the Emperor Louis I (the Pious). Charles received the western Frankish lands that would later become the kingdom of France. Louis received the eastern Frankish lands that would later become Germany. Lothar received the title of emperor and those lands extending from the North Sea to the Mediterranean that would later become the Netherlands, the Rhineland and northern Italy. The territories of Lothar I would be fought over by France and Germany for centuries.

Vernacular is the native or spoken language of a region or country. In medieval and early modern Europe, Latin was the language used for the writing of literary, scientific, legal, and religious texts. With the growth of the modern nation-state, national vernacular languages such as French, German, Spanish, Dutch, and English replaced Latin.

Versailles is a large, opulent palace built outside Paris by Louis XIV where he and the French nobility resided. The palace was a symbol of French power and a triumph of royal centralized authority over the nobility.

Versailles Conference (Paris Peace Conference) (1919–1920) was the peace conference held by the victorious Allies after World War I that resulted in the Treaty of Versailles.

Versailles, Treaty of (1919) was the treaty between Germany and the Allies (Britain, France, and the United States) that ended World War I. It included the controversial "war guilt clause" and that required Germany to pay reparations of $32 billion. The Treaty also required Germany to dismantle its military and also to surrender valuable territories and colonies. The Treaty was greatly resented by many segments of German society.

Vichy or Vichy Government (1940–1944) was the authoritarian and collaborationist government established in France headed by Marshall Petain in 1940 after France's defeat by Germany during World War II.

Victoria, Queen (1819–1901) was the influential British monarch who reigned from 1837 to 1901. She presided over the expansion of the British Empire and instituted significant political and social reforms. "Victorian Age" is the term used by historians to describe the reign of Queen Victoria of Britain as well as European society in the late 1800s. This society displayed rigid moral standards and sharply differentiated roles and values for men and women and for the middle class and working class.

Victorian Morality refers to the social ethic that emerged among the growing middle class in the 1800s in Britain. It emphasized strict moral principles, especially regarding sex and alcohol. The middle class viewed Queen Victoria as the embodiment of such values.

Viet Cong (National Liberation Front) (1959–1975) was the name used by the American military forces and political leaders to refer to the National Liberation Front, the communist guerrilla organization in South Vietnam formed in 1954. The National Liberation Front also sought to overthrow the South Vietnamese government and reunify North and South Vietnam.

Viet Minh (1941–1960) was the communistled resistance movement formed by Ho Chi Minh in 1941 to seek independence for Vietnam from France as well as to oppose the Japanese occupation during World War II. Due to their opposition to the Japanese, the Viet Minh received funding from the Americans and the Chinese. Nevertheless, the Chinese would imprison Ho Chi Minh for more than a year during the Viet Minh's fight against the Japanese military dictatorship because he was a communist. When Japan surrendered in August 1945, the Japanese handed over control of some public buildings in Hanoi to the Viet Minh and Ho Chi Minh declared the Democratic Republic of Vietnam on September 2, 1945. However, within a few days after the formation of the Democratic Republic of Vietnam, the Chinese Kuomintang Army arrived in Vietnam to supervise the repatriation of the Japanese Imperial Army. The Democratic Republic of Vietnam therefore existed only in theory and effectively controlled no territory. A few months later, the Chinese, Vietnamese, and French came to a three-way understanding. The French gave up certain rights in China, the Viet Minh agreed to the return of the French to Vietnam in exchange for promises of independence within the French Union, and the Chinese agreed to leave. Negotiations between the French and Viet Minh broke down quickly. What followed was nearly ten years of war against France. This was known as the French-Indochina War, or to the Vietnamese, the French War, that lasted from 1945 to 1954.

Vietnam War (1955–1975) was the conflict between North Vietnam and the National Liberation Front guerrillas in South Vietnam and the South Vietnamese government supported by the United States. American military involvement in this conflict deepened dramatically after the Gulf of Tonkin incident in August 1964. By the time the U.S. government withdrew the last of the American troops from Vietnam in 1973, over 2 1/2 million American soldiers had fought in what was then the longest war in American history.

Vietnamization (1968–1973) was the name of the American plan adopted after 1968 by the Nixon administration to turn over control of the Vietnam War to the South Vietnamese government while U.S. troops withdrew from Vietnam.

Vikings (also known as Northmen) is a catchall name for those Scandinavian people who raided Western Europe, the islands in the north Atlantic, and the Slavic areas of Europe between 793 and the 1066 CE.

Villa, Francisco "Pancho" (1878–1923) was one of the three revolutionary leaders of the Mexican Revolution from 1910 to 1920, the other two being Francisco Madero and Emiliano Zapata. Villa led a cowboy army based in Mexico that seized land from the large northern landowners in northern Mexico in 1910. The revolutionary forces of Madero, Zapata and Villa defeated Porfirio Diaz, the unpopular dictator of Mexico. In the wake of the defeat of Diaz, Francisco Madero, a more liberal-oriented politician, was elected president. However, in 1913, General Victoriano Huerta, commander of the Mexican army under Madero, led a coup against Madero, whom Huerta had murdered. With Madero's death, a civil war that would last for years arose between the remnants of Madero's army, the armies led by Zapata, and Villa. Zapata and Villa continued their guerrilla war against Huerta, who had instituted a brutal and ruthless dictatorship. Subsequently, Venustiano Carranza, a more moderate politician, who defeated Huerta and forced him into exile, organized a new national army (the Constitutionalist Army). However, efforts by Carranza in 1914 to gain the support of Villa failed and Villa continued the civil war against Carranza. As part of his efforts against Carranza, who was supported by the United States, Villa attacked two towns in New Mexico in 1916, killing thirty-four Americans. In response to those attacks, President Wilson sent a military force led by General John J. Pershing to Mexico to capture Villa, which Pershing was unable to do. After the overthrow of the Carranza government in 1920, Villa was granted a pardon by the new Mexican government for his political activities during the Mexican Revolution as well as a ranch in northern Mexico. Villa was later assassinated on that ranch in 1923.

Villanovans is the name given to the Iron Age peoples from northern Italy that existed from 1000 to 800 BCE. They made iron tools and placed the ashes of their dead in large urns.

Virgil (70–19 BCE) was a Roman poet and author of the *Aeneid*, the great patriotic epic of Rome that was influenced by Homer's *Iliad* and the *Odyssey*. He greatly admired Augustus for ending the civil wars that raged in Rome and bringing order to Rome. As a patron of Virgil, Augustus asked him to write a grand opus that would glorify the imperial achievements of Rome. After ten years of work, Virgil produced the *Aeneid*, but died before it was completed. On his death bed, Virgil asked Augustus to destroy the *Aeneid*, but Augustus refused. In the *Aeneid*, Virgil stated that Augustus was a god and the greatest ruler of the Roman Empire.

Virtus was one of the principal cultural values of ancient Rome, which translated means "manliness" or "toughness." From its founding, Rome was primarily an agricultural and martial culture that stressed manliness, simplicity, strength, and toughness.

Visigoths were a Germanic federation of tribes who served as allied troops for the Romans along the western frontiers of the Roman Empire. After being threatened by the Huns, they crossed the Danube into Roman territory and settled in the Balkans circa 376 CE. They defeated a Roman army in 378 and sacked Rome in 410. They expanded their rule into parts of Spain and southern France.

Vizier was the title of the highest ranking government official in ancient Egypt. A vizier was the chief minister and advisor to the pharaohs who appointed him. In that capacity, a vizier was responsible for administering the daily functioning of the pharaoh's palace and overseeing the daily administration of the pharaoh's government. All government documents issued in ancient Egypt had to have the seal of the vizier in order to be considered authentic and binding. In view of his extensive duties and authority, a vizier was considered to be the second most powerful individual in ancient Egypt after the pharaoh. Viziers were selected by the pharaohs based on their talent and loyalty and were answerable only to the pharaoh. While a vizier was a trusted confidant of the pharaoh, a vizier was neither a member of the royal family nor an heir to the throne. By the time of the New Kingdom, there were two viziers, one for Upper Egypt and one for Lower Egypt. Imhotep, who is considered to be the earliest known architect and engineer in ancient Egypt, designed and built the stepped pyramid and served as vizier under

King Djoser, the second king of the Third Dynasty (27th century BCE). The office of vizier was adopted by Muslim societies beginning with the Abbasid Caliphate (750–1517 CE) during which the vizier was appointed by the caliph. During the Ottoman Empire (1299–1922/23 CE), the office of vizier continued to be an influential governmental position. But, the title of vizier was changed to "Grand Vizier", who was appointed by the sultan.

Vladivostok Accords (1974) was the bilateral arms control agreement signed by President Ford and Premier Brezhnev that set a limit of 2400 offensive nuclear weapons that each side could possess.

Vo Nguyen Giap (1912–2013) was the Vietnamese political and military leader who use of guerrilla and conventional military tactics led the Viet Minh and later the National Liberation Front and North Vietnam to victory over the French in the First Indochina War (1946–1954) and United States in the Second Indochina War (1955–1973)

Volkish Thought was the belief that emerged in the late 1800s in Germany that German culture was superior to all other cultures in the world and that the German people had a universal mission to save Western civilization from inferior races.

Volksgeist, which is a German word meaning "people's spirit" or "soul of the people," was a term developed by Johann Gottfried von Herder, a German philosopher. Herder argued that a nation's spirit would not come to maturity unless people studied their own unique culture and traditions. Herder gave Germans new pride in their origins, rejecting the Greco-Roman cultural traditions that many considered the source of European culture. He urged Germans to glory in their language. His extensive collection of folk-poetry began a great craze in Germany for that neglected topic. Herder was one of the first to argue that language determines thought. Herder's focus on language and cultural traditions as the ties that create a "nation" extended to include folklore, dance, music, and art. He attached great importance to the concepts of nationality and patriotism. Herder carried his folk theory to an extreme by maintaining that "there is only one class in the state, the *Volk*, and the king belongs to this class as well as the peasant."

Voltaire (1694–1778) was the pseudonym of Francois Marie Arouet, a noted French writer and deist who advocated rationalism and the cause of human dignity. His satirical writing and philosophical critiques targeted Christianity, intolerance, and tyranny. He is the author of *Candide*. He became the most prolific and influential of all of the authors of the French Enlightenment. He became internationally renowned for his popularization of natural philosophy and his campaign on behalf of religious toleration. As a result of the publication of his *Philosophical Letters* in 1734, he was banished from Paris. This banishment was not lifted until 1778.

Voluntary Association refers to the idea enunciated by John Calvin that a Protestant church should be regarded as group of people who have willingly decided to become members of that church and that all church members should participate in decisions regarding their church. This innovative concept was based on Martin Luther's belief that the church should be a "priesthood of all believers." According to Luther, since all Christian believers should be free from authority or coercion in religious matters, authority in the church should be vested in all Christians, not simply a select hierarchy of priests, bishops, cardinals, or popes. The ideas of Luther and Calvin had far-reaching unintended social and political consequences in terms of European and American history. The idea that a social organization, such as a church, should be governed by its members contributed to the development of social contract theory, human rights, and representative democracy. These ideas contributed to undercutting the legitimacy of monarchical government.

Vouillé, Battle of (507 CE) was the armed conflict between the Franks and the Visigoths over Visigothic land (Aquitaine, Languedoc and Roussillon) that were considered to be part of Gaul by the Franks. King Clovis I of the Franks defeated King Alaric II of the Visigoths, who was killed in the battle. The defeat contributed to the emergence of political battles, for almost sixty years, among the Visigoths over who would succeed Alaric and control the Visigothic kingdom in the Iberian Peninsula.

Vulgate was the Latin translation of the Hebrew Bible and the Greek New Testament by Jerome in the 300s CE that became the standard bible used by the Catholic Church in the Middle Ages. It was called the Vulgate because it was to be the Bible for the "people" (vulgus), whose language was Latin.

Waldensians were medieval heretics in the 1100s who advocated biblical simplicity in reaction to the increasing worldliness of the Catholic Church. They proposed that the laity had the right to preach and administer the sacraments.

Waldseemuller, Martin (1470–1518/21) published a map in 1507 calling the lands discovered by Columbus the "New World."

Walesa, Lech (1943–present) was the leader of the Polish Solidarity movement. He was president of Poland from 1990–1995.

Wang Mang (33 BCE–23 CE) was an official at the Han court who seized power in the 9 CE and proclaimed his own dynasty, the Xin. He instituted various reforms, but following his death in 23 CE, the Liu family reclaimed the throne.

Wanli (1563–1620) was the Chinese emperor who ruled from 1572 to 1620 during the Ming Dynasty. Refusing to meet with his governmental officials, his inaction contributed to the decline of the Ming Dynasty.

Wannsee Conference (1942) was a meeting held near Berlin on January 20, 1942 to coordinate the implementation of the "Final Solution to the Jewish Problem." This meeting established the administrative apparatus for achieving Hitler's dream of a Europe free of Jews.

War Communism was the economic policy adopted by the Bolsheviks during the Russian Civil War (1918–1921) to nationalize industry and seize banks, railroads, grain stockpiles, and private land.

War Guilt Clause was the section of the Versailles Treaty, Clause 231, that assigned responsibility for starting World War I to Germany and Austria. This clause also required Germany to pay reparations to the Allies for the damages the Allies suffered as a result of World War I.

War of National Liberation is an armed conflict fought by indigenous nationalist military groups against an imperial power in the name of national self-determination. A war of national liberation is fought using guerrilla tactics. The main purpose of these tactics is to increase the political cost of occupation of the imperial/colonial power. A war of national liberation depends on civilians providing crucial intelligence and logistic support. Some historians contend that the first war of national liberation in modern history was the American War for Independence from 1775 to 1783. More recently, the Vietnam War was characterized by the National Liberation Front and North Vietnam as a war of national liberation.

War of the Roses (1455–1485) was the series of civil wars in Britain between the Lancaster and York dynasties for the English throne. Both dynastic families claimed descent from sons of King Edward III. Each side of this civil war was symbolized by either a red (Lancaster) or white (York) rose. Henry VII, a member of the Lancaster family, won the conflict.

War of the Trousers was a phrase used to refer to the increasing influence of Western fashion on the Soviet Union in the late 1950s and early 1960s that was evident in the popularity of "narrow trousers." Special police patrols were organized to root out such influences.

Warlord is a person who uses military force to control a country or region of a country. Warlordism is a term used by historians to describe a period of political chaos and anarchy that developed after the formation of the Republic of China until the victory of the communists in 1949.

Warring States Period (476–221 BCE) refers to that period of Chinese history from the 5th century through the late 3rd century BCE during which there was prolonged warfare. During the

Warring States Period, stronger states began to conquer weaker states until only a few remained. Eventually, the state of Qin defeated the last of its rivals, destroying the southern kingdom of Chu in 221 BCE.

Warsaw Pact (1955–1991) was the military alliance formed by the Soviet Union and other communist states in response to the creation of NATO, the rearmament of West Germany, and West Germany's inclusion in NATO. The purpose of the Warsaw Pact was to act as a buffer against NATO. It permitted the stationing of Soviet troops in Eastern Europe until it was disbanded in 1991.

Water Frame (1769) was a water-powered machine invented by Richard Arkwright to produce a more durable cotton fabric. This invention led to the shift in the production of cotton textiles from rural households to factories.

Water Wheel was a mechanism that harnessed the energy of flowing water to grind grain or power machinery. It was an especially common source of power in Europe between the 1200s and 1900s, before it was replaced by the use of steam power.

Waterloo, Battle of (1815) was the battle that marked the end of Napoleonic domination in Europe. After escaping from Elba and returning to France while the nations of Europe were meeting at the Congress of Vienna, Napoleon again retook the French throne. The British Duke of Wellington led the allied forces of Prussia, Russia, and Austria that defeated Napoleon. The massive size of Wellington's army and the combined tactical mistakes of Napoleon's generals were two of the most important factors contributing to Napoleon's defeat. As a result of his defeat, Napoleon was forced into exile on the island of St, Helena in the Atlantic around 1200 miles from the west coast of Africa.

Watt, James (1736–1819) was a Scottish inventor and scientist who invented the condenser and other improvements that made the steam engine a more practical source of power for industry and transportation.

Weapons of Mass Destruction are nuclear, chemical, and biological weapons, all of which are distinguished from conventional weapons by their enormous potential for indiscriminate human and physical destruction.

Wedgwood, Josiah (1730–1795) was the English industrialist whose pottery factory was the first to mass-produce fine-quality pottery.

Weimar Republic (1919–1933) was the liberal democratic government that was established in Germany at the end of World War I. It would last until Hitler's rise to power in 1933. The German General Staff would use the existence of the Weimar Republic as a scapegoat for the German defeat in World War I and the harsh peace terms to which Germany had to agree at the Versailles Peace Conference. The Weimar constitution called for an elected President, a Chancellor (Prime Minister) appointed by the President, a Cabinet of Ministers appointed by the Chancellor, and an elected house of representatives called the Reichstag, which acted more in an advisory capacity than an actual legislative one. The real governing powers rested with the Chancellor while the President retained veto power over the actions of the Chancellor.

Welfare State is a term used to refer to a government or a society that adopts large-scale social welfare programs while still maintaining a capitalist economy. These types of government programs became prevalent in Western European capitalist countries after World War II.

Weltpolitik (1897), which means "world politics" in German, is the term used to describe the policy of Kaiser Wilhelm II to make Germany a world economic and military power. Wilhelm II used nationalist appeals and threats to implement this policy.

Wergild (800s-1100s CE), which means "money for a man," was a term used in Germanic societies to refer to what an individual was worth in case he or she suffered an injury. It was the amount of compensation that was to be paid in gold by a wrongdoer's family to a victim's family in place of blood vengeance. Germanic tribal leaders used it to reduce internal hostilities.

Western Front (1914–1918) was a series of continuous military trenches and fortifications built during World War I that stretched without break from Switzerland through France and Belgium to the English Channel.

Western World is a term used by historians to refer to the societies of Western, Central, and Eastern Europe and those countries whose ethnic, cultural, and linguistic traditions are derived from European culture. However, the definition of the Western World has changed over time. Ancient Romans distinguished between Oriental (Eastern) cultures that inhabited present-day Egypt and Turkey and Occidental cultures that lived in the West. A thousand years later, the East–West Schism separated the Catholic Church from the Eastern Orthodox Church. Furthermore, the Western World expanded to include Russia when Peter the Great brought back ideas from France. Today, the Western World generally includes the nations of North and South America; Western, Central, and Eastern Europe; Russia; Australia; and New Zealand. Widening this definition, however, invites controversy. Some people add Israel to the definition of Western World because Western culture is rooted in a Jewish-Christian tradition. The Jewish community also has historical and cultural ties with Europe, and Israel is a member of a number of European organizations. South Africa is also considered by some to be part of the Western World because of its languages (English, Afrikaans), its religion (Christianity), its political system (democratic), and its economic system (capitalism). The Philippines are sometimes considered part of the Western World because of the influence on Spanish and English as well as Catholicism on its society.

Westernization is a process by which a country, a society, or a group of people adopts the values, customs, cultural patterns, and political and economic institutions associated with European and American culture. This process has been accelerating throughout the world since the 1400s as a result initially of European global political and economic expansion. Westernization culminated in the 1900s, when, after World War II, many smaller states that had once been colonies of European nations gained their political independence and adopted some aspects of Western culture. Indeed, as a result of technological advances in communication and transportation since the 1400s, many people throughout the world have adopted European languages and customs, sometimes willingly, but generally unwillingly as a result of European and American imperialism and colonialism. During the period of decolonization after World War II, many ex-colonies frequently reacted against the impact of Western culture on their societies by adopting nationalistic and projectionist policies. Today, westernization is often regarded as a part of the ongoing process of globalization. Proponents of globalization often argue that western culture has led to globalization and that globalization leads to greater westernization.

Whigs (1650s–1850s) were members of a political party in Britain in the 1600s that supported the Protestant succession to the British throne and advocated a constitutional monarchy. They were typically associated with social and parliamentary reform. The Tories opposed them.

White House (Moscow) refers to the Russian parliament building that became the rallying point for Boris Yeltsin and crowds of Muscovites during the failed coup to overthrow Mikhail Gorbachev in 1991.

White Russians (Whites) were those Russian counterrevolutionaries opposed to the Bolsheviks, who were known as the "Reds," in the Russian Civil War that lasted from 1918 to 1921. The Whites were comprised of former supporters of the tsarist monarchy, Social Democrats, and socialists.

Wilhelm II (1859–1944) was the German emperor (Kaiser) who ruled Germany from 1888 to 1918. His aggressive international, commercial, and military policies severely aggravated international tensions in Europe and contributed to the outbreak of World War I.

Will to Power is an idea enunciated by Friedrich Nietzsche in which he claimed that human beings have a fundamental biological and psychological drive to control and dominate the personal and social lives of other people. From his perspective, this instinct is both healthy and noble.

William of Occam (1290–1349 CE) was an English Franciscan friar and philosopher whose ideas challenged the legitimacy of the Catholic Church during the Avignon Papacy. After witnessing the conduct of the Avignon Papacy, he argued that the Avignon popes were heretics. He questioned the pope's authority and argued that individual piety should be the cornerstone of religious life. He also questioned the connection between reason and faith that had been developed by Thomas Aquinas. He claimed that all governments should have limited powers, be accountable to those it governs and that the church and state should be separate. Occam's ideas were condemned as heresy by the Catholic Church. By the late 1300s, many thinkers began to agree with Occam. They believed that the Catholic Church should be reformed by holding periodic councils that represented all of the members of the Church. Those individuals would be called "conciliarists."

William the Conqueror (1028–1087 CE) was the Duke of Normandy who crossed the English Channel and defeated King Harold II for the English throne in 1066. He imposed a centralized feudal system on England and introduced French as the official language.

Wilson, Woodrow (1856–1924) was the U.S. president and leading figure at the Paris Peace Conference of 1919 who was unable to persuade the U.S. Congress to ratify the Treaty of Versailles or join the League of Nations after World War I.

Wind Wheels was the name for the prevailing patterns in the Atlantic and Pacific Oceans north and south of the equator, the discovery of which made sailing much safer and quicker.

Window of Vulnerability (1980) was the claim made by President Reagan in his 1980 presidential campaign that the Soviet Union had a nuclear advantage over the United States. Although the claim may have contributed to his victory, (similar to the 1960 missile gap claim), no such window of vulnerability existed.

Winter Solstice occurs at the instant when the sun's position in the sky is at its greatest angular distance on the other side of the equatorial plane as the observer. The winter solstice occurs sometime between December 20 and 23 each year in the Northern Hemisphere and between June 20 and 23 in the Southern Hemisphere. Worldwide, interpretation of the event has varied from culture to culture, but most cultures hold holidays, festivals, gatherings, rituals, or other celebrations around that time.

Witch-Hunt was the name of the judicial prosecutions of alleged witches by secular courts during the 1500s and 1600s in Europe and North America. During that period, there were approximately 100,000 trials. Some scholars estimate that one-third of the accused were executed. Other scholars estimate that between 50-60,000 individuals were killed. Unmarried and widowed women comprised about 75% to 80% of the accused. These women were often tortured to make a confession and required to accuse others of witch-craft.

Witte, Sergei (1849–1915) was the Russian minister for finance in the late 1800s who advocated industrialization. He wrote the October Manifesto of 1905, the precursor to Russia's first constitution.

Wollstonecraft, Mary (1759–1797) was an English feminist and author of *A Vindication of the Rights of Woman,* in which she stated her views of women: "I do not wish them to have power over men; but over themselves." She argued for equality of the sexes and that women should be educated. She applied Enlightenment political ideas to the issue of gender.

Women's Rights Convention (1848) was a meeting of women in Seneca Falls, New York, to discuss women's rights after the women had been excluded from an international anti-slavery meeting.

Women's Suffrage was the political movement that developed in the late 1800s and early 1900s in Europe and the United States that advocated legal and political rights for women, including the right to vote.

World Bank (1944), formally the International Bank for Reconstruction and Development, was established in 1944 as a source of loans to help reconstruct the war-torn European economies and poor countries. Later, the main borrowers of the World Bank were Third World countries and, in the 1990s, Eastern European countries.

World Court (International Court of Justice) (1945) is the judicial arm of the United Nations that is located in The Hague. While it hears only cases between states, it does issue advisory opinions.

World Trade Organization (WTO) (1995) is an international organization composed of 164 members and 22 observer states that seeks to promote freer trade throughout the world. Since its formation, WTO meetings have drawn large demonstrations of anti-globalization groups.

Worldview is a complex, dynamic, and some-times contradictory series of interrelated ideas, observations, symbols, practices, propositions, and perspectives on the social, political, cultural, economic, intellectual, scientific, and religious elements that define a culture and an individual's role within that culture.

Wu Di (circa 156–87 BCE) was an emperor of the Han Dynasty who launched military campaigns to expand the empire and promoted the synthesis of Confucian, Daoist, and Legalist thought. He ruled from 141 to 87 BCE.

Wu Sangui (1612–1678 CE) was a Chinese general who allowed the Manchus to cross the Great Wall in 1644. He was given a large territory to govern in South China, but rebelled in 1673 in the last serious challenge to the new Qing Dynasty.

Wu Zetian (624–705 CE) was a concubine in the harem of Emperor Li Shimin. She assumed the throne for herself in 690 and became the only woman ever to rule China in her own name. She abdicated in 705 when the Tang Dynasty was restored.

Wycliffe, John (1328–1384) was an English religious reformer and theologian who argued against the power of the Catholic Church to make papal levies on Englishmen. He also claimed that the English king and parliament could limit power of the Catholic Church in England. He believed in a doctrine of equality and rejected the concept of transubstantiation.

X

Xenophon (430–350 BCE) was an Athenian aristocrat, soldier, and writer whose literary works included history, biography, and political pamphlets as well as instruction manuals on cavalry tactics, hunting, and household management. He wrote histories of the final years of the Peloponnesian Wars.

Xerxes I of Persia (Xerxes the Great) (519–465 BCE) was the fourth king of the Achaemenid Empire. He was the son of Darius I whose army was defeated at the Battle of Marathon in 490 BCE. Xerxes led the second invasion of Greece in 480–479 BCE in response to that defeat. Using two pontoon bridges that his army constructed across the Hellespont, he invaded Greece in 480 BCE. His invasion is best known for the Battles of Thermopylae, Salamis, and Plataea. After his defeats at Salamis and Plataea, he withdrew his forces from Greece and returned to Persia where he completed a number of unfinished construction projects at Susa and Persepolis. He was murdered by the commander of his royal bodyguard in 465 BCE.

Xia (2070–1600 BCE) was an early Chinese Dynasty known primarily through legend.

Xianyang was the capital of the Qin Dynasty.

Xinjian is a western Chinese province that was conquered in the early years of the Qing Dynasty.

Xiongnu was a confederation of nomadic peoples living on the northwest frontier of ancient China. Chinese officials referred to them as "barbarians."

Xuanzong (685–762 CE) was an emperor of the Tang Dynasty who reigned from 712 to 756. He presided over a long period of growth and stability. Over time, however, he withdrew from active participation in court life and devoted himself to his favorite concubine, Yang Guifei. His jealousy was exploited by officials that led to the rebellion of An Lushan.

Y

Yahweh is the sacred Hebrew name for God, which in Latin became "Jehovah." Yahweh appeared to Moses on Mount Sinai and made a covenant with the Hebrews.

Yalta Conference (1945) was the second meeting during World War II between President Roosevelt, Prime Minister Winston Churchill, and Premier Josef Stalin that occurred in the southern Russian city of Yalta from February 4 to 11, 1945. The three Allied leaders met to discuss the occupation of postwar Germany and Eastern Europe, the preparations for ending the war in the Pacific, and the post–World War II world. They agreed that: (1) Nazi Germany must unconditionally surrender and that after the war Germany would be split into four occupied zones, with a quadripartite occupation of Berlin as well; (2) France would get the fourth occupation zone in Germany and Austria, carved out from the British and American zones, and France would also be granted a seat in the Allied Control Council; (3) Germany would undergo demilitarization and denazification; (4) an Allied reparation council would be established, with its seat in Moscow; (5) the Provisional Government of the Republic of Poland that had been set up by the Red Army would be reorganized by the inclusion of other groups such as the Polish Provisional Government of National Unity, to be followed by democratic elections; (6) the Polish eastern border would basically follow the Curzon Line, and Poland would receive substantial territorial compensation in the west from Germany; (7) the Soviet Union would participate in the United Nations once it was agreed that each of the five permanent members of the Security Council would have veto power; and (8) the Soviet Union would enter the fight against Japan ninety days after the defeat of Germany and the Soviet Union would receive the southern part of Sakhalin and the Kurile islands after the defeat of Japan.

Yang Guifei (died 756 CE) was the daughter of an official who became a consort of the emperor Xuanzong who reigned from 712–756. They became so close that she influenced his decisions on government.

Yang Jian (Wendi) (541–604 CE) was a Chinese general who led a revolt and established his own dynasty, the Sui, in 581.

Yangshao Culture (5000–3000 BCE) was an early Chinese culture and society.

Yangzi is a river in central China around which developed a rice culture.

Yao (circa 2356–2255 BCE) was a legendary ruler in ancient China.

Yellow Badge or Yellow Patch, also referred to as a Jewish badge, was a cloth patch that Jews were ordered to sew on their outer garments in order to mark them as Jews in public. It was intended to be a badge of shame. In both Christian and Islamic countries, persons not of the dominant religion were intermittently compelled by sumptuary laws to wear badges, hats, bells or other items of clothing that distinguished them from members of the dominant religious group. While anti-Judaism was less pronounced in the Muslim countries, Jews were still required to wear distinctive marks. The yellow badge was first introduced by a caliph in Baghdad in the 800s and spread to Europe in 1215 when the Fourth Lateran Council (1215) ruled that Jews must wear a yellow badge. However, the key distinguishing mark of Jewish dress in Europe during the Middle Ages was the Jewish hat (or "Judenhut"), a cone-shaped hat. From the 1500s, onward the use of the Judenhut declined, but the yellow badge continued to be worn in certain countries in Europe until the 1700s. The identifying mark for Jews varied from one country to another and from one period to another. Apart from the Judenhut, the most common form of badge was the "rota" (Latin for "wheel"), which looked like a ring of white or yellow. In England, the Statute of Jewry prescribed "the form of two Tables joined, of yellow felt of the length of six inches and of the breadth of three inches". This shape — two separate strips or two joined round-topped rectangles — was particular to England. In Portugal a red Star of David was used. After the German invasion of Poland in 1939, there were initially different local decrees forcing Jews to wear a distinctive sign such as a white armband with a blue Star of David on it or a yellow badge in the form of a Star of David on the left side of the breast and on the back. The requirement to wear the Star of David with the word *Jude* (German for Jew) inscribed on it was required in 1941 of all Jews over the age of six in Germany and all German-occupied territories in Europe during World War II.

Yellow Press refers to newspapers that arose in the late 1800s in the United States that sought to increase circulation by featuring sensationalist reporting that would supposedly appeal to the masses of people.

Yeoman is the name given to a farmer in England-history who cultivated his own land.

Yin and Yang were complimentary elements in Chinese philosophy that helped to maintain the equilibrium of the world. Yang is associated with masculine, light, and active qualities. Yin is associated with feminine, dark, and passive qualities.

Yongle (1360–1424 CE) was the dynastic name for the reign of Emperor Zhu Di, the third emperor of the Ming Dynasty, who ruled China from 1403 to 1424. He sponsored the building of the Forbidden City in Beijing, the development of a huge encyclopedia project, the reopening of China to trade and travel, and the naval expeditions of Zheng He.

Young Turks (1889–1918), was the name for a group of nationalist Turkish military officers and intellectuals who wanted to transform the Ottoman Empire into a more modern, westernized state. They were also known as the Committee of Union and Progress. They overthrew the Sultan of the Ottoman Empire, Abdul Hamid II. This group of military officers and intellectuals controlled Turkey during World War I. Today, the term is used to refer a group which advocates political, social and economic reform and modernization.

Yu was the legendary founder of the Xia Dynasty circa 2070 BCE.

Yuan Dynasty (1271–1368 CE) was the Chinese dynasty founded by the Mongol leader Khubilai Khan, the grandson of Genghis Khan.

Yuan Shikai (1859–1916) was a military leader of the late Qing Dynasty in China. He commanded the modernized Beiyang Army in northern China. In 1898, he supported the suppression of political reformers in China. In 1911, he negotiated the abdication of the emperor and became the first president of the new Republic of China, which lasted only briefly from 1912 to 1916. He opposed the democratic movement led by Sun Yat-sen and attempted to assume the imperial throne in 1916.

Zaibatsu is a Japanese term that refers to the "financial cliques," or business conglomerates, whose influence and size allowed for control over significant parts of the Japanese economy. The term *zaibatsu* was used in the late 1800s and the first half of the 1900s to refer to large family-controlled banking and industrial combines in Japan. Mitsubishi, Mitsui, Sumitomo, and Yasuda are the four most historically significant zaibatsu groups. After the Russo-Japanese War, a number of so-called "second-tier" zaibatsus also emerged, mostly as the result of business conglomerations. Some more famous second-tier zaibatsu included the Okura, Furukawa, Nakajima, and Nissan groups. The zaibatsu were dissolved during the American occupation of Japan after World War II. Specifically, the assets of the controlling families were seized, holding companies were eliminated, and interlocking directorships were outlawed. Among the zaibatsu that were dissolved in 1946 were: Asano, Furukawa, Nakajima, Nissan, Nomura, Okura, and Matsushita. However, complete dissolution of the zaibatsu was never achieved because American policymakers during the Cold War came to view the reindustrialization of Japan as an important bulwark against the growing influence of communism in Asia.

Zama, Battle of (202 CE) was the decisive battle in the Second Punic War between Rome and Carthage. After Rome's victory, the Carthaginian Empire disappeared and was absorbed into the Roman Empire.

Zapata, Emiliano (1879–1919) was one of the three revolutionary leaders of the Mexican Revolution from 1910 to 1920, the other two being Francisco Madero and Pancho Villa. Zapata led a peasant army based in southern Mexico that sought agrarian reform (land redistribution). Upon the defeat of Porfirio Diaz, the unpopular dictator of Mexico, by Zapata's forces, Francisco Madero, a more liberal-oriented politician, was elected president. However, when Madero failed to redistribute land to the peasants, Zapata began a guerrilla war against the Madero-led central government and established a land reform program in those areas of Mexico that the Zapata forces controlled. In 1913, General Victoriano Huerta, commander of the Mexican army under Madero, led a coup against Madero, whom Huerta had murdered. Zapata continued his guerrilla war against Huerta, who had instituted a brutal and ruthless dictatorship. Subsequently, Venustiano Carranza, a more moderate politician, who defeated Huerta and forced him into exile, organized a new national army (the Constitutionalist Army). However, efforts by Carranza in 1914 to gain the support of Zapata failed, and Zapata continued the civil war against Carranza until 1919, when Carranza's forces ambushed and killed Zapata.

Zealot was the name of a group of Jews from Galilee who fled to Jerusalem during the early stages of the Jewish War against Rome in 666 to 670. They overthrew the governing aristocracy in Jerusalem and urged violent resistance to Roman rule.

Zeitgeist is a German expression that means "the spirit of the age." It is typically used to describe the dominant intellectual and cultural climate of an era. German Romantic writers used the concept extensively. Those German Romantic writers treated the Zeitgeist as a historical character rather than as a generalized description for an era.

Zemstvos were locally elected village or regional assemblies established throughout the Russian Empire during the reign of Alexander II. The landowners, townspeople, and peasants would elect representatives.

Zen Buddhism is the Japanese version of Chan Buddhism.

Zeng Guofan (1811–1872) was a Chinese military leader and government official who led the Hunan army against the Taipings in the 1860s and played a leading role in the SelfStrengthening Movement.

Zeno of Citium (334–262 BCE) was a Greek philosopher who was the founder of Stoicism.

Zero Option refers to the proposal by the Western German peace movement that was later adopted by the Reagan administration that called for the ban of all European intermediaterange nuclear forces.

Zero-Sum Games involve a situation in which one actor's gain is by definition equal to the other's loss, as opposed to a non-zero-sum game, in which it is possible for both actors to gain or lose.

Zhang Xueliang (1901–2001) was a warlord in northwestern China who placed Chiang Kaishek under house arrest in December 1936 in order to coerce him into forming a new alliance with the communists to resist Japanese aggression. After the negotiations concluded and Chiang was released, Chiang placed Zhang under arrest. The Nationalists in Taiwan held him until 1996.

Zheng He (1371–1433) was a Muslim eunuch in the imperial court of Zhu Di in China who led a series of overseas voyages that took the gigantic ships of the Chinese navy through the Indian Ocean to Southeast Asia, India, and the east coast of Africa.

Zhou Dynasty (1046–256 BCE) was the Chinese dynasty that conquered the Shang Dynasty in northern China. The rulers of the Zhou Dynasty developed the concept of the "mandate of Heaven" to justify their rule. The era of the centralized Zhou Dynasty was characterized by respect for Chinese tradition and prosperity. However, during the period from 771 to 221 BCE, the centralized control of the Zhou rulers broke down and warfare became frequent among the many small states that comprised the Zhou Empire. Confucianism, Daoism, and Legalism, the foundational ideas of Chinese social and political thought, were developed during this dynasty.

Zhu Xi (1130–1200) was a philosopher who brought ideas about natural patterns and principles and the nature of moral values together to form the school of *Daoxue*, the "Learning of the Way." His interpretations of the Confucian classics became the standard for the imperial examination system from the mid-1200s on.

Zhu Yuanzhang (1328–1398) was a founding emperor of the Ming Dynasty. He rose from being an impoverished orphan to become leader of the rebels known as the Red Turbans at the end of the Yuan Dynasty. In 1368, he defeated the last Mongol forces and established his new regime. Fearful about the political and social influence of the literati, he launched repeated purges of his officials, which claimed tens of thousands of victims.

Ziggurat was a massive stepped pyramid made of mudbricks. Ziggurats were built as religious complexes in ancient Mesopotamian cities beginning circa 2000 BCE.

Zimbabwe is the present name of the former British colony of Southern Rhodesia. It gained independence in 1980.

Zionism was the nationalist Jewish political movement that was founded in Europe in 1897 to create an independent Jewish state in Palestine, which was considered to be the Biblical home (Zion) of the Jewish people. The movement contended that the Jewish people constituted a nation and that they were entitled to a national homeland. In the late 1800s, some European Jews led by Theodor Herzl argued that in the face of growing anti-Semitism, Jews would only be safe in their own nation. The idea of a Jewish homeland became a reality in 1948 with the creation of Israel.

Zollverein (1834) was a free-trade customs union established by Prussia in 1819 in which member states adopted the Prussian customs regulations. The Hohenzollerns of Prussia sought to use this customs union as a means to overcome the fragmented nature of the German economy and facilitate unification under the auspices of Prussia. By 1860, Prussia had incorporated all of the other German states into this union while excluding Austria. As a result of these efforts by Prussia, it made itself the economic leader of Germany.

Zoroastrianism is a monotheistic religion founded by Zarathustra (Zoroaster in Greek) some during the 6th century BCE that emphasized the duality of good and evil and the role of individuals in determining their own fate. It was the religion of the Achaemenid and Sassanid Persians. It centered on a single benevolent deity—Ahuramazda—who engaged in a twelve-thousand-year struggle with demonic forces before prevailing and restoring a pristine world. Emphasizing truth-telling, purity, and reverence for nature, the religion demanded that humans choose sides in the struggle between good (light) and evil (darkness).

Zulus were an African tribe who, under the leadership of King Shaka, created a warrior state in southern Africa in the early 1800s.

Zwingli, Huldrych (1484–1531) was the town preacher of Zurich who became the leader of the Protestant Reformation in Switzerland and founder of the Swiss Reformed Churches. While a priest, Zwingli publicly started questioning the dogma of the Catholic Church. Independently of Martin Luther, Zwingli arrived at similar conclusions by studying the Scriptures from the point of view of a humanist scholar. His theology emphasized the importance of community in the salvation of individuals. Zwingli was killed in a battle against the Roman Catholics.

Zyklon B was the commercial name for hydrogen cyanide, a poisonous gas used in the Nazi euthanasia program and at Auschwitz. The poison was produced by a firm controlled by I. G. Farben. Zyklon B was delivered to the camps in the form of pellets in air-tight containers. When the pellets were exposed to the air they turned into a deadly gas that would asphyxiate victims within minutes.

Biography

Dr. Meyrowitz is a professor of history and international studies at Macomb Community College. He teaches courses on Western Civilization, modern European history, world history since 1750, international relations, the Holocaust and the Vietnam War. He has also taught this curriculum, plus 20th century American history and international security, at numerous other institutions of higher education, including the University of Pennsylvania, University of Maryland in Japan, Wayne State University and Lawrence Technological University.

After service in Vietnam as an U.S.Armyparatrooper, Dr. Meyrowitz received a B. A. with Honors in Political Science from the University of North Carolina (under the Disabled Veterans Retraining Program), a J.D. from Rutgers University School of Law-Newark, and a M.A. and Ph.D. in History from the University of Pennsylvania.

In 1982, he was an Adjunct Professor of Law at the Benjamin N. Cardozo School of Law at Yeshiva University where he taught one of the first law courses in an American law school dealing with the status of nuclear weapons under international law. In addition, for over 15 years, he was Adjunct Professor of Law at Michigan State University College of Law, where he taught Nuclear Weapons Doctrine, Arms Control and International Law, Laws of War, Weapons of Mass Destruction and International Law, and International Criminal Law.

He is the author of numerous scholarly articles as well as a seminal and comprehensive book, *Prohibition of Nuclear Weapons: The Relevance of International Law*. One of his articles was cited and relied upon by a dissenting Justice on the International Court of Justice with respect to the Court's advisory opinion issued in 1996 on the "Legality of the Threat or Use of Nuclear Weapons. Professor Meyrowitz has also taught a course titled "War and Morality: What is a Just War?" pursuant to a grant awarded by the National Endowment of the Humanities.